THE DOCTRINE
AND COVENANTS
THE PEARL
OF GREAT PRICE

Single-Column Journal Edition

DESERET
BOOK

SALT LAKE CITY, UTAH

DESERET BOOK is a registered trademark of Deseret Book Company.

Visit us at deseretbook.com

ISBN 978-1-62972-966-4 (paperbound)

Printed in the United States of America
LSC Communications, Crawfordsville, IN

10 9 8 7 6 5 4 3 2 1

CONTENTS

Doctrine and Covenants

Pearl of Great Price

THE DOCTRINE AND COVENANTS

OF THE CHURCH OF JESUS CHRIST OF LATTER-DAY SAINTS

CONTAINING REVELATIONS GIVEN TO
JOSEPH SMITH, THE PROPHET

WITH SOME ADDITIONS BY HIS SUCCESSORS
IN THE PRESIDENCY OF THE CHURCH

ABBREVIATIONS

Old Testament

Gen.	Genesis
Ex.	Exodus
Lev.	Leviticus
Num.	Numbers
Deut.	Deuteronomy
Josh.	Joshua
Judg.	Judges
Ruth	Ruth
1 Sam.	1 Samuel
2 Sam.	2 Samuel
1 Kgs.	1 Kings
2 Kgs.	2 Kings
1 Chr.	1 Chronicles
2 Chr.	2 Chronicles
Ezra	Ezra
Neh.	Nehemiah
Esth.	Esther
Job	Job
Ps.	Psalms
Prov.	Proverbs
Eccl.	Ecclesiastes
Song	Song of Solomon
Isa.	Isaiah
Jer.	Jeremiah
Lam.	Lamentations
Ezek.	Ezekiel
Dan.	Daniel
Hosea	Hosea
Joel	Joel
Amos	Amos
Obad.	Obadiah
Jonah	Jonah
Micah	Micah
Nahum	Nahum
Hab.	Habakkuk
Zeph.	Zephaniah
Hag.	Haggai
Zech.	Zechariah
Mal.	Malachi

New Testament

Matt.	Matthew
Mark	Mark
Luke	Luke
John	John
Acts	Acts
Rom.	Romans
1 Cor.	1 Corinthians
2 Cor.	2 Corinthians
Gal.	Galatians
Eph.	Ephesians
Philip.	Philippians
Col.	Colossians
1 Thes.	1 Thessalonians
2 Thes.	2 Thessalonians
1 Tim.	1 Timothy
2 Tim.	2 Timothy
Titus	Titus
Philem.	Philemon
Heb.	Hebrews
James	James
1 Pet.	1 Peter
2 Pet.	2 Peter
1 Jn.	1 John
2 Jn.	2 John
3 Jn.	3 John
Jude	Jude
Rev.	Revelation

Book of Mormon

1 Ne.	1 Nephi
2 Ne.	2 Nephi
Jacob	Jacob
Enos	Enos
Jarom	Jarom
Omni	Omni
W of M	Words of Mormon
Mosiah	Mosiah
Alma	Alma
Hel.	Helaman
3 Ne.	3 Nephi
4 Ne.	4 Nephi
Morm.	Mormon
Ether	Ether
Moro.	Moroni

Doctrine and Covenants

D&C	Doctrine and Covenants
OD	Official Declaration

Pearl of Great Price

Moses	Moses
Abr.	Abraham
JS—M	Joseph Smith—Matthew
JS—H	Joseph Smith—History
A of F	Articles of Faith

Other Abbreviations and Explanations

JST	Joseph Smith Translation
TG	Topical Guide
BD	Bible Dictionary
HEB	An alternate translation from the Hebrew
GR	An alternate translation from the Greek
IE	An explanation of idioms and difficult wording
OR	Alternate words that clarify the meaning of an archaic expression

INTRODUCTION

The Doctrine and Covenants is a collection of divine revelations and inspired declarations given for the establishment and regulation of the kingdom of God on the earth in the last days. Although most of the sections are directed to members of The Church of Jesus Christ of Latter-day Saints, the messages, warnings, and exhortations are for the benefit of all mankind and contain an invitation to all people everywhere to hear the voice of the Lord Jesus Christ, speaking to them for their temporal well-being and their everlasting salvation.

Most of the revelations in this compilation were received through Joseph Smith Jr., the first prophet and president of The Church of Jesus Christ of Latter-day Saints. Others were issued through some of his successors in the Presidency (see headings to D&C 135, 136, and 138, and Official Declarations 1 and 2).

The book of Doctrine and Covenants is one of the standard works of the Church in company with the Holy Bible, the Book of Mormon, and the Pearl of Great Price. However, the Doctrine and Covenants is unique because it is not a translation of an ancient document, but is of modern origin and was given of God through His chosen prophets for the restoration of His holy work and the establishment of the kingdom of God on the earth in these days. In the revelations, one hears the tender but firm voice of the Lord Jesus Christ, speaking anew in the dispensation of the fulness of times; and the work that is initiated herein is preparatory to His Second Coming, in fulfillment of and in concert with the words of all the holy prophets since the world began.

Joseph Smith Jr. was born December 23, 1805, in Sharon, Windsor County, Vermont. During his early life, he moved with his family to present-day Manchester, in western New York. It was while he was living there in the spring of 1820, when he was fourteen years of age, that he experienced his first vision, in which he was visited in person by God, the Eternal Father, and His Son Jesus Christ. He was told in this vision that the true Church of Jesus Christ that had been established in New Testament times, and which had administered the fulness of the gospel, was no longer on the earth. Other divine manifestations followed in which he was taught by many angels; it was shown to him that God had a special work for him to do on the earth and that through him the Church of Jesus Christ would be restored to the earth.

In the course of time, Joseph Smith was enabled by divine assistance to translate and publish the Book of Mormon. In the meantime he and Oliver Cowdery were ordained to the Aaronic Priesthood by John the Baptist in May 1829 (see D&C 13), and soon thereafter they were also ordained to the Melchizedek Priesthood by the ancient Apostles Peter, James, and John (see D&C 27:12). Other ordinations followed in which priesthood keys were conferred by Moses, Elijah, Elias, and many ancient prophets (see D&C 110; 128:18, 21). These ordinations were, in fact, a restoration of divine authority to man on the earth. On April 6, 1830, under heavenly direction, the Prophet Joseph Smith organized the Church, and thus the true Church of Jesus Christ is once again operative as an institution among men, with authority to teach the gospel and administer the ordinances of salvation. (See D&C 20 and the Pearl of Great Price, Joseph Smith—History 1.)

These sacred revelations were received in answer to prayer, in times of need, and came out of real-life situations involving real people. The Prophet and his associates sought for divine guidance, and these revelations certify that they received it. In the revelations, one sees the restoration and unfolding of the gospel of Jesus Christ and the ushering in of the dispensation of the fulness of times. The westward movement of the Church from New York and Pennsylvania to Ohio, to Missouri, to Illinois, and finally to the Great Basin of western America and the mighty struggles of the Saints in attempting to build Zion on the earth in modern times are also shown forth in these revelations.

Several of the earlier sections involve matters regarding the translation and publication of the Book of Mormon (see sections 3, 5, 10, 17, and 19). Some later sections reflect the work of the Prophet Joseph Smith in making an inspired translation of the Bible, during which many of the great doctrinal sections were received (see, for example, sections 37, 45, 73, 76, 77, 86, 91, and 132, each of which has some direct relationship to the Bible translation).

In the revelations, the doctrines of the gospel are set forth with explanations about such fundamental matters as the nature of the Godhead, the origin of man, the reality of Satan, the purpose of mortality, the necessity for obedience, the need for repentance, the workings of the Holy Spirit, the ordinances and performances that pertain to salvation, the destiny of the earth, the future conditions of man after the Resurrection and the Judgment, the eternity of the marriage relationship, and the eternal nature of the family. Likewise, the gradual unfolding of the administrative structure of the Church is shown with the calling of bishops, the First Presidency, the Council of the Twelve, and the Seventy and the establishment of other presiding offices and quorums. Finally, the testimony that is given of Jesus Christ—His divinity, His majesty, His perfection, His love, and His redeeming power—makes this book of great value to the human family and "worth to the Church the riches of the whole Earth" (see heading to D&C 70).

The revelations were originally recorded by Joseph Smith's scribes, and Church members enthusiastically shared handwritten copies with each other. To create a more permanent record, scribes soon copied these revelations into manuscript record books, which Church leaders used in preparing the revelations to be printed. Joseph and the early Saints viewed the revelations as they did the Church: living, dynamic, and subject to refinement with additional revelation. They also recognized that unintentional errors had likely occurred through the process of copying the revelations and preparing them for publication. Thus, a Church conference asked Joseph Smith in 1831 to "correct those errors or mistakes which he may discover by the Holy Spirit."

After the revelations had been reviewed and corrected, Church members in Missouri began printing a book titled *A Book of Commandments for the Government of the Church of Christ*, which contained many of the Prophet's early revelations. This first attempt to publish the revelations ended, however, when a mob destroyed the Saints' printing office in Jackson County on July 20, 1833.

Upon hearing of the destruction of the Missouri printing office, Joseph Smith and other Church leaders began preparations to publish the revelations in Kirtland, Ohio. To again correct errors, clarify wording, and recognize developments in Church doctrine and organization, Joseph Smith oversaw the editing of the text of some revelations to prepare them for publication in 1835 as the *Doctrine and Covenants of the Church of the Latter Day Saints*. Joseph Smith authorized another edition of the Doctrine and Covenants, which was published only months after the Prophet's martyrdom in 1844.

The early Latter-day Saints prized the revelations and viewed them as messages from God. On one occasion in late 1831, several elders of the Church gave solemn testimony that the Lord had borne record to their souls of the truth of the revelations. This testimony was published in the 1835 edition of the Doctrine and Covenants as the written testimony of the Twelve Apostles:

TESTIMONY OF THE
TWELVE APOSTLES TO THE TRUTH OF THE
BOOK OF DOCTRINE AND COVENANTS

The Testimony of the Witnesses to the Book of the Lord's Commandments, which commandments He gave to His Church through Joseph Smith, Jun., who was appointed by the voice of the Church for this purpose:

We, therefore, feel willing to bear testimony to all the world of mankind, to every creature upon the face of the earth, that the Lord has borne record to our souls, through the Holy Ghost shed forth upon us, that these commandments were given by inspiration of God, and are profitable for all men and are verily true.

We give this testimony unto the world, the Lord being our helper; and it is through the grace of God the Father, and His Son, Jesus Christ, that we are permitted to have this privilege of bearing this testimony unto the world, in the which we rejoice exceedingly, praying the Lord always that the children of men may be profited thereby.

The names of the Twelve were:

Thomas B. Marsh	Orson Hyde	William Smith
David W. Patten	William E. McLellin	Orson Pratt
Brigham Young	Parley P. Pratt	John F. Boynton
Heber C. Kimball	Luke S. Johnson	Lyman E. Johnson

In successive editions of the Doctrine and Covenants, additional revelations or other matters of record have been added, as received and as accepted by competent assemblies or conferences of the Church. The 1876 edition, prepared by Elder Orson Pratt under Brigham Young's direction, arranged the revelations chronologically and supplied new headings with historical introductions.

Beginning with the 1835 edition, a series of seven theological lessons was also included; these were titled the *Lectures on Faith.* These had been prepared for use in the School of the Prophets in Kirtland, Ohio, from 1834 to 1835. Although profitable for doctrine and instruction, these lectures have been omitted from the Doctrine and Covenants since the 1921 edition because they were not given or presented as revelations to the whole Church.

In the 1981 edition of the Doctrine and Covenants, three documents were included for the first time. These are sections 137 and 138, setting forth the fundamentals of salvation for the dead; and Official Declaration 2, announcing that all worthy male members of the Church may be ordained to the priesthood without regard for race or color.

Each new edition of the Doctrine and Covenants has corrected past errors and added new information, particularly in the historical portions of the section headings. The present edition further refines dates and place-names and makes other corrections. These changes have been made to bring the material into conformity with the most accurate historical information. Other special features of this latest edition include revised maps showing the major geographical locations in which the revelations were received, plus improved photographs of Church historical sites, cross-references, section headings, and subject-matter summaries, all of which are designed to help readers to understand and rejoice in the message of the Lord as given in the Doctrine and Covenants. Information for the section headings has been taken from the Manuscript History of the Church and the published *History of the Church* (collectively referred to in the headings as Joseph Smith's history) and the *Joseph Smith Papers*.

CHRONOLOGICAL ORDER
OF CONTENTS

* At or near place specified

* At or near place specified

* At or near place specified

SECTION 1

Revelation given through Joseph Smith the Prophet, on November 1, 1831, during a special conference of elders of the Church, held at Hiram, Ohio. Many revelations had been received from the Lord prior to this time, and the compilation of these for publication in book form was one of the principal subjects passed upon at the conference. This section constitutes the Lord's preface to the doctrines, covenants, and commandments given in this dispensation.

1–7, The voice of warning is to all people; 8–16, Apostasy and wickedness precede the Second Coming; 17–23, Joseph Smith is called to restore to earth the Lord's truths and powers; 24–33, The Book of Mormon is brought forth and the true Church is established; 34–36, Peace will be taken from the earth; 37–39, Search these commandments.

1 ^aHearken, O ye people of my ^bchurch, saith the voice of him who dwells on high, and whose ^ceyes are upon all men; yea, verily I say: Hearken ye people from afar; and ye that are upon the islands of the sea, listen together.

2 For verily the ^avoice of the Lord is unto all men, and there is none to ^bescape; and there is no eye that shall not see, neither ^cear that shall not hear, neither ^dheart that shall not be penetrated.

3 And the ^arebellious shall be ^bpierced with much ^csorrow; for their iniquities shall be ^dspoken upon the housetops, and their secret acts shall be revealed.

4 And the ^avoice of warning shall be unto all people, by the mouths of my disciples, whom I have ^bchosen in these ^clast days.

5 And they shall ^ago forth and none shall stay them, for I the Lord have commanded them.

6 Behold, this is mine ^aauthority, and the authority of my servants, and my preface unto the book of my ^bcommandments, which I have given them to ^cpublish unto you, O ^dinhabitants of the earth.

---

1 1 *a* Deut. 32:1; Isa. 1:2; 49:1.
  b 3 Ne. 27:3 (1–8); D&C 20:1; 21:3. TG Jesus Christ, Head of the Church.
  c Ps. 33:18; Amos 9:8; D&C 38:7 (7–8). TG God, Omniscience of.
 2 *a* Ps. 65:2; Micah 1:2; D&C 1:34 (34–35); 18:28 (26–28); 39:15; 42:58; 68:8; 138:30.

  TG Israel, Mission of.
  b Job 34:22; 1 Thes. 5:3.
  c TG Conversion.
  d TG Heart.
 3 *a* TG Rebellion.
  b TG Conscience.
  c Ps. 32:10. TG Sorrow.
  d Prov. 28:13; Isa. 57:12 (11–12); Luke 8:17; 12:3; 2 Ne. 27:11; Morm. 5:8; D&C 88:108; 112:25 (25–26).
 4 *a* Ezek. 3:21 (17–21); D&C

63:37. TG Israel, Mission of; Mission of Latter-day Saints; Warn.
  b TG Priesthood, Authority.
  c TG Last Days.
 5 *a* TG Missionary Work.
 6 *a* TG Jesus Christ, Authority of; Priesthood, Authority.
  b D&C 33:14; 42:13; 51:4.
  c Acts 13:49; D&C 72:21.
  d Joel 1:2; Micah 1:2.

7 Wherefore, ^afear and ^btremble, O ye people, for what I the Lord have ^cdecreed in them shall be ^dfulfilled.

8 And verily I say unto you, that they who go forth, bearing these tidings unto the inhabitants of the earth, to them is power given to ^aseal both on earth and in heaven, the unbelieving and ^brebellious;

9 Yea, verily, to seal them up unto the ^aday when the ^bwrath of God shall be poured out upon the ^cwicked without measure—

10 Unto the ^aday when the Lord shall come to ^brecompense unto every man according to his ^cwork, and ^dmeasure to every man according to the measure which he has measured to his fellow man.

11 Wherefore the voice of the Lord is unto the ends of the earth, that all that will hear may hear:

12 Prepare ye, ^aprepare ye for that which is to come, for the Lord is ^bnigh;

13 And the ^aanger of the Lord is kindled, and his ^bsword is bathed in heaven, and it shall fall upon the inhabitants of the earth.

14 And the ^aarm of the Lord shall be revealed; and the ^bday cometh that they who will not ^chear the voice of the Lord, neither the voice of his ^dservants, neither give ^eheed to the words of the prophets and ^fapostles, shall be ^gcut off from among the people;

15 For they have ^astrayed from mine ^bordinances, and have ^cbroken mine ^deverlasting covenant;

16 They ^aseek not the Lord to establish his righteousness, but every man ^bwalketh in his ^cown ^dway, and after the ^eimage of his own god, whose

---

7 a Deut. 5:29; Eccl. 12:13.
  b Ezra 9:4.
  c Isa. 10:22 (21–34); Matt. 24:34.
  d Isa. 34:16 (16–17).
8 a D&C 68:12. TG Priesthood, Keys of; Sealing.
  b TG Rebellion.
9 a 2 Cor. 1:14.
  b Prov. 11:4 (3–9); Eccl. 8:12 (11–12); Rev. 18:6 (6–8).
  c Nahum 1:3; Mosiah 16:2; JS—M 1:55 (31, 55).
10 a TG Day of the Lord.
  b Prov. 11:31; Isa. 65:6 (6–7, 11); Ezek. 7:4; Mosiah 12:1; D&C 56:19. TG Jesus Christ, Judge.
  c Job 34:11; Prov. 24:12; Isa. 59:18; Alma 9:28; 36:15; 41:3 (2–5); 42:27; D&C 6:33.

  d Matt. 7:2; Luke 6:38.
12 a TG Millennium, Preparing a People for.
  b D&C 2:1; 49:28; 58:65; 68:11; 68:35; 84:119. TG Jesus Christ, Second Coming.
13 a D&C 63:6. TG Anger; God, Indignation of.
  b Ezek. 21:3; D&C 35:14; 84:114; 85:3.
14 a Isa. 40:10 (5–10); D&C 45:47; 56:1.
  b Zech. 14:1.
  c Ezek. 33:31 (30–33); Matt. 11:15; Heb. 5:11 (11–14); 2 Ne. 9:31; Mosiah 26:28; Moses 6:27. TG Hardheartedness; Haughtiness.
  d TG Prophets, Rejection of.
  e D&C 11:2. TG Disobedience.

  f TG Apostles.
  g Acts 3:23 (22–23); Alma 50:20; D&C 5:5; 50:8; 56:3 (1, 3–4).
15 a Josh. 23:16 (15–16); Isa. 24:5; D&C 3:6 (6–8); 104:52.
  b TG Ordinance.
  c TG Apostasy of Individuals; Apostasy of Israel; Apostasy of the Early Christian Church.
  d Ezek. 44:7. TG New and Everlasting Covenant.
16 a Matt. 6:33.
  b TG Walking in Darkness.
  c Isa. 53:6; Jer. 44:17.
  d Gen. 6:12; D&C 82:6; Moses 8:29.
  e Ex. 20:4; Isa. 41:29 (24, 29); 3 Ne. 21:17 (17–19). TG Idolatry.

image is in the likeness of the world, and whose substance is that of an idol, which waxeth *fold and shall perish in *gBabylon, even Babylon the great, which shall fall.

17 Wherefore, I the Lord, *aknowing the calamity which should come upon the *binhabitants of the earth, *ccalled upon my *dservant Joseph Smith, Jun., and *espake unto him from heaven, and gave him *fcommandments;

18 And also gave commandments to others, that they should proclaim these things unto the world; and all this that it might be fulfilled, which was written by the prophets—

19 The *aweak things of the world shall come forth and break down the mighty and strong ones, that man *bshould not counsel his fellow man, neither *ctrust in the arm of flesh—

20 But that every man might *aspeak in the name of God the Lord, even the Savior of the world;

21 That faith also might increase in the earth;

22 That mine everlasting *acovenant might be established;

23 That the *afulness of my *bgospel might be *cproclaimed by the *dweak and the simple unto the ends of the world, and before *ekings and *frulers.

24 Behold, I am God and have spoken it; these *acommandments are of me, and were given unto my servants in their weakness, after the manner of their *blanguage, that they might come to *cunderstanding.

25 And inasmuch as they *aerred it might be made known;

26 And inasmuch as they sought *awisdom they might be *binstructed;

27 And inasmuch as they sinned they might be *achastened, that they might *brepent;

28 And inasmuch as they were *ahumble they might be made strong, and blessed from on high, and receive *bknowledge from time to time.

16f Isa. 50:9.
  g Isa. 21:9; 48:14; D&C 64:24; 133:14. TG Babylon; Worldliness.
17a TG God, Foreknowledge of.
  b Isa. 24:6 (1–6).
  c TG Called of God.
  d TG Servant.
  e TG Revelation.
  f D&C 1:30 (23–28, 30).
19a 1 Chr. 29:1; Acts 4:13; 1 Cor. 1:27; 1 Ne. 7:8 (8–18); D&C 35:13; 124:1. TG Meek.
  b Isa. 8:10.
  c Ps. 44:6 (6–8); Jer.

9:4; 17:5; 2 Ne. 28:31 (30–31). TG Trust Not in the Arm of Flesh.
20a TG Authority.
22a D&C 39:11. TG Covenants; New and Everlasting Covenant.
23a Rom. 15:29.
  b TG Gospel.
  c TG Missionary Work.
  d 1 Cor. 1:27 (26–29). TG Strength.
  e TG Kings, Earthly.
  f Ps. 119:46; Matt. 10:18; Acts 9:15; D&C 124:3 (3, 16, 107).
24a Isa. 51:16; 2 Ne. 33:10

(10–11); Moro. 10:27 (27–29).
  b 2 Ne. 31:3; Ether 12:39; D&C 67:5. TG Language.
  c D&C 50:12. TG Understanding.
25a Isa. 29:24.
26a Eccl. 8:16 (16–17); D&C 42:68. TG Wisdom.
  b TG Teachable.
27a TG Chastening; Reproof.
  b TG Repent.
28a TG Humility; Poor in Spirit.
  b TG Knowledge.

29 And after having received the record of the Nephites, yea, even my servant Joseph Smith, Jun., might have power to ªtranslate through the ᵇmercy of God, by the power of God, the ᶜBook of Mormon.

30 And also those to whom these commandments were given, might have ªpower to lay the foundation of this ᵇchurch, and to bring it forth out of obscurity and out of ᶜdarkness, the only true and living ᵈchurch upon the face of the whole earth, with which I, the Lord, am well ᵉpleased, ᶠspeaking unto the church collectively and not individually—

31 For I the Lord cannot look upon ªsin with the least degree of allowance;

32 Nevertheless, he that ªrepents and does the ᵇcommandments of the Lord shall be ᶜforgiven;

33 And he that ªrepents not, from him shall be ᵇtaken even the light which he has received; for my ᶜSpirit shall not always ᵈstrive with man, saith the Lord of Hosts.

34 And again, verily I say unto you, O inhabitants of the earth: I the Lord am willing to make these things ªknown unto ᵇall flesh;

35 For I am no ªrespecter of persons, and will that all men shall know that the ᵇday speedily cometh; the hour is not yet, but is nigh at hand, when ᶜpeace shall be taken from the earth, and the ᵈdevil shall have power over his own dominion.

36 And also the Lord shall have ªpower over his ᵇsaints, and shall ᶜreign in their ᵈmidst, and shall come down in ᵉjudgment upon ᶠIdumea, or the world.

37 ªSearch these ᵇcommandments, for they are true and ᶜfaithful, and the prophecies and ᵈpromises which are in them shall all be fulfilled.

---

29 a D&C 3:12.
  b TG Mercy.
  c TG Book of Mormon.
30 a D&C 1:17 (4–5, 17–18).
  b TG Restoration of the Gospel.
  c TG Darkness, Spiritual.
  d 1 Cor. 14:33; Eph. 4:5 (3–13). TG Church.
  e D&C 38:10.
  f D&C 50:4.
31 a Lev. 5:17 (17–19); D&C 24:2. TG Sin.
32 a TG Repent.
  b Prov. 19:16.
  c Ps. 65:3; D&C 58:42 (42–43). TG Forgive.
33 a D&C 3:11; 121:37 (34–37).

  b Matt. 25:29 (29–30); D&C 60:3 (2–3).
  c TG God, Spirit of; Holy Ghost, Loss of.
  d Gen. 6:3; 1 Sam. 28:15; Isa. 57:16; Moro. 9:4.
34 a Isa. 45:19. TG Testimony.
  b D&C 1:2; 18:28 (26–28); 39:15; 42:58.
35 a Deut. 1:17; 10:17; Prov. 24:23; Acts 10:34; Col. 3:25; Alma 1:30; 16:14; D&C 38:16; Moses 5:21 (20–21).
  b TG Last Days.
  c Rev. 6:4. TG Peace; War.
  d TG Devil.
36 a TG Protection, Divine.
  b TG Saints.

  c Micah 4:7. TG Jesus Christ, Millennial Reign.
  d Zech. 2:11 (10–12); D&C 29:11 (9–11); 45:59; 84:119 (118–19); 104:59.
  e TG Judgment.
  f TG World, End of. BD Idumea.
37 a TG Priesthood, Magnifying Callings within; Scriptures, Study of; Study.
  b Rev. 21:5.
  c TG Trustworthiness.
  d Rev. 17:17; D&C 58:31; 82:10.

38 What I the Lord have spoken, I have spoken, and I excuse not myself; and though the heavens and the earth pass away, my *word shall not pass away, but shall all be *fulfilled, whether by mine own *voice or by the *voice of my *servants, it is the *same.

39 For behold, and lo, the Lord is God, and the *Spirit beareth record, and the record is true, and the *truth abideth forever and ever. Amen.

SECTION 2

An extract from Joseph Smith's history relating the words of the angel Moroni to Joseph Smith the Prophet, while in the house of the Prophet's father at Manchester, New York, on the evening of September 21, 1823. Moroni was the last of a long line of historians who had made the record that is now before the world as the Book of Mormon. (Compare Malachi 4:5–6; also sections 27:9; 110:13–16; and 128:18.)

1, Elijah is to reveal the priesthood; 2–3, The promises of the fathers are planted in the hearts of the children.

1 Behold, I will reveal unto you the Priesthood, by the hand of *Elijah the prophet, before the coming of the great and *dreadful day of the Lord.

2 And *he shall plant in the hearts of the children the *promises made to the fathers, and the hearts of the children shall turn to their fathers.

3 If it were not so, the whole *earth would be utterly wasted at his coming.

SECTION 3

Revelation given to Joseph Smith the Prophet, at Harmony, Pennsylvania, July 1828, relating to the loss of 116 pages of manuscript translated from the

---

38 *a* 2 Kgs. 10:10; Ps. 33:11;
119:89; Matt. 5:18;
24:35; 2 Ne. 9:16; 10:17;
D&C 5:20; 101:64;
Moses 1:4; JS—M 1:35.
b TG Promise.
c Deut. 18:18; Jer. 7:23
(21–28); D&C 18:35
(33–39); 21:5. TG Obe-
dience; Prophecy;
Revelation.
d Isa. 50:10; 1 Jn. 4:6
(1–6); D&C 25:16.

TG Priesthood, Author-
ity.
e 1 Thes. 4:2. TG Prophets,
Mission of; Servant.
f TG Sustaining Church
Leaders.
39 *a* 1 Jn. 5:6; D&C 20:27;
42:17.
b TG Truth.
2 1 *a* Mal. 4:5 (5–6); 3 Ne.
25:5 (5–6); D&C 35:4;
110:13 (13–15); 128:17;
JS—H 1:38 (38–39).

TG Last Days; Priest-
hood, Keys of.
b 1 Cor. 5:5; D&C 1:12;
34:8 (6–9); 43:17
(17–26).
2 *a* 2 Kgs. 2:15; D&C 27:9;
98:16 (16–17).
b TG Family, Children,
Duties of; Genealogy and
Temple Work; Promise;
Salvation for the Dead.
3 *a* Luke 1:17. TG Earth,
Purpose of.

first part of the Book of Mormon, which was called the book of Lehi. The Prophet had reluctantly allowed these pages to pass from his custody to that of Martin Harris, who had served for a brief period as scribe in the translation of the Book of Mormon. The revelation was given through the Urim and Thummim. (See section 10.)

1–4, The Lord's course is one eternal round; 5–15, Joseph Smith must repent or lose the gift to translate; 16–20, The Book of Mormon comes forth to save the seed of Lehi.

1 The ᵃworks, and the designs, and the purposes of God cannot be ᵇfrustrated, neither can they come to naught.

2 For God doth not ᵃwalk in crooked paths, neither doth he ᵇturn to the right hand nor to the left, neither doth he vary from that which he hath said, therefore his paths are straight, and his ᶜcourse is one eternal round.

3 Remember, remember that it is not the ᵃwork of God that is frustrated, but the work of men;

4 For although a man may have many ᵃrevelations, and have ᵇpower to do many mighty works, yet if he ᶜboasts in his own ᵈstrength, and sets at naught the ᵉcounsels of God, and follows after the dictates of his own will and ᶠcarnal desires, he must fall and incur the ᵍvengeance of a ʰjust God upon him.

5 Behold, you have been ᵃentrusted with these things, but how strict were your commandments; and remember also the promises which were made to you, if you did not transgress them.

6 And behold, how ᵃoft you have ᵇtransgressed the commandments and the laws of God, and have gone on in the ᶜpersuasions of men.

7 For, behold, you should not have ᵃfeared man more than God. Although men set at naught the counsels of God, and ᵇdespise his words—

---

3 1 *a* TG God, Works of.
  b Jer. 1:8 (7–8).
2 *a* Neh. 9:8; Isa. 45:19;
    Alma 7:20. TG God,
    Perfection of.
  b Josh. 1:7; 3 Ne. 18:13
    (12–14).
  c 1 Ne. 10:19 (18–19);
    D&C 35:1.
3 *a* Acts 5:38; Morm. 8:22;
    D&C 10:38 (38–40).
4 *a* TG Revelation.
  b Alma 19:4.
  c Amos 6:13 (13–14); Mo-
    siah 11:19; D&C 84:73.

    TG Boast.
  d TG Strength.
  e Josh. 9:14; Jacob 4:10;
    Alma 37:37. TG Counsel.
  f TG Carnal Mind; Chas-
    tity; Lust.
  g TG Vengeance.
  h 2 Ne. 1:22.
5 *a* Alma 37:14.
6 *a* D&C 5:21; 20:5; JS—H
    1:28 (28–29).
  b Josh. 23:16 (15–16);
    Alma 12:31. TG Trans-
    gress.
  c Titus 1:14; D&C 45:29;

    46:7; JS—H 1:19.
    TG Motivations; Peer
    Influence.
7 *a* Neh. 6:13; Ps. 27:1
    (1–14); Isa. 57:11;
    Luke 9:26; John 12:43
    (42–43); Acts 4:19; D&C
    122:9 (4–9). TG Cour-
    age; Fearful.
  b Num. 15:31 (30–31);
    2 Sam. 12:9 (7–9); 1 Ne.
    19:7; 2 Ne. 33:2; Jacob
    4:14 (8–14). TG Hate.

8 Yet you should have been faithful; and he would have extended his arm and ᵃsupported you against all the fiery ᵇdarts of the ᶜadversary; and he would have been with you in every time of ᵈtrouble.

9 Behold, thou art Joseph, and thou wast chosen to do the work of the Lord, but because of transgression, if thou art not aware thou wilt ᵃfall.

10 But remember, God is merciful; therefore, repent of that which thou hast done which is contrary to the commandment which I gave you, and thou art still chosen, and art ᵃagain called to the work;

11 Except thou ᵃdo this, thou shalt be delivered up and become as other men, and have no more gift.

12 And when thou deliveredst up that which God had given thee sight and power to ᵃtranslate, thou deliveredst up that which was ᵇsacred into the hands of a wicked ᶜman,

13 Who has set at naught the counsels of God, and has broken the most sacred promises which were made before God, and has depended upon his own judgment and ᵃboasted in his own wisdom.

14 And this is the reason that thou hast lost thy privileges for a season—

15 For thou hast suffered the counsel of thy ᵃdirector to be trampled upon from the beginning.

16 Nevertheless, my ᵃwork shall go forth, for inasmuch as the knowledge of a Savior has come unto the world, through the ᵇtestimony of the Jews, even so shall the ᶜknowledge of a ᵈSavior come unto my people—

17 And to the ᵃNephites, and the Jacobites, and the Josephites, and the Zoramites, through the testimony of their fathers—

18 And this ᵃtestimony shall come to the knowledge of the ᵇLamanites, and the Lemuelites, and the Ishmaelites, who ᶜdwindled in unbelief because of the ᵈiniquity of their fathers, whom the Lord has suffered to destroy their ᵉbrethren the Nephites, because of their ᶠiniquities and their abominations.

8a TG God, Power of.
b Eph. 6:16; 1 Ne. 15:24; D&C 27:17.
c TG Devil.
d Ps. 81:7; Alma 9:17; 38:5.
9a Acts 1:25; 1 Cor. 10:12. TG Apostasy of Individuals.
10a D&C 10:3.
11a Luke 13:3; D&C 1:33; 121:37 (34–37).
12a D&C 1:29; 5:4 (4, 30–31).
b TG Sacred; Sacrilege.
c D&C 10:6 (6–8).
13a Jacob 4:10. TG Haughtiness; Pride.
15a IE the Lord; see v. 6.
16a TG Israel, Mission of.
b John 5:39; 1 Ne. 13:25 (23–25); 2 Ne. 29:4 (4–6); D&C 20:26.
c Mosiah 3:20.
d TG Jesus Christ, Savior.
17a 1 Ne. 13:30; 2 Ne. 29:12 (12–13); Alma 45:14
(10–14).
18a TG Testimony.
b Jacob 1:13; Enos 1:13; D&C 10:48 (46–52); 109:65.
c 2 Ne. 26:15; Jacob 3:7. TG Doubt.
d TG Family, Children, Responsibilities toward; Sin.
e Morm. 8:2 (2–3).
f Mosiah 12:7.

19 And for this very *ᵃpurpose are these *ᵇplates *ᶜpreserved, which contain these records—that the *ᵈpromises of the Lord might be fulfilled, which he made to his *ᵉpeople;

20 And that the *ᵃLamanites might come to the knowledge of their fathers, and that they might know the *ᵇpromises of the Lord, and that they may *ᶜbelieve the gospel and *ᵈrely upon the merits of Jesus Christ, and be *ᵉglorified through faith in his name, and that through their repentance they might be saved. Amen.

SECTION 4

Revelation given through Joseph Smith the Prophet to his father, Joseph Smith Sr., at Harmony, Pennsylvania, February 1829.

1–4, Valiant service saves the Lord's ministers; 5–6, Godly attributes qualify them for the ministry; 7, The things of God must be sought after.

1 Now behold, a *ᵃmarvelous work is about to come forth among the children of men.

2 Therefore, O ye that embark in the *ᵃservice of God, see that ye *ᵇserve him with all your heart, might, mind and strength, that ye may stand *ᶜblameless before God at the last day.

3 Therefore, if ye have desires to serve God ye are *ᵃcalled to the work;

4 For behold the *ᵃfield is white already to *ᵇharvest; and lo, he that thrusteth in his sickle with his might, the same layeth up in *ᶜstore that he perisheth not, but bringeth salvation to his soul;

5 And *ᵃfaith, *ᵇhope, *ᶜcharity and *ᵈlove, with an *ᵉeye single to the *ᶠglory of God, *ᵍqualify him for the work.

19 *a* 1 Ne. 9:3 (3, 5).
  b TG Book of Mormon.
  c TG Scriptures, Preservation of.
  d Enos 1:16 (13–18); Mosiah 21:4; 3 Ne. 5:14 (13–15); D&C 10:47 (46–50).
  e TG Israel, Joseph, People of; Israel, Restoration of.
20 *a* 2 Ne. 30:5 (3–6); D&C 28:8 (8–9, 14); 32:2; 49:24.
  b 2 Ne. 10:9 (9, 21); Alma 9:24.
  c Morm. 3:21.
  d 2 Ne. 31:19; Moro. 6:4.
  e Moro. 7:26 (26, 38).

4 1 *a* Isa. 29:14; 1 Ne. 14:7 (7–17); 22:8; D&C 6:1; 11:1; 12:1; 18:44. TG Missionary Work; Restoration of the Gospel.
  2 *a* Acts 20:19. TG Children of Light; Service.
    b Josh. 22:5; Judg. 6:14; 1 Sam. 7:3; D&C 20:19; 76:5. TG Commitment; Dedication; Heart; Mind; Strength.
    c 1 Cor. 1:8; Col. 1:22; Jacob 1:19; Mosiah 3:21; 3 Ne. 27:20; D&C 88:85.
  3 *a* Matt. 8:19 (19–22); D&C 11:4, 15; 36:5;

63:57. TG Called of God; Service.
  4 *a* John 4:35; Alma 26:5; D&C 11:3; 12:3; 14:3; 33:3 (3, 7); 101:64.
    b Joel 3:13; D&C 31:4. TG Harvest.
    c Gen. 41:36 (33–57); 1 Tim. 6:19; 3 Ne. 4:18.
  5 *a* TG Faith.
    b TG Hope.
    c TG Charity.
    d TG Love.
    e Ps. 25:15; 141:8; Matt. 6:22; Morm. 8:15.
    f TG Glory; Motivations.
    g TG Priesthood, Qualifying for.

6 Remember faith, *a*virtue, knowledge, *b*temperance, *c*patience, *d*brotherly *e*kindness, *f*godliness, charity, *g*humility, *h*diligence.

7 *a*Ask, and ye shall receive; *b*knock, and it shall be opened unto you. Amen.

SECTION 5

Revelation given through Joseph Smith the Prophet, at Harmony, Pennsylvania, March 1829, at the request of Martin Harris.

1–10, This generation will receive the Lord's word through Joseph Smith; 11–18, Three witnesses will testify of the Book of Mormon; 19–20, The word of the Lord will be verified as in previous times; 21–35, Martin Harris may repent and be one of the witnesses.

1 Behold, I say unto you, that as my servant *a*Martin Harris has desired a witness at my hand, that you, my servant Joseph Smith, Jun., have got the plates of which you have testified and borne record that you have received of me;

2 And now, behold, this shall you say unto him—he who spake unto you, said unto you: I, the Lord, am God, and have given these things unto you, my servant Joseph Smith, Jun., and have commanded you that you should stand as a *a*witness of these things;

3 And I have caused you that you should enter into a *a*covenant with me, that you should not *b*show them except to those *c*persons to whom I commanded you; and you have no *d*power over them except I grant it unto you.

4 And you have a gift to *a*translate the plates; and this is the first gift that I bestowed upon you; and I have commanded that you should pretend to no other gift until my purpose is fulfilled in this; for I will grant unto you no other gift until it is finished.

5 Verily, I say unto you, that *a*woe shall come unto the inhabitants of the earth if they will not *b*hearken unto my words;

---

6 *a* TG Chastity; Virtue.
  b TG Temperance.
  c TG Patience.
  d TG Brotherhood and
    Sisterhood.
  e TG Benevolence; Courtesy; Kindness.
  f TG Godliness.
  g TG Humility; Meek;
    Poor in Spirit.
  h TG Diligence.

7 *a* Matt. 7:7 (7–8).
    TG Prayer.
  b TG Objectives.
5 1 *a* D&C 5:23 (23–24);
    JS—H 1:61.
2 *a* TG Witness.
3 *a* TG Covenants.
  b Prov. 25:2.
  c 2 Ne. 27:13. See also
    "The Testimony of Three
    Witnesses" and "The

Testimony of Eight
Witnesses" in the preliminary pages of the Book
of Mormon.
  d 2 Ne. 3:11.
4 *a* D&C 3:12; 6:25 (25, 28).
5 *a* Rev. 8:13; Hel. 7:22;
    D&C 1:14.
  b Jer. 26:4; Alma 5:37
    (37–38).

6 For hereafter you shall be *ordained and go forth and deliver my *words unto the children of men.

7 Behold, if they will not *believe my words, they would not believe you, my servant Joseph, if it were possible that you should show them all these things which I have committed unto you.

8 Oh, this *unbelieving and *stiffnecked generation—mine *anger is kindled against them.

9 Behold, verily I say unto you, I have *reserved those things which I have entrusted unto you, my servant Joseph, for a wise purpose in me, and it shall be made known unto future generations;

10 But this generation shall have my word *through you;

11 And in addition to your testimony, the *testimony of three of my servants, whom I shall call and ordain, unto whom I will show these things, and they shall go forth with my words that are given through you.

12 Yea, they shall know of a *surety that these things are true, for from heaven will I declare it unto them.

13 I will give them power that they may behold and view these things as they are;

14 And to *none else will I grant this power, to receive this same testimony among this generation, in this the beginning of the rising up and the coming forth of my *church out of the wilderness—clear as the *moon, and fair as the sun, and terrible as an army with banners.

15 And the testimony of three *witnesses will I send forth of my word.

16 And behold, whosoever *believeth on my words, them will I *visit with the *manifestation of my *Spirit; and they shall be *born of me, even of water and of the Spirit—

17 And you must wait yet a little while, for ye are not yet *ordained—

18 And their testimony shall also go forth unto the *condemnation of this generation if they *harden their hearts against them;

19 For a desolating *scourge shall go forth among the inhabitants of the

---

6 a D&C 20:2 (2–3).
  b 2 Ne. 29:7.
7 a Luke 16:30 (27–31);
    D&C 63:7–12.
8 a TG Unbelief.
  b Morm. 8:33. TG Haughtiness; Stiffnecked.
  c TG Anger; God, Indignation of.
9 a Alma 37:18.
10 a Mosiah 18:19 (18–20);
    D&C 31:4; 42:12; 52:36.
11 a 2 Ne. 27:12; Ether 5:3
    (3–4); D&C 17:3 (1–5);

20:10.
12 a Ether 5:3.
14 a 2 Ne. 27:13.
  b Rev. 12:1 (1–6).
    TG Church; Jesus Christ,
    Head of the Church.
  c Song 6:10; D&C 105:31;
    109:73.
15 a D&C 17:1. TG Witness.
16 a Ether 4:11.
  b Ps. 8:4; 1 Ne. 2:16; 19:11;
    Alma 17:10.
  c D&C 8:1 (1–3); 70:13.
  d TG God, Spirit of.

  e TG Baptism; Holy Ghost,
    Baptism of; Man, New,
    Spiritually Reborn.
17 a TG Priesthood,
    Authority; Priesthood,
    Ordination.
18 a 1 Ne. 14:7; D&C 20:13
    (13–15).
  b TG Hardheartedness.
19 a Isa. 28:18 (15, 18); D&C
    29:8; 35:11 (11–16);
    43:17 (17–27). TG Last
    Days.

earth, and shall continue to be poured out from time to time, if they *bre-pent not, until the earth is *empty, and the inhabitants thereof are *con-sumed away and utterly destroyed by the brightness of my *coming.

20 Behold, I tell you these things, even as I also *told the people of the destruction of Jerusalem; and my *word shall be verified at this time as it hath hitherto been verified.

21 And now I command you, my servant Joseph, to *repent and *walk more uprightly before me, and to yield to the *persuasions of men no more;

22 And that you be *firm in *keeping the commandments wherewith I have commanded you; and if you do this, behold I grant unto you *eternal life, even if you should be *slain.

23 And now, again, I speak unto you, my servant Joseph, concerning the *man that desires the witness—

24 Behold, I say unto him, he exalts himself and does not *humble him-self sufficiently before me; but if he will *bow down before me, and humble himself in mighty *prayer and faith, in the *sincerity of his heart, then will I grant unto him a *view of the things which he desires to see.

25 And then he shall say unto the people of this generation: Behold, I have seen the things which the Lord hath shown unto Joseph Smith, Jun., and I *know of a surety that they are true, for I have seen them, for they have been shown unto me by the power of God and not of man.

26 And I the Lord command him, my servant Martin Harris, that he shall say no more unto them concerning these things, except he shall say: I have seen them, and they have been shown unto me by the power of God; and these are the words which he shall say.

27 But if he deny this he will break the *covenant which he has before covenanted with me, and behold, he is condemned.

28 And now, except he humble himself and acknowledge unto me the things that he has done which are wrong, and covenant with me that he will keep my commandments, and exercise *faith in me, behold, I say unto

19 *b* TG Repent.
  c Isa. 24:1 (1, 5–6).
  d Mal. 3:6 (6–7).
  e Isa. 66:15 (15–16); D&C 133:41. TG Jesus Christ, Prophecies about; Jesus Christ, Second Coming.
20 *a* Lam. 1:8 (7–9); 1 Ne. 1:18; 2 Ne. 25:9.
  b D&C 1:38.
21 *a* D&C 3:6; 20:5; JS—H

1:28 (28–29).
  b 1 Ne. 16:3.
  c TG Peer Influence.
22 *a* Hel. 7:7.
  b TG Obedience.
  c D&C 132:49.
  d Alma 60:13; D&C 6:30; 135:1 (1–7).
23 *a* D&C 5:1.
24 *a* Ether 9:35.
  b Alma 22:17.

TG Reverence.
  c TG Prayer.
  d TG Sincere.
  e D&C 17:1. See also "The Testimony of Three Witnesses" in the prelim-inary pages of the Book of Mormon.
25 *a* Ether 5:3.
27 *a* TG Covenants.
28 *a* Ether 4:7.

him, he shall have no such views, for I will grant unto him no views of the things of which I have spoken.

29 And if this be the case, I command you, my servant Joseph, that you shall say unto him, that he shall do no more, nor trouble me any more concerning this matter.

30 And if this be the case, behold, I say unto thee Joseph, when thou hast translated a few more pages thou shalt stop for a season, even until I command thee again; then thou mayest translate again.

31 And except thou do this, behold, thou shalt have no more gift, and I will take away the things which I have entrusted with thee.

32 And now, because I foresee the lying in wait to destroy thee, yea, I foresee that if my servant Martin Harris humbleth not himself and receive a witness from my hand, that he will fall into *transgression;

33 And there are many that lie in wait to *destroy thee from off the face of the earth; and for this cause, that thy days may be *prolonged, I have given unto thee these commandments.

34 Yea, for this cause I have said: Stop, and *stand still until I command thee, and I will *provide means whereby thou mayest accomplish the thing which I have commanded thee.

35 And if thou art *faithful in keeping my commandments, thou shalt be *lifted up at the last day. Amen.

SECTION 6

Revelation given to Joseph Smith the Prophet and Oliver Cowdery, at Harmony, Pennsylvania, April 1829. Oliver Cowdery began his labors as scribe in the translation of the Book of Mormon, April 7, 1829. He had already received a divine manifestation of the truth of the Prophet's testimony respecting the plates on which was engraved the Book of Mormon record. The Prophet inquired of the Lord through the Urim and Thummim and received this response.

1–6, Laborers in the Lord's field gain salvation; 7–13, There is no gift greater than the gift of salvation; 14–27, A witness of the truth comes by the power of the Spirit; 28–37, Look unto Christ, and do good continually.

---

32 a Enos 1:13.
33 a D&C 10:6 (6, 25); 38:13
(13, 28); 42:64.
 b Ex. 20:12; Deut. 4:40;
11:9 (8–9); Prov. 3:2

(1–2); Hel. 7:24; 15:11
(10–11).
34 a 1 Sam. 9:27; Isa. 30:15.
 b 1 Ne. 3:7.
35 a Ex. 15:26; D&C 11:20.

b John 6:39; 1 Thes. 4:17;
3 Ne. 15:1; D&C 9:14;
17:8; 52:44; 75:16, 22.

1 A great and *marvelous work is about to come forth unto the children of men.

2 Behold, I am God; give heed unto my *word, which is quick and powerful, *sharper than a two-edged sword, to the dividing asunder of both joints and marrow; therefore give heed unto my words.

3 Behold, the *field is white already to harvest; therefore, whoso desireth to reap, let him thrust in his sickle with his might, and reap while the day *lasts, that he may *treasure up for his soul everlasting salvation in the kingdom of God.

4 Yea, whosoever will thrust in his sickle and reap, the same is *called of God.

5 Therefore, if you will *ask of me you shall receive; if you will knock it shall be opened unto you.

6 Now, as you have asked, behold, I say unto you, keep my commandments, and *seek to bring forth and establish the cause of *Zion;

7 *Seek not for *riches but for *wisdom, and behold, the *mysteries of God shall be unfolded unto you, and then shall you be made *rich. Behold, he that hath *eternal life is rich.

8 Verily, verily, I say unto you, even as you *desire of me so it shall be unto you; and if you desire, you shall be the means of doing much *good in this generation.

9 Say nothing but *repentance unto this generation; keep my commandments, and assist to bring forth my work, according to my commandments, and you shall be blessed.

10 Behold thou hast a gift, and blessed art thou because of thy *gift. Remember it is *sacred and cometh from above—

11 And if thou wilt *inquire, thou shalt know *mysteries which are great

6 1 a Isa. 29:14; D&C 4:1
(1–7); 18:44.
2 a Heb. 4:12; Rev. 1:16;
D&C 27:1.
  b Hel. 3:29 (29–30); D&C
  15:2; 33:1; 85:6; 121:43.
3 a Joel 3:13; D&C 101:64.
  b TG Procrastination.
  c TG Treasure.
4 a D&C 11:4 (3–4, 27);
  12:4 (3–4); 14:4 (3–4).
5 a Matt. 7:7.
6 a JST Matt. 6:38 (Matt.
  6:33 note a); JST Luke
  12:34 (Luke 12:31 note a).

  b D&C 35:24. TG Mission
  of Latter-day Saints;
  Objectives; Zion.
7 a Alma 39:14 (12–14);
  D&C 68:31 (31–32).
  TG Study.
  b 1 Kgs. 3:11 (10–13);
  Matt. 19:23 (23–26);
  Jacob 2:18. TG Worldliness.
  c TG Education; Wisdom.
  d Rom. 16:25; D&C 42:65
  (61–65); 121:27 (25–27).
  TG Mysteries of Godliness.

  e 4 Ne. 1:3. TG Treasure.
  f Prov. 13:7; Rev. 3:18.
8 a TG Motivations; Prayer.
  b TG Good Works.
9 a D&C 15:6; 18:14; 34:6.
  TG Missionary Work;
  Prophets, Mission of;
  Repent.
10 a TG God, Gifts of.
  b D&C 63:64.
11 a D&C 46:7; 102:23;
  JS—H 1:18 (18, 26).
  TG Prayer.
  b Matt. 11:25; 13:11; Alma
  12:9.

and marvelous; therefore thou shalt exercise thy ^cgift, that thou mayest find out mysteries, that thou mayest bring ^dmany to the knowledge of the truth, yea, ^econvince them of the error of their ways.

12 Make not thy gift known unto any save it be those who are of thy faith. Trifle not with ^asacred things.

13 If thou wilt do ^agood, yea, and ^bhold out ^cfaithful to the ^dend, thou shalt be saved in the ^ekingdom of God, which is the greatest of all the ^fgifts of God; for there is no gift greater than the gift of ^gsalvation.

14 Verily, verily, I say unto thee, blessed art thou for what thou hast done; for thou hast ^ainquired of me, and behold, as often as thou hast inquired thou hast received instruction of my Spirit. If it had not been so, thou wouldst not have come to the place where thou art at this time.

15 Behold, thou knowest that thou hast inquired of me and I did enlighten thy ^amind; and now I tell thee these things that thou mayest know that thou hast been ^benlightened by the ^cSpirit of truth;

16 Yea, I tell thee, that thou mayest know that there is none else save God that ^aknowest thy thoughts and the ^bintents of thy ^cheart.

17 I tell thee these things as a witness unto thee—that the words or the work which thou hast been writing are ^atrue.

18 Therefore be diligent; ^astand by my ^bservant Joseph, faithfully, in whatsoever difficult circumstances he may be for the word's sake.

19 Admonish him in his faults, and also ^areceive admonition of him. ^bBe patient; be sober; be temperate; have patience, faith, hope and charity.

20 Behold, thou art Oliver, and I have spoken unto thee because of thy desires; therefore ^atreasure up these words in thy heart. Be faithful and ^bdiligent in keeping the commandments of God, and I will encircle thee in the arms of my ^clove.

21 Behold, I am Jesus Christ, the ^aSon of God. I am the same that came

---

c TG Talents.
d 1 Tim. 2:4; Alma 36:26. TG Knowledge.
e James 5:20; Alma 12:1; 62:45; D&C 18:44.
12 a Prov. 23:9; Matt. 7:6; D&C 10:37 (36–37). TG Sacred; Sacrilege.
13 a TG Good Works.
b 1 Tim. 1:19; 1 Ne. 15:24.
c Ps. 31:23; Mosiah 2:41; Ether 4:19; D&C 51:19; 63:47; 138:12. TG Perseverance; Steadfastness.
d Rev. 2:10.

e TG Kingdom of God, in Heaven.
f TG God, Gifts of.
g TG Salvation.
14 a TG Guidance, Divine.
15 a TG Mind.
b Eph. 1:18. TG Holy Ghost, Mission of.
c TG God, Spirit of.
16 a 2 Sam. 7:20; 1 Chr. 28:9; Ps. 139:2; Matt. 12:25; Heb. 4:12; Mosiah 24:12; Morm. 6:22; D&C 15:3. TG God, Omniscience of.
b TG Motivations; Sincere.

c 1 Kgs. 8:39.
17 a D&C 18:2.
18 a TG Diligence; Loyalty.
b D&C 124:95.
19 a TG Teachable.
b See Topical Guide entry on each of the qualities listed here.
20 a D&C 11:26; 84:85. TG Treasure.
b TG Diligence.
c John 15:12 (12–15). TG God, Love of.
21 a TG Jesus Christ, Divine Sonship.

unto mine *b*own, and mine own received me not. I am the *c*light which shineth in *d*darkness, and the darkness comprehendeth it not.

22 Verily, verily, I say unto you, if you desire a further witness, cast your mind upon the night that you cried unto me in your heart, that you might *a*know concerning the truth of these things.

23 Did I not speak *a*peace to your mind concerning the matter? What greater *b*witness can you have than from God?

24 And now, behold, you have received a *a*witness; for if I have *b*told you things which no man knoweth have you not received a witness?

25 And, behold, I grant unto you a gift, if you desire of me, to *a*translate, even as my servant Joseph.

26 Verily, verily, I say unto you, that there are *a*records which contain much of my gospel, which have been kept back because of the *b*wickedness of the people;

27 And now I command you, that if you have good desires—a desire to lay up *a*treasures for yourself in heaven—then shall you assist in bringing to light, with your gift, those parts of my *b*scriptures which have been hidden because of iniquity.

28 And now, behold, I give unto you, and also unto my servant Joseph, the *a*keys of this gift, which shall bring to light this ministry; and in the mouth of two or three *b*witnesses shall every word be established.

29 Verily, verily, I say unto you, if they *a*reject my words, and this part of my gospel and ministry, blessed are ye, for they can do no more unto you than unto me.

30 And even if they *a*do unto you even as they have done unto me, blessed are ye, for you shall *b*dwell with me in *c*glory.

31 But if they *a*reject not my words, which shall be established by the *b*testimony which shall be given, blessed are they, and then shall ye have joy in the fruit of your labors.

21 *b* John 1:11; Acts 3:17 (14–17); 3 Ne. 9:16. TG Prophets, Rejection of.
  c John 1:5; D&C 10:58. TG Jesus Christ, Light of the World; Light [noun]; Light of Christ.
  d TG Darkness, Spiritual.
22 *a* TG Discernment, Spiritual; God, Access to.
23 *a* Gen. 41:16. TG Contentment; Peace; Peace of

God.
  b Rom. 2:15 (14–15); 1 Jn. 5:9.
24 *a* D&C 18:2.
  b TG God, Omniscience of.
25 *a* Mosiah 8:13; D&C 5:4 (4, 30–31); 9:2 (1–3, 5, 10).
26 *a* D&C 8:1; 9:2. TG Record Keeping; Scriptures, Writing of; Scriptures to Come Forth.

  b TG Wickedness.
27 *a* TG Treasure.
  b D&C 35:20.
28 *a* D&C 7:7.
  b Deut. 19:15; 2 Cor. 13:1.
29 *a* John 15:20.
30 *a* D&C 5:22; 135:1 (1–7). TG Martyrdom.
  b Rev. 3:21.
  c TG Glory.
31 *a* 3 Ne. 16:10 (10–14); D&C 20:15 (8–15).
  b TG Testimony.

32 Verily, verily, I say unto you, as I said unto my disciples, where two or three are gathered together in my name, as *a*touching *b*one thing, behold, there will I be in the *c*midst of them—even so am I in the *d*midst of you.

33 *a*Fear not to do *b*good, my sons, for whatsoever ye *c*sow, that shall ye also reap; therefore, if ye sow *d*good ye shall also reap good for your *e*reward.

34 Therefore, fear not, little *a*flock; do good; let earth and hell combine against you, for if ye are *b*built upon my rock, they cannot prevail.

35 Behold, I do not condemn you; go your ways and *a*sin no more; perform with soberness the work which I have commanded you.

36 *a*Look unto me in every *b*thought; *c*doubt not, fear not.

37 *a*Behold the wounds which pierced my side, and also the prints of the *b*nails in my hands and feet; be faithful, keep my commandments, and ye shall *c*inherit the *d*kingdom of heaven. Amen.

SECTION 7

Revelation given to Joseph Smith the Prophet and Oliver Cowdery, at Harmony, Pennsylvania, April 1829, when they inquired through the Urim and Thummim as to whether John, the beloved disciple, tarried in the flesh or had died. The revelation is a translated version of the record made on parchment by John and hidden up by himself.

1–3, John the Beloved will live until the Lord comes; 4–8, Peter, James, and John hold gospel keys.

1 And the Lord said unto me: *a*John, my beloved, what *b*desirest thou? For if you shall ask what you will, it shall be granted unto you.

2 And I said unto him: Lord, give unto me *a*power over *b*death, that I may live and bring souls unto thee.

3 And the Lord said unto me: Verily, verily, I say unto thee, because thou

---

32 *a* Matt. 18:19 (19–20); D&C 29:6; 84:1.
  b TG Unity.
  c D&C 32:3; 38:7.
  d D&C 29:5; 88:63 (62–63).
33 *a* TG Courage; Fearful.
  b TG Good Works.
  c Job 34:11; Ps. 7:16; Hosea 8:7; Gal. 6:7–8; Mosiah 7:30; Alma 9:28; D&C 1:10. TG Harvest.
  d TG Benevolence.

  e TG Reward.
34 *a* TG Church; Sheep.
  b Ps. 71:3; Matt. 7:24 (24–25); Hel. 5:12; D&C 10:69; 11:16 (16, 24); 18:4 (4, 17); 33:13; Moses 7:53. TG Rock.
35 *a* John 8:11.
36 *a* Isa. 45:22; D&C 43:34.
  b TG Motivations.
  c TG Doubt.
37 *a* TG Jesus Christ, Appearances, Postmortal.

  b TG Jesus Christ, Crucifixion of.
  c Matt. 5:10 (3, 10).
  d TG Kingdom of God, in Heaven.
7 1 *a* John 19:26 (26–27); 20:2 (2–9).
  b 2 Chr. 1:7 (7–12); 3 Ne. 28:1 (1–12).
2 *a* TG Death, Power over.
  b Luke 9:27.

desirest this thou shalt ^atarry until I come in my ^bglory, and shalt ^cprophesy before nations, kindreds, tongues and people.

4 And for this cause the Lord said unto Peter: If I will that he tarry till I come, what is that to thee? For he desired of me that he might bring ^asouls unto me, but thou desiredst that thou mightest speedily come unto me in my ^bkingdom.

5 I say unto thee, Peter, this was a good desire; but my beloved has desired that he might do more, or a greater ^awork yet among men than what he has before done.

6 Yea, he has undertaken a greater work; therefore I will make him as flaming fire and a ^aministering angel; he shall minister for those who shall be ^bheirs of salvation who dwell on the earth.

7 And I will make thee to minister for him and for thy brother James; and unto you three I will ^agive this power and the ^bkeys of this ministry until I come.

8 Verily I say unto you, ye shall both have according to your desires, for ye both ^ajoy in that which ye have desired.

SECTION 8

Revelation given through Joseph Smith the Prophet to Oliver Cowdery, at Harmony, Pennsylvania, April 1829. In the course of the translation of the Book of Mormon, Oliver, who continued to serve as scribe, writing at the Prophet's dictation, desired to be endowed with the gift of translation. The Lord responded to his supplication by granting this revelation.

1–5, Revelation comes by the power of the Holy Ghost; 6–12, Knowledge of the mysteries of God and the power to translate ancient records come by faith.

1 ^aOliver Cowdery, verily, verily, I say unto you, that assuredly as the Lord liveth, who is your God and your Redeemer, even so surely shall you receive a ^bknowledge of whatsoever things you shall ^cask in faith, with an ^dhonest heart, believing that you shall receive a ^eknowledge concerning the

---

3 *a* John 21:22 (20–25).
    TG Translated Beings.
 b TG Glory; Jesus Christ,
    Glory of; Jesus Christ,
    Second Coming.
 c Rev. 10:11.
4 *a* TG Conversion; Worth of
    Souls.
 b TG Kingdom of God, in

    Heaven.
5 *a* Philip. 1:24 (23–24);
    3 Ne. 28:9 (1–12).
6 *a* Heb. 1:14; D&C 43:25;
    130:5.
 b D&C 76:88.
7 *a* Matt. 16:19.
 b Acts 15:7; D&C
    6:28; JS—H 1:72.

    TG Priesthood, Keys of.
8 *a* TG Joy.
8 1 *a* JS—H 1:66.
 b Dan. 5:16; Mosiah 8:13
    (13–18); D&C 6:25; 9:5
    (1–5). TG Testimony.
 c Isa. 58:9 (8–9).
 d TG Prayer; Sincere.
 e TG Knowledge.

engravings of old *f*records, which are ancient, which contain those parts of my scripture of which has been spoken by the *g*manifestation of my Spirit.

2 Yea, behold, I will *a*tell you in your mind and in your *b*heart, by the *c*Holy Ghost, which shall come upon you and which shall dwell in your heart.

3 Now, behold, this is the spirit of revelation; behold, this is the spirit by which Moses *a*brought the children of Israel through the Red Sea on dry ground.

4 Therefore this is thy *a*gift; apply unto it, and blessed art thou, for it shall *b*deliver you out of the hands of your *c*enemies, when, if it were not so, they would slay you and bring your soul to destruction.

5 Oh, remember these *a*words, and keep my commandments. Remember, this is your gift.

6 Now this is not all thy *a*gift; for you have another gift, which is the gift of Aaron; behold, it has told you many things;

7 Behold, there is no other power, save the power of God, that can cause this gift of Aaron to be with you.

8 Therefore, *a*doubt not, for it is the gift of God; and you shall hold it in your hands, and do marvelous works; and no power shall be able to take it away out of your hands, for it is the *b*work of God.

9 And, therefore, whatsoever you shall ask me to tell you by that means, that will I grant unto you, and you shall have knowledge concerning it.

10 Remember that without *a*faith you can do nothing; therefore ask in faith. Trifle not with these things; do not *b*ask for that which you ought not.

11 Ask that you may know the mysteries of God, and that you may *a*translate and receive knowledge from all those ancient records which have been hid up, that are *b*sacred; and according to your faith shall it be done unto you.

12 Behold, it is I that have spoken it; and I am the same that spake unto you from the beginning. Amen.

1*f* D&C 6:26; 9:2.
  g D&C 5:16.
2*a* D&C 9:8 (7–9).
  TG Guidance, Divine.
  b Ezek. 40:4. TG Heart;
  Inspiration.
  c Rom. 8:9. TG Holy
  Ghost, Mission of.
3*a* Ex. 3:10 (2–10); 13:14;

14:16; Deut. 11:4; Josh.
2:10; Neh. 9:11; 1 Ne.
4:2; 17:26; Mosiah 7:19;
Hel. 8:11; D&C 17:1.
TG Israel, Deliverance of.
4*a* 2 Tim. 1:6.
  b TG Deliver.
  c Ex. 23:22 (20–23); D&C
105:15; 136:40.

5*a* Deut. 11:18.
6*a* D&C 6:10.
8*a* TG Doubt.
  b TG God, Works of.
10*a* TG Faith.
  b D&C 88:65 (63–65).
11*a* D&C 1:29; 9:1, 10.
  b TG Sacred.

SECTION 9

Revelation given through Joseph Smith the Prophet to Oliver Cowdery, at Harmony, Pennsylvania, April 1829. Oliver is admonished to be patient and is urged to be content to write, for the time being, at the dictation of the translator, rather than to attempt to translate.

1–6, Other ancient records are yet to be translated; 7–14, The Book of Mormon is translated by study and by spiritual confirmation.

1 Behold, I say unto you, my son, that because you did not *a*translate according to that which you desired of me, and did commence again to *b*write for my servant, Joseph Smith, Jun., even so I would that ye should continue until you have finished this record, which I have entrusted unto him.

2 And then, behold, *a*other *b*records have I, that I will give unto you power that you may assist to *c*translate.

3 Be patient, my son, for it is *a*wisdom in me, and it is not expedient that you should translate at this present time.

4 Behold, the work which you are called to do is to *a*write for my servant Joseph.

5 And, behold, it is because that you did not continue as you commenced, when you began to translate, that I have taken away this privilege from you.

6 Do not *a*murmur, my son, for it is wisdom in me that I have dealt with you after this manner.

7 Behold, you have not understood; you have supposed that I would give it unto you, when you took no thought save it was to ask me.

8 But, behold, I say unto you, that you must *a*study it out in your *b*mind; then you must *c*ask me if it be right, and if it is right I will cause that your *d*bosom shall *e*burn within you; therefore, you shall *f*feel that it is right.

9 But if it be not right you shall have no such feelings, but you shall have a *a*stupor of thought that shall cause you to forget the thing which is wrong;

9 1 *a* D&C 8:11 (1, 11).
   b JS—H 1:67.
  2 *a* An allusion to additional translation activity, i.e., the Joseph Smith Translation of the Bible and the Book of Abraham, in which Oliver Cowdery assisted as a scribe. See also BD Joseph Smith Translation.
   b D&C 6:26; 8:1.

    TG Scriptures to Come Forth.
   c D&C 6:25 (25, 28); 10:3 (3, 18, 41, 45).
  3 *a* TG God, Wisdom of; Stewardship.
  4 *a* D&C 18:2; 24:1.
    TG Scribe; Scriptures, Writing of.
  6 *a* TG Murmuring.
  8 *a* Acts 1:24 (22–26).
    TG Knowledge; Meditation; Problem-Solving;

    Study; Testimony.
   b TG Mind.
   c TG Communication; Prayer.
   d Luke 24:32.
   e TG Inspiration; Revelation.
   f D&C 8:2 (2–3). TG Holy Ghost, Source of Testimony.
  9 *a* D&C 10:2.

therefore, you cannot write that which is *b*sacred save it be given you from me.

10 Now, if you had known this you could have *a*translated; nevertheless, it is not expedient that you should translate now.

11 Behold, it was expedient when you commenced; but you *a*feared, and the time is past, and it is not expedient now;

12 For, do you not behold that I have *a*given unto my servant *b*Joseph sufficient strength, whereby it is made up? And neither of you have I condemned.

13 Do this thing which I have commanded you, and you shall *a*prosper. Be faithful, and yield to no *b*temptation.

14 Stand fast in the *a*work wherewith I have *b*called you, and a hair of your head shall not be lost, and you shall be *c*lifted up at the last day. Amen.

SECTION 10

Revelation given to Joseph Smith the Prophet, at Harmony, Pennsylvania, likely around April 1829, though portions may have been received as early as the summer of 1828. Herein the Lord informs Joseph of alterations made by wicked men in the 116 manuscript pages from the translation of the book of Lehi, in the Book of Mormon. These manuscript pages had been lost from the possession of Martin Harris, to whom the sheets had been temporarily entrusted. (See the heading to section 3.) The evil design was to await the expected retranslation of the matter covered by the stolen pages and then to discredit the translator by showing discrepancies created by the alterations. That this wicked purpose had been conceived by the evil one and was known to the Lord even while Mormon, the ancient Nephite historian, was making his abridgment of the accumulated plates, is shown in the Book of Mormon (see Words of Mormon 1:3–7).

1–26, Satan stirs up wicked men to oppose the Lord's work; 27–33, He seeks to destroy the souls of men; 34–52, The gospel is to go to the Lamanites and all nations through the Book of Mormon; 53–63, The Lord will establish His Church and His gospel among men; 64–70, He will gather the repentant into His Church and will save the obedient.

---

9 *b* TG Sacred.
10 *a* D&C 8:11.
11 *a* TG Fearful.
12 *a* D&C 1:29.

b D&C 18:8.
13 *a* Deut. 29:9; Ps. 1:3 (2–3).
   b TG Temptation.
14 *a* 1 Cor. 16:13.

b TG Called of God.
c D&C 5:35; 17:8.

1 Now, behold, I say unto you, that because you *delivered up those writings which you had power given unto you to translate by the means of the *Urim and Thummim, into the hands of a wicked man, you have lost them.

2 And you also lost your gift at the same time, and your *mind became *darkened.

3 Nevertheless, it is now *restored unto you again; therefore see that you are faithful and continue on unto the finishing of the remainder of the work of *translation as you have begun.

4 Do not run *faster or labor more than you have *strength and means provided to enable you to translate; but be *diligent unto the end.

5 *Pray always, that you may come off *conqueror; yea, that you may conquer Satan, and that you may *escape the hands of the servants of Satan that do uphold his work.

6 Behold, they have sought to *destroy you; yea, even the *man in whom you have trusted has sought to destroy you.

7 And for this cause I said that he is a wicked man, for he has sought to take away the things wherewith you have been entrusted; and he has also sought to destroy your gift.

8 And because you have delivered the writings into his hands, behold, wicked men have taken them from you.

9 Therefore, you have delivered them up, yea, that which was *sacred, unto wickedness.

10 And, behold, *Satan hath put it into their hearts to alter the words which you have caused to be *written, or which you have translated, which have gone out of your hands.

11 And behold, I say unto you, that because they have altered the words, they read contrary from that which you translated and caused to be written;

12 And, on this wise, the devil has sought to lay a cunning plan, that he may destroy this work;

13 For he hath put into their hearts to do this, that by lying they may say they have *caught you in the words which you have pretended to translate.

---

10 1 a D&C 3:12 (1–15).
 b TG Urim and Thummim.
2 a Eph. 4:18. TG Mind.
 b D&C 9:9.
3 a D&C 3:10.
 b D&C 9:2 (1–3, 5, 10);
  10:18 (18, 41, 45); 11:19.
4 a Mosiah 4:27; Alma 1:26.

 b Ex. 18:18 (13–26).
  TG Health; Strength.
 c Matt. 10:22. TG Diligence.
5 a TG Prayer.
 b TG Self-Mastery.
 c Ps. 59:2 (1–5).
6 a D&C 5:33 (32–33);

  38:13 (13, 28); 42:64.
 b D&C 3:12 (7–13); 5:2
  (1–18).
9 a TG Sacrilege.
10 a TG Devil.
 b D&C 3:12.
13 a Jer. 5:26.

14 Verily, I say unto you, that I will not suffer that Satan shall accomplish his ^aevil design in this thing.

15 For behold, he has put it into their ^ahearts to get thee to ^btempt the Lord thy God, in asking to translate it over again.

16 And then, behold, they say and think in their hearts—We will see if God has given him power to translate; if so, he will also give him power again;

17 And if God giveth him power again, or if he translates again, or, in other words, if he bringeth forth the same words, behold, we have the same with us, and we have altered them;

18 Therefore they will not agree, and we will say that he has lied in his words, and that he has no ^agift, and that he has no power;

19 Therefore we will destroy him, and also the work; and we will do this that we may not be ashamed in the end, and that we may get ^aglory of the world.

20 Verily, verily, I say unto you, that ^aSatan has great hold upon their hearts; he stirreth them up to ^biniquity against that which is good;

21 And their hearts are ^acorrupt, and ^bfull of wickedness and abominations; and they ^clove ^ddarkness rather than light, because their ^edeeds are evil; therefore they will not ask of me.

22 ^aSatan stirreth them up, that he may ^blead their souls to destruction.

23 And thus he has laid a cunning plan, thinking to ^adestroy the work of God; but I will ^brequire this at their hands, and it shall turn to their shame and condemnation in the day of ^cjudgment.

24 Yea, he stirreth up their hearts to ^aanger against this work.

25 Yea, he saith unto them: ^aDeceive and lie in wait to catch, that ye may destroy; behold, this is no harm. And thus he flattereth them, and telleth them that it is no sin to ^blie that they may catch a man in a lie, that they may destroy him.

26 And thus he ^aflattereth them, and leadeth them along until he draggeth

---

14 a TG Evil.
15 a John 13:2.
　 b TG Test.
18 a D&C 10:3.
19 a Matt. 4:8.
20 a TG Devil.
　 b 2 Ne. 28:20–22. TG Sin.
21 a Gen. 6:5 (5–6, 11); Ps. 14:1; 2 Tim. 3:8; D&C 112:23 (23–24); Moses 8:28 (28–30).
　 b Rev. 17:4.

TG Wickedness.
　 c Moses 5:18 (13–18).
　 d Job 24:13 (13, 16); Mosiah 15:26. TG Darkness, Spiritual.
　 e John 3:19 (18–21); D&C 29:45. TG Evil.
22 a Luke 22:31; 2 Ne. 2:18 (17–18, 27); 3 Ne. 18:18; D&C 50:3.
　 b TG Damnation.
23 a Neh. 6:2 (1–14).

　 b TG Accountability.
　 c Hel. 8:25; D&C 121:24 (23–25).
24 a TG Anger.
25 a Prov. 26:19 (16–19); Luke 20:23; Alma 10:17. TG Lying.
　 b 2 Ne. 2:18; 28:8 (7–23); Moses 4:4. TG Gossip.
26 a TG Apostasy of Individuals.

their souls down to *hell; and thus he causeth them to catch themselves in their own *snare.

27 And thus he goeth up and down, *to and fro in the earth, seeking to *destroy the souls of men.

28 Verily, verily, I say unto you, wo be unto him that *lieth to *deceive because he supposeth that another lieth to deceive, for such are not exempt from the *justice of God.

29 Now, behold, they have altered these words, because Satan saith unto them: He hath deceived you—and thus he *flattereth them away to do iniquity, to get thee to *tempt the Lord thy God.

30 Behold, I say unto you, that you shall not translate again those words which have gone forth out of your hands;

31 For, behold, they shall not accomplish their evil designs in lying against those words. For, behold, if you should bring forth the same words they will say that you have lied and that you have pretended to translate, but that you have contradicted yourself.

32 And, behold, they will publish this, and Satan will *harden the hearts of the people to stir them up to anger against you, that they will not believe my words.

33 Thus *Satan thinketh to overpower your *testimony in this generation, that the work may not come forth in this generation.

34 But behold, here is wisdom, and because I show unto you wisdom, and give you commandments concerning these things, what you shall do, show it not unto the world until you have accomplished the work of translation.

35 Marvel not that I said unto you: Here is *wisdom, show it not unto the world—for I said, show it not unto the world, that you may be preserved.

36 Behold, I do not say that you shall not show it unto the righteous;

37 But as you cannot always judge the *righteous, or as you cannot always tell the wicked from the righteous, therefore I say unto you, hold your *peace until I shall see fit to make all things known unto the world concerning the matter.

---

26 b TG Hell.
  c Esth. 7:10; Ps. 69:22;
    Prov. 29:6 (3–8); Matt.
    7:2 (1–2); 1 Ne. 14:3.
27 a Job 1:7; Prov. 7:12.
  b Rev. 13:7; 2 Ne. 2:18;
    28:20 (19–23); D&C
    76:29.

28 a TG False Doctrine;
    Honesty.
  b TG Deceit.
  c Rom. 2:3.
29 a TG Flatter.
  b Matt. 4:7.
32 a TG Hardheartedness.
33 a TG Devil.

  b TG Testimony.
35 a TG God, Wisdom of.
37 a Prov. 23:9; Matt. 7:6;
    15:26 (26–28); 23:28;
    D&C 6:12 (10–12).
  b Ex. 14:14.

38 And now, verily I say unto you, that an account of those things that you have written, which have gone out of your hands, is engraven upon the *a*plates of Nephi;

39 Yea, and you remember it was said in those writings that a more particular account was given of these things upon the plates of Nephi.

40 And now, because the account which is engraven upon the plates of Nephi is more particular concerning the things which, in my wisdom, I *a*would bring to the knowledge of the people in this account—

41 Therefore, you shall translate the engravings which are on the plates of Nephi, down even till you come to the reign of king Benjamin, or until you come to that which you have translated, which you have retained;

42 And behold, you shall publish it as the record of Nephi; and thus I will *a*confound those who have altered my words.

43 I will not suffer that they shall destroy my *a*work; yea, I will show unto them that my *b*wisdom is greater than the cunning of the devil.

44 Behold, they have only got a part, or an *a*abridgment of the account of Nephi.

45 Behold, there are many things engraven upon the *a*plates of Nephi which do throw greater views upon my gospel; therefore, it is wisdom in me that you should *b*translate this first part of the engravings of Nephi, and send forth in this work.

46 And, behold, all the remainder of this work does contain all those parts of my *a*gospel which my holy prophets, yea, and also my disciples, *b*desired in their prayers should come forth unto this people.

47 And I said unto them, that it should be *a*granted unto them according to their *b*faith in their prayers;

48 Yea, and this was their faith—that my gospel, which I gave unto them that they might preach in their days, might come unto their brethren the *a*Lamanites, and also all that had become Lamanites because of their dissensions.

49 Now, this is not all—their faith in their prayers was that this gospel should be made known also, if it were possible that other nations should possess this land;

---

38 *a* 1 Ne. 9:2 (2–6); W of M 1:3.
40 *a* W of M 1:7 (3–7).
42 *a* TG Book of Mormon. In the Preface to the first edition of the Book of Mormon, the Prophet explained that the material in the 116 pages had been translated from a portion of the plates called the "Book of Lehi."
43 *a* TG God, Works of.
   b TG God, Wisdom of; Wisdom.
44 *a* W of M 1:3.
45 *a* TG Book of Mormon.
   b D&C 10:3.
46 *a* TG Gospel.
   b Enos 1:13 (12–18); Morm. 8:24 (24–26); 9:36 (34–37).
47 *a* Enos 1:16 (13–18); 3 Ne. 5:14 (13–15); D&C 3:19.
   b TG Faith.
48 *a* Moro. 10:1 (1–5); D&C 3:18; 109:65.

50 And thus they did leave a blessing upon this land in their prayers, that whosoever should believe in this ªgospel in this land might have eternal life;

51 Yea, that it might be ªfree unto all of whatsoever nation, kindred, tongue, or people they may be.

52 And now, behold, according to their faith in their prayers will I bring this part of my gospel to the knowledge of my people. Behold, I do not bring it to ªdestroy that which they have received, but to build it up.

53 And for this cause have I said: If this generation ªharden not their hearts, I will establish my ᵇchurch among them.

54 Now I do not say this to destroy my church, but I say this to build up my church;

55 Therefore, whosoever belongeth to my church need not ªfear, for such shall ᵇinherit the ᶜkingdom of heaven.

56 But it is they who do not ªfear me, neither keep my commandments but build up ᵇchurches unto themselves to get ᶜgain, yea, and all those that do wickedly and build up the kingdom of the devil—yea, verily, verily, I say unto you, that it is they that I will disturb, and cause to tremble and shake to the center.

57 Behold, I am Jesus Christ, the ªSon of God. I came unto mine own, and mine own ᵇreceived me not.

58 I am the ªlight which shineth in darkness, and the darkness comprehendeth it not.

59 I am he who said—ªOther ᵇsheep have I which are not of this fold—unto my disciples, and many there were that ᶜunderstood me not.

60 And I will show unto this people that I had other ªsheep, and that they were a ᵇbranch of the house of ᶜJacob;

61 And I will bring to light their marvelous works, which they did in my name;

62 Yea, and I will also bring to light my gospel which was ministered unto them, and, behold, they shall not deny that which you have received, but they shall build it up, and shall bring to light the true points of my ªdoctrine, yea, and the only doctrine which is in me.

---

50 a TG Gospel.
51 a TG Mission of Latter-day Saints.
52 a Matt. 5:17.
53 a TG Hardheartedness.
   b TG Church.
55 a TG Courage; Fearful.
   b Matt. 5:10 (3, 10).
   c TG Kingdom of God, in Heaven.

56 a Eccl. 8:13 (12–13); 12:13–14; Jer. 44:10 (10–11); Rom. 3:18; D&C 45:39.
   b TG Devil, Church of.
   c 4 Ne. 1:26. TG Selfishness.
57 a Rom. 1:4.
   b TG Prophets, Rejection of.

58 a D&C 6:21.
59 a John 10:16.
   b TG Jesus Christ, Good Shepherd.
   c 3 Ne. 15:16–18.
60 a TG Sheep.
   b TG Israel, Joseph, People of; Vineyard of the Lord.
   c TG Israel, Origins of.
62 a 1 Ne. 13:34 (34–42).

63 And this I do that I may establish my gospel, that there may not be so much *a*contention; yea, *b*Satan doth *c*stir up the hearts of the people to *d*contention concerning the points of my doctrine; and in these things they do err, for they do *e*wrest the scriptures and do not understand them.

64 Therefore, I will unfold unto them this great mystery;

65 For, behold, I will *a*gather them as a hen gathereth her chickens under her wings, if they will not harden their hearts;

66 Yea, if they will come, they may, and partake of the *a*waters of life freely.

67 Behold, this is my doctrine—whosoever repenteth and *a*cometh unto me, the same is my *b*church.

68 Whosoever *a*declareth more or less than this, the same is not of me, but is *b*against me; therefore he is not of my church.

69 And now, behold, whosoever is of my church, and *a*endureth of my church to the end, him will I establish upon my *b*rock, and the *c*gates of hell shall not prevail against them.

70 And now, remember the words of him who is the life and *a*light of the *b*world, your Redeemer, your *c*Lord and your God. Amen.

SECTION 11

Revelation given through Joseph Smith the Prophet to his brother Hyrum Smith, at Harmony, Pennsylvania, May 1829. This revelation was received through the Urim and Thummim in answer to Joseph's supplication and inquiry. Joseph Smith's history suggests that this revelation was received after the restoration of the Aaronic Priesthood.

1–6, Laborers in the vineyard will gain salvation; 7–14, Seek wisdom, cry repentance, trust in the Spirit; 15–22, Keep the commandments, and study the Lord's word; 23–27, Deny not the spirit of revelation and of prophecy; 28–30, Those who receive Christ become the sons of God.

1 *a*A great and marvelous work is about to come forth among the children of men.

---

63 a TG Self-Mastery; Strife.
  b TG Devil.
  c TG Provoking.
  d TG Contention; Disputations.
  e 2 Pet. 3:16.
65 a Luke 13:34; D&C 39:22.
  TG Israel, Gathering of;
  Last Days.
66 a TG Living Water.

67 a Matt. 11:28.
  b TG Church; Jesus Christ,
  Head of the Church.
68 a 1 Tim. 6:3.
  b Luke 11:23.
69 a TG Perseverance.
  b D&C 6:34; 11:16 (16,
  24); 18:4 (4, 17); 33:13.
  TG Rock.
  c Matt. 16:18; D&C 17:8;

  18:5; 21:6; 33:13; 98:22;
  109:26.
70 a TG Jesus Christ, Light
  of the World; Light of
  Christ.
  b TG World.
  c TG Jesus Christ, Lord.
11 1 a Isa. 29:14; D&C 4:1
  (1–7).

2 Behold, I am God; give *a*heed to my *b*word, which is quick and *c*powerful, *d*sharper than a two-edged sword, to the dividing asunder of both joints and marrow; therefore give *e*heed unto my word.

3 Behold, the field is *a*white already to harvest; therefore, whoso desireth to reap let him thrust in his sickle with his *b*might, and reap while the day lasts, that he may *c*treasure up for his soul *d*everlasting salvation in the kingdom of God.

4 Yea, whosoever will thrust in his sickle and *a*reap, the same is *b*called of God.

5 Therefore, if you will ask of me you shall receive; if you will *a*knock it shall be opened unto you.

6 Now, as you have asked, behold, I say unto you, keep my commandments, and seek to bring forth and establish the cause of *a*Zion.

7 Seek not for *a*riches but for *b*wisdom; and, behold, the mysteries of God shall be unfolded unto you, and then shall you be made *c*rich. Behold, he that hath eternal life is rich.

8 Verily, verily, I say unto you, even as you desire of me so it shall be done unto you; and, if you desire, you shall be the means of doing much good in this generation.

9 *a*Say nothing but *b*repentance unto this generation. Keep my commandments, and assist to bring forth my *c*work, *d*according to my commandments, and you shall be blessed.

10 Behold, thou hast a *a*gift, or thou shalt have a gift if thou wilt desire of me in faith, with an *b*honest heart, believing in the power of Jesus Christ, or in my power which speaketh unto thee;

11 For, behold, it is I that speak; behold, I am the *a*light which shineth in darkness, and by my *b*power I give these words unto thee.

12 And now, verily, verily, I say unto thee, put your *a*trust in that *b*Spirit which *c*leadeth to do *d*good—yea, to do *e*justly, to walk *f*humbly, to *g*judge righteously; and this is my Spirit.

2 *a* D&C 1:14 (14, 37);
84:43 (43–45).
b Heb. 4:12.
c Alma 4:19; 31:5.
d Hel. 3:29; D&C 6:2.
e 1 Ne. 15:25 (23–25).
3 *a* D&C 4:4.
b TG Dedication.
c TG Treasure.
d 1 Tim. 6:19.
4 *a* TG Harvest.
b Rev. 14:15; D&C 4:3;
6:4; 12:4 (3–4); 14:4
(3–4).
5 *a* TG Objectives; Prayer.

6 *a* Isa. 52:8; D&C 66:11.
TG Zion.
7 *a* 1 Kgs. 3:11 (11–13);
2 Ne. 26:31; Jacob 2:18
(17–19); D&C 38:39.
b TG Education; Wisdom.
c TG Treasure.
9 *a* D&C 19:21 (21–22).
b TG Repent.
c TG God, Works of.
d D&C 105:5.
10 *a* D&C 46:8.
b Luke 8:15. TG Motivations.
11 *a* TG Light of Christ.

b TG Jesus Christ, Authority of.
12 *a* Prov. 28:25 (25–26);
D&C 84:116. TG Trust
in God.
b Rom. 8:1 (1–9); 1 Jn. 4:1
(1–6). TG God, Spirit of.
c TG Guidance, Divine.
d TG Benevolence.
e TG Justice.
f TG Humility.
g Matt. 7:1 (1–5); Rom.
14:4 (4–6); Alma 41:14
(14–15).

13 Verily, verily, I say unto you, I will impart unto you of my Spirit, which shall ^aenlighten your ^bmind, which shall fill your soul with ^cjoy;

14 And then shall ye know, or by this shall you know, all things whatsoever you desire of me, which are pertaining unto things of ^arighteousness, in faith believing in me that you shall receive.

15 Behold, I command you that you need not suppose that you are ^acalled to ^bpreach ^cuntil you are called.

16 Wait a little longer, until you shall have my word, my ^arock, my ^bchurch, and my gospel, that you may know of a surety my doctrine.

17 And then, behold, according to your desires, yea, even according to your ^afaith shall it be done unto you.

18 Keep my commandments; hold your peace; appeal unto my Spirit;

19 Yea, ^acleave unto me with all your heart, that you may assist in bringing to light those things of which has been spoken—yea, the ^btranslation of my work; be patient until you shall accomplish it.

20 Behold, this is your work, to ^akeep my commandments, yea, with all your might, ^bmind and strength.

21 Seek not to ^adeclare my word, but first seek to ^bobtain my ^cword, and then shall your tongue be loosed; then, if you desire, you shall have my ^dSpirit and my word, yea, the power of God unto the ^econvincing of men.

22 But now hold your ^apeace; study ^bmy word which hath gone forth among the children of men, and also ^cstudy my word which shall come forth among the children of men, or that which is ^dnow translating, yea, until you have obtained all which I shall ^egrant unto the children of men in this generation, and then shall all things be added thereto.

23 Behold thou art ^aHyrum, my son; ^bseek the kingdom of God, and all things shall be added according to that which is just.

24 ^aBuild upon my ^brock, which is my ^cgospel;

13a Eph. 1:18; D&C 76:12. TG Discernment, Spiritual; Inspiration; Light of Christ.
b TG Mind.
c TG Joy.
14a TG Righteousness.
15a TG Authority.
b A of F 1:5. TG Preaching.
c D&C 30:5.
16a D&C 6:34; 10:69; 18:4 (4, 17); 33:13. TG Rock.
b TG Church; Jesus Christ, Head of the Church.
17a TG Faith.
19a Josh. 23:8; Jacob 6:5; Hel. 4:25.
b D&C 10:3.
20a Ex. 15:26; D&C 5:35. TG Commitment; Obedience.
b TG Dedication.
21a TG Missionary Work; Preaching.
b Alma 17:2 (2–3); D&C 84:85.
c TG Learn; Scriptures, Value of.
d TG Teaching with the Spirit.
e TG Conversion.
22a Ex. 14:14.
b IE the Bible.
c TG Education; Scriptures, Study of; Study.
d IE the Book of Mormon.
e Alma 29:8; 3 Ne. 26:8 (7–10).
23a JS—H 1:4.
b Matt. 6:33.
24a Matt. 7:24.
b TG Rock.
c TG Gospel.

25 Deny not the spirit of *revelation, nor the spirit of *prophecy, for wo unto him that *denieth these things;

26 Therefore, *treasure up in your *heart until the time which is in my wisdom that you shall go forth.

27 Behold, I speak unto *all who have good desires, and have thrust in their sickle to reap.

28 Behold, I am Jesus Christ, the *Son of God. I am the life and the *light of the world.

29 I am the same who came unto mine own and mine own *received me not;

30 But verily, verily, I say unto you, that as many as receive me, to them will I give *power to become the *sons of God, even to them that *believe on my name. Amen.

SECTION 12

Revelation given through Joseph Smith the Prophet to Joseph Knight Sr., at Harmony, Pennsylvania, May 1829. Joseph Knight believed the declarations of Joseph Smith concerning his possession of the Book of Mormon plates and the work of translation then in progress and several times had given material assistance to Joseph Smith and his scribe, which enabled them to continue translating. At Joseph Knight's request, the Prophet inquired of the Lord and received the revelation.

1–6, Laborers in the vineyard are to gain salvation; 7–9, All who desire and are qualified may assist in the Lord's work.

1 *A great and *marvelous work is about to come forth among the children of men.

2 Behold, I am God; give heed to my *word, which is quick and powerful, sharper than a two-edged sword, to the dividing asunder of both joints and marrow; therefore, give heed unto my word.

3 Behold, the field is *white already to harvest; therefore, whoso desireth

25 a TG Revelation.
  b Rev. 19:10. TG Prophecy.
  c TG Apostasy of Individuals.
26 a Deut. 11:18; D&C 6:20; 43:34; 84:85; JS—M 1:37.
  b Prov. 20:5.
27 a TG Mission of Latter-day

Saints.
28 a Rom. 1:4.
  b TG Jesus Christ, Light of the World; Light [noun].
29 a TG Prophets, Rejection of.
30 a John 1:12.
  b TG Sons and Daughters of God.

  c 1 Jn. 3:23 (19–24).
12 1 a See D&C 11:1–6 for similar concepts and cross-references.
  b Isa. 29:14; D&C 4:1 (1–4).
2 a Heb. 4:12.
3 a D&C 4:4; 14:3; 33:3 (3, 7); 101:64.

to reap let him thrust in his sickle with his might, and reap while the day lasts, that he may treasure up for his soul everlasting salvation in the kingdom of God.

4 Yea, whosoever will thrust in his sickle and ªreap, the same is ᵇcalled of God.

5 Therefore, if you will ask of me you shall receive; if you will knock it shall be opened unto you.

6 Now, as you have asked, behold, I say unto you, keep my commandments, and seek to bring forth and establish the cause of ªZion.

7 Behold, I speak unto you, and also to all those who have desires to bring forth and establish this work;

8 And no one can assist in this work except he shall be ªhumble and full of ᵇlove, having faith, hope, and charity, being temperate in all things, whatsoever shall be ᶜentrusted to his care.

9 Behold, I am the light and the life of the world, that speak these words, therefore give heed with your might, and then you are called. Amen.

SECTION 13

An extract from Joseph Smith's history recounting the ordination of the Prophet and Oliver Cowdery to the Aaronic Priesthood near Harmony, Pennsylvania, May 15, 1829. The ordination was done by the hands of an angel who announced himself as John, the same that is called John the Baptist in the New Testament. The angel explained that he was acting under the direction of Peter, James, and John, the ancient Apostles, who held the keys of the higher priesthood, which was called the Priesthood of Melchizedek. The promise was given to Joseph and Oliver that in due time this higher priesthood would be conferred upon them. (See section 27:7–8, 12.)

The keys and powers of the Aaronic Priesthood are set forth.

1 Upon you my fellow servants, in the name of Messiah I ªconfer the ᵇPriesthood of Aaron, which holds the ᶜkeys of the ministering of ᵈangels,

---

4 *a* Rev. 14:15.
  b D&C 6:4; 11:4 (3–4, 27); 14:4 (3–4).
6 *a* Isa. 52:8.
8 *a* TG Humility.
  b TG Charity; Faith; Hope; Love; Temperance.

c 1 Thes. 2:4; D&C 124:113.
13 1 *a* JS—H 1:69 (68–75). TG Delegation of Responsibility; Ordain; Priesthood, Authority; Restoration of the

Gospel.
  b D&C 27:8. TG Priesthood, Aaronic.
  c D&C 84:26. TG Priesthood, Keys of.
  d TG Angels.

and of the gospel of ^{c}repentance, and of ^{f}baptism by immersion for the remission of sins; and this shall never be taken again from the earth, until the ^{g}sons of Levi do offer again an offering unto the Lord in ^{h}righteousness.

SECTION 14

Revelation given through Joseph Smith the Prophet to David Whitmer, at Fayette, New York, June 1829. The Whitmer family had become greatly interested in the translating of the Book of Mormon. The Prophet established his residence at the home of Peter Whitmer Sr., where he dwelt until the work of translation was carried to completion and the copyright on the forthcoming book was secured. Three of the Whitmer sons, each having received a testimony as to the genuineness of the work, became deeply concerned over the matter of their individual duty. This revelation and the two following (sections 15 and 16) were given in answer to an inquiry through the Urim and Thummim. David Whitmer later became one of the Three Witnesses to the Book of Mormon.

1–6, Laborers in the vineyard will gain salvation; 7–8, Eternal life is the greatest of God's gifts; 9–11, Christ created the heavens and the earth.

1 ^{a}A great and marvelous work is about to come forth unto the children of men.

2 Behold, I am God; give heed to my word, which is quick and powerful, sharper than a two-edged sword, to the dividing asunder of both joints and marrow; therefore give heed unto my word.

3 Behold, the field is white already to harvest; therefore, whoso desireth to reap let him thrust in his sickle with his might, and reap while the day lasts, that he may treasure up for his soul everlasting salvation in the kingdom of God.

4 Yea, whosoever will thrust in his sickle and reap, the same is called of God.

5 Therefore, if you will ask of me you shall receive; if you will ^{a}knock it shall be opened unto you.

---

1 *e* D&C 84:26 (26–28).
　TG Repent.
　f TG Baptism; Remission of Sins.
　g See JS—H 1:71, footnote by Oliver Cowdery on

the restoration of the Aaronic Priesthood. Gen. 49:5; Deut. 10:8; 1 Chr. 6:48; 23:24; D&C 84:31 (18–34); 124:39; 128:24; JS—H 1:69.

h TG Righteousness.
14 1 *a* See D&C 11:1–6 for similar concepts and cross-references.
5 *a* TG Objectives.

6 Seek to bring forth and establish my Zion. Keep my commandments in all things.

7 And, if you *a*keep my commandments and *b*endure to the end you shall have *c*eternal life, which gift is the greatest of all the gifts of God.

8 And it shall come to pass, that if you shall ask the Father in my name, in faith *a*believing, you shall receive the *b*Holy Ghost, which *c*giveth utterance, that you may stand as a *d*witness of the things of which you shall both *e*hear and see, and also that you may declare *f*repentance unto this generation.

9 Behold, I am *a*Jesus Christ, the *b*Son of the *c*living God, who *d*created the heavens and the *e*earth, a *f*light which cannot be hid in *g*darkness;

10 Wherefore, I must bring forth the *a*fulness of my *b*gospel from the *c*Gentiles unto the house of Israel.

11 And behold, thou art David, and thou art called to assist; which thing if ye do, and are faithful, ye shall be blessed both spiritually and temporally, and great shall be your reward. Amen.

SECTION 15

Revelation given through Joseph Smith the Prophet to John Whitmer, at Fayette, New York, June 1829 (see the heading to section 14). The message is intimately and impressively personal in that the Lord tells of what was known only to John Whitmer and Himself. John Whitmer later became one of the Eight Witnesses to the Book of Mormon.

1–2, The Lord's arm is over all the earth; 3–6, To preach the gospel and save souls is the thing of most worth.

1 Hearken, my servant John, and listen to the words of Jesus Christ, your Lord and your Redeemer.

---

7 *a* Ps. 19:11 (9–11); Prov. 7:2; Mosiah 2:22; D&C 58:2.
  b TG Steadfastness.
  c D&C 6:13; 88:4. TG Eternal Life; Exaltation; God, Gifts of; Man, Potential to Become like Heavenly Father.
8 *a* 2 Cor. 4:13. TG Trust in God.
  b Acts 2:4.
  c TG Holy Ghost, Mission of.

d Acts 26:16; 2 Ne. 27:12 (12–14); Ether 5:4 (3–5). TG Witness.
  e See "The Testimony of Three Witnesses" in the preliminary pages of the Book of Mormon.
  f TG Repent.
9 *a* Mosiah 4:2; Morm. 9:11; D&C 76:24 (20–24).
  b Rom. 1:4.
  c Dan. 6:26; Alma 7:6; D&C 20:19.
  d Jer. 14:22; Acts 4:24

(23–24); Mosiah 4:2; 3 Ne. 9:15; D&C 45:1. TG Creation; Jesus Christ, Creator.
  e Abr. 4:12 (12, 24–25).
  f 2 Sam. 22:29. TG Light [noun]; Light of Christ.
  g TG Darkness, Spiritual.
10 *a* Rom. 15:29; D&C 20:9 (8–9); JS—H 1:34.
  b TG Israel, Restoration of.
  c 1 Ne. 10:14; 13:42; 15:13 (13–20).

2 For behold, I speak unto you with *sharpness and with power, for mine arm is over all the *earth.

3 And I will *tell you that which no man *knoweth save me and thee alone—

4 For many times you have desired of me to know that which would be of the most worth unto you.

5 Behold, blessed are you for this thing, and for speaking my words which I have given you according to my commandments.

6 And now, behold, I say unto you, that the thing which will be of the most worth unto you will be to *declare *repentance unto this people, that you may bring *souls unto me, that you may *rest with them in the *kingdom of my *Father. Amen.

SECTION 16

Revelation given through Joseph Smith the Prophet to Peter Whitmer Jr., at Fayette, New York, June 1829 (see the heading to section 14). Peter Whitmer Jr. later became one of the Eight Witnesses to the Book of Mormon.

1–2, The Lord's arm is over all the earth; 3–6, To preach the gospel and save souls is the thing of most worth.

1 *Hearken, my servant Peter, and listen to the words of Jesus Christ, your Lord and your Redeemer.

2 For behold, I speak unto you with sharpness and with power, for mine arm is over all the earth.

3 And I will tell you that which no man knoweth save me and thee alone—

4 For many times you have desired of me to know that which would be of the most worth unto you.

5 Behold, blessed are you for this thing, and for speaking my words which I have given unto you according to my commandments.

---

15 2 *a* Hel. 3:29 (29–30).
TG God, Power of.
b Ex. 9:29; D&C 14:9;
Abr. 4:12 (12, 24–25).
3 *a* TG God, Omniscience of.
b D&C 6:16.

6 *a* D&C 6:6; 18:15 (15–16);
30:9 (9–10).
b TG Missionary Work;
Repent.
c TG Conversion; Soul;
Worth of Souls.
d TG Rest.

e TG Kingdom of God, in Heaven.
f TG God the Father, Elohim.
16 1 *a* See D&C 15 for similar concepts and cross-references.

6 And now, behold, I say unto you, that the thing which will be of the most worth unto you will be to declare repentance unto this people, that you may bring souls unto me, that you may rest with them in the kingdom of my Father. Amen.

SECTION 17

Revelation given through Joseph Smith the Prophet to Oliver Cowdery, David Whitmer, and Martin Harris, at Fayette, New York, June 1829, prior to their viewing the engraved plates that contained the Book of Mormon record. Joseph and his scribe, Oliver Cowdery, had learned from the translation of the Book of Mormon plates that three special witnesses would be designated (see Ether 5:2–4; 2 Nephi 11:3; 27:12). Oliver Cowdery, David Whitmer, and Martin Harris were moved upon by an inspired desire to be the three special witnesses. The Prophet inquired of the Lord, and this revelation was given in answer through the Urim and Thummim.

1–4, By faith the Three Witnesses will see the plates and other sacred items; 5–9, Christ bears testimony of the divinity of the Book of Mormon.

1 Behold, I say unto you, that you must rely upon my word, which if you do with full purpose of heart, you shall have a *a*view of the *b*plates, and also of the *c*breastplate, the *d*sword of Laban, the *e*Urim and Thummim, which were given to the *f*brother of Jared upon the mount, when he talked with the Lord *g*face to face, and the *h*miraculous directors which were given to Lehi while in the wilderness, on the borders of the *i*Red Sea.

2 And it is by your faith that you shall obtain a view of them, even by that faith which was had by the prophets of old.

3 And after that you have obtained faith, and have seen them with your eyes, you shall *a*testify of them, by the power of God;

4 And this you shall do that my servant Joseph Smith, Jun., may not be destroyed, that I may bring about my righteous purposes unto the children of men in this work.

---

17 1 *a* 2 Ne. 27:12; Ether
    5:4 (2–4); D&C 5:15
    (15, 24). See also "The
    Testimony of Three
    Witnesses" in the prelim-
    inary pages of the Book
    of Mormon.
  b Morm. 6:6; Ether 4:5

  (4–7); JS—H 1:52.
c Ex. 25:7.
d 1 Ne. 4:9; 2 Ne. 5:14;
    Jacob 1:10; Mosiah 1:16.
e TG Urim and Thummim.
    BD Urim and Thummim.
f Ether 3:28 (1–28).
g Gen. 32:30; Num. 12:8;
    Moses 1:2.

h 1 Ne. 16:16 (10, 16,
    26); 18:12 (12, 21);
    2 Ne. 5:12; Alma 37:38
    (38–47).
i 1 Ne. 2:5.
3 *a* Ether 5:3 (3–4); D&C
    5:11. TG Witness.

5 And ye shall testify that you have seen them, even as my servant Joseph Smith, Jun., has seen them; for it is by my power that he has seen them, and it is because he had faith.

6 And he has translated the ᵃbook, even that ᵇpart which I have commanded him, and as your Lord and your God liveth it is true.

7 Wherefore, you have received the same power, and the same faith, and the same gift like unto him;

8 And if you do these last ᵃcommandments of mine, which I have given you, the ᵇgates of hell shall not prevail against you; for my ᶜgrace is sufficient for you, and you shall be ᵈlifted up at the last day.

9 And I, Jesus Christ, your ᵃLord and your God, have spoken it unto you, that I might bring about my righteous purposes unto the children of men. Amen.

SECTION 18

Revelation to Joseph Smith the Prophet, Oliver Cowdery, and David Whitmer, given at Fayette, New York, June 1829. According to the Prophet, this revelation made known "the calling of twelve apostles in these last days, and also instructions relative to building up the Church."

1–5, Scriptures show how to build up the Church; 6–8, The world is ripening in iniquity; 9–16, The worth of souls is great; 17–25, To gain salvation, men must take upon themselves the name of Christ; 26–36, The calling and mission of the Twelve are revealed; 37–39, Oliver Cowdery and David Whitmer are to search out the Twelve; 40–47, To gain salvation, men must repent, be baptized, and keep the commandments.

1 Now, behold, because of the thing which you, my servant Oliver Cowdery, have desired to know of me, I give unto you these words:

2 Behold, I have ᵃmanifested unto you, by my Spirit in many instances, that the ᵇthings which you have written are ᶜtrue; wherefore you know that they are true.

3 And if you know that they are true, behold, I give unto you a commandment, that you ᵃrely upon the things which are ᵇwritten;

---

6 a TG Book of Mormon.
  b 2 Ne. 27:8 (7–11, 21);
    3 Ne. 26:9 (7–12, 18);
    Ether 4:5 (4–7); 5:1.
8 a D&C 19:13.
  b Matt. 16:18; 1 Ne. 22:26;
    Alma 48:17 (16–17);
    3 Ne. 11:39 (39–40);

D&C 10:69.
  c TG Grace.
  d 1 Ne. 13:37; 3 Ne. 27:14
    (14–15, 22); D&C 5:35;
    9:14; 27:18.
9 a TG Jesus Christ, Lord.
18 2 a D&C 6:24 (22–24).
  b D&C 9:4.

c D&C 6:17 (15–17).
3 a Prov. 22:21; D&C 98:11.
    TG Dependability; Guidance, Divine; Scriptures, Value of.
  b D&C 18:30 (29–30).

4 For in them are all things *a*written concerning the foundation of my church, my gospel, and my *b*rock.

5 Wherefore, if you shall build up my *a*church, upon the foundation of my gospel and my *b*rock, the *c*gates of hell shall not prevail against you.

6 Behold, the *a*world is *b*ripening in iniquity; and it must needs be that the children of men are stirred up unto repentance, both the *c*Gentiles and also the house of Israel.

7 Wherefore, as thou hast been *a*baptized by the hands of my servant Joseph Smith, Jun., according to that which I have commanded him, he hath fulfilled the thing which I commanded him.

8 And now, marvel not that I have *a*called him unto mine own purpose, which purpose is known in me; wherefore, if he shall be *b*diligent in keeping my commandments he shall be *c*blessed unto eternal life; and his name is *d*Joseph.

9 And now, Oliver Cowdery, I speak unto you, and also unto David Whitmer, by the way of commandment; for, behold, I *a*command all men everywhere to repent, and I speak unto you, even as unto Paul mine *b*apostle, for you are called even with that same calling with which he was called.

10 Remember the *a*worth of *b*souls is great in the sight of God;

11 For, behold, the Lord your *a*Redeemer suffered *b*death in the flesh; wherefore he *c*suffered the *d*pain of all men, that all men might repent and *e*come unto him.

12 And he hath *a*risen again from the dead, that he might bring all men unto him, on conditions of *b*repentance.

13 And how great is his *a*joy in the *b*soul that *c*repenteth!

14 Wherefore, you are called to *a*cry repentance unto this people.

15 And if it so be that you should labor all your days in crying repentance unto this people, and bring, save it be one *a*soul unto me, how great shall be your joy with him in the kingdom of my Father!

---

4 a D&C 20:9 (8–11); 39:11; 68:1. TG Gospel.
 b D&C 6:34; 10:69; 11:16 (16, 24); 33:13.
5 a TG Church; Jesus Christ, Head of the Church.
 b TG Rock.
 c Matt. 16:18; D&C 10:69.
6 a TG World.
 b Rev. 14:15.
 c 1 Ne. 13:42; D&C 18:26; 19:27; 21:12; 90:9 (8–9); 107:33; 112:4. TG Gentiles; Israel, Restoration of; Missionary Work.

7 a JS—H 1:71 (70–71).
8 a D&C 9:12.
 b TG Diligence.
 c TG Blessing.
 d 2 Ne. 3:15 (14–15). TG Joseph Smith.
9 a Acts 17:30.
 b Rom. 1:1.
10 a Isa. 43:4. TG Life, Sanctity of; Worth of Souls.
 b TG Soul.
11 a TG Jesus Christ, Redeemer.
 b TG Death; Jesus Christ, Death of.

 c TG Redemption; Self-Sacrifice.
 d Isa. 53:4 (4–5). TG Jesus Christ, Atonement through; Pain.
 e John 12:32.
12 a TG Jesus Christ, Resurrection.
 b D&C 19:4 (4–18).
13 a Luke 15:7.
 b TG Worth of Souls.
 c TG Repent.
14 a D&C 6:9; 34:6; 63:57.
15 a TG Missionary Work; Worth of Souls.

16 And now, if your joy will be great with one soul that you have brought unto me into the *a*kingdom of my Father, how great will be your *b*joy if you should bring many *c*souls unto me!

17 Behold, you have my gospel before you, and my rock, and my *a*salvation.

18 *a*Ask the Father in my *b*name in faith, believing that you shall receive, and you shall have the Holy Ghost, which manifesteth all things which are *c*expedient unto the children of men.

19 And if you have not *a*faith, *b*hope, and *c*charity, you can do nothing.

20 *a*Contend against no church, save it be the *b*church of the devil.

21 Take upon you the *a*name of Christ, and *b*speak the truth in *c*soberness.

22 And as many as repent and are *a*baptized in my name, which is Jesus Christ, and *b*endure to the end, the same shall be saved.

23 Behold, Jesus Christ is the *a*name which is given of the Father, and there is none other name given whereby man can be *b*saved;

24 Wherefore, all men must take upon them the *a*name which is given of the Father, for in that name shall they be called at the last day;

25 Wherefore, if they *a*know not the *b*name by which they are called, they cannot have place in the *c*kingdom of my Father.

26 And now, behold, there are others who are *a*called to declare my gospel, both unto *b*Gentile and unto Jew;

27 Yea, even twelve; and the *a*Twelve shall be my disciples, and they shall take upon them my name; and the Twelve are they who shall desire to take upon them my *b*name with full purpose of heart.

28 And if they desire to take upon them my name with full purpose of heart, they are called to go into all the *a*world to preach my *b*gospel unto *c*every creature.

16a TG Kingdom of God, in
   Heaven.
  b John 4:36; 1 Thes. 3:9;
   Alma 26:11 (11–13);
   D&C 50:22 (17–22).
   TG Joy.
  c TG Conversion.
17a TG Rock; Salvation.
18a TG Prayer.
  b John 15:16.
  c D&C 88:64 (63–65).
19a TG Faith.
  b TG Hope.
  c TG Charity.
20a 2 Tim. 2:24 (23–24);
   3 Ne. 11:29 (29–30).

  b TG Devil, Church of.
21a TG Jesus Christ, Taking
   the Name of.
  b 2 Cor. 4:13; D&C 100:7
   (5–8).
  c Rom. 12:3; D&C 43:35.
22a TG Baptism, Essential.
  b TG Perseverance; Steadfastness.
23a Mal. 1:11; Acts 4:12.
  b TG Jesus Christ, Atonement through; Jesus
   Christ, Savior; Salvation;
   Salvation, Plan of.
24a TG Jesus Christ, Taking
   the Name of.

25a TG Ignorance.
  b Mosiah 5:12 (9–14).
  c TG Kingdom of God, in
   Heaven.
26a TG Authority.
  b 1 Ne. 13:42; D&C 18:6;
   19:27; 21:12; 90:9 (8–9);
   107:33; 112:4.
27a TG Apostles.
  b Jer. 15:16; D&C 27:12.
28a Mark 16:15 (15–16).
  b TG Gospel.
  c D&C 1:2 (2, 34–35);
   39:15; 42:58.

29 And they are they who are ordained of me to ^abaptize in my name, according to that which is written;

30 And you have that which is written before you; wherefore, you must perform it ^aaccording to the words which are ^bwritten.

31 And now I speak unto you, the ^aTwelve—Behold, my grace is sufficient for you; you must walk uprightly before me and sin not.

32 And, behold, you are they who are ordained of me to ^aordain priests and teachers; to declare my gospel, ^baccording to the power of the Holy Ghost which is in you, and according to the ^ccallings and gifts of God unto men;

33 And I, Jesus Christ, your Lord and your God, have spoken it.

34 These ^awords are not of men nor of man, but of me; wherefore, you shall testify they are of me and not of man;

35 For it is my ^avoice which speaketh them unto you; for they are given by my Spirit unto you, and by my power you can read them one to another; and save it were by my power you could not have them;

36 Wherefore, you can ^atestify that you have ^bheard my voice, and know my words.

37 And now, behold, I give unto you, Oliver Cowdery, and also unto David Whitmer, that you shall search out the Twelve, who shall have the desires of which I have spoken;

38 And by their ^adesires and their ^bworks you shall know them.

39 And when you have found them you shall show these things unto them.

40 And you shall fall down and ^aworship the Father in my ^bname.

41 And you must preach unto the world, saying: You must ^arepent and be baptized, in the name of Jesus Christ;

42 For all men must repent and be baptized, and not only men, but women, and ^achildren who have arrived at the years of ^baccountability.

43 And now, after that you have received this, you must keep my ^acommandments in all things;

---

29 a John 4:2 (1–2); 3 Ne.
  11:22 (21–22); 12:1;
  D&C 20:38.
30 a 3 Ne. 11:22 (22–28);
  D&C 20:72 (72–74).
  b D&C 18:3 (3–4).
31 a D&C 107:23 (23–39).
32 a Moro. 3:4 (1–4); D&C
  20:39 (39, 60); 107:58.
  TG Priesthood, Ordina-
  tion.

  b 2 Pet. 1:21; D&C 68:3
  (3–4).
  c D&C 20:27.
34 a TG Scriptures, Value of.
35 a D&C 1:38. TG Revela-
  tion.
36 a TG Testimony.
  b Ex. 19:9 (7–13).
38 a TG Motivations.
  b TG Good Works.
40 a TG Worship.

  b 1 Kgs. 8:29. TG Name.
41 a TG Baptism, Essential;
  Repent.
42 a TG Children; Family,
  Children, Duties of.
  b D&C 20:71; 29:47;
  68:25 (25–27).
43 a TG Commandments of
  God.

44 And by your hands I will work a *marvelous work among the children of men, unto the *convincing of many of their sins, that they may come unto repentance, and that they may come unto the kingdom of my Father.

45 Wherefore, the blessings which I give unto you are *above all things.

46 And after that you have received this, if you *keep not my commandments you cannot be saved in the kingdom of my Father.

47 Behold, I, Jesus Christ, your Lord and your God, and your *Redeemer, by the *power of my Spirit have spoken it. Amen.

SECTION 19

Revelation given through Joseph Smith, at Manchester, New York, likely in the summer of 1829. In his history, the Prophet introduces it as "a commandment of God and not of man, to Martin Harris, given by him who is Eternal."

1–3, Christ has all power; 4–5, All men must repent or suffer; 6–12, Eternal punishment is God's punishment; 13–20, Christ suffered for all, that they might not suffer if they would repent; 21–28, Preach the gospel of repentance; 29–41, Declare glad tidings.

1 I am *Alpha and Omega, *Christ the Lord; yea, even I am he, the beginning and the end, the Redeemer of the *world.

2 I, having accomplished and *finished the will of him whose I am, even the Father, concerning me—having done this that I might *subdue all things unto myself—

3 Retaining all *power, even to the *destroying of Satan and his works at the *end of the world, and the last great day of judgment, which I shall pass upon the inhabitants thereof, *judging every man according to his *works and the deeds which he hath done.

4 And surely every man must *repent or *suffer, for I, God, am *endless.

---

44 *a* Isa. 29:14; D&C 4:1; 6:1.
  b Job 13:23 (23–28); Alma 12:1; 36:17 (12–19); 62:45; D&C 6:11.
45 *a* D&C 76:92; 84:38 (35–38).
46 *a* 1 Pet. 4:17 (17–18); D&C 82:3.
47 *a* TG Jesus Christ, Redeemer.
  b TG Jesus Christ, Power of.

19 1 *a* Rev. 1:8 (8, 11); D&C 35:1; 45:7; 54:1; 61:1; 68:35; 75:1.
  b TG Jesus Christ, Messiah.
  c TG World.
2 *a* John 17:4; 3 Ne. 11:11.
  b Philip. 3:21. TG Jesus Christ, Mission of.
3 *a* TG Jesus Christ, Power of.
  b Gen. 3:15; Rom. 16:20;

1 Jn. 3:8; Rev. 20:10 (8, 10); D&C 29:28 (27–30, 44); 88:114 (111–15).
  c TG World, End of.
  d TG Jesus Christ, Judge; Judgment, the Last; Justice.
  e TG Good Works.
4 *a* TG Repent.
  b Luke 13:3.
  c Moses 1:3.

5 Wherefore, I ^arevoke not the judgments which I shall pass, but woes shall go forth, weeping, ^bwailing and gnashing of teeth, yea, to those who are found on my ^cleft hand.

6 Nevertheless, it is ^anot written that there shall be no end to this torment, but it is written ^bendless ^ctorment.

7 Again, it is written ^aeternal damnation; wherefore it is more express than other scriptures, that it might work upon the hearts of the children of men, altogether for my name's glory.

8 Wherefore, I will explain unto you this ^amystery, for it is meet unto you to know even as mine apostles.

9 I speak unto you that are chosen in this thing, even as one, that you may enter into my ^arest.

10 For, behold, the ^amystery of godliness, how great is it! For, behold, I am ^bendless, and the punishment which is given from my hand is endless ^cpunishment, for ^dEndless is my name. Wherefore—

11 ^aEternal punishment is God's punishment.

12 Endless punishment is God's punishment.

13 Wherefore, I command you to repent, and keep the ^acommandments which you have received by the hand of my servant Joseph Smith, Jun., in my name;

14 And it is by my almighty power that you have received them;

15 Therefore I command you to repent—repent, lest I ^asmite you by the rod of my mouth, and by my wrath, and by my anger, and your ^bsufferings be sore—how sore you know not, how exquisite you know not, yea, how hard to bear you know not.

16 For behold, I, God, have ^asuffered these things for all, that they ^bmight not suffer if they would ^crepent;

17 But if they would not repent they must ^asuffer even as I;

18 Which ^asuffering caused myself, even God, the greatest of all, to

---

5 a D&C 56:4; 58:32.
  b Matt. 13:42.
  c Matt. 25:41.
6 a D&C 76:106 (105–6); 138:59.
  b D&C 76:44 (33, 44–45).
  c TG Punish.
7 a Hel. 12:26 (25–26); D&C 29:44.
8 a Matt. 13:11.
9 a Heb. 4:3 (3, 5); 2 Ne.

21:10.
10 a 1 Tim. 3:16; Jacob 4:8; D&C 76:114 (114–16).
  b TG God, Eternal Nature of.
  c TG Punish.
  d Ex. 3:15; Moses 1:3; 7:35.
11 a Matt. 25:46. TG Punish.
13 a D&C 5:2 (1–18); 10:6 (6–7); 17:8 (1–9).
15 a Ps. 2:9; Isa. 11:4 (1–4).

  b Alma 36:12 (11–19).
16 a 2 Cor. 5:14; Alma 11:40 (40–41). TG Jesus Christ, Atonement through; Jesus Christ, Redeemer; Redemption.
  b TG Mercy.
  c TG Remission of Sins.
17 a Mark 14:36; Alma 11:40 (40–41); D&C 29:17.
18 a TG Pain; Suffering.

tremble because of pain, and to bleed at every pore, and to suffer both body and spirit—and would that I might *b*not drink the bitter cup, and shrink—

19 Nevertheless, glory be to the Father, and I partook and *a*finished my preparations unto the children of men.

20 Wherefore, I command you again to repent, lest I *a*humble you with my almighty power; and that you *b*confess your sins, lest you suffer these *c*punishments of which I have spoken, of which in the smallest, yea, even in the least degree you have *d*tasted at the time I withdrew my Spirit.

21 And I command you that you *a*preach naught but repentance, and show *b*not these things unto the world until it is wisdom in me.

22 For they cannot *a*bear meat now, but *b*milk they must receive; wherefore, they must not know these things, lest they perish.

23 *a*Learn of me, and listen to my words; *b*walk in the *c*meekness of my Spirit, and you shall have *d*peace in me.

24 I am Jesus Christ; I *a*came by the *b*will of the Father, and I do his will.

25 And again, I command thee that thou shalt not *a*covet thy *b*neighbor's *c*wife; nor seek thy neighbor's life.

26 And again, I command thee that thou shalt not *a*covet thine own property, but impart it freely to the printing of the Book of Mormon, which contains the *b*truth and the word of God—

27 Which is my word to the *a*Gentile, that soon it may go to the *b*Jew, of whom the Lamanites are a *c*remnant, that they may believe the gospel, and look not for a *d*Messiah to come who has already come.

28 And again, I command thee that thou shalt *a*pray *b*vocally as well as in thy heart; yea, before the world as well as in secret, in public as well as in private.

---

18 *b* Luke 22:42 (42–44).
19 *a* John 17:4; 19:30; Heb. 12:2 (1–3).
20 *a* TG God, Indignation of.
  b Num. 5:7 (6–10); D&C 58:43; 64:7. TG Confession.
  c TG Despair; Punish.
  d D&C 10:7 (1–7). TG Holy Ghost, Loss of.
21 *a* D&C 11:9.
  b Moses 1:42; 4:32; JS—H 1:42.
22 *a* D&C 78:18 (17–18).
  b Isa. 28:9; 1 Cor. 3:2 (2–3); Heb. 5:12 (11–14);

D&C 50:40.
23 *a* TG Education; Learn.
  b 1 Jn. 2:6; Moro. 7:4 (3–4).
  c TG Meek.
  d Micah 5:5. TG Peace of God.
24 *a* TG Jesus Christ, Birth of.
  b TG God, Will of; Jesus Christ, Authority of.
25 *a* TG Covet.
  b TG Neighbor.
  c Ex. 20:17; 1 Cor. 7:2 (2–4). TG Adulterer; Lust; Marriage, Husbands; Marriage, Wives.

26 *a* Acts 5:1 (1–11).
  b TG Truth.
27 *a* 1 Ne. 13:42; 3 Ne. 16:7 (4–13); D&C 18:6 (6, 26); 21:12; 90:9 (8–9); 107:33; 112:4.
  b 2 Ne. 26:12; 30:7 (7–8); Morm. 5:14 (12–14).
  c Omni 1:15 (14–19); Mosiah 25:2 (2–4); Hel. 8:21; D&C 52:2; 109:65.
  d TG Jesus Christ, Messiah.
28 *a* 1 Tim. 2:8. TG Prayer.
  b D&C 20:47 (47, 51); 23:6.

29 And thou shalt ªdeclare glad tidings, yea, ᵇpublish it upon the mountains, and upon every high place, and among every people that thou shalt be permitted to see.

30 And thou shalt do it with all humility, ªtrusting in me, ᵇreviling not against revilers.

31 And of ªtenets thou shalt not talk, but thou shalt declare repentance and ᵇfaith on the Savior, and ᶜremission of sins by ᵈbaptism, and by ᵉfire, yea, even the ᶠHoly Ghost.

32 Behold, this is a great and the last ªcommandment which I shall give unto you concerning this matter; for this shall suffice for thy daily walk, even unto the end of thy life.

33 And misery thou shalt receive if thou wilt slight these ªcounsels, yea, even the destruction of thyself and property.

34 ªImpart a portion of thy property, yea, even part of thy lands, and all save the support of thy ᵇfamily.

35 Pay the ªdebt thou hast ᵇcontracted with the printer. Release thyself from ᶜbondage.

36 ªLeave thy house and home, except when thou shalt desire to see thy family;

37 And ªspeak freely to all; yea, preach, exhort, declare the ᵇtruth, even with a loud voice, with a sound of rejoicing, crying—Hosanna, hosanna, blessed be the name of the Lord God!

38 ªPray always, and I will ᵇpour out my Spirit upon you, and great shall be your blessing—yea, even more than if you should obtain ᶜtreasures of earth and corruptibleness to the extent thereof.

39 Behold, canst thou read this without ªrejoicing and lifting up thy heart for ᵇgladness?

40 Or canst thou run about longer as a ªblind guide?

41 Or canst thou be ªhumble and meek, and conduct thyself wisely before me? Yea, ᵇcome unto me thy Savior. Amen.

---

29 a TG Preaching.
  b Mark 13:10.
30 a TG Trust in God.
  b TG Forbear; Retribution; Reviling; Strife.
31 a 2 Tim. 2:23 (23–24).
  b TG Baptism, Qualifications for; Faith.
  c TG Remission of Sins.
  d TG Baptism.
  e Matt. 3:11.
  f TG Holy Ghost, Baptism of.

32 a D&C 58:26 (26–29).
33 a TG Counsel.
34 a Acts 4:37 (34–37).
  b TG Family.
35 a TG Debt.
  b IE to pay for the publication of the first edition of the Book of Mormon.
  c Prov. 22:7. TG Bondage, Physical.
36 a Matt. 19:29.
37 a Ps. 105:2; Heb. 13:16; D&C 58:47; 63:37; 68:8;

  71:7.
  b 2 Cor. 4:2; D&C 75:4.
38 a TG Prayer.
  b Prov. 1:23; Acts 2:17; D&C 95:4.
  c TG Treasure.
39 a TG Joy.
  b TG Cheerful.
40 a Matt. 23:16 (16, 24).
41 a TG Humility; Meek.
  b Matt. 11:28 (28–30).

SECTION 20

Revelation on Church organization and government, given through Joseph Smith the Prophet, at or near Fayette, New York. Portions of this revelation may have been given as early as summer 1829. The complete revelation, known at the time as the Articles and Covenants, was likely recorded soon after April 6, 1830 (the day the Church was organized). The Prophet wrote, "We obtained of Him [Jesus Christ] the following, by the spirit of prophecy and revelation; which not only gave us much information, but also pointed out to us the precise day upon which, according to His will and commandment, we should proceed to organize His Church once more here upon the earth."

1–16, The Book of Mormon proves the divinity of the latter-day work; 17–28, The doctrines of creation, fall, atonement, and baptism are affirmed; 29–37, Laws governing repentance, justification, sanctification, and baptism are set forth; 38–67, Duties of elders, priests, teachers, and deacons are summarized; 68–74, Duties of members, blessing of children, and the mode of baptism are revealed; 75–84, Sacramental prayers and regulations governing Church membership are given.

1 The ^arise of the ^bChurch of Christ in these last days, being one thousand eight hundred and thirty years since the ^ccoming of our Lord and Savior Jesus Christ in the flesh, it being regularly ^dorganized and established agreeable to the ^elaws of our country, by the will and commandments of God, in the fourth month, and on the sixth day of the month which is called April—

2 Which commandments were given to Joseph Smith, Jun., who was ^acalled of God, and ^bordained an ^capostle of Jesus Christ, to be the ^dfirst ^eelder of this church;

3 And to Oliver Cowdery, who was also called of God, an apostle of Jesus Christ, to be the ^asecond elder of this church, and ordained under his hand;

4 And this according to the ^agrace of our Lord and Savior Jesus Christ, to whom be all glory, both now and forever. Amen.

5 After it was truly manifested unto this first elder that he had received a ^aremission of his sins, he was ^bentangled again in the ^cvanities of the world;

---

20 1 *a* JS—H 1:2.
   b 3 Ne. 27:3 (1–8); D&C
     1:1. TG Church.
   c Matt. 1:18. TG Jesus
     Christ, Birth of.
   d D&C 21:3.
   e D&C 58:21; 98:4 (4–5).

2 *a* TG Authority; Called of
     God.
   b D&C 5:6.
   c TG Apostles.
   d D&C 21:11; 30:7.
   e TG Elder, Melchizedek
     Priesthood.
3 *a* D&C 28:1.

4 *a* TG Grace.
5 *a* D&C 21:8; 23:5; JS—H
     1:73 (68–74). TG Remission of Sins.
   b 2 Pet. 2:20; D&C 3:6;
     5:21; 20:32 (31–34);
     JS—H 1:28 (28–29).
   c Ps. 25:7. TG Vanity.

6 But after *repenting, and humbling himself sincerely, through faith, God ministered unto him by an holy *angel, whose *countenance was as lightning, and whose garments were pure and white above all other whiteness;

7 And gave unto him *commandments which inspired him;

8 And *gave him power from on high, by the *means which were before prepared, to translate the Book of Mormon;

9 Which contains a *record of a fallen people, and the *fulness of the *gospel of Jesus Christ to the Gentiles and to the Jews also;

10 Which was given by inspiration, and is confirmed to *others by the ministering of angels, and is *declared unto the world by them—

11 Proving to the world that the holy scriptures are *true, and that God does *inspire men and call them to his *holy work in this age and generation, as well as in generations of old;

12 Thereby showing that he is the *same God yesterday, today, and *forever. Amen.

13 Therefore, having so great witnesses, by *them shall the world be judged, even as many as shall hereafter come to a knowledge of this work.

14 And those who receive it in faith, and work *righteousness, shall receive a *crown of eternal life;

15 But those who *harden their hearts in *unbelief, and *reject it, it shall turn to their own *condemnation—

16 For the Lord God has spoken it; and we, the elders of the church, have heard and bear *witness to the words of the glorious Majesty on high, to whom be glory forever and ever. Amen.

17 By these things we *know that there is a *God in heaven, who is infinite and *eternal, from everlasting to everlasting the same *unchangeable God, the framer of heaven and earth, and all things which are in them;

6 a TG Priesthood, Qualifying for.
  b JS—H 1:30 (29–35). TG Angels.
  c Matt. 28:3.
7 a TG Guidance, Divine.
8 a Luke 24:49.
  b TG Urim and Thummim.
9 a TG Record Keeping.
  b D&C 14:10; 18:4; JS—H 1:34.
  c TG Book of Mormon; Gospel.
10 a Moro. 7:31 (29–32); D&C 5:11.
  b See "The Testimony of

Three Witnesses" and "The Testimony of Eight Witnesses" in the preliminary pages of the Book of Mormon.
11 a D&C 66:11. TG Scriptures, Value of.
  b TG Inspiration.
  c TG Sacred.
12 a Heb. 13:8; 1 Ne. 10:18 (18–19); Morm. 9:9 (9–11); D&C 35:1; 38:1 (1–4); 39:1 (1–3); 76:4.
  b Ps. 48:14.
13 a Dan. 7:22; Rev. 20:4 (4–6); D&C 5:18.

14 a TG Righteousness.
  b Rev. 2:10. TG Exaltation.
15 a TG Hardheartedness.
  b TG Unbelief.
  c D&C 6:31.
  d John 5:24.
16 a D&C 20:36 (35–36); 109:79.
17 a 1 Sam. 17:46; D&C 76:22 (22–23).
  b Josh. 2:11; 2 Ne. 10:14.
  c TG Eternity; God, Eternal Nature of; Immortality.
  d TG God, Perfection of.

18 And that he ^acreated man, male and female, after his own ^bimage and in his own likeness, created he them;

19 And gave unto them commandments that they should ^alove and ^bserve him, the only ^cliving and true ^dGod, and that he should be the only being whom they should worship.

20 But by the ^atransgression of these holy laws man became ^bsensual and ^cdevilish, and became ^dfallen man.

21 Wherefore, the Almighty God gave his ^aOnly Begotten Son, as it is written in those scriptures which have been given of him.

22 He ^asuffered ^btemptations but gave no heed unto them.

23 He was ^acrucified, ^bdied, and ^crose again the third day;

24 And ^aascended into heaven, to sit down on the right hand of the ^bFather, to ^creign with almighty power according to the will of the Father;

25 That as many as would ^abelieve and be baptized in his holy name, and ^bendure in faith to the end, should be saved—

26 Not only those who believed after he came in the ^ameridian of time, in the ^bflesh, but all those from the beginning, even as many as were before he came, who believed in the words of the holy prophets, who ^cspake as they were inspired by the ^dgift of the Holy Ghost, who truly ^etestified of him in all things, should have eternal life,

27 As well as those who should come after, who should believe in the ^agifts and callings of God by the Holy Ghost, which ^bbeareth record of the Father and of the Son;

28 Which Father, Son, and Holy Ghost are ^aone God, infinite and eternal, without end. Amen.

---

18 a TG Creation; God, Creator; Man, Physical Creation of.
  b Gen. 1:26 (26–28); Mosiah 7:27; Ether 3:15 (14–17). TG God, Body of, Corporeal Nature.
19 a Deut. 11:1; Mosiah 2:4; Moro. 10:32; D&C 59:5 (5–6); Moses 7:33. TG God, Love of; Love.
  b Deut. 6:13 (13–15); D&C 4:2. TG Duty; Obedience.
  c Ps. 42:2; Dan. 6:26; 1 Thes. 1:9; Alma 5:13; 7:6; D&C 14:9.
  d Deut. 6:14. TG Worship.
20 a TG Transgress.
  b TG Sensuality.
  c TG Devil.

  d TG Man, Natural, Not Spiritually Reborn.
21 a TG Jesus Christ, Divine Sonship.
22 a Matt. 4:6; 27:40.
  b TG Jesus Christ, Temptation of; Temptation.
23 a TG Jesus Christ, Crucifixion of.
  b TG Jesus Christ, Death of.
  c TG Jesus Christ, Resurrection; Resurrection.
24 a TG Jesus Christ, Ascension of.
  b TG God the Father, Elohim.
  c TG Jesus Christ, Authority of.
25 a D&C 35:2; 38:4; 45:5 (5, 8); 68:9; 76:51.

  b TG Baptism; Faith; Perseverance.
26 a D&C 39:3.
  b TG Jesus Christ, Condescension of.
  c 1 Pet. 1:11; Jacob 4:4; 7:11 (11–12); Mosiah 13:33 (33–35).
  d Moses 5:58 (57–58). TG Holy Ghost, Gift of.
  e John 5:39; D&C 3:16. TG Jesus Christ, Prophecies about; Prophets, Mission of; Testimony.
27 a D&C 18:32.
  b D&C 1:39; 42:17.
28 a John 17:20–22; Alma 11:44; 3 Ne. 11:27 (27–28, 36); 28:10; Morm. 7:7. TG God, Eternal Nature of; Godhead; Unity.

29 And we know that all men must *a*repent and *b*believe on the name of Jesus Christ, and worship the Father in his name, and *c*endure in *d*faith on his name to the end, or they cannot be *e*saved in the kingdom of God.

30 And we know that *a*justification through the *b*grace of our Lord and Savior Jesus Christ is just and true;

31 And we know also, that *a*sanctification through the grace of our Lord and Savior Jesus Christ is just and true, to all those who *b*love and serve God with all their *c*mights, minds, and strength.

32 But there is a possibility that man may *a*fall from *b*grace and depart from the living God;

33 Therefore let the church take heed and pray always, lest they fall into *a*temptation;

34 Yea, and even let those who are *a*sanctified take heed also.

35 And we know that these things are true and according to the revelations of John, neither *a*adding to, nor diminishing from the prophecy of his book, the holy scriptures, or the revelations of God which shall come hereafter by the gift and power of the Holy Ghost, the *b*voice of God, or the ministering of angels.

36 And the Lord God has *a*spoken it; and honor, power and glory be rendered to his holy *b*name, both now and ever. Amen.

37 *And again, by way of commandment to the church concerning the manner of baptism*—All those who *a*humble themselves before God, and desire to be baptized, and come forth with broken hearts and *b*contrite spirits, and witness before the church that they have truly repented of all their sins, and are willing to take upon them the *c*name of Jesus Christ, having a *d*determination to serve him to the end, and truly manifest by their *e*works that they have received of the *f*Spirit of Christ unto the *g*remission of their sins, shall be received by baptism into his church.

---

29 *a* TG Repent.
  b 1 Jn. 3:23 (19–24).
  c TG Perseverance.
  d TG Faith.
  e TG Salvation.
30 *a* Rom. 3:24. TG Justification.
  b Eph. 2:8 (8–9). TG Salvation, Plan of.
31 *a* TG Sanctification.
  b Ps. 18:1; Alma 13:29; D&C 76:116.
  c Deut. 6:5.
32 *a* Gal. 5:4; D&C 20:5; 50:4. TG Apostasy of Individuals.

  b Rom. 6:1 (1–2). TG Grace.
33 *a* Mark 14:38. TG Temptation.
34 *a* TG Sanctification.
35 *a* Rev. 22:18 (18–19); D&C 68:34; 93:25 (24–25). TG Scriptures, Value of.
  b 1 Kgs. 19:12 (11–13).
36 *a* Ezek. 5:13; D&C 20:16; 109:79.
  b 1 Kgs. 8:29; D&C 18:40 (21–41); 97:15 (15–17); 109:26 (16–26). TG Name.

37 *a* TG Baptism, Qualifications for.
  b TG Contrite Heart; Poor in Spirit.
  c Mosiah 5:8 (2–14); 18:8 (8–10). TG Jesus Christ, Taking the Name of.
  d Prov. 24:16. TG Commitment.
  e James 2:18. TG Good Works.
  f TG Light of Christ; Spirituality.
  g TG Remission of Sins.

38 The *a*duty of the elders, priests, teachers, deacons, and members of the church of Christ—An *b*apostle is an *c*elder, and it is his calling to *d*baptize;

39 And to *a*ordain other elders, priests, teachers, and deacons;

40 And to administer *a*bread and wine—the *b*emblems of the flesh and blood of Christ—

41 And to *a*confirm those who are baptized into the church, by the laying on of *b*hands for the baptism of fire and the Holy Ghost, according to the scriptures;

42 And to teach, expound, exhort, baptize, and watch over the church;

43 And to confirm the church by the laying on of the hands, and the giving of the Holy Ghost;

44 And to take the *a*lead of all meetings.

45 The elders are to *a*conduct the *b*meetings as they are *c*led by the Holy Ghost, according to the commandments and revelations of God.

46 The *a*priest's duty is to preach, *b*teach, expound, exhort, and baptize, and administer the sacrament,

47 And visit the house of each member, and exhort them to *a*pray *b*vocally and in secret and attend to all *c*family duties.

48 And he may also *a*ordain other priests, teachers, and deacons.

49 And he is to take the *a*lead of meetings when there is no elder present;

50 But when there is an elder present, he is only to preach, teach, expound, exhort, and baptize,

51 And visit the house of each member, exhorting them to pray vocally and in secret and attend to all family duties.

52 In all these duties the priest is to *a*assist the elder if occasion requires.

53 The *a*teacher's duty is to *b*watch over the *c*church always, and be with and strengthen them;

38 *a* TG Church Organization; Duty; Priesthood, History of; Priesthood, Magnifying Callings within.
  b TG Apostles.
  c TG Elder.
  d 3 Ne. 11:22 (21–22); D&C 18:29.
39 *a* Moro. 3:4 (1–4); D&C 18:32; 107:58.
40 *a* TG Sacrament.
  b TG Jesus Christ, Types of, in Memory.

41 *a* D&C 33:15 (11, 14–15); 55:3.
  b TG Hands, Laying on of; Holy Ghost, Baptism of.
44 *a* TG Leadership.
45 *a* Moro. 6:9; D&C 46:2.
  b TG Meetings.
  c Gal. 5:18.
46 *a* Ezra 6:18; D&C 84:111; 107:61 (20, 61). TG Priest, Aaronic Priesthood; Priesthood, Aaronic.
  b Lev. 10:11. TG Teaching.

47 *a* 1 Tim. 2:8.
  b D&C 19:28; 23:6.
  c TG Family; Family, Children, Responsibilities toward.
48 *a* TG Priesthood, Ordination.
49 *a* TG Leadership.
52 *a* D&C 107:14 (5, 14).
53 *a* TG Teacher, Aaronic Priesthood.
  b D&C 84:111.
  c Prov. 27:23.

54 And see that there is no iniquity in the church, neither ^ahardness with each other, neither lying, ^bbackbiting, nor ^cevil ^dspeaking;

55 And see that the church meet together often, and also see that all the members do their duty.

56 And he is to take the lead of meetings in the absence of the elder or priest—

57 And is to be assisted always, in all his duties in the church, by the ^adeacons, if occasion requires.

58 But neither teachers nor deacons have authority to baptize, administer the ^asacrament, or lay on ^bhands;

59 They are, however, to warn, expound, exhort, and teach, and invite all to come unto Christ.

60 Every ^aelder, ^bpriest, teacher, or deacon is to be ^cordained ^daccording to the gifts and callings of God unto him; and he is to be ^eordained by the power of the Holy Ghost, which is in the one who ordains him.

61 The several elders composing this church of Christ are to ^ameet in conference once in three months, or from time to time as said conferences shall direct or appoint;

62 And said conferences are to do whatever church business is necessary to be done at the time.

63 The elders are to receive their licenses from other elders, by ^avote of the church to which they belong, or from the conferences.

64 Each priest, teacher, or deacon, who is ordained by a priest, may take a certificate from him at the time, which ^acertificate, when presented to an elder, shall entitle him to a license, which shall authorize him to perform the duties of his calling, or he may receive it from a conference.

65 No person is to be ^aordained to any office in this church, where there is a regularly organized branch of the same, without the ^bvote of that church;

66 But the presiding elders, traveling bishops, high councilors, high priests, and elders, may have the privilege of ordaining, where there is no branch of the church that a vote may be called.

67 Every president of the high priesthood (or presiding elder), ^abishop,

54a 1 Thes. 5:13.
  b TG Backbiting; Gossip.
  c TG Evil; Slander.
  d TG Profanity; Reviling.
57a TG Deacon.
58a TG Sacrament.
  b TG Hands, Laying on of.
60a TG Elder, Melchizedek Priesthood.

  b TG Priest, Aaronic Priesthood.
  c TG Called of God.
  d Moro. 3:4 (1–4).
  e TG Priesthood, Ordination.
61a TG Meetings.
63a D&C 73:2. TG Sustaining Church Leaders.

64a D&C 20:84; 52:41; 72:17 (17, 19–26); 112:21.
65a TG Priesthood, Ordination.
  b D&C 26:2; 28:13. TG Common Consent.
67a TG Bishop.

high councilor, and *b*high priest, is to be ordained by the direction of a *c*high council or general conference.

68 The *a*duty of the members after they are received by *b*baptism—The elders or priests are to have a sufficient time to expound all things concerning the church of Christ to their *c*understanding, previous to their partaking of the *d*sacrament and being confirmed by the laying on of the *e*hands of the elders, so that all things may be done in *f*order.

69 And the members shall manifest before the church, and also before the elders, by a *a*godly walk and conversation, that they are worthy of it, that there may be works and *b*faith agreeable to the holy scriptures—walking in *c*holiness before the Lord.

70 Every member of the church of Christ having *a*children is to bring them unto the elders before the church, who are to lay their *b*hands upon them in the name of Jesus Christ, and bless them in his name.

71 No one can be received into the church of Christ unless he has arrived unto the years of *a*accountability before God, and is capable of *b*repentance.

72 *a*Baptism is to be administered in the following manner unto all those who repent—

73 The person who is called of God and has authority from Jesus Christ to baptize, shall go down into the water with the person who has presented himself or herself for baptism, and shall say, calling him or her by name: Having been commissioned of Jesus Christ, I baptize you in the name of the Father, and of the Son, and of the Holy Ghost. Amen.

74 Then shall he *a*immerse him or her in the water, and come forth again out of the water.

75 It is expedient that the church *a*meet together often to *b*partake of *c*bread and wine in the *d*remembrance of the Lord Jesus;

76 And the elder or priest shall administer it; and after this *a*manner shall he administer it—he shall kneel with the church and call upon the Father in solemn prayer, saying:

---

67 b TG Church Organi-
zation; High Priest,
Melchizedek Priesthood.
  c D&C 102:2 (1–3).
68 a TG Duty.
  b TG Baptism.
  c TG Understanding.
  d TG Sacrament.
  e TG Hands, Laying on of.
  f TG Order.
69 a TG Godliness.

  b James 2:14.
  c TG Holiness.
70 a TG Blessing; Children;
Family, Love within.
  b TG Hands, Laying on of.
71 a D&C 18:42; 29:47;
68:25 (25–27). TG Ac-
countability; Baptism,
Qualifications for; Salvation of Little Children.
  b TG Repent.

72 a 3 Ne. 11:22 (22–28);
D&C 18:30.
74 a TG Baptism, Immersion;
Jesus Christ, Types of, in
Memory.
75 a TG Assembly for Wor-
ship; Meetings.
  b Acts 20:7.
  c TG Bread.
  d TG Sacrament.
76 a Moro. 4:1 (1–3).

77 O God, the Eternal Father, we ask thee in the name of thy Son, Jesus Christ, to bless and sanctify this ^abread to the souls of all those who partake of it, that they may eat in remembrance of the body of thy Son, and ^bwitness unto thee, O God, the Eternal Father, that they are willing to take upon them the name of thy Son, and always remember him and keep his ^ccommandments which he has given them; that they may always have his ^dSpirit to be with them. Amen.

78 The ^amanner of administering the wine—he shall take the ^bcup also, and say:

79 O God, the Eternal Father, we ask thee in the name of thy Son, Jesus Christ, to bless and sanctify this ^awine to the souls of all those who drink of it, that they may do it in remembrance of the blood of thy Son, which was shed for them; that they may witness unto thee, O God, the Eternal Father, that they do always remember him, that they may have his Spirit to be with them. Amen.

80 Any member of the church of Christ ^atransgressing, or being ^bovertaken in a fault, shall be dealt with as the scriptures direct.

81 It shall be the duty of the several churches, composing the church of Christ, to send one or more of their teachers to attend the several conferences held by the elders of the church,

82 With a list of the ^anames of the several members uniting themselves with the church since the last conference; or send by the hand of some priest; so that a regular list of all the names of the whole church may be kept in a book by one of the elders, whomsoever the other elders shall appoint from time to time;

83 And also, if any have been ^aexpelled from the church, so that their names may be blotted out of the general church ^brecord of names.

84 All members removing from the church where they reside, if going to a church where they are not known, may take a letter ^acertifying that they are regular members and in good standing, which certificate may be signed by any elder or priest if the member receiving the letter is personally acquainted with the elder or priest, or it may be signed by the teachers or deacons of the church.

---

77 a Luke 22:19 (15–20).
   b Mosiah 5:8 (8–12); 18:8
     (8–10); D&C 20:37.
     TG Commitment.
   c TG Obedience.
   d John 14:16.
78 a Moro. 5:1 (1–2).

   b Luke 22:20.
79 a D&C 27:2–4.
80 a TG Offense.
   b Gal. 6:1.
82 a Moro. 6:4; D&C 85:3
     (3–5, 11–12).
83 a Ex. 32:33; Deut. 9:14;

     Ps. 109:13; Alma 5:57;
     Moro. 6:7. TG Excommunication.
   b TG Record Keeping.
84 a D&C 20:64; 52:41;
     72:17 (17, 19–26);
     112:21.

SECTION 21

Revelation given to Joseph Smith the Prophet, at Fayette, New York, April 6, 1830. This revelation was given at the organization of the Church, on the date named, in the home of Peter Whitmer Sr. Six men, who had previously been baptized, participated. By unanimous vote these persons expressed their desire and determination to organize, according to the commandment of God (see section 20). They also voted to accept and sustain Joseph Smith Jr. and Oliver Cowdery as the presiding officers of the Church. With the laying on of hands, Joseph then ordained Oliver an elder of the Church, and Oliver similarly ordained Joseph. After administration of the sacrament, Joseph and Oliver laid hands upon the participants individually for the bestowal of the Holy Ghost and for the confirmation of each as a member of the Church.

1–3, Joseph Smith is called to be a seer, translator, prophet, apostle, and elder; 4–8, His word will guide the cause of Zion; 9–12, The Saints will believe his words as he speaks by the Comforter.

1 Behold, there shall be a ^arecord kept among you; and in it thou shalt be called a ^bseer, a translator, a prophet, an ^capostle of Jesus Christ, an elder of the church through the will of God the Father, and the grace of your Lord Jesus Christ,

2 Being ^ainspired of the Holy Ghost to lay the foundation thereof, and to ^bbuild it up unto the most holy faith.

3 Which ^achurch was ^borganized and established in the year of your Lord eighteen hundred and thirty, in the fourth month, and on the sixth day of the month which is called April.

4 Wherefore, meaning the church, thou shalt give ^aheed unto all his words and ^bcommandments which he shall give unto you as he receiveth them, walking in all ^choliness before me;

5 For his ^aword ye shall receive, as if from mine own mouth, in all patience and faith.

6 For by doing these things the ^agates of hell shall not prevail against you; yea, and the Lord God will disperse the powers of ^bdarkness from before you, and cause the heavens to ^cshake for your ^dgood, and his name's ^eglory.

---

21 1 *a* D&C 47:1; 69:3 (3–8);
 85:1. TG Record Keeping.
 b TG Seer.
 c 2 Cor. 1:1. TG Apostles.
 2 *a* TG Inspiration.
 b Jude 1:20.
 3 *a* D&C 1:1. TG Church
 Organization.

b D&C 20:1.
4 *a* Heb. 2:1. TG Priesthood,
 Magnifying Callings
 within.
 b TG Scriptures, Study of.
 c TG Holiness.
5 *a* D&C 1:38. TG Prophets,
 Mission of; Sustaining

Church Leaders.
6 *a* Matt. 16:18; D&C 10:69.
 b Col. 1:13.
 c Joel 3:16; Hag. 2:7; D&C
 35:24; 45:48 (22, 48);
 49:23; 84:118.
 d Deut. 10:13; D&C 61:13.
 e TG Glory.

7 For thus saith the Lord God: Him have I inspired to move the cause of ^aZion in mighty power for good, and his diligence I know, and his prayers I have heard.

8 Yea, his weeping for Zion I have seen, and I will cause that he shall mourn for her no longer; for his days of rejoicing are come unto the ^aremission of his sins, and the manifestations of my blessings upon his works.

9 For, behold, I will ^abless all those who labor in my vineyard with a mighty blessing, and they shall believe on his words, which are given him through me by the ^bComforter, which ^cmanifesteth that Jesus was ^dcrucified by ^esinful men for the sins of the ^fworld, yea, for the remission of sins unto the ^gcontrite heart.

10 Wherefore it behooveth me that he should be ^aordained by you, Oliver Cowdery mine apostle;

11 This being an ordinance unto you, that you are an elder under his hand, he being the ^afirst unto you, that you might be an elder unto this church of Christ, bearing my name—

12 And the first ^apreacher of this church unto the church, and before the world, yea, before the Gentiles; yea, and thus saith the Lord God, lo, lo! to the ^bJews also. Amen.

SECTION 22

Revelation given through Joseph Smith the Prophet, at Manchester, New York, April 16, 1830. This revelation was given to the Church in consequence of some who had previously been baptized desiring to unite with the Church without rebaptism.

1, Baptism is a new and everlasting covenant; 2–4, Authoritative baptism is required.

1 Behold, I say unto you that all ^aold covenants have I caused to be done away in this thing; and this is a ^bnew and an everlasting ^ccovenant, even that which was from the beginning.

---

7 a TG Zion.
8 a D&C 20:5 (5–6); JS—H 1:73 (68–74).
9 a 1 Ne. 13:37; Jacob 5:75 (70–76).
　b TG Holy Ghost, Comforter.
　c TG Testimony.
　d Lev. 16:9 (7–10). TG Jesus

Christ, Crucifixion of.
　e TG Sin.
　f 1 Jn. 2:2. TG World.
　g TG Contrite Heart.
10 a TG Priesthood, Ordination.
11 a D&C 20:2 (2, 5).
12 a TG Missionary Work; Mission of Latter-day

Saints.
　b 1 Ne. 13:42; D&C 18:6, 26; 19:27; 90:9 (8–9); 107:33; 112:4.
22 1 a Heb. 8:13; 3 Ne. 9:17; 12:47 (46–47).
　b D&C 66:2. TG New and Everlasting Covenant.
　c TG Covenants.

2 Wherefore, although a man should be baptized an hundred times it availeth him nothing, for you cannot enter in at the strait gate by the *a*law of Moses, neither by your *b*dead works.

3 For it is because of your dead works that I have caused this last covenant and this church to be built up unto me, even as in days of old.

4 Wherefore, enter ye in at the *a*gate, as I have commanded, and *b*seek not to counsel your God. Amen.

SECTION 23

A series of five revelations given through Joseph Smith the Prophet, at Manchester, New York, April 1830, to Oliver Cowdery, Hyrum Smith, Samuel H. Smith, Joseph Smith Sr., and Joseph Knight Sr. As the result of earnest desire on the part of the five persons named to know of their respective duties, the Prophet inquired of the Lord and received a revelation for each person.

1–7, These early disciples are called to preach, exhort, and strengthen the Church.

1 Behold, I speak unto you, Oliver, a few words. Behold, thou art blessed, and art under no condemnation. But beware of *a*pride, lest thou shouldst enter into *b*temptation.

2 Make known thy calling unto the church, and also before the *a*world, and thy heart shall be opened to preach the truth from henceforth and forever. Amen.

3 Behold, I speak unto you, Hyrum, a few words; for thou also art under no condemnation, and thy heart is opened, and thy tongue *a*loosed; and thy calling is to exhortation, and to *b*strengthen the church continually. Wherefore thy duty is unto the church forever, and this because of thy family. Amen.

4 Behold, I speak a few words unto you, *a*Samuel; for thou also art under no condemnation, and thy calling is to exhortation, and to strengthen the church; and thou art not as yet called to preach before the world. Amen.

5 Behold, I speak a few words unto you, Joseph; for thou also art under no *a*condemnation, and thy calling also is to exhortation, and to strengthen the church; and this is thy duty from henceforth and forever. Amen.

2*a* Gal. 2:16. TG Law of Moses.
  b Moro. 8:23 (23–26).
4*a* Matt. 7:13 (13–14);
  Luke 13:24; 2 Ne. 9:41;
  31:9 (9, 17–18); 3 Ne.
  14:14 (13–14); 27:33;

D&C 43:7. TG Baptism, Essential.
  b Rom. 11:34; 1 Cor. 2:16; Jacob 4:10.
23 1*a* TG Pride.
  b Mark 14:38. TG Temptation.

2*a* Rom. 10:18.
3*a* 3 Ne. 26:14 (14, 16).
  b D&C 81:5 (4–5); 108:7.
4*a* JS—H 1:4.
5*a* D&C 20:5.

6 Behold, I manifest unto you, Joseph Knight, by these words, that you must take up your *cross, in the which you must *pray *vocally before the world as well as in secret, and in your family, and among your friends, and in all places.

7 And, behold, it is your duty to unite with the true *church, and give your language to exhortation continually, that you may receive the reward of the *laborer. Amen.

SECTION 24

Revelation given to Joseph Smith the Prophet and Oliver Cowdery, at Harmony, Pennsylvania, July 1830. Though less than four months had elapsed since the Church was organized, persecution had become intense, and the leaders had to seek safety in partial seclusion. The following three revelations were given at this time to strengthen, encourage, and instruct them.

1–9, Joseph Smith is called to translate, preach, and expound scriptures; 10–12, Oliver Cowdery is called to preach the gospel; 13–19, The law is revealed relative to miracles, cursings, casting off the dust of one's feet, and going without purse or scrip.

1 Behold, thou wast called and chosen to *write the Book of Mormon, and to my ministry; and I have *lifted thee up out of thine afflictions, and have counseled thee, that thou hast been delivered from all thine enemies, and thou hast been *delivered from the powers of Satan and from *darkness!

2 Nevertheless, thou art not excusable in thy *transgressions; nevertheless, go thy way and sin no more.

3 *Magnify thine office; and after thou hast *sowed thy fields and secured them, go speedily unto the church which is in *Colesville, Fayette, and Manchester, and they shall *support thee; and I will bless them both spiritually and *temporally;

4 But if they receive thee not, I will send upon them a *cursing instead of a blessing.

---

6 a Matt. 10:38; 3 Ne. 12:30.
  b 1 Tim. 2:8. TG Prayer.
  c D&C 19:28; 20:47 (47, 51).
7 a TG Baptism, Essential; Commitment.
  b TG Industry.
24 1 a D&C 9:4. TG Scribe;

Scriptures, Writing of.
  b Acts 7:10.
  c TG Deliver.
  d TG Darkness, Spiritual.
2 a D&C 1:31 (31–33).
3 a Rom. 11:13; Jacob 1:19; 2:2.

  b TG Industry; Labor.
  c D&C 26:1; 37:2.
  d D&C 42:71 (70–73); 70:12.
  e Deut. 28:8; Luke 12:31.
4 a TG Curse.

5 And thou shalt continue in calling upon God in my name, and writing the things which shall be given thee by the *Comforter, and expounding all scriptures unto the church.

6 And it shall be given thee in the very moment what thou shalt *speak and *write, and they shall hear it, or I will send unto them a cursing instead of a blessing.

7 For thou shalt devote all thy *service in Zion; and in this thou shalt have strength.

8 Be *patient in *afflictions, for thou shalt have many; but *endure them, for, lo, I am with thee, even unto the *end of thy days.

9 And in temporal labors thou shalt not have strength, for this is not thy calling. Attend to thy *calling and thou shalt have wherewith to magnify thine office, and to expound all scriptures, and continue in laying on of the hands and *confirming the churches.

10 And thy brother Oliver shall continue in bearing my name before the *world, and also to the church. And he shall not suppose that he can say enough in my cause; and lo, I am with him to the end.

11 In me he shall have glory, and not of himself, whether in weakness or in strength, whether in *bonds or free;

12 And at all times, and in all places, he shall open his mouth and *declare my gospel as with the voice of a *trump, both day and night. And I will give unto him strength such as is not known among men.

13 Require not *miracles, except I shall *command you, except *casting out *devils, *healing the sick, and against *poisonous serpents, and against deadly poisons;

14 And these things ye shall not do, except it be required of you by them who *desire it, that the scriptures might be *fulfilled; for ye shall do according to that which is written.

---

5 a TG Holy Ghost, Comforter; Scriptures, Writing of.
6 a Ex. 4:12 (12–16); Matt. 10:19 (19–20); Luke 12:12 (11–12); Hel. 5:18 (18–19); D&C 28:4; 84:85; 100:5 (5–8); Moses 6:8 (8, 32). TG Prophets, Mission of.
  b TG Scribe.
7 a TG Service.

8 a Rom. 12:12. TG Patience.
  b Job 2:13; Hel. 5:12. TG Affliction.
  c TG Steadfastness.
  d Matt. 28:20.
9 a TG Stewardship.
  b Acts 15:41.
10 a Rom. 10:18.
11 a 1 Cor. 12:13.
12 a TG Preaching.
  b D&C 34:6.
13 a Matt. 4:7 (5–7).

TG Miracle; Sign Seekers.
  b 1 Ne. 7:12; 17:50.
  c Mark 16:17 (17–18).
  d TG Devil.
  e TG Heal.
  f Acts 28:3 (3–9); D&C 84:72 (71–72); 124:99 (98–100).
14 a TG Administrations to the Sick.
  b Matt. 4:14.

15 And in whatsoever place ye shall ^aenter, and they receive you not in my name, ye shall leave a cursing instead of a blessing, by casting off the ^bdust of your feet against them as a testimony, and cleansing your feet by the wayside.

16 And it shall come to pass that whosoever shall lay their hands upon you by violence, ye shall command to be smitten in my name; and, behold, I will ^asmite them according to your words, in mine own due time.

17 And whosoever shall go to law with thee shall be cursed by the law.

18 And thou shalt take no ^apurse nor scrip, neither staves, neither two coats, for the church shall give unto thee in the very hour what thou needest for food and for raiment, and for shoes and for money, and for scrip.

19 For thou art called to ^aprune my vineyard with a mighty pruning, yea, even for the last time; yea, and also all those whom thou hast ^bordained, and they shall do even according to this pattern. Amen.

SECTION 25

Revelation given through Joseph Smith the Prophet, at Harmony, Pennsylvania, July 1830 (see the heading to section 24). This revelation manifests the will of the Lord to Emma Smith, the Prophet's wife.

1–6, Emma Smith, an elect lady, is called to aid and comfort her husband; 7–11, She is also called to write, to expound scriptures, and to select hymns; 12–14, The song of the righteous is a prayer unto the Lord; 15–16, Principles of obedience in this revelation are applicable to all.

1 Hearken unto the voice of the Lord your God, while I speak unto you, Emma Smith, my daughter; for verily I say unto you, all those who ^areceive my gospel are sons and daughters in my ^bkingdom.

2 A revelation I give unto you concerning my will; and if thou art faithful and ^awalk in the paths of ^bvirtue before me, I will preserve thy life, and thou shalt receive an ^cinheritance in Zion.

15a Matt. 10:11 (11–15).
 b Mark 6:11; Luke 10:11 (11–12); Acts 13:51; 18:6 (5–6); D&C 60:15 (13–15); 75:20 (19–22); 99:4 (4–5).
16a TG Retribution.
18a Matt. 10:9 (9–10); Luke 10:4; D&C 84:78

(78–80, 86).
19a Jacob 5:61 (61–74); D&C 39:17; 71:4; 95:4. TG Millennium, Preparing a People for.
 b TG Priesthood, Ordination.
25 1a John 1:12. TG Sons and Daughters of God.

 b TG Kingdom of God, on Earth.
2a Deut. 30:16.
 b TG Virtue; Zion.
 c D&C 52:42 (2, 5, 42); 58:51 (17, 28, 51); 63:48 (29, 31, 48); 64:30; 85:7 (1–3, 7, 9); 99:7; 101:18 (1, 6, 18); 103:14 (11, 14).

3 Behold, thy *a*sins are forgiven thee, and thou art an *b*elect *c*lady, whom I have *d*called.

4 *a*Murmur not because of the *b*things which thou hast not seen, for they are *c*withheld from thee and from the world, which is wisdom in me in a time to come.

5 And the office of thy calling shall be for a *a*comfort unto my servant, Joseph Smith, Jun., thy *b*husband, in his *c*afflictions, with consoling words, in the spirit of *d*meekness.

6 And thou shalt go with him at the time of his going, and be unto him for a scribe, while there is no one to be a scribe for him, that I may send my servant, Oliver Cowdery, whithersoever I will.

7 And thou shalt be *a*ordained under his hand to expound scriptures, and to exhort the church, according as it shall be given thee by my *b*Spirit.

8 For he shall lay his *a*hands upon thee, and thou shalt receive the Holy Ghost, and thy time shall be given to writing, and to learning much.

9 And thou needest not fear, for thy *a*husband shall support thee in the church; for unto them is his *b*calling, that all things might be *c*revealed unto them, whatsoever I will, according to their faith.

10 And verily I say unto thee that thou shalt lay aside the *a*things of this *b*world, and *c*seek for the things of a *d*better.

11 And it shall be given thee, also, to make a selection of *a*sacred *b*hymns, as it shall be given thee, which is pleasing unto me, to be had in my church.

12 For my soul *a*delighteth in the *b*song of the *c*heart; yea, the *d*song of the righteous is a prayer unto me, and it shall be answered with a blessing upon their heads.

13 Wherefore, *a*lift up thy heart and *b*rejoice, and cleave unto the covenants which thou hast made.

---

3 *a* Matt. 9:2.
  b IE one chosen or set apart. 2 Jn. 1:1 (1, 13).
  c TG Woman.
  d TG Authority; Called of God.
4 *a* TG Murmuring.
  b TG Knowledge.
  c Luke 24:16 (10–24); Alma 40:3; Ether 3:25. TG God, Wisdom of.
5 *a* TG Comfort; Compassion; Family, Love within.
  b TG Marriage, Wives.

  c TG Affliction.
  d 2 Cor. 10:1.
7 *a* OR set apart.
  b 1 Cor. 12:8. TG God, Spirit of.
8 *a* TG Hands, Laying on of.
9 *a* TG Marriage, Husbands.
  b TG Called of God; Stewardship.
  c TG Prophets, Mission of; Revelation.
10 *a* TG Covet.
  b 2 Cor. 6:17; D&C 30:2. TG Treasure; World.
  c Ether 12:4.

  d TG Reward.
11 *a* TG Sacred.
  b Eph. 5:19 (19–20).
12 *a* TG God, the Standard of Righteousness.
  b TG Communication.
  c TG Heart.
  d 1 Chr. 16:9; Ps. 33:3; 96:1; D&C 25:11; 136:28. TG Prayer; Singing.
13 *a* Lam. 3:41.
  b TG Joy.

14 Continue in the spirit of meekness, and beware of *a*pride. Let thy soul delight in thy *b*husband, and the *c*glory which shall come upon him.

15 Keep my commandments continually, and a *a*crown of *b*righteousness thou shalt receive. And except thou do this, where I am you *c*cannot come.

16 And verily, verily, I say unto you, that this is my *a*voice unto all. Amen.

SECTION 26

Revelation given to Joseph Smith the Prophet, Oliver Cowdery, and John Whitmer, at Harmony, Pennsylvania, July 1830 (see the heading to section 24).

1, They are instructed to study the scriptures and to preach; 2, The law of common consent is affirmed.

1 Behold, I say unto you that you shall let your *a*time be devoted to the *b*studying of the scriptures, and to preaching, and to confirming the church at *c*Colesville, and to performing your *d*labors on the land, such as is required, until after you shall go to the west to hold the next conference; and then it shall be made *e*known what you shall do.

2 And all things shall be done by *a*common consent in the *b*church, by much prayer and faith, for all things you shall receive by faith. Amen.

SECTION 27

Revelation given to Joseph Smith the Prophet, at Harmony, Pennsylvania, August 1830. In preparation for a religious service at which the sacrament of bread and wine was to be administered, Joseph set out to procure wine. He was met by a heavenly messenger and received this revelation, a portion of which was written at the time and the remainder in the September following. Water is now used instead of wine in the sacramental services of the Church.

1–4, The emblems to be used in partaking of the sacrament are set forth; 5–14, Christ and His servants from all dispensations are to partake of the sacrament; 15–18, Put on the whole armor of God.

14a TG Meek; Pride.
 b TG Family, Love within;
   Marriage, Continuing
   Courtship in.
 c TG Glory.
15a TG Exaltation.
 b TG Righteousness.
 c John 7:34.

16a Jer. 42:6; D&C 1:38.
26 1a TG Time.
 b TG Scriptures, Study of;
   Study.
 c D&C 24:3; 37:2.
 d TG Industry.
 e TG Guidance, Divine.
2a 1 Sam. 8:7; Mosiah

29:26; Alma 29:4.
 TG Common Consent;
 Sustaining Church
 Leaders.
 b 1 Chr. 13:4. TG Church;
 Church Organization.

1 Listen to the *a*voice of Jesus Christ, your Lord, your God, and your Redeemer, whose word is *b*quick and powerful.

2 For, behold, I say unto you, that it mattereth not what ye shall *a*eat or what ye shall drink when ye partake of the sacrament, if it so be that ye do it with an eye single to my *b*glory—*c*remembering unto the Father my *d*body which was laid down for you, and my *e*blood which was shed for the *f*remission of your sins.

3 Wherefore, a commandment I give unto you, that you shall not purchase *a*wine neither strong drink of your enemies;

4 Wherefore, you shall partake of none except it is made *a*new among you; yea, in this my Father's kingdom which shall be built up on the earth.

5 Behold, this is wisdom in me; wherefore, marvel not, for the hour cometh that I will *a*drink of the fruit of the *b*vine with you on the earth, and with *c*Moroni, whom I have sent unto you to reveal the Book of Mormon, containing the fulness of my everlasting gospel, to whom I have committed the keys of the *d*record of the *e*stick of *f*Ephraim;

6 And also with *a*Elias, to whom I have committed the keys of bringing to pass the restoration of all things spoken by the mouth of all the holy prophets since the world began, concerning the last days;

7 And also John the son of Zacharias, which Zacharias he *a*(Elias) visited and gave promise that he should have a son, and his name should be *b*John, and he should be filled with the spirit of Elias;

8 Which John I have sent unto you, my servants, Joseph Smith, Jun., and Oliver Cowdery, to ordain you unto the first *a*priesthood which you have received, that you might be called and *b*ordained even as *c*Aaron;

9 And also *a*Elijah, unto whom I have committed the keys of the power of turning the hearts of the fathers to the children, and the hearts of the children to the *b*fathers, that the whole earth may not be smitten with a *c*curse;

---

27 1 *a* TG Revelation.
  b Hel. 3:29; D&C 6:2.
2 *a* TG Sacrament.
  b TG Glory.
  c TG Jesus Christ, Types of, in Memory.
  d TG Sacrifice.
  e TG Blood, Symbolism of.
  f TG Remission of Sins.
3 *a* D&C 89:5 (4–7).
4 *a* Isa. 65:8; Joel 1:5; 3:18; Hag. 1:11; Matt. 26:29.
5 *a* Mark 14:25; Luke 22:18.

  b Deut. 32:14.
  c D&C 27:16; 128:20 (19–21).
  d TG Book of Mormon.
  e Ezek. 37:16.
  f TG Israel, Joseph, People of.
6 *a* BD Elias.
7 *a* Luke 1:19 (17–19).
  b Luke 1:13 (13–19); D&C 84:27 (27–28).
8 *a* D&C 13. TG Priesthood, Aaronic.

  b TG Authority; Priesthood, Ordination.
  c Ex. 28:1 (1–3, 41); D&C 107:13.
9 *a* 1 Kgs. 17:1 (1–22); 2 Kgs. 1:1–2:15; D&C 2:2 (1–3); JS—H 1:38 (38–39). TG Genealogy and Temple Work.
  b TG Honoring Father and Mother.
  c TG Earth, Curse of.

10 And also with Joseph and *Jacob, and *Isaac, and Abraham, your *fathers, by whom the *promises remain;

11 And also with Michael, or *Adam, the father of all, the prince of all, the *ancient of days;

12 And also with Peter, and James, and John, whom I have sent unto you, by whom I have *ordained you and confirmed you to be *apostles, and especial *witnesses of my *name, and bear the keys of your ministry and of the same things which I revealed unto them;

13 Unto whom I have *committed the *keys of my kingdom, and a *dispensation of the *gospel for the *last times; and for the *fulness of times, in the which I will gather together in *one all things, both which are in heaven, and which are on earth;

14 And also with all those whom my Father hath *given me out of the world.

15 Wherefore, *lift up your hearts and *rejoice, and *gird up your loins, and take upon you my whole *armor, that ye may be able to withstand the evil day, having done all, that ye may be able to *stand.

16 Stand, therefore, having your loins *girt about with *truth, having on the *breastplate of *righteousness, and your feet shod with the preparation of the *gospel of *peace, which I have sent mine *angels to commit unto you;

17 Taking the shield of faith wherewith ye shall be able to quench all the *fiery darts of the wicked;

18 And take the helmet of salvation, and the sword of my *Spirit, which I will pour out upon you, and my word which I reveal unto you, and be agreed as touching all things whatsoever ye ask of me, and be faithful until I come, and ye shall be *caught up, that where I am ye shall be *also. Amen.

---

10 a Alma 7:25.
  b Gen. 21:12; Heb. 11:18
    (17–18); 1 Ne. 17:40.
  c Deut. 11:9; D&C 98:32.
    TG Israel, Origins of.
  d Ex. 32:13 (11–13).
11 a 1 Cor. 15:45 (45–48);
    2 Ne. 2:20 (19–20);
    Moses 1:34. TG Adam.
  b Dan. 7:22 (13, 22).
12 a JS—H 1:72. TG Priesthood, Authority;
    Priesthood, History of;
    Priesthood, Melchizedek;
    Priesthood, Ordination.
  b TG Apostles.
  c Luke 24:48; Acts 1:8.
    TG Witness.
  d D&C 18:27.

13 a Matt. 16:19.
  b D&C 113:6. TG Priesthood, Keys of.
  c TG Dispensations.
  d TG Gospel.
  e Jacob 5:71 (71–75);
    D&C 43:28 (28–30).
  f Eph. 1:10 (9–10); D&C
    76:106; 112:30; 124:41.
  g D&C 84:100.
14 a John 6:37; 17:9 (9, 11,
    14); 3 Ne. 15:24; D&C
    50:41 (41–42); 84:63.
15 a Lam. 3:41.
  b TG Joy.
  c Hag. 2:4; D&C 75:22.
  d Ex. 12:11; Rom. 13:12;
    Eph. 6:11. TG Children
    of Light; Protection,

Divine; War.
  e Mal. 3:2; D&C 87:8
    (1–8).
16 a Isa. 11:5.
  b TG Truth.
  c Lev. 8:8 (7–9); Isa. 59:17;
    JS—H 1:35.
  d TG Righteousness.
  e Rev. 14:6 (6–7).
  f Micah 5:5; 2 Ne. 19:6;
    D&C 111:8.
  g D&C 27:5 (5–14);
    128:20 (19–21).
17 a 1 Ne. 15:24; D&C 3:8.
18 a TG God, Spirit of.
  b 1 Ne. 13:37; 3 Ne. 27:14
    (14–15, 22); D&C 17:8.
  c John 14:3.

SECTION 28

Revelation given through Joseph Smith the Prophet to Oliver Cowdery, at Fayette, New York, September 1830. Hiram Page, a member of the Church, had a certain stone and professed to be receiving revelations by its aid concerning the upbuilding of Zion and the order of the Church. Several members had been deceived by these claims, and even Oliver Cowdery was wrongly influenced thereby. Just prior to an appointed conference, the Prophet inquired earnestly of the Lord concerning the matter, and this revelation followed.

1–7, Joseph Smith holds the keys of the mysteries, and only he receives revelations for the Church; 8–10, Oliver Cowdery is to preach to the Lamanites; 11–16, Satan deceived Hiram Page and gave him false revelations.

1 Behold, I say unto thee, ªOliver, that it shall be given unto thee that thou shalt be heard by the church in all things whatsoever thou shalt teach them by the ᵇComforter, concerning the revelations and commandments which I have given.

2 But, behold, verily, verily, I say unto thee, ªno one shall be appointed to receive commandments and ᵇrevelations in this church excepting my servant ᶜJoseph Smith, Jun., for he receiveth them even as ᵈMoses.

3 And thou shalt be obedient unto the things which I shall give unto him, even as ªAaron, to ᵇdeclare faithfully the commandments and the revelations, with power and ᶜauthority unto the church.

4 And if thou art ªled at any time by the Comforter to ᵇspeak or teach, or at all times by the way of commandment unto the church, thou mayest do it.

5 But thou shalt not write by way of ªcommandment, but by wisdom;

6 And thou shalt not command him who is at thy head, and at the head of the church;

7 For I have given him the ªkeys of the ᵇmysteries, and the revelations which are sealed, until I shall appoint unto them another in his stead.

---

28 1 *a* D&C 20:3 (3, 38).
  b TG Holy Ghost, Comforter; Teaching with the Spirit.
 2 *a* D&C 32:4; 35:17 (17–18); 43:4. TG Church Organization; Order.
  b TG Revelation.

 c 2 Ne. 3:15 (14–20). TG Joseph Smith.
 d Lev. 1:1.
 3 *a* Ex. 4:30 (14–16, 30); 28:1 (1–5).
  b Jer. 26:2.
  c TG Priesthood, Authority.
 4 *a* Gal. 5:18.

 b Ex. 4:12 (12–16); D&C 24:6 (5–6); Moses 6:8 (8, 32).
 5 *a* D&C 43:5; 63:22 (22–23).
 7 *a* D&C 35:18; 64:5; 84:19. TG Priesthood, Keys of.
  b TG Mysteries of Godliness.

8 And now, behold, I say unto you that you shall go unto the ^aLamanites and preach my ^bgospel unto them; and inasmuch as they ^creceive thy teachings thou shalt cause my ^dchurch to be established among them; and thou shalt have revelations, but write them not by way of commandment.

9 And now, behold, I say unto you that it is not revealed, and no man knoweth where the ^acity ^bZion shall be built, but it shall be given hereafter. Behold, I say unto you that it shall be on the borders by the Lamanites.

10 Thou shalt not leave this place until after the conference; and my servant Joseph shall be appointed to preside over the conference by the voice of it, and what he saith to thee thou shalt tell.

11 And again, thou shalt take thy brother, Hiram Page, ^abetween him and thee alone, and tell him that those things which he hath written from that ^bstone are not of me and that ^cSatan ^ddeceiveth him;

12 For, behold, these things have not been appointed unto him, neither shall anything be appointed unto any of this church contrary to the church covenants.

13 For all things must be done in ^aorder, and by common ^bconsent in the church, by the prayer of faith.

14 And thou shalt assist to settle all these things, according to the covenants of the church, before thou shalt take thy journey among the Lamanites.

15 And it shall be ^agiven thee from the time thou shalt go, until the time thou shalt return, what thou shalt do.

16 And thou must open thy mouth at all times, declaring my gospel with the sound of rejoicing. Amen.

SECTION 29

Revelation given through Joseph Smith the Prophet, in the presence of six elders, at Fayette, New York, September 1830. This revelation was given some days prior to the conference, beginning September 26, 1830.

1–8, Christ gathers His elect; 9–11, His coming ushers in the Millennium; 12–13, The Twelve will judge all Israel; 14–21, Signs, plagues, and desolations will

8 *a* 2 Ne. 3:19 (18–22); Alma
  17:1; D&C 30:5; 32:2
  (1–3); 49:24.
  b D&C 3:20.
  c TG Teachable.
  d Ether 13:6 (6–10).
9 *a* D&C 57:2; 103:24
  (22–24).
  b D&C 52:42 (42–43).
  TG Zion.
11 *a* Matt. 18:15.
  b TG Sorcery;
Superstitions.
  c Rev. 20:10; D&C 50:4.
  d D&C 43:6 (5–7); 46:7.
13 *a* TG Order.
  b TG Common Consent.
15 *a* 2 Ne. 32:5 (3, 5).

precede the Second Coming; 22–28, The last resurrection and final judgment follow the Millennium; 29–35, All things are spiritual unto the Lord; 36–39, The devil and his hosts were cast out of heaven to tempt man; 40–45, The Fall and Atonement bring salvation; 46–50, Little children are redeemed through the Atonement.

1 Listen to the voice of Jesus Christ, your Redeemer, the Great *a*I Am, whose arm of *b*mercy hath *c*atoned for your sins;

2 Who will *a*gather his people even as a hen gathereth her chickens under her wings, even as many as will hearken to my voice and *b*humble themselves before me, and call upon me in mighty prayer.

3 Behold, verily, verily, I say unto you, that at this time your *a*sins are *b*forgiven you, therefore ye receive these things; but remember to sin no more, lest perils shall come upon you.

4 Verily, I say unto you that ye are chosen out of the world to declare my gospel with the sound of rejoicing, as with the *a*voice of a trump.

5 Lift up your hearts and be *a*glad, for I am in your *b*midst, and am your *c*advocate with the Father; and it is his good will to give you the *d*kingdom.

6 And, as it is written—Whatsoever ye shall *a*ask in *b*faith, being *c*united in prayer according to my command, ye shall receive.

7 And ye are called to bring to pass the *a*gathering of mine *b*elect; for mine elect *c*hear my voice and *d*harden not their *e*hearts;

8 Wherefore the decree hath gone forth from the Father that they shall be *a*gathered in unto one place upon the face of this land, to *b*prepare their hearts and be prepared in all things against the day when *c*tribulation and desolation are sent forth upon the wicked.

9 For the hour is nigh and the *a*day soon at hand when the earth is ripe;

29 1 *a* TG Jesus Christ, Jehovah.
 b TG Mercy.
 c TG Jesus Christ, Atonement through.
 2 *a* Matt. 23:37. TG Israel, Gathering of.
 b TG Humility; Submissiveness.
 3 *a* 3 Ne. 8:1; D&C 50:29 (28–29).
 b TG Forgive.
 4 *a* Isa. 58:1; Rev. 1:10; Alma 29:1 (1–2); D&C 19:37; 30:9; 33:2.
 5 *a* Rom. 8:35 (35–39).
 b Matt. 18:20; D&C 6:32; 38:7; 88:63 (62–63).

 c TG Jesus Christ, Advocate; Jesus Christ, Relationships with the Father.
 d Luke 12:31 (22–34); D&C 35:27. TG Kingdom of God, on Earth.
 6 *a* Matt. 21:22; John 14:13.
 b Mark 11:24.
 c 3 Ne. 27:1 (1–2); D&C 84:1.
 7 *a* TG Israel, Gathering of; Mission of Latter-day Saints.
 b Matt. 24:24; Mark 13:21; John 6:44 (44, 63–65); D&C 84:34; JS—M 1:23.

 TG Election; Foreordination.
 c 1 Jn. 4:6 (1–6); Alma 5:41 (37–41). TG Missionary Work.
 d TG Hardheartedness.
 e TG Heart.
 8 *a* Matt. 24:28; D&C 45:66 (64–66); 52:2 (2, 42); 57:1; 103:24.
 b 3 Ne. 17:3; D&C 58:6; 78:7; 132:3. TG Millennium, Preparing a People for.
 c Isa. 47:11; D&C 5:19 (19–20); 35:11 (11–16); 43:17 (17–27).
 9 *a* TG Day of the Lord.

and all the *b*proud and they that do wickedly shall be as *c*stubble; and I will *d*burn them up, saith the Lord of Hosts, that wickedness shall not be upon the earth;

10 For the hour is nigh, and that which was *a*spoken by mine *b*apostles must be fulfilled; for as they spoke so shall it come to pass;

11 For I will reveal *a*myself from heaven with power and great glory, with all the *b*hosts thereof, and *c*dwell in *d*righteousness with men on earth a *e*thousand years, and the wicked shall not stand.

12 And again, verily, verily, I say unto you, and it hath gone forth in a firm decree, by the will of the Father, that mine *a*apostles, the Twelve which were with me in my ministry at Jerusalem, shall stand at my right hand at the day of my coming in a pillar of *b*fire, being clothed with robes of righteousness, with crowns upon their heads, in *c*glory even as I am, to *d*judge the whole house of Israel, even as many as have loved me and kept my commandments, and none else.

13 For a *a*trump shall sound both long and loud, even as upon Mount Sinai, and all the *b*earth shall quake, and they shall *c*come forth—yea, even the *d*dead which died in me, to receive a *e*crown of righteousness, and to be clothed upon, *f*even as I am, to be with me, that we may be one.

14 But, behold, I say unto you that before this great *a*day shall come the *b*sun shall be *c*darkened, and the moon shall be turned into blood, and the stars shall fall from heaven, and there shall be greater *d*signs in heaven above and in the earth beneath;

15 And there shall be weeping and *a*wailing among the hosts of men;

16 And there shall be a great *a*hailstorm sent forth to destroy the *b*crops of the earth.

---

9 *b* Ps. 18:27; 2 Ne. 20:33;
3 Ne. 25:1. TG Pride.
c Ex. 15:7 (7–8); Ps. 37:2;
Nahum 1:10; Mal. 4:1;
1 Ne. 22:23 (15, 23);
2 Ne. 26:6 (4–6); JS—H
1:37.
d Ps. 21:9 (8–10); 1 Ne.
22:15; D&C 45:57; 63:34
(34, 54); 64:24; 88:94;
101:24 (23–25); 133:64.
TG Earth, Cleansing of.
10 *a* Matt. 16:27. TG Jesus
Christ, Prophecies about;
Jesus Christ, Second
Coming.
b D&C 45:16 (15–16).
11 *a* D&C 101:23.
b JS—M 1:37.
c D&C 1:36 (35–36);

45:59; 84:119 (118–19);
104:59.
d TG Righteousness.
e TG Jesus Christ, Millennial Reign; Millennium.
12 *a* TG Apostles.
b Ex. 3:2; Isa. 66:15
(15–16); D&C 130:7;
133:41.
c TG Glory; Jesus Christ,
Glory of.
d Matt. 19:28; Luke 22:30;
1 Ne. 12:9 (9–10);
Morm. 3:18 (18–19).
13 *a* Ex. 19:13, 19; D&C
43:18; 45:45 (45–46).
b TG Earth, Destiny of.
c D&C 76:50 (17, 50).
d Rev. 11:18 (18–19); D&C
88:97 (96–97); 133:56.

e TG Exaltation.
f D&C 76:95; 78:5 (5–7);
84:38 (35–39); 132:20
(18–20).
14 *a* TG Last Days.
b Joel 2:10; JS—M 1:33.
c TG Darkness, Physical.
d Gen. 1:14. TG World,
End of.
15 *a* Matt. 13:42. TG Mourning.
16 *a* Ex. 9:18 (13–35); Isa.
32:19 (15–19); Ezek.
13:13; 38:22; Rev. 11:19;
16:21; Mosiah 12:6;
D&C 109:30. TG Last
Days.
b TG Famine.

17 And it shall come to pass, because of the wickedness of the world, that I will take *vengeance upon the *wicked, for they will not repent; for the *cup of mine *indignation is full; for behold, my *blood shall not *cleanse them if they hear me not.

18 Wherefore, I the Lord God will send forth *flies upon the face of the earth, which shall take hold of the inhabitants thereof, and shall eat their flesh, and shall cause maggots to come in upon them;

19 And their tongues shall be stayed that they shall not *utter against me; and their flesh shall fall from off their bones, and their eyes from their sockets;

20 And it shall come to pass that the *beasts of the forest and the fowls of the air shall devour them up.

21 And the great and *abominable church, which is the *whore of all the earth, shall be cast down by *devouring fire, according as it is spoken by the mouth of Ezekiel the prophet, who spoke of these things, which have not come to pass but surely *must, as I live, for *abominations shall not reign.

22 And again, verily, verily, I say unto you that when the *thousand years are ended, and men again begin to deny their God, then will I spare the earth but for a *little season;

23 And the *end shall come, and the heaven and the earth shall be consumed and *pass away, and there shall be a new heaven and a *new earth.

24 For all *old things shall *pass away, and all things shall become new, even the heaven and the earth, and all the fulness thereof, both men and *beasts, the fowls of the air, and the fishes of the sea;

25 And not one *hair, neither mote, shall be lost, for it is the *workmanship of mine hand.

26 But, behold, verily I say unto you, before the earth shall pass away, *Michael, mine archangel, shall sound his *trump, and then shall all the

17 a Ps. 73:17 (3–17); Rev.
    16:9–11; 2 Ne. 30:10;
    JS—M 1:55. TG God,
    Justice of; Vengeance.
  b TG Wickedness.
  c Jer. 25:15.
  d TG God, Indignation of.
  e 1 Jn. 1:7; Alma 11:40
    (40–41); D&C 19:17
    (16–18).
  f TG Purification.
18 a TG Plague.
19 a Ex. 16:8; Zech. 14:12;
    Rev. 16:9 (9, 11, 21);
    1 Ne. 16:22 (20–25).

20 a Isa. 18:6; Jer. 15:3; Ezek.
    39:17 (17–20); Rev. 19:17
    (17–18).
21 a TG Devil, Church of.
  b Rev. 19:2. TG Whore.
  c Ezek. 38:22; Joel 1:19
    (19–20); 2:3; D&C 45:41
    (40–41); 97:26 (25–26).
    TG Earth, Cleansing of.
  d D&C 1:38.
  e Ezek. 5:9 (9–11).
22 a TG Millennium.
  b Rev. 20:3 (3–10); Jacob
    5:77 (76–77); D&C
    43:31 (30–31); 88:111

    (110–12).
23 a Matt. 24:14. TG Earth,
    Destiny of; World, End
    of.
  b Matt. 24:35; JS—M
    1:35.
  c TG Earth, Renewal of.
24 a Rev. 20:11 (11–15).
  b 2 Cor. 5:17.
  c D&C 77:3 (2–4); Moses
    3:19.
25 a Luke 21:18; Alma 40:23.
  b Eph. 2:10.
26 a TG Adam.
  b 1 Cor. 15:52.

dead ᶜawake, for their graves shall be opened, and they shall ᵈcome forth—yea, even all.

27 And the ᵃrighteous shall be gathered on my ᵇright hand unto eternal life; and the wicked on my left hand will I be ashamed to own before the Father;

28 Wherefore I will say unto them—ᵃDepart from me, ye cursed, into everlasting ᵇfire, prepared for the ᶜdevil and his angels.

29 And now, behold, I say unto you, never at any time have I declared from mine own mouth that they should return, for ᵃwhere I am they cannot come, for they have no power.

30 But remember that all my judgments are not given unto men; and as the words have gone forth out of my mouth even so shall they be fulfilled, that the ᵃfirst shall be last, and that the last shall be first in all things whatsoever I have created by the word of my power, which is the power of my ᵇSpirit.

31 For by the power of my Spirit ᵃcreated I them; yea, all things both ᵇspiritual and temporal—

32 ᵃFirst ᵇspiritual, secondly temporal, which is the beginning of my work; and again, first temporal, and secondly spiritual, which is the last of my work—

33 ᵃSpeaking unto you that you may naturally understand; but unto myself my works have no ᵇend, neither beginning; but it is given unto you that ye may understand, because ye have asked it of me and are agreed.

34 Wherefore, verily I say unto you that all things unto me are spiritual, and not at any time have I given unto you a ᵃlaw which was ᵇtemporal; neither any man, nor the children of men; neither Adam, your father, whom I created.

35 Behold, I gave unto him that he should be an ᵃagent unto himself; and I gave unto him commandment, but no temporal commandment gave I

---

26 c TG Immortality; Resurrection.
  d John 5:29 (28–29).
27 a Ps. 5:12. TG Righteousness.
  b Matt. 25:33. TG Judgment, the Last.
28 a Matt. 25:41; Luke 13:27; Rom. 16:20; 1 Jn. 3:8; D&C 19:3; 29:41; 76:37; 88:114 (111–15).
  b Dan. 7:11; D&C 43:33.

  c TG Devil.
29 a John 7:34 (33–36); D&C 76:112 (51–112).
30 a Matt. 19:30; Luke 13:30.
  b TG God, Spirit of.
31 a TG Creation; Jesus Christ, Creator.
  b Moses 3:5.
32 a 1 Cor. 15:46 (44–46); D&C 128:14; Moses 3:5 (5–7).
  b TG Resurrection; Spirit

  Creation.
33 a TG Communication; Language.
  b Ps. 111:8 (7–8); 1 Ne. 14:7; Moses 1:4.
34 a Rom. 7:14. TG God, Law of.
  b TG God, Eternal Nature of.
35 a TG Agency.

unto him, for my *b*commandments are *c*spiritual; they are not natural nor temporal, neither carnal nor sensual.

36 And it came to pass that Adam, being tempted of the *a*devil—for, behold, the *b*devil was before Adam, for he *c*rebelled against me, saying, Give me thine *d*honor, which is my *e*power; and also a *f*third part of the *g*hosts of heaven turned he away from me because of their *h*agency;

37 And they were thrust down, and thus came the *a*devil and his *b*angels;

38 And, behold, there is a place *a*prepared for them from the beginning, which place is *b*hell.

39 And it must needs be that the *a*devil should *b*tempt the children of men, or they could not be *c*agents unto themselves; for if they never should have *d*bitter they could not know the sweet—

40 Wherefore, it came to pass that the devil tempted Adam, and he partook of the forbidden *a*fruit and *b*transgressed the commandment, wherein he became *c*subject to the will of the devil, because he yielded unto temptation.

41 Wherefore, I, the Lord God, caused that he should be *a*cast out from the Garden of *b*Eden, from my presence, because of his transgression, wherein he became *c*spiritually *d*dead, which is the first death, even that same death which is the last *e*death, which is spiritual, which shall be pronounced upon the wicked when I shall say: Depart, ye *f*cursed.

42 But, behold, I say unto you that I, the Lord God, gave unto Adam and unto his seed, that they should not *a*die as to the temporal death, until I, the Lord God, should send forth *b*angels to declare unto them *c*repentance and *d*redemption, through faith on the name of mine *e*Only Begotten Son.

43 And thus did I, the Lord God, appoint unto man the days of his

---

35 *b* TG Commandments of
   God.
   c TG Spirituality.
36 *a* TG Devil.
   b D&C 76:25 (25–26);
   Moses 4:1 (1–4).
   c TG Council in Heaven;
   Rashness.
   d TG Honor.
   e Isa. 14:14; D&C 76:28
   (25–29).
   f Luke 8:30; Rev. 12:4
   (3–4); Moses 4:6.
   g Gen. 2:1; D&C 38:1;
   45:1; Moses 3:1; Abr. 5:1.
   TG Man, Antemortal
   Existence of.
   h TG Agency; Initiative.

37 *a* TG Devil.
   b 2 Pet. 2:4; Jude 1:6;
   Moses 7:26. TG Angels.
38 *a* Moses 6:29.
   b Prov. 9:18; Alma 12:11;
   D&C 76:84 (84–86).
   TG Hell.
39 *a* TG Devil.
   b 1 Thes. 3:5; Moses 4:4
   (3–4). TG Opposition;
   Temptation.
   c TG Agency.
   d Moses 6:55.
40 *a* Gen. 3:6; Moses 4:12
   (7–13).
   b John 8:34. TG Transgress.
   c 2 Ne. 10:24; Mosiah

16:3 (3–5); Alma 5:41
   (41–42).
41 *a* TG Fall of Man.
   b TG Eden.
   c TG Man, Natural, Not
   Spiritually Reborn.
   d TG Death, Spiritual,
   First.
   e Alma 40:26. TG Death,
   Spiritual, Second.
   f D&C 29:28; 76:37;
   Moses 5:36.
42 *a* 2 Ne. 2:21. TG Death.
   b Alma 12:29 (28–30).
   c TG Repent.
   d TG Redemption.
   e TG Jesus Christ, Divine
   Sonship.

*a*probation—that by his *b*natural death he might be *c*raised in *d*immortality unto eternal life, even as many as would believe;

44 And they that believe not unto eternal *a*damnation; for they cannot be redeemed from their spiritual *b*fall, because they repent not;

45 For they love darkness rather than light, and their *a*deeds are evil, and they receive their *b*wages of *c*whom they list to obey.

46 But behold, I say unto you, that little *a*children are *b*redeemed from the foundation of the world through mine Only Begotten;

47 Wherefore, they cannot *a*sin, for power is not given unto Satan to *b*tempt little children, until they *c*begin to become *d*accountable before me;

48 For it is given unto them even as I will, according to mine own *a*pleasure, that great things may be required at the hand of their *b*fathers.

49 And, again, I say unto you, that whoso having knowledge, have I not commanded to *a*repent?

50 And he that hath no *a*understanding, it remaineth in me to do according as it is written. And now I declare no more unto you at this time. Amen.

SECTION 30

Revelation given through Joseph Smith the Prophet to David Whitmer, Peter Whitmer Jr., and John Whitmer, at Fayette, New York, September 1830, following the three-day conference at Fayette, but before the elders of the Church had separated. Originally this material was published as three revelations; it was combined into one section by the Prophet for the 1835 edition of the Doctrine and Covenants.

1–4, David Whitmer is chastened for failure to serve diligently; 5–8, Peter Whitmer Jr. is to accompany Oliver Cowdery on a mission to the Lamanites; 9–11, John Whitmer is called to preach the gospel.

43 *a* TG Earth, Purpose of; Mortality; Probation.
 b 1 Cor. 15:44.
 c TG Resurrection.
 d Matt. 5:48; Rom. 8:17 (14–21); 2 Ne. 2:15 (14–30); Alma 42:26; Moses 1:39. TG Immortality.
44 *a* D&C 19:7. TG Damnation; Hell.
 b TG Death, Spiritual, Second.
45 *a* John 3:19 (18–21);

Jude 1:4; D&C 10:21; 84:46–48; 93:31–32.
 b Mosiah 2:32 (32–33); Alma 3:27 (26–27); 5:42 (41–42); 30:60. TG Wages.
 c D&C 58:33.
46 *a* Moro. 8:12 (8, 12, 22); D&C 93:38. TG Children; Conceived in Sin; Salvation of Little Children.
 b D&C 74:7. TG Jesus Christ, Redeemer;

Redemption.
47 *a* TG Sin.
 b TG Temptation.
 c Moses 6:55.
 d D&C 18:42; 20:71; 68:25 (25–27). TG Accountability.
48 *a* TG Pleasure.
 b D&C 68:25. TG Family, Children, Responsibilities toward.
49 *a* TG Repent.
50 *a* D&C 137:7 (7–10). TG Understanding.

1 Behold, I say unto you, David, that you have *a*feared man and have not *b*relied on me for strength as you ought.

2 But your mind has been on the things of the *a*earth more than on the things of me, your Maker, and the ministry whereunto you have been called; and you have not given heed unto my *b*Spirit, and to those who were set over you, but have been persuaded by those whom I have not commanded.

3 Wherefore, you are left to inquire for yourself at my hand, and *a*ponder upon the things which you have received.

4 And your home shall be at your *a*father's house, until I give unto you further commandments. And you shall attend to the *b*ministry in the church, and before the world, and in the regions round about. Amen.

5 Behold, I say unto you, Peter, that you shall take your *a*journey with your brother Oliver; for the *b*time has come that it is expedient in me that you shall open your mouth to declare my gospel; therefore, fear not, but give *c*heed unto the words and advice of your brother, which he shall give you.

6 And be you afflicted in all his *a*afflictions, ever *b*lifting up your heart unto me in prayer and faith, for his and your *c*deliverance; for I have given unto him power to *d*build up my *e*church among the *f*Lamanites;

7 And none have I appointed to be his counselor *a*over him in the church, concerning church matters, except it is his brother, Joseph Smith, Jun.

8 Wherefore, give heed unto these things and be diligent in keeping my commandments, and you shall be blessed unto eternal life. Amen.

9 Behold, I say unto you, my servant John, that thou shalt commence from this time forth to *a*proclaim my gospel, as with the *b*voice of a trump.

10 And your labor shall be at your brother Philip Burroughs', and in that region round about, yea, wherever you can be heard, until I command you to go from hence.

11 And your whole labor shall be in Zion, with all your soul, from henceforth; yea, you shall ever open your mouth in my cause, not *a*fearing what *b*man can do, for I am *c*with you. Amen.

---

30 1 *a* Acts 5:29. TG Peer Influ-
    ence.
  b 2 Chr. 16:7.
  2 *a* D&C 25:10.
    b TG God, Spirit of.
  3 *a* TG Meditation.
  4 *a* D&C 128:21.
    b TG Ministry; Service.

5 *a* D&C 28:8; 32:2 (1–3).
  b D&C 11:15; 16:6.
  c TG Sustaining Church
    Leaders.
6 *a* TG Affliction.
  b Lam. 3:41.
  c TG Deliver.
  d D&C 39:13; 42:8.
  e TG Jesus Christ, Head of

    the Church.
  f D&C 3:20; 49:24.
7 *a* D&C 20:3 (2–3).
9 *a* Jer. 3:12; D&C 15:6
    (1–6).
  b D&C 19:37; 29:4; 33:2.
11 *a* TG Courage.
  b Isa. 51:7.
  c Matt. 28:20.

SECTION 31

Revelation given through Joseph Smith the Prophet to Thomas B. Marsh, September 1830. The occasion was immediately following a conference of the Church (see the heading to section 30). Thomas B. Marsh had been baptized earlier in the month and had been ordained an elder in the Church before this revelation was given.

1–6, Thomas B. Marsh is called to preach the gospel and is assured of his family's well-being; 7–13, He is counseled to be patient, pray always, and follow the Comforter.

1 ^aThomas, my son, blessed are you because of your faith in my work.

2 Behold, you have had many afflictions because of your family; nevertheless, I will bless you and your ^afamily, yea, your little ones; and the day cometh that they will believe and know the truth and be one with you in my church.

3 Lift up your heart and rejoice, for the hour of your mission is come; and your tongue shall be loosed, and you shall declare ^aglad tidings of great joy unto this generation.

4 You shall ^adeclare the things which have been revealed to my servant, Joseph Smith, Jun. You shall begin to preach from this time forth, yea, to reap in the field which is ^bwhite already to be burned.

5 Therefore, ^athrust in your sickle with all your soul, and your sins are ^bforgiven you, and you shall be laden with ^csheaves upon your back, for the ^dlaborer is worthy of his hire. Wherefore, your family shall live.

6 Behold, verily I say unto you, go from them only for a little ^atime, and declare my word, and I will prepare a place for them.

7 Yea, I will ^aopen the hearts of the people, and they will receive you. And I will establish a church by your hand;

8 And you shall ^astrengthen them and prepare them against the time when they shall be gathered.

9 Be ^apatient in ^bafflictions, ^crevile not against those that revile. Govern your ^dhouse in meekness, and be ^esteadfast.

---

31 1 *a* D&C 52:22; 56:5 (5–6); 75:31.
2 *a* TG Family; Unity.
3 *a* Isa. 52:7 (7–10); Luke 2:10 (10–11); Rom. 10:15; Mosiah 3:3 (3–5).
4 *a* Mosiah 18:19 (18–20); D&C 5:10; 42:12; 52:36.

b D&C 4:4 (4–6).
5 *a* Rev. 14:15.
b TG Forgive.
c Ps. 126:6; D&C 79:3.
d Luke 10:7 (3–11); D&C 51:14; 75:24; 84:79. TG Consecration; Wages.
6 *a* TG Family, Children, Responsibilities toward.

7 *a* TG Conversion.
8 *a* Zech. 10:12; D&C 81:5; 108:7.
9 *a* Rom. 12:12. TG Patience.
b TG Affliction.
c TG Forbear; Malice; Retribution; Reviling.
d TG Family, Love within.
e TG Steadfastness.

10 Behold, I say unto you that you shall be a physician unto the church, but not unto the world, for they will not receive you.

11 Go your way whithersoever I will, and it shall be given you by the [a]Comforter what you shall do and whither you shall go.

12 [a]Pray always, lest you enter into [b]temptation and lose your [c]reward.

13 Be [a]faithful unto the [b]end, and lo, I am [c]with you. These words are not of man nor of men, but of me, even Jesus Christ, your Redeemer, by the [d]will of the Father. Amen.

SECTION 32

Revelation given through Joseph Smith the Prophet to Parley P. Pratt and Ziba Peterson, in Manchester, New York, early October 1830. Great interest and desires were felt by the elders respecting the Lamanites, of whose predicted blessings the Church had learned from the Book of Mormon. In consequence, supplication was made that the Lord would indicate His will as to whether elders should be sent at that time to the Indian tribes in the West. The revelation followed.

1–3, Parley P. Pratt and Ziba Peterson are called to preach to the Lamanites and to accompany Oliver Cowdery and Peter Whitmer Jr.; 4–5, They are to pray for an understanding of the scriptures.

1 And now concerning my servant [a]Parley P. Pratt, behold, I say unto him that as I live I will that he shall declare my gospel and [b]learn of me, and be meek and lowly of heart.

2 And that which I have appointed unto him is that he shall [a]go with my servants, Oliver Cowdery and Peter Whitmer, Jun., into the wilderness among the [b]Lamanites.

3 And [a]Ziba Peterson also shall go with them; and I myself will go with them and be in their [b]midst; and I am their [c]advocate with the Father, and nothing shall [d]prevail against them.

---

11 *a* TG Holy Ghost, Comforter.
12 *a* TG Prayer.
  b Mark 14:38. TG Temptation.
  c TG Reward.
13 *a* TG Steadfastness.
  b Rev. 2:10.
  c Matt. 28:20.

d TG Jesus Christ, Authority of.
32 1 *a* D&C 50:37; 52:26; 97:3; 103:30 (30–37).
  b Matt. 11:29.
2 *a* D&C 28:8; 30:5.
  b D&C 3:20 (18–20).
3 *a* D&C 58:60.
  b Matt. 18:20; D&C 6:32;

38:7.
c TG Jesus Christ, Advocate; Jesus Christ, Relationships with the Father.
d Mosiah 28:7 (6–7); Moses 8:18 (18–19).

4 And they shall give ᵃheed to that which is written, and pretend to no other ᵇrevelation; and they shall pray always that I may ᶜunfold the same to their ᵈunderstanding.

5 And they shall give heed unto these words and trifle not, and I will bless them. Amen.

SECTION 33

Revelation given through Joseph Smith the Prophet to Ezra Thayre and Northrop Sweet, at Fayette, New York, October 1830. In introducing this revelation, Joseph Smith's history affirms that "the Lord . . . is ever ready to instruct such as diligently seek in faith."

1–4, Laborers are called to declare the gospel in the eleventh hour; 5–6, The Church is established, and the elect are to be gathered; 7–10, Repent, for the kingdom of heaven is at hand; 11–15, The Church is built upon the gospel rock; 16–18, Prepare for the coming of the Bridegroom.

1 Behold, I say unto you, my servants ᵃEzra and Northrop, open ye your ears and hearken to the voice of the Lord your God, whose ᵇword is quick and powerful, sharper than a two-edged sword, to the dividing asunder of the joints and marrow, soul and spirit; and is a discerner of the thoughts and ᶜintents of the heart.

2 For verily, verily, I say unto you that ye are called to lift up your voices as with the ᵃsound of a trump, to declare my gospel unto a crooked and ᵇperverse generation.

3 For behold, the ᵃfield is ᵇwhite already to harvest; and it is the ᶜeleventh hour, and the last time that I shall call ᵈlaborers into my vineyard.

4 And my ᵃvineyard has become ᵇcorrupted every whit; and there is none which doeth ᶜgood save it be a few; and they ᵈerr in many instances because of ᵉpriestcrafts, all having corrupt minds.

5 And verily, verily, I say unto you, that this ᵃchurch have I ᵇestablished and called forth out of the ᶜwilderness.

---

4 *a* 1 Ne. 15:25 (23–25);
D&C 84:43 (43–44).
b D&C 28:2.
c JS—H 1:74.
d TG Understanding.
33 1 *a* D&C 52:22; 56:5 (5–8).
b Heb. 4:12; Hel. 3:29
(29–30).
c Amos 4:13.
2 *a* Isa. 58:1; D&C 19:37;
29:4; 30:9.

b Deut. 32:5.
3 *a* John 4:35.
b D&C 4:4; 12:3; 14:3;
101:64.
c Matt. 20:6 (1–16).
d Jacob 5:71 (71–75);
D&C 43:28.
4 *a* TG Vineyard of the Lord.
b 2 Ne. 28:11 (2–14);
Morm. 8:28 (28–41);
D&C 38:11.

c Eccl. 7:20; Jer. 13:23;
Rom. 3:12; D&C 35:12.
d 2 Ne. 27:35 (34–35);
28:14.
e TG Priestcraft.
5 *a* TG Church; Jesus Christ,
Head of the Church.
b TG Mission of Latter-day
Saints.
c Rev. 12:6 (1–6).

6 And even so will I ^agather mine elect from the ^bfour quarters of the earth, even as many as will believe in me, and hearken unto my voice.

7 Yea, verily, verily, I say unto you, that the field is ^awhite already to harvest; wherefore, thrust in your sickles, and reap with all your might, mind, and strength.

8 ^aOpen your mouths and they shall be filled, and you shall become even as ^bNephi of old, who journeyed from Jerusalem in the wilderness.

9 Yea, open your mouths and spare not, and you shall be laden with ^asheaves upon your backs, for lo, I am with you.

10 Yea, open your mouths and they shall be filled, saying: ^aRepent, repent, and prepare ye the way of the Lord, and make his paths straight; for the ^bkingdom of heaven is at hand;

11 Yea, ^arepent and be baptized, every one of you, for a ^bremission of your sins; yea, be baptized even by water, and then cometh the baptism of fire and of the Holy Ghost.

12 Behold, verily, verily, I say unto you, this is my ^agospel; and remember that they shall have faith in me or they can in nowise be saved;

13 And upon this ^arock I will build my church; yea, upon this rock ye are built, and if ye continue, the ^bgates of hell shall not prevail against you.

14 And ye shall remember the church ^aarticles and covenants to keep them.

15 And whoso having faith you shall ^aconfirm in my church, by the laying on of the ^bhands, and I will bestow the ^cgift of the Holy Ghost upon them.

16 And the Book of Mormon and the holy scriptures are given of me for your ^ainstruction; and the power of my ^bSpirit ^cquickeneth all things.

17 Wherefore, be faithful, praying always, having your ^alamps ^btrimmed and burning, and oil with you, that you may be ^cready at the coming of the ^dBridegroom—

18 For behold, verily, verily, I say unto you, that I ^acome quickly. Even so. Amen.

6 a Deut. 30:3. TG Israel, Gathering of.
  b Jer. 49:36; Rev. 20:8; D&C 45:46.
7 a D&C 4:4 (2–4).
8 a TG Missionary Work.
  b 2 Ne. 1:27 (27–28).
9 a Ps. 126:6; Alma 26:5; D&C 75:5.
10 a Matt. 3:2.
  b Mark 1:15.
11 a TG Baptism, Qualifications for; Repent.

  b TG Remission of Sins.
12 a TG Gospel; Salvation, Plan of.
13 a TG Rock.
  b Matt. 16:18; D&C 10:69.
14 a IE D&C 20 (see the section 20 heading). D&C 1:6 (6, 37); 42:13; 51:4.
15 a D&C 20:41.
  b TG Hands, Laying on of.
  c TG Holy Ghost, Gift of.
16 a TG Scriptures, Study of; Scriptures, Value of.

  b TG God, Spirit of.
  c Ps. 71:20; 1 Tim. 6:13.
17 a D&C 88:92; 133:19 (10, 19).
  b Matt. 25:7 (1–13).
  c TG Procrastination.
  d TG Jesus Christ, Prophecies about.
18 a Rev. 22:20; D&C 34:12. TG Jesus Christ, Second Coming.

SECTION 34

Revelation given through Joseph Smith the Prophet to Orson Pratt, at Fayette, New York, November 4, 1830. Brother Pratt was nineteen years old at the time. He had been converted and baptized when he first heard the preaching of the restored gospel by his older brother, Parley P. Pratt, six weeks before. This revelation was received in the Peter Whitmer Sr. home.

1–4, The faithful become the sons of God through the Atonement; 5–9, The preaching of the gospel prepares the way for the Second Coming; 10–12, Prophecy comes by the power of the Holy Ghost.

1 My son ^aOrson, hearken and hear and behold what I, the Lord God, shall say unto you, even Jesus Christ your Redeemer;

2 The ^alight and the life of the world, a light which shineth in darkness and the darkness comprehendeth it not;

3 Who so ^aloved the world that he ^bgave his own life, that as many as would believe might become the ^csons of God. Wherefore you are my son;

4 And ^ablessed are you because you have believed;

5 And more blessed are you because you are ^acalled of me to preach my gospel—

6 To lift up your voice as with the sound of a ^atrump, both long and loud, and ^bcry repentance unto a crooked and perverse generation, ^cpreparing the way of the Lord for his ^dsecond coming.

7 For behold, verily, verily, I say unto you, the ^atime is soon at hand that I shall ^bcome in a ^ccloud with power and great glory.

8 And it shall be a ^agreat day at the time of my coming, for all nations shall ^btremble.

9 But before that great day shall come, the ^asun shall be darkened, and the moon be turned into blood; and the stars shall refuse their shining, and some shall fall, and great destructions await the wicked.

10 Wherefore, lift up your voice and ^aspare not, for the Lord God hath

---

34 1 a D&C 52:26; 103:40;
    124:129; 136:13.
  2 a John 1:5.
  3 a John 3:16; 15:13.
    TG Love.
    b TG Jesus Christ,
    Redeemer.
    c Luke 8:21; John 1:12
    (9–13); Rom. 8:17
    (12–17); Moses 6:68

(64–68). TG Sons and
    Daughters of God.
  4 a John 20:29.
  5 a TG Called of God.
  6 a D&C 24:12.
    b D&C 3:20; 6:9; 18:14.
    c Matt. 3:3.
    d TG Jesus Christ, Second
    Coming; Millennium,
    Preparing a People for.
  7 a Rev. 1:3.

b TG Jesus Christ, Prophe-
    cies about.
    c Num. 11:25; Luke 21:27;
    Ether 2:4 (4–5, 14);
    JS—H 1:68 (68–71).
  8 a Joel 2:11; Mal. 4:5;
    D&C 2:1; 43:17 (17–26).
    TG Day of the Lord.
    b Isa. 64:2.
  9 a TG Last Days.
  10 a Isa. 58:1.

spoken; therefore *b*prophesy, and it shall be given by the *c*power of the Holy Ghost.

11 And if you are faithful, behold, I am with you until I come—

12 And verily, verily, I say unto you, I come *a*quickly. I am your *b*Lord and your Redeemer. Even so. Amen.

SECTION 35

Revelation given to Joseph Smith the Prophet and Sidney Rigdon, at or near Fayette, New York, December 7, 1830. At this time, the Prophet was engaged almost daily in making a translation of the Bible. The translation was begun as early as June 1830, and both Oliver Cowdery and John Whitmer had served as scribes. Since they had now been called to other duties, Sidney Rigdon was called by divine appointment to serve as the Prophet's scribe in this work (see verse 20). As a preface to the record of this revelation, Joseph Smith's history states: "In December Sidney Rigdon came [from Ohio] to inquire of the Lord, and with him came Edward Partridge. . . . Shortly after the arrival of these two brethren, thus spake the Lord."

1–2, How men may become the sons of God; 3–7, Sidney Rigdon is called to baptize and to confer the Holy Ghost; 8–12, Signs and miracles are wrought by faith; 13–16, The Lord's servants will thresh the nations by the power of the Spirit; 17–19, Joseph Smith holds the keys of the mysteries; 20–21, The elect will abide the day of the Lord's coming; 22–27, Israel will be saved.

1 Listen to the voice of the *a*Lord your God, even *b*Alpha and Omega, the beginning and the end, whose *c*course is one *d*eternal round, the *e*same today as yesterday, and forever.

2 I am Jesus Christ, the Son of God, who was *a*crucified for the sins of the world, even as many as will *b*believe on my name, that they may become the *c*sons of God, even *d*one in *e*me as I am *f*one in the Father, as the Father is one in me, that we may be one.

3 Behold, verily, verily, I say unto my servant Sidney, I have looked upon

---

10 *b* TG Prophets, Mission of.
  c 2 Pet. 1:21; D&C 18:32;
    42:16; 68:3.
12 *a* D&C 33:18.
  b TG Jesus Christ, Lord.
35 1 *a* TG Jesus Christ, Lord.
  b Rev. 1:8; D&C 19:1.
  c 1 Ne. 10:19; D&C 3:2.

d TG God, Eternal Nature
    of.
  e Heb. 13:8; D&C 20:12;
    38:1 (1–4); 39:1 (1–3);
    76:4.
2 *a* TG Jesus Christ, Cruci-
    fixion of.
  b D&C 20:25; 38:4; 45:5

  (5, 8).
  c TG Sons and Daughters
    of God.
  d John 17:21; Moses 6:68.
    TG Unity.
  e TG Jesus Christ, Exem-
    plar.
  f TG Godhead.

thee and thy works. I have *heard thy prayers, and prepared thee for a greater work.

4 Thou art blessed, for thou shalt do great things. Behold thou wast sent forth, even as *John, to prepare the way before me, and before *Elijah which should come, and thou knewest it not.

5 Thou didst baptize by water unto repentance, but they *received not the Holy Ghost;

6 But now I give unto thee a commandment, that thou shalt *baptize by water, and they shall receive the *Holy Ghost by the laying on of the *hands, even as the apostles of old.

7 And it shall come to pass that there shall be a great work in the land, even among the *Gentiles, for their *folly and their abominations shall be made manifest in the eyes of all people.

8 For I am God, and mine arm is not *shortened; and I will show *miracles, *signs, and wonders, unto all those who *believe on my name.

9 And whoso shall ask it in my name in *faith, they shall *cast out *devils; they shall heal the *sick; they shall cause the blind to receive their *sight, and the deaf to hear, and the dumb to speak, and the lame to walk.

10 And the time *speedily cometh that great things are to be shown forth unto the children of men;

11 But *without faith shall not anything be shown forth except *desolations upon *Babylon, the same which has made *all nations drink of the wine of the wrath of her *fornication.

12 And there are *none that doeth good except those who are ready to *receive the fulness of my gospel, which I have sent forth unto this generation.

13 Wherefore, I call upon the *weak things of the world, those who are *unlearned and despised, to thresh the *nations by the power of my *Spirit;

---

3 *a* Ex. 2:24 (23–24); Mosiah 9:18 (17–18); Abr. 1:15 (15–16).
4 *a* Mal. 3:1; Matt. 11:10; John 5:33; 1 Ne. 11:27; D&C 84:27 (27–28).
   b 3 Ne. 25:5 (5–6); D&C 2:1; 110:13 (13–15); 128:17.
5 *a* Acts 19:2 (1–6).
6 *a* TG Baptism.
   b TG Holy Ghost, Gift of.
   c TG Hands, Laying on of.
7 *a* Isa. 66:12. TG Gentiles.
   b Eccl. 10:12 (1–3, 12);

2 Tim. 3:9; 2 Ne. 9:28 (28–29); 19:17.
8 *a* Isa. 50:2 (2–4); 59:1.
   b TG Miracle.
   c TG Signs.
   d TG Believe; Trust in God.
9 *a* TG Faith.
   b Mark 16:17.
   c Mark 1:39 (21–45).
   d TG Heal; Sickness.
   e TG Sight.
10 *a* JS—H 1:41.
11 *a* D&C 63:11 (7–12).
   b Jer. 51:62; D&C 5:19

(19–20); 29:8; 43:17 (17–27).
   c TG Babylon.
   d 1 Ne. 14:11 (10–13).
   e Rev. 18:3.
12 *a* Rom. 3:12; Moro. 7:13 (12–13); D&C 33:4; 38:11; 84:47 (47–51).
   b TG Missionary Work; Teachable.
13 *a* 1 Cor. 1:27; D&C 1:19 (19, 23); 124:1.
   b Acts 4:13.
   c TG Nations.
   d TG God, Spirit of.

14 And their arm shall be my arm, and I will be their ᵃshield and their buckler; and I will gird up their loins, and they shall fight manfully for me; and their ᵇenemies shall be under their feet; and I will let ᶜfall the ᵈsword in their behalf, and by the ᵉfire of mine indignation will I preserve them.

15 And the ᵃpoor and the ᵇmeek shall have the gospel preached unto them, and they shall be ᶜlooking forth for the time of my coming, for it is ᵈnigh at hand—

16 And they shall learn the parable of the ᵃfig tree, for even now already summer is nigh.

17 And I have sent forth the ᵃfulness of my gospel by the hand of my servant Joseph; and in weakness have I blessed him;

18 And I have given unto him the ᵃkeys of the mystery of those things which have been ᵇsealed, even things which were from the ᶜfoundation of the world, and the things which shall come from this time until the time of my coming, if he ᵈabide in me, and if not, ᵉanother will I plant in his stead.

19 Wherefore, watch over him that his faith fail not, and it shall be given by the ᵃComforter, the ᵇHoly Ghost, that knoweth all things.

20 And a commandment I give unto thee—that thou shalt ᵃwrite for him; and the ᵇscriptures shall be given, even as they are in mine own bosom, to the salvation of mine own ᶜelect;

21 For they will hear my ᵃvoice, and shall ᵇsee me, and shall not be ᶜasleep, and shall ᵈabide the day of my ᵉcoming; for they shall be ᶠpurified, even as I am pure.

22 And now I say unto you, ᵃtarry with him, and he shall journey with you; forsake him not, and surely these things shall be fulfilled.

---

14 a 2 Sam. 22:3; Ps. 33:20;
      91:4.
   b D&C 98:37 (34–38).
   c D&C 1:14 (13–14);
      45:47.
   d D&C 1:13.
   e Num. 11:1 (1, 10); D&C
      128:24; Moses 7:34.
15 a Matt. 11:5.
   b TG Meek.
   c 2 Pet. 3:12 (10–13);
      D&C 39:23; 45:39;
      Moses 7:62.
   d D&C 63:53.
16 a Matt. 24:32; Luke 21:29
      (29–30); D&C 45:37
      (36–38); JS—M 1:38.
      TG Last Days.

17 a Rom. 15:29; D&C 42:12;
      135:3.
18 a D&C 28:7; 84:19.
   b Dan. 12:9; Matt. 13:35;
      1 Ne. 14:26; 2 Ne. 27:10;
      Ether 4:5 (4–7); JS—H
      1:65.
   c D&C 128:18.
   d John 15:4 (4, 7).
   e D&C 42:10; 64:40;
      104:77; 107:99 (99–100).
19 a John 14:16, 26; 15:26;
      1 Cor. 12:8.
   b 1 Cor. 2:10.
20 a The Prophet was at
      this time engaged in a
      revelatory translation
      of the Bible, to which

Sidney Rigdon was called
as scribe.
   b D&C 6:27; 37:1; 42:15
      (15, 56–58).
   c TG Election.
21 a Joel 2:11; John 10:3;
      D&C 43:18 (17–25);
      88:90; 133:50 (50–52).
   b John 16:16. TG God,
      Privilege of Seeing.
   c Matt. 25:5.
   d Mal. 3:2.
   e TG Jesus Christ, Prophe-
      cies about; Jesus Christ,
      Second Coming.
   f TG Purification.
22 a D&C 90:6; 100:9 (9–11).

23 And *inasmuch as ye do not write, behold, it shall be *given unto him to prophesy; and thou shalt preach my gospel and call on *the holy prophets to prove his words, as they shall be given him.

24 *Keep all the commandments and covenants by which ye are bound; and I will cause the heavens to *shake for your *good, and *Satan shall tremble and *Zion shall *rejoice upon the hills and *flourish;

25 And *Israel shall be *saved in mine own due time; and by the *keys which I have given shall they be led, and no more be confounded at all.

26 *Lift up your hearts and be glad, your *redemption draweth nigh.

27 Fear not, little *flock, the *kingdom is yours until I come. Behold, I *come quickly. Even so. Amen.

SECTION 36

Revelation given through Joseph Smith the Prophet to Edward Partridge, near Fayette, New York, December 9, 1830 (see the heading to section 35). Joseph Smith's history states that Edward Partridge "was a pattern of piety, and one of the Lord's great men."

1–3, The Lord lays His hand upon Edward Partridge by the hand of Sidney Rigdon; 4–8, Every man who receives the gospel and the priesthood is to be called to go forth and preach.

1 Thus saith the Lord God, the *Mighty One of Israel: Behold, I say unto you, my servant *Edward, that you are blessed, and your sins are forgiven you, and you are called to preach my gospel as with the voice of a trump;

2 And I will lay my *hand upon you by the hand of my servant Sidney Rigdon, and you shall receive my Spirit, the Holy Ghost, even the *Comforter, which shall *teach you the peaceable things of the kingdom;

3 And you shall declare it with a loud voice, saying: Hosanna, *blessed be the name of the most high God.

---

23 *a* IE whenever you are not occupied with writing.
  b 1 Cor. 12:8.
  c IE the scriptures.
24 *a* D&C 66:11; 103:7.
  b D&C 21:6.
  c TG Blessing.
  d 1 Ne. 22:26; Alma 48:17.
  e D&C 6:6.
  f TG Joy.
  g D&C 39:13; 49:25; 117:7 (7–8).
25 *a* TG Israel, Blessings of; Israel, Restoration of;

Israel, Ten Lost Tribes of; Israel, Twelve Tribes of.
  b Ps. 94:14; Isa. 45:17; 1 Ne. 19:16 (15–16); 22:12. TG Israel, Deliverance of.
  c TG Priesthood, Keys of.
26 *a* Lam. 3:41.
  b Luke 21:28; Rom. 13:11.
27 *a* Luke 12:32. TG Church; Sheep.
  b D&C 29:5; 38:9. TG Jesus Christ, Second Coming; Kingdom of

God, on Earth.
  c Rev. 22:10.
36 1 *a* TG Jesus Christ, Jehovah.
  b D&C 41:9 (9–11). See also Partridge, Edward, in Index.
2 *a* TG Hands, Laying on of.
  b TG Holy Ghost, Comforter.
  c D&C 39:6; 42:61. TG Holy Ghost, Mission of.
3 *a* Gen. 14:20.

4 And now this calling and commandment give I unto you concerning all men—

5 That as many as shall come before my servants Sidney Rigdon and Joseph Smith, Jun., embracing this calling and commandment, shall be ^aordained and sent forth to ^bpreach the everlasting gospel among the nations—

6 Crying repentance, saying: ^aSave yourselves from this untoward generation, and come forth out of the fire, hating even the ^bgarments spotted with the flesh.

7 And this commandment shall be given unto the elders of my church, that every man which will ^aembrace it with ^bsingleness of heart may be ordained and sent forth, even as I have spoken.

8 I am Jesus Christ, the Son of God; wherefore, gird up your loins and I will ^asuddenly ^bcome to my ^ctemple. Even so. Amen.

SECTION 37

Revelation given to Joseph Smith the Prophet and Sidney Rigdon, near Fayette, New York, December 1830. Herein is given the first commandment concerning a gathering in this dispensation.

1–4, The Saints are called to gather at the Ohio.

1 Behold, I say unto you that it is not expedient in me that ye should ^atranslate any more until ye shall go to the Ohio, and this because of the enemy and for your sakes.

2 And again, I say unto you that ye shall not go until ye have preached my gospel in those parts, and have ^astrengthened up the church whithersoever it is found, and more especially in ^bColesville; for, behold, they pray unto me in much faith.

3 And again, a commandment I give unto the church, that it is expedient in me that they should assemble together at ^athe Ohio, against the time that my servant Oliver Cowdery shall return unto them.

4 Behold, here is wisdom, and let every man ^achoose for himself until I come. Even so. Amen.

---

5 *a* D&C 4:3 (3–6); 63:57.
  TG Priesthood, Ordination.
  b TG Missionary Work;
  Mission of Latter-day
  Saints.
6 *a* Acts 2:40.
  b Jude 1:23.
7 *a* TG Commitment;

Priesthood, Magnifying
Callings within; Priesthood, Qualifying for.
  b TG Sincere.
8 *a* D&C 42:36.
  b TG Jesus Christ, Second
  Coming.
  c Mal. 3:1.
37 1 *a* IE the translation of the

Bible already in process.
  D&C 1:29; 35:20.
2 *a* Zech. 10:12.
  b D&C 24:3; 26:1.
3 *a* IE the state of Ohio.
  D&C 38:32.
4 *a* TG Agency.

SECTION 38

Revelation given through Joseph Smith the Prophet, at Fayette, New York, January 2, 1831. The occasion was a conference of the Church.

1–6, Christ created all things; 7–8, He is in the midst of His Saints, who will soon see Him; 9–12, All flesh is corrupted before Him; 13–22, He has reserved a land of promise for His Saints in time and in eternity; 23–27, The Saints are commanded to be one and esteem each other as brethren; 28–29, Wars are predicted; 30–33, The Saints are to be given power from on high and to go forth among all nations; 34–42, The Church is commanded to care for the poor and needy and to seek the riches of eternity.

1 Thus saith the Lord your God, even Jesus Christ, the Great *a*I Am, Alpha and Omega, the *b*beginning and the end, the *c*same which looked upon the *d*wide expanse of eternity, and all the seraphic *e*hosts of heaven, *f*before the world was *g*made;

2 The same which *a*knoweth all things, for *b*all things are *c*present before mine eyes;

3 I am the same which *a*spake, and the world was made, and all things came by me.

4 I am the same which have taken the *a*Zion of *b*Enoch into mine own bosom; and verily, I say, even as many as have *c*believed in my name, for I am Christ, and in mine own name, by the virtue of the *d*blood which I have spilt, have I pleaded before the Father for them.

5 But behold, the residue of the *a*wicked have I kept in *b*chains of darkness until the *c*judgment of the great day, which shall come at the end of the earth;

6 And even so will I cause the wicked to be kept, that will not hear my voice but *a*harden their hearts, and wo, wo, wo, is their doom.

7 But behold, verily, verily, I say unto you that mine *a*eyes are upon you. I am in your *b*midst and ye cannot *c*see me;

38 1 *a* TG Jesus Christ, Jehovah.
 b Rev. 1:8.
 c Heb. 13:8; D&C 20:12; 35:1; 39:1 (1–3); 76:4.
 d Isa. 57:15.
 e Gen. 2:1; D&C 45:1.
 f TG Man, Antemortal Existence of.
 g Ps. 90:2.
 2 *a* D&C 88:41; Moses 1:35 (35–37); 7:36. TG God, Omniscience of.
 b Prov. 5:21; 2 Ne. 9:20.

 c TG God, Foreknowledge of.
 3 *a* Ps. 33:9. TG Jesus Christ, Creator.
 4 *a* JST Gen. 14:30–34 (Bible Appendix); D&C 45:11 (11–12); 76:67; 84:100 (99–100); 133:54; Moses 7:18 (18, 21). TG Zion.
 b Gen. 5:23.
 c D&C 20:25; 35:2; 45:3 (3–8).
 d TG Jesus Christ,

 Atonement through.
 5 *a* TG Wickedness.
 b 2 Pet. 2:4 (4–9); Jude 1:6. TG Hell; Spirits in Prison.
 c TG Judgment, the Last.
 6 *a* TG Hardheartedness.
 7 *a* Ps. 33:18; Amos 9:8; D&C 1:1.
 b Josh. 1:9; D&C 6:32; 29:5; 32:3; 88:63 (62–63).
 c Isa. 45:15.

8 But the day soon cometh that ye shall ^asee me, and know that I am; for the ^bveil of darkness shall soon be rent, and he that is not ^cpurified shall not ^dabide the day.

9 Wherefore, gird up your loins and be prepared. Behold, the ^akingdom is yours, and the enemy shall not overcome.

10 Verily I say unto you, ye are ^aclean, but not all; and there is none else with whom I am well ^bpleased;

11 For all ^aflesh is corrupted before me; and the powers of ^bdarkness prevail upon the earth, among the children of men, in the presence of all the hosts of heaven—

12 Which causeth ^asilence to reign, and all eternity is ^bpained, and the ^cangels are waiting the great command to ^dreap down the earth, to ^egather the ^ftares that they may be ^gburned; and, behold, the enemy is combined.

13 And now I show unto you a mystery, a thing which is had in secret chambers, to bring to pass even your ^adestruction in process of time, and ye knew it not;

14 But now I tell it unto you, and ye are blessed, not because of your iniquity, neither your hearts of unbelief; for verily some of you are ^aguilty before me, but I will be merciful unto your ^bweakness.

15 Therefore, be ye ^astrong from henceforth; ^bfear not, for the kingdom is yours.

16 And for your salvation I give unto you a commandment, for I have heard your ^aprayers, and the ^bpoor have complained before me, and the ^crich have I made, and all flesh is mine, and I am no ^drespecter of persons.

17 And I have made the earth rich, and behold it is my ^afootstool, wherefore, again I will stand upon it.

18 And I hold forth and deign to give unto you greater riches, even a land

---

8 a John 16:16; Rev. 22:4
  (1–5). TG Jesus Christ,
  Second Coming.
 b TG Veil.
 c TG Purification; Worthiness.
 d Mal. 3:2.
9 a Luke 6:20; D&C 35:27;
  45:1. TG Kingdom of
  God, on Earth.
10 a John 13:10. TG Cleanliness.
 b D&C 1:30.
11 a Gen. 6:12; Ex. 32:7; Isa.
  1:4 (3–4); Hosea 9:9
  (7–9); D&C 33:4; 35:12
  (7, 12). TG Filthiness.

 b Micah 3:6; Col. 1:13;
  D&C 112:23; Moses 7:61
  (61–62).
12 a Lam. 2:10; D&C 88:95.
  TG Silence.
 b Moses 7:41.
 c D&C 86:5 (3–7).
 d TG Harvest.
 e TG Last Days.
 f D&C 86:7; 88:94;
  101:66.
 g Matt. 13:30.
13 a Ether 8:21 (20–22);
  D&C 5:33 (32–33); 10:6
  (6, 25); 38:28; 42:64.
14 a TG Guilt.
 b Heb. 8:12.

15 a Deut. 11:8. TG Courage.
 b TG Courage; Fearful.
16 a Ex. 3:7.
 b Isa. 10:2; Mosiah 4:16
  (16–18).
 c Gen. 14:23; 1 Sam. 2:7.
  TG Treasure.
 d Deut. 1:17; Isa. 56:7
  (3–8); Acts 10:34; Eph.
  6:9; Col. 3:25; Alma
  1:30; Moro. 8:12; D&C
  1:35 (34–35). TG Judgment.
17 a Lam. 2:1; 1 Ne. 17:39;
  Abr. 2:7.

of ^apromise, a land ^bflowing with milk and honey, upon which there shall be no ^ccurse when the Lord cometh;

19 And I will give it unto you for the land of your inheritance, if you seek it with all your hearts.

20 And this shall be my covenant with you, ye shall have it for the land of your inheritance, and for the ^ainheritance of your children forever, while the earth shall stand, and ye shall possess it again in eternity, no more to pass away.

21 But, verily I say unto you that in time ye shall have no ^aking nor ruler, for I will be your king and watch over you.

22 Wherefore, hear my voice and ^afollow me, and you shall be a ^bfree people, and ye shall have no laws but my laws when I come, for I am your ^clawgiver, and what can stay my hand?

23 But, verily I say unto you, ^ateach one another according to the office wherewith I have appointed you;

24 And let every man ^aesteem his brother as himself, and practice ^bvirtue and holiness before me.

25 And again I say unto you, let every man esteem his ^abrother as himself.

26 For what man among you having twelve sons, and is no respecter of them, and they serve him obediently, and he saith unto the one: Be thou clothed in robes and sit thou here; and to the other: Be thou clothed in rags and sit thou there—and looketh upon his sons and saith I am ^ajust?

27 Behold, this I have given unto you as a parable, and it is even as I am. I say unto you, be ^aone; and if ye are not one ye are not mine.

28 And again, I say unto you that the enemy in the secret chambers seeketh your ^alives.

29 Ye hear of ^awars in far countries, and you say that there will soon be great wars in far countries, but ye know not the hearts of men in your own land.

30 I tell you these things because of your prayers; wherefore, ^atreasure up ^bwisdom in your bosoms, lest the wickedness of men reveal these things

---

18a Heb. 11:9.
  b Ex. 3:8; Lev. 20:24.
  c TG Earth, Curse of.
20a Isa. 29:19; Matt. 5:5;
    D&C 45:58.
21a 1 Sam. 8:5 (4–22); 12:12
    (12–15); Ps. 44:4; Zech.
    14:9; 2 Ne. 10:14; Alma
    5:50. TG Kingdom of
    God, on Earth.
22a John 10:27.
  b TG Liberty.
  c Gen. 49:10; Isa. 33:22;

    Micah 4:2; D&C 45:59.
23a Ex. 35:34; Heb. 3:13;
    Moro. 10:9 (9–10);
    D&C 88:77 (77–79,
    118); 107:85 (85–89).
    TG Teaching.
24a Deut. 17:20; 1 Cor. 4:6
    (6–7). TG Brotherhood
    and Sisterhood.
  b D&C 46:33. TG Holi-
    ness; Virtue.
25a Acts 17:26 (26–34).
26a TG God, Justice of.

27a John 17:21 (21–23);
    1 Cor. 1:10; Eph. 4:13
    (11–14); 3 Ne. 11:28
    (28–30); Moses 7:18.
    TG Unity.
28a D&C 5:33 (32–33); 10:6
    (6, 25); 38:13; 42:64.
29a D&C 42:64; 45:63 (26,
    63); 87:2 (1–5); 130:12.
30a JS—M 1:37.
  b TG Study; Wisdom.

unto you by their wickedness, in a manner which shall speak in your ears with a voice louder than that which shall shake the earth; but if ye are prepared ye shall not fear.

31 And that ye might escape the power of the *enemy, and be gathered unto me a righteous people, without *spot and blameless—

32 Wherefore, for this cause I gave unto you the *commandment that ye should go to the *Ohio; and there I will give unto you my *law; and there you shall be *endowed with power from on high;

33 And from thence, whosoever I will shall *go forth among all nations, and it shall be told them what they shall do; for I have a great work laid up in store, for Israel shall be *saved, and I will *lead them whithersoever I will, and no power shall *stay my hand.

34 And now, I give unto the church in these parts a commandment, that certain men among them shall be appointed, and they shall be *appointed by the *voice of the church;

35 And they shall look to the poor and the needy, and administer to their *relief that they shall not suffer; and send them forth to the place which I have commanded them;

36 And this shall be their work, to govern the affairs of the property of this *church.

37 And they that have farms that cannot be sold, let them be left or rented as seemeth them good.

38 See that all things are preserved; and when men are *endowed with power from on high and sent forth, all these things shall be gathered unto the bosom of the church.

39 And if ye seek the *riches which it is the will of the Father to give unto you, ye shall be the richest of all people, for ye shall have the riches of eternity; and it must needs be that the *riches of the earth are mine to give; but beware of *pride, lest ye become as the *Nephites of old.

40 And again, I say unto you, I give unto you a commandment, that every man, both elder, priest, teacher, and also member, go to with his might,

31 a TG Enemies.
  b 2 Pet. 3:14.
32 a D&C 42:3.
  b D&C 37:3.
  c D&C 42:2 (1–93).
  d Luke 24:49; D&C 39:15; 43:16; 95:8 (8–9); 110:9 (9–10).
33 a TG Missionary Work.
  b Isa. 45:17; Jer. 30:10; 31:7

(6–7); Hosea 13:9; D&C 136:22.
  c TG Guidance, Divine.
  d Dan. 4:35.
34 a TG Delegation of Responsibility.
  b TG Sustaining Church Leaders.
35 a TG Welfare.
36 a TG Church

Organization.
38 a TG Endowment; Genealogy and Temple Work.
39 a 2 Ne. 26:31; Jacob 2:18 (17–19); D&C 11:7. TG Objectives.
  b Hag. 2:8.
  c Prov. 11:2; 2 Ne. 26:20 (20–22). TG Pride.
  d Moro. 8:27.

with the *labor of his *hands, to prepare and accomplish the things which I have commanded.

41 And let your *preaching be the *warning voice, every man to his neighbor, in mildness and in *meekness.

42 And go ye *out from among the *wicked. Save yourselves. Be ye *clean that bear the vessels of the Lord. Even so. Amen.

SECTION 39

Revelation given through Joseph Smith the Prophet to James Covel, at Fayette, New York, January 5, 1831. James Covel, who had been a Methodist minister for about forty years, covenanted with the Lord that he would obey any command that the Lord would give to him through Joseph the Prophet.

1–4, The Saints have power to become the sons of God; 5–6, To receive the gospel is to receive Christ; 7–14, James Covel is commanded to be baptized and labor in the Lord's vineyard; 15–21, The Lord's servants are to preach the gospel before the Second Coming; 22–24, Those who receive the gospel will be gathered in time and in eternity.

1 Hearken and listen to the voice of him who is from all *eternity to all eternity, the Great *I Am, even Jesus Christ—

2 The *light and the life of the world; a light which shineth in darkness and the darkness comprehendeth it not;

3 The same which came in the *meridian of time unto mine own, and mine own *received me not;

4 But to as many as received me, gave I power to become my *sons; and even so will I give unto as many as will receive me, power to become my sons.

5 And verily, verily, I say unto you, he that receiveth my gospel *receiveth me; and he that *receiveth not my gospel receiveth not me.

6 And this is my *gospel—repentance and baptism by water, and then cometh the *baptism of fire and the Holy Ghost, even the Comforter, which showeth all things, and *teacheth the peaceable things of the kingdom.

---

40 *a* TG Industry.
  b 1 Cor. 4:12.
41 *a* TG Preaching.
  b TG Warn.
  c Titus 3:2.
42 *a* Isa. 52:11.
  b Ps. 26:4; Rom. 12:9.
  c Lev. 21:6; Ether 12:37.
39 1 *a* Heb. 13:8; D&C 20:12;
  35:1; 38:1 (1–4); 76:4.
  TG Eternity.

  b Ex. 3:14; Isa. 44:6; Rev.
  1:8. TG Jesus Christ,
  Jehovah.
2 *a* TG Jesus Christ, Light of
  the World.
3 *a* D&C 20:26; Moses 5:57;
  6:57 (57, 62); 7:46.
  b TG Prophets, Rejection
  of.
4 *a* John 1:12. TG Sons and
  Daughters of God.

5 *a* John 13:20.
  b TG Teachable.
6 *a* TG Baptism; Gospel;
  Repent.
  b TG Holy Ghost, Baptism of; Holy Ghost,
  Comforter; Holy Ghost,
  Mission of.
  c D&C 36:2; 42:61.

7 And now, behold, I say unto you, my servant [a]James, I have looked upon thy works and I [b]know thee.

8 And verily I say unto thee, thine heart is now right before me at this time; and, behold, I have bestowed great [a]blessings upon thy head;

9 Nevertheless, thou hast seen great [a]sorrow, for thou hast [b]rejected me many times because of pride and the cares of the [c]world.

10 But, behold, the days of thy [a]deliverance are come, if thou wilt [b]hearken to my voice, which saith unto thee: Arise and be baptized, and [c]wash away your sins, calling on my name, and you shall receive my Spirit, and a blessing so great as you never have known.

11 And if thou do this, I have prepared thee for a greater work. Thou shalt preach the [a]fulness of my gospel, which I have sent forth in these last days, the [b]covenant which I have sent forth to [c]recover my people, which are of the house of Israel.

12 And it shall come to pass that power shall [a]rest upon thee; thou shalt have great faith, and I will be with thee and go before thy face.

13 Thou art called to [a]labor in my vineyard, and to [b]build up my [c]church, and to bring forth [d]Zion, that it may rejoice upon the hills and [e]flourish.

14 Behold, verily, verily, I say unto thee, thou art not called to go into the eastern countries, but thou art called to go to the Ohio.

15 And inasmuch as my people shall assemble themselves at the Ohio, I have kept in store a [a]blessing such as is not known among the children of men, and it shall be poured forth upon their heads. And from thence men shall go forth into [b]all [c]nations.

16 Behold, verily, verily, I say unto you, that the people in Ohio call upon me in much faith, thinking I will [a]stay my hand in judgment upon the nations, but I cannot [b]deny my word.

17 Wherefore lay to with your might and call faithful laborers into my vineyard, that it may be [a]pruned for the last time.

18 And inasmuch as they do repent and receive the fulness of my gospel, and become sanctified, I will stay mine hand in [a]judgment.

7 a D&C 40:1.
  b Gen. 18:19.
8 a Prov. 10:6.
9 a Mosiah 7:29.
  b John 12:48; Alma 10:6.
  c Matt. 13:22; Hel. 7:5.
10 a TG Deliver.
  b D&C 40:3 (1–3).
  c TG Baptism, Essential;
    Purity; Repent.
11 a Rom. 15:29; D&C 18:4.

  b D&C 1:22.
  c TG Israel, Restoration of.
12 a 2 Cor. 12:9. TG Deliver;
    Guidance, Divine.
13 a Matt. 20:8 (1–16).
  b D&C 30:6; 42:8.
  c TG Jesus Christ, Head of
    the Church.
  d Isa. 52:8.
  e D&C 35:24; 49:25; 117:7
    (7–8).

15 a D&C 38:32; 43:16; 95:8
    (8–9); 110:9 (8–10).
  b D&C 1:2, 34 (34–35);
    18:28 (26–28); 42:58.
  c TG Missionary Work.
16 a 2 Sam. 24:16; Moses
    7:51.
  b 2 Tim. 2:13.
17 a Jacob 5:61 (61–75);
    D&C 24:19; 95:4.
18 a TG Jesus Christ, Judge.

19 Wherefore, go forth, crying with a loud voice, saying: The kingdom of heaven is at ªhand; crying: Hosanna! blessed be the name of the Most High God.

20 Go forth ªbaptizing with water, preparing the way before my face for the time of my ᵇcoming;

21 For the time is at hand; the ªday or the hour no man ᵇknoweth; but it surely shall ᶜcome.

22 And he that receiveth these things receiveth me; and they shall be ªgathered unto me in time and in eternity.

23 And again, it shall come to pass that on as many as ye shall baptize with water, ye shall lay your ªhands, and they shall receive the ᵇgift of the Holy Ghost, and shall be ᶜlooking forth for the signs of my ᵈcoming, and shall know me.

24 Behold, I come quickly. Even so. Amen.

SECTION 40

Revelation given to Joseph Smith the Prophet and Sidney Rigdon, at Fayette, New York, January 6, 1831. Preceding the record of this revelation, the Prophet's history states, "As James [Covel] rejected the word of the Lord, and returned to his former principles and people, the Lord gave unto me and Sidney Rigdon the following revelation" (see section 39).

1–3, Fear of persecution and cares of the world cause rejection of the gospel.

1 Behold, verily I say unto you, that the heart of my servant ªJames Covel was right before me, for he covenanted with me that he would obey my word.

2 And he ªreceived the word with gladness, but straightway Satan ᵇtempted him; and the fear of ᶜpersecution and the cares of the world caused him to ᵈreject the word.

3 Wherefore he ªbroke my covenant, and it remaineth with me to do with him as seemeth me good. Amen.

---

19 *a* Matt. 3:2.
20 *a* TG Baptism, Essential.
   b TG Jesus Christ, Prophecies about; Jesus Christ, Second Coming.
21 *a* Matt. 24:36; 1 Cor. 5:5.
   b JS—M 1:40.
   c Hab. 2:3.

22 *a* D&C 10:65.
23 *a* TG Hands, Laying on of.
   b TG Holy Ghost, Gift of.
   c Rev. 3:3; D&C 35:15; 45:39.
   d 2 Pet. 3:12.
40 1 *a* D&C 39:7.
   2 *a* Mark 4:16.

b TG Test.
c Matt. 13:21 (20–22). TG Persecution.
d TG Apostasy of Individuals.
3 *a* D&C 39:10 (7–24).

SECTION 41

Revelation given through Joseph Smith the Prophet to the Church, at Kirtland, Ohio, February 4, 1831. This revelation instructs the Prophet and Church elders to pray to receive God's "law" (see section 42). Joseph Smith had just arrived in Kirtland from New York, and Leman Copley, a Church member in nearby Thompson, Ohio, "requested Brother Joseph and Sidney [Rigdon] . . . live with him and he would furnish them houses and provisions." The following revelation clarifies where Joseph and Sidney should live and also calls Edward Partridge to be the Church's first bishop.

1–3, The elders will govern the Church by the spirit of revelation; 4–6, True disciples will receive and keep the Lord's law; 7–12, Edward Partridge is named as a bishop unto the Church.

1 Hearken and *a*hear, O ye my people, saith the Lord and your God, ye whom I delight to bless with the greatest of all *b*blessings, ye that hear me; and ye that hear me not will I *c*curse, that have *d*professed my *e*name, with the heaviest of all cursings.

2 Hearken, O ye elders of my church whom I have called, behold I give unto you a commandment, that ye shall assemble yourselves together to *a*agree upon my word;

3 And by the prayer of your faith ye shall receive my *a*law, that ye may know how to govern my *b*church and have all things right before me.

4 And I will be your *a*ruler when I *b*come; and behold, I come quickly, and ye shall see that my law is kept.

5 He that *a*receiveth my *b*law and *c*doeth it, the same is my disciple; and he that saith he receiveth it and *d*doeth it not, the same is not my disciple, and shall be *e*cast out from among you;

6 For it is not meet that the things which belong to the children of the kingdom should be given to them that are not worthy, or to *a*dogs, or the *b*pearls to be cast before swine.

---

41 1*a* Deut. 32:1.
  b TG Blessing.
  c Deut. 11:28; 1 Ne. 2:23;
    D&C 50:8. TG Curse.
  d D&C 50:4; 56:1; 112:26.
  e TG Jesus Christ, Taking
    the Name of.
  2*a* TG Unity.
  3*a* D&C 42:2 (1–93).
    TG God, Law of.

  b TG Jesus Christ, Head of
    the Church.
  4*a* Zech. 14:9; 1 Tim. 6:15
    (14–15); D&C 45:59.
    TG Governments.
  b TG Jesus Christ, Second
    Coming.
  5*a* Matt. 7:24.
  b Josh. 1:8; Jer. 26:4; Mosiah 3:14 (14–15); 13:29
    (29–32); Alma 25:15

    (15–16).
  c Rom. 2:13; James 1:22
    (22–25); D&C 42:60.
  d Matt. 21:30. TG Hypocrisy.
  e D&C 42:37; 50:8 (8–9);
    64:35. TG Excommunication.
  6*a* Matt. 15:26; Mark 7:27
    (25–30).
  b Matt. 7:6. TG Holiness.

7 And again, it is meet that my servant Joseph Smith, Jun., should have a *a*house built, in which to live and *b*translate.

8 And again, it is meet that my servant Sidney Rigdon should live as seemeth him good, inasmuch as he keepeth my commandments.

9 And again, I have called my servant *a*Edward Partridge; and I give a commandment, that he should be appointed by the voice of the church, and ordained a *b*bishop unto the church, to leave his merchandise and to *c*spend all his time in the labors of the church;

10 To see to all things as it shall be appointed unto him in my laws in the day that I shall give them.

11 And this because his heart is pure before me, for he is like unto *a*Nathanael of old, in whom there is no *b*guile.

12 These words are given unto you, and they are pure before me; wherefore, beware how you hold them, for they are to be answered upon your *a*souls in the day of judgment. Even so. Amen.

SECTION 42

Revelation given in two parts through Joseph Smith the Prophet, at Kirtland, Ohio, February 9 and 23, 1831. The first part, consisting of verses 1 through 72, was received in the presence of twelve elders and in fulfillment of the Lord's promise previously made that the "law" would be given in Ohio (see section 38:32). The second portion consists of verses 73 through 93. The Prophet specifies this revelation as "embracing the law of the Church."

1–10, The elders are called to preach the gospel, baptize converts, and build up the Church; 11–12, They must be called and ordained and are to teach the principles of the gospel found in the scriptures; 13–17, They are to teach and prophesy by the power of the Spirit; 18–29, The Saints are commanded not to kill, steal, lie, lust, commit adultery, or speak evil against others; 30–39, Laws governing the consecration of properties are set forth; 40–42, Pride and idleness are condemned; 43–52, The sick are to be healed through administrations and by faith; 53–60, The scriptures govern the Church and are to be proclaimed to the world; 61–69, The site of the New Jerusalem and the mysteries of the kingdom will be revealed; 70–73, Consecrated properties are to be used to support Church officers; 74–93, Laws governing fornication, adultery, killing, stealing, and confession of sins are set forth.

---

7 *a* D&C 42:71 (70–73).
   b IE translate the Bible.
      D&C 37:1; 45:60–62;
      73:3; 76:15; 93:53.
9 *a* D&C 36:1; 42:10.

b D&C 58:24 (14–24);
   68:14; 72:6 (6, 9–12);
   107:69 (69–75).
   TG Bishop.
c D&C 51:1 (1–20); 57:7;

58:17 (14–18).
11 *a* John 1:47.
   b TG Guile.
12 *a* TG Accountability;
   Responsibility.

1 Hearken, O ye elders of my ªchurch, who have assembled yourselves together in my name, even Jesus Christ the Son of the living God, the Savior of the world; inasmuch as ye believe on my name and keep my commandments.

2 Again I say unto you, hearken and hear and obey the ªlaw which I shall give unto you.

3 For verily I say, as ye have assembled yourselves together according to the ªcommandment wherewith I commanded you, and are agreed as ᵇtouching this one thing, and have asked the Father in my name, even so ye shall receive.

4 Behold, verily I say unto you, I give unto you this first commandment, that ye shall ªgo forth in my name, every one of you, excepting my servants Joseph Smith, Jun., and Sidney Rigdon.

5 And I give unto them a commandment that they shall go forth for a little season, and it shall be ªgiven by the power of the Spirit when they shall return.

6 And ye shall go forth in the power of my Spirit, preaching my gospel, ªtwo by two, in my name, lifting up your voices as with the sound of a ᵇtrump, declaring my word like unto angels of God.

7 And ye shall go forth baptizing with water, saying: Repent ye, repent ye, for the kingdom of heaven is at hand.

8 And from this place ye shall go forth into the regions westward; and inasmuch as ye shall find them that will receive you ye shall ªbuild up my church in every region—

9 Until the time shall come when it shall be revealed unto you from on high, when the ªcity of the ᵇNew Jerusalem shall be prepared, that ye may be ᶜgathered in one, that ye may be my ᵈpeople and I will be your God.

10 And again, I say unto you, that my servant ªEdward Partridge shall stand in the office whereunto I have ᵇappointed him. And it shall come to pass, that if he transgress ᶜanother shall be appointed in his stead. Even so. Amen.

42 1a TG Jesus Christ, Head of the Church.
 2a Jer. 26:4; D&C 41:3; 43:2; 58:23. TG God, Law of.
 3a D&C 38:32.
 b Matt. 18:19.
 4a TG Mission of Latter-day Saints.
 5a TG Guidance, Divine;

Holy Ghost, Mission of.
 6a Mark 6:7; Rom. 10:14. TG Gospel; Missionary Work.
 b Isa. 58:1.
 8a D&C 30:6; 39:13.
 9a D&C 57:2.
 b Ether 13:6 (2–11); D&C 45:66 (66–71); 48:4; 64:30; 84:2, 4 (2–5); Moses 7:62; A of F 1:10.

TG Jerusalem, New.
 c TG Israel, Gathering of.
 d Zech. 8:8.
10a D&C 41:9 (9–11); 50:39; 124:19.
 b TG Delegation of Responsibility.
 c D&C 35:18 (17–18); 64:40; 104:77; 107:99 (99–100).

11 Again I say unto you, that it shall not be given to any one to go forth to ᵃpreach my gospel, or to build up my church, except he be ᵇordained by some one who has ᶜauthority, and it is known to the church that he has authority and has been regularly ordained by the heads of the church.

12 And again, the ᵃelders, priests and teachers of this church shall ᵇteach the principles of my gospel, which are in the Bible and the ᶜBook of Mormon, in the which is the ᵈfulness of the ᵉgospel.

13 And they shall ᵃobserve the ᵇcovenants and church articles to ᶜdo them, and these shall be their teachings, as they shall be ᵈdirected by the Spirit.

14 And the Spirit shall be given unto you ᵃby the prayer of faith; and if ye receive not the ᵇSpirit ye shall not teach.

15 And all this ye shall observe to do as I have ᵃcommanded concerning your teaching, until the fulness of my ᵇscriptures is given.

16 And as ye shall lift up your voices by the ᵃComforter, ye shall speak and prophesy as seemeth me good;

17 For, behold, the ᵃComforter knoweth all things, and ᵇbeareth record of the Father and of the Son.

18 And now, behold, I speak unto the church. Thou shalt not ᵃkill; and he that ᵇkills shall ᶜnot have forgiveness in this world, nor in the world to come.

19 And again, I say, thou shalt not kill; but he that ᵃkilleth shall ᵇdie.

20 Thou shalt not steal; and he that ᵃstealeth and will not repent shall be ᵇcast out.

21 Thou shalt not ᵃlie; he that lieth and will not repent shall be cast out.

---

11 a TG Missionary Work; Preaching.
  b TG Called of God; Priesthood, Authority; Priesthood, Ordination; Priesthood, Qualifying for.
  c Acts 18:27. TG Authority; Leadership.
12 a TG Elder, Melchizedek Priesthood.
  b Mosiah 18:19 (19–20); D&C 5:10; 31:4; 52:9 (9, 36). TG Education; Mission of Latter-day Saints; Priesthood, Magnifying Callings within.
  c TG Book of Mormon.
  d Rom. 15:29; D&C 35:17; 135:3. TG Scriptures, Value of.

13 a TG Commitment.
  b IE D&C 20 (see the section 20 heading). D&C 1:6 (6, 37); 33:14; 51:4; 68:24.
  c D&C 84:57.
  d Gal. 5:18.
14 a D&C 63:64. TG Prayer.
  b Ex. 35:34; 1 Cor. 4:20. TG Holy Ghost, Mission of; Missionary Work; Teacher; Teaching; Teaching with the Spirit.
15 a TG Commandments of God.
  b D&C 35:20; 42:56 (56–58).
16 a 2 Pet. 1:21; D&C 18:32; 34:10; 68:3.
17 a 1 Cor. 2:10. TG Holy

Ghost, Comforter.
  b D&C 1:39; 20:27. TG Holy Ghost, Source of Testimony.
18 a Ex. 20:13 (13–17); Deut. 5:17 (17–21); Matt. 5:21 (21–37); Mosiah 13:21 (21–24); 3 Ne. 12:21 (21–37).
  b TG Life, Sanctity of; Murder.
  c D&C 76:34; 84:41; 132:27.
19 a TG Blood, Shedding of.
  b TG Capital Punishment.
20 a TG Stealing.
  b Zech. 5:3.
21 a Luke 18:20. TG Honesty; Lying.

22 Thou shalt ᵃlove thy wife with all thy heart, and shalt ᵇcleave unto her and none else.

23 And he that ᵃlooketh upon a woman to lust after her shall deny the faith, and shall not have the ᵇSpirit; and if he repents not he shall be cast out.

24 Thou shalt not commit ᵃadultery; and he that committeth ᵇadultery, and repenteth not, shall be ᶜcast out.

25 But he that has committed adultery and repents with all his heart, and forsaketh it, and doeth it ᵃno more, thou shalt forgive;

26 But if he doeth it ᵃagain, he shall not be forgiven, but shall be cast out.

27 Thou shalt not ᵃspeak evil of thy neighbor, nor do him any harm.

28 Thou knowest my laws concerning these things are given in my scriptures; he that sinneth and ᵃrepenteth not shall be ᵇcast out.

29 If thou ᵃlovest me thou shalt ᵇserve me and ᶜkeep all my commandments.

30 And behold, thou wilt remember the ᵃpoor, and ᵇconsecrate of thy properties for their ᶜsupport that which thou hast to impart unto them, with a covenant and a deed which cannot be broken.

31 And inasmuch as ye ᵃimpart of your ᵇsubstance unto the ᶜpoor, ye will do it unto me; and they shall be ᵈlaid before the ᵉbishop of my church and his ᶠcounselors, two of the elders, or high priests, such as he shall appoint or has appointed and ᵍset apart for that purpose.

32 And it shall come to pass, that after they are laid before the bishop of my church, and after that he has received these testimonies concerning the ᵃconsecration of the properties of my church, that they cannot be taken from the church, agreeable to my commandments, every man shall

---

22 a TG Family, Love within; Love; Marriage, Continuing Courtship in; Marriage, Husbands; Marriage, Wives.
   b Gen. 2:24 (23–24); D&C 49:15 (15–16); Moses 3:24 (23–24); Abr. 5:18 (17–18). TG Divorce.
23 a 2 Sam. 11:2. TG Carnal Mind; Lust.
   b D&C 63:16. TG Holy Ghost, Loss of.
24 a Ezek. 18:6; Luke 18:20; D&C 63:14.

   b TG Adulterer; Sexual Immorality.
   c Prov. 6:33 (32–33).
25 a John 8:11. TG Forgive.
26 a Ps. 85:8; 2 Pet. 2:20.
27 a Prov. 3:29. TG Gossip; Slander.
28 a TG Repent.
   b TG Excommunication; Punish.
29 a John 14:15 (15, 21). TG Love.
   b TG Service.
   c TG Obedience.
30 a Prov. 31:20; Mosiah 4:26

(16–26); Alma 1:27; Hel. 4:12. TG Poor.
   b Micah 4:13; D&C 72:15; 85:3. TG Consecration.
   c TG Welfare.
31 a Dan. 4:27; Mosiah 2:17.
   b Lev. 19:9. TG Generosity.
   c Job 29:12. TG Almsgiving; Poor.
   d D&C 58:35.
   e TG Bishop.
   f TG Counselor.
   g TG Setting Apart.
32 a D&C 51:4; 64:15.

be made *b*accountable unto me, a *c*steward over his own property, or that which he has received by consecration, as much as is sufficient for himself and *d*family.

33 And again, if there shall be properties in the hands of the church, or any individuals of it, more than is necessary for their support after this first consecration, which is a *a*residue to be consecrated unto the bishop, it shall be kept to administer to those who have not, from time to time, that every man who has need may be amply supplied and receive according to his wants.

34 Therefore, the residue shall be kept in my *a*storehouse, to administer to the poor and the needy, as shall be appointed by the *b*high council of the church, and the bishop and his council;

35 And for the purpose of *a*purchasing lands for the public benefit of the church, and building houses of *b*worship, and building up of the *c*New Jerusalem which is hereafter to be revealed—

36 That my covenant people may be gathered in one in that day when I shall *a*come to my *b*temple. And this I do for the salvation of my people.

37 And it shall come to pass, that he that sinneth and repenteth not shall be *a*cast out of the church, and shall not receive again that which he has *b*consecrated unto the poor and the needy of my church, or in other words, unto me—

38 For inasmuch as ye *a*do it unto the least of these, ye do it unto me.

39 For it shall come to pass, that which I spake by the mouths of my prophets shall be fulfilled; for I will consecrate of the *a*riches of those who embrace my gospel among the Gentiles unto the *b*poor of my people who are of the house of Israel.

40 And again, thou shalt not be *a*proud in thy *b*heart; let all thy *c*garments be plain, and their *d*beauty the beauty of the *e*work of thine own hands;

41 And let all things be done in *a*cleanliness before me.

42 Thou shalt not be *a*idle; for he that is idle shall not eat the *b*bread nor wear the garments of the *c*laborer.

---

32 *b* D&C 72:3 (3–11).
　TG Accountability;
　Judgment.
　c D&C 72:17 (17, 22).
　TG Stewardship.
　d D&C 51:3.
33 *a* D&C 42:55; 51:13; 82:18
　(17–19); 119:1 (1–3).
34 *a* D&C 42:55; 51:13.
　b D&C 102:1 (1–30).
35 *a* D&C 57:5 (5–7); 58:49
　(49–51); 101:70 (68–74);
　103:23 (22–24).
　b TG Worship.

c TG Zion.
36 *a* D&C 36:8.
　b Mal. 3:1.
37 *a* D&C 41:5; 50:8 (8–9);
　64:35. TG Excommuni-
　cation.
　b D&C 51:5.
38 *a* Matt. 25:40 (34–40).
　TG Love.
39 *a* TG Treasure.
　b TG Poor.
40 *a* Prov. 16:5. TG Haughti-
　ness; Pride.
　b TG Hardheartedness.

c TG Apparel; Clothing;
　Modesty.
　d TG Beauty.
　e TG Industry.
41 *a* TG Cleanliness; Purifica-
　tion.
42 *a* D&C 60:13; 68:30–32;
　75:29. TG Idleness;
　Laziness; Welfare.
　b TG Bread.
　c TG Labor; Work, Value
　of.

43 And whosoever among you are *sick, and have not faith to be healed, but believe, shall be *nourished with all tenderness, with herbs and mild *food, and that not by the hand of an enemy.

44 And the elders of the church, two or more, shall be called, and shall pray for and *lay their *hands upon them in my name; and if they *die they shall *die unto me, and if they live they shall live unto me.

45 Thou shalt *live together in *love, insomuch that thou shalt *weep for the loss of them that die, and more especially for those that have not *hope of a glorious resurrection.

46 And it shall come to pass that those that die in me shall not *taste of *death, for it shall be *sweet unto them;

47 And they that die not in me, wo unto them, for their death is bitter.

48 And again, it shall come to pass that he that hath *faith in me to be *healed, and is not *appointed unto death, shall be *healed.

49 He who hath faith to see shall see.

50 He who hath faith to hear shall hear.

51 The lame who hath faith to leap shall leap.

52 And they who have not faith to do these things, but believe in me, have *power to become my *sons; and inasmuch as they break not my laws thou shalt *bear their infirmities.

53 Thou shalt *stand in the place of thy stewardship.

54 Thou shalt not take thy brother's *garment; thou shalt *pay for that which thou shalt receive of thy brother.

55 And if thou *obtainest more than that which would be for thy support, thou shalt give it into my *storehouse, that all things may be done according to that which I have said.

56 Thou shalt ask, and my *scriptures shall be given as I have appointed, and they shall be *preserved in safety;

43 a TG Sickness.
 b TG Health.
 c TG Food.
44 a TG Hands, Laying on of.
 b TG Administrations to the Sick.
 c Rom. 14:8 (5–9); D&C 63:49.
 d Rev. 14:13.
45 a 1 Jn. 4:16.
 b John 11:36 (35–36). TG Family, Love within; Love.
 c Gen. 50:1; Alma 28:11 (11–12); 48:23. TG Mourning.

 d 1 Cor. 15:19 (19–22). TG Hope.
46 a John 8:52 (51–52).
 b John 11:26; 1 Cor. 15:56. TG Death.
 c Job 13:15 (15–16); Rev. 14:13.
48 a D&C 46:19. TG Faith.
 b Luke 18:42 (35–43). TG Heal.
 c 2 Kgs. 20:1 (1–6); Job 7:1; Isa. 38:5; 1 Cor. 4:9; Alma 12:27 (26–28); D&C 121:25.
 d TG Death, Power over.
52 a TG Initiative.

 b TG Sons and Daughters of God.
 c Rom. 15:1. TG Fellowshipping.
53 a TG Stewardship; Trustworthiness.
54 a Ex. 22:26.
 b D&C 51:11.
55 a D&C 82:18 (17–19); 119:1 (1–3).
 b D&C 42:34; 51:13.
56 a D&C 42:15; 45:60 (60–61).
 b TG Scriptures, Preservation of.

57 And it is expedient that thou shouldst hold thy peace concerning them, and *not teach them until ye have received them in full.

58 And I give unto you a commandment that then ye shall teach them unto all men; for they shall be *taught unto *all *nations, kindreds, tongues and people.

59 Thou shalt take the things which thou hast received, which have been given unto thee in my scriptures for a law, to be my *law to govern my *church;

60 And he that *doeth according to these things shall be saved, and he that doeth them not shall be *damned if he so continue.

61 If thou shalt ask, thou shalt receive *revelation upon revelation, *knowledge upon knowledge, that thou mayest know the *mysteries and *peaceable things—that which bringeth *joy, that which bringeth life eternal.

62 Thou shalt ask, and it shall be revealed unto you in mine own due time where the *New Jerusalem shall be built.

63 And behold, it shall come to pass that my servants shall be sent forth to the east and to the west, to the north and to the south.

64 And even now, let him that goeth to the east teach them that shall be converted to flee to the *west, and this in consequence of *that which is coming on the earth, and of *secret combinations.

65 Behold, thou shalt observe all these things, and great shall be thy *reward; for unto you it is given to know the *mysteries of the kingdom, but unto the world it is not given to know them.

66 Ye shall observe the laws which ye have received and be faithful.

67 And ye shall hereafter receive church *covenants, such as shall be sufficient to establish you, both here and in the New Jerusalem.

68 Therefore, he that lacketh *wisdom, let him ask of me, and I will give him liberally and upbraid him not.

---

57 a Moses 1:42; 4:32.
58 a D&C 124:89.
  b D&C 1:2, 34 (34–35);
    18:28 (26–28); 39:15.
  c TG Nations.
59 a Josh. 1:8.
  b TG God, Law of;
    Jesus Christ, Head of the
    Church.
60 a D&C 41:5. TG Salvation.
  b Moses 5:15. TG Damnation.
61 a D&C 59:4; 76:7; 98:12;

101:32; 121:28 (26–33).
  TG Revelation.
  b Prov. 19:2; Abr. 1:2.
    TG Knowledge; Learn;
    Testimony.
  c D&C 63:23; 71:1.
    TG Mysteries of Godliness.
  d D&C 36:2; 39:6.
  e TG Joy.
62 a D&C 57:2 (1–5).
64 a D&C 45:64; 48:2.
  b D&C 38:29 (28–30).

c Ether 8:24 (22–25);
    D&C 5:33 (32–33); 10:6
    (6, 25); 38:13, 28.
65 a TG Reward.
  b Rom. 16:25; Alma 12:9;
    D&C 6:7 (7–11); 121:27
    (25–27).
67 a D&C 82:11 (11–15);
    84:39; 132:4 (4–7).
68 a James 1:5; D&C 1:26.
    TG God, Wisdom of.

69 Lift up your hearts and rejoice, for unto you the ªkingdom, or in other words, the ᵇkeys of the church have been given. Even so. Amen.

70 The priests and ªteachers shall have their ᵇstewardships, even as the members.

71 And the elders or high priests who are appointed to assist the bishop as counselors in all things, are to have their families ªsupported out of the property which is ᵇconsecrated to the bishop, for the good of the poor, and for other purposes, as before mentioned;

72 Or they are to receive a just remuneration for all their services, either a stewardship or otherwise, as may be thought best or decided by the counselors and bishop.

73 And the bishop, also, shall receive his support, or a just remuneration for all his services in the church.

74 Behold, verily I say unto you, that whatever persons among you, having put away their ªcompanions for the cause of ᵇfornication, or in other words, if they shall testify before you in all lowliness of heart that this is the case, ye shall not cast them out from among you;

75 But if ye shall find that any persons have left their companions for the sake of ªadultery, and they themselves are the offenders, and their companions are living, they shall be ᵇcast out from among you.

76 And again, I say unto you, that ye shall be ªwatchful and careful, with all inquiry, that ye receive none such among you if they are married;

77 And if they are not married, they shall repent of all their sins or ye shall not receive them.

78 And again, every person who belongeth to this church of Christ, shall observe to keep all the commandments and covenants of the church.

79 And it shall come to pass, that if any persons among you shall ªkill they shall be delivered up and dealt with according to the laws of the land; for remember that he hath no forgiveness; and it shall be proved according to the laws of the land.

80 And if any man or woman shall commit ªadultery, he or she shall be tried before two elders of the church, or more, and every word shall be

---

69 a TG Kingdom of God, on Earth.
  b Matt. 16:19; D&C 65:2. TG Priesthood, Keys of.
70 a TG Priest, Aaronic Priesthood; Teacher, Aaronic Priesthood.

  b TG Stewardship.
71 a D&C 41:7.
  b TG Consecration.
74 a Matt. 5:32.
  b TG Fornication; Sexual Immorality.
75 a TG Adulterer.

  b TG Excommunication.
76 a TG Watch.
79 a Luke 18:20. TG Blood, Shedding of; Murder.
80 a TG Adulterer.

established against him or her by two *b*witnesses of the church, and not of the enemy; but if there are more than two witnesses it is better.

81 But he or she shall be condemned by the mouth of two witnesses; and the elders shall lay the case before the *a*church, and the church shall lift up their hands against him or her, that they may be dealt with according to the *b*law of God.

82 And if it can be, it is necessary that the *a*bishop be present also.

83 And thus ye shall do in all cases which shall come before you.

84 And if a man or woman shall rob, he or she shall be delivered up unto the law of the land.

85 And if he or she shall *a*steal, he or she shall be delivered up unto the law of the land.

86 And if he or she shall *a*lie, he or she shall be delivered up unto the law of the land.

87 And if he or she do any manner of *a*iniquity, he or she shall be delivered up unto the law, even that of God.

88 And if thy *a*brother or sister *b*offend thee, thou shalt take him or her between him or her and thee alone; and if he or she *c*confess thou shalt be *d*reconciled.

89 And if he or she confess not thou shalt deliver him or her up unto the church, not to the members, but to the elders. And it shall be done in a *a*meeting, and that not before the world.

90 And if thy brother or sister offend many, he or she shall be *a*chastened before many.

91 And if any one offend *a*openly, he or she shall be rebuked openly, that he or she may be *b*ashamed. And if he or she confess not, he or she shall be delivered up unto the law of God.

92 If any shall offend in secret, he or she shall be rebuked in secret, that he or she may have opportunity to confess in secret to him or her whom he or she has offended, and to God, that the church may not speak reproachfully of him or her.

93 And thus shall ye conduct in all things.

80 b TG Witness.
81 a Matt. 18:17 (16–17).
  b D&C 64:12.
82 a TG Bishop.
85 a TG Stealing.
86 a TG Honesty; Lying.

87 a D&C 43:11.
88 a TG Brotherhood and
  Sisterhood.
  b Matt. 18:15 (15–18).
  TG Offense.
  c TG Confession.

d TG Reconciliation.
89 a TG Judgment; Justice.
90 a TG Chastening; Reproof.
91 a Ezek. 5:8; 1 Tim. 5:20
  (19–21).
  b TG Shame.

SECTION 43

Revelation given through Joseph Smith the Prophet, at Kirtland, Ohio, in February 1831. At this time some members of the Church were disturbed by people making false claims as revelators. The Prophet inquired of the Lord and received this communication addressed to the elders of the Church. The first part deals with matters of Church polity; the latter part contains a warning that the elders are to give to the nations of the earth.

1–7, Revelations and commandments come only through the one appointed; 8–14, The Saints are sanctified by acting in all holiness before the Lord; 15–22, Elders are sent forth to cry repentance and prepare men for the great day of the Lord; 23–28, The Lord calls upon men by His own voice and through the forces of nature; 29–35, The Millennium and the binding of Satan will come.

1 O hearken, ye elders of my church, and give ear to the words which I shall speak unto you.

2 For behold, verily, verily, I say unto you, that ye have received a commandment for a *a*law unto my church, through him whom I have appointed unto you to receive commandments and *b*revelations from my hand.

3 And this ye shall know assuredly—that there is *a*none other appointed unto you to receive *b*commandments and revelations until he be taken, if he *c*abide in me.

4 But verily, verily, I say unto you, that *a*none else shall be appointed unto this gift except it be through him; for if it be taken from him he shall not have power except to appoint another in his stead.

5 And this shall be a law unto you, that ye *a*receive not the *b*teachings of any that shall come before you as revelations or commandments;

6 And this I give unto you that you may not be *a*deceived, that you may know they are not of me.

7 For verily I say unto you, that he that is *a*ordained of me shall come in at the *b*gate and be ordained as I have told you before, to teach those *c*revelations which you have received and shall receive through him whom I have appointed.

---

43 2 *a* D&C 42:2 (1–93).
  b TG Commandments
     of God; God, Law of;
     Revelation.
 3 *a* TG False Prophets.
  b TG Prophets, Mission of.
  c John 15:4.

 4 *a* D&C 28:2 (1–3, 11–13).
 5 *a* D&C 28:5 (3–8).
  b TG False Doctrine.
 6 *a* D&C 28:11; 46:7.
     TG Deceit.
 7 *a* TG Authority; Called of
     God.

  b Matt. 7:13; 2 Ne. 9:41;
     31:9 (9, 17–18); 3 Ne.
     14:14 (13–14); D&C
     22:4.
  c TG Scriptures to Come
     Forth.

8 And now, behold, I give unto you a *a*commandment, that when ye are *b*assembled together ye shall *c*instruct and *d*edify each other, that ye may know *e*how to act and direct my church, how to act upon the points of my law and commandments, which I have given.

9 And thus ye shall become instructed in the law of my church, and be *a*sanctified by that which ye have received, and ye shall bind yourselves to act in all holiness before me—

10 That inasmuch as ye do this, glory shall be *a*added to the kingdom which ye have received. Inasmuch as ye do it not, it shall be *b*taken, even that which ye have received.

11 *a*Purge ye out the *b*iniquity which is among you; sanctify yourselves before me;

12 And if ye desire the glories of the kingdom, *a*appoint ye my servant Joseph Smith, Jun., and uphold him before me by the prayer of faith.

13 And again, I say unto you, that if ye desire the *a*mysteries of the kingdom, provide for him food and raiment, and whatsoever thing he needeth to accomplish the work wherewith I have commanded him;

14 And if ye do it not he shall remain unto them that have received him, that I may reserve unto myself a *a*pure *b*people before me.

15 Again I say, hearken ye elders of my *a*church, whom I have appointed: Ye are not sent forth to be *b*taught, but to *c*teach the children of men the things which I have put into your hands by the power of my *d*Spirit;

16 And ye are to be *a*taught from on high. *b*Sanctify yourselves and ye shall be *c*endowed with power, that ye may give even as I have spoken.

17 Hearken ye, for, behold, the *a*great *b*day of the Lord is nigh at hand.

18 For the day cometh that the Lord shall utter his *a*voice out of heaven; the heavens shall *b*shake and the earth shall *c*tremble, and the *d*trump of

8 *a* TG Commandments of God.
  b TG Assembly for Worship; Meetings.
  c D&C 88:77 (77–79).
  d TG Edification.
  e D&C 82:9; JS—H 1:12.
9 *a* TG Sanctification.
10 *a* Alma 12:10 (9–11).
  b Mark 4:25.
11 *a* 1 Cor. 5:7.
  b D&C 42:87. TG Sin.
12 *a* TG Sustaining Church Leaders.
13 *a* TG Mysteries of Godliness.

14 *a* TG Purity.
  b TG Millennium, Preparing a People for.
15 *a* TG Jesus Christ, Head of the Church.
  b 1 Jn. 2:27. TG Teaching.
  c D&C 50:13. TG Missionary Work; Mission of Latter-day Saints; Priesthood, Ordination.
  d TG Teaching with the Spirit.
16 *a* TG Inspiration; Teachable.
  b Josh. 3:5. TG Sanctification.

  c Luke 24:49; D&C 38:32; 39:15; 95:8 (8–9); 110:9 (8–10).
17 *a* Mal. 4:5; D&C 2:1; 34:8 (6–9).
  b D&C 5:19 (19–20); 29:8; 35:11 (11–16).
18 *a* Joel 2:11; D&C 35:21; 88:90; 133:50 (50–52).
  b Joel 2:10; 3:16; D&C 45:48. TG Last Days.
  c D&C 45:33 (33, 48); 84:118; 88:87 (87, 90).
  d D&C 29:13; 45:45.

God shall sound both long and loud, and shall say to the sleeping nations: Ye saints *arise and live; ye sinners* stay and *sleep until I shall call again.

19 Wherefore gird up your loins lest ye be found among the wicked.

20 Lift up your voices and spare not. Call upon the nations to repent, both old and young, both *bond and free, saying: Prepare yourselves for the great day of the Lord;

21 For if I, who am a man, do lift up my voice and call upon you to repent, and ye *hate me, what will ye say when the *day cometh when the *thunders shall utter their voices from the ends of the earth, speaking to the ears of all that live, saying—Repent, and prepare for the great day of the Lord?

22 Yea, and again, when the *lightnings shall streak forth from the east unto the west, and shall utter forth their voices unto all that live, and make the ears of all tingle that hear, saying these words—Repent ye, for the great day of the Lord is come?

23 And again, the Lord shall utter his voice out of heaven, saying: Hearken, O ye nations of the earth, and hear the words of that God who *made you.

24 O, ye nations of the earth, how often would I have gathered you together as a *hen gathereth her chickens under her wings, but ye *would not!

25 How oft have I *called upon you by the mouth of my *servants, and by the *ministering of angels, and by mine own voice, and by the voice of *thunderings, and by the voice of lightnings, and by the voice of tempests, and by the voice of earthquakes, and great hailstorms, and by the voice of *famines and pestilences of every kind, and by the great sound of a *trump, and by the voice of judgment, and by the voice of *mercy all the day long, and by the voice of glory and honor and the *riches of eternal life, and would have saved you with an *everlasting salvation, but ye would not!

26 Behold, the day has come, when the *cup of the *wrath of mine indignation is full.

---

18 *e* TG Resurrection.
  f Rev. 20:13 (12–13);
    Alma 11:41; D&C 76:85;
    88:100 (100–101).
  g Dan. 12:2; Morm. 9:13
    (13–14).
20 *a* 1 Cor. 12:13.
21 *a* TG Hate.
  b TG Day of the Lord.
  c 2 Ne. 27:2; D&C 88:90.
22 *a* Amos 4:6 (6–10).
23 *a* Deut. 32:6; 1 Ne. 2:12.

24 *a* Matt. 23:37; Luke 13:34;
    3 Ne. 10:6 (4–6).
  b TG Rebellion.
25 *a* Lev. 26:16; Ezek. 26:6;
    1 Ne. 21:26 (25–26);
    Mosiah 7:29; 11:22
    (20–22); Hel. 12:3 (2–4).
  b Matt. 23:34. TG Prophets, Mission of.
  c D&C 7:6; 130:5.
  d Rev. 16:18; 2 Ne. 6:15.
    TG Nature, Earth.

  e Jer. 24:10; Joel 1:10;
    Amos 4:6; D&C 87:6
    (1–8); JS—M 1:29.
    TG Drought; Famine.
  f Ex. 19:19 (13, 16, 19).
  g TG Mercy.
  h TG Treasure.
  i TG Eternal Life; Immortality; Salvation.
26 *a* Lam. 4:21.
  b Ezek. 21:31. TG God, Indignation of.

27 Behold, verily I say unto you, that these are the words of the Lord your God.

28 Wherefore, labor ye, *a*labor ye in my vineyard for the last time—for the last time call upon the inhabitants of the earth.

29 For in mine own due time will I *a*come upon the earth in *b*judgment, and my people shall be *c*redeemed and shall *d*reign with me on earth.

30 For the great *a*Millennium, of which I have spoken by the mouth of my servants, shall come.

31 For *a*Satan shall be *b*bound, and when he is loosed again he shall only reign for a *c*little season, and then cometh the *d*end of the earth.

32 And he that liveth in *a*righteousness shall be *b*changed in the twinkling of an eye, and the earth shall pass away so as by *c*fire.

33 And the wicked shall go away into unquenchable *a*fire, and their end no man knoweth on earth, nor ever shall know, until they come before me in *b*judgment.

34 Hearken ye to these words. Behold, I am Jesus Christ, the *a*Savior of the world. *b*Treasure these things up in your hearts, and let the *c*solemnities of *d*eternity *e*rest upon your *f*minds.

35 Be *a*sober. Keep all my commandments. Even so. Amen.

SECTION 44

Revelation given to Joseph Smith the Prophet and Sidney Rigdon, at Kirtland, Ohio, in the latter part of February 1831. In compliance with the requirement herein set forth, the Church appointed a conference to be held early in the month of June following.

1–3, Elders are to assemble in conference; 4–6, They are to organize according to the laws of the land and to care for the poor.

---

28 *a* Jacob 5:71 (71–75);
   D&C 27:13; 33:3.
   TG Vineyard of the Lord.
29 *a* TG Jesus Christ, Second
   Coming.
   b TG Judgment, the Last.
   c Rev. 14:4 (2–5).
   d TG Jesus Christ, Millennial Reign.
30 *a* TG Millennium.
31 *a* 1 Ne. 22:26. TG Devil.
   b D&C 45:55; 84:100;
   88:110 (110–12); 101:28.

c Rev. 20:3 (3–10); Jacob
   5:77 (76–77); D&C
   29:22; 88:111 (110–12).
   d Matt. 24:14. TG World,
   End of.
32 *a* TG Righteousness.
   b 1 Cor. 15:51 (51–52);
   D&C 63:51; 88:28 (20,
   28); 101:31. TG Resurrection.
   c Matt. 3:12.
33 *a* Dan. 7:11; D&C 29:28
   (21, 26–30). TG Hell.

b TG Jesus Christ, Judge.
34 *a* TG Jesus Christ, Savior.
   b Isa. 45:22; D&C 6:36;
   11:26; JS—M 1:37.
   TG Treasure.
   c D&C 84:61; 88:121;
   100:7. TG Levity.
   d TG Eternity.
   e TG Meditation.
   f TG Mind.
35 *a* Rom. 12:3; D&C 18:21.

1 Behold, thus saith the Lord unto you my servants, it is expedient in me that the elders of my church should be *called together, from the east and from the west, and from the north and from the south, by letter or some other way.

2 And it shall come to pass, that inasmuch as they are faithful, and exercise faith in me, I will pour out my *Spirit upon them in the day that they assemble themselves together.

3 And it shall come to pass that they shall go forth into the regions round about, and *preach repentance unto the people.

4 And many shall be *converted, insomuch that ye shall obtain *power to organize yourselves *according to the laws of man;

5 That your *enemies may not have power over you; that you may be preserved in all things; that you may be enabled to keep my laws; that every bond may be broken wherewith the enemy seeketh to destroy my people.

6 Behold, I say unto you, that ye must *visit the poor and the needy and administer to their relief, that they may be kept until all things may be done according to my law which ye have received. Amen.

SECTION 45

Revelation given through Joseph Smith the Prophet to the Church, at Kirtland, Ohio, March 7, 1831. Prefacing the record of this revelation, Joseph Smith's history states that "at this age of the Church . . . many false reports . . . and foolish stories, were published . . . and circulated, . . . to prevent people from investigating the work, or embracing the faith. . . . But to the joy of the Saints, . . . I received the following."

1–5, Christ is our advocate with the Father; 6–10, The gospel is a messenger to prepare the way before the Lord; 11–15, Enoch and his brethren were received by the Lord unto Himself; 16–23, Christ revealed signs of His coming as given on the Mount of Olives; 24–38, The gospel will be restored, the times of the Gentiles will be fulfilled, and a desolating sickness will cover the land; 39–47, Signs, wonders, and the Resurrection are to attend the Second Coming; 48–53, Christ will stand on the Mount of Olives, and the Jews will see the wounds in His hands and feet; 54–59, The Lord will reign during the Millennium; 60–62, The Prophet is instructed to begin the translation of the New Testament, through which important information

---

44 1 a TG Assembly for Worship; Meetings.
  2 a Acts 2:17.
  3 a TG Preaching.

4 a TG Conversion.
  b TG Authority; Church Organization.
  c 1 Pet. 2:13 (13–14); D&C 51:6; 98:5 (5–7);

    109:54.
5 a Lev. 26:7 (1–13); 2 Ne. 4:33 (16–35).
6 a James 1:27. TG Compassion; Service; Welfare.

will be made known; 63–75, The Saints are commanded to gather and build the New Jerusalem, to which people from all nations will come.

1 Hearken, O ye people of my ᵃchurch, to whom the ᵇkingdom has been given; hearken ye and give ear to him who laid the foundation of the earth, who ᶜmade the heavens and all the ᵈhosts thereof, and by whom all things were made which ᵉlive, and move, and have a being.

2 And again I say, hearken unto my voice, lest ᵃdeath shall overtake you; in an ᵇhour when ye think not the summer shall be past, and the ᶜharvest ended, and your souls not saved.

3 Listen to him who is the ᵃadvocate with the Father, who is pleading your cause before him—

4 Saying: Father, behold the ᵃsufferings and ᵇdeath of him who did no ᶜsin, in whom thou wast well pleased; behold the blood of thy Son which was shed, the blood of him whom thou gavest that thyself might be ᵈglorified;

5 Wherefore, Father, spare these my ᵃbrethren that ᵇbelieve on my name, that they may come unto me and have ᶜeverlasting life.

6 Hearken, O ye people of my church, and ye elders listen together, and hear my voice while it is called ᵃtoday, and harden not your hearts;

7 For verily I say unto you that I am ᵃAlpha and Omega, the beginning and the end, the light and the life of the world—a ᵇlight that shineth in darkness and the darkness comprehendeth it not.

8 I came unto mine own, and mine own ᵃreceived me not; but unto as many as received me gave I ᵇpower to do many ᶜmiracles, and to become the ᵈsons of God; and even unto them that ᵉbelieved on my name gave I power to obtain eternal ᶠlife.

9 And even so I have sent mine ᵃeverlasting ᵇcovenant into the world, to be a ᶜlight to the world, and to be a ᵈstandard for my people, and for the

---

45 1 *a* TG Jesus Christ, Head of the Church.
  b D&C 38:9; 50:35.
  c Jer. 14:22; Mosiah 4:2; 3 Ne. 9:15; D&C 14:9. TG Jesus Christ, Creator.
  d Gen. 2:1; D&C 38:1; Moses 3:1; Abr. 5:1.
  e Acts 17:28.
2 *a* Alma 34:33 (33–35).
  b Matt. 24:44.
  c Jer. 8:20; D&C 56:16; 76:79 (71–79). TG Harvest.
3 *a* Isa. 59:16; D&C 62:1. TG Jesus Christ, Advocate.

4 *a* TG Jesus Christ, Atonement through; Jesus Christ, Redeemer; Pain; Suffering.
  b TG Jesus Christ, Death of.
  c Heb. 4:15; 7:26.
  d John 12:28.
5 *a* 1 Jn. 3:14 (10–18).
  b John 17:20; D&C 20:25; 35:2; 38:4.
  c John 3:16.
6 *a* John 9:4; Heb. 3:13; D&C 64:23 (23–25).
7 *a* Rev. 1:8; 21:6; D&C 19:1.

  b John 1:5.
8 *a* TG Prophets, Rejection of.
  b TG Priesthood, Power of.
  c TG Miracle.
  d TG Sons and Daughters of God.
  e TG Believe; Faith.
  f 2 Pet. 1:3 (2–4).
9 *a* TG New and Everlasting Covenant.
  b Jer. 31:33 (31–34); Hosea 2:18 (14–23); Morm. 5:20. TG Covenants.
  c 2 Cor. 4:6.
  d TG Ensign; Israel, Gathering of.

^eGentiles to seek to it, and to be a ^fmessenger before my face to prepare the way before me.

10 Wherefore, come ye unto it, and with him that cometh I will ^areason as with men in days of old, and I will show unto you my strong reasoning.

11 Wherefore, hearken ye together and let me show unto you even my ^awisdom—the wisdom of him whom ye say is the God of ^bEnoch, and his brethren,

12 Who were ^aseparated from the earth, and were received unto myself—a ^bcity reserved until a ^cday of righteousness shall come—a day which was sought for by all holy men, and they found it not because of wickedness and abominations;

13 And confessed they were ^astrangers and pilgrims on the earth;

14 But obtained a ^apromise that they should find it and see it in their flesh.

15 Wherefore, hearken and I will reason with you, and I will ^aspeak unto you and prophesy, as unto men in days of old.

16 And I will show it plainly as I showed it unto my ^adisciples as I stood before them in the flesh, and spake unto them, saying: As ye have asked of me concerning the ^bsigns of my coming, in the day when I shall come in my ^cglory in the clouds of heaven, to fulfil the promises that I have made unto your fathers,

17 For as ye have looked upon the long ^aabsence of your ^bspirits from your bodies to be a bondage, I will show unto you how the day of redemption shall come, and also the ^crestoration of the ^dscattered Israel.

18 And now ye ^abehold this temple which is in Jerusalem, which ye call the house of God, and your enemies say that this house shall never fall.

19 But, verily I say unto you, that ^adesolation shall come upon this generation as a thief in the night, and this people shall be destroyed and ^bscattered among all nations.

9 e Isa. 42:6; Matt. 8:11
     (11–12); Luke 13:29
     (28–30); Acts 10:45;
     2 Ne. 10:18 (9–18).
  f Mal. 3:1; Matt. 11:10;
     Luke 7:27.
10 a Isa. 41:21; D&C 50:10
     (10–12).
11 a TG God, Wisdom of.
   b D&C 38:4; 76:67;
     84:100 (99–100); 133:54.
12 a JST Gen. 14:30–34 (Bible
     Appendix); D&C 38:4;
     Moses 7:21.
   b Heb. 11:16; D&C

     84:100; Moses 7:63
     (62–64). TG Translated
     Beings; Zion.
   c 1 Cor. 5:5.
13 a IE sojourners; see Gen.
     15:13. 1 Pet. 2:11.
     TG Stranger.
14 a Heb. 11:13 (8–13); Moses
     7:63.
15 a TG Scriptures to Come
     Forth.
16 a D&C 29:10.
   b Matt. 24:3 (3–46); Luke
     21:7 (7–36); JS—M 1:4
     (4–55). TG Last Days.

   c TG Jesus Christ, Glory
     of; Jesus Christ, Second
     Coming.
17 a Luke 1:79; D&C 138:50.
   b TG Spirit Body; Spirits,
     Disembodied.
   c TG Israel, Restoration of.
   d Dan. 12:7; 1 Ne. 10:12
     (12–14); 22:3 (3–8).
18 a Matt. 24:2 (1–2).
19 a Ps. 79:3 (1–4); Luke
     21:20 (20–24).
   b TG Israel, Scattering of.

20 And this ªtemple which ye now see shall be thrown down that there shall not be left one stone upon another.

21 And it shall come to pass, that this ªgeneration of Jews shall not pass away until every desolation which I have told you concerning them shall come ᵇto pass.

22 Ye say that ye know that the ªend of the world cometh; ye say also that ye know that the heavens and the earth shall pass away;

23 And in this ye say truly, for so it is; but these things which I have told you shall not ªpass away until all shall be fulfilled.

24 And this I have told you concerning Jerusalem; and when that day shall come, shall a remnant be ªscattered among all ᵇnations;

25 But they shall be ªgathered again; but they shall remain until the times of the ᵇGentiles be fulfilled.

26 And in ªthat day shall be heard of ᵇwars and rumors of wars, and the whole earth shall be in commotion, and men's hearts shall ᶜfail them, and they shall say that Christ ᵈdelayeth his coming until the end of the earth.

27 And the ªlove of men shall wax cold, and ᵇiniquity shall abound.

28 And when the times of the ªGentiles is come in, a ᵇlight shall break forth among them that sit in darkness, and it shall be the fulness of my ᶜgospel;

29 But they ªreceive it not; for they perceive not the light, and they turn their ᵇhearts from me because of the ᶜprecepts of men.

30 And in that generation shall the ªtimes of the Gentiles be fulfilled.

31 And there shall be men standing in that ªgeneration, that shall not pass until they shall see an overflowing ᵇscourge; for a desolating ᶜsickness shall cover the land.

32 But my disciples shall ªstand in holy places, and shall not be moved; but among the wicked, men shall lift up their voices and ᵇcurse God and die.

20 a Matt. 24:1 (1–3); Luke 21:6 (5–6).
21 a Mark 13:30; JS—M 1:34.
  b Matt. 24:34.
22 a Matt. 24:3. TG World, End of.
23 a Matt. 24:35.
24 a Zech. 2:6; 1 Ne. 10:12 (12–13); 22:4 (3–8); 2 Ne. 25:15 (15–16).
  b Gen. 48:19.
25 a Neh. 1:9; 1 Ne. 22:12 (10–12); 2 Ne. 21:12 (11–16). TG Israel, Gathering of.

  b Luke 21:24; Rom. 11:25 (25–27).
26 a TG Day of the Lord.
  b D&C 63:33; 87:1 (1–8); 88:91; JS—M 1:23.
  c Luke 21:26.
  d Matt. 24:48; 2 Pet. 3:4 (3–10); JS—M 1:51.
27 a JS—M 1:10.
  b Matt. 24:12.
28 a TG Gentiles.
  b D&C 45:36. TG Light [noun].
  c TG Restoration of the Gospel.
29 a John 1:5.

  b Matt. 15:8 (8–9). TG Hardheartedness.
  c Titus 1:14; D&C 3:6 (6–7); 46:7; JS—H 1:19.
30 a 2 Pet. 3:12.
31 a JS—M 1:34.
  b Isa. 28:15; D&C 29:18 (14–21).
  c TG Sickness.
32 a Ex. 3:5; 2 Chr. 35:5; Matt. 24:15; D&C 87:8; 101:22 (21–22, 64); 115:7.
  b Job 2:9; Rev. 16:11, 21.

33 And there shall be ᵃearthquakes also in divers places, and many desolations; yet men will harden their hearts against me, and they will take up the ᵇsword, one against another, and they will kill one another.

34 And now, when I the Lord had spoken these words unto my disciples, they were troubled.

35 And I said unto them: Be not ᵃtroubled, for, when all these things shall come to pass, ye may know that the promises which have been made unto you shall be fulfilled.

36 And when the ᵃlight shall begin to break forth, it shall be with them like unto a parable which I will show you—

37 Ye look and behold the ᵃfig trees, and ye see them with your eyes, and ye say when they begin to shoot forth, and their leaves are yet tender, that summer is now nigh at hand;

38 Even so it shall be in that day when they shall see all these things, then shall they know that the hour is nigh.

39 And it shall come to pass that he that ᵃfeareth me shall be ᵇlooking forth for the great ᶜday of the Lord to ᵈcome, even for the ᵉsigns of the coming of the ᶠSon of Man.

40 And they shall see signs and ᵃwonders, for they shall be shown forth in the heavens above, and in the earth beneath.

41 And they shall behold blood, and ᵃfire, and vapors of ᵇsmoke.

42 And before the day of the Lord shall come, the ᵃsun shall be darkened, and the moon be turned into blood, and the stars fall from heaven.

43 And the ᵃremnant shall be gathered unto this place;

44 And then they shall look for me, and, behold, I will come; and they shall see me in the ᵃclouds of heaven, clothed with power and great ᵇglory; with all the holy angels; and he that ᶜwatches not for me shall be cut off.

45 But before the arm of the Lord shall fall, an angel shall sound his ᵃtrump, and the ᵇsaints that have slept shall ᶜcome forth to meet me in the ᵈcloud.

33a D&C 43:18; 84:118; 88:87 (87, 90).
b D&C 63:33.
35a Matt. 24:6.
36a Matt. 24:27; D&C 45:28.
37a Mark 13:28; Luke 21:29 (29–31); D&C 35:16.
39a Job 1:1; D&C 10:56 (55–56). TG Reverence.
b 2 Pet. 3:12 (10–13); D&C 35:15 (15–16); 49:23; Moses 7:62.
c TG Day of the Lord.
d TG Jesus Christ, Second Coming.
e D&C 68:11. TG Signs.
f TG Jesus Christ, Son of Man.
40a Joel 2:30.
41a Joel 1:19 (19–20); D&C 29:21; 97:26 (25–26).
b Gen. 19:28; 1 Ne. 19:11; 3 Ne. 10:13 (13–14); Morm. 8:29 (29–30).
42a Joel 2:10; Rev. 6:12; D&C 88:87; 133:49.
43a TG Israel, Gathering of; Israel, Remnant of.
44a Ex. 19:9 (9, 16).
b TG Glory; Jesus Christ, Glory of; Jesus Christ, Second Coming.
c Matt. 24:50 (43–51); Mark 13:33 (32–37); 1 Cor. 1:7 (7–8).
45a D&C 29:13; 43:18.
b TG Resurrection; Saints.
c D&C 88:97 (96–97); 133:56.
d 1 Thes. 4:17.

46 Wherefore, if ye have slept in *a*peace blessed are you; for as you now behold me and know that I am, even so shall ye *b*come unto me and your souls shall *c*live, and your redemption shall be perfected; and the saints shall come forth from the *d*four quarters of the earth.

47 Then shall the *a*arm of the Lord fall upon the nations.

48 And then shall the Lord set his foot upon this *a*mount, and it shall cleave in twain, and the earth shall *b*tremble, and reel to and fro, and the *c*heavens also *d*shall shake.

49 And the Lord shall utter his voice, and all the ends of the earth shall hear it; and the nations of the earth shall *a*mourn, and they that have *b*laughed shall see their *c*folly.

50 And calamity shall cover the *a*mocker, and the scorner shall be consumed; and they that have watched for iniquity shall be hewn down and *b*cast into the *c*fire.

51 And then shall the *a*Jews *b*look upon me and say: What are these *c*wounds in thine hands and in thy feet?

52 Then shall they know that I am the Lord; for I will say unto them: These wounds are the wounds with which I was *a*wounded in the house of my friends. I am he who was lifted up. I am Jesus that was *b*crucified. I am the *c*Son of God.

53 And then shall they *a*weep because of their iniquities; then shall they *b*lament because they *c*persecuted their *d*king.

54 And then shall the *a*heathen nations be *b*redeemed, and they that *c*knew no *d*law shall have part in the *e*first *f*resurrection; and it shall be *g*tolerable for them.

55 And *a*Satan shall be *b*bound, that he shall have no place in the hearts of the children of men.

---

46 *a* Alma 40:12.
   b Isa. 55:3; Amos 5:6;
      D&C 88:63; 101:38.
   c Ps. 121:7. TG Immortality.
   d D&C 33:6.
47 *a* D&C 1:14 (13–14);
      35:14.
48 *a* Zech. 14:4 (4–7).
   b D&C 43:18; 84:118;
      88:87 (87, 90).
   c TG Last Days.
   d Joel 3:16; D&C 21:6;
      49:23.
49 *a* D&C 29:15 (14–21);
      87:6.
   b TG Laughter.
   c 2 Tim. 3:9. TG Foolishness.

50 *a* TG Mocking.
   b Isa. 29:20.
   c TG Earth, Cleansing of.
51 *a* TG Israel, Judah, People of.
   b Zech. 12:10.
   c TG Jesus Christ, Second Coming.
52 *a* Zech. 13:6. TG Jesus Christ, Mission of.
   b TG Jesus Christ, Appearances, Postmortal.
   c Rom. 1:4.
53 *a* Rev. 1:7 (7–8).
   b Ps. 4:6; 119:135; Zech. 12:10.
   c TG Jesus Christ, Betrayal of.

d Luke 23:38; John 19:3 (3, 14–15).
54 *a* Ezek. 36:23 (23, 36);
      37:28; 38:16 (16, 23); 39:21 (7, 21, 23).
      TG Heathen.
   b TG Conversion.
   c TG Ignorance.
   d TG Accountability.
   e Rev. 20:2; 1 Ne. 22:26;
      D&C 76:71 (71–80).
   f TG Resurrection.
   g Matt. 11:22; D&C 75:22.
55 *a* TG Devil.
   b D&C 43:31; 84:100;
      88:110; 101:28.

56 And at that day, when I shall come in my *glory, shall the parable be fulfilled which I spake concerning the ten *virgins.

57 For they that are wise and have received the *truth, and have taken the Holy Spirit for their *guide, and have not been deceived—verily I say unto you, they shall not be hewn down and cast into the *fire, but shall abide the day.

58 And the *earth shall be given unto them for an *inheritance; and they shall *multiply and wax strong, and their *children shall *grow up without *sin unto *salvation.

59 For the Lord shall be in their *midst, and his *glory shall be upon them, and he will be their *king and their *lawgiver.

60 And now, behold, I say unto you, it shall not be given unto you to know any further concerning this chapter, until the *New Testament be translated, and in it all these things shall be made known;

61 Wherefore I give unto you that ye may now translate it, that ye may be prepared for the things to come.

62 For verily I say unto you, that great things await you;

63 Ye hear of *wars in foreign lands; but, behold, I say unto you, they are nigh, even at your *doors, and not many years hence ye shall hear of wars in your own lands.

64 Wherefore I, the Lord, have said, gather ye out from the *eastern lands, assemble ye yourselves together ye elders of my church; go ye forth into the western countries, call upon the inhabitants to repent, and inasmuch as they do repent, build up churches unto me.

65 And with one heart and with one mind, gather up your riches that ye may *purchase an inheritance which shall hereafter be appointed unto you.

---

56 a TG Jesus Christ, Second Coming.
  b Matt. 25:1 (1–13); D&C 63:54.
57 a TG Truth.
  b TG Guidance, Divine; Holy Ghost, Mission of; Motivations; Testimony.
  c D&C 29:9 (9, 21, 23); 63:34 (34, 54); 64:24; 88:94; 101:24 (23–25).
58 a TG Earth, Destiny of.
  b Isa. 29:19; Matt. 5:5; Col. 1:12; 2 Ne. 9:18; D&C 38:20 (16–20);

56:20.
  c Gen. 1:22 (20–25); Jer. 30:19.
  d TG Children.
  e D&C 63:51; 101:30 (29–31).
  f TG Sin.
  g TG Salvation; Salvation of Little Children.
59 a Matt. 18:20; D&C 1:36 (35–36); 29:11 (9–11); 84:119 (118–19); 104:59.
  b TG Glory.
  c TG Kingdom of God, on Earth.

  d Gen. 49:10; Zech. 14:9; D&C 38:22; 41:4.
60 a See an excerpt in the Pearl of Great Price, in Joseph Smith—Matthew. See also Bible, footnotes and Appendix, excerpts from the Joseph Smith Translation. D&C 42:56; 73:3 (3–4).
63 a D&C 38:29; 87:2 (1–5); 130:12.
  b Matt. 24:33.
64 a D&C 42:64; 48:2.
65 a D&C 63:27.

66 And it shall be called the *a*New Jerusalem, a *b*land of *c*peace, a city of *d*refuge, a place of *e*safety for the saints of the Most High God;

67 And the *a*glory of the Lord shall be there, and the *b*terror of the Lord also shall be there, insomuch that the wicked will not come unto it, and it shall be called Zion.

68 And it shall come to pass among the wicked, that every man that will not take his sword against his *a*neighbor must needs flee unto *b*Zion for safety.

69 And there shall be *a*gathered unto it out of every *b*nation under heaven; and it shall be the only people that shall not be at *c*war one with another.

70 And it shall be said among the wicked: Let us not go up to battle against Zion, for the inhabitants of Zion are *a*terrible; wherefore we cannot stand.

71 And it shall come to pass that the righteous shall be gathered out from among all nations, and shall come to Zion, singing with *a*songs of everlasting *b*joy.

72 And now I say unto you, keep these things from going abroad unto the world until it is expedient in me, that ye may accomplish this work in the eyes of the people, and in the eyes of your enemies, that they may not know your works until ye have accomplished the thing which I have commanded you;

73 That when they shall know it, that they may consider these things.

74 For when the Lord shall appear he shall be *a*terrible unto them, that fear may seize upon them, and they shall stand afar off and tremble.

75 And all nations shall be afraid because of the terror of the Lord, and the power of his might. Even so. Amen.

SECTION 46

Revelation given through Joseph Smith the Prophet to the Church, at Kirtland, Ohio, March 8, 1831. In this early time of the Church, a

---

66 a Isa. 35:10; Ether 13:6
(2–11); D&C 42:9 (9, 35,
62); Moses 7:62; A of F
1:10. TG Jerusalem, New;
Zion.
b D&C 29:8 (7–8); 52:2
(2, 42); 57:1; 103:24.
c Ps. 72:7; D&C 54:10.
TG Peace.
d Isa. 4:6; Joel 2:32.

TG Refuge.
e TG Protection, Divine.
67 a D&C 64:41 (41–43);
84:5 (4–5, 31); 97:15
(15–20). TG Jesus Christ,
Glory of.
b D&C 64:43.
68 a Zech. 14:13. TG Neighbor.
b Isa. 31:9. TG Zion.

69 a Deut. 30:3; Jer. 32:37.
b Zech. 2:11 (10–12);
D&C 49:10; 97:19
(18–21).
c TG War.
70 a Mal. 1:14.
71 a D&C 66:11.
b TG Joy.
74 a Zeph. 2:11.

unified pattern for the conducting of Church services had not yet developed. However, a custom of admitting only members and earnest investigators to the sacrament meetings and other assemblies of the Church had become somewhat general. This revelation expresses the will of the Lord relative to governing and conducting meetings and His direction on seeking and discerning the gifts of the Spirit.

1–2, Elders are to conduct meetings as guided by the Holy Spirit; 3–6, Truth seekers should not be excluded from sacramental services; 7–12, Ask of God and seek the gifts of the Spirit; 13–26, An enumeration of some of these gifts is given; 27–33, Church leaders are given power to discern the gifts of the Spirit.

1 Hearken, O ye people of my church; for verily I say unto you that these things were spoken unto you for your *a*profit and learning.

2 But notwithstanding those things which are written, it always has been given to the *a*elders of my church from the beginning, and ever shall be, to *b*conduct all meetings as they are directed and guided by the Holy Spirit.

3 Nevertheless ye are commanded never to *a*cast any one out from your public *b*meetings, which are held before the world.

4 Ye are also commanded not to cast any one who belongeth to the church out of your sacrament meetings; nevertheless, if any have trespassed, let him *a*not *b*partake until he makes reconciliation.

5 And again I say unto you, ye shall not cast any out of your sacrament meetings who are earnestly *a*seeking the kingdom—I speak this concerning those who are not of the church.

6 And again I say unto you, concerning your *a*confirmation meetings, that if there be any that are not of the church, that are earnestly seeking after the kingdom, ye shall not cast them out.

7 But ye are commanded in all things to *a*ask of God, who giveth liberally; and that which the Spirit testifies unto you even so I would that ye should do in all *b*holiness of heart, walking uprightly before me, *c*considering the end of your salvation, doing all things with prayer and *d*thanksgiving, that ye may not be *e*seduced by evil *f*spirits, or doctrines of devils, or the *g*commandments of men; for some are of men, and others of devils.

---

46 1 *a* Deut. 10:13 (12–13).
  2 *a* Lev. 9:1; Alma 6:1.
    b Moro. 6:9; D&C 20:45.
  3 *a* 3 Ne. 18:22 (22–34).
    b TG Church; Fellowshipping; Meetings.
  4 *a* 3 Ne. 12:24 (23–26).
    b TG Reconciliation; Sacrament.
  5 *a* TG Missionary Work.

6 *a* IE for confirmation of those recently baptized, commonly done now in sacrament meeting.
7 *a* James 1:5 (5–6); D&C 6:11; 88:62 (62–65); 102:23. TG Problem-Solving.
    b TG Holiness.
    c TG Meditation; Prayer.

d Ps. 34:1 (1–3); 69:30 (30–31); Alma 34:38. TG Thanksgiving.
    e 1 Tim. 4:1 (1–4); D&C 28:11; 43:6 (5–7).
    f TG Spirits, Evil or Unclean.
    g Col. 2:22 (18–22); Titus 1:14; D&C 3:6 (6–7); 45:29; JS—H 1:19.

8 Wherefore, beware lest ye are deceived; and that ye may not be deceived *seek ye earnestly the best gifts, always remembering for what they are given;

9 For verily I say unto you, they are given for the benefit of those who love me and keep all my commandments, and him that seeketh so to do; that all may be benefited that seek or that ask of me, that ask and not for a *sign that they may *consume it upon their lusts.

10 And again, verily I say unto you, I would that ye should always remember, and always retain in your *minds what those *gifts are, that are given unto the church.

11 For all have not every *gift given unto them; for there are many gifts, and to every man is given a gift by the Spirit of God.

12 To some is given one, and to some is given another, that all may be profited thereby.

13 To some it is given by the *Holy Ghost to know that Jesus Christ is the Son of God, and that he was crucified for the sins of the world.

14 To others it is given to *believe on their words, that they also might have eternal life if they continue faithful.

15 And again, to some it is given by the Holy Ghost to know the *differences of administration, as it will be pleasing unto the same Lord, according as the Lord will, suiting his *mercies according to the conditions of the children of men.

16 And again, it is given by the Holy Ghost to some to know the diversities of operations, whether they be of God, that the manifestations of the *Spirit may be given to every man to profit withal.

17 And again, verily I say unto you, to some is given, by the Spirit of God, the word of *wisdom.

18 To another is given the word of *knowledge, that all may be taught to be wise and to have knowledge.

19 And again, to some it is given to have *faith to be healed;

20 And to others it is given to have faith to *heal.

21 And again, to some is given the working of *miracles;

---

8 a 1 Cor. 12:31; D&C 11:10.
9 a TG Sign Seekers.
  b James 4:3.
10 a TG Mind.
  b 1 Cor. 14:12.
11 a Rom. 1:11. TG Holy Ghost, Gifts of.
13 a TG Holy Ghost, Source

of Testimony.
14 a Rom. 10:10 (4–11); Mosiah 26:15 (15–16); Alma 19:9; 56:48 (47–48); 3 Ne. 12:2.
15 a Moro. 10:8.
  b Gen. 32:10; 1 Ne. 1:20; Alma 34:38.
16 a 1 Cor. 12:7 (3–8).

17 a 1 Kgs. 5:12; Moro. 10:9 (9–10).
18 a TG Education; Knowledge.
19 a Mark 5:34 (34–36); Hel. 15:9 (9–10); D&C 42:48 (48–52). TG Faith.
20 a TG Heal.
21 a TG Miracle.

22 And to others it is given to ªprophesy;

23 And to others the ªdiscerning of spirits.

24 And again, it is given to some to speak with ªtongues;

25 And to another is given the interpretation of tongues.

26 And all these ªgifts come from God, for the benefit of the ᵇchildren of God.

27 And unto the ªbishop of the church, and unto such as God shall appoint and ordain to watch over the church and to be elders unto the church, are to have it given unto them to ᵇdiscern all those gifts lest there shall be any among you professing and yet be not of God.

28 And it shall come to pass that he that asketh in ªSpirit shall receive in Spirit;

29 That unto some it may be given to have all those gifts, that there may be a head, in order that every member may be profited thereby.

30 He that ªasketh in the ᵇSpirit asketh according to the ᶜwill of God; wherefore it is done even as he asketh.

31 And again, I say unto you, all things must be done in the name of Christ, whatsoever you do in the Spirit;

32 And ye must give ªthanks unto God in the Spirit for whatsoever blessing ye are blessed with.

33 And ye must practice ªvirtue and holiness before me continually. Even so. Amen.

SECTION 47

Revelation given through Joseph Smith the Prophet, at Kirtland, Ohio, March 8, 1831. John Whitmer, who had already served as a clerk to the Prophet, initially hesitated when he was asked to serve as the Church historian and recorder, replacing Oliver Cowdery. He wrote, "I would rather not do it but observed that the will of the Lord be done, and if he desires it, I desire that he would manifest it through Joseph the Seer." After Joseph Smith received this revelation, John Whitmer accepted and served in his appointed office.

---

22 a TG Prophecy.
23 a Acts 16:18 (16–18);
    Moses 1:15 (13–15).
24 a TG Language.
26 a TG God, Gifts of.
   b TG Man, a Spirit Child
    of Heavenly Father; Sons
    and Daughters of God.

27 a TG Bishop.
   b TG Discernment, Spiritual.
28 a Ezek. 36:27; Rom. 8:26
    (26–27); D&C 88:65
    (64–65).
30 a Hel. 10:5; 3 Ne. 19:24;
    D&C 50:29. TG Holy

    Ghost, Mission of.
   b James 4:3.
   c TG God, Will of.
32 a 1 Chr. 16:8 (7–36);
    1 Thes. 1:2; Alma 37:37;
    D&C 59:7. TG Thanksgiving.
33 a TG Holiness; Virtue.

1–4, John Whitmer is designated to keep the history of the Church and to write for the Prophet.

1 Behold, it is expedient in me that my servant John should write and keep a regular *a*history, and assist you, my servant Joseph, in transcribing all things which shall be given you, until he is called to further duties.

2 Again, verily I say unto you that he can also *a*lift up his voice in meetings, whenever it shall be expedient.

3 And again, I say unto you that it shall be appointed unto him to keep the church *a*record and history continually; for Oliver Cowdery I have appointed to another office.

4 Wherefore, it shall be given him, inasmuch as he is faithful, by the *a*Comforter, to write these things. Even so. Amen.

SECTION 48

Revelation given through Joseph Smith the Prophet, at Kirtland, Ohio, March 10, 1831. The Prophet had inquired of the Lord as to the mode of procedure in procuring lands for the settlement of the Saints. This was an important matter in view of the migration of members of the Church from the eastern United States, in obedience to the Lord's command that they should assemble in Ohio (see sections 37:1–3; 45:64).

1–3, The Saints in Ohio are to share their lands with their brethren; 4–6, The Saints are to purchase lands, build a city, and follow the counsel of their presiding officers.

1 It is necessary that ye should remain for the present time in your places of abode, as it shall be suitable to your circumstances.

2 And inasmuch as ye have lands, ye shall *a*impart to the *b*eastern brethren;

3 And inasmuch as ye have not lands, let them buy for the present time in those regions round about, as seemeth them good, for it must needs be necessary that they have places to live for the present time.

4 It must needs be necessary that ye *a*save all the money that ye can, and that ye obtain all that ye can in righteousness, that in time ye may be enabled to *b*purchase *c*land for an *d*inheritance, even the city.

---

47 1 *a* D&C 21:1; 69:3 (3–8);
     85:1.
   2 *a* TG Preaching.
   3 *a* TG Record Keeping.

4 *a* TG Holy Ghost, Comforter.
48 2 *a* TG Welfare.
     b D&C 42:64; 45:64.
   4 *a* TG Family, Managing

Finances in.
   b D&C 57:4.
   c D&C 57:8.
   d D&C 42:9 (9, 35, 62);
     45:66 (66–71); 64:30.

5 The *place is not yet to be *revealed; but after your brethren come from the east there are to be certain men appointed, and to them it shall be given to know the place, or to them it shall be revealed.

6 And they shall be appointed to *purchase the lands, and to make a commencement to lay the foundation of the city; and then shall ye begin to be gathered with your families, every man according to his *family, according to his circumstances, and as is appointed to him by the presidency and the bishop of the church, according to the laws and commandments which ye have received, and which ye shall hereafter receive. Even so. Amen.

SECTION 49

Revelation given through Joseph Smith the Prophet to Sidney Rigdon, Parley P. Pratt, and Leman Copley, at Kirtland, Ohio, May 7, 1831. Leman Copley had embraced the gospel but still held to some of the teachings of the Shakers (United Society of Believers in Christ's Second Appearing), to which he had formerly belonged. Some of the beliefs of the Shakers were that Christ's Second Coming had already occurred and that He had appeared in the form of a woman, Ann Lee. They did not consider baptism by water essential. They rejected marriage and believed in a life of total celibacy. Some Shakers also forbade the eating of meat. In prefacing this revelation, Joseph Smith's history states, "In order to have [a] more perfect understanding on the subject, I inquired of the Lord, and received the following." The revelation refutes some of the basic concepts of the Shaker group. The aforementioned brethren took a copy of the revelation to the Shaker community (near Cleveland, Ohio) and read it to them in its entirety, but it was rejected.

1–7, The day and hour of Christ's coming will remain unknown until He comes; 8–14, Men must repent, believe the gospel, and obey the ordinances to gain salvation; 15–16, Marriage is ordained of God; 17–21, The eating of meat is approved; 22–28, Zion will flourish and the Lamanites blossom as the rose before the Second Coming.

1 Hearken unto my word, my servants Sidney, and Parley, and Leman; for behold, verily I say unto you, that I give unto you a commandment that you shall go and *preach my gospel which ye have received, even as ye have received it, unto the Shakers.

---

5 a D&C 51:16.
  b D&C 57:2 (1–3).

6 a TG Jerusalem, New;
    Zion.
  b Num. 1:2; Mosiah 6:3;

Ether 1:41.
49 1 a TG Preaching.

2 Behold, I say unto you, that they desire to know the truth in part, but not all, for they are not ^aright before me and must needs repent.

3 Wherefore, I send you, my servants Sidney and Parley, to preach the gospel unto them.

4 And my servant Leman shall be ordained unto this work, that he may reason with them, not according to that which he has received of them, but according to that which shall be ^ataught him by you my servants; and by so doing I will bless him, otherwise he shall not prosper.

5 Thus saith the Lord; for I am God, and have ^asent mine ^bOnly Begotten Son into the world for the ^credemption of the world, and have decreed that he that receiveth him shall be saved, and he that receiveth him not shall be ^ddamned—

6 And they have done unto the ^aSon of Man even as they listed; and he has taken his power on the ^bright hand of his ^cglory, and now reigneth in the heavens, and will reign till he descends on the earth to put all enemies ^dunder his feet, which time is nigh at hand—

7 I, the Lord God, have spoken it; but the hour and the ^aday no man knoweth, neither the angels in heaven, nor shall they know until he comes.

8 Wherefore, I will that all men shall repent, for all are under ^asin, except those which I have ^breserved unto myself, ^choly men that ye know not of.

9 Wherefore, I say unto you that I have sent unto you mine everlasting ^acovenant, even that which was from the beginning.

10 And that which I have promised I have so fulfilled, and the ^anations of the earth shall ^bbow to it; and, if not of themselves, they shall come down, for that which is now exalted of itself shall be laid ^clow of power.

11 Wherefore, I give unto you a commandment that ye ^ago among this people, and say unto them, like unto mine apostle of old, whose name was ^bPeter:

12 ^aBelieve on the name of the Lord Jesus, who was on the earth, and is to come, the beginning and the end;

2 a Acts 8:21.
4 a TG Gospel; Truth.
5 a John 3:17 (16–17); D&C 132:24 (24, 59). TG Jesus Christ, Authority of.
  b TG Jesus Christ, Divine Sonship.
  c TG Jesus Christ, Redeemer; Redemption.
  d TG Damnation.
6 a TG Jesus Christ, Son of Man.
  b Acts 7:56; D&C 76:20 (20–23); 104:7.

  c TG Jesus Christ, Glory of.
  d Ps. 66:3; D&C 76:61.
7 a Matt. 24:36; 25:13; Mark 13:32; Rev. 16:15 (15–16); D&C 133:11; JS—M 1:40.
8 a Gal. 3:22; Mosiah 16:3.
  b Rom. 11:4.
  c Ex. 22:31; Heb. 13:2; W of M 1:17; Alma 13:26; D&C 107:29.
9 a Ps. 74:20; Isa. 59:21 (20–21); Rom. 11:27;

Heb. 10:16 (16–17). TG New and Everlasting Covenant.
10 a Zech. 2:11 (10–12); D&C 45:69 (66–69); 97:19 (18–21).
  b Isa. 60:14.
  c Matt. 23:12.
11 a TG Missionary Work.
  b Acts 2:38 (37–38).
12 a TG Baptism, Qualifications for.

13 ᵃRepent and be baptized in the name of Jesus Christ, according to the holy commandment, for the remission of sins;

14 And whoso doeth this shall receive the ᵃgift of the Holy Ghost, by the laying on of the ᵇhands of the elders of the church.

15 And again, verily I say unto you, that whoso ᵃforbiddeth to marry is not ordained of God, for ᵇmarriage is ordained of God unto man.

16 Wherefore, it is lawful that he should have one ᵃwife, and they twain shall be ᵇone flesh, and all this that the ᶜearth might answer the end of its creation;

17 And that it might be filled with the measure of man, according to his ᵃcreation ᵇbefore the world was made.

18 And whoso ᵃforbiddeth to ᵇabstain from ᶜmeats, that man should not eat the same, is not ordained of God;

19 For, behold, the ᵃbeasts of the field and the fowls of the air, and that which cometh of the earth, is ᵇordained for the use of man for food and for ᶜraiment, and that he might have in abundance.

20 But it is not given that one man should ᵃpossess that which is above another, wherefore the ᵇworld lieth in ᶜsin.

21 And wo be unto man that ᵃsheddeth blood or that ᵇwasteth ᶜflesh and hath no need.

22 And again, verily I say unto you, that the Son of Man ᵃcometh not in the form of a woman, neither of a man traveling on the earth.

23 Wherefore, be not ᵃdeceived, but continue in steadfastness, ᵇlooking forth for the heavens to be ᶜshaken, and the earth to tremble and to reel to and fro as a drunken man, and for the ᵈvalleys to be exalted, and for the ᵉmountains to be made low, and for the rough places to become smooth— and all this when the angel shall sound his ᶠtrumpet.

---

13 a TG Repent.
14 a TG Holy Ghost, Gift of.
 b TG Hands, Laying on of.
15 a 1 Tim. 4:3.
 b Gen. 2:24 (23–24);
  D&C 42:22; Moses
  3:24 (23–24); Abr. 5:18
  (17–18). TG Marriage,
  Celestial; Marriage,
  Marry.
16 a TG Marriage, Husbands;
  Marriage, Wives.
 b TG Family, Love within.
 c TG Earth, Purpose of.
17 a TG Creation; Foreordination.
 b TG Man, Antemortal
  Existence of.

18 a IE biddeth to abstain; see
  v. 19 and Gen. 9:3–4.
 b TG Abstain.
 c TG Food; Meat; Word of
  Wisdom.
19 a Gen. 1:26; D&C 89:12.
 b 1 Tim. 4:3. TG Food.
 c TG Clothing.
20 a Acts 4:32; D&C 51:3;
  70:14; 78:6 (5–6).
  TG Consecration; Covet.
 b TG World.
 c TG Sin.
21 a TG Life, Sanctity of.
  JST Gen. 9:11 And surely,
  blood shall not be shed,
  only for meat, to save your
  lives; and the blood of

every beast will I require
  at your hands.
 b TG Cruelty; Waste.
 c TG Food; Meat.
22 a Matt. 24:23 (23–27).
  TG Jesus Christ, Second
  Coming.
23 a Matt. 24:4 (4–5).
 b 2 Pet. 3:12; D&C 45:39.
 c D&C 21:6; 45:48 (22,
  48).
 d Isa. 40:4; D&C 109:74;
  133:22.
 e Micah 1:4. TG Earth,
  Renewal of.
 f Isa. 27:13; Matt. 24:31.

24 But before the great day of the Lord shall come, ^aJacob shall flourish in the wilderness, and the Lamanites shall ^bblossom as the rose.

25 Zion shall ^aflourish upon the ^bhills and rejoice upon the mountains, and shall be assembled together unto the place which I have appointed.

26 Behold, I say unto you, go forth as I have commanded you; repent of all your sins; ^aask and ye shall receive; knock and it shall be opened unto you.

27 Behold, I will go before you and be your ^arearward; and I will be in your ^bmidst, and you shall not be ^cconfounded.

28 Behold, I am Jesus Christ, and I come ^aquickly. Even so. Amen.

SECTION 50

Revelation given through Joseph Smith the Prophet, at Kirtland, Ohio, May 9, 1831. Joseph Smith's history states that some of the elders did not understand the manifestations of different spirits abroad in the earth and that this revelation was given in response to his special inquiry on the matter. So-called spiritual phenomena were not uncommon among the members, some of whom claimed to be receiving visions and revelations.

1–5, Many false spirits are abroad in the earth; 6–9, Wo unto the hypocrites and those who are cut off from the Church; 10–14, Elders are to preach the gospel by the Spirit; 15–22, Both preachers and hearers need to be enlightened by the Spirit; 23–25, That which doth not edify is not of God; 26–28, The faithful are possessors of all things; 29–36, The prayers of the purified are answered; 37–46, Christ is the Good Shepherd and the Stone of Israel.

1 Hearken, O ye elders of my church, and give ear to the ^avoice of the living God; and attend to the words of wisdom which shall be given unto you, according as ye have asked and are agreed as touching the church, and the ^bspirits which have gone abroad in the earth.

2 Behold, verily I say unto you, that there are many spirits which are false ^aspirits, which have gone forth in the earth, deceiving the world.

3 And also ^aSatan hath sought to deceive you, that he might overthrow you.

---

24 a 3 Ne. 5:21 (21–26); D&C 52:2 (1–3).
   b Isa. 35:1 (1–2); 2 Ne. 30:6; 3 Ne. 21:25 (22–25); D&C 3:20; 30:6; 109:65.
25 a D&C 35:24; 39:13; 117:7 (7–8).

   b Gen. 49:26; 2 Ne. 12:2 (2–3).
26 a D&C 88:63 (62–64).
27 a Isa. 52:12.
   b Matt. 18:20.
   c Ps. 22:5; 1 Pet. 2:6; D&C 84:116.
28 a D&C 1:12.

50 1 a Josh. 3:10; Jer. 23:36.
   b Rev. 16:14. TG Sorcery.
  2 a TG False Doctrine; Spirits, Evil or Unclean.
  3 a Luke 22:31; 2 Ne. 2:18 (17–18); 3 Ne. 18:18; D&C 10:22 (22–27). TG Devil.

4 Behold, I, the Lord, have looked upon you, and have seen ªabominations in the church that ᵇprofess my name.

5 But blessed are they who are faithful and ªendure, whether in life or in death, for they shall inherit eternal life.

6 But wo unto them that are ªdeceivers and hypocrites, for, thus saith the Lord, I will bring them to judgment.

7 Behold, verily I say unto you, there are ªhypocrites among you, who have deceived some, which has given the ᵇadversary ᶜpower; but behold ᵈsuch shall be reclaimed;

8 But the ªhypocrites shall be detected and shall be ᵇcut off, either in life or in death, even as I will; and wo unto them who are cut off from my church, for the same are overcome of the world.

9 Wherefore, let every man beware lest he do that which is not in truth and righteousness before me.

10 And now come, saith the Lord, by the Spirit, unto the elders of his church, and let us ªreason together, that ye may understand;

11 Let us reason even as a man reasoneth one with another face to face.

12 Now, when a man reasoneth he is understood of man, because he reasoneth as a man; even so will I, the Lord, reason with you that you may ªunderstand.

13 Wherefore, I the Lord ask you this question—unto what were ye ªordained?

14 To preach my gospel by the ªSpirit, even the ᵇComforter which was sent forth to teach the truth.

15 And then received ye ªspirits which ye could not understand, and received them to be of God; and in this are ye justified?

16 Behold ye shall answer this question yourselves; nevertheless, I will be ªmerciful unto you; he that is weak among you hereafter shall be made ᵇstrong.

17 Verily I say unto you, he that is ordained of me and sent forth to ªpreach the word of truth by the Comforter, in the Spirit of truth, doth he ᵇpreach it by the Spirit of truth or some other way?

---

4 a D&C 1:30; 20:32
   (32–34); 28:11 (11–12).
  b D&C 41:1; 56:1; 112:26.
   TG Jesus Christ, Taking
   the Name of.
5 a TG Adversity; Steadfastness.
6 a TG Deceit.
7 a Prov. 11:9 (5–11).
  b TG Devil.
  c Mosiah 27:9 (8–9); D&C
   93:39 (37, 39).
  d IE those who have been

   deceived.
8 a TG Hypocrisy.
  b D&C 1:14; 41:1 (1, 5);
   42:37; 56:3 (1, 3–4);
   64:35. TG Excommuni-
   cation.
10 a Isa. 1:18; 41:1; D&C
   45:10.
12 a Ps. 119:27; D&C 1:24.
13 a TG Priesthood, Ordination.
14 a D&C 43:15. TG Teach-
   ing with the Spirit.

  b TG Holy Ghost, Com-
   forter.
15 a 1 Cor. 2:12. TG Discernment, Spiritual.
16 a Ps. 67:1.
  b 2 Cor. 12:10.
   TG Strength.
17 a TG Missionary Work;
   Priesthood, Magnifying
   Callings within.
  b TG Holy Ghost, Mission
   of.

18 And if it be by some other way it is not of God.

19 And again, he that receiveth the word of truth, doth he receive it by the Spirit of truth or some other way?

20 If it be some other way it is not of God.

21 Therefore, why is it that ye cannot understand and know, that he that receiveth the word by the ^aSpirit of truth receiveth it as it is preached by the Spirit of truth?

22 Wherefore, he that preacheth and he that receiveth, understand one another, and both are ^aedified and ^brejoice together.

23 And that which doth not ^aedify is not of God, and is ^bdarkness.

24 That which is of God is ^alight; and he that ^breceiveth ^clight, and ^dcontinueth in God, receiveth more ^elight; and that light groweth brighter and brighter until the perfect day.

25 And again, verily I say unto you, and I say it that you may know the ^atruth, that you may chase darkness from among you;

26 He that is ^aordained of God and sent forth, the same is appointed to be the ^bgreatest, notwithstanding he is the ^cleast and the ^dservant of all.

27 Wherefore, he is possessor of all things; for all things are ^asubject unto him, both in heaven and on the earth, the life and the light, the Spirit and the ^bpower, sent forth by the will of the Father through Jesus Christ, his Son.

28 But no man is possessor of ^aall things except he be ^bpurified and ^ccleansed from all sin.

29 And if ye are ^apurified and cleansed from all ^bsin, ye shall ^cask whatsoever you will in the name of Jesus and it shall be done.

30 But know this, it shall be given you what you shall ^aask; and as ye are appointed to the ^bhead, the spirits shall be subject unto you.

31 Wherefore, it shall come to pass, that if you behold a ^aspirit manifested

---

21 a TG Truth.
22 a TG Edification.
   b Neh. 8:12; John 4:36;
     D&C 18:16 (13–16).
     TG Joy.
23 a 1 Cor. 14:26.
   b TG Darkness, Spiritual.
24 a Eccl. 8:1; 1 Jn. 2:8;
     Moro. 7:18 (14–19);
     D&C 67:9; 84:45
     (45–47); 88:49 (40–41,
     49). TG Light of Christ.
   b TG Learn; Teachable.
   c Ps. 97:11; Dan. 2:21.
     TG Children of Light.
   d John 15:4 (4–5, 10).

   e Isa. 28:13 (9–13); 2 Ne.
     28:30. TG Light [noun];
     Man, Potential to
     Become like Heavenly
     Father; Perfection.
25 a John 8:32.
26 a TG Leadership.
   b Luke 22:24 (24–30).
   c Matt. 11:11; Luke 7:28.
   d Mark 10:43 (43–44).
     TG Self-Sacrifice; Servant; Service.
27 a Dan. 7:14 (13–14); Matt.
     28:18; John 3:35; D&C
     63:59; 76:55 (5–10,
     53–60).

   b TG Priesthood, Power of.
28 a D&C 76:55 (55, 59).
   b TG Man, New, Spiritually Reborn; Purity.
   c 1 Jn. 1:7.
29 a Neh. 12:30; 3 Ne. 8:1;
     19:28 (28–29); D&C
     29:3; 88:74 (74–75).
   b TG Sin.
   c Hel. 10:5; D&C 46:30.
30 a TG Prayer.
   b TG Authority.
31 a Luke 11:24 (24–26);
     1 Jn. 4:1 (1–6). TG Spirits, Evil or Unclean.

that you cannot understand, and you receive not that spirit, ye shall ask of the Father in the name of Jesus; and if he give not unto you that spirit, then you may know that it is not of God.

32 And it shall be given unto you, ^apower over that spirit; and you shall proclaim against that spirit with a loud voice that it is ^bnot of God—

33 Not with ^arailing accusation, that ye be not overcome, neither with ^bboasting nor rejoicing, lest you be seized therewith.

34 He that receiveth of God, let him ^aaccount it of God; and let him rejoice that he is accounted of God worthy to receive.

35 And by giving heed and doing these things which ye have received, and which ye shall hereafter receive—and the ^akingdom is given ^byou of the Father, and ^cpower to ^dovercome all things which are not ordained of him—

36 And behold, verily I say unto you, blessed are you who are now hearing these words of mine from the mouth of my servant, for your sins are ^aforgiven you.

37 Let my servant Joseph Wakefield, in whom I am well pleased, and my servant ^aParley P. Pratt go forth among the churches and strengthen them by the word of ^bexhortation;

38 And also my servant John Corrill, or as many of my servants as are ordained unto this office, and let them labor in the ^avineyard; and let no man hinder them doing that which I have appointed unto them—

39 Wherefore, in this thing my servant ^aEdward Partridge is not justified; nevertheless let him repent and he shall be forgiven.

40 Behold, ye are little children and ye cannot ^abear all things now; ye must ^bgrow in ^cgrace and in the knowledge of the truth.

41 ^aFear not, little ^bchildren, for you are mine, and I have ^covercome the world, and you are of them that my Father hath ^dgiven me;

42 And none of them that my Father hath given me shall be ^alost.

32 a Matt. 10:1.
  b 1 Jn. 4:3 (1–3).
33 a Jude 1:9.
  b Luke 10:20 (17–20);
    D&C 84:73; 105:24.
    TG Boast.
34 a TG Ingratitude; Thanksgiving.
35 a D&C 45:1; 61:37.
    TG Kingdom of God, on Earth.
  b D&C 6:4; 35:27.
  c TG Initiative.

  d 1 Jn. 4:4.
36 a TG Forgive.
37 a D&C 32:1; 52:26; 97:3;
    103:30 (30–37).
  b TG Preaching.
38 a TG Vineyard of the Lord.
39 a D&C 42:10; 51:1 (1–18).
40 a John 16:12; 3 Ne. 17:2
    (2–4); D&C 78:18
    (17–18).
  b 1 Cor. 3:2 (2–3); Heb.
    5:12 (11–14); D&C
    19:22.

  c TG Grace; Knowledge; Truth.
41 a John 14:1 (1–3); 1 Jn.
    2:1–13; 4:18 (7–21).
  b TG Sons and Daughters of God.
  c John 16:33.
  d John 6:37; 10:29 (27–29);
    17:2 (2–12); 3 Ne. 15:24;
    D&C 27:14; 84:63.
42 a John 17:12.

43 And the Father and I are ^aone. I am ^bin the Father and the Father in me; and inasmuch as ye have received me, ye are in me and I in you.

44 Wherefore, I am in your midst, and I am the ^agood ^bshepherd, and the ^cstone of Israel. He that buildeth upon this ^drock shall never ^efall.

45 And the ^aday cometh that you shall hear my voice and ^bsee me, and ^cknow that I am.

46 ^aWatch, therefore, that ye may be ^bready. Even so. Amen.

SECTION 51

Revelation given through Joseph Smith the Prophet, at Thompson, Ohio, May 20, 1831. At this time the Saints migrating from the eastern states began to arrive in Ohio, and it became necessary to make definite arrangements for their settlement. As this undertaking belonged particularly to the bishop's office, Bishop Edward Partridge sought instruction on the matter, and the Prophet inquired of the Lord.

1–8, Edward Partridge is appointed to regulate stewardships and properties; 9–12, The Saints are to deal honestly and receive alike; 13–15, They are to have a bishop's storehouse and to organize properties according to the Lord's law; 16–20, Ohio is to be a temporary gathering place.

1 Hearken unto me, saith the Lord your God, and I will speak unto my servant ^aEdward Partridge, and give unto him directions; for it must needs be that he receive directions how to organize this people.

2 For it must needs be that they be ^aorganized according to my ^blaws; if otherwise, they will be cut off.

3 Wherefore, let my servant Edward Partridge, and those whom he has chosen, in whom I am well pleased, appoint unto this people their ^aportions, every man ^bequal according to his family, according to his circumstances and his wants and ^cneeds.

4 And let my servant Edward Partridge, when he shall appoint a man his

---

43 *a* TG Jesus Christ, Relationships with the Father; Unity.
　b John 14:11.
44 *a* Ezra 3:11; Alma 5:40.
　b TG Jesus Christ, Good Shepherd; Shepherd.
　c Gen. 49:24. TG Cornerstone; Jesus Christ, Prophecies about.
　d 1 Pet. 2:4 (4–8).

　　TG Rock.
　e 2 Pet. 1:10; Hel. 5:12.
　　TG Apostasy of Individuals.
45 *a* TG Day of the Lord.
　b D&C 67:10. TG God, Privilege of Seeing.
　c Acts 7:56.
46 *a* TG Watch.
　b TG Procrastination.
51 1 *a* D&C 50:39; 52:24.

2 *a* TG Church Organization.
　b D&C 42:30 (30–39); 51:15; 105:5.
3 *a* TG Family, Managing Finances in.
　b D&C 49:20. TG Consecration.
　c Acts 2:45.

*portion, give unto him a writing that shall secure unto him his portion, that he shall hold it, even this right and this inheritance in the church, until he transgresses and is not accounted worthy by the voice of the church, according to the *laws and *covenants of the church, to belong to the church.

5 And if he shall transgress and is not accounted worthy to belong to the church, he shall not have power to *claim that portion which he has consecrated unto the bishop for the poor and needy of my church; therefore, he shall not retain the gift, but shall only have *claim on that portion that is deeded unto him.

6 And thus all things shall be made sure, *according to the *laws of the land.

7 And let that which belongs to this people be appointed unto this people.

8 And the *money which is left unto this people—let there be an *agent appointed unto this people, to take the *money to provide food and raiment, according to the wants of this people.

9 And let every man deal *honestly, and be alike among this people, and receive alike, that ye may be *one, even as I have commanded you.

10 And let that which belongeth to this people not be taken and given unto that of *another church.

11 Wherefore, if another church would receive money of this church, let them *pay unto this church again according as they shall agree;

12 And this shall be done through the bishop or the agent, which shall be appointed by the *voice of the church.

13 And again, let the bishop appoint a *storehouse unto this church; and let all things both in money and in meat, which are more than is *needful for the wants of this people, be kept in the hands of the bishop.

14 And let him also reserve unto *himself for his own wants, and for the wants of his family, as he shall be employed in doing this business.

15 And thus I grant unto this people a privilege of organizing themselves according to my *laws.

16 And I consecrate unto them this land for a *little season, until I, the Lord, shall provide for them otherwise, and command them to go hence;

4 a D&C 83:5.
  b D&C 42:32 (30–39).
  c D&C 1:6 (6, 37); 33:14;
    42:13.
5 a D&C 42:37 (30–39). See
    also section 83.
  b D&C 56:10.
6 a 1 Pet. 2:13 (13–14);
    D&C 44:4; 98:5 (5–7);
    109:54.
  b D&C 58:21.

8 a D&C 58:51 (49–51);
    60:10; 84:104.
  b D&C 84:113.
  c D&C 63:40 (40, 43, 46).
9 a TG Honesty.
  b TG Unity.
10 a IE another branch of the
    Church, not another
    denomination. D&C
    60:9.
11 a D&C 42:54 (42, 53–54).

12 a TG Common Consent.
13 a D&C 42:55; 58:24 (24,
    37). TG Welfare.
  b D&C 42:33 (33–34,
    55); 82:18 (17–19); 119:1
    (1–3).
14 a D&C 31:5.
15 a D&C 42:30 (30–39);
    51:2.
16 a D&C 48:5.

17 And the hour and the day is not given unto them, wherefore let them act upon this land as for years, and this shall turn unto them for their good.

18 Behold, this shall be ^aan example unto my servant Edward Partridge, in other places, in all churches.

19 And whoso is found a ^afaithful, a ^bjust, and a wise ^csteward shall enter into the ^djoy of his Lord, and shall inherit eternal life.

20 Verily, I say unto you, I am Jesus Christ, who ^acometh quickly, in an ^bhour you think not. Even so. Amen.

SECTION 52

Revelation given through Joseph Smith the Prophet to the elders of the Church, at Kirtland, Ohio, June 6, 1831. A conference had been held at Kirtland, beginning on the 3rd and closing on the 6th of June. At this conference the first distinctive ordinations to the office of high priest were made, and certain manifestations of false and deceiving spirits were discerned and rebuked.

1–2, The next conference is designated to be held in Missouri; 3–8, Appointments of certain elders to travel together are made; 9–11, The elders are to teach what the apostles and prophets have written; 12–21, Those enlightened by the Spirit bring forth fruits of praise and wisdom; 22–44, Various elders are appointed to go forth preaching the gospel while traveling to Missouri for the conference.

1 Behold, thus saith the Lord unto the elders whom he hath called and chosen in these last days, by the ^avoice of his Spirit—

2 Saying: I, the Lord, will make known unto you what I will that ye shall do from this time until the next conference, which shall be held in Missouri, upon the ^aland which I will ^bconsecrate unto my people, which are a ^cremnant of Jacob, and those who are heirs according to the ^dcovenant.

3 Wherefore, verily I say unto you, let my servants Joseph Smith, Jun., and Sidney Rigdon take their journey as soon as preparations can be made to leave their homes, and journey to the land of ^aMissouri.

4 And inasmuch as they are faithful unto me, it shall be made known unto them what they shall do;

---

18 *a* IE a pattern. D&C 72:23
(19–26).
19 *a* Matt. 24:45; Luke 16:10;
D&C 6:13; 138:12.
TG Trustworthiness.
b Prov. 11:9 (9–11).
c TG Stewardship.

d TG Joy.
20 *a* Rev. 22:7 (6–16).
b Matt. 24:44.
52 1 *a* TG Called of God.
2 *a* D&C 29:8 (7–8); 45:66
(64–66); 57:1; 103:24.
b D&C 58:57; 84:3 (3–4,

31); 103:35; 105:15.
c Ps. 135:4; 3 Ne. 5:21
(21–26); D&C 19:27;
49:24 (23–25); 109:65.
d TG Abrahamic Covenant;
Covenants.
3 *a* D&C 54:8 (7–8); 57:1.

5 And it shall also, inasmuch as they are faithful, be made *a*known unto them the *b*land of your inheritance.

6 And inasmuch as they are not faithful, they shall be cut off, even as I will, as seemeth me good.

7 And again, verily I say unto you, let my servant Lyman Wight and my servant John Corrill take their journey speedily;

8 And also my servant John Murdock, and my servant Hyrum Smith, take their journey unto the same place by the way of Detroit.

9 And let them journey from thence preaching the word by the way, saying *a*none other things than that which the *b*prophets and apostles have written, and that which is taught them by the *c*Comforter through the prayer of faith.

10 Let them go *a*two by two, and thus let them preach by the way in every congregation, baptizing by *b*water, and the laying on of the *c*hands by the water's side.

11 For thus saith the Lord, I will cut my work short in *a*righteousness, for the days come that I will send forth *b*judgment unto victory.

12 And let my servant Lyman Wight beware, for Satan desireth to *a*sift him as chaff.

13 And behold, he that is *a*faithful shall be made ruler over many things.

14 And again, I will give unto you a pattern in all things, that ye may not be deceived; for Satan is abroad in the land, and he goeth forth *a*deceiving the nations—

15 Wherefore he that prayeth, whose spirit is *a*contrite, the same is *b*accepted of me if he obey mine *c*ordinances.

16 He that *a*speaketh, whose spirit is contrite, whose language is meek and *b*edifieth, the same is of God if he obey mine ordinances.

17 And again, he that trembleth under my power shall be made *a*strong, and shall bring forth fruits of praise and *b*wisdom, according to the revelations and truths which I have given you.

18 And again, he that is overcome and *a*bringeth not forth fruits, even according to this pattern, is not of me.

---

5 a D&C 57:2 (1–3).
  b TG Lands of Inheritance.
9 a Mosiah 18:19 (19–20);
    D&C 42:12; 52:36.
  b TG Prophets, Mission of;
    Scriptures, Value of.
  c TG Holy Ghost, Com-
    forter; Teaching with the
    Spirit.
10 a Mark 6:7; Luke 10:1;
    D&C 61:35; 62:5.
  b John 1:26.
  c TG Hands, Laying on of.
11 a Rom. 9:28.
  b Matt. 12:20.
12 a Luke 22:31.
13 a Neh. 7:2; Matt. 25:23;
    D&C 132:53.
14 a Rev. 13:14 (11–18).
15 a TG Contrite Heart.
  b Gen. 4:7.
  c TG Ordinance.
16 a TG Communication.
  b TG Edification.
17 a D&C 66:8; 133:58.
  b TG Wisdom.
18 a Matt. 3:10.

19 Wherefore, by this pattern ye shall ^aknow the spirits in all cases under the whole heavens.

20 And the days have come; according to men's faith it shall be ^adone unto them.

21 Behold, this commandment is given unto all the elders whom I have chosen.

22 And again, verily I say unto you, let my servant ^aThomas B. Marsh and my servant ^bEzra Thayre take their journey also, preaching the word by the way unto this same land.

23 And again, let my servant Isaac Morley and my servant Ezra Booth take their journey, also preaching the word by the way unto this same land.

24 And again, let my servants ^aEdward Partridge and Martin Harris take their journey with my servants Sidney Rigdon and Joseph Smith, Jun.

25 Let my servants David Whitmer and Harvey Whitlock also take their journey, and preach by the way unto this same land.

26 And let my servants ^aParley P. Pratt and ^bOrson Pratt take their journey, and preach by the way, even unto this same land.

27 And let my servants Solomon Hancock and Simeon Carter also take their journey unto this same land, and preach by the way.

28 Let my servants Edson Fuller and Jacob Scott also take their journey.

29 Let my servants Levi W. Hancock and Zebedee Coltrin also take their journey.

30 Let my servants Reynolds Cahoon and Samuel H. Smith also take their journey.

31 Let my servants Wheeler Baldwin and William Carter also take their journey.

32 And let my servants ^aNewel Knight and ^bSelah J. Griffin both be ordained, and also take their journey.

33 Yea, verily I say, let all these take their journey unto one place, in their several courses, and one man shall not build upon another's ^afoundation, neither journey in another's track.

34 He that is faithful, the same shall be kept and blessed with much ^afruit.

---

19 a TG Discernment, Spiritual.
20 a Matt. 8:13.
22 a D&C 31:1; 56:5 (5–6); 75:31.
   b D&C 33:1.

24 a D&C 51:1 (1–18); 57:7.
26 a D&C 32:1; 50:37; 97:3; 103:30 (30–37).
   b D&C 34:1; 103:40; 124:129; 136:13.
32 a D&C 54:2.

   b D&C 56:6.
33 a Rom. 15:20.
34 a Col. 1:6; Alma 32:42 (28–42); 3 Ne. 14:16.

35 And again, I say unto you, let my servants Joseph Wakefield and Solomon Humphrey take their journey into the eastern lands;

36 Let them labor with their families, *declaring none other things than the prophets and apostles, that which they have *seen and heard and most assuredly *believe, that the prophecies may be fulfilled.

37 In consequence of transgression, let that which was bestowed upon Heman Basset be *taken from him, and placed upon the head of Simonds Ryder.

38 And again, verily I say unto you, let Jared Carter be *ordained a priest, and also George James be ordained a *priest.

39 Let the residue of the elders *watch over the churches, and declare the word in the regions round about them; and let them *labor with their own hands that there be no *idolatry nor wickedness practiced.

40 And remember in all things the *poor and the *needy, the *sick and the afflicted, for he that doeth not these things, the same is not my disciple.

41 And again, let my servants Joseph Smith, Jun., and Sidney Rigdon and Edward Partridge take with them a *recommend from the church. And let there be one obtained for my servant Oliver Cowdery also.

42 And thus, even as I have said, if ye are faithful ye shall assemble yourselves together to rejoice upon the land of *Missouri, which is the land of your *inheritance, which is now the land of your enemies.

43 But, behold, I, the Lord, will hasten the city in its time, and will crown the faithful with *joy and with rejoicing.

44 Behold, I am Jesus Christ, the Son of God, and I will *lift them up at the last day. Even so. Amen.

SECTION 53

Revelation given through Joseph Smith the Prophet to Algernon Sidney Gilbert, at Kirtland, Ohio, June 8, 1831. At Sidney Gilbert's request, the Prophet inquired of the Lord as to Brother Gilbert's work and appointment in the Church.

---

36 *a* Mosiah 18:19 (18–20);
      D&C 5:10; 31:4; 42:12;
      52:9.
   b John 3:11 (11, 32).
   c TG Believe.
37 *a* Matt. 13:12 (10–13);
      25:29 (25–30).
38 *a* D&C 79:1.
   b TG Priest, Aaronic Priest-
      hood.

39 *a* Alma 6:1.
   b Neh. 4:6; 1 Cor. 4:12;
      D&C 75:3; 115:10.
   c TG Idolatry.
40 *a* Prov. 14:21; Isa. 3:15;
      D&C 104:18. TG Gener-
      osity; Poor.
   b TG Compassion; Welfare.
   c TG Sickness.
41 *a* Acts 14:26; 15:40; D&C

20:64, 84; 72:17 (17, 19);
      112:21.
42 *a* D&C 28:9. TG Zion.
   b Num. 32:18; D&C 25:2;
      57:2 (1–3); 58:51 (17, 28,
      51).
43 *a* TG Joy.
44 *a* D&C 5:35.

1–3, Sidney Gilbert's calling and election in the Church is to be ordained an elder; 4–7, He is also to serve as a bishop's agent.

1 Behold, I say unto you, my servant Sidney Gilbert, that I have heard your prayers; and you have called upon me that it should be made known unto you, of the Lord your God, concerning your *ᵃcalling* and *ᵇelection* in the church, which I, the Lord, have raised up in these last days.

2 Behold, I, the Lord, who was *ᵃcrucified* for the sins of the world, give unto you a commandment that you shall *ᵇforsake* the world.

3 Take upon you mine ordination, even that of an elder, to preach faith and repentance and *ᵃremission* of sins, according to my word, and the reception of the Holy Spirit by the laying on of *ᵇhands;*

4 And also to be an *ᵃagent* unto this church in the place which shall be appointed by the bishop, according to commandments which shall be given hereafter.

5 And again, verily I say unto you, you shall take your journey with my servants Joseph Smith, Jun., and Sidney Rigdon.

6 Behold, these are the first ordinances which you shall receive; and the residue shall be made known in a time to come, according to your labor in my vineyard.

7 And again, I would that ye should learn that he only is saved who *ᵃendureth* unto the end. Even so. Amen.

SECTION 54

Revelation given through Joseph Smith the Prophet to Newel Knight, at Kirtland, Ohio, June 10, 1831. Members of the Church living in Thompson, Ohio, were divided on questions having to do with the consecration of properties. Selfishness and greed were manifest. Following his mission to the Shakers (see the heading to section 49), Leman Copley had broken his covenant to consecrate his large farm as a place of inheritance for the Saints arriving from Colesville, New York. As a consequence, Newel Knight (leader of the members living in Thompson) and other elders had come to the Prophet asking how to proceed. The Prophet inquired of the Lord and received this revelation, which commands the members in Thompson to leave Leman Copley's farm and journey to Missouri.

---

53 1 *a* Compare with sections 12; 14; 15; 16.
   b TG Election.
2 *a* TG Jesus Christ,

Crucifixion of.
   b 2 Cor. 6:17. TG World; Worldliness.
3 *a* TG Remission of Sins.

   b TG Hands, Laying on of.
4 *a* D&C 57:6 (6–15); 84:113.
7 *a* Matt. 10:22.

1–6, The Saints must keep the gospel covenant to gain mercy; 7–10, They must be patient in tribulation.

1 Behold, thus saith the Lord, even *a*Alpha and Omega, the beginning and the end, even he who was *b*crucified for the sins of the world—

2 Behold, verily, verily, I say unto you, my servant Newel Knight, you shall stand fast in the office whereunto I have appointed you.

3 And if your brethren desire to escape their enemies, let them repent of all their sins, and become truly *a*humble before me and contrite.

4 And as the covenant which they made unto me has been *a*broken, even so it has become *b*void and of none effect.

5 And wo to him by whom this *a*offense cometh, for it had been better for him that he had been drowned in the depth of the sea.

6 But blessed are they who have kept the *a*covenant and observed the *b*commandment, for they shall obtain *c*mercy.

7 Wherefore, go to now and flee the land, lest your enemies come upon you; and take your journey, and appoint whom you will to be your leader, and to pay moneys for you.

8 And thus you shall take your journey into the regions westward, unto the land of *a*Missouri, unto the borders of the Lamanites.

9 And after you have done journeying, behold, I say unto you, seek ye a *a*living like unto men, until I prepare a place for you.

10 And again, be *a*patient in tribulation until I *b*come; and, behold, I come quickly, and my *c*reward is with me, and they who have *d*sought me early shall find *e*rest to their souls. Even so. Amen.

SECTION 55

Revelation given through Joseph Smith the Prophet to William W. Phelps, at Kirtland, Ohio, June 14, 1831. William W. Phelps, a printer, and his family had just arrived at Kirtland, and the Prophet sought the Lord for information concerning him.

54 1 *a* Rev. 1:8; D&C 19:1; 75:1.
  b 1 Cor. 15:3. TG Jesus Christ, Crucifixion of.
3 *a* Jer. 44:10.
4 *a* Josh. 23:16 (15–16).
  b D&C 58:32 (32–33).

5 *a* Matt. 18:6 (6–7); Luke 17:2 (1–2). TG Offense.
6 *a* 1 Kgs. 8:23. TG Covenants.
  b 1 Kgs. 3:14 (12–14).
  c TG Mercy.
8 *a* D&C 52:3 (3, 42).
9 *a* 1 Thes. 4:11.

10 *a* TG Patience; Test; Tribulation.
  b Rev. 22:12. TG Jesus Christ, Second Coming.
  c TG Reward.
  d Prov. 8:17. TG Prayer.
  e Ps. 72:7; Matt. 11:29; D&C 45:66. TG Rest.

1–3, William W. Phelps is called and chosen to be baptized, to be ordained an elder, and to preach the gospel; 4, He is also to write books for children in Church schools; 5–6, He is to travel to Missouri, which will be the area of his labors.

1 Behold, thus saith the Lord unto you, my servant William, yea, even the Lord of the whole *a*earth, thou art called and chosen; and after thou hast been *b*baptized by water, which if you do with an eye single to my glory, you shall have a remission of your sins and a reception of the Holy Spirit by the laying on of *c*hands;

2 And then thou shalt be ordained by the hand of my servant Joseph Smith, Jun., to be an elder unto this church, to preach repentance and *a*remission of sins by way of baptism in the name of Jesus Christ, the Son of the living God.

3 And on whomsoever you shall *a*lay your hands, if they are contrite before me, you shall have power to give the Holy Spirit.

4 And again, you shall be ordained to assist my servant Oliver Cowdery to do the work of printing, and of selecting and writing *a*books for *b*schools in this church, that little *c*children also may receive *d*instruction before me as is pleasing unto me.

5 And again, verily I say unto you, for this cause you shall take your journey with my servants Joseph Smith, Jun., and Sidney Rigdon, that you may be *a*planted in the land of your inheritance to do this work.

6 And again, let my servant *a*Joseph Coe also take his journey with them. The residue shall be made known hereafter, even as I will. Amen.

SECTION 56

Revelation given through Joseph Smith the Prophet, at Kirtland, Ohio, June 15, 1831. This revelation chastises Ezra Thayre for not obeying a former revelation (the "commandment" referred to in verse 8), which Joseph Smith had received for him, instructing Thayre concerning his duties on Frederick G. Williams' farm, where he lived. The following revelation also revokes Thayre's call to travel to Missouri with Thomas B. Marsh (see section 52:22).

---

55 1 *a* Deut. 10:14; 1 Ne. 11:6;
    2 Ne. 29:7.
   b TG Baptism, Essential.
   c TG Hands, Laying on of.

2 *a* TG Remission of Sins.
3 *a* D&C 20:41.
4 *a* D&C 88:118; 97:3 (3–6);
    109:7 (7, 14).
   b TG Education.

   c TG Children.
   d TG Family, Children,
    Responsibilities toward.
5 *a* Amos 9:15.
6 *a* D&C 102:3 (3, 34).

1–2, The Saints must take up their cross and follow the Lord to gain salvation; 3–13, The Lord commands and revokes, and the disobedient are cast off; 14–17, Wo unto the rich who will not help the poor, and wo unto the poor whose hearts are not broken; 18–20, Blessed are the poor who are pure in heart, for they will inherit the earth.

1 Hearken, O ye people who ªprofess my name, saith the Lord your God; for behold, mine anger is ᵇkindled against the rebellious, and they shall know mine arm and mine indignation, in the day of ᶜvisitation and of wrath upon the nations.

2 And he that will not take up his ªcross and ᵇfollow me, and keep my commandments, the same shall not be saved.

3 Behold, I, the Lord, command; and he that will not ªobey shall be ᵇcut off in mine own due time, after I have commanded and the commandment is broken.

4 Wherefore I, the Lord, command and ªrevoke, as it seemeth me good; and all this to be answered upon the heads of the ᵇrebellious, saith the Lord.

5 Wherefore, I revoke the commandment which was given unto my servants ªThomas B. Marsh and Ezra Thayre, and give a new commandment unto my servant Thomas, that he shall take up his journey speedily to the land of Missouri, and my servant Selah J. Griffin shall also go with him.

6 For behold, I revoke the commandment which was given unto my servants ªSelah J. Griffin and Newel Knight, in consequence of the ᵇstiffneckedness of my people which are in Thompson, and their rebellions.

7 Wherefore, let my servant Newel Knight remain with them; and as many as will go may go, that are contrite before me, and be led by him to the land which I have appointed.

8 And again, verily I say unto you, that my servant Ezra Thayre must repent of his ªpride, and of his ᵇselfishness, and obey the former commandment which I have given him concerning the place upon which he lives.

9 And if he will do this, as there shall be no divisions made upon the land, he shall be appointed still to go to the land of Missouri;

---

56 1 *a* D&C 41:1; 50:4; 112:26.
  b TG Provoking.
  c Jer. 10:15; Hosea 9:7; D&C 1:14 (13–14).
 2 *a* Luke 14:27.
  b Matt. 8:19; 2 Ne. 31:10 (10–13); Moro. 7:11.

  TG Jesus Christ, Exemplar.
 3 *a* TG Disobedience; Obedience.
  b D&C 1:14; 50:8; 64:35 (35–36).
 4 *a* Num. 14:34; Jer. 18:10 (6–10); D&C 19:5; 58:32

(31–33); 75:6.
  b TG Rebellion.
 5 *a* D&C 31:1; 52:22; 75:31.
 6 *a* D&C 52:32.
  b TG Stiffnecked.
 8 *a* TG Pride.
  b TG Selfishness.

10 Otherwise he shall receive the ^amoney which he has paid, and shall leave the place, and shall be ^bcut off out of my church, saith the Lord God of hosts;

11 And though the heaven and the earth pass away, these words shall not ^apass away, but shall be fulfilled.

12 And if my servant Joseph Smith, Jun., must needs pay the money, behold, I, the Lord, will pay it unto him again in the land of Missouri, that those of whom he shall receive may be rewarded again according to that which they do;

13 For according to that which they do they shall receive, even in lands for their inheritance.

14 Behold, thus saith the Lord unto my people—you have many things to do and to repent of; for behold, your ^asins have come up unto me, and are not ^bpardoned, because you seek to ^ccounsel in your own ways.

15 And your hearts are not satisfied. And ye obey not the truth, but have ^apleasure in unrighteousness.

16 Wo unto you ^arich men, that will not ^bgive your substance to the ^cpoor, for your ^driches will canker your souls; and this shall be your lamentation in the day of visitation, and of judgment, and of indignation: The ^eharvest is past, the summer is ended, and my soul is not saved!

17 Wo unto you ^apoor men, whose hearts are not broken, whose spirits are not contrite, and whose bellies are not satisfied, and whose hands are not stayed from laying hold upon other men's goods, whose eyes are full of ^bgreediness, and who will not ^clabor with your own hands!

18 But blessed are the ^apoor who are pure in heart, whose hearts are broken, and whose spirits are ^bcontrite, for they shall see the ^ckingdom of God coming in power and great glory unto their deliverance; for the fatness of the ^dearth shall be theirs.

19 For behold, the Lord shall come, and his ^arecompense shall be with him, and he shall ^breward every man, and the poor shall rejoice;

---

10 *a* D&C 51:5.
  b TG Apostasy of Individu-
     als.
11 *a* 2 Ne. 9:16.
14 *a* Jonah 1:2.
  b Ex. 34:7. TG Forgive.
  c Moses 6:43.
15 *a* Luke 21:34.
16 *a* Jer. 17:11; Luke 21:1
     (1–4); 2 Ne. 9:30; Mo-
     siah 4:23; D&C 84:112.
     TG Treasure.
  b TG Almsgiving;

Generosity.
  c Prov. 14:20 (20, 31);
     Alma 5:55 (54–56); Hel.
     6:39 (39–40). TG Poor.
  d Ps. 62:10; James 5:3;
     Alma 5:53 (53–56).
  e Jer. 8:20; D&C 45:2.
17 *a* Ex. 23:3 (1–3); Mosiah
     4:25 (24–27); D&C
     42:42; 68:30 (30–32).
  b TG Covet.
  c TG Labor; Laziness.
18 *a* Ps. 35:10; 86:1; 109:31;

Isa. 25:4; Matt. 5:3 (3,
8); Luke 6:20; 3 Ne.
12:3. TG Poor.
  b TG Contrite Heart;
     Humility; Meek.
  c TG Kingdom of God, on
     Earth.
  d TG Earth, Destiny of.
19 *a* Prov. 11:31; Rev. 22:12;
     D&C 1:10.
  b TG Reward.

20 And their generations shall *a*inherit the earth from generation to generation, forever and ever. And now I make an end of speaking unto you. Even so. Amen.

SECTION 57

Revelation given through Joseph Smith the Prophet, in Zion, Jackson County, Missouri, July 20, 1831. In compliance with the Lord's command to travel to Missouri, where He would reveal "the land of your inheritance" (section 52), the elders had journeyed from Ohio to Missouri's western border. Joseph Smith contemplated the state of the Lamanites and wondered: "When will the wilderness blossom as the rose? When will Zion be built up in her glory, and where will Thy temple stand, unto which all nations shall come in the last days?" Subsequently he received this revelation.

1–3, Independence, Missouri, is the place for the City of Zion and the temple; 4–7, The Saints are to purchase lands and receive inheritances in that area; 8–16, Sidney Gilbert is to establish a store, William W. Phelps is to be a printer, and Oliver Cowdery is to edit material for publication.

1 Hearken, O ye elders of my church, saith the Lord your God, who have assembled yourselves together, according to my commandments, in this land, which is the land of *a*Missouri, which is the *b*land which I have appointed and *c*consecrated for the *d*gathering of the saints.

2 Wherefore, this is the *a*land of promise, and the *b*place for the city of *c*Zion.

3 And thus saith the Lord your God, if you will receive wisdom here is wisdom. Behold, the place which is now called Independence is the *a*center place; and a spot for the *b*temple is lying westward, upon a lot which is not far from the courthouse.

4 Wherefore, it is wisdom that the land should be *a*purchased by the saints, and also every tract lying westward, even unto the line running directly *b*between Jew and Gentile;

5 And also every tract bordering by the prairies, inasmuch as my disciples

---

20 *a* Isa. 29:19; Matt. 5:5;
D&C 45:58; 57:5.
57 1 *a* D&C 52:3 (3, 42).
  b D&C 29:8 (7–8); 45:66
  (64–66); 52:2 (2, 42);
  58:1; 103:24.
  c D&C 61:17.
  d TG Mission of Latter-day

Saints.
2 *a* D&C 48:5; 52:5 (5, 42).
  b D&C 28:9; 42:9 (9, 62);
  103:24 (22–24).
  c D&C 62:4; 78:3.
  TG Zion.
3 *a* D&C 69:6.
  b D&C 58:57; 84:3

(3–5, 31); 97:10 (10–20);
124:51 (49–51).
4 *a* D&C 48:4. TG Jerusalem, New; Zion.
  b IE by metonymy "Jew"
  here refers to the Lamanites, and "Gentile" to
  the white settlers.

are enabled to *buy lands. Behold, this is wisdom, that they may *obtain it for an everlasting inheritance.

6 And let my servant Sidney Gilbert stand in the office to which I have appointed him, to receive moneys, to be an *agent unto the church, to buy land in all the regions round about, inasmuch as can be done in righteousness, and as wisdom shall direct.

7 And let my servant *Edward Partridge stand in the *office to which I have appointed him, and *divide unto the saints their inheritance, even as I have commanded; and also those whom he has appointed to assist him.

8 And again, verily I say unto you, let my servant Sidney Gilbert plant himself in this place, and establish a *store, that he may sell goods *without fraud, that he may obtain money to buy *lands for the good of the saints, and that he may obtain whatsoever things the disciples may need to plant them in their inheritance.

9 And also let my servant Sidney Gilbert obtain a license—behold here is *wisdom, and whoso readeth let him *understand—that he may send goods also unto the people, even by whom he will as clerks employed in his service;

10 And thus provide for my saints, that my gospel may be preached unto those who sit in *darkness and in the region and *shadow of death.

11 And again, verily I say unto you, let my servant *William W. Phelps be planted in this place, and be established as a *printer unto the church.

12 And lo, if the world receive his writings—behold here is wisdom—let him obtain whatsoever he can obtain in righteousness, for the good of the saints.

13 And let my servant *Oliver Cowdery assist him, even as I have commanded, in whatsoever place I shall appoint unto him, to copy, and to correct, and select, that all things may be right before me, as it shall be proved by the Spirit through him.

14 And thus let those of whom I have spoken be planted in the land of Zion, as speedily as can be, with their *families, to do those things even as I have spoken.

---

5 a D&C 42:35; 58:49 (49–51); 101:70 (68–74); 103:23 (22–24).
  b Matt. 5:5; D&C 56:20; 59:2. TG Lands of Inheritance.
6 a D&C 53:4; 64:18; 70:11.
7 a D&C 52:24; 58:14 (14, 19, 24).

  b D&C 58:40 (40–41); 61:7 (7–12).
  c D&C 41:9 (9–11); 51:1 (1–20); 58:17 (14–18).
8 a D&C 63:42; 64:26.
  b TG Honesty.
  c D&C 48:4.
9 a Rev. 13:18.
  b Matt. 24:15.

10 a Matt. 4:16. TG Darkness, Spiritual.
  b Job 3:5; Ps. 23:4.
11 a D&C 58:40; 61:7 (7–9); 70:1.
  b D&C 58:37 (37, 40–41).
13 a See Index for many references to Oliver Cowdery.
14 a TG Family.

15 And now concerning the gathering—Let the bishop and the agent make preparations for those families which have been commanded to come to this land, as soon as possible, and plant them in their inheritance.

16 And unto the residue of both elders and members further directions shall be given hereafter. Even so. Amen.

SECTION 58

Revelation given through Joseph Smith the Prophet, in Zion, Jackson County, Missouri, August 1, 1831. Earlier, on the first Sabbath after the arrival of the Prophet and his party in Jackson County, Missouri, a religious service had been held, and two members had been received by baptism. During that week, some of the Colesville Saints from the Thompson Branch and others arrived (see section 54). Many were eager to learn the will of the Lord concerning them in the new place of gathering.

1–5, Those who endure tribulation will be crowned with glory; 6–12, The Saints are to prepare for the marriage of the Lamb and the supper of the Lord; 13–18, Bishops are judges in Israel; 19–23, The Saints are to obey the laws of the land; 24–29, Men should use their agency to do good; 30–33, The Lord commands and revokes; 34–43, To repent, men must confess and forsake their sins; 44–58, The Saints are to purchase their inheritance and gather in Missouri; 59–65, The gospel must be preached unto every creature.

1 Hearken, O ye elders of my church, and give ^aear to my word, and learn of me what I will concerning you, and also concerning ^bthis land unto which I have sent you.

2 For verily I say unto you, blessed is he that ^akeepeth my commandments, whether in life or in ^bdeath; and he that is ^cfaithful in ^dtribulation, the ^ereward of the same is greater in the kingdom of heaven.

3 Ye cannot behold with your natural ^aeyes, for the present time, the design of your God concerning those things which shall come hereafter, and the ^bglory which shall follow after much tribulation.

4 For after much ^atribulation come the ^bblessings. Wherefore the day cometh that ye shall be ^ccrowned with much ^dglory; the hour is not yet, but is nigh at hand.

---

58 1 a Isa. 50:5 (5–7).
    b D&C 57:1 (1–8).
  2 a Ps. 19:11 (9–11); Mosiah 2:22.
    b 1 Pet. 4:6.
    c 2 Thes. 1:4.

TG Steadfastness.
    d TG Adversity.
    e TG Reward.
  3 a TG God, Privilege of Seeing.
    b 1 Pet. 1:11. TG Glory.
  4 a Ps. 30:5; D&C 101:2

(2–7); 103:12 (11–14); 109:76. TG Tribulation.
    b TG Blessing.
    c TG Exaltation.
    d Rom. 8:18; D&C 63:66; 136:31.

5 Remember this, which I tell you before, that you may ^alay it to heart, and receive that which is to follow.

6 Behold, verily I say unto you, for this cause I have sent you—that you might be obedient, and that your hearts might be ^aprepared to ^bbear ^ctestimony of the things which are to come;

7 And also that you might be honored in laying the foundation, and in bearing record of the land upon which the ^aZion of God shall stand;

8 And also that a feast of fat things might be prepared for the ^apoor; yea, a feast of fat things, of wine on the ^blees well refined, that the earth may know that the mouths of the prophets shall not fail;

9 Yea, a supper of the house of the Lord, well prepared, unto which all ^anations shall be invited.

10 First, the rich and the learned, the wise and the noble;

11 And after that cometh the day of my power; then shall the ^apoor, the lame, and the blind, and the deaf, come in unto the ^bmarriage of the Lamb, and partake of the ^csupper of the Lord, prepared for the great day to come.

12 Behold, I, the Lord, have spoken it.

13 And that the ^atestimony might go forth from Zion, yea, from the mouth of the city of the heritage of God—

14 Yea, for this cause I have sent you hither, and have selected my servant ^aEdward Partridge, and have appointed unto him his mission in this land.

15 But if he repent not of his sins, which are ^aunbelief and blindness of ^bheart, let him take heed lest he ^cfall.

16 Behold his mission is given unto him, and it shall not be given again.

17 And whoso standeth in this mission is appointed to be a ^ajudge in Israel, like as it was in ancient days, to ^bdivide the lands of the heritage of God unto his ^cchildren;

18 And to judge his people by the testimony of the just, and by the assistance of his ^acounselors, according to the laws of the kingdom which are given by the ^bprophets of God.

19 For verily I say unto you, my law shall be kept on this land.

---

5 a Deut. 11:18.
6 a 3 Ne. 17:3; D&C 29:8; 132:3.
   b Isa. 43:10 (10–12); 44:8.
   c TG Testimony.
7 a TG Zion.
8 a Ps. 132:15 (13–16). TG Poor.
   b Isa. 25:6.
9 a TG Nations.

11 a TG Poor.
    b Matt. 22:2 (1–14); Rev. 19:9; D&C 65:3.
    c Luke 14:16 (16–24).
13 a Micah 4:2. TG Testimony.
14 a D&C 57:7; 60:10.
15 a TG Doubt.
    b TG Hardheartedness.
    c 1 Cor. 10:12.

17 a Deut. 16:18; D&C 64:40; 107:72 (72–74). TG Bishop.
    b D&C 41:9 (9–11); 51:1 (1–20); 57:7.
    c TG Sons and Daughters of God.
18 a TG Counselor.
    b TG Prophets, Mission of.

20 Let no man think he is ªruler; but let God rule him that judgeth, according to the counsel of his own ᵇwill, or, in other words, him that counseleth or sitteth upon the judgment seat.

21 Let no man break the ªlaws of the land, for he that keepeth the laws of God hath no need to break the laws of the land.

22 Wherefore, be ªsubject to the powers that be, ᵇuntil he reigns whose right it is to reign, and subdues all enemies under his feet.

23 Behold, the ªlaws which ye have received from my hand are the laws of the church, and in this light ye shall hold them forth. Behold, here is wisdom.

24 And now, as I spake concerning my servant Edward Partridge, this land is the land of his ªresidence, and those whom he has appointed for his counselors; and also the land of the residence of him whom I have appointed to keep my ᵇstorehouse;

25 Wherefore, let them bring their families to this land, as they shall ªcounsel between themselves and me.

26 For behold, it is not meet that I should command in all things; for he that is ªcompelled in all things, the same is a ᵇslothful and not a wise servant; wherefore he receiveth no reward.

27 Verily I say, men should be ªanxiously engaged in a good cause, and do many things of their own free will, and bring to pass much righteousness;

28 For the power is in them, wherein they are ªagents unto themselves. And inasmuch as men do good they shall in nowise lose their ᵇreward.

29 But he that ªdoeth not anything until he is commanded, and receiveth a commandment with ᵇdoubtful heart, and keepeth it with slothfulness, the same is ᶜdamned.

30 Who am I that ªmade man, saith the Lord, that will hold him ᵇguiltless that obeys not my commandments?

31 Who am I, saith the Lord, that have ªpromised and have not fulfilled?

---

20 a TG Unrighteous Domin-
      ion.
   b TG God, Will of.
21 a Matt. 17:24 (24–27);
      Luke 20:22 (22–26);
      D&C 20:1; 51:6; 98:9
      (4–10); A of F 1:12.
      TG Citizenship; Govern-
      ments.
22 a Rom. 13:1 (1–7).
      TG Governments; Sub-
      missiveness.
   b Gen. 49:10; Ezek. 21:27;

Zech. 9:10; D&C 76:63.
      TG Jesus Christ, Messiah;
      Jesus Christ, Millennial
      Reign.
23 a D&C 42:2 (2–28).
24 a D&C 41:9; 72:6.
   b D&C 51:13; 70:7 (7–11).
25 a TG Guidance, Divine.
26 a TG Initiative.
   b Matt. 24:45 (45–51);
      D&C 107:100 (99–100).
      TG Apathy; Laziness.
27 a TG Dedication;

Diligence; Good Works;
      Industry; Zeal.
28 a Amos 5:14. TG Agency.
   b TG Reward.
29 a Moro. 7:6 (6–9).
   b TG Doubt.
   c TG Damnation.
30 a Isa. 45:9 (9–10); Hel.
      12:6 (6–22).
   b Ex. 20:7; Mosiah 13:15;
      Morm. 7:7.
31 a D&C 1:37 (37–38);
      82:10.

32 I command and men *obey not; I *revoke and they receive not the blessing.

33 Then they *say in their hearts: This is not the work of the Lord, for his promises are not fulfilled. But wo unto such, for their *reward lurketh *beneath, and not from above.

34 And now I give unto you further directions concerning this land.

35 It is wisdom in me that my servant Martin Harris should be an example unto the church, in *laying his moneys before the bishop of the church.

36 And also, this is a law unto every man that cometh unto this land to receive an inheritance; and he shall do with his moneys according as the law directs.

37 And it is wisdom also that there should be lands purchased in Independence, for the place of the storehouse, and also for the house of the *printing.

38 And other directions concerning my servant Martin Harris shall be given him of the Spirit, that he may receive his inheritance as seemeth him good;

39 And let him repent of his sins, for he seeketh the *praise of the world.

40 And also let my servant *William W. Phelps stand in the office to which I have appointed him, and receive his inheritance in the land;

41 And also he hath need to repent, for I, the Lord, am not well pleased with him, for he seeketh to excel, and he is not sufficiently meek before me.

42 Behold, he who has *repented of his *sins, the same is *forgiven, and I, the Lord, remember them no more.

43 By this ye may know if a man repenteth of his sins—behold, he will *confess them and *forsake them.

44 And now, verily, I say concerning the residue of the elders of my *church, the time has not yet come, for many years, for them to receive their *inheritance in this land, except they desire it through the prayer of faith, only as it shall be appointed unto them of the Lord.

45 For, behold, they shall *push the people together from the *ends of the earth.

32 a 1 Sam. 28:18. TG Disobedience.
   b Jer. 18:10 (6–10); D&C
   19:5; 54:4; 56:4 (3–4).
33 a 1 Ne. 15:9 (7–11).
   b TG Reward.
   c D&C 29:45.
35 a D&C 42:31 (30–32).
37 a D&C 57:11 (11–12).

39 a 2 Ne. 26:29; D&C
   121:35 (34–37).
40 a D&C 57:11; 61:7 (7–9);
   70:1.
42 a TG Repent.
   b Ps. 25:7.
   c Isa. 1:18; Jer. 31:34.
   TG Forgive.
43 a Num. 5:7 (6–10); D&C

19:20; 64:7. TG Confes-
   sion.
   b D&C 82:7.
44 a TG Jesus Christ, Head of
   the Church.
   b TG Lands of Inheritance.
45 a Deut. 33:17.
   b TG Israel, Gathering of.

46 Wherefore, assemble yourselves together; and they who are not appointed to stay in this land, let them preach the gospel in the regions round about; and after that let them return to their homes.

47 Let them preach by the way, and *a*bear testimony of the truth in all places, and call upon the rich, the high and the low, and the poor to repent.

48 And let them build up *a*churches, inasmuch as the inhabitants of the earth will repent.

49 And let there be an agent appointed by the voice of the church, unto the church in Ohio, to receive moneys to *a*purchase lands in *b*Zion.

50 And I give unto my servant Sidney Rigdon a commandment, that he shall *a*write a description of the land of Zion, and a statement of the will of God, as it shall be made known by the Spirit unto him;

51 And an epistle and subscription, to be presented unto all the churches to obtain moneys, to be put into the hands of the bishop, of himself or the agent, as seemeth him good or as he shall direct, to *a*purchase lands for an *b*inheritance for the children of God.

52 For, behold, verily I say unto you, the Lord willeth that the disciples and the children of men should open their hearts, even to purchase this whole region of country, as soon as time will permit.

53 Behold, here is wisdom. Let them do this lest they *a*receive none inheritance, save it be by the shedding of blood.

54 And again, inasmuch as there is land obtained, let there be workmen sent forth of all kinds unto this land, to labor for the saints of God.

55 Let all these things be done in *a*order; and let the privileges of the lands be made known from time to time, by the bishop or the agent of the church.

56 And let the work of the *a*gathering be not in *b*haste, nor by flight; but let it be done as it shall be *c*counseled by the elders of the church at the conferences, according to the knowledge which they receive from time to time.

57 And let my servant Sidney Rigdon *a*consecrate and *b*dedicate this land, and the spot for the *c*temple, unto the Lord.

58 And let a conference meeting be called; and after that let my servants Sidney Rigdon and Joseph Smith, Jun., return, and also Oliver Cowdery

47 *a* D&C 19:37; 63:37; 68:8;
  71:7.
48 *a* IE branches of the
  Church.
49 *a* D&C 42:35; 57:5 (5–7);
  101:70 (68–74); 103:23
  (22–24).
  b TG Zion.
50 *a* D&C 63:56 (55–56);

  100:9.
51 *a* D&C 51:8 (8–13);
  84:104.
  b D&C 25:2; 52:42 (2, 5,
  42).
53 *a* D&C 63:29 (27–31);
  101:70 (70–75).
55 *a* D&C 101:68. TG Order.
56 *a* D&C 63:24; 101:68.

  b TG Haste; Rashness.
  c D&C 72:24.
57 *a* D&C 52:2; 103:35;
  105:15.
  b TG Dedication.
  c D&C 57:3; 84:3
  (3–5, 31); 97:10 (10–20);
  124:51 (49–51).

with them, to accomplish the residue of the work which I have appointed unto them in their own land, and the residue as shall be *ruled by the conferences.

59 And let no man return from this land except he bear *record by the way, of that which he knows and most assuredly believes.

60 Let that which has been bestowed upon *Ziba Peterson be taken from him; and let him stand as a member in the church, and labor with his own hands, with the brethren, until he is sufficiently *chastened for all his sins; for he confesseth them not, and he thinketh to hide them.

61 Let the residue of the elders of this church, who are coming to this land, some of whom are exceedingly blessed even above measure, also hold a *conference upon this land.

62 And let my servant Edward Partridge direct the conference which shall be held by them.

63 And let them also return, preaching the gospel by the way, bearing record of the things which are revealed unto them.

64 For, verily, the sound must go forth from this place into all the world, and unto the uttermost parts of the earth—the gospel must be *preached unto every creature, with *signs following them that believe.

65 And behold the Son of Man *cometh. Amen.

SECTION 59

Revelation given through Joseph Smith the Prophet, in Zion, Jackson County, Missouri, August 7, 1831. Preceding this revelation, the land was consecrated, as the Lord had directed, and the site for the future temple was dedicated. On the day this revelation was received, Polly Knight, the wife of Joseph Knight Sr., died, the first Church member to die in Zion. Early members characterized this revelation as "instructing the Saints how to keep the sabbath and how to fast and pray."

1–4, The faithful Saints in Zion will be blessed; 5–8, They are to love and serve the Lord and keep His commandments; 9–19, By keeping the Lord's day holy, the Saints are blessed temporally and spiritually; 20–24, The righteous are promised peace in this world and eternal life in the world to come.

---

58 a TG Church Organization; Common Consent.
59 a TG Mission of Latter-day Saints; Testimony.
60 a D&C 32:3.

b TG Chastening; Forgive; Repent.
61 a TG Meetings.
64 a TG Mission of Latter-day Saints.

b TG Holy Ghost, Gifts of; Miracle; Signs.
65 a D&C 1:12.

1 Behold, blessed, saith the Lord, are they who have come up unto this land with an *a*eye single to my glory, according to my commandments.

2 For those that live shall *a*inherit the earth, and those that *b*die shall rest from all their labors, and their works shall follow them; and they shall receive a *c*crown in the *d*mansions of my Father, which I have prepared for them.

3 Yea, blessed are they whose feet stand upon the land of Zion, who have obeyed my gospel; for they shall receive for their reward the good things of the earth, and it shall bring forth in its *a*strength.

4 And they shall also be crowned with blessings from above, yea, and with *a*commandments not a few, and with *b*revelations in their time—they that are *c*faithful and *d*diligent before me.

5 Wherefore, I give unto them a commandment, saying thus: Thou shalt *a*love the Lord thy God with all thy *b*heart, with all thy might, mind, and strength; and in the name of Jesus Christ thou shalt *c*serve him.

6 Thou shalt *a*love thy *b*neighbor as thyself. Thou shalt not *c*steal; neither commit *d*adultery, nor *e*kill, nor do anything *f*like unto it.

7 Thou shalt *a*thank the Lord thy God in all things.

8 Thou shalt offer a *a*sacrifice unto the Lord thy God in *b*righteousness, even that of a broken heart and a *c*contrite spirit.

9 And that thou mayest more fully keep thyself *a*unspotted from the world, thou shalt go to the house of *b*prayer and offer up thy *c*sacraments upon my *d*holy day;

10 For verily this is a *a*day appointed unto you to rest from your labors, and to pay thy devotions unto the Most High;

59 1*a* Matt. 6:22 (22–24).
  2*a* Matt. 5:5; D&C 57:5;
      63:20 (20, 48–49).
    b Isa. 57:1 (1–2); Rev.
      14:13. TG Paradise.
    c TG Celestial Glory;
      Exaltation.
    d Ps. 65:4; John 14:2;
      D&C 72:4; 76:111; 81:6;
      98:18; 106:8.
  3*a* Gen. 4:12; Moses
      4:23 (23–24); 5:37.
      TG Strength.
  4*a* Alma 29:9.
    b D&C 42:61; 76:7; 98:12;
      101:32; 121:28 (26–33).
      TG Revelation.
    c TG Steadfastness; Wor-
      thiness.

    d TG Diligence.
  5*a* Deut. 11:1; Matt. 22:37;
      Mosiah 2:4; Moro. 10:32;
      D&C 20:19. TG God,
      Love of; Love.
    b TG Heart.
    c TG Service; Worship.
  6*a* TG Love.
    b Prov. 11:12 (12–17).
      TG Fellowshipping;
      Neighbor.
    c TG Stealing.
    d TG Adulterer; Chastity.
    e TG Murder.
    f Ex. 22:19; Lev. 18:22;
      1 Cor. 6:9; 1 Tim. 1:10.
  7*a* Ezra 3:11; Ps. 34:1
      (1–3); 92:1; Alma 37:37;
      Ether 6:9; D&C 46:32.

      TG Communication;
      Thanksgiving.
  8*a* TG Jesus Christ, Types
      of, in Memory; Self-
      Sacrifice.
    b TG Righteousness.
    c TG Contrite Heart; Poor
      in Spirit.
  9*a* James 1:27. TG Abstain;
      Self-Mastery.
    b TG Assembly for Wor-
      ship; Prayer.
    c D&C 62:4. TG Sacra-
      ment.
    d Lev. 19:3; 23:3; Alma
      1:26 (26–27); D&C
      68:29. TG Sabbath.
 10*a* Ex. 35:2; Lev. 23:25.
      TG Rest; Worship.

11 Nevertheless thy ^avows shall be offered up in righteousness on all days and at all times;

12 But remember that on this, the ^aLord's day, thou shalt offer thine ^boblations and thy sacraments unto the Most High, ^cconfessing thy sins unto thy brethren, and before the Lord.

13 And on this day thou shalt do none other thing, only let thy food be prepared with singleness of heart that thy ^afasting may be perfect, or, in other words, that thy ^bjoy may be full.

14 Verily, this is fasting and prayer, or in other words, rejoicing and prayer.

15 And inasmuch as ye do these things with ^athanksgiving, with ^bcheerful ^chearts and countenances, not with ^dmuch ^elaughter, for this is sin, but with a glad heart and a cheerful countenance—

16 Verily I say, that inasmuch as ye do this, the ^afulness of the earth is yours, the beasts of the field and the fowls of the air, and that which climbeth upon the trees and walketh upon the earth;

17 Yea, and the herb, and the ^agood things which come of the earth, whether for food or for ^braiment, or for houses, or for barns, or for orchards, or for gardens, or for vineyards;

18 Yea, all things which come of the earth, in the season thereof, are made for the ^abenefit and the ^buse of man, both to please the eye and to ^cgladden the heart;

19 Yea, for ^afood and for raiment, for taste and for smell, to ^bstrengthen the body and to enliven the soul.

20 And it pleaseth God that he hath given all these things unto man; for unto this end were they made to be used, with judgment, not to ^aexcess, neither by extortion.

21 And in nothing doth man ^aoffend God, or against none is his ^bwrath ^ckindled, save those who ^dconfess not his hand in all things, and ^eobey not his commandments.

11 a TG Commitment; Vow.
12 a Neh. 8:10; Rev. 1:10.
  b IE offerings, whether of time, talents, or means, in service of God and fellowman. TG Sacrifice.
  c TG Confession.
13 a IE hungering and thirsting after righteousness; see Matt. 5:6; 3 Ne. 12:6. TG Fast, Fasting.
  b TG Joy.
15 a TG Thanksgiving.

  b Ex. 25:2 (1–7); 35:5; D&C 64:22 (22, 34); 97:8. TG Cheerful.
  c Prov. 17:22.
  d 1 Pet. 4:3; D&C 88:69.
  e TG Laughter.
16 a TG Abundant Life.
17 a Gen. 1:31; Moro. 7:12; Moses 2:31.
  b D&C 70:16 (15–16).
18 a TG Earth, Purpose of; Meat.
  b Gen. 1:29; 9:3 (3–4).

  c TG Happiness.
19 a TG Food.
  b TG Health.
20 a TG Temperance.
21 a TG Offense.
  b TG God, Indignation of.
  c TG Provoking.
  d Neh. 12:24; Job 1:21; Ps. 97:12; Mosiah 2:20 (20–22); D&C 62:7. TG Ingratitude.
  e TG Disobedience.

22 Behold, this is according to the law and the prophets; wherefore, trouble me no more concerning this matter.

23 But learn that he who doeth the works of *a*righteousness shall receive his *b*reward, even *c*peace in this world, and *d*eternal life in the world to come.

24 I, the Lord, have spoken it, and the Spirit beareth record. Amen.

SECTION 60

Revelation given through Joseph Smith the Prophet, in Independence, Jackson County, Missouri, August 8, 1831. On this occasion the elders who had traveled to Jackson County and participated in the dedication of the land and the temple site desired to know what they were to do.

1–9, The elders are to preach the gospel in the congregations of the wicked; 10–14, They should not idle away their time, nor bury their talents; 15–17, They may wash their feet as a testimony against those who reject the gospel.

1 Behold, thus saith the Lord unto the elders of his church, who are to return speedily to the land from whence they came: Behold, it pleaseth me, that you have come up hither;

2 But with some I am not well pleased, for they will not open their *a*mouths, but they hide the *b*talent which I have given unto them, because of the *c*fear of man. Wo unto such, for mine *d*anger is *e*kindled against them.

3 And it shall come to pass, if they are not more faithful unto me, it shall be *a*taken away, even that which they have.

4 For I, the Lord, *a*rule in the heavens above, and among the *b*armies of the earth; and in the day when I shall make up my *c*jewels, all men shall know what it is that bespeaketh the power of God.

5 But, verily, I will speak unto you concerning your journey unto the land from whence you came. Let there be a craft made, or bought, as *a*seemeth

---

23 *a* TG Righteousness.
  b TG Blessing; Reward.
  c Matt. 11:29 (28–30).
    TG Happiness; Objectives; Peace; Peace of God.
  d D&C 14:7.
60 2 *a* Ex. 4:10 (10–12); Jer. 1:6 (6–9); Luke 8:16 (16–18);

Eph. 6:20 (19–20).
  b Matt. 25:25 (24–30).
    TG Talents.
  c TG Courage; Fearful; Peer Influence.
  d TG Anger; God, Indignation of.
  e TG Provoking.
3 *a* Matt. 25:29 (29–30);

Mark 4:25; D&C 1:33.
4 *a* Judg. 8:23 (22–23); Hel. 12:6.
  b 2 Chr. 25:8. TG War.
  c Isa. 62:3; Zech. 9:16; Mal. 3:17; D&C 101:3.
5 *a* TG Agency; Initiative.

you good, it mattereth not unto me, and take your journey speedily for the place which is called St. Louis.

6 And from thence let my servants, Sidney Rigdon, Joseph Smith, Jun., and Oliver Cowdery, take their journey for Cincinnati;

7 And in this place let them lift up their voice and declare my word with loud voices, without wrath or *doubting, lifting up holy hands upon them. For I am able to make you *holy, and your sins are *forgiven you.

8 And let the residue take their journey from St. Louis, *two by two, and preach the word, not in haste, among the congregations of the wicked, until they return to the churches from whence they came.

9 And all this for the good of the *churches; for this intent have I sent them.

10 And let my servant *Edward Partridge impart of the *money which I have given him, a portion unto mine elders who are commanded to return;

11 And he that is able, let him return it by the way of the agent; and he that is not, of him it is not required.

12 And now I speak of the residue who are to come unto this land.

13 Behold, they have been sent to preach my gospel among the congregations of the wicked; wherefore, I give unto them a commandment, thus: Thou shalt not *idle away thy time, neither shalt thou bury thy *talent that it may not be known.

14 And after thou hast come up unto the land of Zion, and hast proclaimed my word, thou shalt speedily return, proclaiming my word among the congregations of the wicked, not in *haste, neither in *wrath nor with *strife.

15 And shake off the *dust of thy feet against those who receive thee not, not in their presence, lest thou *provoke them, but in secret; and *wash thy feet, as a testimony against them in the day of judgment.

16 Behold, this is sufficient for you, and the will of him who hath sent you.

17 And by the mouth of my servant Joseph Smith, Jun., it shall be made known concerning Sidney Rigdon and Oliver Cowdery. The residue hereafter. Even so. Amen.

---

7 a TG Doubt.
  b TG Holiness.
  c TG Forgive.
8 a Mark 6:7.
9 a D&C 51:10.
10 a D&C 58:14 (14, 19, 24);
   64:17.
  b D&C 51:8 (8–13).

13 a D&C 42:42. TG Apathy;
   Idleness; Laziness;
   Priesthood, Magnifying
   Callings within; Procras-
   tination; Waste; Zeal.
  b Matt. 25:25 (14–30);
   D&C 82:18.
14 a TG Rashness.

  b Prov. 14:29.
  c TG Strife.
15 a Matt. 10:14; Luke 9:5;
   Acts 13:51; 18:6 (5–6);
   D&C 24:15; 75:20;
   84:92 (92–95).
  b TG Provoking.
  c TG Wash.

SECTION 61

Revelation given through Joseph Smith the Prophet, on the bank of the Missouri River, McIlwaine's Bend, August 12, 1831. On their return trip to Kirtland, the Prophet and ten elders had traveled down the Missouri River in canoes. On the third day of the journey, many dangers were experienced. Elder William W. Phelps, in a daylight vision, saw the destroyer riding in power upon the face of the waters.

1–12, The Lord has decreed many destructions upon the waters; 13–22, The waters were cursed by John, and the destroyer rides upon their face; 23–29, Some have power to command the waters; 30–35, Elders are to journey two by two and preach the gospel; 36–39, They are to prepare for the coming of the Son of Man.

1 Behold, and hearken unto the voice of him who has all ᵃpower, who is from everlasting to everlasting, even ᵇAlpha and Omega, the beginning and the end.

2 Behold, verily thus saith the Lord unto you, O ye elders of my church, who are assembled upon this spot, whose sins are now forgiven you, for I, the Lord, ᵃforgive sins, and am ᵇmerciful unto those who ᶜconfess their sins with humble hearts;

3 But verily I say unto you, that it is not needful for this whole company of mine elders to be moving swiftly upon the waters, whilst the inhabitants on either side are perishing in unbelief.

4 Nevertheless, I suffered it that ye might bear record; behold, there are many dangers upon the waters, and more especially hereafter;

5 For I, the Lord, have decreed in mine anger many destructions upon the waters; yea, and especially upon these waters.

6 Nevertheless, all flesh is in mine hand, and he that is faithful among you shall not ᵃperish by the waters.

7 Wherefore, it is expedient that my servant Sidney Gilbert and my servant ᵃWilliam W. Phelps be in haste upon their errand and mission.

8 Nevertheless, I would not suffer that ye should part until you were ᵃchastened for all your sins, that you might be one, that you might not perish in ᵇwickedness;

9 But now, verily I say, it behooveth me that ye should part. Wherefore let my servants Sidney Gilbert and William W. Phelps take their former

---

61 1a TG God, Power of.
    b D&C 19:1.
  2a Mosiah 4:10 (10–11).

    TG Forgive.
    b TG God, Mercy of.
    c TG Confession.
  6a TG Protection, Divine.

  7a D&C 57:11 (6–12);
    58:40 (40–41); 70:1.
  8a TG Chastening.
    b TG Wickedness.

company, and let them take their journey in haste that they may fill their mission, and through faith they shall overcome;

10 And inasmuch as they are ^afaithful they shall be preserved, and I, the Lord, will be ^bwith them.

11 And let the residue take that which is needful for clothing.

12 Let my servant Sidney Gilbert take that which is not needful with him, as you shall agree.

13 And now, behold, for your ^agood I gave unto you a ^bcommandment concerning these things; and I, the Lord, will reason with you as with men in days of old.

14 Behold, I, the Lord, in the beginning blessed the ^awaters; but in the last days, by the mouth of my servant John, I ^bcursed the waters.

15 Wherefore, the days will come that no flesh shall be safe upon the waters.

16 And it shall be said in days to come that none is able to go up to the land of Zion upon the waters, but he that is upright in heart.

17 And, as I, the Lord, in the beginning ^acursed the land, even so in the last days have I ^bblessed it, in its time, for the use of my saints, that they may partake the fatness thereof.

18 And now I give unto you a commandment that what I say unto one I say unto all, that you shall forewarn your brethren concerning these waters, that they come not in journeying upon them, lest their faith fail and they are caught in snares;

19 I, the Lord, have decreed, and the destroyer rideth upon the face thereof, and I revoke not the decree.

20 I, the Lord, was ^aangry with you yesterday, but today mine anger is turned away.

21 Wherefore, let those concerning whom I have spoken, that should take their journey in haste—again I say unto you, let them take their journey in haste.

22 And it mattereth not unto me, after a little, if it so be that they fill their mission, whether they go by water or by land; let this be as it is made known unto them ^aaccording to their judgments hereafter.

23 And now, concerning my servants, Sidney Rigdon, Joseph Smith, Jun., and Oliver Cowdery, let them come not again upon the waters, save it be

---

10 a Ps. 31:23.
  b Matt. 28:20.
13 a Deut. 10:13; D&C 21:6.
  b TG Commandments of
    God.
14 a Gen. 1:20.
  b Rev. 8:10 (8–11).
    TG Curse; Last Days.
17 a Moses 4:23.
  b D&C 57:1 (1–5).
20 a TG God, Indignation of;
    God, Love of.
22 a TG Agency; Initiative.

upon the canal, while journeying unto their homes; or in other words they shall not come upon the waters to journey, save upon the canal.

24 Behold, I, the Lord, have appointed a way for the journeying of my saints; and behold, this is the way—that after they leave the canal they shall journey by land, inasmuch as they are commanded to journey and go up unto the land of Zion;

25 And they shall do *like unto the children of Israel, *pitching their tents by the way.

26 And, behold, this commandment you shall give unto all your brethren.

27 Nevertheless, unto whom is given *power to command the waters, unto him it is given by the Spirit to know all his ways;

28 Wherefore, let him do as the Spirit of the living God commandeth him, whether upon the land or upon the waters, as it remaineth with me to do hereafter.

29 And unto you is given the course for the saints, or the way for the saints of the camp of the Lord, to journey.

30 And again, verily I say unto you, my servants, Sidney Rigdon, Joseph Smith, Jun., and Oliver Cowdery, shall not open their mouths in the *congregations of the wicked until they arrive at Cincinnati;

31 And in that place they shall lift up their voices unto God against that people, yea, unto him whose anger is *kindled against their wickedness, a people who are well-nigh *ripened for destruction.

32 And from thence let them journey for the congregations of their brethren, for their labors even now are wanted more abundantly among them than among the congregations of the wicked.

33 And now, concerning the residue, let them journey and *declare the word among the congregations of the wicked, inasmuch as it is given;

34 And inasmuch as they do this they shall *rid their garments, and they shall be spotless before me.

35 And let them journey together, or *two by two, as seemeth them good, only let my servant Reynolds Cahoon, and my servant Samuel H. Smith, with whom I am well pleased, be not separated until they return to their homes, and this for a wise purpose in me.

36 And now, verily I say unto you, and what I say unto one I say unto all,

---

25 a Num. 9:18.
  b Num. 2:34 (32–34).
27 a TG Holy Ghost, Gifts of; Priesthood, Power of.
30 a Micah 6:10 (10–15);

D&C 62:5; 68:1.
31 a TG Provoking.
  b Alma 37:31; Hel. 13:14; D&C 101:11.
33 a TG Preaching.

34 a 2 Ne. 9:44; Jacob 2:2 (2, 16); Mosiah 2:28.
35 a Mark 6:7; Luke 10:1; D&C 52:10; 62:5.
    TG Missionary Work.

be of good *a*cheer, *b*little children; for I am in your *c*midst, and I have not *d*forsaken you;

37 And inasmuch as you have humbled yourselves before me, the blessings of the *a*kingdom are yours.

38 Gird up your loins and be *a*watchful and be sober, looking forth for the coming of the Son of Man, for he cometh in an hour you think not.

39 Pray always that you enter not into *a*temptation, that you may abide the day of his coming, whether in life or in death. Even so. Amen.

SECTION 62

Revelation given through Joseph Smith the Prophet, on the bank of the Missouri River at Chariton, Missouri, August 13, 1831. On this day the Prophet and his group, who were on their way from Independence to Kirtland, met several elders who were on their way to the land of Zion, and, after joyful salutations, received this revelation.

1–3, Testimonies are recorded in heaven; 4–9, The elders are to travel and preach according to judgment and as directed by the Spirit.

1 Behold, and hearken, O ye elders of my church, saith the Lord your God, even Jesus Christ, your *a*advocate, who knoweth the weakness of man and how to *b*succor them who are *c*tempted.

2 And verily mine eyes are upon those who have not as yet gone up unto the land of Zion; wherefore your mission is not yet full.

3 Nevertheless, ye are *a*blessed, for the *b*testimony which ye have borne is *c*recorded in heaven for the angels to look upon; and they rejoice over you, and your *d*sins are forgiven you.

4 And now continue your journey. Assemble yourselves upon the land of *a*Zion; and hold a meeting and rejoice together, and offer a *b*sacrament unto the Most High.

5 And then you may return to bear record, yea, even altogether, or *a*two by two, as seemeth you good, it mattereth not unto me; only be faithful,

---

36 *a* TG Cheerful.
   b John 13:33.
   c Matt. 18:20; 28:20 (19–20).
   d Isa. 41:17 (15–17); 1 Ne. 21:15 (14–15).
37 *a* D&C 50:35; 62:9.
38 *a* TG Watch.
39 *a* TG Temptation.

62 1 *a* D&C 45:3. TG Jesus Christ, Advocate; Jesus Christ, Relationships with the Father.
   b Heb. 2:18; Alma 7:12.
   c Luke 4:2.
3 *a* TG Blessing.
   b Luke 12:8 (8–9).

   TG Testimony.
   c TG Book of Life.
   d Matt. 9:2; D&C 84:61.
4 *a* D&C 57:2 (1–2).
   b TG Assembly for Worship; Sacrament.
5 *a* Mark 6:7; Luke 10:1; D&C 52:10; 61:35.

and ^b declare glad tidings unto the inhabitants of the earth, or among the ^c congregations of the wicked.

6 Behold, I, the Lord, have brought you together that the promise might be fulfilled, that the faithful among you should be preserved and rejoice together in the land of Missouri. I, the Lord, ^a promise the faithful and cannot ^b lie.

7 I, the Lord, am willing, if any among you ^a desire to ride upon horses, or upon mules, or in chariots, he shall receive this blessing, if he receive it from the hand of the Lord, with a ^b thankful heart in all things.

8 These things remain with you to do according to judgment and the directions of the Spirit.

9 Behold, the ^a kingdom is yours. And behold, and lo, I am ^b with the faithful always. Even so. Amen.

SECTION 63

Revelation given through Joseph Smith the Prophet, at Kirtland, Ohio, August 30, 1831. The Prophet, Sidney Rigdon, and Oliver Cowdery had arrived in Kirtland on August 27 from their visit to Missouri. Joseph Smith's history describes this revelation: "In these infant days of the Church, there was a great anxiety to obtain the word of the Lord upon every subject that in any way concerned our salvation; and as the land of Zion was now the most important temporal object in view, I enquired of the Lord for further information upon the gathering of the Saints, and the purchase of the land, and other matters."

1–6, A day of wrath will come upon the wicked; 7–12, Signs come by faith; 13–19, The adulterous in heart will deny the faith and be cast into the lake of fire; 20, The faithful will receive an inheritance upon the transfigured earth; 21, A full account of the events on the Mount of Transfiguration has not yet been revealed; 22–23, The obedient receive the mysteries of the kingdom; 24–31, Inheritances in Zion are to be purchased; 32–35, The Lord decrees wars, and the wicked slay the wicked; 36–48, The Saints are to gather to Zion and provide moneys to build it up; 49–54, Blessings are assured the faithful at the Second Coming, in the Resurrection, and during the Millennium; 55–58, This is a day of warning; 59–66, The Lord's name is taken in vain by those who use it without authority.

---

5 *b* TG Missionary Work.
  c D&C 61:30.
6 *a* Ezek. 36:36.
  b TG God, Perfection of;

Honesty.
7 *a* TG Agency.
  b Job 1:21; Mosiah 2:20
    (20–22); D&C 59:21.

TG Thanksgiving.
9 *a* D&C 61:37; 64:4.
  b Matt. 28:20.

1 Hearken, O ye people, and open your hearts and give ear from afar; and listen, you that call yourselves the *a*people of the Lord, and hear the word of the Lord and his will concerning you.

2 Yea, verily, I say, hear the word of him whose anger is *a*kindled against the wicked and *b*rebellious;

3 Who willeth to take even them whom he will *a*take, and *b*preserveth in life them whom he will preserve;

4 Who buildeth up at his own will and *a*pleasure; and destroyeth when he pleases, and is able to *b*cast the soul down to hell.

5 Behold, I, the Lord, utter my voice, and it shall be *a*obeyed.

6 Wherefore, verily I say, let the wicked take heed, and let the *a*rebellious *b*fear and tremble; and let the unbelieving hold their lips, for the *c*day of wrath shall come upon them as a *d*whirlwind, and all flesh shall *e*know that I am God.

7 And he that seeketh *a*signs shall see *b*signs, but not unto salvation.

8 Verily, I say unto you, there are those among you who seek signs, and there have been such even from the beginning;

9 But, behold, faith cometh not by signs, but *a*signs follow those that believe.

10 Yea, *a*signs come by *b*faith, not by the will of men, nor as they please, but by the will of God.

11 Yea, signs come by faith, unto mighty works, for without *a*faith no man pleaseth God; and with whom God is *b*angry he is not well pleased; wherefore, unto such he showeth no signs, only in *c*wrath unto their *d*condemnation.

12 Wherefore, I, the Lord, am not pleased with those among you who have sought after signs and wonders for faith, and not for the good of men unto my glory.

13 Nevertheless, I give commandments, and many have turned away from my commandments and have *a*not kept them.

14 There were among you *a*adulterers and adulteresses; some of whom

---

63 1 *a* Lev. 26:12; 3 Ne. 20:19.
　　2 *a* TG Provoking.
　　　 b TG Rebellion.
　　3 *a* Job 1:21; Isa. 57:1.
　　　　 TG Death.
　　　 b Mosiah 2:20 (20–21).
　　4 *a* TG God, Justice of;
　　　　 Judgment.
　　　 b Hel. 12:21 (20–22).
　　5 *a* TG Obedience.

6 *a* TG Rebellion.
　 b TG Day of the Lord.
　 c D&C 1:13 (13–14).
　 d Jer. 30:23; Dan. 11:40.
　 e Isa. 49:26.
7 *a* TG Sign Seekers.
　 b Mark 8:11 (11–21); D&C 46:9.
9 *a* Mark 16:17. TG Holy Ghost, Gifts of; Miracle; Signs.

10 *a* John 12:18 (9, 17–18); Rom. 15:19 (18–19); Morm. 9:19 (19–21).
　 b TG Faith.
11 *a* Heb. 11:6.
　 b TG God, Indignation of.
　 c D&C 35:11.
　 d D&C 88:65.
13 *a* TG Disobedience.
14 *a* D&C 42:24 (24–25).

have turned away from you, and others remain with you that hereafter shall be revealed.

15 Let such beware and repent speedily, lest judgment shall come upon them as a *a*snare, and their *b*folly shall be made manifest, and their works shall follow them in the eyes of the people.

16 And verily I say unto you, as I have said before, he that *a*looketh on a woman to *b*lust after her, or if any shall commit *c*adultery in their hearts, they shall not have the *d*Spirit, but shall deny the faith and shall fear.

17 Wherefore, I, the Lord, have said that the *a*fearful, and the *b*unbelieving, and all *c*liars, and whosoever loveth and maketh a lie, and the *d*whoremonger, and the *e*sorcerer, shall have their part in that *f*lake which burneth with fire and brimstone, which is the *g*second death.

18 Verily I say, that they shall not have part in the *a*first resurrection.

19 And now behold, I, the Lord, say unto you that ye are not *a*justified, because these things are among you.

20 Nevertheless, he that *a*endureth in faith and doeth my *b*will, the same shall overcome, and shall receive an *c*inheritance upon the earth when the day of transfiguration shall come;

21 When the *a*earth shall be *b*transfigured, even according to the pattern which was shown unto mine apostles upon the *c*mount; of which account the fulness ye have not yet received.

22 And now, verily I say unto you, that as I said that I would make known my will unto you, behold I will make it known unto you, *a*not by the way of commandment, for there are many who observe not to keep my commandments.

23 But unto him that keepeth my commandments I will give the *a*mysteries of my kingdom, and the same shall be in him a well of living *b*water, *c*springing up unto everlasting life.

24 And now, behold, this is the will of the Lord your God concerning his saints, that they should *a*assemble themselves together unto the land

15 *a* Luke 21:35.
  b 2 Tim. 3:9. TG Foolishness.
16 *a* Matt. 5:28 (27–28).
  b 2 Sam. 13:4 (2–4). TG Lust; Sensuality; Sexual Immorality.
  c TG Adulterer; Chastity.
  d TG Holy Ghost, Loss of.
17 *a* Rev. 21:8. TG Fearful.
  b TG Unbelief.
  c TG Honesty; Lying.
  d Rev. 22:15 (14–15); D&C 76:103. TG Whore.

  e TG Sorcery.
  f Rev. 19:20; 2 Ne. 9:16 (8–19, 26); 28:23; Jacob 6:10; Alma 12:17 (16–18); D&C 76:36. TG Hell.
  g TG Death, Spiritual, Second.
18 *a* Rev. 20:6.
19 *a* TG Justification.
20 *a* 2 Cor. 1:6; D&C 101:35. TG Steadfastness.
  b TG God, Will of.
  c Isa. 29:19; Matt. 5:5;

  D&C 59:2; 88:26 (25–26). TG Inheritance.
21 *a* TG Earth, Destiny of.
  b TG Transfiguration; World, End of.
  c Matt. 17:3 (1–3).
22 *a* 2 Cor. 8:8; D&C 28:5.
23 *a* Alma 12:9 (9–11); D&C 42:61; 84:19; 107:19 (18–19).
  b TG Living Water.
  c John 4:14.
24 *a* D&C 58:56; 101:68.

of Zion, not in haste, lest there should be confusion, which bringeth pestilence.

25 Behold, the land of *Zion—I, the Lord, hold it in mine own hands;

26 Nevertheless, I, the Lord, render unto *Cæsar the things which are Cæsar's.

27 Wherefore, I the Lord will that you should *purchase the lands, that you may have advantage of the world, that you may have claim on the world, that they may not be *stirred up unto anger.

28 For *Satan *putteth it into their hearts to anger against you, and to the shedding of blood.

29 Wherefore, the land of Zion shall not be obtained but by *purchase or by blood, otherwise there is none inheritance for you.

30 And if by purchase, behold you are blessed;

31 And if by *blood, as you are forbidden to shed blood, lo, your enemies are upon you, and ye shall be scourged from city to city, and from synagogue to synagogue, and but *few shall stand to receive an inheritance.

32 I, the Lord, am *angry with the *wicked; I am holding my *Spirit from the inhabitants of the earth.

33 I have sworn in my wrath, and *decreed wars upon the face of the earth, and the wicked shall *slay the wicked, and fear shall come upon every man;

34 And the *saints also shall *hardly *escape; nevertheless, I, the Lord, am with them, and will *come down in heaven from the presence of my Father and *consume the wicked with unquenchable fire.

35 And behold, this is not yet, but *by and by.

36 Wherefore, seeing that I, the Lord, have decreed all these things upon the face of the earth, I will that my saints should be assembled upon the land of Zion;

37 *And that every man should take *righteousness in his hands and

---

25 a TG Zion.
26 a Luke 20:25; 23:2; D&C
     58:22 (21–23). TG Gov-
     ernments.
27 a D&C 45:65.
   b TG Provoking.
28 a TG Devil.
   b John 13:2; 2 Ne. 28:20.
29 a D&C 58:53; 101:70
     (70–75).
31 a TG Blood, Shedding of.
   b D&C 95:5 (5–6); 121:34
     (34–40).

32 a Deut. 32:21; 2 Ne. 15:25;
     Moses 6:27. TG God,
     Indignation of.
   b Isa. 57:17.
   c TG God, Spirit of.
33 a D&C 45:26 (26, 33);
     87:2; 88:91. TG War.
   b Ps. 139:19 (17–24); Isa.
     11:4 (3–4).
34 a TG Saints.
   b Matt. 24:22; Luke 21:36.
   c TG Protection, Divine.
   d TG Jesus Christ, Second

Coming.
   e Jer. 8:13; Matt. 3:12;
     2 Ne. 26:6; D&C 29:9
     (9, 21, 23); 45:57; 64:24;
     88:94; 101:24 (23–25,
     66). TG Earth, Cleansing
     of.
35 a JS—H 1:41.
37 a D&C 19:37; 58:47; 68:8;
     71:7.
   b TG Righteousness.

faithfulness upon his loins, and lift a warning ^dvoice unto the inhabitants of the earth; and declare both by word and by flight that ^edesolation shall come upon the wicked.

38 Wherefore, let my disciples in Kirtland arrange their temporal concerns, who dwell upon this farm.

39 Let my servant Titus Billings, who has the care thereof, dispose of the land, that he may be prepared in the coming spring to take his journey up unto the land of Zion, with those that dwell upon the face thereof, excepting those whom I shall reserve unto myself, that shall ^anot go until I shall command them.

40 And let all the moneys which can be spared, it mattereth not unto me whether it be little or much, be sent up unto the land of Zion, unto them whom I have appointed to ^areceive.

41 Behold, I, the Lord, will give unto my servant Joseph Smith, Jun., power that he shall be enabled to ^adiscern by the Spirit those who shall go up unto the land of Zion, and those of my disciples who shall tarry.

42 Let my servant ^aNewel K. Whitney retain his ^bstore, or in other words, the store, yet for a little season.

43 Nevertheless, let him impart all the money which he can impart, to be sent up unto the land of Zion.

44 Behold, these things are in his own hands, let him do ^aaccording to wisdom.

45 Verily I say, let him be ordained as an agent unto the disciples that shall tarry, and let him be ^aordained unto this power;

46 And now speedily visit the churches, expounding these things unto them, with my servant Oliver Cowdery. Behold, this is my will, obtaining moneys even as I have directed.

47 He that is ^afaithful and ^bendureth shall overcome the world.

48 He that sendeth up treasures unto the land of Zion shall receive an ^ainheritance in this world, and his works shall follow him, and also a ^breward in the world to come.

49 Yea, and blessed are the dead that ^adie in the Lord, from henceforth,

37 c Isa. 11:5.
　d D&C 1:4.
　e Isa. 47:11. TG Judgment.
39 a D&C 66:6.
40 a D&C 51:8 (3–9).
41 a TG Discernment, Spiritual.
42 a D&C 64:26.
　b D&C 57:8.
44 a TG Agency; Initiative.
45 a TG Delegation of Responsibility; Stewardship.
47 a Ps. 31:23; Mosiah 2:41; Ether 4:19; D&C 6:13.
　b TG Perseverance.
48 a D&C 25:2; 64:30; 85:7
(1–3, 7, 9); 99:7; 101:18 (1, 6, 18); 103:14 (11, 14).
　b TG Reward.
49 a Rom. 14:8 (5–9); Rev. 14:13; D&C 42:44 (44–47).

when the Lord shall come, and old things shall *b*pass away, and all things become new, they shall *c*rise from the dead and shall not *d*die after, and shall receive an inheritance before the Lord, in the *e*holy city.

50 And he that liveth when the Lord shall come, and hath kept the faith, *a*blessed is he; nevertheless, it is appointed to him to *b*die at the age of man.

51 Wherefore, *a*children shall *b*grow up until they become old; old men shall die; but they shall not sleep in the dust, but they shall be *c*changed in the twinkling of an eye.

52 Wherefore, for this cause preached the apostles unto the world the resurrection of the dead.

53 These things are the things that ye must look for; and, speaking after the manner of the Lord, they are now *a*nigh at hand, and in a time to come, even in the day of the coming of the Son of Man.

54 And until that hour there will be foolish *a*virgins among the wise; and at that hour cometh an entire *b*separation of the righteous and the wicked; and in that day will I send mine angels to *c*pluck out the wicked and cast them into unquenchable fire.

55 And now behold, verily I say unto you, I, the Lord, am not pleased with my servant *a*Sidney Rigdon; he *b*exalted himself in his heart, and received not counsel, but *c*grieved the Spirit;

56 Wherefore his *a*writing is not acceptable unto the Lord, and he shall make another; and if the Lord receive it not, behold he standeth no longer in the office to which I have appointed him.

57 And again, verily I say unto you, *a*those who desire in their hearts, in meekness, to *b*warn sinners to repentance, let them be ordained unto this power.

58 For this is a day of *a*warning, and not a day of many words. For I, the Lord, am not to be *b*mocked in the last days.

59 Behold, I am from above, and my power lieth beneath. I am over all, and in all, and through all, and *a*search all things, and the day cometh that all things shall be *b*subject unto me.

49 *b* 2 Cor. 5:17.
   c TG Resurrection.
   d John 5:24; 8:51; 11:26;
     Rev. 21:4; Alma 11:45;
     12:18 (18, 20); D&C
     88:116. TG Immortality.
   e Jer. 31:40 (38–40).
50 *a* TG Blessing.
   b TG Death.
51 *a* TG Children; Millennium.
   b Isa. 65:20 (20–22); D&C

45:58; 101:30 (29–31).
   TG Mortality; Old Age.
   c 1 Cor. 15:52 (51–52);
     D&C 43:32; 88:28 (20,
     28).
53 *a* D&C 35:15.
54 *a* Matt. 25:1; D&C 45:56
     (56–59).
   b TG Separation.
   c Ps. 52:5; Matt. 13:40 (30,
     39–41); Mosiah 16:2.
55 *a* Lev. 4:22.

   b TG Haughtiness; Pride.
   c TG Holy Ghost, Loss of.
56 *a* D&C 58:50 (50–51).
57 *a* D&C 4:3 (3–6); 36:5.
   b D&C 18:14. TG Missionary Work.
58 *a* TG Warn.
   b TG Mocking.
59 *a* 1 Cor. 2:10.
   b D&C 50:27.

60 Behold, I am ^aAlpha and Omega, even Jesus Christ.

61 Wherefore, let all men ^abeware how they take my ^bname in their lips—

62 For behold, verily I say, that many there be who are under this condemnation, who use the name of the Lord, and use it in vain, having not ^aauthority.

63 Wherefore, let the church repent of their sins, and I, the Lord, will ^aown them; otherwise they shall be cut off.

64 Remember that that which cometh from above is ^asacred, and must be ^bspoken with care, and by constraint of the Spirit; and in this there is no condemnation, and ye receive the Spirit ^cthrough prayer; wherefore, without this there remaineth condemnation.

65 Let my servants, Joseph Smith, Jun., and Sidney Rigdon, seek them a home, as they are ^ataught through prayer by the Spirit.

66 These things remain to overcome through patience, that such may receive a more exceeding and eternal ^aweight of ^bglory, otherwise, a greater condemnation. Amen.

SECTION 64

Revelation given through Joseph Smith the Prophet to the elders of the Church, at Kirtland, Ohio, September 11, 1831. The Prophet was preparing to move to Hiram, Ohio, to renew his work on the translation of the Bible, which had been laid aside while he had been in Missouri. A company of brethren who had been commanded to journey to Zion (Missouri) was earnestly engaged in making preparations to leave in October. At this busy time, the revelation was received.

1–11, The Saints are commanded to forgive one another, lest there remain in them the greater sin; 12–22, The unrepentant are to be brought before the Church; 23–25, He that is tithed will not be burned at the Lord's coming; 26–32, The Saints are warned against debt; 33–36, The rebellious will be cut off out of Zion; 37–40, The Church will judge the nations; 41–43, Zion will flourish.

1 Behold, thus saith the Lord your God unto you, O ye elders of my ^achurch, hearken ye and hear, and receive my will concerning you.

---

60 a D&C 35:1.
61 a TG Self-Mastery.
  b Ezek. 43:8 (8–11).
    TG Jesus Christ, Taking
    the Name of; Profanity.
62 a TG Authority.

63 a Rev. 3:5.
64 a TG Sacred.
  b TG Reverence.
  c D&C 42:14.
65 a TG God, Spirit of;
    Prayer; Teaching.

66 a 2 Cor. 4:17.
  b Rom. 8:18; D&C 58:4;
    136:31.
64 1 a TG Jesus Christ, Head of
    the Church.

2 For verily I say unto you, I will that ye should *a*overcome the world; wherefore I will have *b*compassion upon you.

3 There are those among you who have sinned; but verily I say, for this once, for mine own *a*glory, and for the salvation of souls, I have *b*forgiven you your sins.

4 I will be merciful unto you, for I have given unto you the *a*kingdom.

5 And the *a*keys of the mysteries of the kingdom shall not be taken from my servant Joseph Smith, Jun., through the means I have appointed, while he liveth, inasmuch as he obeyeth mine *b*ordinances.

6 There are those who have sought occasion against him without cause;

7 Nevertheless, he has sinned; but verily I say unto you, I, the Lord, *a*forgive sins unto those who *b*confess their sins before me and ask forgiveness, who have not *c*sinned unto *d*death.

8 My disciples, in days of old, sought *a*occasion against one another and forgave not one another in their hearts; and for this *b*evil they were *c*afflicted and sorely *d*chastened.

9 Wherefore, I say unto you, that ye ought to *a*forgive one another; for he that *b*forgiveth not his brother his trespasses standeth condemned before the Lord; for there remaineth in him the greater sin.

10 I, the Lord, will *a*forgive whom I will forgive, but of you it is required to *b*forgive all men.

11 And ye ought to say in your hearts—let God *a*judge between me and thee, and *b*reward thee according to thy *c*deeds.

12 And him that *a*repenteth not of his sins, and *b*confesseth them not, ye shall bring before the *c*church, and do with him as the *d*scripture saith unto you, either by commandment or by revelation.

13 And this ye shall do that God may be glorified—not because ye forgive not, having not compassion, but that ye may be justified in the eyes of the law, that ye may not *a*offend him who is your lawgiver—

---

2 *a* 1 Jn. 5:4.
  b Micah 7:19. TG Compassion.
3 *a* Moses 1:39.
  b Isa. 43:25; Luke 5:21.
4 *a* D&C 62:9; 82:24.
5 *a* D&C 28:7; 84:19. TG Priesthood, Keys of.
  b TG Ordinance.
7 *a* Dan. 9:9. TG Remission of Sins.
  b Num. 5:7 (6–10); D&C 19:20; 58:43. TG Confession.

  c 1 Jn. 3:15; 5:17; Alma 5:42 (41–42).
  d D&C 76:33 (31–37).
8 *a* Dan. 6:4. TG Contention; Disputations.
  b TG Evil.
  c TG Affliction.
  d TG Chastening.
9 *a* Prov. 17:9; Mark 11:26 (25–26); D&C 82:1. TG Reconciliation.
  b Matt. 6:15 (14–15); Eph. 4:32.
10 *a* Ex. 33:19; 34:7; Rom.

9:18; Alma 39:6; D&C 56:14. TG Forgive.
  b Mosiah 26:31 (29–31). TG Benevolence; Forbear.
11 *a* 1 Sam. 24:12; Ps. 75:7. TG Judgment.
  b TG Reward.
  c 2 Tim. 4:14.
12 *a* TG Repent.
  b TG Confession.
  c 1 Cor. 6:1.
  d D&C 42:81 (80–93).
13 *a* TG Offense.

14 Verily I say, for this cause ye shall do these things.

15 Behold, I, the Lord, was angry with him who was my servant Ezra Booth, and also my servant Isaac Morley, for they ^akept not the law, neither the commandment;

16 They sought ^aevil in their hearts, and I, the Lord, ^bwithheld my Spirit. They ^ccondemned for evil that thing in which there was no evil; nevertheless I have forgiven my servant Isaac Morley.

17 And also my servant ^aEdward Partridge, behold, he hath sinned, and ^bSatan seeketh to destroy his soul; but when these things are made known unto them, and they repent of the evil, they shall be forgiven.

18 And now, verily I say that it is expedient in me that my servant Sidney Gilbert, after a few weeks, shall return upon his business, and to his ^aagency in the land of Zion;

19 And that which he hath seen and heard may be made known unto my disciples, that they perish not. And for this cause have I spoken these things.

20 And again, I say unto you, that my servant Isaac Morley may not be ^atempted above that which he is able to bear, and counsel wrongfully to your hurt, I gave commandment that his farm should be sold.

21 I will not that my servant Frederick G. Williams should sell his farm, for I, the Lord, will to retain a strong hold in the land of Kirtland, for the space of five years, in the which I will not overthrow the wicked, that thereby I may save some.

22 And after that day, I, the Lord, will not hold any ^aguilty that shall go with an open heart up to the land of Zion; for I, the Lord, require the ^bhearts of the children of men.

23 Behold, now it is called ^atoday until the ^bcoming of the Son of Man, and verily it is a day of ^csacrifice, and a day for the tithing of my people; for he that is ^dtithed shall not be ^eburned at his coming.

24 For after today cometh the ^aburning—this is speaking after the manner of the Lord—for verily I say, tomorrow all the ^bproud and they that do

15 a D&C 42:32 (32–35).
16 a Prov. 1:16; 2 Ne. 19:17.
   TG Evil.
   b TG Holy Ghost, Loss of.
   c 2 Ne. 15:20; D&C
     121:16.
17 a D&C 60:10; 115:2 (2–6).
   b TG Devil.
18 a D&C 57:6.
20 a TG Temptation.
22 a TG Guilt.

   b Ex. 35:5; D&C 59:15;
     64:34.
23 a John 9:4; D&C 45:6;
     64:25 (24–25).
   b TG Jesus Christ, Second
     Coming.
   c TG Sacrifice.
   d Mal. 3:10 (10–11). See
     note on tithing in head-
     ing to section 119.
   e Isa. 9:5 (5, 18–19); Mal.

   4:1; 3 Ne. 25:1; JS—H
     1:37.
24 a Isa. 66:15 (15–16); Joel
     2:5; 2 Ne. 15:24; 26:6 (4,
     6). TG Earth, Cleansing
     of; World, End of.
   b Job 40:11; Prov. 15:25;
     Mal. 3:15; 2 Ne. 12:12;
     23:11. TG Pride.

wickedly shall be as ^cstubble; and I will burn them up, for I am the Lord of Hosts; and I will not ^dspare any that remain in ^eBabylon.

25 Wherefore, if ye believe me, ye will labor while it is called ^atoday.

26 And it is not meet that my servants, ^aNewel K. Whitney and Sidney Gilbert, should sell their ^bstore and their possessions here; for this is not wisdom until the residue of the church, which remaineth in this place, shall go up unto the land of Zion.

27 Behold, it is said in my laws, or forbidden, to get in ^adebt to thine enemies;

28 But behold, it is not said at any time that the Lord should not take when he please, and pay as seemeth him good.

29 Wherefore, as ye are agents, ye are on the Lord's errand; and whatever ye do according to the will of the Lord is the Lord's business.

30 And he hath set you to provide for his saints in these last days, that they may obtain an ^ainheritance in the land of Zion.

31 And behold, I, the Lord, declare unto you, and my ^awords are sure and shall not ^bfail, that they shall obtain it.

32 But all things must come to pass in their time.

33 Wherefore, be not ^aweary in ^bwell-doing, for ye are laying the foundation of a great work. And out of ^csmall things proceedeth that which is great.

34 Behold, the Lord ^arequireth the ^bheart and a ^cwilling mind; and the willing and ^dobedient shall ^eeat the good of the land of Zion in these last days.

35 And the ^arebellious shall be ^bcut off out of the land of Zion, and shall be sent away, and shall not inherit the land.

36 For, verily I say that the rebellious are not of the blood of ^aEphraim, wherefore they shall be plucked out.

---

24 c Rev. 18:8 (6–8).
   d Gen. 18:23; 1 Ne. 22:16; Hel. 13:13 (12–14).
   e D&C 1:16. TG Babylon.
25 a John 9:4; D&C 45:6; 64:23. TG Procrastination.
26 a D&C 63:42.
   b D&C 57:8.
27 a TG Debt.
30 a D&C 63:48 (29, 31, 48); 85:7 (1–3, 7, 9).
31 a Ps. 19:4; Mark 13:31; 2 Ne. 31:15.

   b 1 Ne. 20:14; D&C 76:3.
33 a Gal. 6:9. TG Dedication; Laziness.
   b TG Benevolence; Good Works; Self-Sacrifice.
   c D&C 123:16 (16–17).
34 a Micah 6:8.
   b Deut. 32:46; Josh. 22:5; 1 Kgs. 2:4; Morm. 9:27. TG Heart.
   c Isa. 1:19; 2 Cor. 8:12; Moro. 7:8; D&C 64:22; 97:8.
   d TG Loyalty; Obedience.

   e D&C 101:101. TG Abundant Life.
35 a TG Rebellion.
   b Gen. 6:13; Obad. 1:9; D&C 41:5; 42:37; 50:8 (8–9); 56:3; Moses 8:30 (26, 30). TG Excommunication.
36 a Gen. 48:16; 49:26 (22–26); Deut. 33:17 (16–17); Hosea 7:1 (1–16); Zech. 10:7 (7–12).

37 Behold, I, the Lord, have made my church in these last days like unto a ^ajudge sitting on a hill, or in a high place, to ^bjudge the nations.

38 For it shall come to pass that the inhabitants of Zion shall ^ajudge all things pertaining to Zion.

39 And ^aliars and hypocrites shall be proved by them, and they who are ^bnot ^capostles and prophets shall be ^dknown.

40 And even the ^abishop, who is a ^bjudge, and his counselors, if they are not faithful in their ^cstewardships shall be condemned, and ^dothers shall be planted in their ^estead.

41 For, behold, I say unto you that ^aZion shall flourish, and the ^bglory of the Lord shall be upon her;

42 And she shall be an ^aensign unto the people, and there shall come unto her out of every ^bnation under heaven.

43 And the day shall come when the nations of the earth shall ^atremble because of her, and shall fear because of her terrible ones. The Lord hath spoken it. Amen.

SECTION 65

Revelation on prayer given through Joseph Smith the Prophet, at Hiram, Ohio, October 30, 1831.

1–2, The keys of the kingdom of God are committed to man on earth, and the gospel cause will triumph; 3–6, The millennial kingdom of heaven will come and join the kingdom of God on earth.

1 Hearken, and lo, a voice as of one sent down from on high, who is mighty and powerful, whose going forth is unto the ends of the earth, yea, whose voice is unto men—^aPrepare ye the way of the Lord, make his paths straight.

---

37 a Obad. 1:21.
  b TG Judgment.
38 a Isa. 2:3; Joel 3:16; D&C
     133:21.
39 a TG Honesty; Lying.
  b TG False Prophets.
  c Rev. 2:2. TG Apostles.
  d Deut. 18:21 (21–22).
40 a TG Bishop.
  b D&C 58:17; 107:72

(72–74).
  c TG Stewardship.
  d D&C 35:18 (17–18);
     42:10; 104:77; 107:99
     (99–100).
  e D&C 93:50 (47–50).
41 a TG Zion.
  b D&C 45:67; 84:5
     (4–5, 31); 97:15 (15–20).
     TG Glory.

42 a TG Ensign; Mission of
     Latter-day Saints.
  b 1 Kgs. 8:41; Isa. 60:9.
43 a Isa. 60:14; D&C 45:67;
     97:19 (19–20).
65 1 a Isa. 40:3; Matt. 3:3; John
     1:23. TG Millennium,
     Preparing a People for.

2 The ᵃkeys of the ᵇkingdom of God are committed unto man on the earth, and from thence shall the ᶜgospel roll forth unto the ends of the earth, as the ᵈstone which is cut out of the mountain without hands shall roll forth, until it has ᵉfilled the whole earth.

3 Yea, a voice crying—ᵃPrepare ye the way of the Lord, prepare ye the ᵇsupper of the Lamb, make ready for the ᶜBridegroom.

4 Pray unto the Lord, ᵃcall upon his holy name, make known his wonderful ᵇworks among the people.

5 Call upon the Lord, that his kingdom may go forth upon the earth, that the inhabitants thereof may receive it, and be prepared for the days to come, in the which the Son of Man shall ᵃcome down in heaven, ᵇclothed in the brightness of his ᶜglory, to meet the ᵈkingdom of God which is set up on the earth.

6 Wherefore, may the ᵃkingdom of God go forth, that the ᵇkingdom of heaven may come, that thou, O God, mayest be ᶜglorified in heaven so on earth, that thine ᵈenemies may be subdued; for ᵉthine is the honor, power and glory, forever and ever. Amen.

SECTION 66

Revelation given through Joseph Smith the Prophet, at Hiram, Ohio, October 29, 1831. William E. McLellin had petitioned the Lord in secret to make known through the Prophet the answer to five questions, which were unknown to Joseph Smith. At McLellin's request, the Prophet inquired of the Lord and received this revelation.

1–4, The everlasting covenant is the fulness of the gospel; 5–8, Elders are to preach, testify, and reason with the people; 9–13, Faithful ministerial service ensures an inheritance of eternal life.

---

2 a Matt. 16:19; D&C 42:69.
TG Priesthood, Keys of;
Priesthood, Melchize-
dek; Restoration of the
Gospel.
  b Micah 4:7; Luke 17:21
(20–21); D&C 90:3
(1–5).
  c TG Mission of Latter-day
Saints.
  d Dan. 2:45 (34–45); 8:25.
  e Num. 14:21; Ps. 72:19.

TG Last Days.
3 a Matt. 3:3; D&C 88:66.
  b Matt. 22:2 (1–14); Rev.
19:9; D&C 58:11.
  c Mark 2:19 (19–20).
4 a Gen. 4:26; 1 Chr. 16:8;
Ps. 116:17.
  b 1 Chr. 16:24. TG God,
Works of.
5 a Matt. 16:27; 24:30.
  b Ps. 93:1.
  c TG Glory.

d Dan. 2:44.
6 a TG Kingdom of God,
in Heaven; Kingdom of
God, on Earth.
  b Rev. 11:15.
  c John 17:4.
  d 1 Chr. 17:10; Ps. 89:10;
Micah 4:10. TG Enemies.
  e 1 Chr. 29:11; Matt. 6:13;
Rev. 11:15.

1 Behold, thus saith the Lord unto my servant ^aWilliam E. McLellin— Blessed are you, inasmuch as you have ^bturned away from your iniquities, and have received my truths, saith the Lord your Redeemer, the ^cSavior of the world, even of as many as believe on my name.

2 Verily I say unto you, blessed are you for receiving mine ^aeverlasting covenant, even the fulness of my gospel, sent forth unto the children of men, that they might have ^blife and be made ^cpartakers of the ^dglories which are to be revealed in the last days, as it was written by the prophets and apostles in days of old.

3 Verily I say unto you, my servant William, that you are clean, but not ^aall; repent, therefore, of those things which are not pleasing in my sight, saith the Lord, for the Lord will ^bshow them unto you.

4 And now, verily, I, the Lord, will show unto you what I ^awill concerning you, or what is my will concerning you.

5 Behold, verily I say unto you, that it is my will that you should ^aproclaim my gospel from land to land, and from ^bcity to city, yea, in those regions round about where it has not been proclaimed.

6 Tarry not many days in this place; go ^anot up unto the land of Zion as yet; but inasmuch as you can ^bsend, send; otherwise, think not of thy property.

7 ^aGo unto the eastern lands, bear ^btestimony in every place, unto every people and in their ^csynagogues, reasoning with the people.

8 Let my servant Samuel H. Smith go with you, and forsake him not, and give him thine instructions; and he that is ^afaithful shall be made ^bstrong in every place; and I, the Lord, will go with you.

9 Lay your ^ahands upon the ^bsick, and they shall ^crecover. Return not till I, the Lord, shall send you. Be patient in affliction. ^dAsk, and ye shall receive; knock, and it shall be opened unto you.

10 Seek not to be ^acumbered. Forsake all ^bunrighteousness. Commit not ^cadultery—a temptation with which thou hast been troubled.

---

66 1 a D&C 68:7; 75:6; 90:35.
   b Mal. 2:6.
   c John 1:12; 4:42; 1 Jn. 4:14.
  2 a TG New and Everlasting Covenant.
   b John 5:40; 10:10.
   c 1 Pet. 5:1.
   d 1 Pet. 4:13. TG Glory.
  3 a John 13:11 (10–11).
   b Jacob 4:7.

4 a TG God, Will of; Guidance, Divine.
5 a Mark 16:15.
   b Luke 8:1; Alma 23:4; D&C 75:18.
6 a D&C 63:39 (24–39).
   b D&C 63:40 (40–46).
7 a D&C 75:6.
   b John 1:7.
   c Acts 9:20; 18:4 (4–26); Alma 21:4; D&C 68:1.
8 a Ps. 31:23.

   b D&C 52:17; 133:58.
9 a TG Administrations to the Sick; Hands, Laying on of.
   b TG Sickness.
   c Matt. 9:18.
   d John 16:24.
10 a Luke 10:40.
   b Prov. 9:6.
   c Mark 10:19. TG Adulterer.

11 ^aKeep these sayings, for they are true and ^bfaithful; and thou shalt ^cmagnify thine office, and push many people to ^dZion with ^esongs of everlasting joy upon their heads.

12 ^aContinue in these things even unto the end, and you shall have a ^bcrown of eternal life at the right hand of my Father, who is full of ^cgrace and truth.

13 Verily, thus saith the Lord your ^aGod, your Redeemer, even Jesus Christ. Amen.

SECTION 67

Revelation given through Joseph Smith the Prophet, at Hiram, Ohio, early November 1831. The occasion was that of a special conference, and the publication of the revelations already received from the Lord through the Prophet was considered and acted upon (see the heading to section 1). William W. Phelps had recently established the Church printing press in Independence, Missouri. The conference decided to publish the revelations in the Book of Commandments and to print 10,000 copies (which because of unforeseen difficulties was later reduced to 3,000 copies). Many of the brethren bore solemn testimony that the revelations then compiled for publication were verily true, as was witnessed by the Holy Ghost shed forth upon them. Joseph Smith's history records that after the revelation known as section 1 had been received, some conversation was had concerning the language used in the revelations. The present revelation followed.

1–3, The Lord hears the prayers of and watches over His elders; 4–9, He challenges the wisest person to duplicate the least of His revelations; 10–14, Faithful elders will be quickened by the Spirit and see the face of God.

1 Behold and hearken, O ye ^aelders of my church, who have assembled yourselves together, whose ^bprayers I have heard, and whose ^chearts I know, and whose desires have come up before me.

2 Behold and lo, mine ^aeyes are upon you, and the heavens and the earth are in mine ^bhands, and the riches of eternity are mine to give.

3 Ye endeavored to ^abelieve that ye should receive the blessing which was

---

11 *a* D&C 35:24; 103:7.
  b 2 Ne. 31:15.
  c Rom. 11:13.
  d D&C 11:6.
  e Isa. 35:10; D&C 45:71.
    TG Singing.
12 *a* 2 Tim. 3:14.

  b Isa. 62:3; Matt. 25:21;
    1 Pet. 5:4; Rev. 2:10.
  c John 1:14.
13 *a* Isa. 43:12 (11–14); 44:6.
67 1 *a* TG Elder, Melchizedek
    Priesthood.
  b 1 Kgs. 9:3.

  c Acts 1:24. TG God,
    Omniscience of.
2 *a* Ps. 34:15; Amos 9:8.
  b Ps. 112:8 (7–8); Heb.
    1:10. TG God, Works of.
3 *a* TG Faith.

offered unto you; but behold, verily I say unto you there were *b*fears in your hearts, and verily this is the reason that ye did not receive.

4 And now I, the Lord, give unto you a *a*testimony of the truth of these commandments which are lying before you.

5 Your eyes have been upon my servant Joseph Smith, Jun., and his *a*language you have known, and his imperfections you have known; and you have sought in your hearts knowledge that you might express beyond his language; this you also know.

6 Now, seek ye out of the Book of Commandments, even the least that is among them, and appoint him that is the most *a*wise among you;

7 Or, if there be any among you that shall make one *a*like unto it, then ye are justified in saying that ye do not know that they are true;

8 But if ye cannot make one like unto it, ye are under condemnation if ye do not *a*bear record that they are true.

9 For ye know that there is no unrighteousness in them, and that which is *a*righteous cometh down from above, from the Father of *b*lights.

10 And again, verily I say unto you that it is your privilege, and a *a*promise I give unto you that have been ordained unto this ministry, that inasmuch as you *b*strip yourselves from *c*jealousies and *d*fears, and *e*humble yourselves before me, for ye are not sufficiently humble, the *f*veil shall be rent and you shall *g*see me and know that I am—not with the carnal neither natural mind, but with the spiritual.

11 For no *a*man has seen God at any time in the flesh, except quickened by the Spirit of God.

12 Neither can any *a*natural man abide the presence of God, neither after the carnal mind.

13 Ye are not able to abide the presence of God now, neither the ministering of angels; wherefore, *a*continue in patience until ye are *b*perfected.

14 Let not your minds *a*turn back; and when ye are *b*worthy, in mine own due time, ye shall see and know that which was conferred upon you by the hands of my servant Joseph Smith, Jun. Amen.

---

3 *b* TG Fearful.
4 *a* TG Testimony; Truth.
5 *a* D&C 1:24 (18–24).
6 *a* 2 Ne. 9:29 (28–29, 42).
7 *a* Prov. 30:5 (5–6).
8 *a* TG Testimony; Witness.
9 *a* Ps. 119:138; Isa. 45:19; James 1:17; Moro. 7:16 (15–18).
  b D&C 50:24; 84:45; 88:49.
10 *a* TG Promise.
  b TG Humility; Purity.

c TG Jealous.
d TG Courage; Fearful.
e Prov. 6:3. TG Teachable.
f TG Veil.
g Lev. 9:4; D&C 50:45; 88:68; 93:1; 97:16; Moses 1:11.
11 *a* Ex. 19:21; 33:20; JST Ex. 33:20 (Bible Appendix); John 1:18 (JST 1 Jn. 4:12 No man hath seen God at any time, *except them who believe . . .*); D&C

84:22; Moses 1:11 (11, 14). TG God, Privilege of Seeing.
12 *a* JST Ex. 33:20 (Bible Appendix); Mosiah 3:19. TG Man, Natural, Not Spiritually Reborn.
13 *a* Rom. 2:7. TG Patience.
  b Matt. 5:48.
14 *a* D&C 133:15 (14–15).
  b TG Worthiness.

SECTION 68

Revelation given through Joseph Smith the Prophet, at Hiram, Ohio, November 1, 1831, in response to prayer that the mind of the Lord be made known concerning Orson Hyde, Luke S. Johnson, Lyman E. Johnson, and William E. McLellin. Although part of this revelation was directed toward these four men, much of the content pertains to the whole Church. This revelation was expanded under Joseph Smith's direction when it was published in the 1835 edition of the Doctrine and Covenants.

1–5, The words of the elders when moved upon by the Holy Ghost are scripture; 6–12, Elders are to preach and baptize, and signs will follow true believers; 13–24, The firstborn among the sons of Aaron may serve as the Presiding Bishop (that is, hold the keys of presidency as a bishop) under the direction of the First Presidency; 25–28, Parents are commanded to teach the gospel to their children; 29–35, The Saints are to observe the Sabbath, labor diligently, and pray.

1 My servant, Orson Hyde, was called by his ordination to proclaim the *^a*everlasting gospel, by the *^b*Spirit of the living God, from people to people, and from land to land, in the *^c*congregations of the wicked, in their *^d*synagogues, reasoning with and *^e*expounding all scriptures unto them.

2 And, behold, and lo, this is an ensample unto all those who were ordained unto this priesthood, whose mission is appointed unto them to go forth—

3 And this is the *^a*ensample unto them, that they shall *^b*speak as they are moved upon by the Holy Ghost.

4 And whatsoever they shall speak when moved upon by the *^a*Holy Ghost shall be scripture, shall be the will of the Lord, shall be the mind of the Lord, shall be the word of the Lord, shall be the voice of the Lord, and the *^b*power of God unto salvation.

5 Behold, this is the promise of the Lord unto you, O ye my servants.

6 Wherefore, be of good *^a*cheer, and do not *^b*fear, for I the Lord am with you, and will stand by you; and ye shall bear record of me, even Jesus Christ, that I am the Son of the living God, that I *^c*was, that I am, and that I am to come.

7 This is the word of the Lord unto you, my servant Orson Hyde, and also

68 1 *a* D&C 18:4.
  b TG God, Spirit of.
  c Ps. 26:5; D&C 61:30.
  d D&C 66:7.
  e Acts 28:23.
  3 *a* TG Example.

  b Ex. 4:12 (12–16); 2 Pet.
    1:21; D&C 18:32; 34:10;
    42:16; 100:5.
  4 *a* Acts 4:31. TG Revelation.
  b Rom. 1:16.
  6 *a* Matt. 9:2.

  b Gen. 26:24; Isa. 41:10;
    Dan. 10:12; Philip. 1:14
    (12–17); D&C 98:1;
    JS—H 1:32.
  c Rev. 1:4.

unto my servant Luke Johnson, and unto my servant Lyman Johnson, and unto my servant *William E. McLellin, and unto all the faithful elders of my church—

8 *Go ye into all the world, *preach the gospel to every *creature, acting in the *authority which I have given you, *baptizing in the name of the Father, and of the Son, and of the Holy Ghost.

9 And *he that believeth and is baptized shall be saved, and he that believeth not shall be *damned.

10 And he that believeth shall be blest with *signs following, even as it is written.

11 And unto you it shall be given to know the signs of the *times, and the *signs of the coming of the Son of Man;

12 And of as many as the Father shall bear record, to you shall be given power to *seal them up unto eternal life. Amen.

13 And now, concerning the items in addition to the *covenants and commandments, they are these—

14 There remain hereafter, in the due time of the Lord, other *bishops to be set apart unto the *church, to minister even according to the first;

15 Wherefore they shall be *high priests who are worthy, and they shall be appointed by the *First Presidency of the Melchizedek Priesthood, except they be literal descendants of *Aaron.

16 And if they be literal descendants of *Aaron they have a legal right to the bishopric, if they are the *firstborn among the sons of Aaron;

17 For the firstborn holds the right of the presidency over this priesthood, and the *keys or authority of the same.

18 No man has a legal right to this office, to hold the keys of this priesthood, except he be a *literal descendant and the firstborn of Aaron.

19 But, as a *high priest of the Melchizedek Priesthood has authority to officiate in all the lesser offices he may officiate in the office of *bishop when no literal descendant of Aaron can be found, provided he is called

7 a D&C 66:1; 75:6; 90:35.
8 a D&C 1:2; 19:37; 58:47;
    63:37; 71:7.
  b TG Preaching.
  c Mark 16:15.
  d TG Authority; Priest-
    hood, Authority.
  e TG Baptism.
9 a Mark 16:16; D&C 20:25.
  b TG Damnation.
10 a TG Signs.
11 a Acts 1:7; D&C 121:12
    (12, 27, 31).

b D&C 1:12.
12 a D&C 1:8; 132:19, 49.
    TG Sealing.
13 a D&C 1:6. See also D&C
    "Introduction."
14 a D&C 41:9. TG Bishop.
  b TG Church Organiza-
    tion.
15 a D&C 72:1.
  b D&C 81:2; 107:17 (9, 17,
    22).
  c Lev. 1:7; D&C 84:30;
    132:59.

16 a D&C 107:16 (15–17,
    68–69). TG Priesthood,
    Aaronic.
  b TG Firstborn.
17 a TG Priesthood, Keys of.
18 a Ex. 40:15 (12–15); D&C
    84:18 (18, 30); 107:16
    (13–16, 70–76).
19 a TG High Priest,
    Melchizedek Priesthood.
  b TG Bishop.

and set apart and ordained unto this power, under the hands of the First Presidency of the Melchizedek Priesthood.

20 And a literal descendant of Aaron, also, must be designated by this Presidency, and found worthy, and ªanointed, and ordained under the hands of this Presidency, otherwise they are not legally authorized to officiate in their priesthood.

21 But, by virtue of the decree concerning their right of the priesthood descending from father to son, they may claim their ªanointing if at any time they can prove their lineage, or do ascertain it by revelation from the Lord under the ᵇhands of the above named Presidency.

22 And again, no bishop or high priest who shall be set apart for this ministry shall be tried or ªcondemned for any crime, save it be before the ᵇFirst Presidency of the church;

23 And inasmuch as he is found ªguilty before this Presidency, by testimony that cannot be impeached, he shall be condemned;

24 And if he repent he shall be ªforgiven, according to the covenants and ᵇcommandments of the church.

25 And again, inasmuch as ªparents have children in Zion, or in any of her ᵇstakes which are organized, that ᶜteach them not to understand the ᵈdoctrine of repentance, faith in Christ the Son of the living God, and of baptism and the gift of the Holy Ghost by the laying on of the hands, when ᵉeight years old, the ᶠsin be upon the heads of the parents.

26 For this shall be a law unto the ªinhabitants of Zion, or in any of her stakes which are organized.

27 And their children shall be ªbaptized for the ᵇremission of their sins when ᶜeight years old, and receive the laying on of the hands.

28 And they shall also ªteach their children to pray, and to walk uprightly before the Lord.

29 And the inhabitants of Zion shall also observe the ªSabbath day to keep it holy.

<hr />

20 a D&C 109:35.
  TG Anointing; Priesthood, Ordination.
21 a Num. 18:8.
  b TG Hands, Laying on of.
22 a TG Excommunication.
  b D&C 107:78 (76–84).
23 a TG Guilt.
24 a TG Forgive.
  b D&C 42:13 (13–29).
25 a TG Family, Patriarchal;

Marriage, Fatherhood; Marriage, Motherhood.
  b TG Stake.
  c 1 Sam. 3:13; Ps. 78:4 (4–6). TG Family, Children, Responsibilities toward.
  d Heb. 6:2.
  e D&C 18:42; 20:71.
  f Ezek. 33:4 (2–8); Jacob 1:19; D&C 29:48.

26 a TG Zion.
27 a TG Baptism, Essential; Salvation of Little Children.
  b TG Remission of Sins.
  c TG Baptism, Qualifications for.
28 a Prov. 13:24. TG Learn; Prayer; Teaching.
29 a Alma 1:26 (26–27); D&C 59:9. TG Sabbath.

30 And the inhabitants of Zion also shall remember their ^alabors, inasmuch as they are appointed to labor, in all faithfulness; for the ^bidler shall be had in remembrance before the Lord.

31 Now, I, the Lord, am not well ^apleased with the inhabitants of Zion, for there are ^bidlers among them; and their ^cchildren are also growing up in ^dwickedness; they also ^eseek not earnestly the riches of eternity, but their eyes are full of ^fgreediness.

32 These things ought not to be, and must be done away from among them; wherefore, let my servant Oliver Cowdery ^acarry these sayings unto the land of Zion.

33 And a commandment I give unto them—that he that observeth not his ^aprayers before the Lord in the season thereof, let him be had in ^bremembrance before the judge of my people.

34 These sayings are ^atrue and faithful; wherefore, transgress them not, neither ^btake therefrom.

35 Behold, I am ^aAlpha and Omega, and I ^bcome quickly. Amen.

SECTION 69

Revelation given through Joseph Smith the Prophet, at Hiram, Ohio, November 11, 1831. The compilation of revelations intended for early publication had been passed upon at the special conference of November 1–2. On November 3, the revelation herein appearing as section 133, later called the Appendix, was added. Oliver Cowdery had previously been appointed to carry the manuscript of the compiled revelations and commandments to Independence, Missouri, for printing. He was also to take with him money that had been contributed for the building up of the Church in Missouri. This revelation instructs John Whitmer to accompany Oliver Cowdery and also directs Whitmer to travel and collect historical material in his calling as Church historian and recorder.

1–2, John Whitmer is to accompany Oliver Cowdery to Missouri; 3–8, He is also to preach and to collect, record, and write historical data.

30a TG Industry; Work, Value of.
  b TG Laziness.
31a 1 Cor. 10:5.
  b TG Idleness.
  c Prov. 15:5. TG Children.
  d TG Wickedness.
  e Matt. 6:33 (25–34); Alma 39:14 (12–14); D&C 6:7 (6–7). TG Objectives; Treasure.
  f TG Greediness.
32a D&C 69:1.
33a TG Prayer.
  b TG Chastening; Reproof.
34a Rev. 22:6.
  b D&C 20:35; 93:25 (24–25).
35a Rev. 1:8; D&C 19:1.
  b D&C 1:12.

1 Hearken unto me, saith the Lord your God, for my servant Oliver Cowdery's sake. It is not wisdom in me that he should be entrusted with the commandments and the moneys which he shall ^acarry unto the land of Zion, except one go with him who will be ^btrue and faithful.

2 Wherefore, I, the Lord, will that my servant, John Whitmer, should go with my servant Oliver Cowdery;

3 And also that he shall continue in ^awriting and making a ^bhistory of all the important things which he shall observe and know concerning my church;

4 And also that he receive ^acounsel and assistance from my servant Oliver Cowdery and others.

5 And also, my servants who are abroad in the earth should send forth the accounts of their ^astewardships to the land of Zion;

6 For the land of Zion shall be a ^aseat and a place to receive and do all these things.

7 Nevertheless, let my servant John Whitmer travel many times from place to place, and from church to church, that he may the more easily obtain knowledge—

8 Preaching and expounding, writing, copying, selecting, and obtaining all things which shall be for the good of the church, and for the rising generations that shall grow up on the land of Zion, to ^apossess it from generation to generation, forever and ever. Amen.

SECTION 70

Revelation given through Joseph Smith the Prophet, at Hiram, Ohio, November 12, 1831. The Prophet's history states that four special conferences were held from the 1st to the 12th of November, inclusive. In the last of these assemblies, the great importance of the revelations that would later be published as the Book of Commandments and then the Doctrine and Covenants was considered. This revelation was given after the conference voted that the revelations were "worth to the Church the riches of the whole Earth." Joseph Smith's history refers to the revelations as "the foundation of the Church in these last days, and a benefit to the world, showing that the keys of the mysteries of the kingdom of our Savior are again entrusted to man."

---

69 1 *a* D&C 68:32.
    b TG Dependability; Trustworthiness.
3 *a* TG Record Keeping.
    b D&C 21:1; 47:1 (1–3); 85:1.
4 *a* Prov. 20:18. TG Counsel.
5 *a* TG Stewardship.
6 *a* D&C 57:3.
8 *a* TG Zion.

1–5, Stewards are appointed to publish the revelations; 6–13, Those who labor in spiritual things are worthy of their hire; 14–18, The Saints should be equal in temporal things.

1 Behold, and hearken, O ye inhabitants of Zion, and all ye people of my church who are afar off, and ^ahear the word of the Lord which I give unto my servant Joseph Smith, Jun., and also unto my servant Martin Harris, and also unto my servant Oliver Cowdery, and also unto my servant John Whitmer, and also unto my servant Sidney Rigdon, and also unto my servant ^bWilliam W. Phelps, by the way of commandment unto them.

2 For I give unto them a commandment; wherefore hearken and hear, for thus saith the Lord unto them—

3 I, the Lord, have appointed them, and ordained them to be ^astewards over the revelations and commandments which I have given unto them, and which I shall hereafter give unto them;

4 And an account of this ^astewardship will I require of them in the day of judgment.

5 Wherefore, I have appointed unto them, and this is their business in the church of God, to ^amanage them and the concerns thereof, yea, the benefits thereof.

6 Wherefore, a commandment I give unto them, that they shall not give these things unto the church, neither unto the ^aworld;

7 Nevertheless, inasmuch as they ^areceive more than is needful for their necessities and their wants, it shall be given into my ^bstorehouse;

8 And the ^abenefits shall be consecrated unto the inhabitants of Zion, and unto their generations, inasmuch as they become ^bheirs according to the laws of the kingdom.

9 Behold, this is what the Lord requires of every man in his ^astewardship, even as I, the Lord, have appointed or shall hereafter appoint unto any man.

10 And behold, none are exempt from this ^alaw who belong to the church of the living God;

11 Yea, neither the bishop, neither the ^aagent who keepeth the Lord's storehouse, neither he who is appointed in a stewardship over ^btemporal things.

---

70 1 *a* Isa. 39:5.
    b D&C 57:11; 58:40; 61:7 (7–9).
  3 *a* 1 Cor. 4:1; D&C 72:20.
  4 *a* TG Scriptures, Preservation of; Stewardship.

5 *a* TG Accountability; Delegation of Responsibility.
6 *a* Moses 1:42; 4:32.
7 *a* D&C 42:55.
  b D&C 58:24 (24, 37); 72:10.

8 *a* D&C 72:21. TG Wages.
  b D&C 38:20.
9 *a* TG Stewardship.
10 *a* D&C 85:3.
11 *a* D&C 57:6.
  b D&C 107:68 (68–71).

12 He who is appointed to administer spiritual things, the same is *worthy of his hire, even as those who are appointed to a stewardship to administer in temporal things;

13 Yea, even more abundantly, which abundance is multiplied unto them through the *manifestations of the Spirit.

14 Nevertheless, in your temporal things you shall be *equal, and this not grudgingly, otherwise the abundance of the manifestations of the Spirit shall be *withheld.

15 Now, this commandment I give unto my servants for their *benefit while they remain, for a manifestation of my blessings upon their heads, and for a *reward of their *diligence and for their security;

16 For food and for *raiment; for an inheritance; for houses and for lands, in whatsoever circumstances I, the Lord, shall place them, and whithersoever I, the Lord, shall send them.

17 For they have been faithful over *many things, and have done well inasmuch as they have not sinned.

18 Behold, I, the Lord, am *merciful and will bless them, and they shall enter into the joy of these things. Even so. Amen.

SECTION 71

Revelation given to Joseph Smith the Prophet and Sidney Rigdon, at Hiram, Ohio, December 1, 1831. The Prophet had continued to translate the Bible with Sidney Rigdon as his scribe until this revelation was received, at which time it was temporarily laid aside so as to enable them to fulfill the instruction given herein. The brethren were to go forth to preach in order to allay the unfriendly feelings that had developed against the Church as a result of the publication of letters written by Ezra Booth, who had apostatized.

1–4, Joseph Smith and Sidney Rigdon are sent forth to proclaim the gospel; 5–11, Enemies of the Saints will be confounded.

1 Behold, thus saith the Lord unto you my servants Joseph Smith, Jun., and Sidney Rigdon, that the time has verily come that it is necessary and expedient in me that you should open your mouths in *proclaiming my gospel, the things of the kingdom, expounding the *mysteries thereof out

---

12 *a* Luke 10:7.
13 *a* D&C 5:16.
14 *a* D&C 49:20. TG Consecration; Selfishness.
  b TG Holy Ghost, Loss of.
15 *a* Deut. 10:13.

b TG Reward.
  c TG Dependability; Diligence.
16 *a* D&C 59:17 (16–20).
17 *a* Matt. 25:21 (21–23).
18 *a* Ps. 34:8; Lam. 3:25;

Nahum 1:7.
71 1 *a* Matt. 4:23. TG Missionary Work.
  b D&C 42:61 (61–65).

of the scriptures, according to that portion of Spirit and power which shall be given unto you, even as I will.

2 Verily I say unto you, proclaim unto the world in the regions round about, and in the church also, for the space of a season, even until it shall be *made known unto you.

3 Verily this is a mission for a season, which I give unto you.

4 Wherefore, *labor ye in my vineyard. Call upon the inhabitants of the earth, and bear record, and prepare the way for the commandments and revelations which are to come.

5 Now, behold this is wisdom; whoso readeth, let him *understand and *receive also;

6 For unto him that receiveth it shall be given more *abundantly, even power.

7 Wherefore, *confound your *enemies; call upon them to *meet you both in public and in private; and inasmuch as ye are faithful their *shame shall be made manifest.

8 Wherefore, let them bring forth their *strong reasons against the Lord.

9 Verily, thus saith the Lord unto you—there is no *weapon that is formed against you shall prosper;

10 And if any man lift his voice against you he shall be *confounded in mine own due time.

11 Wherefore, *keep my commandments; they are true and faithful. Even so. Amen.

SECTION 72

Revelation given through Joseph Smith the Prophet, at Kirtland, Ohio, December 4, 1831. Several elders and members had assembled to learn their duty and to be further edified in the teachings of the Church. This section is a compilation of three revelations received on the same day. Verses 1 through 8 make known the calling of Newel K. Whitney as a bishop. He was then called and ordained, after which verses 9 through 23 were received, giving additional information as to a bishop's duties. Thereafter, verses 24 through 26 were given, providing instructions concerning the gathering to Zion.

2 a D&C 73:3.
4 a D&C 24:19.
5 a TG Understanding.
  b Alma 12:10 (9–11).
6 a Matt. 13:12.
7 a Ps. 83:17 (2–17); 2 Ne.

25:14; Moses 7:15
(14–16).
  b TG Enemies.
  c D&C 19:37; 58:47;
63:37; 68:8.
  d TG Shame.

8 a Isa. 41:21.
9 a Isa. 54:17.
10 a Jer. 17:18 (15–18).
11 a Ex. 16:28.

1–8, Elders are to render an account of their stewardship unto the bishop; 9–15, The bishop keeps the storehouse and cares for the poor and needy; 16–26, Bishops are to certify the worthiness of elders.

1 Hearken, and listen to the voice of the Lord, O ye who have assembled yourselves together, who are the *a*high priests of my church, to whom the *b*kingdom and power have been given.

2 For verily thus saith the Lord, it is expedient in me for a *a*bishop to be appointed unto you, or of you, unto the church in this part of the Lord's vineyard.

3 And verily in this thing ye have done wisely, for it is required of the Lord, at the hand of every *a*steward, to render an *b*account of his *c*stewardship, both in time and in eternity.

4 For he who is faithful and *a*wise in time is accounted worthy to inherit the *b*mansions prepared for him of my Father.

5 Verily I say unto you, the elders of the church in this part of my vineyard shall render an account of their stewardship unto the *a*bishop, who shall be appointed of me in this part of my vineyard.

6 These things shall be had on *a*record, to be handed over unto the *b*bishop in Zion.

7 And the duty of the *a*bishop shall be made known by the commandments which have been given, and the voice of the conference.

8 And now, verily I say unto you, my servant Newel K. Whitney is the man who shall be appointed and ordained unto this power. This is the will of the Lord your God, your Redeemer. Even so. Amen.

9 The word of the Lord, in addition to the *a*law which has been given, making known the *b*duty of the *c*bishop who has been ordained unto the church in this part of the vineyard, which is verily this—

10 To keep the Lord's *a*storehouse; to receive the funds of the church in this part of the vineyard;

11 To take an account of the elders as before has been commanded; and to *a*administer to their wants, who shall pay for that which they receive, inasmuch as they have wherewith to pay;

---

72 1 *a* D&C 68:15 (15–19).
  b D&C 35:27. TG Kingdom of God, on Earth.
  2 *a* TG Bishop.
  3 *a* Ezek. 34:10; Matt. 25:19; D&C 51:19; 70:9 (9–11); 104:13 (11–13).
  b D&C 42:32 (30–42).

  c Luke 19:15 (11–27). TG Stewardship.
  4 *a* Matt. 24:45.
  b D&C 59:2.
  5 *a* TG Bishop.
  6 *a* TG Record Keeping.
  b D&C 41:9; 58:14 (14–24).
  7 *a* D&C 41:9; 42:31

  (30–31); 46:27; 58:17 (17–18); 68:16; 107:88 (87–88).
  9 *a* TG Bishop.
  b TG Duty.
  c D&C 58:14–24.
  10 *a* D&C 70:7 (7–11); 78:3. TG Welfare.
  11 *a* D&C 75:24 (24–26).

12 That this also may be consecrated to the good of the church, to the poor and needy.

13 And he who *hath not wherewith to pay, an account shall be taken and handed over to the bishop of Zion, who shall pay the debt out of that which the Lord shall put into his hands.

14 And the labors of the faithful who labor in spiritual things, in administering the gospel and the *things of the kingdom unto the church, and unto the world, shall answer the debt unto the bishop in Zion;

15 Thus it cometh out of the church, for according to the *law every man that cometh up to Zion must lay all things before the bishop in Zion.

16 And now, verily I say unto you, that as every elder in this part of the vineyard must give an account of his stewardship unto the bishop in this part of the vineyard—

17 A *certificate from the judge or bishop in this part of the vineyard, unto the bishop in Zion, rendereth every man acceptable, and answereth all things, for an inheritance, and to be received as a wise *steward and as a faithful *laborer;

18 Otherwise he shall not be *accepted of the bishop of Zion.

19 And now, verily I say unto you, let every elder who shall give an account unto the bishop of the church in this part of the vineyard be *recommended by the church or churches, in which he labors, that he may render himself and his accounts approved in all things.

20 And again, let my servants who are appointed as stewards over the *literary concerns of my church have claim for assistance upon the bishop or bishops in all things—

21 That the revelations may be *published, and go forth unto the ends of the earth; that they also may obtain *funds which shall benefit the church in all things;

22 That they also may render themselves approved in all things, and be accounted as *wise stewards.

23 And now, behold, this shall be an *ensample for all the extensive branches of my church, in whatsoever land they shall be established. And now I make an end of my sayings. Amen.

24 A few words in addition to the laws of the kingdom, respecting the

13 a D&C 58:14. TG Poor.
14 a TG Almsgiving; Generosity.
15 a D&C 42:30.
17 a D&C 20:64 (64, 84); 52:41; 72:19 (18–26);

112:21.
 b D&C 42:32.
 c TG Work, Value of.
18 a D&C 72:26.
19 a D&C 20:64.
20 a D&C 70:3 (3–5).

21 a D&C 67:6 (6–9).
 b D&C 70:8 (5–8).
22 a D&C 42:32.
23 a D&C 51:18. TG Example.

members of the church—they that are ^aappointed by the Holy Spirit to go up unto Zion, and they who are ^bprivileged to go up unto Zion—

25 Let them carry up unto the bishop a ^acertificate from three elders of the church, or a certificate from the bishop;

26 Otherwise he who shall go up unto the land of Zion shall not be accounted as a wise steward. This is also an ensample. Amen.

SECTION 73

Revelation given to Joseph Smith the Prophet and Sidney Rigdon, at Hiram, Ohio, January 10, 1832. Since the early part of the preceding December, the Prophet and Sidney had been engaged in preaching, and by this means much was accomplished in diminishing the unfavorable feelings that had arisen against the Church (see the heading to section 71).

1–2, Elders are to continue to preach; 3–6, Joseph Smith and Sidney Rigdon are to continue to translate the Bible until it is finished.

1 For verily, thus saith the Lord, it is expedient in me that ^athey should continue preaching the gospel, and in exhortation to the churches in the regions round about, until conference;

2 And then, behold, it shall be made known unto them, by the ^avoice of the conference, their several missions.

3 Now, verily I say unto you my servants, Joseph Smith, Jun., and Sidney Rigdon, saith the Lord, it is ^aexpedient to ^btranslate again;

4 And, inasmuch as it is practicable, to preach in the regions round about until conference; and after that it is expedient to continue the work of ^atranslation until it be finished.

5 And let this be a pattern unto the elders until further knowledge, even as it is written.

6 Now I give no more unto you at this time. ^aGird up your loins and be sober. Even so. Amen.

SECTION 74

Revelation given to Joseph Smith the Prophet, at Wayne County, New York, in 1830. Even before the organization of the Church, questions had arisen

24 a TG Holy Ghost, Mission of.
   b D&C 58:56.
25 a D&C 72:17 (17–18).
73 1 a IE the others who were

on missions; see D&C 57–68.
2 a D&C 20:63.
3 a D&C 71:2.
   b IE the translation of

the Bible. D&C 45:60 (60–61); 76:15.
4 a D&C 90:13.
6 a 1 Pet. 1:13.

about the proper mode of baptism, leading the Prophet to seek answers on the subject. Joseph Smith's history states that this revelation is an explanation of 1 Corinthians 7:14, a scripture that had often been used to justify infant baptism.

1–5, Paul counsels the Church of his day not to keep the law of Moses; 6–7, Little children are holy and are sanctified through the Atonement.

1 For the ᵃunbelieving ᵇhusband is ᶜsanctified by the wife, and the unbelieving wife is sanctified by the husband; else were your children unclean, but now are they holy.

2 Now, in the days of the apostles the law of circumcision was had among all the Jews who believed not the gospel of Jesus Christ.

3 And it came to pass that there arose a great ᵃcontention among the people concerning the law of ᵇcircumcision, for the unbelieving husband was desirous that his children should be circumcised and become subject to the ᶜlaw of Moses, which law was fulfilled.

4 And it came to pass that the children, being brought up in subjection to the law of Moses, gave heed to the ᵃtraditions of their fathers and believed not the gospel of Christ, wherein they became unholy.

5 Wherefore, for this cause the apostle wrote unto the church, giving unto them a commandment, not of the Lord, but of himself, that a believer should not be ᵃunited to an ᵇunbeliever; except the ᶜlaw of Moses should be done away among them,

6 That their children might remain without circumcision; and that the ᵃtradition might be done away, which saith that little children are unholy; for it was had among the Jews;

7 But little ᵃchildren are ᵇholy, being ᶜsanctified through the ᵈatonement of Jesus Christ; and this is what the scriptures mean.

SECTION 75

Revelation given through Joseph Smith the Prophet, at Amherst, Ohio, January 25, 1832. This section comprises two separate revelations (the first in verses 1 through 22 and the second in verses 23 through 36) given on the

---

74 1 *a* 1 Cor. 7:14 (14–19).
   b TG Marriage, Marry.
   c TG Family, Love within;
     Sanctification.
  3 *a* Acts 15:1 (1–35); Gal. 2:3
    (1–5); 5:6 (1–14).
   b TG Circumcision.

   c TG Law of Moses.
  4 *a* TG Traditions of Men.
  5 *a* TG Marriage, Interfaith.
   b TG Unbelief.
   c Rom. 7:4 (4–6); 2 Ne.
    25:25 (24–27).
  6 *a* TG Traditions of Men.

  7 *a* TG Children; Family.
   b Moro. 8:8 (8–15); D&C
    29:46. TG Holiness.
   c TG Salvation of Little
    Children.
   d TG Jesus Christ, Atonement through.

same day. The occasion was a conference at which Joseph Smith was sustained and ordained President of the High Priesthood. Certain elders desired to learn more about their immediate duties. These revelations followed.

1–5, Faithful elders who preach the gospel will gain eternal life; 6–12, Pray to receive the Comforter, who teaches all things; 13–22, Elders will sit in judgment on those who reject their message; 23–36, Families of missionaries are to receive help from the Church.

1 Verily, verily, I say unto you, I who speak even by the ^avoice of my Spirit, even ^bAlpha and Omega, your Lord and your God—

2 Hearken, O ye who have ^agiven your names to go forth to proclaim my gospel, and to ^bprune my vineyard.

3 Behold, I say unto you that it is my will that you should go forth and not tarry, neither be ^aidle but ^blabor with your might—

4 Lifting up your voices as with the sound of a trump, ^aproclaiming the ^btruth according to the revelations and commandments which I have given you.

5 And thus, if ye are faithful ye shall be laden with many ^asheaves, and ^bcrowned with honor, and glory, and immortality, and eternal life.

6 Therefore, verily I say unto my servant ^aWilliam E. McLellin, I ^brevoke the commission which I gave unto him to go unto the eastern countries;

7 And I give unto him a new commission and a new commandment, in the which I, the Lord, ^achasten him for the ^bmurmurings of his heart;

8 And he sinned; nevertheless, I forgive him and say unto him again, Go ye into the south countries.

9 And let my servant Luke Johnson go with him, and proclaim the things which I have commanded them—

10 Calling on the name of the Lord for the ^aComforter, which shall teach them all things that are expedient for them—

11 ^aPraying always that they ^bfaint not; and inasmuch as they do this, I will be with them even unto the end.

12 Behold, this is the will of the Lord your God concerning you. Even so. Amen.

13 And again, verily thus saith the Lord, let my servant Orson Hyde and my servant Samuel H. Smith take their journey into the eastern countries,

75 1*a* TG Revelation.
  b Rev. 1:8; D&C 68:35.
 2*a* D&C 75:23. TG Initiative; Zeal.
  b Jacob 5:62 (62–69).
 3*a* TG Idleness.
  b Neh. 4:6. TG Diligence;

Industry.
 4*a* TG Missionary Work.
  b 2 Cor. 4:2; D&C 19:37.
 5*a* Ps. 126:6; Alma 26:5; D&C 4:4; 33:9.
  b TG Eternal Life; Exaltation; Glory; Honor.
 6*a* D&C 68:7; 90:35.

  b D&C 66:7 (1–13).
 7*a* TG Chastening.
  b Num. 11:1 (1–2); 1 Ne. 17:2.
10*a* TG Holy Ghost, Comforter.
11*a* 2 Ne. 32:9.
  b Luke 18:1.

and proclaim the things which I have commanded them; and inasmuch as they are faithful, lo, I will be *with them even unto the end.

14 And again, verily I say unto my servant Lyman Johnson, and unto my servant Orson Pratt, they shall also take their journey into the eastern countries; and behold, and lo, I am with them also, even unto the end.

15 And again, I say unto my servant Asa Dodds, and unto my servant Calves Wilson, that they also shall take their journey unto the western countries, and proclaim my gospel, even as I have commanded them.

16 And he who is faithful shall overcome all things, and shall be *lifted up at the last day.

17 And again, I say unto my servant Major N. Ashley, and my servant Burr Riggs, let them take their journey also into the south country.

18 Yea, let all those take their journey, as I have commanded them, going from *house to house, and from village to village, and from city to city.

19 And in whatsoever house ye enter, and they receive you, leave your blessing upon that house.

20 And in whatsoever house ye enter, and they receive you not, ye shall depart speedily from that house, and *shake off the dust of your feet as a testimony against them.

21 And you shall be filled with *joy and gladness; and know this, that in the day of judgment you shall be *judges of that house, and condemn them;

22 And it shall be more *tolerable for the *heathen in the day of judgment, than for that house; therefore, *gird up your loins and be faithful, and ye shall overcome all things, and be *lifted up at the last day. Even so. Amen.

23 And again, thus saith the Lord unto you, O ye elders of my church, who have *given your names that you might know his will concerning you—

24 Behold, I say unto you, that it is the *duty of the church to assist in *supporting the families of those, and also to support the families of those who are called and must needs be sent unto the world to proclaim the gospel unto the world.

25 Wherefore, I, the Lord, give unto you this commandment, that ye obtain places for your *families, inasmuch as your brethren are willing to open their hearts.

13a Matt. 28:20.
16a D&C 5:35.
18a Luke 8:1; Alma 23:4;
    D&C 66:5.
20a Matt. 10:14 (12–14);
    Luke 10:11 (11–12);
    D&C 24:15; 60:15; 99:4

(4–5).
21a Matt. 5:12 (11–12).
    b TG Priesthood, Author-
    ity.
22a Matt. 11:22; D&C
    45:54.
    b TG Heathen.

c D&C 27:15 (15–18).
    d D&C 5:35.
23a D&C 75:2.
24a D&C 72:11 (11–12).
    b D&C 31:5.
25a D&C 83:2 (2–4).

26 And let all such as can obtain places for their families, and support of the church for them, not fail to go into the world, whether to the east or to the west, or to the north, or to the south.

27 Let them ^aask and they shall receive, knock and it shall be opened unto them, and be made known from on high, even by the ^bComforter, whither they shall go.

28 And again, verily I say unto you, that every ^aman who is obliged to ^bprovide for his own ^cfamily, let him provide, and he shall in nowise lose his crown; and let him labor in the church.

29 Let every man be ^adiligent in all things. And the ^bidler shall not have place in the church, except he repent and mend his ways.

30 Wherefore, let my servant Simeon Carter and my servant Emer Harris be united in the ministry;

31 And also my servant Ezra Thayre and my servant ^aThomas B. Marsh;

32 Also my servant Hyrum Smith and my servant Reynolds Cahoon;

33 And also my servant Daniel Stanton and my servant Seymour Brunson;

34 And also my servant Sylvester Smith and my servant Gideon Carter;

35 And also my servant Ruggles Eames and my servant ^aStephen Burnett;

36 And also my servant Micah B. Welton and also my servant ^aEden Smith. Even so. Amen.

SECTION 76

A vision given to Joseph Smith the Prophet and Sidney Rigdon, at Hiram, Ohio, February 16, 1832. Prefacing the record of this vision, Joseph Smith's history states: "Upon my return from Amherst conference, I resumed the translation of the Scriptures. From sundry revelations which had been received, it was apparent that many important points touching the salvation of man had been taken from the Bible, or lost before it was compiled. It appeared self-evident from what truths were left, that if God rewarded every one according to the deeds done in the body the term 'Heaven,' as intended for the Saints' eternal home, must include more kingdoms than one.

---

27 *a* D&C 4:7.
  b TG Holy Ghost, Comforter.
28 *a* TG Marriage, Husbands.
  b 1 Tim. 5:8. TG Family,

Managing Finances in; Marriage, Fatherhood.
  c TG Family; Family, Love within.
29 *a* TG Diligence; Zeal.

  b TG Idleness; Laziness.
31 *a* D&C 56:5 (5–6).
35 *a* D&C 80:1.
36 *a* D&C 80:2.

Accordingly, . . . while translating St. John's Gospel, myself and Elder Rigdon saw the following vision." At the time this vision was given, the Prophet was translating John 5:29.

1–4, The Lord is God; 5–10, The mysteries of the kingdom will be revealed to all the faithful; 11–17, All will come forth in the resurrection of the just or the unjust; 18–24, The inhabitants of many worlds are begotten sons and daughters unto God through the Atonement of Jesus Christ; 25–29, An angel of God fell and became the devil; 30–49, Sons of perdition suffer eternal damnation; all others gain some degree of salvation; 50–70, The glory and reward of exalted beings in the celestial kingdom is described; 71–80, Those who will inherit the terrestrial kingdom are described; 81–113, The status of those in the telestial, terrestrial, and celestial glories is explained; 114–19, The faithful may see and understand the mysteries of God's kingdom by the power of the Holy Spirit.

1 *ᵃ*Hear, O ye heavens, and give ear, O earth, and rejoice ye inhabitants thereof, for the Lord is *ᵇ*God, and beside him there is *ᶜ*no *ᵈ*Savior.

2 *ᵃ*Great is his wisdom, *ᵇ*marvelous are his ways, and the extent of his doings none can find out.

3 His *ᵃ*purposes fail not, neither are there any who can stay his hand.

4 From eternity to eternity he is the *ᵃ*same, and his years never *ᵇ*fail.

5 For thus saith the Lord—I, the Lord, am *ᵃ*merciful and gracious unto those who *ᵇ*fear me, and delight to honor those who *ᶜ*serve me in righteousness and in truth unto the end.

6 Great shall be their reward and eternal shall be their *ᵃ*glory.

7 And to them will I *ᵃ*reveal all *ᵇ*mysteries, yea, all the hidden mysteries of my kingdom from days of old, and for ages to come, will I make known unto them the good pleasure of my will concerning all things pertaining to my kingdom.

8 Yea, even the wonders of *ᵃ*eternity shall they know, and things to come will I show them, even the things of many generations.

9 And their *ᵃ*wisdom shall be great, and their *ᵇ*understanding reach to

---

76 1 *a* Isa. 1:2.
  b Josh. 22:34; Jer. 10:10.
  c Ex. 8:10 (8–10); 1 Kgs.
    8:60; Isa. 43:11; Hosea
    13:4.
  d TG Jesus Christ, Savior.
2 *a* Ex. 15:11. TG God, Intel-
    ligence of; God, Wisdom
    of.
  b Ps. 25:4 (1–5); 118:23;
    Rev. 15:3 (1–3).

3 *a* 1 Kgs. 8:56; 1 Ne. 20:14;
    D&C 64:31.
4 *a* Heb. 13:8; D&C 20:12;
    35:1; 38:1 (1–4); 39:1
    (1–3). TG God, Eternal
    Nature of; God, Perfec-
    tion of.
  b Ps. 102:27 (25–27); Heb.
    1:12.
5 *a* Ex. 34:6; Ps. 103:8; Prov.
    8:17. TG God, Mercy of.
  b Deut. 6:13; Josh. 4:24;

1 Kgs. 18:3. TG Rever-
    ence.
  c 1 Sam. 7:3; Ps. 34:15;
    D&C 4:2.
6 *a* TG Celestial Glory.
7 *a* D&C 42:61; 59:4; 98:12;
    101:32; 121:28 (26–33).
  b 2 Pet. 1:2. TG Mysteries
    of Godliness.
8 *a* TG Eternity.
9 *a* TG Wisdom.
  b TG Understanding.

heaven; and before them the wisdom of the wise shall ^cperish, and the understanding of the ^dprudent shall come to naught.

10 For by my ^aSpirit will I ^benlighten them, and by my ^cpower will I make known unto them the ^dsecrets of my ^ewill—yea, even those things which ^feye has not seen, nor ear heard, nor yet entered into the heart of man.

11 We, Joseph Smith, Jun., and Sidney Rigdon, being ^ain the Spirit on the sixteenth day of February, in the year of our Lord one thousand eight hundred and thirty-two—

12 By the power of the ^aSpirit our ^beyes were opened and our understandings were enlightened, so as to see and understand the things of God—

13 Even those things which were from the beginning before the world was, which were ordained of the Father, through his Only Begotten Son, who was in the bosom of the Father, even from the ^abeginning;

14 Of whom we bear record; and the record which we bear is the fulness of the gospel of Jesus Christ, who is the Son, whom we saw and with whom we ^aconversed in the heavenly ^bvision.

15 For while we were doing the work of ^atranslation, which the Lord had appointed unto us, we came to the twenty-ninth verse of the fifth chapter of John, which was given unto us as follows—

16 Speaking of the resurrection of the dead, concerning those who shall ^ahear the voice of the ^bSon of Man:

17 And shall come forth; ^athey who have done ^bgood, in the ^cresurrection of the ^djust; and they who have done evil, in the resurrection of the unjust.

18 Now this caused us to marvel, for it was given unto us of the Spirit.

19 And while we ^ameditated upon these things, the Lord touched the eyes of our understandings and they were opened, and the ^bglory of the Lord shone round about.

20 And we beheld the ^aglory of the Son, on the ^bright hand of the ^cFather, and received of his fulness;

---

9 c Isa. 29:14; 2 Ne. 9:28.
  d TG Prudence.
10 a TG God, Spirit of.
   b TG Testimony.
   c TG Jesus Christ, Power of.
   d Dan. 2:28.
   e TG God, Will of.
   f Isa. 64:4; 1 Cor. 2:9; 3 Ne. 17:16 (15–25); D&C 76:116 (114–19).
11 a Rev. 1:10; 4:2.
12 a TG Transfiguration.
   b Eph. 1:18; D&C 11:13; 110:1; 137:1; 138:11 (11,

29). TG God, Privilege of Seeing.
13 a TG Jesus Christ, Foreordained.
14 a D&C 109:57.
   b TG Vision.
15 a D&C 73:3 (3–4); 93:53.
16 a John 5:28.
   b TG Jesus Christ, Son of Man.
17 a Joseph Smith Translation has the same wording as used here, which differs from the King James Version of John 5:29.

b TG Good Works.
   c TG Resurrection.
   d Dan. 12:2 (1–3); Acts 24:15; D&C 76:65 (50, 64–65).
19 a 1 Ne. 11:1; D&C 138:11 (1, 11); JS—H 1:44. TG Meditation.
   b TG God, Glory of.
20 a TG Jesus Christ, Glory of.
   b Acts 7:56; D&C 49:6; 104:7.
   c TG God the Father, Elohim.

21 And saw the holy *angels, and them who are *sanctified before his throne, worshiping God, and the Lamb, who *worship him forever and ever.

22 And now, after the many testimonies which have been given of him, this is the *testimony, last of all, which we give of him: That he *lives!

23 For we *saw him, even on the *right hand of *God; and we heard the voice bearing record that he is the *Only Begotten of the Father—

24 That by *him, and through him, and of him, the *worlds are and were created, and the *inhabitants thereof are begotten *sons and daughters unto God.

25 And this we saw also, and bear record, that an *angel of God who was in authority in the presence of God, who *rebelled against the Only Begotten *Son whom the Father *loved and who was in the bosom of the Father, was thrust down from the presence of God and the Son,

26 And was called *Perdition, for the heavens *wept over him—he was *Lucifer, a son of the morning.

27 And we beheld, and lo, he is *fallen! is fallen, even a son of the morning!

28 And while we were yet in the Spirit, the Lord commanded us that we should write the vision; for we beheld Satan, that old *serpent, even the *devil, who rebelled against God, and sought to take the kingdom of our *God and his Christ—

29 Wherefore, he maketh *war with the saints of God, and encompasseth them round about.

30 And we saw a vision of the *sufferings of those with whom he made war and overcame, for thus came the voice of the Lord unto us:

---

21 a Matt. 25:31; 2 Thes. 1:7; Heb. 12:22; D&C 130:7; 136:37.
 b TG Sanctification.
 c TG Worship.
22 a TG Testimony; Witness.
 b Josh. 3:10; 2 Sam. 22:47; D&C 20:17. TG Jesus Christ, Resurrection.
23 a TG God, Privilege of Seeing; Jesus Christ, Appearances, Postmortal.
 b Heb. 1:3.
 c TG Godhead.
 d John 1:14.
24 a Gen. 1:1; John 1:3 (1–3); Rom. 11:36 (34–36); Heb. 1:2 (1–3); Mosiah 4:2; Morm. 9:11; D&C

14:9; 93:10 (8–10).
 b Job 9:9 (7–9); Ps. 8:3 (3–4); Moses 1:33 (31–33); 7:30 (29–31). TG Astronomy; Creation; Jesus Christ, Creator; Jesus Christ, Power of.
 c D&C 88:61.
 d Mal. 2:10; 1 Cor. 15:45 (45–48); 2 Ne. 2:20 (19–20); D&C 27:11; Moses 1:34. TG Sons and Daughters of God.
25 a D&C 29:36 (36–39); Moses 4:1 (1–3).
 b TG Council in Heaven; Rebellion.
 c TG Jesus Christ, Divine Sonship.

d TG Jesus Christ, Relationships with the Father.
26 a D&C 76:32 (32–48); Moses 5:24. TG Sons of Perdition.
 b Moses 7:29 (28–31).
 c Isa. 14:12.
27 a Luke 10:18.
28 a Rev. 12:9.
 b TG Devil.
 c Isa. 14:14; D&C 29:36 (36–37); Moses 4:1 (1–4).
29 a Rev. 12:9 (7–9); 13:7; 2 Ne. 2:18; 28:20 (19–23); D&C 10:27. TG War.
30 a Jude 1:6 (6–8); D&C 76:44 (36, 44–49).

31 Thus saith the Lord concerning all those who know my power, and have been made partakers thereof, and *suffered themselves through the power of the devil to be overcome, and to deny the truth and defy my power—

32 They are they who are the *sons of *perdition, of whom I say that it had been better for them never to have been born;

33 For they are *vessels of wrath, doomed to suffer the wrath of God, with the devil and his angels in eternity;

34 Concerning whom I have said there is *no *forgiveness in this world nor in the world to come—

35 Having *denied the Holy Spirit after having received it, and having denied the Only Begotten Son of the Father, having *crucified him unto themselves and put him to an open *shame.

36 These are they who shall go away into the *lake of fire and brimstone, with the devil and his angels—

37 And the *only ones on whom the *second *death shall have any power;

38 Yea, verily, the only ones who shall *not be redeemed in the due time of the Lord, after the sufferings of his wrath.

39 For all the rest shall be *brought forth by the resurrection of the dead, through the *triumph and the glory of the Lamb, who was slain, who was in the bosom of the Father *before the worlds were made.

40 And this is the *gospel, the glad *tidings, which the voice out of the heavens bore record unto us—

41 That he *came into the world, even Jesus, to be *crucified for the world, and to *bear the sins of the *world, and to *sanctify the world, and to *cleanse it from all unrighteousness;

---

31 a TG Apostasy of Individuals.
32 a TG Sons of Perdition.
  b D&C 76:26; Moses 5:24.
33 a Rom. 9:22 (20–23); Rev. 2:27 (26–27).
34 a D&C 42:18; 84:41; 132:27.
  b TG Forgive.
35 a 2 Pet. 2:20 (20–22); Alma 39:6; D&C 76:83. TG Holy Ghost, Loss of; Holy Ghost, Unpardonable Sin against.
  b Heb. 6:6 (4–6); 1 Ne. 19:7; D&C 132:27.
  c TG Shame.
36 a Dan. 7:11; Rev. 19:20;

20:10; 21:8; 2 Ne. 9:16 (8–19, 26); 28:23; Jacob 6:10; Mosiah 3:27; Alma 12:17 (16–18); D&C 63:17.
37 a D&C 76:44 (44–49).
  b D&C 29:28 (28, 41).
  c D&C 64:7. TG Death, Spiritual, Second.
38 a TG Sons of Perdition.
39 a IE redeemed; see v. 38. All will be resurrected. See Alma 11:41–45; D&C 88:32.
  b TG Jesus Christ, Resurrection.
  c John 1:1 (1–3, 10); Rev. 13:8; D&C 93:7.

40 a 3 Ne. 27:13 (13–22). TG Gospel; Salvation, Plan of.
  b Luke 8:1.
41 a TG Jesus Christ, Birth of; Jesus Christ, Mission of.
  b TG Jesus Christ, Crucifixion of.
  c Isa. 53:12 (4–12); Heb. 9:28.
  d 1 Jn. 2:2 (1–2); Alma 11:41 (40–41).
  e TG Salvation, Plan of; Sanctification.
  f TG Purification; Redemption.

42 That through him all might be ᵃsaved whom the Father had put into his ᵇpower and made by him;

43 Who ᵃglorifies the Father, and saves all the works of his hands, except those sons of ᵇperdition who deny the Son after the Father has revealed him.

44 Wherefore, he saves all ᵃexcept them—they shall go away into ᵇeverlasting ᶜpunishment, which is endless punishment, which is eternal punishment, to ᵈreign with the ᵉdevil and his angels in eternity, where their ᶠworm dieth not, and the fire is not quenched, which is their torment—

45 And the ᵃend thereof, neither the place thereof, nor their torment, no man knows;

46 Neither was it revealed, neither is, neither will be revealed unto man, except to them who are made partakers thereof;

47 Nevertheless, I, the Lord, show it by ᵃvision unto many, but straightway shut it up again;

48 Wherefore, the end, the width, the height, the ᵃdepth, and the misery thereof, they understand not, neither any man except those who are ᵇordained unto this ᶜcondemnation.

49 And we heard the voice, saying: ᵃWrite the vision, for lo, this is the end of the vision of the sufferings of the ungodly.

50 And again we bear record—for we ᵃsaw and heard, and this is the ᵇtestimony of the ᶜgospel of Christ concerning them who shall come forth in the resurrection of the ᵈjust—

51 They are they who received the ᵃtestimony of Jesus, and ᵇbelieved on his name and were ᶜbaptized after the ᵈmanner of his burial, being ᵉburied in the water in his name, and this according to the commandment which he has given—

52 That by ᵃkeeping the commandments they might be ᵇwashed and

---

42 a TG Salvation.
  b TG Jesus Christ, Authority of.
43 a John 17:4. TG Jesus Christ, Relationships with the Father.
  b TG Sons of Perdition.
44 a D&C 76:37.
  b D&C 19:6.
  c D&C 76:30. TG Damnation; Punish.
  d D&C 88:24.

e TG Devil.
f Isa. 66:24; Mark 9:48 (43–48).
45 a D&C 29:28 (28–29).
47 a Moses 1:20. TG Vision.
48 a Rev. 20:1.
  b IE sentenced, consigned.
  c Alma 42:22.
49 a TG Scriptures, Writing of.
50 a TG Vision.
  b TG Testimony.

c TG Gospel.
d D&C 29:13; 76:17.
51 a 1 Pet. 1:9 (1–16).
  TG Baptism, Qualifications for.
  b D&C 20:25.
  c TG Baptism, Essential.
  d D&C 124:29; 128:13.
  e Rom. 6:4 (3–5). TG Baptism, Immersion.
52 a D&C 138:12.
  b 2 Ne. 9:23; Moro. 8:25.

^ccleansed from all their sins, and receive the Holy Spirit by the laying on of the ^dhands of him who is ^eordained and sealed unto this power;

53 And who ^aovercome by faith, and are ^bsealed by the Holy Spirit of ^cpromise, which the Father ^dsheds forth upon all those who are just and true.

54 They are they who are the ^achurch of the ^bFirstborn.

55 They are they into whose hands the Father has given ^aall things—

56 They are they who are ^apriests and ^bkings, who have received of his fulness, and of his glory;

57 And are ^apriests of the Most High, after the order of Melchizedek, which was after the order of ^bEnoch, which was after the ^corder of the Only Begotten Son.

58 Wherefore, as it is written, they are ^agods, even the ^bsons of ^cGod—

59 Wherefore, ^aall things are theirs, whether life or death, or things present, or things to come, all are theirs and they are Christ's, and Christ is God's.

60 And they shall ^aovercome all things.

61 Wherefore, let no man ^aglory in man, but rather let him ^bglory in God, who shall ^csubdue all enemies under his feet.

62 These shall ^adwell in the ^bpresence of God and his Christ forever and ever.

63 These are they whom he shall bring with him, when he shall ^acome in the ^bclouds of heaven to ^creign on the earth over his people.

64 These are they who shall have part in the ^afirst resurrection.

---

52 c TG Purification.
  d TG Hands, Laying on of; Holy Ghost, Gift of.
  e TG Authority.
53 a TG Self-Mastery.
  b TG Holy Ghost, Mission of; Sealing.
  c Eph. 1:13; D&C 88:3 (3–4); 124:124; 132:19 (18–26). TG Promise.
  d Acts 2:33.
54 a D&C 84:34.
  b Heb. 12:23; D&C 93:22 (21–22). TG Jesus Christ, Firstborn.
55 a Dan. 7:14 (13–14); Matt. 28:18; John 3:35; 2 Pet. 1:3; Rev. 2:7; D&C 50:28 (26–28); 84:38.
56 a Ex. 19:6; Rev. 1:6 (1–6); 5:10; 20:6; D&C 78:15 (15, 18); 132:19 (19–20).

  b D&C 104:7.
57 a TG High Priest, Melchizedek Priesthood; Priesthood, Melchizedek.
  b Gen. 5:23; Moses 6:27 (27–68); 7:1 (1–69).
  c D&C 107:3 (2–4).
58 a Ps. 82:6 (1, 6); John 10:34 (34–36); 1 Cor. 8:6 (5–6); D&C 121:28. TG Exaltation; Man, Potential to Become like Heavenly Father.
  b Luke 6:35. TG Sons and Daughters of God.
  c Deut. 10:17 (17–21); D&C 121:32 (28–32).
59 a Ps. 84:11; Luke 12:44; John 16:15; 3 Ne. 28:10; D&C 84:38 (37–38).
60 a Rev. 3:5; 21:7.
61 a John 5:44 (41–44);

  1 Cor. 3:21 (21–23); 1 Thes. 2:6.
  b Ps. 44:8 (4–8); 2 Ne. 33:6; Alma 26:16 (11–16).
  c Ps. 66:3; D&C 49:6.
62 a Ps. 15:1 (1–5); 24:3 (3–4); 27:4; 1 Ne. 10:21; 15:33 (19–26); Mosiah 15:23 (19–26); Morm. 7:7; Moses 6:57 (55–59).
  b D&C 76:94 (94, 119); 130:7. TG Eternal Life; God, Presence of.
63 a TG Jesus Christ, Second Coming.
  b Matt. 24:30.
  c Zech. 9:10; D&C 58:22. TG Jesus Christ, Millennial Reign.
64 a Rev. 20:6 (5–6).

65 These are they who shall come forth in the resurrection of the *just.

66 These are they who are come unto *Mount *Zion, and unto the city of the living God, the heavenly place, the holiest of all.

67 These are they who have come to an innumerable company of *angels, to the general assembly and church of *Enoch, and of the *Firstborn.

68 These are they whose names are *written in heaven, where God and Christ are the *judge of all.

69 These are they who are *just men made *perfect through Jesus the mediator of the *new covenant, who wrought out this perfect *atonement through the shedding of his own *blood.

70 These are they whose bodies are *celestial, whose *glory is that of the *sun, even the glory of God, the *highest of all, whose glory the sun of the firmament is written of as being typical.

71 And again, we saw the *terrestrial world, and behold and lo, these are they who are of the terrestrial, whose glory differs from that of the church of the *Firstborn who have received the fulness of the Father, even as that of the *moon differs from the sun in the firmament.

72 Behold, these are they who died *without *law;

73 And also they who are the *spirits of men kept in *prison, whom the Son visited, and *preached the *gospel unto them, that they might be judged according to men in the flesh;

74 Who *received not the *testimony of Jesus in the flesh, but afterwards received it.

75 These are they who are *honorable men of the earth, who were *blinded by the craftiness of men.

---

65 *a* D&C 76:17.
66 *a* Isa. 24:23; Joel 2:32;
    Obad. 1:21; Heb. 11:10;
    12:22 (22, 24); Rev. 14:1;
    D&C 84:2 (2, 18, 32);
    133:56 (18, 56).
  b TG Zion.
67 *a* TG Angels.
  b D&C 38:4; 45:11
    (11–12); 84:100
    (99–100); 133:54.
  c D&C 76:54 (53–54).
68 *a* TG Book of Life.
  b TG Jesus Christ, Judge;
    Judgment.
69 *a* Ezek. 18:9 (5–9); Heb.
    12:23; D&C 129:3
    (3–6); 138:12.
  b TG Man, New, Spiritu-
    ally Reborn; Perfection.

  c TG New and Everlasting
    Covenant.
  d TG Jesus Christ, Atone-
    ment through.
  e TG Blood, Symbolism of.
70 *a* D&C 88:29; 131:1
    (1–4); 137:7. TG Celestial
    Glory.
  b Dan. 12:3; D&C 137:2
    (2–4).
  c Matt. 13:43; 1 Cor. 15:41
    (40–42).
  d TG God, Perfection of.
71 *a* D&C 88:30. TG Terres-
    trial Glory.
  b D&C 76:54.
  c 1 Cor. 15:41.
72 *a* Rom. 2:12; D&C 137:7
    (7–10).
  b Acts 17:30.

  TG Accountability;
    Ignorance.
73 *a* Job 14:10; Alma 11:45;
    40:11 (11–14); Moses
    7:57. TG Spirit Body;
    Spirits, Disembodied;
    Spirits in Prison.
  b D&C 88:99; 138:8.
    TG Genealogy and
    Temple Work; Salvation
    for the Dead.
  c 1 Pet. 3:19 (19–20); 4:6;
    D&C 138:19.
  d TG Gospel.
74 *a* D&C 138:32.
  b TG Salvation for the
    Dead; Testimony.
75 *a* TG Honorable.
  b TG Spiritual Blindness.

76 These are they who receive of his glory, but not of his fulness.

77 These are they who receive of the *presence of the Son, but not of the fulness of the Father.

78 Wherefore, they are *bodies terrestrial, and not bodies celestial, and differ in glory as the moon differs from the sun.

79 These are they who are not *valiant in the *testimony of Jesus; wherefore, they obtain not the crown over the kingdom of our God.

80 And now this is the end of the *vision which we saw of the terrestrial, that the Lord commanded us to *write while we were yet in the Spirit.

81 And again, we *saw the glory of the *telestial, which glory is that of the lesser, even as the *glory of the stars differs from that of the glory of the moon in the firmament.

82 These are they who received not the gospel of Christ, neither the *testimony of Jesus.

83 These are they who *deny not the Holy Spirit.

84 These are they who are thrust down to *hell.

85 These are they who shall not be redeemed from the *devil until the *last resurrection, until the Lord, even Christ the *Lamb, shall have finished his work.

86 These are they who receive not of his fulness in the eternal world, but of the Holy Spirit through the ministration of the terrestrial;

87 And the terrestrial through the *ministration of the celestial.

88 And also the telestial receive it of the administering of angels who are appointed to minister for them, or who are appointed to be *ministering spirits for them; for they shall be *heirs of salvation.

89 And thus we saw, in the heavenly vision, the glory of the *telestial, which surpasses all understanding;

90 And no man knows it except him to whom God has revealed it.

91 And thus we saw the glory of the *terrestrial which excels in all things the glory of the telestial, even in glory, and in power, and in might, and in dominion.

---

77 a TG God, Presence of.
78 a 1 Cor. 15:40 (40–42).
79 a Jer. 8:20; D&C 45:2;
   56:16; 121:29. TG Apathy; Diligence; Trustworthiness.
   b TG Testimony.
80 a TG Vision.
   b Moses 2:1. TG Record Keeping; Scriptures, Writing of.

81 a TG Vision.
   b D&C 88:31. TG Telestial Glory.
   c TG Glory.
82 a D&C 138:21. TG Testimony.
83 a D&C 76:35.
84 a Prov. 9:18; 2 Ne. 9:12 (11–12); Alma 12:11; D&C 29:38. TG Hell.
85 a TG Devil.

   b Rev. 20:13 (12–13); Alma 11:41; D&C 43:18; 88:100 (100–101).
   c Gen. 22:8 (8–14); 1 Ne. 13:35.
87 a D&C 138:37.
88 a TG Angels.
   b D&C 7:6.
89 a TG Telestial Glory.
91 a TG Terrestrial Glory.

92 And thus we saw the ^aglory of the celestial, which ^bexcels in all things—where God, even the Father, reigns upon his ^cthrone forever and ever;

93 Before whose throne all things bow in humble ^areverence, and give him glory forever and ever.

94 They who dwell in his ^apresence are the church of the ^bFirstborn; and they see as they are seen, and ^cknow as they are known, having received of his fulness and of his ^dgrace;

95 And he makes them ^aequal in power, and in might, and in dominion.

96 And the glory of the celestial is one, even as the glory of the ^asun is one.

97 And the glory of the terrestrial is one, even as the glory of the moon is one.

98 And the glory of the telestial is one, even as the glory of the stars is one; for as one star differs from another star in glory, even so differs one from another in glory in the telestial world;

99 For these are they who are of ^aPaul, and of Apollos, and of Cephas.

100 These are they who say they are some of one and some of another—some of Christ and some of John, and some of Moses, and some of Elias, and some of ^aEsaias, and some of Isaiah, and some of Enoch;

101 But ^areceived not the gospel, neither the testimony of Jesus, neither the prophets, neither the ^beverlasting covenant.

102 Last of all, these all are they who will not be ^agathered with the saints, to be ^bcaught up unto the ^cchurch of the Firstborn, and received into the cloud.

103 These are ^athey who are ^bliars, and ^csorcerers, and ^dadulterers, and ^ewhoremongers, and whosoever loves and makes a lie.

104 These are they who suffer the ^awrath of God on earth.

105 These are they who suffer the ^avengeance of eternal fire.

92a TG Celestial Glory.
  b D&C 18:45; 84:38
    (35–38).
  c TG Kingdom of God, in
    Heaven.
93a TG Reverence.
94a D&C 76:62; 130:7.
    TG God, Presence of.
  b D&C 76:54.
  c 1 Cor. 13:12.
  d TG Grace.
95a D&C 29:13 (12–13);

78:5 (5–7); 84:38
  (35–39); 88:107; 132:20
  (18–20).
96a 1 Cor. 15:41 (40–41).
99a 1 Cor. 3:22.
100a D&C 84:13 (11–13).
101a TG Prophets, Rejection
    of.
  b TG New and Everlasting
    Covenant.
102a TG Separation.
  b 1 Thes. 4:16 (16–17);

D&C 84:100; 88:96
  (96–98); 101:31.
  c D&C 78:21.
103a Rev. 21:8; 22:15 (14–15);
    D&C 63:17 (17–18).
  b TG Lying.
  c TG Sorcery.
  d TG Adulterer; Sexual
    Immorality.
  e TG Whore.
104a TG Damnation.
105a Jude 1:7.

106 These are they who are cast down to ^ahell and ^bsuffer the wrath of ^cAlmighty God, until the ^dfulness of times, when Christ shall have ^esubdued all enemies under his ^ffeet, and shall have ^gperfected his work;

107 When he shall ^adeliver up the ^bkingdom, and present it unto the Father, spotless, saying: I have ^covercome and have ^dtrodden the ^ewine-press ^falone, even the wine-press of the fierceness of the wrath of Almighty God.

108 Then shall he be ^acrowned with the crown of his glory, to sit on the ^bthrone of his power to reign forever and ever.

109 But behold, and lo, we saw the glory and the inhabitants of the telestial world, that they were as ^ainnumerable as the stars in the firmament of heaven, or as the sand upon the seashore;

110 And heard the voice of the Lord saying: These all shall bow the knee, and every tongue shall ^aconfess to him who sits upon the throne forever and ever;

111 For they shall be judged according to their ^aworks, and every man shall receive according to his own ^bworks, his own ^cdominion, in the ^dmansions which are prepared;

112 And they shall be ^aservants of the Most High; but ^bwhere God and Christ ^cdwell they ^dcannot come, ^eworlds without end.

113 This is the end of the vision which we saw, which we were commanded to write while we were yet in the Spirit.

114 But ^agreat and marvelous are the works of the Lord, and the ^bmysteries of his kingdom which he showed unto us, which surpass all understanding in glory, and in might, and in dominion;

115 Which he commanded us we should not write while we were yet in the Spirit, and are not ^alawful for man to utter;

116 Neither is man ^acapable to make them known, for they are only to be

106 a TG Damnation; Hell.
  b D&C 19:6.
  c D&C 87:6.
  d Eph. 1:10 (9–10).
  e 1 Cor. 15:28; Philip. 3:21.
  f Heb. 2:8.
  g Heb. 10:14 (12–14).
107 a 1 Cor. 15:24 (24–28).
  b TG Jesus Christ, Relationships with the Father; Kingdom of God, on Earth.
  c John 16:33.
  d Rev. 14:20 (15–20); 19:15; D&C 88:106;

133:50 (46–53).
  e Gen. 49:11 (11–12); Isa. 63:2 (1–3); Joel 3:13; D&C 133:48.
  f Mark 14:37 (37, 40–41); D&C 122:8 (7–8).
108 a Rev. 19:16.
  b D&C 137:3.
109 a Matt. 7:13.
110 a Philip. 2:10 (9–11).
111 a TG Good Works.
  b Rev. 20:12 (12–13).
  c Dan. 7:27.
  d John 14:2; D&C 59:2; 81:6.
112 a TG Servant.

  b D&C 29:29.
  c Rev. 21:27 (9–27).
  d D&C 43:33 (18, 33).
  e Eph. 3:21.
114 a 1 Chr. 16:9; Ps. 9:1; 26:7; 40:5; 92:5; Rev. 15:3; Morm. 9:16 (16–20); D&C 88:47; Moses 1:4 (3–5).
  b Jacob 4:8; D&C 19:10.
115 a 2 Cor. 12:4; 3 Ne. 28:14 (12–14).
116 a 3 Ne. 5:18; 17:16 (15–25); 19:32 (30–36); D&C 76:10.

*b*seen and *c*understood by the power of the Holy Spirit, which God bestows on those who *d*love him, and purify themselves before him;

117 To whom he grants this privilege of *a*seeing and knowing for themselves;

118 That through the power and manifestation of the Spirit, while in the flesh, they may be able to *a*bear his *b*presence in the world of glory.

119 And to God and the Lamb be *a*glory, and honor, and dominion forever and ever. Amen.

SECTION 77

Revelation given to Joseph Smith the Prophet, at Hiram, Ohio, about March 1832. Joseph Smith's history states, "In connection with the translation of the Scriptures, I received the following explanation of the Revelation of St. John."

1–4, Beasts have spirits and will dwell in eternal felicity; 5–7, This earth has a temporal existence of 7,000 years; 8–10, Various angels restore the gospel and minister on earth; 11, The sealing of the 144,000; 12–14, Christ will come in the beginning of the seventh thousand years; 15, Two prophets will be raised up to the Jewish nation.

1 Q. What is the *a*sea of glass spoken of by John, 4th chapter, and 6th verse of the Revelation?

A. It is the *b*earth, in its *c*sanctified, *d*immortal, and *e*eternal state.

2 Q. What are we to understand by the four beasts, spoken of in the same verse?

A. They are *a*figurative expressions, used by the Revelator, John, in describing *b*heaven, the *c*paradise of God, the *d*happiness of man, and of beasts, and of creeping things, and of the fowls of the air; that which is spiritual being in the likeness of that which is temporal; and that which is temporal in the likeness of that which is spiritual; the *e*spirit of man in the likeness of his person, as also the spirit of the *f*beast, and every other creature which God has created.

---

116 *b* Ezek. 12:2.
   c 1 Cor. 2:11 (10–12).
   TG Holy Ghost, Mission of.
   d D&C 20:31.
117 *a* TG God, Privilege of Seeing.
118 *a* D&C 88:22.
   b TG God, Presence of.

119 *a* Matt. 6:13.
77 1 *a* Ezek. 1:22; Rev. 4:6.
   b TG Earth, Destiny of.
   c D&C 130:9. TG Sanctification.
   d TG Immortality.
   e TG Celestial Glory.
2 *a* TG Symbolism.
   b TG Heaven.

   c TG Paradise.
   d TG Happiness.
   e D&C 93:33; Abr. 5:7 (7–8). TG Man, a Spirit Child of Heavenly Father; Spirit Body.
   f D&C 29:24 (24–25); Moses 3:19.

3 Q. Are the four beasts limited to individual beasts, or do they represent classes or [a]orders?

A. They are limited to four individual beasts, which were shown to John, to represent the glory of the classes of beings in their destined [b]order or [c]sphere of creation, in the enjoyment of their [d]eternal [e]felicity.

4 Q. What are we to understand by the [a]eyes and [b]wings, which the beasts had?

A. Their eyes are a representation of light and knowledge, that is, they are full of [c]knowledge; and their wings are a [d]representation of [e]power, to move, to act, etc.

5 Q. What are we to understand by the four and twenty [a]elders, spoken of by John?

A. We are to understand that these elders whom John saw, were elders who had been [b]faithful in the work of the ministry and were dead; who belonged to the [c]seven churches, and were then in the paradise of God.

6 Q. What are we to understand by the book which John saw, which was [a]sealed on the back with seven seals?

A. We are to understand that it contains the revealed will, [b]mysteries, and the works of God; the hidden things of his economy concerning this [c]earth during the seven thousand years of its continuance, or its temporal existence.

7 Q. What are we to understand by the seven [a]seals with which it was sealed?

A. We are to understand that the first seal contains the things of the [b]first thousand years, and the [c]second also of the second thousand years, and so on until the seventh.

8 Q. What are we to understand by the four [a]angels, spoken of in the 7th chapter and 1st verse of Revelation?

A. We are to understand that they are four angels sent forth from God, to whom is given power over the four parts of the earth, to save life and to destroy; these are they who have the [b]everlasting gospel to commit to every nation, kindred, tongue, and people; having power to [c]shut up the heavens, to seal up unto life, or to cast down to the [d]regions of darkness.

---

3 a D&C 88:42 (37–42);
  Abr. 3:9.
 b TG Order.
 c D&C 93:30; Moses 3:9.
 d D&C 29:24.
 e TG Joy.
4 a Zech. 3:9; Rev. 5:6.
 b 2 Chr. 5:8; Isa. 6:2 (2–7);
  Ezek. 1:11.
 c TG God, Omniscience of.

d TG Symbolism.
 e TG God, Power of.
5 a Rev. 4:4 (4, 10).
 b Rev. 14:4 (2–5).
 c Rev. 1:4.
6 a Rev. 5:1.
 b TG Mysteries of Godli-
  ness.
 c TG Earth, Destiny of.
7 a TG Seal.

b D&C 88:108 (108–10).
 c Rev. 6:3 (3–4); Moses
  8:28 (22, 28–29).
8 a Rev. 7:1 (1–8).
 b Rev. 14:6.
 c 1 Kgs. 8:35; Ether 4:9.
 d Matt. 8:12 (11–12); 22:13
  (1–14); D&C 133:72
  (71–73).

9 Q. What are we to understand by the angel [a]ascending from the east, Revelation 7th chapter and 2nd verse?

A. We are to understand that the angel ascending from the east is he to whom is given the seal of the living God over the twelve tribes of [b]Israel; wherefore, he crieth unto the four angels having the everlasting gospel, saying: Hurt not the earth, neither the sea, nor the trees, till we have sealed the servants of our God in their [c]foreheads. And, if you will receive it, this is [d]Elias which was to come to gather together the tribes of Israel and [e]restore all things.

10 Q. What time are the things spoken of in this chapter to be accomplished?

A. They are to be accomplished in the [a]sixth thousand years, or the opening of the sixth seal.

11 Q. What are we to understand by sealing the [a]one hundred and forty-four thousand, out of all the tribes of Israel—twelve thousand out of every tribe?

A. We are to understand that those who are sealed are [b]high priests, ordained unto the holy order of God, to administer the everlasting gospel; for they are they who are ordained out of every nation, kindred, tongue, and people, by the angels to whom is given power over the nations of the earth, to bring as many as will come to the church of the [c]Firstborn.

12 Q. What are we to understand by the sounding of the [a]trumpets, mentioned in the 8th chapter of Revelation?

A. We are to understand that as God [b]made the world in six days, and on the seventh day he finished his work, and [c]sanctified it, and also formed man out of the [d]dust of the earth, even so, in the beginning of the seventh thousand years will the Lord God [e]sanctify the earth, and complete the salvation of man, and [f]judge all things, and shall [g]redeem all things, except that which he hath not put into his power, when he shall have sealed all things, unto the end of all things; and the sounding of the trumpets of the seven angels are the preparing and finishing of his work, in the beginning of the seventh thousand years—the [h]preparing of the way before the time of his coming.

---

9 a Rev. 7:2.
　b Rev. 7:4.
　c Ezek. 9:4.
　d BD Elias.
　e TG Restoration of the Gospel.
10 a Rev. 6:12 (12–17).
11 a Rev. 7:4 (1–8); 14:3.
　b TG High Priest, Melchizedek Priesthood.

　c D&C 76:54 (54, 67, 71, 102). TG Jesus Christ, Firstborn.
12 a Rev. 8:2.
　b TG Creation.
　c Gen. 2:3 (1–3); Ex. 20:11; Mosiah 13:19 (16–19); Moses 3:3 (1–3); Abr. 5:3 (1–3).
　d Gen. 2:7; Morm. 9:17;

D&C 93:35 (33–35).
　e TG Sanctification.
　f TG Jesus Christ, Judge; Judgment, the Last.
　g TG Jesus Christ, Redeemer.
　h TG Millennium, Preparing a People for.

13 Q. When are the things to be accomplished, which are written in the 9th chapter of Revelation?

A. They are to be accomplished after the [a]opening of the seventh seal, [b]before the coming of Christ.

14 Q. What are we to understand by the little book which was [a]eaten by John, as mentioned in the 10th chapter of Revelation?

A. We are to understand that it was a mission, and an ordinance, for him to [b]gather the tribes of Israel; behold, this is Elias, who, as it is written, must come and [c]restore all things.

15 Q. What is to be understood by the two [a]witnesses, in the eleventh chapter of Revelation?

A. They are two prophets that are to be raised up to the [b]Jewish nation in the last days, at the time of the [c]restoration, and to prophesy to the Jews after they are gathered and have built the city of Jerusalem in the [d]land of their fathers.

SECTION 78

Revelation given through Joseph Smith the Prophet, at Kirtland, Ohio, March 1, 1832. On that day, the Prophet and other leaders had assembled to discuss Church business. This revelation originally instructed the Prophet, Sidney Rigdon, and Newel K. Whitney to travel to Missouri and organize the Church's mercantile and publishing endeavors by creating a "firm" that would oversee these efforts, generating funds for the establishment of Zion and for the benefit of the poor. This firm, known as the United Firm, was organized in April 1832 and disbanded in 1834 (see section 82). Sometime after its dissolution, under the direction of Joseph Smith, the phrase "the affairs of the storehouse for the poor" replaced "mercantile and publishing establishments" in the revelation, and the word "order" replaced the word "firm."

1–4, The Saints should organize and establish a storehouse; 5–12, Wise use of their properties will lead to salvation; 13–14, The Church should be independent of earthly powers; 15–16, Michael (Adam) serves under the direction of the Holy One (Christ); 17–22, Blessed are the faithful, for they will inherit all things.

---

13 a Rev. 8:1.
  b Mal. 4:5.
14 a Ezek. 2:9 (9–10); 3:2
    (1–3); Rev. 10:10.
  b TG Israel, Gathering of.

  c Matt. 17:11. TG Resto-
    ration of the Gospel.
15 a Zech. 4:14 (12–14); Rev.
    11:3 (1–14).
  b TG Israel, Judah,

People of.
  c TG Last Days; Resto-
    ration of the Gospel.
  d Amos 9:15 (14–15).
    TG Israel, Land of.

1 The Lord spake unto Joseph Smith, Jun., saying: Hearken unto me, saith the Lord your God, who are ordained unto the ªhigh priesthood of my church, who have assembled yourselves together;

2 And listen to the ªcounsel of him who has ᵇordained you from on high, who shall speak in your ears the words of ᶜwisdom, that salvation may be unto you in that thing which you have presented before me, saith the Lord God.

3 For verily I say unto you, the time has come, and is now at hand; and behold, and lo, it must needs be that there be an ªorganization of my people, in regulating and establishing the affairs of the ᵇstorehouse for the ᶜpoor of my people, both in this place and in the land of ᵈZion—

4 For a permanent and everlasting establishment and order unto my church, to advance the cause, which ye have espoused, to the salvation of man, and to the glory of your Father who is in heaven;

5 That you may be ªequal in the bonds of heavenly things, yea, and earthly things also, for the obtaining of heavenly things.

6 For if ye are not equal in earthly things ye cannot be ªequal in obtaining heavenly things;

7 For if you will that I give unto you a place in the ªcelestial world, you must ᵇprepare yourselves by ᶜdoing the things which I have commanded you and required of you.

8 And now, verily thus saith the Lord, it is expedient that all things be done unto my ªglory, by you who are joined together in this ᵇorder;

9 Or, in other words, let my servant Newel K. Whitney and my servant Joseph Smith, Jun., and my servant Sidney Rigdon sit in council with the saints which are in ªZion;

10 Otherwise ªSatan seeketh to turn their ᵇhearts away from the truth, that they become ᶜblinded and understand not the things which are prepared for them.

11 Wherefore, a commandment I give unto you, to prepare and organize yourselves by a ªbond or everlasting ᵇcovenant that cannot be broken.

78 1 a TG Priesthood, Melchizedek.
  2 a TG Counsel.
    b TG Priesthood, Authority; Priesthood, Ordination.
    c TG God, Wisdom of; Wisdom.
  3 a D&C 51:3; 82:11 (11,

15–21).
    b D&C 72:10; 83:5.
    c D&C 42:30 (30–42). TG Poor; Welfare.
    d D&C 57:2.
  5 a TG Consecration; Zion.
  6 a D&C 49:20.
  7 a TG Celestial Glory; Objectives.
    b D&C 29:8; 58:6; 132:3.

    c TG Commitment.
  8 a TG Glory.
    b D&C 92:1.
  9 a D&C 72:6 (1–26).
  10 a TG Devil.
    b TG Hardheartedness.
    c TG Spiritual Blindness.
  11 a D&C 82:11 (11, 15).
    b TG Covenants.

12 And he who breaketh it shall lose his office and standing in the church, and shall be *delivered over to the *buffetings of Satan until the day of redemption.

13 Behold, this is the preparation wherewith I prepare you, and the foundation, and the *ensample which I give unto you, whereby you may accomplish the commandments which are given you;

14 That through my providence, notwithstanding the *tribulation which shall descend upon you, that the church may stand independent above all other creatures beneath the celestial world;

15 That you may come up unto the *crown prepared for you, and be made *rulers over many kingdoms, saith the Lord God, the Holy One of Zion, who hath established the foundations of *Adam-ondi-Ahman;

16 Who hath appointed *Michael your prince, and established his feet, and set him upon high, and given unto him the keys of salvation under the counsel and direction of the *Holy One, who is without beginning of days or end of life.

17 Verily, verily, I say unto you, ye are *little children, and ye have not as yet understood how great blessings the Father hath in his own hands and prepared for you;

18 And ye cannot *bear all things now; nevertheless, be of good *cheer, for I will *lead you along. The kingdom is yours and the blessings thereof are yours, and the *riches of *eternity are yours.

19 And he who receiveth all things with *thankfulness shall be made glorious; and the things of this earth shall be added unto him, even an *hundred fold, yea, more.

20 Wherefore, do the things which I have commanded you, saith your Redeemer, even the Son *Ahman, who prepareth all things before he *taketh you;

21 For ye are the *church of the *Firstborn, and he will take you up in a *cloud, and appoint every man his portion.

22 And he that is a faithful and *wise *steward shall inherit *all things. Amen.

---

12 a 1 Tim. 1:20.
  b 1 Cor. 5:5 (1–7); D&C 82:21; 104:10 (8–10).
13 a TG Millennium, Preparing a People for.
14 a D&C 58:4 (3–4). TG Tribulation.
15 a TG Exaltation.
  b Ex. 19:6; Rev. 5:10; 20:6; D&C 76:56; 132:19 (19–20).
  c D&C 107:53; 116; 117:8

(8, 11).
16 a D&C 27:11. TG Adam.
  b D&C 107:54 (54–55).
17 a John 13:33; 1 Cor. 2:9; 1 Jn. 2:1 (1, 12–13).
18 a John 16:12; 3 Ne. 17:2 (2–4); D&C 50:40.
  b TG Cheerful.
  c TG Guidance, Divine.
  d TG Treasure.
  e TG Eternity.
19 a Ps. 34:1 (1–3);

Mosiah 2:20 (20–21). TG Thanksgiving.
  b Matt. 19:29 (27–29).
20 a D&C 95:17; 107:53; 116.
  b 1 Thes. 4:17; Rev. 11:12.
21 a D&C 76:102.
  b D&C 76:54 (53–54).
  c D&C 88:97.
22 a D&C 101:61.
  b TG Stewardship.
  c D&C 84:38.

SECTION 79

Revelation given through Joseph Smith the Prophet, at Hiram, Ohio, March 12, 1832.

1–4, Jared Carter is called to preach the gospel by the Comforter.

1 Verily I say unto you, that it is my will that my servant Jared Carter should go again into the eastern countries, from place to place, and from city to city, in the power of the ᵃordination wherewith he has been ordained, proclaiming glad tidings of great joy, even the ᵇeverlasting gospel.

2 And I will send upon him the ᵃComforter, which shall teach him the truth and the ᵇway whither he shall go;

3 And inasmuch as he is faithful, I will crown him again with ᵃsheaves.

4 Wherefore, let your heart be glad, my servant Jared Carter, and ᵃfear not, saith your Lord, even Jesus Christ. Amen.

SECTION 80

Revelation given through Joseph Smith the Prophet to Stephen Burnett, at Hiram, Ohio, March 7, 1832.

1–5, Stephen Burnett and Eden Smith are called to preach in whatever place they choose.

1 Verily, thus saith the Lord unto you my servant ᵃStephen Burnett: Go ye, go ye into the world and preach the gospel to every ᵇcreature that cometh under the sound of your voice.

2 And inasmuch as you desire a companion, I will give unto you my servant ᵃEden Smith.

3 Wherefore, go ye and preach my gospel, whether to the north or to the south, to the east or to the west, it mattereth not, for ye cannot go amiss.

4 Therefore, declare the things which ye have heard, and verily believe, and ᵃknow to be true.

5 Behold, this is the will of him who hath ᵃcalled you, your Redeemer, even Jesus Christ. Amen.

---

79 1 *a* D&C 52:38 (38–39).
  b Rev. 14:6.
  2 *a* TG Holy Ghost, Comforter.
    b Ps. 25:4 (1–5).
  3 *a* D&C 31:5.
  4 *a* TG Courage; Fearful; Joy.
80 1 *a* D&C 75:35.
  b Mark 16:15.
  2 *a* D&C 75:36.
  4 *a* D&C 20:17. TG Testimony.
  5 *a* TG Called of God.

SECTION 81

Revelation given through Joseph Smith the Prophet, at Hiram, Ohio, March 15, 1832. Frederick G. Williams is called to be a high priest and a counselor in the Presidency of the High Priesthood. The historical records show that when this revelation was received in March 1832, it called Jesse Gause to the office of counselor to Joseph Smith in the Presidency. However, when he failed to continue in a manner consistent with this appointment, the call was subsequently transferred to Frederick G. Williams. The revelation (dated March 1832) should be regarded as a step toward the formal organization of the First Presidency, specifically calling for the office of counselor in that body and explaining the dignity of the appointment. Brother Gause served for a time but was excommunicated from the Church in December 1832. Brother Williams was ordained to the specified office on March 18, 1833.

1–2, The keys of the kingdom are always held by the First Presidency; 3–7, If Frederick G. Williams is faithful in his ministry, he will have eternal life.

1 Verily, verily, I say unto you my servant Frederick G. Williams: Listen to the voice of him who speaketh, to the word of the Lord your God, and hearken to the calling wherewith you are called, even to be a *a*high priest in my church, and a *b*counselor unto my servant Joseph Smith, Jun.;

2 Unto whom I have given the *a*keys of the kingdom, which belong always unto the *b*Presidency of the High Priesthood:

3 Therefore, verily I acknowledge him and will bless him, and also thee, inasmuch as thou art faithful in counsel, in the office which I have appointed unto you, in prayer always, vocally and in thy heart, in public and in private, also in thy *a*ministry in proclaiming the gospel in the *b*land of the living, and among thy brethren.

4 And in doing these things thou wilt do the greatest *a*good unto thy fellow beings, and wilt promote the *b*glory of him who is your Lord.

5 Wherefore, be faithful; stand in the office which I have appointed unto you; *a*succor the *b*weak, lift up the hands which hang down, and *c*strengthen the *d*feeble knees.

6 And if thou art *a*faithful unto the end thou shalt have a *b*crown of

---

81 1 *a* D&C 68:15. TG High
 Priest, Melchizedek
 Priesthood.
 b D&C 35:22 (3–23);
 90:6; 107:24. TG Coun-
 selor.
2 *a* TG Priesthood, Keys of.

b D&C 68:15; 107:17 (9,
 17, 22).
3 *a* TG Mission of Latter-day
 Saints.
 b Ps. 27:13.
4 *a* TG Good Works.
 b D&C 124:18; Moses

1:39.
5 *a* TG Service.
 b Rom. 14:1 (1–3).
 c D&C 23:3; 31:8; 108:7.
 d Isa. 35:3.
6 *a* TG Steadfastness.
 b TG Exaltation.

*c*immortality, and eternal life in the *d*mansions which I have prepared in the house of my Father.

7 Behold, and lo, these are the words of Alpha and Omega, even Jesus Christ. Amen.

SECTION 82

Revelation given to Joseph Smith the Prophet, in Independence, Jackson County, Missouri, April 26, 1832. The occasion was a council of high priests and elders of the Church. At the council, Joseph Smith was sustained as the President of the High Priesthood, to which office he had previously been ordained at a conference of high priests, elders, and members, at Amherst, Ohio, January 25, 1832 (see the heading to section 75). This revelation reiterates instructions given in an earlier revelation (section 78) to establish a firm—known as the United Firm (under Joseph Smith's direction, the term "order" later replaced "firm")—to govern the Church's mercantile and publishing endeavors.

1–4, Where much is given, much is required; 5–7, Darkness reigns in the world; 8–13, The Lord is bound when we do what He says; 14–18, Zion must increase in beauty and holiness; 19–24, Every man should seek the interest of his neighbor.

1 Verily, verily, I say unto you, my servants, that inasmuch as you have *a*forgiven one another your trespasses, even so I, the Lord, forgive you.

2 Nevertheless, there are those among you who have sinned exceedingly; yea, even *a*all of you have sinned; but verily I say unto you, beware from henceforth, and *b*refrain from sin, lest sore judgments fall upon your heads.

3 For of him unto whom *a*much is *b*given much is *c*required; and he who *d*sins against the greater *e*light shall *f*receive the greater *g*condemnation.

4 Ye call upon my name for *a*revelations, and I give them unto you; and inasmuch as ye keep not my sayings, which I give unto you, ye become transgressors; and *b*justice and judgment are the penalty which is affixed unto my law.

---

6 *c* TG Immortality.
  d John 14:2 (2–3); D&C 59:2; 76:111; 98:18; 106:8.
82 1 *a* Matt. 6:14. TG Forgive.
  2 *a* Rom. 3:23.
    b TG Abstain.
  3 *a* Luke 12:48; James 4:17. TG Accountability;

Talents.
  b Matt. 25:29. TG Stewardship.
  c TG Mission of Latter-day Saints.
  d TG Apostasy of Individuals; Sin.
  e John 15:22 (22–24); Rom. 7:7 (7–8).

TG Intelligence; Light [noun].
  f Luke 12:47 (47–48); James 3:1.
  g D&C 18:46. TG Punish.
4 *a* TG Revelation.
  b TG God, Justice of; Justice.

5 Therefore, what I say unto one I say unto all: *a*Watch, for the *b*adversary *c*spreadeth his dominions, and *d*darkness reigneth;

6 And the anger of God kindleth against the inhabitants of the earth; and *a*none doeth good, for all have gone out of the *b*way.

7 And now, verily I say unto you, I, the Lord, will not lay any *a*sin to your charge; go your ways and sin no more; but unto that soul who sinneth shall the *b*former sins return, saith the Lord your God.

8 And again, I say unto you, I give unto you a *a*new commandment, that you may understand my will concerning you;

9 Or, in other words, I give unto you directions how you may *a*act before me, that it may *b*turn to you for your salvation.

10 I, the Lord, am *a*bound when ye do what I say; but when ye do not what I say, ye have no *b*promise.

11 Therefore, verily I say unto you, that it is expedient for my servants Edward Partridge and Newel K. Whitney, A. Sidney Gilbert and Sidney Rigdon, and my servant Joseph Smith, and John Whitmer and Oliver Cowdery, and W. W. Phelps and Martin Harris to be bound *a*together by a bond and covenant that cannot be *b*broken by transgression, except judgment shall immediately follow, in your several *c*stewardships—

12 To manage the affairs of the poor, and all things pertaining to the bishopric *a*both in the land of Zion and in the land of Kirtland;

13 For I have consecrated the land of Kirtland in mine own due time for the benefit of the saints of the Most High, and for a *a*stake to Zion.

14 For *a*Zion must increase in *b*beauty, and in *c*holiness; her borders must be enlarged; her *d*stakes must be strengthened; yea, verily I say unto you, Zion must *e*arise and put on her *f*beautiful garments.

15 Therefore, I give unto you this commandment, that ye bind yourselves by this covenant, and it shall be done according to the laws of the Lord.

16 Behold, here is *a*wisdom also in me for your good.

---

5 a TG Watch.
  b TG Devil.
  c Isa. 60:2; D&C 38:11
    (11–12).
  d TG Darkness, Spiritual.
6 a Eccl. 7:20; Matt. 19:17.
  b Gen. 6:12; Rom. 3:12;
    D&C 1:16; Moses 8:29.
7 a John 8:11 (2–11). TG Sin.
  b Ps. 79:8; Matt. 12:45
    (43–45); 18:32–34;
    D&C 1:33 (32–33);
    58:43.
8 a John 13:34.

9 a D&C 43:8; 103:1.
  b Philip. 1:19.
10 a Josh. 23:14; 1 Kgs. 8:23;
    Ps. 97:10; 145:20 (1–21);
    Prov. 12:2; 1 Ne. 17:35
    (33–35); D&C 1:37
    (37–38); 58:31; 130:20
    (20–21). TG Blessing;
    Obedience.
  b TG Promise.
11 a D&C 78:3 (3–7, 11–15);
    92:1.
  b D&C 78:11.
  c TG Stewardship.

12 a D&C 104:47.
13 a Isa. 33:20; 54:2; D&C
    68:26; 94:1.
14 a TG Mission of Latter-day
    Saints.
  b TG Beauty.
  c Lev. 19:2 (2–37).
  d TG Stake.
  e TG Israel, Restoration of.
  f Isa. 52:1; D&C 113:8
    (7–8).
16 a TG God, Wisdom of.

17 And you are to be *equal, or in other words, you are to have equal *claims on the *properties, for the benefit of *managing the concerns of your stewardships, every man according to his wants and his needs, inasmuch as his wants are just—

18 And all this for the benefit of the church of the living God, that every man may *improve upon his *talent, that every man may *gain other *talents, yea, even an hundred fold, to be cast into the Lord's *storehouse, to become the common *property of the whole church—

19 *Every man seeking the interest of his *neighbor, and doing all things with an *eye single to the glory of God.

20 This order I have appointed to be an *everlasting *order unto you, and unto your successors, inasmuch as you sin not.

21 And the soul that sins against this covenant, and *hardeneth his heart against it, shall be dealt with according to the laws of my church, and shall be delivered over to the *buffetings of Satan until the day of redemption.

22 And now, verily I say unto you, and this is wisdom, make unto yourselves friends with the *mammon of unrighteousness, and they will not destroy you.

23 Leave judgment alone with me, for it is mine and I will *repay. Peace be with you; my blessings continue with you.

24 For even yet the *kingdom is yours, and shall be forever, if you fall not from your *steadfastness. Even so. Amen.

SECTION 83

Revelation given through Joseph Smith the Prophet, at Independence, Missouri, April 30, 1832. This revelation was received as the Prophet sat in council with his brethren.

1–4, Women and children have claim upon their husbands and fathers for their support; 5–6, Widows and orphans have claim upon the Church for their support.

17 a D&C 51:3.
  b TG Consecration.
  c TG Wages.
  d TG Family, Managing Finances in.
18 a TG Industry.
  b Matt. 25:25 (14–30); D&C 60:13.
  c TG Work, Value of.
  d TG Talents.
  e D&C 42:33 (33–34, 55);

51:13; 119:1 (1–3).
  f D&C 42:30.
19 a 1 Cor. 10:24.
  b TG Neighbor.
  c Prov. 4:21; D&C 88:67. TG Motivations.
20 a D&C 104:47.
  b D&C 78:3 (3–6).
21 a TG Apostasy of Individuals; Hardheartedness.
  b D&C 78:12; 104:9

(8–10); 132:26.
22 a Luke 16:9.
23 a Rom. 12:19; Morm. 3:15.
24 a Luke 12:32; D&C 64:4. TG Kingdom of God, on Earth.
  b TG Dedication; Dependability.

1 Verily, thus saith the Lord, in addition to the *a*laws of the church concerning women and children, those who belong to the church, who have *b*lost their husbands or fathers:

2 *a*Women have *b*claim on their husbands for their maintenance, until their *c*husbands are taken; and if they are not found transgressors they shall have fellowship in the church.

3 And if they are not faithful they shall not have fellowship in the church; yet they may remain upon their inheritances according to the laws of the land.

4 All *a*children have claim upon their *b*parents for their *c*maintenance until they are of age.

5 And after that, they have *a*claim upon the church, or in other words upon the Lord's *b*storehouse, if their parents have not wherewith to give them inheritances.

6 And the storehouse shall be kept by the consecrations of the church; and *a*widows and orphans shall be provided for, as also the *b*poor. Amen.

SECTION 84

Revelation given through Joseph Smith the Prophet, at Kirtland, Ohio, September 22 and 23, 1832. During the month of September, elders had begun to return from their missions in the eastern states and to make reports of their labors. It was while they were together in this season of joy that the following communication was received. The Prophet designated it a revelation on priesthood.

1–5, The New Jerusalem and the temple will be built in Missouri; 6–17, The line of priesthood from Moses to Adam is given; 18–25, The greater priesthood holds the key of the knowledge of God; 26–32, The lesser priesthood holds the key of the ministering of angels and of the preparatory gospel; 33–44, Men gain eternal life through the oath and covenant of the priesthood; 45–53, The Spirit of Christ enlightens men, and the world lies in sin; 54–61, The Saints must testify of those things they have received; 62–76, They are to preach the gospel, and signs will follow; 77–91, Elders are to go forth without purse or scrip, and the Lord will care for their needs;

---

83 1 *a* D&C 51:8 (7–14).
   b Deut. 10:18; Isa. 1:17 (16–17); James 1:27.
  2 *a* D&C 75:25.
   b 1 Tim. 5:8 (8–16).
   c TG Family, Patriarchal;

Marriage, Husbands.
  4 *a* Mosiah 4:14 (14–15).
   b TG Children.
   b TG Birth Control.
   c TG Family, Children, Responsibilities toward.
  5 *a* D&C 51:4 (3–4).

b D&C 78:3. TG Welfare.
  6 *a* Deut. 14:29; Mal. 3:5; Acts 4:35. TG Widows.
   b Zech. 7:10; Mosiah 4:26 (16–26); Hel. 4:12; D&C 42:30 (30–39, 71).

92–97, Plagues and cursings await those who reject the gospel; 98–102, The new song of the redemption of Zion is given; 103–10, Let every man stand in his own office and labor in his own calling; 111–20, The Lord's servants are to proclaim the abomination of desolation of the last days.

1 A ªrevelation of Jesus Christ unto his servant Joseph Smith, Jun., and six elders, as they ᵇunited their hearts and ᶜlifted their voices on high.

2 Yea, the word of the Lord concerning his church, established in the last days for the ªrestoration of his people, as he has spoken by the mouth of his ᵇprophets, and for the ᶜgathering of his ᵈsaints to stand upon ᵉMount Zion, which shall be the city of ᶠNew Jerusalem.

3 Which city shall be ªbuilt, beginning at the ᵇtemple lot, which is appointed by the finger of the Lord, in the western boundaries of the State of Missouri, and ᶜdedicated by the hand of Joseph Smith, Jun., and others with whom the Lord was well pleased.

4 Verily this is the word of the Lord, that the city ªNew Jerusalem shall be built by the gathering of the saints, beginning at this place, even the place of the temple, which ᵇtemple shall be ᶜreared in this ᵈgeneration.

5 For verily this generation shall not all ªpass away until an ᵇhouse shall be built unto the Lord, and a ᶜcloud shall rest upon it, which cloud shall be even the ᵈglory of the Lord, which shall fill the house.

6 ªAnd the ᵇsons of Moses, according to the Holy Priesthood which he received under the ᶜhand of his father-in-law, ᵈJethro;

7 And Jethro received it under the hand of Caleb;

8 And Caleb received it under the hand of Elihu;

9 And Elihu under the hand of Jeremy;

10 And Jeremy under the hand of Gad;

11 And Gad under the hand of Esaias;

12 And Esaias received it under the hand of God.

---

84 1 a Gal. 1:12.
  b 3 Ne. 27:1 (1–2); D&C 29:6.
  c TG Prayer.
  2 a TG Israel, Restoration of.
  b Acts 3:21.
  c D&C 10:65.
  d TG Saints.
  e Isa. 2:3 (2–5); 18:7; 24:23; Heb. 12:22 (22, 24); Rev. 14:1; 3 Ne. 20:33 (22–34); D&C 76:66; 84:32; 133:56 (18, 56).
  f Ether 13:6 (2–11); D&C 42:9; 45:66 (66–67); A of F 1:10.

TG Jerusalem, New.
  3 a D&C 101:18; 103:11.
  b D&C 57:3; 58:57; 97:10 (10–20); 124:51 (49–51).
  c D&C 52:2.
  4 a D&C 45:66; Moses 7:62. TG Mission of Latter-day Saints.
  b TG Temple.
  c D&C 124:51 (49–54).
  d Matt. 23:36; 24:34; JS—M 1:34.
  5 a D&C 45:31.
  b D&C 124:31 (25–55).
  c Ex. 33:9; 40:34; Num. 14:14; 1 Kgs. 8:10; 2 Chr.

5:14 (11–14); 3 Ne. 18:38. TG God, Presence of.
  d 2 Chr. 7:2 (2–3); D&C 45:67; 64:41 (41–43); 97:15 (15–20); 109:12, 37. TG God, Manifestations of.
  6 a D&C 84:31 (31–34).
  b Lev. 8:13; D&C 84:34 (18–41).
  c TG Hands, Laying on of.
  d Ex. 2:18 (16–18); 3:1; 18:1; Num. 10:29. TG Priesthood, History of.

13 ^aEsaias also lived in the days of Abraham, and was blessed of him—

14 Which ^aAbraham received the priesthood from ^bMelchizedek, who received it through the lineage of his fathers, even till ^cNoah;

15 And from Noah till ^aEnoch, through the lineage of their fathers;

16 And from Enoch to ^aAbel, who was slain by the ^bconspiracy of his brother, who ^creceived the priesthood by the commandments of God, by the hand of his father ^dAdam, who was the first man—

17 Which ^apriesthood ^bcontinueth in the church of God in all generations, and is without ^cbeginning of days or end of years.

18 And the Lord confirmed a ^apriesthood also upon ^bAaron and his ^cseed, throughout all their generations, which priesthood also continueth and ^dabideth forever with the priesthood which is after the holiest order of God.

19 And this greater ^apriesthood administereth the gospel and holdeth the ^bkey of the ^cmysteries of the kingdom, even the key of the ^dknowledge of God.

20 Therefore, in the ^aordinances thereof, the power of ^bgodliness is manifest.

21 And without the ordinances thereof, and the ^aauthority of the priesthood, the power of godliness is ^bnot manifest unto men in the flesh;

22 For without this no ^aman can see the face of God, even the Father, and live.

23 Now this ^aMoses plainly taught to the children of Israel in the wilderness, and sought diligently to ^bsanctify his people that they might ^cbehold the face of God;

24 But they ^ahardened their hearts and could not endure his ^bpresence;

13a D&C 76:100.
14a Abr. 1:3 (1–4, 19, 31).
  b Gen. 14:18 (17–20); JST Gen. 14:25–40 (Bible Appendix); Alma 13:14 (1–19); D&C 107:2. BD Melchizedek.
  c Gen. 5:29.
15a Gen. 5:21 (21–31); Moses 6:21 (21–68); 7:1 (1–69).
16a Gen. 4:25 (2, 25).
  b Moses 5:29 (29–32).
  c D&C 107:42 (1, 40–57); Moses 6:2.
  d 1 Cor. 15:45. TG Adam.
17a Alma 13:1 (1–19); Moses 6:7; Abr. 2:9 (9, 11). TG Priesthood, Melchizedek.
  b D&C 13; 90:3; 122:9; 124:130.
  c Heb. 7:3.
18a TG Priesthood, History of.
  b Ex. 40:15 (12–15); Num. 16:40; 2 Chr. 26:18; D&C 68:18; 107:13 (13–16, 70–76).
  c Lev. 8:13; D&C 84:6 (6–26, 33–41).
  d Num. 25:13; D&C 13.
19a TG Priesthood, Melchizedek.
  b D&C 28:7; 35:18; 64:5. TG Priesthood, Keys of.
  c D&C 63:23; 107:19 (18–19). TG Mysteries of Godliness.
  d Abr. 1:2.
20a TG Ordinance.
  b TG Godliness.
21a TG Authority;
  Priesthood, Authority.
  b John 14:21 (21–23).
22a John 1:18; D&C 67:11. TG God, Privilege of Seeing.
23a Ex. 19:11 (5–11); 32:19 (19–29); Deut. 4:14; 30:11 (11–14); 1 Ne. 20:16; D&C 93:31.
  b Lev. 8:10. TG Sanctification.
  c TG God, Privilege of Seeing.
24a Ex. 20:19 (18–21); 32:8; Deut. 9:23; 1 Ne. 17:30 (30–31, 42). TG Hardheartedness.
  b Ex. 33:3 (1–4); D&C 103:19. TG God, Presence of.

therefore, the Lord in his ᶜwrath, for his ᵈanger was kindled against them, swore that they should not ᵉenter into his rest while in the wilderness, which rest is the fulness of his glory.

25 Therefore, he took ᵃMoses out of their midst, and the Holy ᵇPriesthood also;

26 And the lesser ᵃpriesthood continued, which priesthood holdeth the ᵇkey of the ᶜministering of angels and the ᵈpreparatory gospel;

27 Which ᵃgospel is the gospel of ᵇrepentance and of ᶜbaptism, and the ᵈremission of sins, and the ᵉlaw of ᶠcarnal commandments, which the Lord in his wrath caused to continue with the house of Aaron among the children of Israel until ᵍJohn, whom God raised up, being ʰfilled with the Holy Ghost from his mother's womb.

28 For he was baptized while he was yet in his childhood, and was ᵃordained by the angel of God at the time he was ᵇeight days old unto this power, to overthrow the kingdom of the Jews, and to ᶜmake straight the way of the Lord before the face of his people, to prepare them for the ᵈcoming of the Lord, in whose hand is given ᵉall power.

29 And again, the ᵃoffices of elder and bishop are necessary ᵇappendages belonging unto the high priesthood.

30 And again, the offices of ᵃteacher and deacon are necessary appendages belonging to the lesser priesthood, which priesthood was confirmed upon ᵇAaron and his sons.

31 Therefore, as I said ᵃconcerning the sons of Moses—for the sons of Moses and also the sons of Aaron shall offer an acceptable ᵇoffering and sacrifice in the house of the Lord, which house shall be built unto the Lord in this generation, upon the consecrated ᶜspot as I have appointed—

32 And the sons of Moses and of Aaron shall be filled with the ᵃglory of

24 c Ex. 32:10.
  d TG Anger; God, Indignation of.
  e JST Ex. 34:1 (1–2) (Bible Appendix); Num. 14:23; Heb. 3:11; 4:1 (1–11); Jacob 1:7 (7–8).
25 a Deut. 34:5 (1–5).
  b TG Priesthood, History of; Priesthood, Melchizedek.
26 a 2 Chr. 23:6. TG Priesthood, Aaronic.
  b D&C 13. TG Priesthood, Keys of.
  c D&C 107:20.

  d Matt. 3:3 (1–3); 1 Ne. 10:8 (7–10).
27 a D&C 107:20.
  b TG Repent.
  c TG Baptism.
  d TG Remission of Sins.
  e TG Law of Moses.
  f Heb. 7:16 (11–16).
  g John 5:33; D&C 27:7; 35:4.
  h Luke 1:15.
28 a TG Priesthood, Ordination.
  b Gen. 17:12.
  c Isa. 40:3; Matt. 3:3; Luke 3:4; John 1:23.

  d TG Jesus Christ, Prophecies about.
  e Matt. 28:18; John 17:2; 1 Cor. 15:27; Heb. 1:2; 1 Pet. 3:22; D&C 93:17.
29 a TG Church Organization.
  b D&C 107:5 (5, 7–88).
30 a TG Deacon; Teacher.
  b Lev. 1:7; D&C 132:59.
31 a D&C 13; 84:6; 124:39.
  b D&C 128:24.
  c D&C 57:3.
32 a TG Glory.

the Lord, upon [b]Mount Zion in the Lord's house, whose sons are ye; and also many whom I have called and sent forth to build up my [c]church.

33 For whoso is [a]faithful unto the obtaining these two [b]priesthoods of which I have spoken, and the [c]magnifying their calling, are [d]sanctified by the Spirit unto the [e]renewing of their bodies.

34 They become the [a]sons of Moses and of Aaron and the [b]seed of [c]Abraham, and the church and kingdom, and the [d]elect of God.

35 And also all they who receive this priesthood [a]receive me, saith the Lord;

36 For he that receiveth my servants [a]receiveth me;

37 And he that [a]receiveth me receiveth my Father;

38 And he that receiveth my Father receiveth my Father's [a]kingdom; therefore [b]all that my Father hath shall be given unto him.

39 And this is according to the [a]oath and covenant which belongeth to the priesthood.

40 Therefore, all those who receive the [a]priesthood, receive this [b]oath and covenant of my Father, which he cannot break, neither can it be moved.

41 But whoso breaketh this [a]covenant after he hath received it, and altogether turneth therefrom, shall [b]not have forgiveness of sins in this world nor in the world to come.

42 And wo unto all those who come not unto this priesthood which ye have received, which I now confirm upon you who are present this day, by mine own voice out of the heavens; and even I have given the heavenly hosts and mine angels [a]charge concerning you.

43 And I now give unto you a commandment to beware concerning yourselves, to give [a]diligent [b]heed to the words of eternal life.

---

32 b Isa. 24:23; Heb. 12:22
(22, 24); Rev. 14:1; D&C
76:66; 84:2 (2, 18);
133:56 (18, 56).
  c TG Jesus Christ, Head of
the Church.
33 a TG Loyalty; Worthiness.
  b TG Priesthood.
  c TG Israel, Mission of;
Priesthood, Magnifying
Callings within.
  d TG Sanctification.
  e Rom. 8:11.
34 a D&C 84:6 (6–26).
  b Gal. 3:29; Abr. 2:10
(9–16). TG Seed of
Abraham.

c Lev. 26:42; D&C 132:30
(30–32). TG Abrahamic
Covenant.
  d Matt. 24:24; Mark
13:20; D&C 29:7.
TG Election.
35 a D&C 112:20.
36 a Matt. 10:40 (40–42);
Luke 9:48; 10:16; 1 Jn.
4:6 (1–6).
37 a John 13:20.
38 a TG Exaltation; Kingdom
of God, in Heaven.
  b Matt. 5:12 (3–12); Luke
12:44; 15:31 (31–32);
John 16:15; Rom. 8:32
(22–34); Rev. 21:7; 3 Ne.

28:10; D&C 78:5 (5–7);
132:20 (18–20).
39 a TG Covenants; Oath.
40 a TG Priesthood, Melchizedek.
  b Ezek. 16:59 (44–63).
TG Priesthood, Oath and
Covenant; Promise.
41 a TG Apostasy of Individuals.
  b D&C 41:1; 42:18; 76:34;
132:27.
42 a D&C 84:88.
43 a TG Diligence.
  b 1 Kgs. 2:4; 1 Ne. 15:25
(23–25); D&C 1:14 (14,
37).

44 For you shall *a*live by every word that proceedeth forth from the mouth of God.

45 For the *a*word of the Lord is truth, and whatsoever is truth is *b*light, and whatsoever is light is *c*Spirit, even the Spirit of Jesus Christ.

46 And the *a*Spirit giveth *b*light to *c*every man that cometh into the world; and the Spirit enlighteneth every man through the world, that hearkeneth to the voice of the Spirit.

47 And every one that hearkeneth to the voice of the Spirit *a*cometh unto God, even the Father.

48 And the Father *a*teacheth him of the covenant which he has *b*renewed and confirmed upon you, which is confirmed upon you for your sakes, and not for your sakes only, but for the sake of the *c*whole world.

49 And the whole *a*world lieth in sin, and groaneth under *b*darkness and under the *c*bondage of sin.

50 And by this you may know they are under the *a*bondage of sin, because they come not unto me.

51 For whoso cometh not unto me is under the *a*bondage of sin.

52 And whoso receiveth not my voice is not acquainted with *a*my voice, and is not of me.

53 And by this you may know the righteous from the wicked, and that the whole *a*world *b*groaneth under sin and darkness even now.

54 And your *a*minds in times past have been *b*darkened because of *c*unbelief, and because you have treated *d*lightly the things you have received—

55 Which *a*vanity and unbelief have brought the whole church under condemnation.

56 And this condemnation resteth upon the children of *a*Zion, even all.

57 And they shall remain under this condemnation until they repent and

44*a* Lev. 18:5; Deut. 8:3;
     Matt. 4:4; D&C 98:11.
45*a* Ps. 33:4; 117:2.
     TG Truth.
   b D&C 67:9; 88:7 (6–13).
     TG Jesus Christ, Light of
     the World.
   c TG God, Spirit of.
46*a* Ezek. 36:27.
   b Rom. 2:15 (6–16).
     TG Conscience; Intelli-
     gence; Light of Christ.
   c John 1:9; D&C 93:2.
47*a* Moro. 7:13 (12–13);

     D&C 35:12. TG Guid-
     ance, Divine.
48*a* TG Inspiration; Teach-
     ing.
   b D&C 1:22. TG Cove-
     nants.
   c Isa. 49:6.
49*a* 1 Jn. 5:19 (10–21).
   b TG Darkness, Spiritual.
   c TG Bondage, Spiritual.
50*a* Matt. 13:19 (18–19);
     2 Cor. 6:17; D&C 93:39
     (38–39).
51*a* Gal. 4:9. TG Sin.

52*a* John 10:27 (7–27).
53*a* TG World.
   b Rom. 8:22.
54*a* TG Mind.
   b TG Darkness, Spiritual;
     Light [noun].
   c TG Apostasy of Individu-
     als; Doubt; Unbelief.
   d TG Levity.
55*a* Isa. 3:16. TG Vanity.
56*a* Ps. 149:2; Joel 2:23;
     D&C 97:21.

remember the new ᵃcovenant, even the ᵇBook of Mormon and the ᶜformer commandments which I have given them, not only to say, but to ᵈdo according to that which I have written—

58 That they may bring forth ᵃfruit meet for their Father's kingdom; otherwise there remaineth a ᵇscourge and judgment to be poured out upon the children of Zion.

59 For shall the children of the kingdom ᵃpollute my holy land? Verily, I say unto you, Nay.

60 Verily, verily, I say unto you who now hear my ᵃwords, which are my voice, blessed are ye inasmuch as you receive these things;

61 For I will ᵃforgive you of your sins with this commandment—that you remain ᵇsteadfast in your minds in ᶜsolemnity and the spirit of prayer, in bearing ᵈtestimony to all the world of those things which are communicated unto you.

62 Therefore, ᵃgo ye into all the world; and unto whatsoever place ye cannot go ye shall send, that the testimony may go from you into all the world unto every creature.

63 And as I said unto mine apostles, even so I say unto you, for you are mine ᵃapostles, even God's high priests; ye are they whom my Father hath ᵇgiven me; ye are my ᶜfriends;

64 Therefore, as I said unto mine apostles I say unto you again, that every ᵃsoul who ᵇbelieveth on your words, and is baptized by water for the ᶜremission of sins, shall ᵈreceive the Holy Ghost.

65 And these ᵃsigns shall follow them that believe—

66 In my name they shall do many wonderful ᵃworks;

67 In my ᵃname they shall cast out devils;

68 In my name they shall ᵃheal the sick;

---

57 a Jer. 31:31 (31–34).
  b TG Book of Mormon.
  c Zech. 7:7; Luke 16:29 (29–31); 1 Ne. 13:40.
  d James 1:22 (22–25); D&C 42:13 (13–29).
58 a Luke 6:44. TG Good Works; Mission of Latter-day Saints.
  b D&C 90:36. TG Punish.
59 a TG Pollution.
60 a D&C 18:34 (34–36).
61 a Ex. 34:7; Dan. 9:9; D&C 62:3. TG Forgive.
  b TG Dedication;

Steadfastness.
  c D&C 43:34; 88:121; 100:7.
  d TG Missionary Work.
62 a Mark 16:15; Acts 11:18; D&C 1:2. TG Israel, Mission of; Priesthood, Magnifying Callings within.
63 a TG Apostles.
  b John 6:37; 17:9; 3 Ne. 15:24; D&C 27:14; 50:41 (41–42).
  c Ex. 33:11; John 15:14 (13–15); Ether 12:39;

D&C 84:77; 88:62; 93:45.
64 a TG Soul.
  b Mark 16:16 (15–18). TG Believe.
  c TG Remission of Sins.
  d TG Holy Ghost, Gift of.
65 a Mark 16:17. TG Holy Ghost, Gifts of; Miracle; Signs.
66 a TG God, Works of.
67 a Matt. 7:22; 10:8; 17:21 (14–21).
68 a Luke 4:39. TG Heal.

69 In my name they shall ^aopen the eyes of the blind, and unstop the ears of the deaf;

70 And the tongue of the dumb shall speak;

71 And if any man shall administer ^apoison unto them it shall not hurt them;

72 And the ^apoison of a serpent shall not have power to harm them.

73 But a commandment I give unto them, that they shall not ^aboast themselves of these things, neither speak them before the world; for these things are given unto you for your profit and for salvation.

74 Verily, verily, I say unto you, they who believe not on your words, and are not ^abaptized in water in my name, for the ^bremission of their sins, that they may receive the Holy Ghost, shall be ^cdamned, and shall not come into my Father's kingdom where my Father and I am.

75 And this revelation unto you, and commandment, is in force from this very hour upon all the ^aworld, and the gospel is unto all who have not received it.

76 But, verily I say unto all those to whom the kingdom has been given— from you it ^amust be ^bpreached unto them, that they shall repent of their former evil works; for they are to be upbraided for their evil ^chearts of unbelief, and your brethren in Zion for their ^drebellion against you at the time I sent you.

77 And again I say unto you, my friends, for from henceforth I shall call you ^afriends, it is expedient that I give unto you this commandment, that ye become even as my friends in days when I was with them, traveling to preach the gospel in my power;

78 For I suffered them not to have ^apurse or scrip, neither two coats.

79 Behold, I ^asend you out to ^bprove the world, and the laborer is worthy of his ^chire.

80 And any man that shall go and preach this ^agospel of the kingdom, and fail not to continue ^bfaithful in all things, shall not be weary in mind,

---

69 a Matt. 9:28 (28–31);
20:30 (30–34); John 9:1
(1–4); Mosiah 3:5; 3 Ne.
17:9 (7–10). TG Sight.
71 a Mark 16:18.
72 a Acts 28:3 (3–9); D&C
24:13; 124:99 (98–100).
73 a Prov. 4:24; Rom. 3:27;
D&C 105:24. TG Boast.
74 a 2 Ne. 9:23; D&C
76:52 (50–52); 137:6.

TG Baptism, Essential.
b TG Remission of Sins.
c John 3:18; 12:48.
75 a TG Missionary Work;
Revelation; World.
76 a Isa. 49:6 (5–7).
b TG Priesthood, Magnify-
ing Callings within.
c TG Hardheartedness.
d IE in April 1832.
77 a D&C 84:63.

TG Friendship.
78 a Matt. 10:9 (9–10); Luke
10:4; 22:35 (35–36);
D&C 24:18.
79 a TG Delegation of Re-
sponsibility.
b TG Test.
c D&C 31:5.
80 a Matt. 9:35; JS—M 1:31.
b TG Dependability.

neither darkened, neither in body, limb, nor joint; and a ^chair of his head shall not fall to the ground unnoticed. And they shall not go hungry, neither athirst.

81 Therefore, take ye no ^athought for the morrow, for what ye shall eat, or what ye shall drink, or wherewithal ye shall be clothed.

82 For, ^aconsider the ^blilies of the field, how they grow, they toil not, neither do they spin; and the kingdoms of the world, in all their glory, are not arrayed like one of these.

83 For your ^aFather, who is in heaven, ^bknoweth that you have need of all these things.

84 Therefore, let the morrow take ^athought for the things of itself.

85 Neither take ye thought beforehand ^awhat ye shall say; but ^btreasure up in your minds continually the words of life, and it shall be ^cgiven you in the very hour that portion that shall be meted unto every man.

86 Therefore, let no man among you, for this commandment is unto all the ^afaithful who are called of God in the church unto the ministry, from this hour take purse or scrip, that goeth forth to proclaim this gospel of the kingdom.

87 Behold, I send you out to ^areprove the world of all their unrighteous deeds, and to teach them of a judgment which is to come.

88 And whoso ^areceiveth you, there I will be also, for I will go ^bbefore your face. I will be on your right hand and on your left, and my ^cSpirit shall be in your hearts, and mine ^dangels round about you, to bear you up.

89 Whoso receiveth you receiveth me; and the same will feed you, and clothe you, and give you money.

90 And he who feeds you, or clothes you, or gives you money, shall in nowise ^alose his reward.

91 And he that doeth not these things is not my disciple; by this you may know ^amy disciples.

92 He that receiveth you not, go away from him alone by yourselves, and ^acleanse your feet even with water, pure water, whether in heat or in cold,

---

80 c Luke 21:18.
81 a Matt. 6:25; Luke 12:22.
82 a Matt. 6:28.
   b TG Nature, Earth.
83 a TG Man, a Spirit Child
     of Heavenly Father.
   b Matt. 6:8, 32.
84 a Matt. 6:34.
85 a Matt. 10:19 (19–20);
     Luke 12:11 (11–12);
     21:14; D&C 100:6.
   b Alma 17:2 (2–3); Hel.

5:18 (18–19); D&C 6:20;
11:26 (21–26); 24:6;
100:5 (5–8). TG Meditation; Mind; Motivations;
Study.
   c TG Teaching with the
     Spirit.
86 a Matt. 24:45; D&C
     58:26 (26–29); 107:100
     (99–100).
87 a TG Missionary Work.
88 a Matt. 10:40 (40–42);

John 13:20; 3 Jn. 1:5
(1–14).
   b Ex. 23:23; Lev. 26:12
     (3–13); Judg. 4:14; Ether
     1:42 (42–43).
   c TG God, Spirit of.
   d D&C 84:42. TG Angels.
90 a Matt. 10:42; Mark 9:41.
91 a John 13:35.
92 a Matt. 10:14; Luke 9:5;
     D&C 60:15. TG Wash.

and bear testimony of it unto your Father which is in heaven, and return not again unto that man.

93 And in whatsoever village or city ye enter, do likewise.

94 Nevertheless, search diligently and spare not; and wo unto that house, or that village or city that rejecteth you, or your words, or your testimony concerning me.

95 Wo, I say again, unto that house, or that village or city that rejecteth you, or your words, or your testimony of me;

96 For I, the ^aAlmighty, have laid my hands upon the nations, to ^bscourge them for their ^cwickedness.

97 And ^aplagues shall go forth, and they shall not be taken from the earth until I have completed my work, which shall be cut ^bshort in righteousness—

98 Until all shall ^aknow me, who remain, even from the least unto the greatest, and shall be filled with the knowledge of the Lord, and shall ^bsee eye to eye, and shall lift up their voice, and with the voice together ^csing this new song, saying:

99 The Lord hath brought again Zion;
    The Lord hath ^aredeemed his people, ^bIsrael,
    According to the ^celection of ^dgrace,
    Which was brought to pass by the faith
    And ^ecovenant of their fathers.

100 The Lord hath redeemed his people;
    And Satan is ^abound and ^btime is no longer.
    The Lord hath gathered all things in ^cone.
    The Lord hath brought down ^dZion from above.
    The Lord hath ^ebrought up Zion from beneath.

101 The ^aearth hath travailed and ^bbrought forth her strength;
    And truth is established in her bowels;
    And the heavens have smiled upon her;
    And she is clothed with the ^cglory of her God;
    For he ^dstands in the midst of his ^epeople.

---

96 a TG God, Power of.
  b D&C 1:14 (13–14).
  c TG Wickedness.
97 a TG Plague.
  b Matt. 24:22.
98 a TG God, Knowledge about.
  b Isa. 52:8.
  c Ps. 96:1; Rev. 15:3; D&C 25:12; 133:56. TG Singing.

99 a Deut. 21:8; Ps. 25:22; Rom. 11:26 (25–28); D&C 43:29; 100:13; 136:18.
  b TG Israel, Restoration of.
  c TG Election.
  d TG Grace.
  e TG Abrahamic Covenant.
100 a Rev. 20:2 (2–3); D&C 43:31; 45:55; 88:110; 101:28.

  b Alma 40:8. TG Time.
  c Eph. 1:10; D&C 27:13.
  d D&C 45:12 (11–14); Moses 7:63 (62–64). TG Zion.
  e D&C 76:102; 88:96.
101 a TG Earth, Destiny of.
  b Moses 7:64 (54–67).
  c TG Glory.
  d TG God, Presence of.
  e Jer. 30:22.

102 Glory, and honor, and power, and might,

Be ascribed to our God; for he is full of ^amercy,

Justice, grace and truth, and ^bpeace,

Forever and ever, Amen.

103 And again, verily, verily, I say unto you, it is expedient that every man who goes forth to proclaim mine everlasting gospel, that inasmuch as they have ^afamilies, and receive ^bmoney by gift, that they should send it unto them or make use of it for their benefit, as the Lord shall direct them, for thus it seemeth me good.

104 And let all those who have not families, who receive ^amoney, send it up unto the bishop in Zion, or unto the bishop in Ohio, that it may be consecrated for the bringing forth of the revelations and the printing thereof, and for establishing Zion.

105 And if any man shall give unto any of you a coat, or a suit, take the old and cast it unto the ^apoor, and go on your way rejoicing.

106 And if any man among you be ^astrong in the Spirit, let him take with him him that is ^bweak, that he may be ^cedified in all ^dmeekness, that he may become strong also.

107 Therefore, take with you those who are ordained unto the ^alesser priesthood, and send them ^bbefore you to make appointments, and to prepare the way, and to fill appointments that you yourselves are not able to fill.

108 Behold, this is the way that mine apostles, in ancient days, built up my church unto me.

109 Therefore, let every man stand in his own ^aoffice, and ^blabor in his own calling; and let not the ^chead say unto the feet it hath no need of the feet; for without the feet how shall the body be able to stand?

110 Also the body hath need of every ^amember, that all may be ^bedified together, that the system may be kept perfect.

111 And behold, the ^ahigh priests should travel, and also the elders, and also the lesser ^bpriests; but the ^cdeacons and ^dteachers should be appointed to ^ewatch over the church, to be standing ministers unto the church.

---

102 *a* TG God, Mercy of.
    b TG Peace of God.
103 *a* TG Family.
    b TG Family, Managing Finances in.
104 *a* D&C 51:8 (8–13); 58:51 (49–51).
105 *a* TG Poor.
106 *a* TG Fellowshipping.
    b Rom. 14:1 (1–4, 10, 13).

    c TG Edification.
    d TG Meek.
107 *a* TG Priesthood, Aaronic.
    b Luke 10:1 (1–12).
109 *a* TG Church Organization.
    b TG Priesthood, Magnifying Callings within.
    c 1 Cor. 12:21.
110 *a* TG Church.

    b TG Edification.
111 *a* TG High Priest, Melchizedek Priesthood.
    b TG Priest, Aaronic Priesthood.
    c TG Deacon.
    d TG Teacher.
    e TG Watch.

112 And the bishop, Newel K. Whitney, also should travel round about and among all the churches, searching after the poor to "administer to their wants by "humbling the rich and the proud.

113 He should also employ an "agent to take charge and to do his secular business as he shall direct.

114 Nevertheless, let the bishop go unto the city of New York, also to the city of Albany, and also to the city of Boston, and warn the people of those "cities with the sound of the gospel, with a loud voice, of the "desolation and utter abolishment which await them if they do reject these things.

115 For if they do reject these things the hour of their judgment is nigh, and their house shall be left unto them "desolate.

116 Let him "trust in me and he shall not be "confounded; and a "hair of his head shall not fall to the ground unnoticed.

117 And verily I say unto you, the rest of my servants, go ye forth as your circumstances shall permit, in your several callings, unto the great and notable cities and villages, "reproving the world in righteousness of all their unrighteous and ungodly deeds, setting forth clearly and understandingly the desolation of "abomination in the last days.

118 For, with you saith the Lord "Almighty, I will "rend their "kingdoms; I will not only "shake the earth, but the "starry heavens shall tremble.

119 For I, the Lord, have put forth my hand to exert the "powers of heaven; ye cannot see it now, yet a "little while and ye shall see it, and know that I am, and that "I will "come and reign with my people.

120 I am "Alpha and Omega, the beginning and the end. Amen.

SECTION 85

Revelation given through Joseph Smith the Prophet, at Kirtland, Ohio, November 27, 1832. This section is an extract from a letter of the Prophet to William W. Phelps, who was living in Independence, Missouri. It answers questions about those Saints who had moved to Zion but who had not

112a TG Poor; Welfare.
 b D&C 56:16.
113a D&C 51:8 (8–12); 53:4;
 90:22.
114a Matt. 11:20; Alma 34:31
 (31–36); 3 Ne. 9:3.
 b D&C 1:13 (13–14).
115a Luke 13:35.
116a Prov. 28:25 (25–26);
 Isa. 50:10; D&C 11:12.
 TG Trust in God.
 b Ps. 22:5; 1 Pet. 2:6;

D&C 49:27.
 c Matt. 10:30; Luke 21:18.
117a Titus 1:13.
 b TG Abomination of
 Desolation; Warn.
118a TG God, Power of.
 b Dan. 2:44 (34–35,
 44–45).
 c TG Kings, Earthly.
 d Joel 2:10; D&C 43:18;
 45:33 (33, 48); 88:87 (87,
 90). TG Last Days.

e D&C 21:6.
119a Matt. 24:29.
 b Heb. 10:37.
 c Ex. 15:18.
 d D&C 1:36 (12, 35–36);
 29:11 (9–11); 45:59;
 104:59. TG Jesus Christ,
 Millennial Reign; Jesus
 Christ, Second Coming.
120a D&C 35:1.

followed the commandment to consecrate their properties and had thus not received their inheritances according to the established order in the Church.

1–5, Inheritances in Zion are to be received through consecration; 6–12, One mighty and strong will give the Saints their inheritance in Zion.

1 It is the duty of the Lord's clerk, whom he has appointed, to keep a *a*history, and a general church *b*record of all things that transpire in Zion, and of all those who *c*consecrate properties, and receive *d*inheritances legally from the bishop;

2 And also their manner of life, their faith, and works; and also of the *a*apostates who apostatize after receiving their inheritances.

3 It is contrary to the will and commandment of God that those who receive not their *a*inheritance by *b*consecration, agreeable to his *c*law, which he has given, that he may *d*tithe his people, to prepare them against the day of *e*vengeance and burning, should have their *f*names enrolled with the people of God.

4 Neither is their *a*genealogy to be kept, or to be had where it may be found on any of the records or history of the church.

5 Their names shall not be found, neither the names of the fathers, nor the names of the children written in the *a*book of the law of God, saith the Lord of Hosts.

6 Yea, thus saith the *a*still small voice, which whispereth through and *b*pierceth all things, and often times it maketh my bones to quake while it maketh manifest, saying:

7 And it shall come to pass that I, the Lord God, will send one mighty and strong, holding the scepter of power in his hand, clothed with light for a covering, whose mouth shall utter words, eternal words; while his bowels shall be a fountain of truth, to set in *a*order the house of God, and to arrange by *b*lot the *c*inheritances of the saints whose names are found, and the names of their fathers, and of their children, enrolled in the book of the law of God;

8 While that man, who was called of God and appointed, that putteth

85 1 *a* D&C 21:1; 47:1; 69:3 (3–8).
b TG Record Keeping.
c D&C 42:30 (30–35).
d D&C 51:3 (1–3); 90:30 (30–31).
2 *a* TG Apostasy of Individuals.
3 *a* Num. 34:13.
b D&C 42:30. TG Consecration.
c D&C 70:10.
d TG Tithing.
e Mal. 3:11 (11, 17); D&C 1:13 (13–14); 97:26.
f Mal. 3:16; D&C 20:82.
4 *a* Ezra 2:62 (62–63).
5 *a* TG Book of Life; Record Keeping.
6 *a* 1 Kgs. 19:12 (11–13); Job 4:16 (12–21); Hel. 5:30 (30–31); 3 Ne. 11:3 (3–6).
b Heb. 4:12.
7 *a* TG Order.
b Num. 33:54.
c D&C 64:30; 99:7.

forth his hand to ªsteady the ᵇark of God, shall fall by the shaft of death, like as a tree that is smitten by the vivid shaft of lightning.

9 And all they who are not found written in the ªbook of remembrance shall find none inheritance in that day, but they shall be cut asunder, and their portion shall be appointed them among ᵇunbelievers, where are ᶜwailing and gnashing of teeth.

10 These things I say not of ªmyself; therefore, as the Lord speaketh, he will also fulfil.

11 And they who are of the High Priesthood, whose names are not found written in the ªbook of the law, or that are found to have ᵇapostatized, or to have been ᶜcut off from the church, as well as the lesser priesthood, or the members, in that day shall ᵈnot find an inheritance among the saints of the Most High;

12 Therefore, it shall be done unto them as unto the ªchildren of the ᵇpriest, as will be found recorded in the second chapter and sixty-first and second verses of Ezra.

SECTION 86

Revelation given through Joseph Smith the Prophet, at Kirtland, Ohio, December 6, 1832. This revelation was received while the Prophet was reviewing and editing the manuscript of the translation of the Bible.

1–7, The Lord gives the meaning of the parable of the wheat and tares; 8–11, He explains priesthood blessings to those who are lawful heirs according to the flesh.

1 Verily, thus saith the Lord unto you my servants, concerning the ªparable of the ᵇwheat and of the tares:

2 Behold, verily I say, the field was the world, and the apostles were the ªsowers of the seed;

3 And after they have fallen asleep the great persecutor of the church, the apostate, the ªwhore, even ᵇBabylon, that maketh all nations to drink of

---

8 *a* Num. 1:51; D&C 64:17.
  b 2 Sam. 6:6 (6–7); 1 Chr. 13:10 (9–12). TG Ark of the Covenant.
9 *a* 3 Ne. 24:16; Moses 6:5. TG Book of Remembrance.
  b TG Unbelief.
  c D&C 19:5.
10 *a* D&C 1:38.

11 *a* TG Book of Life.
  b TG Apostasy of Individuals.
  c TG Excommunication; Worthiness.
  d D&C 51:5 (4–5).
12 *a* Ezra 2:61 (61–62); Neh. 7:63 (63–64).
  b TG Priesthood, Qualifying for.

86 1 *a* D&C 101:65 (64–75).
  b Matt. 13:36 (6–43).
2 *a* Matt. 13:37; Mark 4:3. TG Mission of Early Saints.
3 *a* TG Whore.
  b Rev. 17:5 (1–9). TG Babylon.

her cup, in whose hearts the enemy, even Satan, sitteth to reign—behold he soweth the ᶜtares; wherefore, the tares choke the wheat and drive the ᵈchurch into the wilderness.

4 But behold, in the ᵃlast days, even now while the Lord is beginning to bring forth the word, and the blade is springing up and is yet tender—

5 Behold, verily I say unto you, the ᵃangels are crying unto the Lord day and night, who are ready and waiting to be sent forth to ᵇreap down the fields;

6 But the Lord saith unto them, pluck not up the tares while the blade is yet tender (for verily your faith is weak), lest you destroy the wheat also.

7 Therefore, let the wheat and the ᵃtares grow together until the harvest is fully ripe; then ye shall first gather out the wheat from among the tares, and after the gathering of the wheat, behold and lo, the tares are bound in bundles, and the field remaineth to be ᵇburned.

8 Therefore, thus saith the Lord unto you, with whom the ᵃpriesthood hath continued through the lineage of your fathers—

9 For ye are lawful ᵃheirs, according to the flesh, and have been ᵇhid from the world with Christ in God—

10 Therefore your life and the ᵃpriesthood have remained, and must needs remain through you and your lineage until the ᵇrestoration of all things spoken by the mouths of all the holy prophets since the world began.

11 Therefore, blessed are ye if ye continue in my ᵃgoodness, a ᵇlight unto the Gentiles, and through this priesthood, a ᶜsavior unto my people ᵈIsrael. The Lord hath said it. Amen.

SECTION 87

Revelation and prophecy on war, given through Joseph Smith the Prophet, at or near Kirtland, Ohio, December 25, 1832. At this time disputes in the United States over slavery and South Carolina's nullification of federal tariffs were prevalent. Joseph Smith's history states that "appearances of troubles

3 c TG Apostasy of the Early
    Christian Church.
  d Rev. 12:6 (6, 14).
4 a TG Last Days.
5 a D&C 38:12.
  b TG Harvest.
7 a D&C 101:66.
  b Matt. 13:40; Rev. 18:8
    (6–8).
8 a D&C 113:8.

  TG Priesthood, History
    of.
9 a Abr. 2:9 (9–11). TG Abra-
    hamic Covenant; Birth-
    right; Seed of Abraham.
  b Col. 3:3 (3–4).
10 a TG Priesthood, Melchize-
    dek.
  b Acts 3:21; D&C 132:45.
    TG Restoration of the

    Gospel.
11 a Ex. 34:6 (5–7); 2 Ne.
    4:17; 9:10.
  b Isa. 49:6. TG Mission
    of Latter-day Saints;
    Peculiar People.
  c Obad. 1:21.
  d Neh. 1:10; D&C 109:59
    (59–67).

among the nations" were becoming "more visible" to the Prophet "than they had previously been since the Church began her journey out of the wilderness."

1–4, War is foretold between the Northern States and the Southern States; 5–8, Great calamities will fall upon all the inhabitants of the earth.

1 Verily, thus saith the Lord concerning the *a*wars that will *b*shortly come to pass, beginning at the rebellion of *c*South Carolina, which will eventually terminate in the death and misery of many souls;

2 And the *a*time will come that *b*war will be poured out upon all nations, beginning at this place.

3 For behold, the Southern States shall be divided against the Northern States, and the Southern States will call on other nations, even the nation of Great Britain, as it is called, and they shall also call upon other nations, in order to defend themselves against other nations; and then *a*war shall be poured out upon all nations.

4 And it shall come to pass, after many days, *a*slaves shall rise up against their masters, who shall be marshaled and disciplined for war.

5 And it shall come to pass also that the *a*remnants who are left of the land will marshal themselves, and shall become exceedingly angry, and shall vex the Gentiles with a sore vexation.

6 And thus, with the *a*sword and by bloodshed the inhabitants of the earth shall *b*mourn; and with *c*famine, and plague, and earthquake, and the thunder of heaven, and the fierce and vivid lightning also, shall the inhabitants of the earth be made to feel the wrath, and indignation, and *d*chastening *e*hand of an Almighty God, until the consumption decreed hath made a full *f*end of all *g*nations;

7 That the cry of the saints, and of the *a*blood of the saints, shall cease to come up into the ears of the Lord of *b*Sabaoth, from the earth, to be avenged of their enemies.

8 Wherefore, *a*stand ye in holy places, and be not moved, until the day of the Lord come; for behold, it cometh *b*quickly, saith the Lord. Amen.

---

87 1 *a* D&C 45:26.
  b JS—H 1:41 (40–41).
  c D&C 130:12 (12–13).
 2 *a* TG Last Days.
  b Joel 3:9 (9–16); Matt.
    24:6 (6–7); D&C 38:29;
    45:63 (26, 63); 63:33;
    130:12.
 3 *a* D&C 45:69.
 4 *a* D&C 134:12.
 5 *a* Micah 5:8 (8–15); 3 Ne.

  16:15 (7–15); 20:16
    (15–21); 21:12 (12–21);
    D&C 109:65 (65–67).
    TG Israel, Remnant of.
 6 *a* Deut. 32:41; 2 Ne. 1:12.
  b D&C 29:15 (14–21);
    45:49. TG Mourning.
  c Joel 1:10; D&C 43:25
    (24–25); JS—M 1:29.
    TG Drought; Famine;
    Plague.
  d TG Chastening.

  e Ether 1:1.
  f TG World, End of.
  g Mark 13:8; 1 Ne. 14:15.
 7 *a* Rev. 6:10 (1, 10); 19:2;
    2 Ne. 28:10; Morm. 8:27
    (27, 40–41); Ether 8:22
    (22–24).
  b James 5:4; D&C 88:2;
    95:7.
 8 *a* Matt. 24:15; D&C 45:32;
    101:22 (21–22, 64).
  b Rev. 3:11; D&C 1:12.

SECTION 88

Revelation given through Joseph Smith the Prophet at Kirtland, Ohio, December 27 and 28, 1832, and January 3, 1833. The Prophet designated it as the "'olive leaf'... plucked from the Tree of Paradise, the Lord's message of peace to us." The revelation was given after high priests at a conference prayed "separately and vocally to the Lord to reveal his will unto us concerning the upbuilding of Zion."

1–5, Faithful Saints receive that Comforter, which is the promise of eternal life; 6–13, All things are controlled and governed by the Light of Christ; 14–16, The Resurrection comes through the Redemption; 17–31, Obedience to celestial, terrestrial, or telestial law prepares men for those respective kingdoms and glories; 32–35, Those who will to abide in sin remain filthy still; 36–41, All kingdoms are governed by law; 42–45, God has given a law unto all things; 46–50, Man will comprehend even God; 51–61, The parable of the man sending his servants into the field and visiting them in turn; 62–73, Draw near unto the Lord, and ye will see His face; 74–80, Sanctify yourselves and teach one another the doctrines of the kingdom; 81–85, Every man who has been warned should warn his neighbor; 86–94, Signs, upheavals of the elements, and angels prepare the way for the coming of the Lord; 95–102, Angelic trumps call forth the dead in their order; 103–16, Angelic trumps proclaim the restoration of the gospel, the fall of Babylon, and the battle of the great God; 117–26, Seek learning, establish a house of God (a temple), and clothe yourselves with the bond of charity; 127–41, The order of the School of the Prophets is set forth, including the ordinance of washing of feet.

1 Verily, thus saith the Lord unto you who have assembled yourselves together to receive his will concerning you:

2 Behold, this is pleasing unto your Lord, and the angels *a*rejoice over you; the *b*alms of your prayers have come up into the ears of the Lord of *c*Sabaoth, and are recorded in the *d*book of the names of the sanctified, even them of the celestial world.

3 Wherefore, I now send upon you another *a*Comforter, even upon you my friends, that it may abide in your hearts, even the Holy Spirit of *b*promise; which other Comforter is the same that I promised unto my disciples, as is recorded in the testimony of John.

4 This Comforter is the *a*promise which I give unto you of *b*eternal life, even the *c*glory of the celestial kingdom;

---

88 2 *a* Luke 15:7 (7–10).
  b Acts 10:2 (1–4); D&C 112:1. TG Almsgiving; Prayer.
  c James 5:4; D&C 87:7;

95:7.
  d TG Book of Life.
3 *a* John 14:16.
  b 2 Pet. 1:19; D&C 76:53; 132:19 (19, 26, 49).

4 *a* 1 Jn. 2:25.
  b D&C 14:7; 131:5.
  c TG Celestial Glory.

5 Which glory is that of the church of the *Firstborn, even of God, the holiest of all, through Jesus Christ his Son—

6 He that *ascended up on high, as also he *descended below all things, in that he *comprehended all things, that he might be in all and through all things, the *light of truth;

7 Which truth shineth. This is the *light of Christ. As also he is in the sun, and the light of the sun, and the power thereof by which it was *made.

8 As also he is in the moon, and is the light of the moon, and the power thereof by which it was made;

9 As also the light of the stars, and the power thereof by which they were made;

10 And the earth also, and the power thereof, even the earth upon which you *stand.

11 And the light which shineth, which giveth you light, is through him who enlighteneth your eyes, which is the same light that quickeneth your *understandings;

12 Which *light proceedeth forth from the presence of God to *fill the immensity of space—

13 The *light which is in all things, which giveth *life to all things, which is the *law by which all things are governed, even the *power of God who *sitteth upon his throne, who is in the bosom of eternity, who is in the midst of all things.

14 Now, verily I say unto you, that through the *redemption which is made for you is brought to pass the resurrection from the dead.

15 And the *spirit and the *body are the *soul of man.

16 And the *resurrection from the dead is the redemption of the soul.

17 And the redemption of the soul is through him that *quickeneth all

---

5 *a* D&C 77:11.
6 *a* Ps. 68:18; Eph. 4:8.
  b D&C 122:8. TG Jesus Christ, Condescension of.
  c TG God, Omniscience of.
  d D&C 93:2 (2, 8–39). TG Light [noun]; Truth.
7 *a* Moro. 7:19 (15–19); D&C 84:45; 93:36. TG God, Spirit of; Light of Christ.
  b Gen. 1:16. TG Creation; Jesus Christ, Creator;

Jesus Christ, Power of.
10 *a* Moses 2:1.
11 *a* TG Understanding.
12 *a* 1 Tim. 6:16. TG Light of Christ.
  b Ps. 139:7 (7–12); Jer. 23:24.
13 *a* Col. 1:17 (16–17).
  b Deut. 30:20; D&C 10:70. TG Jesus Christ, Creator.
  c Job 38:33 (1–41); D&C 88:38 (36–38). TG God, Law of.
  d 2 Cor. 4:7. TG Jesus

Christ, Power of.
  e Ps. 47:8; Rev. 7:15.
14 *a* TG Jesus Christ, Atonement through; Redemption; Resurrection.
15 *a* TG Man, a Spirit Child of Heavenly Father; Spirit Body; Spirit Creation.
  b TG Body, Sanctity of.
  c Gen. 2:7; Ezek. 37:14 (6–14); Alma 40:23 (16–24). TG Soul.
16 *a* Alma 11:45 (40–45).
17 *a* 1 Tim. 6:13.

things, in whose bosom it is decreed that the [b]poor and the [c]meek of the [d]earth shall inherit it.

18 Therefore, it must needs be [a]sanctified from all [b]unrighteousness, that it may be prepared for the [c]celestial glory;

19 For after it hath filled the measure of its creation, it shall be crowned with [a]glory, even with the presence of God the Father;

20 That bodies who are of the [a]celestial kingdom may [b]possess it forever and ever; for, for this [c]intent was it made and created, and for this intent are they [d]sanctified.

21 And they who are not [a]sanctified through the [b]law which I have given unto you, even the law of Christ, must inherit [c]another kingdom, even that of a terrestrial kingdom, or that of a telestial kingdom.

22 For he who is not able to abide the [a]law of a celestial kingdom cannot [b]abide a [c]celestial glory.

23 And he who cannot abide the law of a [a]terrestrial kingdom cannot abide a terrestrial glory.

24 And he who cannot abide the law of a [a]telestial [b]kingdom cannot abide a telestial [c]glory; therefore he is not meet for a kingdom of glory. Therefore he must abide a kingdom which is not a kingdom of glory.

25 And again, verily I say unto you, the [a]earth abideth the law of a celestial kingdom, for it filleth the [b]measure of its creation, and transgresseth not the law—

26 Wherefore, it shall be [a]sanctified; yea, notwithstanding it shall [b]die, it shall be [c]quickened again, and shall abide the power by which it is quickened, and the [d]righteous shall [e]inherit it.

27 For notwithstanding they die, they also shall [a]rise again, a [b]spiritual body.

28 They who are of a celestial [a]spirit shall receive the same [b]body which

17 b Luke 6:20; D&C 104:16.
   TG Poor.
   c Zeph. 2:3 (1–3); Matt. 5:5; D&C 38:20.
   TG Meek.
   d TG Earth, Destiny of.
18 a TG Earth, Purpose of.
   b Gen. 6:11; Moses 8:28 (28–30).
   c TG Celestial Glory.
19 a D&C 130:7 (7–9).
   TG Earth, Destiny of.
20 a TG Earth, Purpose of.
   b D&C 38:20.
   c Moses 1:39. TG Man,

Potential to Become like Heavenly Father.
   d TG Man, New, Spiritually Reborn.
21 a TG Sanctification.
   b TG God, Law of.
   c D&C 43:33 (18, 33); 76:112 (102, 112).
22 a D&C 105:5.
   b D&C 76:118.
   c TG Celestial Glory.
23 a TG Terrestrial Glory.
24 a TG Telestial Glory.
   b D&C 76:44 (44–48).
   c Moses 1:13.

25 a TG Earth, Destiny of.
   b 2 Ne. 2:12.
26 a TG Sanctification.
   b TG World, End of.
   c TG Earth, Renewal of.
   d 2 Pet. 3:13 (11–13).
   TG Righteousness.
   e Matt. 5:5; D&C 38:20; 45:58; 56:20; 57:5; 59:2; 63:20 (20, 48–49).
27 a TG Resurrection.
   b 1 Cor. 15:44.
28 a TG Spirit Body.
   b TG Body, Sanctity of.

was a natural body; even ye shall receive your bodies, and your ^cglory shall be that glory by which your bodies are ^dquickened.

29 Ye who are ^aquickened by a portion of the ^bcelestial glory shall then receive of the same, even a fulness.

30 And they who are quickened by a portion of the ^aterrestrial glory shall then receive of the same, even a fulness.

31 And also they who are quickened by a portion of the ^atelestial glory shall then receive of the same, even a fulness.

32 And they who remain shall also be ^aquickened; nevertheless, they shall return again to their own place, to enjoy that which they are ^bwilling to receive, because they were not willing to enjoy that which they might have received.

33 For what doth it profit a man if a gift is bestowed upon him, and he receive not the gift? Behold, he rejoices not in that which is given unto him, neither rejoices in him who is the giver of the gift.

34 And again, verily I say unto you, that which is ^agoverned by law is also preserved by law and perfected and ^bsanctified by the same.

35 That which ^abreaketh a law, and ^babideth not by ^claw, but seeketh to become a law unto itself, and willeth to abide in sin, and altogether abideth in sin, cannot be sanctified by law, neither by mercy, ^djustice, nor ^ejudgment. Therefore, they must remain ^ffilthy still.

36 All kingdoms have a law given;

37 And there are many ^akingdoms; for there is no ^bspace in the which there is no ^ckingdom; and there is no kingdom in which there is no space, either a greater or a lesser kingdom.

38 And unto every kingdom is given a ^alaw; and unto every law there are certain bounds also and conditions.

39 All beings who abide not in those ^aconditions are not ^bjustified.

40 For ^aintelligence cleaveth unto intelligence; ^bwisdom receiveth wisdom;

---

28 c TG Judgment, the Last.
   d 1 Cor. 15:35; D&C
      43:32; 63:51; 101:31.
29 a D&C 76:70 (50–70).
   TG Celestial Glory.
   b TG Man, Potential to
      Become like Heavenly
      Father.
30 a D&C 76:71 (71–80).
   TG Terrestrial Glory.
31 a D&C 76:81 (81–90, 98).
   TG Telestial Glory.

32 a Alma 11:41 (41–45);
      D&C 76:39.
   b TG Agency.
34 a TG Governments; Order.
   b TG Sanctification.
35 a TG Disobedience.
   b TG Rebellion.
   c Prov. 28:9.
   d TG God, Justice of.
   e TG Judgment.
   f Rev. 22:11; 1 Ne. 15:33
      (33–35); 2 Ne. 9:16;

Alma 7:21; Morm. 9:14.
      TG Filthiness.
37 a D&C 76:24; Moses 1:33.
   b TG Astronomy.
   c TG Order.
38 a Job 38:33 (1–41); D&C
      88:13. TG God, Law of.
39 a D&C 130:21 (20–21).
   b TG Justification.
40 a TG Intelligence.
   b TG Wisdom.

*truth embraceth truth; *virtue loveth virtue; *light cleaveth unto light; *mercy hath *compassion on mercy and claimeth her own; *justice continueth its course and claimeth its own; judgment goeth before the face of him who sitteth upon the throne and governeth and executeth all things.

41 He *comprehendeth all things, and all things are before him, and all things are round about him; and he is above all things, and in all things, and is through all things, and is round about all things; and all things are by him, and of him, even God, forever and ever.

42 And again, verily I say unto you, he hath given a *law unto all things, by which they move in their *times and their seasons;

43 And their courses are fixed, even the courses of the heavens and the earth, which comprehend the earth and all the planets.

44 And they give *light to each other in their times and in their seasons, in their minutes, in their hours, in their days, in their weeks, in their months, in their years—all these are *one year with God, but not with man.

45 The earth *rolls upon her wings, and the *sun giveth his light by day, and the moon giveth her light by night, and the stars also give their light, as they roll upon their wings in their glory, in the midst of the *power of God.

46 Unto what shall I liken these kingdoms, that ye may understand?

47 Behold, all these are *kingdoms, and any man who hath *seen any or the least of these hath *seen God *moving in his majesty and power.

48 I say unto you, he hath seen him; nevertheless, he who came unto his *own was not comprehended.

49 The *light shineth in darkness, and the darkness comprehendeth it not; nevertheless, the day shall come when you shall *comprehend even God, being quickened in him and by him.

50 Then shall ye know that ye have *seen me, that I am, and that I am the true *light that is in you, and that you are in me; otherwise ye could not abound.

---

40 c TG Truth.
  d TG Chastity; Virtue.
  e TG Light [noun].
  f TG Mercy.
  g TG Compassion.
  h TG God, Justice of;
    Justice.
41 a Job 22:13 (13–14); Ps.
    94:9 (7–10); D&C 38:2;
    Moses 1:35 (35–37);
    7:36; Abr. 3:2 (1–16).
    TG God, Intelligence of;
    God, Omniscience of;
    God, Perfection of.

42 a Dan. 2:21 (19–22, 28);
    Abr. 3:9. TG God, Law
    of; Order.
  b Abr. 3:4 (4–19). TG Na-
    ture, Earth; Time.
44 a TG Light [noun].
  b Ps. 90:4; 2 Pet. 3:8.
45 a Hel. 12:15 (8–15).
  b Gen. 1:16; D&C 76:71
    (70–71); Abr. 4:16.
  c D&C 88:13 (7–13).
47 a D&C 88:61.
  b Moses 1:27 (27–28);
    7:23; Abr. 3:21 (21–23).

  c Alma 30:44; Moses 6:63.
  d D&C 76:114.
48 a John 1:11.
49 a D&C 6:21; 50:24
    (23–24); 67:9; 84:45
    (45–47).
  b John 17:3; D&C 93:28;
    101:32 (32–34). TG Rev-
    elation.
50 a John 14:7.
  b Dan. 2:22. TG Light of
    Christ.

51 Behold, I will liken these kingdoms unto a man having a field, and he sent forth his servants into the field to dig in the field.

52 And he said unto the first: Go ye and labor in the field, and in the first hour I will come unto you, and ye shall behold the joy of my countenance.

53 And he said unto the second: Go ye also into the field, and in the second hour I will visit you with the joy of my countenance.

54 And also unto the third, saying: I will visit you;

55 And unto the fourth, and so on unto the twelfth.

56 And the lord of the field went unto the first in the first hour, and tarried with him all that hour, and he was made glad with the light of the countenance of his lord.

57 And then he withdrew from the first that he might visit the second also, and the third, and the fourth, and so on unto the twelfth.

58 And thus they all received the light of the countenance of their lord, every man in his hour, and in his time, and in his season—

59 Beginning at the first, and so on unto the *a*last, and from the last unto the first, and from the first unto the last;

60 Every man in his own *a*order, until his hour was finished, even according as his lord had commanded him, that his lord might be glorified in him, and he in his lord, that they all might be glorified.

61 Therefore, unto this parable I will liken all these *a*kingdoms, and the *b*inhabitants thereof—every kingdom in its hour, and in its time, and in its season, even according to the decree which God hath made.

62 And again, verily I say unto you, my *a*friends, I leave these *b*sayings with you to *c*ponder in your hearts, with this commandment which I give unto you, that ye shall *d*call upon me while I am near—

63 *a*Draw *b*near unto me and I will draw near unto you; *c*seek me diligently and ye shall *d*find me; ask, and ye shall receive; knock, and it shall be opened unto you.

64 Whatsoever ye *a*ask the Father in my name it shall be given unto you, that is *b*expedient for you;

---

59 *a* Matt. 20:8 (1–16).
60 *a* TG Order.
61 *a* D&C 88:47.
    b D&C 76:24.
62 *a* Ex. 33:11; Ether 12:39;
      D&C 84:63; 93:45.
    b Deut. 6:6.
    c TG Meditation.
    d Isa. 55:6; James 1:5

      (5–6); D&C 46:7.
63 *a* Ps. 69:18; Zech. 1:3
      (3–4); James 4:8; Rev.
      3:20 (20–21). TG God,
      Access to; God, Presence
      of.
    b Deut. 4:7; Lam. 3:57;
      Ezek. 36:9 (8–15).
    c 1 Chr. 28:9; Ezra 8:22

      (22–23); Ether 12:41;
      D&C 101:38; Abr. 2:12.
    d 2 Chr. 15:15; D&C 4:7;
      49:26.
64 *a* TG Communication;
      Prayer.
    b D&C 18:18.

65 And if ye ask anything that is not *expedient for you, it shall turn unto your *condemnation.

66 Behold, that which you hear is as the *voice of one crying in the wilderness—in the wilderness, because you cannot see him—my voice, because my voice is *Spirit; my Spirit is truth; *truth abideth and hath no end; and if it be in you it shall abound.

67 And if your eye be *single to my *glory, your whole bodies shall be filled with light, and there shall be no darkness in you; and that body which is filled with light *comprehendeth all things.

68 Therefore, *sanctify yourselves that your *minds become *single to God, and the days will come that you shall *see him; for he will unveil his face unto you, and it shall be in his own time, and in his own way, and according to his own will.

69 Remember the great and last promise which I have made unto you; cast away your *idle thoughts and your *excess of *laughter far from you.

70 Tarry ye, tarry ye in this place, and call a *solemn assembly, even of those who are the first *laborers in this last kingdom.

71 And let those whom they have warned in their traveling call on the Lord, and *ponder the *warning in their hearts which they have received, for a little season.

72 Behold, and lo, I will take care of your *flocks, and will raise up elders and send unto them.

73 Behold, I will *hasten my work in its time.

74 And I give unto you, who are the first *laborers in this last kingdom, a commandment that you assemble yourselves together, and organize yourselves, and prepare yourselves, and *sanctify yourselves; yea, purify your

---

65 *a* Rom. 8:26 (26–27);
James 4:3; D&C 46:28
(28–30).
 b D&C 63:11 (7–12).
66 *a* Ps. 95:7; Isa. 40:3;
1 Ne. 17:13; Alma 5:37
(37–38); D&C 65:3;
97:1; 128:20.
 b TG God, Spirit of.
 c TG Truth.
67 *a* Matt. 6:22; D&C
82:19. TG Dedication;
Motivations; Priesthood,
Magnifying Callings
within.
 b John 7:18.
 c Prov. 28:5; D&C 93:28.

TG Discernment, Spiritual.
68 *a* TG Man, New, Spiritually Reborn; Sanctification.
 b TG Mind.
 c Luke 11:34 (34–36).
TG Commitment.
 d Lev. 9:4; D&C 67:10
(10–12); 93:1; 97:16.
TG God, Privilege of
Seeing.
69 *a* Matt. 12:36; Alma 12:14.
 b TG Rioting and Reveling;
Temperance.
 c 1 Pet. 4:3; D&C 59:15;
88:121. TG Laughter;

Levity.
70 *a* D&C 88:117 (117–19);
124:39. TG Solemn
Assembly.
 b TG Missionary Work.
71 *a* D&C 101:78.
TG Agency.
 b TG Warn.
72 *a* TG Church; Sheep;
Shepherd.
73 *a* Isa. 60:22 (1–22).
74 *a* Matt. 9:37; 20:1.
 b Lev. 20:7 (7–8); 2 Chr.
35:6; Neh. 12:30; 3 Ne.
19:28 (28–29); D&C
50:29 (28–29); 133:62.

hearts, and ^ccleanse your hands and your feet before me, that I may make you ^dclean;

75 That I may testify unto your ^aFather, and your God, and my ^bGod, that you are clean from the ^cblood of this wicked generation; that I may fulfil this promise, this great and last ^dpromise, which I have made unto you, when I will.

76 Also, I give unto you a commandment that ye shall continue in ^aprayer and fasting from this time forth.

77 And I give unto you a commandment that you shall ^ateach one another the ^bdoctrine of the kingdom.

78 Teach ye diligently and my ^agrace shall attend you, that you may be ^binstructed more perfectly in theory, in principle, in doctrine, in the law of the gospel, in all things that pertain unto the kingdom of God, that are expedient for you to understand;

79 Of things both in ^aheaven and in the earth, and under the earth; things which have been, things which are, things which must ^bshortly come to pass; things which are at home, things which are abroad; the wars and the perplexities of the ^cnations, and the judgments which are on the land; and a ^dknowledge also of countries and of kingdoms—

80 That ye may be prepared in all things when I shall send you again to ^amagnify the calling whereunto I have called you, and the ^bmission with which I have commissioned you.

81 Behold, I sent you out to ^atestify and warn the people, and it becometh every man who hath been warned to ^bwarn his neighbor.

82 Therefore, they are left ^awithout excuse, and their sins are upon their ^bown heads.

83 He that ^aseeketh me ^bearly shall find me, and shall not be forsaken.

84 Therefore, tarry ye, and labor diligently, that you may be perfected in your ministry to go forth among the ^aGentiles for the last time, as many

---

74 c D&C 88:139; 124:37.
  TG Cleanliness; Wash.
  d Ether 12:37; D&C 135:5
  (4–5).
75 a TG Man, a Spirit Child
  of Heavenly Father.
  b TG Jesus Christ, Relationships with the Father.
  c Acts 2:40; D&C 88:138.
  d TG Promise.
76 a 4 Ne. 1:12; Moro. 6:5.
  TG Fast, Fasting; Prayer.
77 a Ex. 35:34; Moro. 10:9
  (9–10); D&C 38:23;

43:8; 107:85 (85–89).
  TG Teaching.
  b Titus 2:1.
78 a TG Grace.
  b D&C 88:118; 90:15;
  93:53. TG Education.
79 a TG Heaven.
  b Rev. 1:1; 22:6.
  c TG Nations; War.
  d TG Knowledge.
80 a TG Priesthood, Magnifying Callings within.
  b TG Mission of Latter-day
  Saints.

81 a TG Testimony.
  b Ex. 18:20; Ezra 7:25;
  Ezek. 33:6 (6–9); D&C
  63:58. TG Warn; Watch-
  man.
82 a Rom. 1:20 (17–21).
  b Acts 18:6.
83 a Deut. 4:29 (29–31); Isa.
  26:9; Jer. 29:13 (10–14);
  D&C 54:10.
  b TG Procrastination.
84 a Isa. 42:6; D&C 133:37
  (37–60); JS—H 1:41.

as the mouth of the Lord shall name, to [b]bind up the law and [c]seal up the testimony, and to prepare the saints for the hour of judgment which is to come;

85 That their souls may escape the wrath of God, the [a]desolation of abomination which awaits the wicked, both in this world and in the world to come. Verily, I say unto you, let those who are not the [b]first elders continue in the vineyard until the mouth of the Lord shall [c]call them, for their time is not yet come; their garments are not [d]clean from the blood of this generation.

86 Abide ye in the [a]liberty wherewith ye are made [b]free; [c]entangle not yourselves in [d]sin, but let your hands be [e]clean, until the Lord comes.

87 For not many days hence and the [a]earth shall [b]tremble and reel to and fro as a drunken man; and the [c]sun shall [d]hide his face, and shall refuse to give light; and the moon shall be bathed in [e]blood; and the stars shall become exceedingly angry, and shall [f]cast themselves down as a fig that falleth from off a fig tree.

88 And after your [a]testimony cometh wrath and indignation upon the people.

89 For after your testimony cometh the testimony of [a]earthquakes, that shall cause groanings in the midst of her, and men shall fall upon the ground and shall not be able to stand.

90 And also cometh the testimony of the [a]voice of thunderings, and the voice of lightnings, and the voice of tempests, and the voice of the waves of the sea heaving themselves beyond their bounds.

91 And all things shall be in [a]commotion; and surely, men's [b]hearts shall fail them; for fear shall come upon all people.

92 And [a]angels shall fly through the midst of heaven, crying with a loud voice, sounding the trump of God, saying: Prepare ye, prepare ye, O

84 b Isa. 8:16 (16–17).
  c TG Seal.
85 a Dan. 9:27; Matt. 24:15.
    TG Abomination of Desolation.
  b D&C 20:2 (2, 5); 105:7 (7, 33).
  c D&C 11:15.
  d Lev. 6:11 (10–11); 1 Ne. 12:10 (10–11); Jacob 1:19; 2:2; D&C 4:2; 112:33. TG Purification.
86 a 1 Cor. 7:22; Mosiah 5:8. TG Liberty.

  b John 8:36; Alma 61:9 (9, 21). TG Agency.
  c Gal. 5:1.
  d TG Bondage, Spiritual; Sin.
  e Job 17:9; 2 Ne. 25:16. TG Chastity; Cleanliness; Purification; Worthiness.
87 a Isa. 13:13 (4–13); 14:26 (22–26).
  b D&C 43:18; 45:33; 84:118; 133:22.
  c Joel 2:10; D&C 45:42; 133:49.

  d D&C 29:14.
  e Rev. 6:12.
  f Joel 3:15; Rev. 8:12.
88 a TG Testimony.
89 a Rev. 11:13 (13–14); D&C 45:33.
90 a Joel 2:11; Rev. 8:5; D&C 35:21; 43:18 (17–25); 133:50 (50–52).
91 a D&C 45:26; 63:33.
  b Luke 21:26. TG Fearful; Last Days.
92 a Rev. 8:13; D&C 43:18 (18, 25); 133:17.

inhabitants of the earth; for the [b]judgment of our God is come. Behold, and lo, the [c]Bridegroom cometh; go ye out to meet him.

93 And immediately there shall appear a [a]great sign in heaven, and all people shall see it together.

94 And another angel shall sound his trump, saying: That [a]great [b]church, the [c]mother of abominations, that made all nations drink of the wine of the wrath of her [d]fornication, that [e]persecuteth the saints of God, that shed their blood—she who sitteth upon many waters, and upon the islands of the sea—behold, she is the [f]tares of the earth; she is bound in bundles; her bands are made strong, no man can loose them; therefore, she is ready to be burned. And he shall sound his trump both long and loud, and all nations shall hear it.

95 And there shall be [a]silence in [b]heaven for the space of half an hour; and immediately after shall the curtain of heaven be unfolded, as a [c]scroll is unfolded after it is rolled up, and the [d]face of the Lord shall be unveiled;

96 And the saints that are upon the earth, who are alive, shall be quickened and be [a]caught up to meet him.

97 And they who have slept in their graves shall [a]come forth, for their graves shall be opened; and they also shall be caught up to meet him in the midst of the [b]pillar of heaven—

98 They are Christ's, the [a]first fruits, they who shall descend with him first, and they who are on the earth and in their graves, who are first caught up to meet him; and all this by the voice of the sounding of the trump of the angel of God.

99 And after this another angel shall sound, which is the second trump; and then cometh the redemption of those who are Christ's at his [a]coming; who have received their part in that [b]prison which is prepared for them, that they might receive the gospel, and be [c]judged according to men in the flesh.

100 And again, another trump shall sound, which is the third trump; and

---

92 b TG Jesus Christ, Judge.
  c Matt. 25:6; D&C 33:17;
    133:19 (10, 19).
93 a Matt. 24:30; Luke 21:25
    (25–27). TG Signs.
94 a 1 Ne. 13:6 (4–9).
  b TG Devil, Church of.
  c Rev. 17:5 (5–15).
  d Rev. 14:8.
  e TG Hate; Persecution.
  f Matt. 13:38; D&C 64:24

(23–24); 101:24 (23–25).
    TG Earth, Cleansing of.
95 a D&C 38:12.
  b D&C 133:40 (40–46).
  c Rev. 6:14.
  d TG Jesus Christ, Second
    Coming.
96 a 1 Thes. 4:16 (16–17);
    D&C 76:102; 84:100;
    101:31.
97 a 1 Thes. 2:19; D&C

29:13; 45:45 (45–46);
    133:56. TG Resurrection.
  b D&C 78:21.
98 a 1 Cor. 15:23 (1–58).
99 a TG Jesus Christ, Second
    Coming.
  b D&C 76:73 (71–74);
    138:8; Moses 7:57.
    TG Salvation for the
    Dead; Spirits in Prison.
  c 1 Pet. 4:6.

then come the *aspirits of men who are to be judged, and are found under *bcondemnation;

101 And these are the rest of the *adead; and they live not again until the *bthousand years are ended, neither again, until the end of the earth.

102 And another trump shall sound, which is the fourth trump, saying: There are found among those who are to remain until that great and last day, even the end, who shall *aremain *bfilthy still.

103 And another trump shall sound, which is the fifth trump, which is the fifth angel who committeth the *aeverlasting gospel—flying through the midst of heaven, unto all nations, kindreds, tongues, and people;

104 And this shall be the sound of his trump, saying to all people, both in heaven and in earth, and that are under the earth—for *aevery ear shall hear it, and every knee shall *bbow, and every tongue shall confess, while they hear the sound of the trump, saying: *cFear God, and give glory to him who sitteth upon the throne, *dforever and ever; for the hour of his judgment is come.

105 And again, another angel shall sound his trump, which is the sixth angel, saying: She is *afallen who made all nations drink of the wine of the wrath of her fornication; she is fallen, is fallen!

106 And again, another angel shall sound his trump, which is the seventh angel, saying: It is finished; it is finished! The *aLamb of God hath *bovercome and *ctrodden the wine-press alone, even the wine-press of the fierceness of the wrath of Almighty God.

107 And then shall the angels be crowned with the glory of his might, and the *asaints shall be filled with his *bglory, and receive their *cinheritance and be made *dequal with him.

108 And then shall the first angel again sound his trump in the ears of all living, and *areveal the secret acts of men, and the mighty works of God in the *bfirst thousand years.

109 And then shall the second angel sound his trump, and reveal the secret acts of men, and the thoughts and intents of their hearts, and the mighty *aworks of God in the second thousand years—

---

100 a Rev. 20:13 (12–13);
    Alma 11:41; D&C 43:18;
    76:85.
  b TG Damnation.
101 a Rev. 20:5.
  b TG Millennium.
102 a D&C 43:18.
  b TG Filthiness.
103 a Rev. 14:6 (6–7). TG Res-
    toration of the Gospel.
104 a Ps. 86:9; Rev. 5:13.

  b Ps. 66:4; 72:9 (9–10);
    Mal. 1:11; Philip. 2:10
    (9–11).
  c Rev. 14:7. TG Reverence.
  d Heb. 1:8.
105 a Rev. 14:8; D&C 1:16.
106 a TG Jesus Christ, Lamb of
    God.
  b 1 Cor. 15:25.
  c Isa. 63:3 (3–4); Rev.
    14:20 (15–20); 19:15;

    D&C 76:107; 133:50
    (46–53).
107 a TG Angels; Saints.
  b TG Celestial Glory.
  c TG Exaltation.
  d John 5:18; D&C 76:95.
108 a Ps. 64:5 (4–6); Alma
    37:25; D&C 1:3.
  b D&C 77:6 (6–7, 12).
109 a TG God, Works of.

110 And so on, until the seventh angel shall sound his trump; and he shall ^astand forth upon the land and upon the sea, and ^bswear in the name of him who sitteth upon the throne, that there shall be ^ctime no longer; and ^dSatan shall be bound, that old serpent, who is called the devil, and shall not be loosed for the space of a ^ethousand years.

111 And then he shall be ^aloosed for a little season, that he may gather together his armies.

112 And ^aMichael, the seventh angel, even the archangel, shall gather together his armies, even the hosts of heaven.

113 And the devil shall gather together his ^aarmies; even the hosts of hell, and shall come up to battle against Michael and his armies.

114 And then cometh the ^abattle of the great God; and the devil and his armies shall be ^bcast away into their own place, that they shall not have power over the saints any more at all.

115 For Michael shall fight their battles, and shall overcome him who ^aseeketh the throne of him who sitteth upon the throne, even the Lamb.

116 This is the glory of God, and the ^asanctified; and they shall not any more see ^bdeath.

117 Therefore, verily I say unto you, my ^afriends, call your solemn assembly, as I have ^bcommanded you.

118 And as all have not ^afaith, seek ye diligently and ^bteach one another words of ^cwisdom; yea, seek ye out of the best ^dbooks words of wisdom; seek learning, even by study and also by faith.

119 ^aOrganize yourselves; prepare every needful thing; and establish a ^bhouse, even a house of prayer, a house of fasting, a house of faith, a house of learning, a house of glory, a house of order, a house of God;

120 That your ^aincomings may be in the name of the Lord; that your outgoings may be in the name of the Lord; that all your salutations may be in the name of the Lord, with ^buplifted hands unto the Most High.

---

110 a Rev. 10:5.
  b Dan. 12:7.
  c D&C 84:100.
  d Rev. 20:2 (1–10); 1 Ne. 22:26; D&C 101:28. TG Devil.
  e TG Millennium.
111 a Rev. 20:3 (3–10); Jacob 5:77 (76–77); D&C 29:22; 43:31 (30–31).
112 a TG Adam.
113 a Rev. 20:8.
114 a Rev. 16:14.
  b Rom. 16:20; 1 Jn. 3:8;

Rev. 20:10 (9–10); D&C 19:3; 29:28 (27–30, 44).
115 a Isa. 14:14 (12–15); Moses 4:1 (1–4).
116 a TG Saints; Sanctification.
  b Rev. 21:4; Alma 11:45; 12:18 (18, 20); D&C 63:49. TG Immortality.
117 a D&C 109:6.
  b D&C 88:70 (70–75).
118 a TG Faith.
  b Prov. 9:9; 23:12; D&C 88:78 (76–80); 90:15; 93:53. TG Education;

Learn; Study; Teaching.
  c TG Wisdom.
  d D&C 55:4; 97:3 (3–6); 109:7 (7, 14).
119 a TG Family, Managing Finances in; Priesthood, Magnifying Callings within.
  b Hag. 1:8; D&C 95:3; 97:12 (10–17); 109:8 (2–9); 115:8. TG Temple.
120 a Ezek. 43:11 (11–12).
  b Ps. 63:4; 134:2 (1–3).

121 Therefore, *a*cease from all your light speeches, from all *b*laughter, from all your *c*lustful desires, from all your *d*pride and light-mindedness, and from all your wicked doings.

122 Appoint among yourselves a teacher, and let *a*not all be spokesmen at once; but let one speak at a time and let all listen unto his sayings, that when all have spoken that all may be *b*edified of all, and that every man may have an equal privilege.

123 See that ye *a*love one another; cease to be *b*covetous; learn to impart one to another as the gospel requires.

124 Cease to be *a*idle; cease to be *b*unclean; cease to *c*find fault one with another; cease to *d*sleep longer than is needful; retire to thy bed early, that ye may not be weary; arise early, that your bodies and your minds may be *e*invigorated.

125 And above all things, clothe yourselves with the bond of *a*charity, as with a mantle, which is the bond of perfectness and *b*peace.

126 *a*Pray always, that ye may not faint, until I *b*come. Behold, and lo, I will come quickly, and receive you unto myself. Amen.

127 And again, the order of the house prepared for the *a*presidency of the *b*school of the *c*prophets, established for their instruction in all things that are expedient for them, even for all the *d*officers of the church, or in other words, those who are called to the ministry in the church, beginning at the high priests, even down to the deacons—

128 And this shall be the order of the house of the presidency of the school: He that is appointed to be president, or teacher, shall be found standing in his place, in the house which shall be prepared for him.

129 Therefore, he shall be first in the house of God, in a place that the congregation in the house may hear his words carefully and distinctly, not with loud speech.

130 And when he cometh into the house of God, for he should be first in the house—behold, this is *a*beautiful, that he may be an *b*example—

---

121 *a* D&C 43:34; 84:61;
     100:7.
   b D&C 59:15; 88:69.
   c TG Carnal Mind; Lust;
     Sensuality.
   d TG Levity; Pride.
122 *a* TG Order.
   b TG Edification.
123 *a* TG Love.
   b TG Covet.
124 *a* TG Idleness; Laziness.

   b TG Uncleanness.
   c Isa. 29:20; D&C 64:8
     (7–10). TG Backbiting;
     Gossip.
   d TG Sleep.
   e TG Health.
125 *a* TG Charity.
   b TG Peace; Peacemakers.
126 *a* TG Prayer.
   b Rev. 22:7 (7, 20); D&C
     1:12.

127 *a* D&C 90:13.
   b D&C 90:7; 95:10 (10,
     17); 97:5 (5–6). TG Edu-
     cation.
   c 2 Kgs. 2:3 (3–15).
   d Num. 11:16; D&C
     107:21.
130 *a* Isa. 52:7.
   b TG Example.

131 Let him offer himself in prayer upon his knees before God, in ᵃtoken or remembrance of the everlasting covenant.

132 And when any shall come in after him, let the teacher arise, and, with ᵃuplifted hands to heaven, yea, even directly, salute his brother or brethren with these words:

133 Art thou a brother or brethren? I salute you in the name of the Lord Jesus Christ, in token or remembrance of the everlasting covenant, in which covenant I receive you to ᵃfellowship, in a determination that is fixed, immovable, and unchangeable, to be your ᵇfriend and ᶜbrother through the grace of God in the bonds of love, to walk in all the commandments of God blameless, in thanksgiving, forever and ever. Amen.

134 And he that is found ᵃunworthy of this salutation shall not have place among you; for ye shall not suffer that mine house shall be ᵇpolluted by him.

135 And he that cometh in and is faithful before me, and is a brother, or if they be brethren, they shall salute the president or teacher with uplifted hands to heaven, with this same prayer and covenant, or by saying Amen, in token of the same.

136 Behold, verily, I say unto you, this is an ensample unto you for a salutation to one another in the house of God, in the school of the prophets.

137 And ye are called to do this by prayer and thanksgiving, as the Spirit shall give utterance in all your doings in the house of the Lord, in the school of the prophets, that it may become a sanctuary, a tabernacle of the Holy Spirit to your ᵃedification.

138 And ye shall not receive any among you into this school save he is clean from the ᵃblood of this generation;

139 And he shall be received by the ordinance of the ᵃwashing of feet, for unto this end was the ordinance of the washing of feet instituted.

140 And again, the ordinance of washing feet is to be administered by the president, or presiding elder of the church.

141 It is to be commenced with prayer; and after partaking of ᵃbread and wine, he is to gird himself according to the ᵇpattern given in the thirteenth chapter of John's testimony concerning me. Amen.

---

131 a TG New and Everlasting Covenant; Prayer; Worship.
132 a Lev. 9:22.
133 a 2 Cor. 8:4. TG Fellowshipping.

b TG Friendship.
c TG Brotherhood and Sisterhood.
134 a Jer. 7:10 (9–10).
b D&C 97:15 (15–17); 110:8 (7–8).

137 a TG Edification; Worship.
138 a D&C 88:75 (75, 85).
139 a D&C 88:74. TG Wash.
141 a TG Sacrament.
b John 13:5 (4–17).

SECTION 89

Revelation given through Joseph Smith the Prophet, at Kirtland, Ohio, February 27, 1833. As a consequence of the early brethren using tobacco in their meetings, the Prophet was led to ponder upon the matter; consequently, he inquired of the Lord concerning it. This revelation, known as the Word of Wisdom, was the result.

1–9, The use of wine, strong drinks, tobacco, and hot drinks is proscribed; 10–17, Herbs, fruits, flesh, and grain are ordained for the use of man and of animals; 18–21, Obedience to gospel law, including the Word of Wisdom, brings temporal and spiritual blessings.

1 A *a*Word of Wisdom, for the benefit of the council of high priests, assembled in Kirtland, and the church, and also the saints in Zion—

2 To be sent greeting; not by commandment or constraint, but by revelation and the *a*word of wisdom, showing forth the order and *b*will of God in the temporal salvation of all saints in the last days—

3 Given for a principle with *a*promise, adapted to the capacity of the *b*weak and the weakest of all *c*saints, who are or can be called saints.

4 Behold, verily, thus saith the Lord unto you: In consequence of *a*evils and designs which do and will exist in the hearts of *b*conspiring men in the last days, I have *c*warned you, and forewarn you, by giving unto you this word of wisdom by revelation—

5 That inasmuch as any man *a*drinketh *b*wine or strong drink among you, behold it is not good, neither meet in the sight of your Father, only in assembling yourselves together to offer up your sacraments before him.

6 And, behold, this should be wine, yea, *a*pure wine of the grape of the vine, of your own make.

7 And, again, *a*strong drinks are not for the belly, but for the washing of your bodies.

8 And again, tobacco is not for the *a*body, neither for the belly, and is not

---

89 1 *a* TG Word of Wisdom.
  2 *a* 1 Cor. 12:8; D&C 84:44.
    b D&C 29:34. TG Commandments of God; God, Will of.
  3 *a* Eph. 2:12; 6:2; D&C 89:18 (18–21).
    b 2 Cor. 12:10; D&C 1:19.

    TG Humility.
    c TG Saints.
  4 *a* TG Deceit; Evil.
    b TG Conspiracy; Wickedness.
    c TG Warn.
  5 *a* TG Abstain.
    b Lev. 10:9 (9–11); Isa. 5:22 (11, 22); Rom.

    14:21 (20–23); D&C 27:3. TG Drunkenness; Temperance; Word of Wisdom.
  6 *a* D&C 27:3 (1–14).
  7 *a* Prov. 20:1; 23:30 (29–35); Luke 1:15.
  8 *a* TG Body, Sanctity of; Health.

good for man, but is an herb for bruises and all sick cattle, to be used with judgment and skill.

9 And again, hot drinks are not for the body or belly.

10 And again, verily I say unto you, all wholesome *herbs God hath ordained for the constitution, nature, and use of man—

11 Every herb in the season thereof, and every fruit in the season thereof; all these to be used with *prudence and *thanksgiving.

12 Yea, *flesh also of *beasts and of the fowls of the air, I, the Lord, have ordained for the use of man with thanksgiving; nevertheless they are to be used *sparingly;

13 And it is pleasing unto me that they should not be *used, only in times of winter, or of cold, or *famine.

14 All *grain is ordained for the use of man and of beasts, to be the staff of life, not only for man but for the beasts of the field, and the fowls of heaven, and all wild animals that run or creep on the earth;

15 And *these hath God made for the use of man only in times of famine and excess of hunger.

16 All grain is good for the *food of man; as also the *fruit of the vine; that which yieldeth fruit, whether in the ground or above the ground—

17 Nevertheless, wheat for man, and corn for the ox, and oats for the horse, and rye for the fowls and for swine, and for all beasts of the field, and barley for all useful animals, and for mild drinks, as also other grain.

18 And all saints who remember to keep and do these sayings, walking in obedience to the commandments, *shall receive *health in their navel and marrow to their bones;

19 And shall *find *wisdom and great *treasures of *knowledge, even hidden treasures;

20 And shall *run and not be *weary, and shall walk and not faint.

21 And I, the Lord, give unto them a promise, that the *destroying angel shall *pass by them, as the children of Israel, and not slay them. Amen.

---

10 a IE plants. Gen. 1:29;
D&C 59:17 (17–20).
11 a TG Prudence; Temperance.
b 1 Tim. 4:3 (3–4).
TG Thanksgiving.
12 a Gen. 9:3; Lev. 11:2 (1–8).
TG Meat.
b D&C 49:19.
c TG Temperance.
13 a D&C 59:20 (16–20).

b TG Famine.
14 a Dan. 1:12 (6–20).
BD Corn.
15 a D&C 49:18; 89:13.
16 a TG Food.
b Gen. 1:29.
18 a D&C 89:3.
b Prov. 3:8; Dan. 1:13
(6–20). TG Health.
19 a D&C 84:80.
b TG Wisdom.

c TG Treasure.
d Dan. 1:17 (6–20).
TG Knowledge; Testimony.
20 a Prov. 4:12; Isa. 40:31.
TG Strength.
b Prov. 24:10 (10–12);
D&C 84:80.
21 a TG Protection, Divine.
b Ex. 12:23 (23, 29).

SECTION 90

Revelation to Joseph Smith the Prophet, given at Kirtland, Ohio, March 8, 1833. This revelation is a continuing step in the establishment of the First Presidency (see the heading to section 81); as a consequence thereof, the counselors mentioned were ordained on March 18, 1833.

1–5, The keys of the kingdom are committed to Joseph Smith and through him to the Church; 6–7, Sidney Rigdon and Frederick G. Williams are to serve in the First Presidency; 8–11, The gospel is to be preached to the nations of Israel, to the Gentiles, and to the Jews, every man hearing in his own tongue; 12–18, Joseph Smith and his counselors are to set the Church in order; 19–37, Various individuals are counseled by the Lord to walk uprightly and serve in His kingdom.

1 Thus saith the Lord, verily, verily I say unto you my son, thy sins are *a*forgiven thee, according to thy petition, for thy prayers and the prayers of thy brethren have come up into my ears.

2 Therefore, thou art blessed from henceforth that bear the *a*keys of the kingdom given unto you; which *b*kingdom is coming forth for the last time.

3 Verily I say unto you, the keys of this *a*kingdom shall *b*never be taken from you, while thou art in the world, neither in the world to come;

4 Nevertheless, through you shall the *a*oracles be given to another, yea, even unto the church.

5 And all they who receive the *a*oracles of God, let them beware how they hold them lest they are accounted as a light thing, and are brought under condemnation thereby, and stumble and fall when the storms descend, and the winds blow, and the *b*rains descend, and beat upon their house.

6 And again, verily I say unto thy brethren, Sidney Rigdon and *a*Frederick G. Williams, their sins are forgiven them also, and they are accounted as *b*equal with thee in holding the keys of this last kingdom;

7 As also through your administration the keys of the *a*school of the prophets, which I have commanded to be organized;

8 That thereby they may be *a*perfected in their ministry for the salvation of Zion, and of the nations of Israel, and of the Gentiles, as many as will believe;

---

90 1 *a* TG Forgive.
  2 *a* TG Priesthood, Keys of.
    b TG Jesus Christ, Prophecies about.
  3 *a* Matt. 21:43; D&C 65:2.
    b D&C 43:3 (3–4); 84:17;

122:9; 124:130.
  4 *a* Acts 7:38; Rom. 3:2;
    Heb. 5:12; D&C 124:39,
    126. TG Prophets, Mission of.
  5 *a* Acts 7:38. TG Prophets,
    Rejection of.

b Matt. 7:25.
  6 *a* D&C 92:1.
    b D&C 35:22 (3–23); 81:1
    (1–7); 107:24 (22–24).
  7 *a* D&C 88:127.
  8 *a* Eph. 4:12 (11–13).

9 That through your administration they may receive the word, and through their administration the word may go forth unto the ends of the earth, unto the *a*Gentiles *b*first, and then, behold, and lo, they shall turn unto the Jews.

10 And then cometh the day when the arm of the Lord shall be *a*revealed in power in convincing the nations, the *b*heathen nations, the house of *c*Joseph, of the gospel of their salvation.

11 For it shall come to pass in that day, that every man shall *a*hear the fulness of the gospel in his own tongue, and in his own *b*language, through those who are *c*ordained unto this *d*power, by the administration of the *e*Comforter, shed forth upon them for the *f*revelation of Jesus Christ.

12 And now, verily I say unto you, I give unto you a commandment that you continue in the *a*ministry and presidency.

13 And when you have finished the *a*translation of the prophets, you shall from thenceforth *b*preside over the affairs of the church and the school;

14 And from time to time, as shall be manifested by the Comforter, receive *a*revelations to unfold the *b*mysteries of the kingdom;

15 And set in order the churches, and *a*study and *b*learn, and become acquainted with all good books, and with *c*languages, tongues, and people.

16 And this shall be your business and mission in all your lives, to preside in council, and set in *a*order all the affairs of this church and kingdom.

17 Be not *a*ashamed, neither confounded; but be admonished in all your high-mindedness and *b*pride, for it bringeth a snare upon your souls.

18 Set in *a*order your houses; keep *b*slothfulness and *c*uncleanness far from you.

19 Now, verily I say unto you, let there be a *a*place provided, as soon as it is possible, for the family of thy counselor and scribe, even Frederick G. Williams.

9 *a* 1 Ne. 13:42; D&C 18:6 (6, 26–27); 19:27; 21:12; 107:33; 112:4; 133:8.
  b Matt. 19:30; Acts 13:46 (46–51); Ether 13:12 (10–12).
10 *a* D&C 42:58 (58–60); 43:25 (23–27); 58:64 (63–64); 88:84 (84, 87–92); 133:37 (37–60).
  b Ps. 98:2; 1 Ne. 15:13. TG Heathen.
  c Gen. 49:22 (22–26); Deut. 33:17 (13–17); Hosea 14:8 (4–9); D&C 133:26 (26–30).
11 *a* TG Missionary Work.

  b TG Language.
  c TG Called of God.
  d TG Priesthood, Power of.
  e TG Holy Ghost, Comforter.
  f TG Testimony.
12 *a* TG Leadership; Service.
13 *a* D&C 73:4 (3–4).
  b D&C 88:127 (127–38); 90:32 (32–33); 107:91.
14 *a* TG Revelation.
  b TG Mysteries of Godliness.
15 *a* D&C 88:78 (76–80), 118; 93:53. TG Education; Scriptures, Study of; Study.

  b Mal. 2:7 (7–9); D&C 107:99 (99–100); 131:6. TG Learn.
  c D&C 90:11. TG Language.
16 *a* Titus 1:5. TG Order.
17 *a* Micah 3:7 (6–7); 2 Ne. 6:13 (7, 13). TG Shame.
  b D&C 88:121. TG Pride.
18 *a* TG Order.
  b TG Apathy; Idleness; Laziness; Procrastination.
  c D&C 94:9; 97:15. TG Uncleanness.
19 *a* D&C 41:7 (7–8).

20 And let mine aged servant, ^aJoseph Smith, Sen., continue with his family upon the place where he now lives; and let it not be sold until the mouth of the Lord shall name.

21 And let my counselor, even ^aSidney Rigdon, remain where he now resides until the mouth of the Lord shall name.

22 And let the bishop search diligently to obtain an ^aagent, and let him be a man who has got ^briches in store—a man of God, and of strong faith—

23 That thereby he may be enabled to discharge every debt; that the storehouse of the Lord may not be brought into disrepute before the eyes of the people.

24 Search ^adiligently, ^bpray always, and be believing, and ^call things shall work together for your good, if ye walk uprightly and remember the ^dcovenant wherewith ye have covenanted one with another.

25 Let your families be ^asmall, especially mine aged servant Joseph Smith's, Sen., as pertaining to those who do not belong to your families;

26 That those things that are provided for you, to bring to pass my work, be not taken from you and given to those that are not worthy—

27 And thereby you be hindered in accomplishing those things which I have commanded you.

28 And again, verily I say unto you, it is my will that my handmaid Vienna Jaques should receive ^amoney to bear her expenses, and go up unto the land of Zion;

29 And the residue of the money may be consecrated unto me, and she be rewarded in mine own due time.

30 Verily I say unto you, that it is meet in mine eyes that she should go up unto the land of Zion, and receive an ^ainheritance from the hand of the bishop;

31 That she may settle down in peace inasmuch as she is faithful, and not be idle in her days from thenceforth.

32 And behold, verily I say unto you, that ye shall ^awrite this commandment, and say unto your brethren in Zion, in love greeting, that I have called you also to ^bpreside over Zion in mine own due time.

33 Therefore, let them cease wearying me concerning this matter.

---

20 a D&C 124:19.
21 a D&C 93:51.
22 a D&C 84:113.
   b Jacob 2:19 (17–19).
24 a TG Dedication; Diligence.
   b TG Prayer.

c Deut. 23:5; Ezra 8:22; Rom. 8:28; D&C 97:18 (18–20); 100:15.
   d Ps. 132:12. TG Commitment; Covenants.
25 a Mosiah 4:27 (26–27).
28 a D&C 60:10 (10–11).

30 a D&C 51:3 (1–3); 85:1 (1–3).
32 a TG Record Keeping; Scriptures, Writing of.
   b D&C 90:13; 107:91.

34 Behold, I say unto you that your brethren in Zion begin to repent, and the angels rejoice over them.

35 Nevertheless, I am not well pleased with many things; and I am not well pleased with my servant ^aWilliam E. McLellin, neither with my servant Sidney Gilbert; and the bishop also, and others have many things to repent of.

36 But verily I say unto you, that I, the Lord, will contend with ^aZion, and plead with her strong ones, and ^bchasten her until she overcomes and is ^cclean before me.

37 For she shall not be removed out of her place. I, the Lord, have spoken it. Amen.

SECTION 91

Revelation given through Joseph Smith the Prophet, at Kirtland, Ohio, March 9, 1833. The Prophet was at this time engaged in the translation of the Old Testament. Having come to that portion of the ancient writings called the Apocrypha, he inquired of the Lord and received this instruction.

1–3, The Apocrypha is mostly translated correctly but contains many interpolations by the hands of men that are not true; 4–6, It benefits those enlightened by the Spirit.

1 Verily, thus saith the Lord unto you concerning the ^aApocrypha—There are many things contained therein that are true, and it is mostly translated correctly;

2 There are many things contained therein that are not true, which are ^ainterpolations by the hands of men.

3 Verily, I say unto you, that it is not needful that the Apocrypha should be ^atranslated.

4 Therefore, whoso readeth it, let him ^aunderstand, for the Spirit manifesteth truth;

5 And whoso is enlightened by the ^aSpirit shall obtain benefit therefrom;

6 And whoso receiveth not by the Spirit, cannot be benefited. Therefore it is not needful that it should be translated. Amen.

---

35 *a* D&C 66:1; 68:7; 75:6.
36 *a* TG Zion.
　b D&C 84:58. TG Chastening.
　c TG Cleanliness;

Purification.
91 1 *a* BD Apocrypha.
　2 *a* TG Record Keeping; Scriptures, Preservation of.

3 *a* D&C 45:60 (60–61); 93:53.
4 *a* TG Understanding.
5 *a* TG Holy Ghost, Mission of; Inspiration.

SECTION 92

Revelation given to Joseph Smith the Prophet, at Kirtland, Ohio, March 15, 1833. The revelation instructs Frederick G. Williams, who had recently been appointed a counselor to Joseph Smith, on his duties in the United Firm (see the headings to sections 78 and 82).

1–2, The Lord gives a commandment relative to admission to the united order.

1 Verily, thus saith the Lord, I give unto the ^aunited order, organized agreeable to the commandment previously given, a revelation and commandment concerning my servant ^bFrederick G. Williams, that ye shall receive him into the order. What I say unto one I say unto all.

2 And again, I say unto you my servant Frederick G. Williams, you shall be a lively member in this order; and inasmuch as you are faithful in keeping all former commandments you shall be blessed forever. Amen.

SECTION 93

Revelation given through Joseph Smith the Prophet, at Kirtland, Ohio, May 6, 1833.

1–5, All who are faithful will see the Lord; 6–18, John bore record that the Son of God went from grace to grace until He received a fulness of the glory of the Father; 19–20, Faithful men, going from grace to grace, will also receive of His fulness; 21–22, Those who are begotten through Christ are the Church of the Firstborn; 23–28, Christ received a fulness of all truth, and man by obedience may do likewise; 29–32, Man was in the beginning with God; 33–35, The elements are eternal, and man may receive a fulness of joy in the Resurrection; 36–37, The glory of God is intelligence; 38–40, Children are innocent before God because of the redemption of Christ; 41–53, The leading brethren are commanded to set their families in order.

1 Verily, thus saith the Lord: It shall come to pass that every soul who ^aforsaketh his ^bsins and cometh unto me, and ^ccalleth on my name, and ^dobeyeth my voice, and keepeth my commandments, shall ^esee my ^fface and ^gknow that I am;

---

92 1 *a* D&C 82:11 (11, 15–21);
   96:8 (6–9).
  b D&C 90:6.
93 1 *a* Rom. 12:1 (1–3).
  b TG Worthiness.
  c Joel 2:32.

d TG Obedience.
e Lev. 9:4; John 14:23
 (18, 21–23); D&C 38:8;
 67:10 (10–12); 88:68;
 101:23; 130:3. TG God,
 Presence of; Jesus Christ,
 Appearances, Postmortal.

f 1 Jn. 4:12 (7–21);
 JST 1 Jn. 4:12 (1 Jn.
 4:12 note *a*). TG God,
 Privilege of Seeing.
g TG God, Access to; God,
 Knowledge about.

2 And that I am the true *light that lighteth every man that cometh into the world;

3 And that I am *in the Father, and the Father in me, and the Father and I are one—

4 The Father *because he *gave me of his fulness, and the Son because I was in the world and made *flesh my *tabernacle, and dwelt among the sons of men.

5 I was in the world and received of my Father, and the *works of him were plainly manifest.

6 And *John saw and bore record of the fulness of my *glory, and the fulness of *John's record is hereafter to be revealed.

7 And he bore record, saying: I saw his glory, that he was in the *beginning, before the world was;

8 Therefore, in the beginning the *Word was, for he was the Word, even the messenger of salvation—

9 The *light and the Redeemer of the world; the Spirit of truth, who came into the world, because the world was made by him, and in him was the life of men and the light of men.

10 The worlds were *made by him; men were made by him; all things were made by him, and through him, and of him.

11 And I, John, *bear record that I beheld his *glory, as the glory of the Only Begotten of the Father, full of grace and truth, even the Spirit of truth, which came and dwelt in the flesh, and dwelt among us.

12 And I, John, saw that he received not of the *fulness at the first, but received *grace for grace;

13 And he received not of the fulness at first, but continued from *grace to grace, until he received a fulness;

14 And thus he was called the *Son of God, because he received not of the fulness at the first.

---

2 *a* John 1:4 (4, 7–9); D&C 14:9; 84:46 (45–47); 88:6. TG Light of Christ.
3 *a* John 10:30 (28–31); 14:10; 17:22; D&C 50:43.
4 *a* Mosiah 15:3 (2–5).
  b TG Jesus Christ, Authority of; Jesus Christ, Relationships with the Father.
  c TG Flesh and Blood; Jesus Christ, Birth of; Jesus Christ, Condescension of.

d 2 Pet. 1:13.
5 *a* John 5:36; 10:25; 14:10 (10–12).
6 *a* John 1:34.
  b TG Jesus Christ, Glory of.
  c John 20:30 (30–31).
7 *a* John 1:1 (1–3, 14); D&C 76:39.
8 *a* TG Jesus Christ, Jehovah; Jesus Christ, Messenger of the Covenant; Salvation.
9 *a* TG Jesus Christ, Creator; Jesus Christ, Light of

the World; Jesus Christ, Mission of.
10 *a* John 1:3 (1–3); Rom. 11:36; Heb. 1:2 (1–3); D&C 76:24.
11 *a* John 1:14 (14, 32).
  b TG Jesus Christ, Glory of.
12 *a* Philip. 2:8 (6–9); Heb. 5:8 (8–9).
  b John 1:16.
13 *a* Luke 2:52. TG Grace.
14 *a* Matt. 1:16 (1–16); Luke 20:41. TG Jesus Christ, Divine Sonship.

15 And I, *John, bear record, and lo, the heavens were opened, and the Holy Ghost descended upon him in the form of a dove, and sat upon him, and there came a voice out of heaven saying: This is my *beloved Son.

16 And I, John, bear record that he received a fulness of the glory of the Father;

17 And he received *all *power, both in heaven and on earth, and the glory of the Father was with him, for he dwelt in him.

18 And it shall come to pass, that if you are faithful you shall receive the *fulness of the record of John.

19 I give unto you these sayings that you may understand and know how to worship, and *know what you worship, that you may come unto the Father in my name, and in due time receive of his fulness.

20 For if you keep my *commandments you shall receive of his *fulness, and be *glorified in me as I am in the Father; therefore, I say unto you, you shall receive *grace for grace.

21 And now, verily I say unto you, I was in the *beginning with the Father, and am the *Firstborn;

22 And all those who are begotten through me are *partakers of the *glory of the same, and are the *church of the Firstborn.

23 Ye were also in the beginning with the Father; that which is *Spirit, even the Spirit of truth;

24 And *truth is *knowledge of things as they are, and as they were, and as they are to come;

25 And whatsoever is *more or less than this is the spirit of that wicked one who was a *liar from the beginning.

26 The Spirit of *truth is of God. I am the Spirit of truth, and John bore record of me, saying: He *received a fulness of truth, yea, even of all truth;

---

15 a John 1:32 (15–32).
  TG Holy Ghost, Dove,
  Sign of.
  b TG Witness of the Father.
17 a Matt. 28:18; John 17:2;
  1 Cor. 15:27; Heb. 1:2;
  1 Pet. 3:22; D&C 84:28.
  b TG God, Power of; God
  the Father, Elohim; Jesus
  Christ, Authority of;
  Jesus Christ, Power of.
18 a TG Scriptures to Come
  Forth.
19 a Luke 4:8; John 4:22
  (5–26); Acts 17:23
  (22–25); Alma 21:22
  (21–22); D&C 43:8

(8–9); 134:4 (1–4);
  A of F 1:11. TG Discernment, Spiritual; Worship.
20 a Deut. 8:1 (1–2).
  b John 1:16.
  c John 17:22 (5, 22).
  TG Man, Potential to
  Become like Heavenly
  Father.
  d Isa. 28:13 (9–13).
  TG Grace.
21 a TG Jesus Christ, Foreordained; Jesus Christ,
  Relationships with the
  Father.
  b TG Jesus Christ, Divine
  Sonship; Jesus Christ,

Firstborn.
22 a 1 Pet. 5:1; D&C 133:57.
  b TG Celestial Glory.
  c D&C 76:54 (53–54).
23 a TG Man, a Spirit Child
  of Heavenly Father;
  Spirit Creation.
24 a Ps. 117:2. TG Truth.
  b TG Knowledge.
25 a D&C 20:35; 68:34.
  b John 8:44; Moses 4:4
  (1–4).
26 a John 14:6. TG God,
  Intelligence of.
  b John 1:16 (16–17).

27 And no man receiveth a *fulness unless he keepeth his commandments.

28 He that *keepeth his commandments receiveth *truth and *light, until he is glorified in truth and *knoweth all things.

29 Man was also in the *beginning with God. *Intelligence, or the *light of *truth, was not *created or made, neither indeed can be.

30 All truth is independent in that *sphere in which God has placed it, to *act for itself, as all intelligence also; otherwise there is no existence.

31 Behold, here is the *agency of man, and here is the condemnation of man; because that which was from the beginning is *plainly manifest unto them, and they receive not the light.

32 And every man whose spirit receiveth not the *light is under condemnation.

33 For man is *spirit. The elements are *eternal, and *spirit and element, inseparably connected, receive a fulness of joy;

34 And when *separated, man cannot receive a fulness of joy.

35 The *elements are the *tabernacle of God; yea, man is the tabernacle of God, even *temples; and whatsoever temple is *defiled, God shall destroy that temple.

36 The *glory of God is *intelligence, or, in other words, *light and truth.

37 Light and truth forsake that *evil one.

38 Every *spirit of man was *innocent in the beginning; and God having *redeemed man from the *fall, men became again, in their infant state, *innocent before God.

---

27 a TG Abundant Life;
    Perfection.
28 a TG Obedience.
  b TG Truth.
  c Matt. 6:22 (22–23);
    D&C 50:24.
  d John 17:3; 2 Pet. 1:4;
    D&C 88:67 (49, 67);
    101:32 (32–34). TG Mys-
    teries of Godliness.
29 a Prov. 8:23; Abr. 3:18.
    TG Man, Antemortal Ex-
    istence of; Man, Potential
    to Become like Heavenly
    Father.
  b TG God, Intelligence of;
    Intelligence.
  c TG Light [noun].
  d TG Truth.
  e TG Creation.
30 a D&C 77:3.
  b 2 Ne. 2:14 (13–26).
31 a TG Agency.

  b Deut. 30:11 (11–14);
    1 Ne. 20:16; D&C
    84:23.
32 a TG Conscience; Igno-
    rance.
33 a John 4:24; D&C 77:2;
    Abr. 5:7 (7–8). TG Man,
    a Spirit Child of Heav-
    enly Father; Spirit Body;
    Spirit Creation.
  b TG Eternity.
  c D&C 138:17. TG Eternal
    Life; Joy; Resurrection.
34 a 2 Ne. 9:8 (8–10).
    TG Spirits, Disembodied.
35 a Gen. 2:7; Morm. 9:17;
    D&C 77:12.
  b 2 Pet. 1:13; D&C 88:41
    (12, 41, 45).
  c TG Body, Sanctity of.
  d Mark 7:15; 1 Cor. 3:17
    (16–17); Titus 1:15;
    2 Ne. 19:17.

36 a TG God, Glory of; Jesus
    Christ, Glory of.
  b D&C 130:18; Abr. 3:19.
    TG God, Intelligence of;
    Intelligence.
  c D&C 88:7 (6–13).
37 a 2 Ne. 30:18; Moses 1:15
    (12–16). TG Devil.
38 a TG Spirit Body.
  b TG Conceived in Sin;
    Purity.
  c Ps. 49:15; Mosiah 27:24
    (24–26); Moses 5:9;
    A of F 1:3. TG Redemp-
    tion.
  d TG Fall of Man.
  e Moro. 8:12 (8, 12, 22);
    D&C 29:46. TG Justifi-
    cation; Salvation of Little
    Children; Sanctification.

39 And that ªwicked one cometh and ᵇtaketh away light and truth, through ᶜdisobedience, from the children of men, and because of the ᵈtradition of their fathers.

40 But I have commanded you to bring up your ªchildren in ᵇlight and truth.

41 But verily I say unto you, my servant Frederick G. Williams, you have continued under this condemnation;

42 You have not ªtaught your children light and truth, according to the commandments; and that wicked one hath power, as yet, over you, and this is the cause of your ᵇaffliction.

43 And now a commandment I give unto you—if you will be delivered you shall set in ªorder your own house, for there are many things that are not right in your house.

44 Verily, I say unto my servant Sidney Rigdon, that in some things he hath not kept the commandments concerning his children; therefore, first set in order thy house.

45 Verily, I say unto my servant Joseph Smith, Jun., or in other words, I will call you ªfriends, for you are my friends, and ye shall have an inheritance with me—

46 I called you ªservants for the world's sake, and ye are their servants for my sake—

47 And now, verily I say unto Joseph Smith, Jun.—You have not kept the commandments, and must needs stand ªrebuked before the Lord;

48 Your ªfamily must needs repent and forsake some things, and give more earnest heed unto your sayings, or be removed out of their place.

49 What I say unto one I say unto all; ªpray always lest that wicked one have power in you, and remove you out of your place.

50 My servant Newel K. Whitney also, a bishop of my church, hath need to be ªchastened, and set in ᵇorder his family, and see that they are more ᶜdiligent and concerned at home, and pray always, or they shall be removed out of their ᵈplace.

39a TG Devil.
  b Matt. 13:19 (18–19);
    2 Cor. 4:4 (3–4); Mosiah
    27:9 (8–9); Alma 12:10
    (9–11); D&C 50:7; 84:50
    (49–53).
  c TG Disobedience.
  d Jer. 16:19; Ezek. 20:18;
    Alma 3:8. TG Traditions
    of Men.
40a TG Family, Children,
    Responsibilities toward;

Marriage, Fatherhood;
    Marriage, Motherhood.
  b TG Children of Light.
42a Ex. 10:2 (1–2); 1 Sam.
    3:13 (11–13); D&C
    68:25 (25–31); Moses
    6:58.
  b TG Accountability.
43a Esth. 1:22; 1 Tim. 3:5
    (4–5). TG Order.
45a Ex. 33:11; D&C
    84:63; 88:62; 94:1.

TG Friendship.
46a Lev. 25:55; 1 Ne. 21:3
    (3–6). TG Servant.
47a D&C 95:1 (1–2).
    TG Chastening.
48a TG Family, Children,
    Duties of.
49a 3 Ne. 18:15 (15–21).
50a TG Reproof; Warn.
  b TG Order.
  c TG Diligence.
  d D&C 64:40.

51 Now, I say unto you, my friends, let my servant Sidney Rigdon go on his journey, and make haste, and also proclaim the ªacceptable year of the Lord, and the ᵇgospel of salvation, as I shall give him utterance; and by your prayer of faith with one consent I will uphold him.

52 And let my servants Joseph Smith, Jun., and Frederick G. Williams make haste also, and it shall be given them even according to the prayer of faith; and inasmuch as you keep my sayings you shall not be confounded in this world, nor in the world to come.

53 And, verily I say unto you, that it is my will that you should ªhasten to ᵇtranslate my scriptures, and to ᶜobtain a ᵈknowledge of history, and of countries, and of kingdoms, of ᵉlaws of God and man, and all this for the salvation of Zion. Amen.

SECTION 94

Revelation given through Joseph Smith the Prophet, at Kirtland, Ohio, August 2, 1833. Hyrum Smith, Reynolds Cahoon, and Jared Carter are appointed as a Church building committee.

1–9, The Lord gives a commandment relative to the erection of a house for the work of the Presidency; 10–12, A printing house is to be built; 13–17, Certain inheritances are assigned.

1 And again, verily I say unto you, my ªfriends, a commandment I give unto you, that ye shall commence a work of laying out and preparing a beginning and foundation of the city of the ᵇstake of Zion, here in the land of Kirtland, beginning at my house.

2 And behold, it must be done according to the ªpattern which I have given unto you.

3 And let the first lot on the south be consecrated unto me for the building of a house for the presidency, for the work of the presidency, in obtaining revelations; and for the work of the ministry of the ªpresidency, in all things pertaining to the church and kingdom.

4 Verily I say unto you, that it shall be built fifty-five by sixty-five feet in the width thereof and in the length thereof, in the inner court.

---

51 *a* Luke 4:19; 2 Cor. 6:2.
   b Eph. 1:13.
53 *a* D&C 45:60 (60–61);
    73:3; 76:15; 91:3; 94:10.
   b IE the translation of the
    Bible.

   c D&C 88:78 (76–80),
    118; 90:15.
   d TG Education; Knowledge; Learn.
   e TG God, Law of.
94 1 *a* D&C 93:45.

   b D&C 68:26; 82:13; 96:1;
    104:48; 109:59.
2 *a* Heb. 8:5; D&C 52:14;
    95:14; 97:10; 115:14
    (14–16).
3 *a* D&C 107:9 (8–78).

5 And there shall be a lower court and a higher court, according to the pattern which shall be given unto you hereafter.

6 And it shall be ^adedicated unto the Lord from the foundation thereof, according to the ^border of the priesthood, according to the pattern which shall be given unto you hereafter.

7 And it shall be wholly dedicated unto the Lord for the work of the ^apresidency.

8 And ye shall not suffer any ^aunclean thing to come in unto it; and my ^bglory shall be there, and my ^cpresence shall be there.

9 But if there shall come into it any ^aunclean thing, my glory shall not be there; and my presence shall not come into it.

10 And again, verily I say unto you, the second lot on the south shall be dedicated unto me for the building of a house unto me, for the work of the ^aprinting of the ^btranslation of my scriptures, and all things whatsoever I shall command you.

11 And it shall be fifty-five by sixty-five feet in the width thereof and the length thereof, in the inner court; and there shall be a lower and a higher court.

12 And this house shall be wholly dedicated unto the Lord from the foundation thereof, for the work of the printing, in all things whatsoever I shall command you, to be holy, undefiled, according to the pattern in all things as it shall be given unto you.

13 And on the third lot shall my servant Hyrum Smith receive his ^ainheritance.

14 And on the first and second lots on the north shall my servants Reynolds Cahoon and Jared Carter receive their inheritances—

15 That they may do the work which I have appointed unto them, to be a committee to build mine houses, according to the commandment, which I, the Lord God, have given unto you.

16 These two houses are not to be built until I give unto you a commandment concerning them.

17 And now I give unto you no more at this time. Amen.

---

6 *a* TG Dedication; Sacred.
  b 1 Chr. 6:32.
7 *a* D&C 107:9 (8–78).
8 *a* Luke 19:46 (46–48);
    D&C 109:20 (19–20).
    TG Uncleanness.
  b 1 Kgs. 8:11 (10–11);

Ezek. 43:2; D&C 101:25.
  TG Glory.
  c TG God, Presence of.
9 *a* Lev. 15:31; D&C 90:18;
    97:15.
10 *a* D&C 104:58. TG Scrip-
    tures, Writing of.

b IE the translation of
  the Bible. D&C 93:53;
  124:89.
13 *a* TG Inheritance. See also
    "Inherit" in Index.

SECTION 95

Revelation given through Joseph Smith the Prophet, at Kirtland, Ohio, June 1, 1833. This revelation is a continuation of divine directions to build a house for worship and instruction, the house of the Lord (see section 88:119–36).

1–6, The Saints are chastened for their failure to build the house of the Lord; 7–10, The Lord desires to use His house to endow His people with power from on high; 11–17, The house is to be dedicated as a place of worship and for the school of the Apostles.

1 Verily, thus saith the Lord unto you whom I love, and whom I *ᵃ*love I also chasten that their sins may be *ᵇ*forgiven, for with the *ᶜ*chastisement I prepare a way for their *ᵈ*deliverance in all things out of *ᵉ*temptation, and I have loved you—

2 Wherefore, ye must needs be chastened and stand rebuked before my face;

3 For ye have sinned against me a very grievous sin, in that ye have not considered the great commandment in all things, that I have given unto you concerning the building of mine *ᵃ*house;

4 For the preparation wherewith I design to prepare mine apostles to *ᵃ*prune my vineyard for the last time, that I may bring to pass my *ᵇ*strange act, that I may *ᶜ*pour out my Spirit upon all flesh—

5 But behold, verily I say unto you, that there are many who have been ordained among you, whom I have called but few of them are *ᵃ*chosen.

6 They who are not chosen have sinned a very grievous sin, in that they are *ᵃ*walking in *ᵇ*darkness at noon-day.

7 And for this cause I gave unto you a commandment that you should call your *ᵃ*solemn assembly, that your *ᵇ*fastings and your *ᶜ*mourning might come up into the ears of the Lord of *ᵈ*Sabaoth, which is by interpretation, the *ᵉ*creator of the first day, the beginning and the end.

---

95 1 *a* 2 Sam. 7:14; Prov. 13:18;
Heb. 12:6 (5–12); Hel.
15:3; D&C 101:4 (4–5);
103:4. TG Chastening;
God, Love of.
b TG Forgive.
c Deut. 11:2 (1–8); D&C
105:6.
d 2 Sam. 14:14; 1 Cor.
10:13. TG Deliver;
Forgive.
e TG Temptation.

3 *a* Hag. 1:8; D&C 88:119.
4 *a* Jacob 5:61 (61–75);
D&C 24:19; 33:3 (3–4);
39:17.
b Isa. 28:21; D&C 101:95.
c Prov. 1:23; Ezek. 36:27;
Joel 2:28; Acts 2:17;
D&C 19:38. TG Holy
Ghost, Gifts of.
5 *a* Matt. 20:16; D&C 63:31;
105:36 (35–36); 121:34
(34–40). TG Called
of God; Election;

Worthiness.
6 *a* TG Walking in Darkness.
b Deut. 28:29 (15–45).
TG Darkness, Spiritual.
7 *a* D&C 88:117 (70–119).
TG Solemn Assembly.
b TG Fast, Fasting.
c TG Mourning; Repent.
d James 5:4; D&C 87:7;
88:2.
e TG Jesus Christ, Creator.

8 Yea, verily I say unto you, I gave unto you a commandment that you should ^abuild a house, in the which house I design to ^bendow those whom I have ^cchosen with power from on high;

9 For this is the ^apromise of the Father unto you; therefore I command you to tarry, even as mine apostles at Jerusalem.

10 Nevertheless, my servants sinned a very grievous sin; and ^acontentions arose in the ^bschool of the prophets; which was very grievous unto me, saith your Lord; therefore I sent them forth to be chastened.

11 Verily I say unto you, it is my will that you should build a house. ^aIf you keep my commandments you shall have power to build it.

12 If you ^akeep not my commandments, the ^blove of the Father shall not continue with you, therefore you shall ^cwalk in darkness.

13 Now here is wisdom, and the ^amind of the Lord—let the house be built, not after the manner of the world, for I give not unto you that ye shall live after the manner of the world;

14 Therefore, let it be built after the ^amanner which I shall show unto three of you, whom ye shall appoint and ordain unto this power.

15 And the size thereof shall be fifty and five feet in width, and let it be sixty-five feet in length, in the inner court thereof.

16 And let the lower part of the inner court be dedicated unto me for your sacrament offering, and for your preaching, and your fasting, and your praying, and the ^aoffering up of your most holy desires unto me, saith your Lord.

17 And let the higher part of the inner court be dedicated unto me for the ^aschool of mine apostles, saith Son ^bAhman; or, in other words, Alphus; or, in other words, Omegus; even Jesus Christ your ^cLord. Amen.

SECTION 96

Revelation given to Joseph Smith the Prophet, showing the order of the city or stake of Zion at Kirtland, Ohio, June 4, 1833, as an example to the Saints in Kirtland. The occasion was a conference of high priests, and the

---

8 *a* D&C 88:119; 104:43;
　115:8.
　b D&C 38:32; 39:15;
　43:16; 110:9 (9–10).
　TG Genealogy and
　Temple Work.
　c TG Election.
9 *a* Luke 24:49; Acts 1:4.

10 *a* D&C 88:134 (133–34).
　TG Contention; Disputa-
　tions.
　b D&C 88:127; 97:5 (5–6).
11 *a* Hag. 1:8 (2–11).
12 *a* John 15:10; Mosiah 2:4.
　b 1 Jn. 2:10 (10, 15).
　c 2 Pet. 2:17. TG Walking

in Darkness.
13 *a* D&C 68:4.
14 *a* D&C 94:2; 124:42.
16 *a* D&C 59:9 (9–14).
17 *a* D&C 88:127 (127–41).
　b D&C 78:20.
　c TG Jesus Christ, Lord.

chief subject of consideration was the disposal of certain lands, known as the French farm, possessed by the Church near Kirtland. Since the conference could not agree who should take charge of the farm, all agreed to inquire of the Lord concerning the matter.

1, The Kirtland Stake of Zion is to be made strong; 2–5, The bishop is to divide the inheritances for the Saints; 6–9, John Johnson is to be a member of the united order.

1 Behold, I say unto you, here is wisdom, whereby ye may know how to act concerning this matter, for it is expedient in me that this ^astake that I have set for the strength of Zion should be made strong.

2 Therefore, let my servant ^aNewel K. Whitney take charge of the place which is named among you, upon which I design to build mine ^bholy house.

3 And again, let it be divided into lots, according to wisdom, for the benefit of those who seek ^ainheritances, as it shall be determined in council among you.

4 Therefore, take heed that ye see to this matter, and that portion that is necessary to benefit mine ^aorder, for the purpose of bringing forth my word to the children of men.

5 For behold, verily I say unto you, this is the most expedient in me, that my word should go forth unto the children of men, for the purpose of subduing the hearts of the children of men for your good. Even so. Amen.

6 And again, verily I say unto you, it is wisdom and expedient in me, that my servant ^aJohn Johnson whose offering I have accepted, and whose prayers I have heard, unto whom I give a promise of eternal life inasmuch as he keepeth my commandments from henceforth—

7 For he is a descendant of ^aJoseph and a partaker of the blessings of the promise made unto his fathers—

8 Verily I say unto you, it is expedient in me that he should become a member of the ^aorder, that he may assist in bringing forth my word unto the children of men.

9 Therefore ye shall ordain him unto this blessing, and he shall seek diligently to take away ^aincumbrances that are upon the house named among you, that he may dwell therein. Even so. Amen.

---

96 1 *a* Isa. 33:20; 54:2; D&C 94:1; 104:48.
2 *a* D&C 72:8 (7–8).
  b 2 Chr. 3:8.

3 *a* D&C 38:20.
4 *a* D&C 78:3.
6 *a* D&C 102:3 (3, 34).
7 *a* Gen. 49:26 (22–26); Rev. 7:8; 1 Ne. 5:14 (14–16);

D&C 133:32.
8 *a* D&C 92:1; 104:1 (1, 47–53).
9 *a* D&C 90:23 (22–23).

SECTION 97

Revelation given through Joseph Smith the Prophet, at Kirtland, Ohio, August 2, 1833. This revelation deals particularly with the affairs of the Saints in Zion, Jackson County, Missouri, in response to the Prophet's inquiry of the Lord for information. Members of the Church in Missouri were at this time subjected to severe persecution and, on July 23, 1833, had been forced to sign an agreement to leave Jackson County.

1–2, Many of the Saints in Zion (Jackson County, Missouri) are blessed for their faithfulness; 3–5, Parley P. Pratt is commended for his labors in the school in Zion; 6–9, Those who observe their covenants are accepted by the Lord; 10–17, A house is to be built in Zion in which the pure in heart will see God; 18–21, Zion is the pure in heart; 22–28, Zion will escape the Lord's scourge if she is faithful.

1 Verily I say unto you my friends, I speak unto you with my ^avoice, even the voice of my Spirit, that I may show unto you my will concerning your brethren in the land of ^bZion, many of whom are truly humble and are seeking diligently to learn wisdom and to find truth.

2 Verily, verily I say unto you, blessed are such, for they shall obtain; for I, the Lord, show mercy unto all the ^ameek, and upon all whomsoever I will, that I may be ^bjustified when I shall bring them unto judgment.

3 Behold, I say unto you, concerning the school in Zion, I, the Lord, am well pleased that there should be a ^aschool in Zion, and also with my servant ^bParley P. Pratt, for he abideth in me.

4 And inasmuch as he continueth to abide in me he shall continue to preside over the school in the land of Zion until I shall give unto him other commandments.

5 And I will bless him with a multiplicity of blessings, in expounding all scriptures and mysteries to the edification of the ^aschool, and of the church in Zion.

6 And to the residue of the school, I, the Lord, am willing to show mercy; nevertheless, there are those that must needs be ^achastened, and their works shall be made known.

7 The ^aax is laid at the root of the trees; and every tree that bringeth not forth good fruit shall be hewn down and cast into the fire. I, the Lord, have spoken it.

---

97 1 *a* TG Revelation; Wisdom.
  b D&C 64:26 (18–41);
    66:6.
  2 *a* Matt. 5:5.

  b Ps. 51:4.
3 *a* D&C 55:4; 88:118; 109:7
    (7, 14).
  b D&C 32:1; 50:37; 52:26;
    103:30 (30–37).

5 *a* D&C 88:127.
6 *a* TG Chastening.
7 *a* Matt. 3:10; 7:19; Luke
    3:9; 6:44; Alma 5:52
    (36–52); 3 Ne. 14:19.

8 Verily I say unto you, all among them who know their hearts are *honest, and are broken, and their spirits contrite, and are *willing to observe their covenants by *sacrifice—yea, every sacrifice which I, the Lord, shall command—they are *accepted of me.

9 For I, the Lord, will cause them to bring forth as a very fruitful *tree which is planted in a goodly land, by a pure stream, that yieldeth much precious fruit.

10 Verily I say unto you, that it is my will that a *house should be built unto me in the land of Zion, like unto the *pattern which I have given you.

11 Yea, let it be built speedily, by the tithing of my people.

12 Behold, this is the *tithing and the *sacrifice which I, the Lord, require at their hands, that there may be a *house built unto me for the salvation of Zion—

13 For a place of *thanksgiving for all saints, and for a place of instruction for all those who are called to the work of the ministry in all their several callings and offices;

14 That they may be perfected in the *understanding of their ministry, in theory, in principle, and in doctrine, in all things pertaining to the *kingdom of God on the earth, the *keys of which kingdom have been *conferred upon you.

15 And inasmuch as my people *build a *house unto me in the *name of the Lord, and do not suffer any *unclean thing to come into it, that it be not defiled, my *glory shall rest upon it;

16 Yea, and my *presence shall be there, for I will come into it, and all the *pure in heart that shall come into it shall see God.

17 But if it be defiled I will not come into it, and my glory shall not be there; for I will not come into *unholy temples.

18 And, now, behold, if Zion do these things she shall *prosper, and spread herself and become very glorious, very great, and very terrible.

---

8 a TG Contrite Heart;
     Honesty.
  b Ex. 25:2 (1–7); D&C
     64:34.
  c TG Commitment; Sacrifice.
  d Gen. 4:7; D&C 52:15;
     132:50; Moses 5:23.
9 a Ps. 1:3 (1–3); Jer. 17:8.
10 a D&C 57:3; 58:57; 84:3
     (3–5, 31); 88:119; 124:31
     (25–51).
   b Num. 8:4; D&C 52:14;
     94:2; 115:14 (14–16).
12 a TG Tithing.

  b TG Sacrifice.
  c 1 Kgs. 5:5.
13 a 2 Chr. 5:13. TG Thanksgiving.
14 a TG Understanding.
   b TG Kingdom of God, on
     Earth.
   c TG Priesthood, Keys of.
   d TG Delegation of Responsibility.
15 a 2 Chr. 2:4.
   b TG Temple.
   c 1 Kgs. 8:29.
   d D&C 94:9; 109:20;
     110:8 (7–8).

  e 2 Chr. 5:14 (13–14);
     Hag. 2:7; D&C 84:5
     (4–5, 31). TG Glory.
16 a Lev. 16:2; D&C 124:27.
     TG God, Presence of.
   b Matt. 5:8; D&C 67:10;
     88:68. TG God, Knowledge about; God, Privilege of Seeing; Purity.
17 a 1 Cor. 3:16 (16–17); Eph.
     5:5.
18 a Josh. 1:7; D&C 90:24;
     100:15.

19 And the *nations of the earth shall honor her, and shall say: Surely *Zion is the city of our God, and surely Zion cannot fall, neither be moved out of her place, for God is there, and the hand of the Lord is there;

20 And he hath sworn by the power of his might to be her salvation and her high *tower.

21 Therefore, verily, thus saith the Lord, let Zion rejoice, for this is *Zion—THE PURE IN HEART; therefore, let Zion rejoice, while all the wicked shall mourn.

22 For behold, and lo, *vengeance cometh speedily upon the ungodly as the whirlwind; and who shall escape it?

23 The Lord's *scourge shall pass over by night and by day, and the report thereof shall vex all people; yea, it shall not be stayed until the Lord come;

24 For the *indignation of the Lord is kindled against their abominations and all their wicked works.

25 Nevertheless, Zion shall *escape if she observe to do all things whatsoever I have commanded her.

26 But if she *observe not to do whatsoever I have commanded her, I will *visit her *according to all her works, with sore affliction, with *pestilence, with *plague, with sword, with *vengeance, with *devouring fire.

27 Nevertheless, let it be read this once to her ears, that I, the Lord, have accepted of her offering; and if she sin no more *none of these things shall come upon her;

28 And I will bless her with *blessings, and multiply a multiplicity of blessings upon her, and upon her generations forever and ever, saith the Lord your God. Amen.

SECTION 98

Revelation given through Joseph Smith the Prophet, at Kirtland, Ohio, August 6, 1833. This revelation came in consequence of the persecution upon the Saints in Missouri. Increased settlement of Church members in Missouri

19 a Isa. 60:14; Zech. 2:11 (10–12); D&C 45:69 (66–69); 49:10.
b TG Jerusalem, New.
20 a 2 Sam. 22:3.
21 a Moses 7:18 (18–19). TG Purity; Zion.
22 a Prov. 10:25; Isa. 66:15; Jer. 23:19. TG Vengeance.
23 a Isa. 28:15; D&C 45:31. TG World, End of.
24 a TG God, Indignation of; Wickedness.
25 a D&C 63:34; JS—M 1:20. TG Protection, Divine.
26 a Deut. 28:15.
b TG Punish; Reproof.
c D&C 84:58.
d Luke 21:11 (10–13); 2 Ne. 6:15; Mosiah 12:4.
e TG Plague.
f Isa. 34:8; 61:2; Mal. 4:1 (1, 3); 3 Ne. 21:21 (20–21).
g Isa. 29:6; Joel 1:19 (19–20); Mal. 3:11; D&C 85:3.
27 a Jer. 18:8; Jonah 3:10 (9–10).
28 a TG Blessing.

troubled some other settlers, who felt threatened by the Saints' numbers, political and economic influence, and cultural and religious differences. In July 1833, a mob destroyed Church property, tarred and feathered two Church members, and demanded that the Saints leave Jackson County. Although some news of the problems in Missouri had no doubt reached the Prophet in Kirtland (nine hundred miles away), the seriousness of the situation could have been known to him at this date only by revelation.

1–3, The afflictions of the Saints will be for their good; 4–8, The Saints are to befriend the constitutional law of the land; 9–10, Honest, wise, and good men should be supported for secular government; 11–15, Those who lay down their lives in the Lord's cause will have eternal life; 16–18, Renounce war and proclaim peace; 19–22, The Saints in Kirtland are reproved and commanded to repent; 23–32, The Lord reveals His laws governing the persecutions and afflictions imposed on His people; 33–38, War is justified only when the Lord commands it; 39–48, The Saints are to forgive their enemies, who, if they repent, will also escape the Lord's vengeance.

1 Verily I say unto you my friends, ᵃfear not, let your hearts be comforted; yea, rejoice evermore, and in everything give ᵇthanks;

2 ᵃWaiting patiently on the Lord, for your prayers have entered into the ears of the Lord of Sabaoth, and are recorded with this seal and testament—the Lord hath sworn and decreed that they shall be granted.

3 Therefore, he giveth this promise unto you, with an immutable covenant that they shall be fulfilled; and all things wherewith you have been ᵃafflicted shall work together for your ᵇgood, and to my name's glory, saith the Lord.

4 And now, verily I say unto you concerning the ᵃlaws of the land, it is my will that my people should observe to do all things whatsoever I command them.

5 And that ᵃlaw of the land which is ᵇconstitutional, supporting that principle of freedom in maintaining rights and privileges, belongs to all mankind, and is justifiable before me.

6 Therefore, I, the Lord, justify you, and your brethren of my church, in befriending that law which is the ᵃconstitutional law of the land;

---

98 1 *a* D&C 68:6.
  b TG Thanksgiving.
 2 *a* Gen. 49:18; Ps. 27:14;
   37:34; 40:1; Prov. 20:22;
   Isa. 30:18 (18–19); 1 Ne.

21:23; 2 Ne. 6:13; D&C
   133:45.
 3 *a* TG Affliction.
  b D&C 122:7.
 4 *a* D&C 20:1; 58:21.
   TG Citizenship.

5 *a* 1 Pet. 2:13 (13–14);
   D&C 44:4; 51:6; 58:21;
   109:54; 134:5.
  b TG Governments; Liberty.
 6 *a* D&C 44:4; 101:80.

7 And as pertaining to law of man, whatsoever is more or less than this, cometh of evil.

8 I, the Lord God, make you *free, therefore ye are free indeed; and the law also maketh you free.

9 Nevertheless, when the *wicked *rule the people mourn.

10 Wherefore, *honest men and wise men should be sought for diligently, and good men and wise men ye should observe to uphold; otherwise whatsoever is less than these cometh of evil.

11 And I give unto you a commandment, that ye shall forsake all evil and cleave unto all *good, that ye shall live by every *word which proceedeth forth out of the mouth of God.

12 For he will *give unto the faithful line upon line, precept upon precept; and I will *try you and prove you herewith.

13 And whoso *layeth down his life in my cause, for my name's sake, shall find it again, even life eternal.

14 Therefore, be not *afraid of your enemies, for I have decreed in my heart, saith the Lord, that I will *prove you in all things, whether you will abide in my covenant, *even unto death, that you may be found worthy.

15 For if ye will not abide in my covenant ye are not worthy of me.

16 Therefore, *renounce war and proclaim peace, and seek diligently to *turn the hearts of the children to their fathers, and the hearts of the fathers to the children;

17 And again, the hearts of the *Jews unto the prophets, and the prophets unto the Jews; lest I come and smite the whole earth with a curse, and all flesh be consumed before me.

18 Let not your hearts be troubled; for in my Father's house are *many mansions, and I have prepared a place for you; and where my Father and I am, there ye shall be also.

19 Behold, I, the Lord, am not well *pleased with many who are in the church at Kirtland;

---

8 a John 8:32; 2 Cor. 3:17.
  TG Agency; Liberty.
9 a Prov. 28:28; 29:2.
  b TG Tyranny.
10 a TG Citizenship; Honesty.
11 a TG Good Works.
  b Deut. 8:3; Matt. 4:4;
    D&C 84:44 (43–44).
12 a Isa. 28:10; D&C 42:61;
    59:4; 76:7; 101:32;
    121:28 (26–33).

  b Judg. 7:4; Alma 27:15;
    Abr. 3:25.
13 a Luke 9:24; 21:17 (15–19);
    Philip. 2:17; D&C
    101:35; 103:27 (27–28).
    TG Martyrdom.
14 a Neh. 4:14; D&C 122:9.
  b D&C 124:55; 132:51.
    TG Test.
  c Rev. 2:10; D&C 136:39
    (31, 39).

16 a Alma 48:14. TG Peace;
    Peacemakers; War.
  b Mal. 4:6 (5–6); D&C
    2:2.
17 a TG Israel, Judah, People
    of; Israel, Restoration of.
18 a John 14:2; D&C 59:2;
    76:111; 81:6; 106:8.
19 a Rom. 8:8 (5–9); 1 Cor.
    10:5 (1–6).

20 For they do not ªforsake their sins, and their wicked ways, the pride of their hearts, and their covetousness, and all their detestable things, and observe the words of wisdom and eternal life which I have given unto them.

21 Verily I say unto you, that I, the Lord, will ªchasten them and will do whatsoever I list, if they do not repent and observe all things whatsoever I have said unto them.

22 And again I say unto you, if ye observe to ªdo whatsoever I command you, I, the Lord, will turn away all ᵇwrath and indignation from you, and the ᶜgates of hell shall not prevail against you.

23 Now, I speak unto you concerning your families—if men will ªsmite you, or your families, once, and ye ᵇbear it patiently and ᶜrevile not against them, neither seek ᵈrevenge, ye shall be ᵉrewarded;

24 But if ye bear it not patiently, it shall be accounted unto you as being ªmeted out as a just measure unto you.

25 And again, if your enemy shall smite you the second time, and you revile not against your enemy, and bear it patiently, your reward shall be an ªhundred-fold.

26 And again, if he shall smite you the third time, and ye bear it ªpatiently, your reward shall be doubled unto you four-fold;

27 And these three ªtestimonies shall stand against your enemy if he repent not, and shall not be blotted out.

28 And now, verily I say unto you, if that enemy shall escape my vengeance, that he be not brought into judgment before me, then ye shall see to it that ye ªwarn him in my name, that he come no more upon you, neither upon your family, even your children's children unto the third and fourth generation.

29 And then, if he shall come upon you or your children, or your children's children unto the third and fourth generation, I have delivered thine ªenemy into thine hands;

30 And then if thou wilt spare him, thou shalt be rewarded for thy ªrighteousness; and also thy children and thy children's children unto the third and fourth generation.

20a TG Repent.
21a Deut. 11:2 (1–8); Mosiah 23:21; Hel. 12:3.
22a TG Obedience.
  b Isa. 60:10; D&C 101:9.
  c Matt. 16:18; D&C 33:13; 109:26.
23a Luke 6:29; Alma 43:46

(46–47). TG Persecution.
  b TG Forbear.
  c TG Reviling.
  d Deut. 19:6. TG Retribution.
  e 2 Sam. 16:12. TG Reward.
24a Matt. 7:2 (1–2).

25a Gen. 26:12.
26a TG Patience.
27a TG Judgment.
28a TG Warn.
29a Deut. 7:23 (16–23).
30a TG Reward; Righteousness.

31 Nevertheless, thine enemy is in thine hands; and if thou rewardest him according to his works thou art justified; if he has sought thy life, and thy life is endangered by him, thine enemy is in thine hands and thou art justified.

32 Behold, this is the law I gave unto my servant Nephi, and thy *fathers, Joseph, and Jacob, and Isaac, and Abraham, and all mine ancient prophets and apostles.

33 And again, this is the *law that I gave unto mine ancients, that they should not go out unto battle against any nation, kindred, tongue, or people, save I, the Lord, commanded them.

34 And if any nation, tongue, or people should proclaim war against them, they should first lift a standard of *peace unto that people, nation, or tongue;

35 And if that people did not accept the offering of peace, neither the second nor the third time, they should bring these testimonies before the Lord;

36 Then I, the Lord, would give unto them a commandment, and justify them in going out to battle against that nation, tongue, or people.

37 And I, the Lord, would *fight their battles, and their children's battles, and their children's children's, until they had avenged themselves on all their enemies, to the third and fourth generation.

38 Behold, this is an *ensample unto all people, saith the Lord your God, for justification before me.

39 And again, verily I say unto you, if after thine *enemy has come upon thee the first time, he repent and come unto thee praying thy forgiveness, thou shalt forgive him, and shalt hold it no more as a testimony against thine enemy—

40 And so on unto the second and third time; and as oft as thine enemy repenteth of the trespass wherewith he has trespassed against thee, thou shalt *forgive him, until seventy times seven.

41 And if he trespass against thee and repent not the first time, nevertheless thou shalt forgive him.

42 And if he trespass against thee the second time, and repent not, nevertheless thou shalt forgive him.

---

32 a D&C 27:10.
33 a Deut. 20:10 (10–12);
 Josh. 8:2 (1–29); 1 Kgs.
 8:44; Alma 48:16
 (10–25).

34 a TG Peace; Peacemakers.
37 a Josh. 23:5 (5–11); Ps.
 35:1; Isa. 49:25; D&C
 105:14. TG Protection,
 Divine.

38 a TG Example.
39 a TG Enemies.
40 a Matt. 18:22 (21–22).
 TG Forgive.

43 And if he trespass against thee the third time, and repent not, thou shalt also forgive him.

44 But if he trespass against thee the fourth time thou shalt not forgive him, but shalt bring these testimonies before the Lord; and they shall not be blotted out until he repent and *reward thee four-fold in all things wherewith he has trespassed against thee.

45 And if he do this, thou shalt forgive him with all thine heart; and if he do not this, I, the Lord, will *avenge thee of thine enemy an hundred-fold;

46 And upon his children, and upon his children's *children of all them that *hate me, unto the *third and fourth generation.

47 But if the *children shall repent, or the children's children, and *turn to the Lord their God, with all their hearts and with all their might, mind, and strength, and *restore four-fold for all their trespasses wherewith they have trespassed, or wherewith their fathers have trespassed, or their fathers' fathers, then thine indignation shall be turned away;

48 And vengeance shall *no more come upon them, saith the Lord thy God, and their trespasses shall never be brought any more as a testimony before the Lord against them. Amen.

SECTION 99

Revelation given through Joseph Smith the Prophet to John Murdock, August 29, 1832, at Hiram, Ohio. For over a year, John Murdock had been preaching the gospel while his children—motherless after the death of his wife, Julia Clapp, in April 1831—resided with other families in Ohio.

1–8, John Murdock is called to proclaim the gospel, and those who receive him receive the Lord and will obtain mercy.

1 Behold, thus saith the Lord unto my servant John Murdock—thou art *called to go into the eastern countries from house to house, from village to village, and from city to city, to proclaim mine everlasting gospel unto the inhabitants thereof, in the midst of *persecution and wickedness.

2 And who *receiveth you receiveth me; and you shall have power to declare my word in the *demonstration of my Holy Spirit.

---

44 a TG Recompence.
45 a Deut. 32:35.
46 a TG Accountability.
  b TG Hate.
  c Deut. 5:9.
47 a Ex. 20:5 (5–6); Ezek.

18:20 (19–23).
  b Lam. 5:21; Mosiah 7:33;
    Morm. 9:6.
  c Lev. 5:16; 6:4; 24:21
    (18–21).
48 a TG Forgive.

99 1 a Luke 10:1 (1–20).
  b TG Persecution.
2 a Matt. 10:40 (40–42).
  b 1 Cor. 2:4.

3 And who receiveth you ^aas a little child, receiveth my ^bkingdom; and blessed are they, for they shall obtain ^cmercy.

4 And whoso rejecteth you shall be ^arejected of my Father and his house; and you shall cleanse your ^bfeet in the secret places by the way for a testimony against them.

5 And behold, and lo, I ^acome quickly to ^bjudgment, to convince all of their ungodly deeds which they have committed against me, as it is written of me in the volume of the book.

6 And now, verily I say unto you, that it is not expedient that you should go until your children are ^aprovided for, and sent up kindly unto the bishop of Zion.

7 And after a few years, if thou desirest of me, thou mayest go up also unto the goodly land, to possess thine ^ainheritance;

8 Otherwise thou shalt continue proclaiming my gospel ^auntil thou be taken. Amen.

SECTION 100

Revelation given to Joseph Smith the Prophet and Sidney Rigdon, at Perrysburg, New York, October 12, 1833. The two brethren, having been absent from their families for several days, felt some concern about them.

1–4, Joseph and Sidney to preach the gospel for the salvation of souls; 5–8, It will be given them in the very hour what they should say; 9–12, Sidney is to be a spokesman and Joseph is to be a revelator and mighty in testimony; 13–17, The Lord will raise up a pure people, and the obedient will be saved.

1 Verily, thus saith the Lord unto you, my friends Sidney and Joseph, your families are well; they are in ^amine hands, and I will do with them as seemeth me good; for in me there is all power.

2 Therefore, follow me, and listen to the counsel which I shall give unto you.

3 Behold, and lo, I have much people in this place, in the regions round about; and an effectual door shall be opened in the regions round about in this eastern land.

4 Therefore, I, the Lord, have suffered you to come unto this place; for thus it was expedient in me for the ^asalvation of souls.

---

3 a Matt. 18:4 (1–14).
  b TG Kingdom of God,
    in Heaven; Kingdom of
    God, on Earth.
  c TG Mercy.
4 a John 12:49 (44–49).

  b D&C 75:20 (19–22).
5 a D&C 1:12.
  b Jude 1:15 (14–15).
    TG Jesus Christ, Judge.
6 a D&C 75:24 (24–26).
7 a D&C 85:7 (1–3, 7, 9);

    101:18 (1, 6, 18).
8 a Matt. 19:29. TG Self-
    Sacrifice.
100 1 a TG Protection, Divine.
  4 a TG Mission of Latter-
    day Saints.

5 Therefore, verily I say unto you, lift up your voices unto this people; ^aspeak the thoughts that I shall put into your hearts, and you shall not be ^bconfounded before men;

6 For it shall be ^agiven you in the very hour, yea, in the very moment, what ye shall say.

7 But a commandment I give unto you, that ye shall declare whatsoever thing ye ^adeclare in my name, in solemnity of heart, in the spirit of meekness, in all things.

8 And I give unto you this promise, that inasmuch as ye do this the ^aHoly Ghost shall be shed forth in bearing record unto all things whatsoever ye shall say.

9 And it is expedient in me that you, my servant Sidney, should be a ^aspokesman unto this people; yea, verily, I will ordain you unto this calling, even to be a spokesman unto my servant Joseph.

10 And I will give unto him power to be mighty in ^atestimony.

11 And I will give unto thee power to be ^amighty in expounding all scriptures, that thou mayest be a spokesman unto him, and he shall be a ^brevelator unto thee, that thou mayest know the certainty of all things ^cpertaining to the things of my kingdom on the earth.

12 Therefore, continue your journey and let your hearts rejoice; for behold, and lo, I am with you even unto the end.

13 And now I give unto you a word concerning Zion. ^aZion shall be ^bredeemed, although she is chastened for a little season.

14 Thy brethren, my servants Orson Hyde and John Gould, are in my hands; and inasmuch as they keep my commandments they shall be saved.

15 Therefore, let your hearts be comforted; for ^aall things shall work together for good to them that walk uprightly, and to the sanctification of the church.

16 For I will raise up unto myself a ^apure people, that will serve me in righteousness;

17 And all that ^acall upon the name of the Lord, and keep his commandments, shall be saved. Even so. Amen.

5 a Ex. 4:12 (12–16); Prov. 16:1; Hel. 5:18 (18–19); 13:3; D&C 68:3 (3–4).
  b Acts 6:10.
6 a Matt. 10:19 (19–20); D&C 84:85.
7 a D&C 18:21; 43:34; 84:61; 88:121. TG Meek; Sincere.
8 a Rom. 10:17 (13–17);

2 Ne. 33:1 (1–4).
9 a Ex. 4:16 (14–16); 2 Ne. 3:17 (17–18); D&C 124:104.
10 a TG Testimony.
11 a Acts 18:24; Alma 17:3 (2–3).
  b TG Revelation.
  c Acts 1:3.
13 a TG Zion.

  b D&C 84:99; 103:15 (15, 20, 29).
15 a Rom. 8:28; D&C 90:24; 105:40.
16 a TG Peculiar People; Purity.
17 a Ps. 50:15; Joel 2:32; Alma 38:5 (4–5).

SECTION 101

Revelation given to Joseph Smith the Prophet, at Kirtland, Ohio, December 16 and 17, 1833. At this time the Saints who had gathered in Missouri were suffering great persecution. Mobs had driven them from their homes in Jackson County; and some of the Saints had tried to establish themselves in Van Buren, Lafayette, and Ray Counties, but persecution followed them. The main body of the Saints was at that time in Clay County, Missouri. Threats of death against individuals of the Church were many. The Saints in Jackson County had lost household furniture, clothing, livestock, and other personal property; and many of their crops had been destroyed.

1–8, The Saints are chastened and afflicted because of their transgressions; 9–15, The Lord's indignation will fall upon the nations, but His people will be gathered and comforted; 16–21, Zion and her stakes will be established; 22–31, The nature of life during the Millennium is set forth; 32–42, The Saints will be blessed and rewarded then; 43–62, The parable of the nobleman and the olive trees signifies the troubles and eventual redemption of Zion; 63–75, The Saints are to continue gathering together; 76–80, The Lord established the Constitution of the United States; 81–101, The Saints are to importune for the redress of grievances, according to the parable of the woman and the unjust judge.

1 Verily I say unto you, concerning your brethren who have been afflicted, and *a*persecuted, and *b*cast out from the land of their inheritance—

2 I, the Lord, have suffered the *a*affliction to come upon them, wherewith they have been afflicted, in consequence of their *b*transgressions;

3 Yet I will own them, and they shall be *a*mine in that day when I shall come to make up my jewels.

4 Therefore, they must needs be *a*chastened and tried, even as *b*Abraham, who was commanded to offer up his only son.

5 For all those who will not *a*endure chastening, but *b*deny me, cannot be sanctified.

6 Behold, I say unto you, there were jarrings, and *a*contentions, and *b*envyings, and *c*strifes, and *d*lustful and covetous desires among them; therefore by these things they polluted their inheritances.

---

101 1*a* TG Persecution.
  b D&C 103:2 (2, 11);
    104:51; 109:47; 121:23.
  2*a* Ps. 119:67; D&C 58:4.
    TG Affliction.
  b Jer. 30:15; 40:3; Lam.
    1:5; Mosiah 7:29; D&C
    103:4; 105:9 (2–10).

3*a* Isa. 62:3; Mal. 3:17;
  D&C 60:4.
4*a* 2 Sam. 7:14; D&C 95:1
  (1–2); 136:31.
  b Gen. 22:2 (1–14); Jacob
    4:5; D&C 132:51.
5*a* Prov. 5:12; Alma 61:9.
  b Prov. 30:9; Matt. 10:33
    (32–33); Rom. 1:16

(15–18); 2 Tim. 2:12
(10–15); 2 Ne. 31:14
(12–21).
6*a* TG Contention; Disputations.
  b TG Envy.
  c TG Strife.
  d TG Carnal Mind; Lust;
    Sensuality.

7 They were slow to ªhearken unto the voice of the Lord their God; therefore, the Lord their God is slow to hearken unto their prayers, to answer them in the day of their trouble.

8 In the day of their peace they esteemed lightly my counsel; but, in the day of their ªtrouble, of necessity they ᵇfeel after me.

9 Verily I say unto you, notwithstanding their sins, my bowels are filled with ªcompassion towards them. I will not utterly ᵇcast them off; and in the day of ᶜwrath I will remember mercy.

10 I have sworn, and the decree hath gone forth by a former commandment which I have given unto you, that I would let fall the ªsword of mine indignation in behalf of my people; and even as I have said, it shall come to pass.

11 Mine indignation is soon to be poured out without measure upon all nations; and this will I do when the cup of their iniquity is ªfull.

12 And in that day all who are found upon the ªwatch-tower, or in other words, all mine Israel, shall be saved.

13 And they that have been scattered shall be ªgathered.

14 And all they who have ªmourned shall be comforted.

15 And all they who have given their ªlives for my name shall be crowned.

16 Therefore, let your hearts be comforted concerning Zion; for all flesh is in mine ªhands; be still and ᵇknow that I am God.

17 ªZion shall not be moved out of her place, notwithstanding her children are scattered.

18 They that remain, and are pure in heart, shall return, and come to their ªinheritances, they and their children, with ᵇsongs of everlasting joy, to ᶜbuild up the waste places of Zion—

19 And all these things that the prophets might be fulfilled.

20 And, behold, there is none other ªplace appointed than that which I have appointed; neither shall there be any other place appointed than that which I have appointed, for the work of the gathering of my saints—

7 a Lev. 26:14 (14–20);
    1 Sam. 8:18; Isa. 1:15;
    59:2; Jer. 2:27; 11:11;
    Ezek. 20:3; Mosiah
    11:24 (22–25); 21:15;
    Alma 5:38 (38–42).
8 a Neh. 9:33; Mosiah
    13:29; Alma 46:8; Hel.
    12:3.
  b Hosea 5:15; Acts 17:27;
    Alma 32:6.
9 a TG Compassion; Mercy.
  b Jer. 30:11.

  c Isa. 60:10; D&C 98:22
    (21–22).
10 a D&C 1:13 (13–14).
11 a Gen. 15:16; Alma 37:31;
    Hel. 13:14; D&C 61:31.
12 a Ezek. 3:17; 33:9 (6–10).
13 a Deut. 30:3; Ps. 60:1
    (1–3); Micah 7:12
    (11–12); 1 Ne. 10:14.
14 a Matt. 5:4. TG Comfort;
    Israel, Restoration of;
    Mourning.
15 a Matt. 5:10 (10–11);

    10:39. TG Martyrdom.
16 a Moses 6:32.
  b Ex. 14:13; Ps. 46:10;
    Jer. 9:3.
17 a D&C 101:20 (20–22).
    TG Zion.
18 a D&C 99:7; 103:14 (11,
    14).
  b Isa. 35:10; D&C 45:71.
    TG Singing.
  c Amos 9:14; D&C 84:3
    (2–5); 103:11.
20 a D&C 57:2 (1–4).

21 Until the day cometh when there is found no more room for them; and then I have other places which I will appoint unto them, and they shall be called *stakes, for the curtains or the strength of Zion.

22 Behold, it is my will, that all they who call on my name, and worship me according to mine everlasting gospel, should *gather together, and *stand in holy places;

23 And *prepare for the revelation which is to come, when the *veil of the covering of my temple, in my tabernacle, which hideth the earth, shall be taken off, and all flesh shall *see me together.

24 And every *corruptible thing, both of man, or of the beasts of the field, or of the fowls of the heavens, or of the fish of the sea, that dwells upon all the face of the earth, shall be *consumed;

25 And also that of element shall *melt with fervent heat; and all things shall become *new, that my knowledge and *glory may dwell upon all the *earth.

26 And in that day the enmity of man, and the *enmity of beasts, yea, the *enmity of all flesh, shall cease from before my face.

27 And in that day *whatsoever any man shall ask, it shall be given unto him.

28 And in that day *Satan shall not have power to tempt any man.

29 And there shall be no *sorrow because there is no death.

30 In that day an *infant shall not die until he is old; and his life shall be as the age of a tree;

31 And when he dies he shall not sleep, that is to say in the earth, but shall be *changed in the twinkling of an eye, and shall be *caught up, and his rest shall be glorious.

32 Yea, verily I say unto you, in that *day when the Lord shall come, he shall *reveal all things—

---

21 a D&C 82:13; 115:18 (6, 17–18). TG Stake.
22 a D&C 10:65. TG Israel, Gathering of; Mission of Latter-day Saints.
  b 2 Chr. 35:5; Matt. 24:15; D&C 45:32; 87:8; JS—M 1:12.
23 a TG Millennium, Preparing a People for.
  b TG Veil.
  c Isa. 40:5; D&C 38:8; 93:1.
24 a Ps. 72:4; D&C 29:24.
  b Zeph. 1:2 (2–3); Mal. 4:1; D&C 88:94;

JS—H 1:37.
25 a Amos 9:5; 2 Pet. 3:10 (10–12). TG Earth, Cleansing of; World, End of.
  b Rev. 21:5. TG Earth, Renewal of.
  c Isa. 6:3; Ezek. 43:2; Rev. 18:1; D&C 94:8. TG Glory.
  d TG Earth, Destiny of.
26 a Isa. 11:9 (6–9).
  b TG Peace.
27 a Isa. 65:24; D&C 4:7.
28 a Rev. 20:2 (2–3); 1 Ne. 22:26; D&C 88:110.

29 a TG Immortality; Sorrow.
30 a Isa. 65:20 (20–22); D&C 45:58; 63:50 (49–50).
31 a 1 Cor. 15:52; D&C 43:32; 88:28 (20, 28). TG Resurrection.
  b 1 Thes. 4:16 (16–17); D&C 76:102; 88:96 (96–98).
32 a D&C 29:11; 43:30. TG Jesus Christ, Second Coming; Millennium.
  b D&C 98:12; 121:28 (26–33).

33 Things which have passed, and ^ahidden things which no man knew, things of the ^bearth, by which it was made, and the purpose and the end thereof—

34 Things most precious, things that are above, and things that are beneath, things that are in the earth, and upon the earth, and in heaven.

35 And all they who suffer ^apersecution for my name, and endure in faith, though they are called to lay down their lives for my ^bsake yet shall they partake of all this glory.

36 Wherefore, ^afear not even unto death; for in this world your joy is not full, but in me your ^bjoy is full.

37 Therefore, care not for the body, neither the life of the body; but care for the ^asoul, and for the life of the soul.

38 And ^aseek the face of the Lord always, that in ^bpatience ye may possess your souls, and ye shall have eternal life.

39 When men are called unto mine ^aeverlasting gospel, and covenant with an everlasting covenant, they are accounted as the ^bsalt of the earth and the savor of men;

40 They are called to be the savor of men; therefore, if that ^asalt of the earth lose its savor, behold, it is thenceforth good for nothing only to be cast out and trodden under the feet of men.

41 Behold, here is wisdom concerning the children of Zion, even many, but not all; they were found transgressors, therefore they must needs be ^achastened—

42 He that ^aexalteth himself shall be abased, and he that ^babaseth himself shall be exalted.

43 And now, I will show unto you a parable, that you may know my will concerning the ^aredemption of Zion.

44 A certain ^anobleman had a spot of land, very choice; and he said unto

33 a TG Mysteries of Godliness.
  b TG Earth, Destiny of; Earth, Purpose of.
35 a 2 Cor. 1:6; 4:9; D&C 63:20. TG Malice; Persecution; Perseverance.
  b Luke 21:17 (15–19); D&C 98:13.
36 a D&C 98:13. TG Comfort; Death, Power over.
  b 2 Ne. 27:30. TG Joy.

37 a TG Soul; Worth of Souls.
38 a 2 Chr. 7:14; Ps. 27:8; 69:32; Amos 5:6; D&C 45:46.
  b TG Patience.
39 a TG New and Everlasting Covenant.
  b Matt. 5:13; 1 Tim. 4:16; D&C 103:10. TG Mission of Latter-day Saints; Peculiar

People; Salt.
40 a D&C 103:10.
41 a TG Chastening; Reproof.
42 a Obad. 1:3 (3–4); Luke 14:11; 2 Ne. 20:33; Hel. 4:12 (12–13). TG Leadership.
  b Luke 18:14; D&C 67:10; 104:82; 124:114.
43 a D&C 103:1.
44 a D&C 103:21 (21–22).

his servants: Go ye unto my [b]vineyard, even upon this very choice piece of land, and plant twelve olive trees;

45 And set [a]watchmen round about them, and build a tower, that one may overlook the land round about, to be a watchman upon the tower, that mine olive trees may not be broken down when the enemy shall come to spoil and take upon themselves the fruit of my vineyard.

46 Now, the servants of the nobleman went and did as their lord commanded them, and planted the olive trees, and built a hedge round about, and set watchmen, and began to build a tower.

47 And while they were yet laying the foundation thereof, they began to say among themselves: And what need hath my lord of this tower?

48 And consulted for a long time, saying among themselves: What need hath my lord of this tower, seeing this is a time of peace?

49 Might not this money be given to the exchangers? For there is no need of these things.

50 And while they were at variance one with another they became very [a]slothful, and they hearkened not unto the commandments of their lord.

51 And the enemy came by night, and broke down the [a]hedge; and the servants of the nobleman arose and were affrighted, and fled; and the enemy destroyed their works, and broke down the olive trees.

52 Now, behold, the nobleman, the lord of the [a]vineyard, called upon his servants, and said unto them, Why! what is the cause of this great evil?

53 Ought ye not to have done even as I commanded you, and—after ye had planted the vineyard, and built the hedge round about, and set watchmen upon the walls thereof—built the tower also, and set a [a]watchman upon the tower, and watched for my vineyard, and not have fallen asleep, lest the enemy should come upon you?

54 And behold, the watchman upon the tower would have seen the enemy while he was yet afar off; and then ye could have made ready and kept the enemy from breaking down the hedge thereof, and saved my vineyard from the hands of the destroyer.

55 And the lord of the vineyard said unto one of his [a]servants: Go and gather together the residue of my servants, and take [b]all the strength of mine house, which are my warriors, my young men, and they that are of

---

44b Isa. 5:1 (1–7); Matt. 21:33 (33–41); Jacob 5:3 (3–77).
45a Ezek. 33:2 (2, 7); 3 Ne. 16:18. TG Watchman.
50a TG Dependability;

Laziness.
51a Isa. 5:5 (1–7).
52a TG Vineyard of the Lord.
53a Ezek. 33:2 (2–7).
55a D&C 103:21.

TG Stewardship.
b D&C 103:22 (22, 29–30); 105:30 (16, 29–30).

middle age also among all my servants, who are the strength of mine house, save those only whom I have appointed to tarry;

56 And go ye straightway unto the land of my vineyard, and redeem my vineyard; for it is mine; I have bought it with money.

57 Therefore, get ye straightway unto my land; break down the *walls of mine enemies; throw down their tower, and scatter their watchmen.

58 And inasmuch as they gather together against you, *avenge me of mine enemies, that by and by I may come with the residue of mine house and possess the land.

59 And the servant said unto his lord: When shall these things be?

60 And he said unto his servant: When I will; go ye straightway, and do all things whatsoever I have commanded you;

61 And this shall be my seal and *blessing upon you—a faithful and *wise steward in the midst of mine house, a *ruler in my kingdom.

62 And his servant went straightway, and did all things whatsoever his lord commanded him; and *after many days all things were fulfilled.

63 Again, verily I say unto you, I will show unto you wisdom in me concerning all the churches, inasmuch as they are *willing to be guided in a right and proper way for their salvation—

64 That the work of the *gathering together of my saints may continue, that I may build them up unto my name upon *holy places; for the time of *harvest is come, and my word must needs be *fulfilled.

65 Therefore, I must gather together my people, according to the parable of the wheat and the *tares, that the wheat may be secured in the garners to possess eternal life, and be crowned with celestial *glory, when I shall come in the kingdom of my Father to reward every man according as his work shall be;

66 While the *tares shall be bound in bundles, and their bands made strong, that they may be *burned with unquenchable fire.

67 Therefore, a commandment I give unto all the churches, that they shall continue to gather together unto the places which I have appointed.

68 Nevertheless, as I have said unto you in a former commandment, let not your *gathering be in haste, nor by flight; but let all things be prepared before you.

57 a Josh. 6:20.
58 a Num. 31:2; Isa. 1:24; D&C 97:22; 103:26; 105:30 (15, 30).
61 a TG Blessing; Reward.
  b D&C 78:22.
  c Matt. 25:21 (20–23).
62 a D&C 105:37 (15, 37).

63 a TG Teachable.
64 a D&C 10:65.
  b D&C 87:8.
  c Joel 3:13; D&C 33:3 (3, 7). TG Harvest.
  d D&C 1:38.
65 a Matt. 13:36 (6–43); D&C 86:1 (1–7).

  b TG Celestial Glory; Glory; Reward.
66 a D&C 38:12.
  b Nahum 1:5; Matt. 3:12; D&C 63:34 (33–34).
68 a D&C 58:56; 63:24.

69 And in order that all things be prepared before you, observe the commandment which I have given concerning these things—

70 Which saith, or teacheth, to ^apurchase all the lands with money, which can be purchased for money, in the region round about the land which I have appointed to be the land of Zion, for the beginning of the gathering of my saints;

71 All the land which can be purchased in Jackson county, and the counties round about, and leave the residue in mine hand.

72 Now, verily I say unto you, let all the churches gather together all their moneys; let these things be done in their time, but not in ^ahaste; and observe to have all things prepared before you.

73 And let honorable men be appointed, even ^awise men, and send them to purchase these lands.

74 And the churches in the ^aeastern countries, when they are built up, if they will hearken unto this counsel they may buy lands and gather together upon them; and in this way they may establish Zion.

75 There is even now already in store sufficient, yea, even an abundance, to redeem Zion, and establish her waste places, no more to be thrown down, were the churches, who call themselves after my name, ^awilling to hearken to my voice.

76 And again I say unto you, those who have been scattered by their enemies, it is my will that they should continue to importune for redress, and redemption, by the hands of those who are placed as rulers and are in authority over you—

77 According to the laws and ^aconstitution of the people, which I have suffered to be established, and should be maintained for the ^brights and protection of all flesh, according to just and holy principles;

78 That every man may act in doctrine and principle pertaining to futurity, according to the moral ^aagency which I have given unto him, that every man may be ^baccountable for his own sins in the day of ^cjudgment.

79 Therefore, it is not right that any man should be in ^abondage one to another.

80 And for this purpose have I established the ^aConstitution of this land,

---

70a D&C 42:35; 57:5
   (5–7); 58:49 (49–53);
   63:27 (27–29); 103:23
   (22–24).
72a Isa. 52:12 (10–12);
   D&C 58:56. TG Haste;
   Rashness.
73a D&C 105:28 (28–30).

74a D&C 100:3.
75a Alma 5:37 (37–39);
   D&C 105:2.
77a TG Citizenship; Governments.
   b TG Liberty.
78a TG Agency.
   b TG Accountability;

   Punish.
   c TG Judgment, the Last.
79a 2 Chr. 28:11; 1 Ne.
   17:25; Mosiah 11:21.
   TG Bondage, Physical;
   Slavery.
80a 2 Ne. 1:7 (7–9); D&C
   98:5 (5–6).

by the hands of wise men whom I raised up unto this very purpose, and redeemed the land by the *b*shedding of blood.

81 Now, unto what shall I liken the children of Zion? I will liken them unto the *a*parable of the woman and the unjust judge, for men ought always to *b*pray and not to faint, which saith—

82 There was in a city a judge which feared not God, neither regarded man.

83 And there was a widow in that city, and she came unto him, saying: Avenge me of mine adversary.

84 And he would not for a while, but afterward he said within himself: Though I fear not God, nor regard man, yet because this widow troubleth me I will avenge her, lest by her continual coming she weary me.

85 Thus will I liken the children of Zion.

86 Let them importune at the *a*feet of the judge;

87 And if he heed them not, let them importune at the feet of the governor;

88 And if the governor heed them not, let them importune at the feet of the president;

89 And if the president heed them not, then will the Lord arise and come forth out of his *a*hiding place, and in his fury vex the nation;

90 And in his hot displeasure, and in his fierce anger, in his time, will cut off those wicked, unfaithful, and *a*unjust *b*stewards, and appoint them their portion among *c*hypocrites, and *d*unbelievers;

91 Even in outer darkness, where there is *a*weeping, and wailing, and gnashing of teeth.

92 Pray ye, therefore, that their ears may be opened unto your cries, that I may be *a*merciful unto them, that these things may not come upon them.

93 What I have said unto you must needs be, that all men may be left without *a*excuse;

94 That wise men and rulers may hear and know that which they have never *a*considered;

95 That I may proceed to bring to pass my act, my *a*strange act, and perform my work, my strange work, that men may *b*discern between the righteous and the wicked, saith your God.

80*b* 1 Ne. 13:18 (13–19).
81*a* Luke 18:1 (1–8).
  b TG Prayer.
86*a* TG Humility.
89*a* Isa. 45:15 (15–17);
   Zech. 2:13; D&C 121:1
   (1, 4); 123:6.

90*a* TG Injustice.
  b TG Stewardship.
  c TG Hypocrisy.
  d Rev. 21:8. TG Unbelief.
91*a* Matt. 25:30; D&C
   19:5; 29:15 (15–20);
   124:8.

92*a* TG God, Mercy of.
93*a* Rom. 1:20 (18–21).
94*a* Isa. 52:15 (13–15);
   3 Ne. 20:45; 21:8.
95*a* Isa. 28:21; D&C 95:4.
  b Mal. 3:18. TG Discernment, Spiritual.

96 And again, I say unto you, it is contrary to my commandment and my will that my servant Sidney Gilbert should sell my ᵃstorehouse, which I have appointed unto my people, into the hands of mine enemies.

97 Let not that which I have appointed be polluted by mine enemies, by the consent of those who ᵃcall themselves after my name;

98 For this is a very sore and grievous sin against me, and against my people, in consequence of those things which I have decreed and which are soon to befall the nations.

99 Therefore, it is my will that my people should claim, and hold claim upon that which I have appointed unto them, though they should not be permitted to dwell thereon.

100 Nevertheless, I do not say they shall not dwell thereon; for inasmuch as they bring forth fruit and works meet for my kingdom they ᵃshall dwell thereon.

101 They shall build, and another shall not ᵃinherit it; they shall plant vineyards, and they shall eat the fruit thereof. Even so. Amen.

SECTION 102

Minutes of the organization of the first high council of the Church, at Kirtland, Ohio, February 17, 1834. The original minutes were recorded by Elders Oliver Cowdery and Orson Hyde. The Prophet revised the minutes the following day, and the next day the corrected minutes were unanimously accepted by the high council as "a form and constitution of the high council" of the Church. Verses 30 through 32, having to do with the Council of the Twelve Apostles, were added in 1835 under Joseph Smith's direction when this section was prepared for publication in the Doctrine and Covenants.

1–8, A high council is appointed to settle important difficulties that arise in the Church; 9–18, Procedures are given for hearing cases; 19–23, The president of the council renders the decision; 24–34, Appellate procedure is set forth.

1 This day a general council of twenty-four high priests assembled at the house of Joseph Smith, Jun., by revelation, and proceeded to organize the ᵃhigh council of the church of Christ, which was to consist of twelve high priests, and one or three presidents as the case might require.

2 The ᵃhigh council was appointed by revelation for the purpose of ᵇsettling important difficulties which might arise in the church, which could

---

96a D&C 58:37; 72:10
  (8–10); 90:35 (35–37).
97a D&C 103:4; 112:26;
  125:2.

100a D&C 103:15 (15–28).
101a Isa. 65:21; D&C 64:34.
  TG Millennium.
102 1a D&C 42:34.

2a D&C 20:67.
  b TG Judgment.

not be settled by the church or the ᶜbishop's council to the satisfaction of the parties.

3 Joseph Smith, Jun., Sidney Rigdon and Frederick G. Williams were acknowledged presidents by the voice of the council; and Joseph Smith, Sen., John Smith, Joseph Coe, John Johnson, Martin Harris, John S. Carter, Jared Carter, Oliver Cowdery, Samuel H. Smith, Orson Hyde, Sylvester Smith, and Luke Johnson, high priests, were chosen to be a standing council for the church, by the unanimous voice of the council.

4 The above-named councilors were then asked whether they accepted their appointments, and whether they would act in that office according to the ᵃlaw of heaven, to which they all answered that they accepted their appointments, and would fill their offices according to the grace of God bestowed upon them.

5 The number composing the council, who voted in the name and for the church in appointing the above-named councilors were forty-three, as follows: nine high priests, seventeen elders, four priests, and thirteen members.

6 Voted: that the high council cannot have power to act without seven of the above-named councilors, or their regularly appointed successors are present.

7 These seven shall have power to appoint other high priests, whom they may consider worthy and capable to act in the place of absent councilors.

8 Voted: that whenever any vacancy shall occur by the death, removal from office for transgression, or removal from the bounds of this church government, of any one of the above-named councilors, it shall be filled by the nomination of the ᵃpresident or presidents, and sanctioned by the voice of a general council of high priests, convened for that purpose, to act in the name of the church.

9 The president of the church, who is also the president of the council, is appointed by ᵃrevelation, and ᵇacknowledged in his administration by the voice of the church.

10 And it is according to the dignity of his office that he should preside over the council of the church; and it is his privilege to be assisted by two other presidents, appointed after the same manner that he himself was appointed.

11 And in case of the absence of one or both of those who are appointed to assist him, he has power to preside over the council without an assistant;

2 c D&C 107:73 (72–75).
4 a TG God, Law of.
8 a D&C 68:15 (15, 19, 22).

9 a TG Called of God. See also the headings to sections 81 and 90.

b TG Sustaining Church Leaders.

and in case he himself is absent, the other presidents have power to preside in his stead, both or either of them.

12 Whenever a high council of the church of Christ is regularly organized, according to the foregoing pattern, it shall be the duty of the twelve councilors to cast lots by numbers, and thereby ascertain who of the twelve shall speak first, commencing with number one and so in succession to number twelve.

13 Whenever this council convenes to act upon any case, the twelve councilors shall consider whether it is a difficult one or not; if it is not, two only of the councilors shall speak upon it, according to the form above written.

14 But if it is thought to be difficult, four shall be appointed; and if more difficult, six; but in no case shall more than six be appointed to speak.

15 The accused, in all cases, has a right to one-half of the council, to prevent insult or *injustice.

16 And the councilors appointed to speak before the council are to present the case, after the evidence is examined, in its true light before the council; and every man is to speak according to equity and *justice.

17 Those councilors who *draw even numbers, that is, 2, 4, 6, 8, 10, and 12, are the individuals who are to stand up in behalf of the accused, and prevent insult and *injustice.

18 In all cases the accuser and the accused shall have a privilege of speaking for themselves before the council, after the evidences are *heard and the councilors who are appointed to speak on the case have finished their remarks.

19 After the evidences are heard, the councilors, accuser and accused have spoken, the president shall give a decision according to the understanding which he shall have of the case, and call upon the twelve councilors to *sanction the same by their vote.

20 But should the remaining councilors, who have not spoken, or any one of them, after hearing the evidences and pleadings impartially, discover an *error in the decision of the president, they can manifest it, and the case shall have a re-hearing.

21 And if, after a careful re-hearing, any additional light is shown upon the case, the decision shall be altered accordingly.

22 But in case no additional light is given, the first decision shall stand, the majority of the council having power to determine the same.

23 In case of difficulty respecting *doctrine or principle, if there is not a sufficiency written to make the case clear to the minds of the council, the president may inquire and obtain the *mind of the Lord by revelation.

---

15 *a* TG Injustice.
16 *a* TG Justice.
17 *a* BD Lots, casting of.
   b TG Injustice.
18 *a* John 7:51; Acts 25:16.
19 *a* TG Common Consent.
20 *a* Isa. 56:1.
23 *a* Num. 9:8.
b Lev. 24:12; D&C 68:4.
   TG Revelation.

24 The high priests, when abroad, have power to call and organize a council after the manner of the foregoing, to settle difficulties, when the parties or either of them shall request it.

25 And the said council of high priests shall have power to appoint one of their own number to preside over such council for the time being.

26 It shall be the duty of said council to *transmit, immediately, a copy of their proceedings, with a full statement of the testimony accompanying their decision, to the high council of the seat of the First Presidency of the Church.

27 Should the parties or either of them be dissatisfied with the decision of said council, they may appeal to the high council of the seat of the First Presidency of the Church, and have a re-hearing, which case shall there be conducted, according to the former pattern written, as though no such decision had been made.

28 This council of high priests abroad is only to be called on the most *difficult cases of church matters; and no common or ordinary case is to be sufficient to call such council.

29 The traveling or located high priests abroad have power to say whether it is necessary to call such a council or not.

30 There is a distinction between the *high council or traveling high priests abroad, and the traveling high council composed of the twelve *apostles, in their decisions.

31 From the decision of the former there can be an appeal; but from the decision of the latter there cannot.

32 The latter can only be called in question by the general authorities of the church in case of transgression.

33 Resolved: that the president or presidents of the seat of the First Presidency of the Church shall have power to determine whether any such case, as may be appealed, is justly entitled to a re-hearing, after examining the appeal and the evidences and statements accompanying it.

34 The twelve councilors then proceeded to cast lots or ballot, to ascertain who should speak first, and the following was the result, namely: 1, Oliver Cowdery; 2, Joseph Coe; 3, Samuel H. Smith; 4, Luke Johnson; 5, John S. Carter; 6, Sylvester Smith; 7, John Johnson; 8, Orson Hyde; 9, Jared Carter; 10, Joseph Smith, Sen.; 11, John Smith; 12, Martin Harris.

After prayer the conference adjourned.

OLIVER COWDERY,
ORSON HYDE,
Clerks

---

26 *a* TG Church Organiza-
　　tion; Order.
28 *a* D&C 107:78.
30 *a* D&C 107:23–24, 31,
35–38.
b TG Apostles.

SECTION 103

Revelation given through Joseph Smith the Prophet, at Kirtland, Ohio, February 24, 1834. This revelation was received after the arrival in Kirtland, Ohio, of Parley P. Pratt and Lyman Wight, who had come from Missouri to counsel with the Prophet as to the relief and restoration of the Saints to their lands in Jackson County.

1–4, Why the Lord permitted the Saints in Jackson County to be persecuted; 5–10, The Saints will prevail if they keep the commandments; 11–20, The redemption of Zion will come by power, and the Lord will go before His people; 21–28, The Saints are to gather in Zion, and those who lay down their lives will find them again; 29–40, Various brethren are called to organize Zion's Camp and go to Zion; they are promised victory if they are faithful.

1 Verily I say unto you, my friends, behold, I will give unto you a revelation and commandment, that you may know how to ᵃact in the discharge of your duties concerning the salvation and ᵇredemption of your brethren, who have been scattered on the land of Zion;

2 Being ᵃdriven and smitten by the hands of mine enemies, on whom I will pour out my ᵇwrath without measure in mine own time.

3 For I have suffered them thus far, that they might ᵃfill up the measure of their iniquities, that their cup might be full;

4 And that those who call themselves after my name might be ᵃchastened for a little season with a sore and grievous chastisement, because they did not ᵇhearken altogether unto the precepts and commandments which I gave unto them.

5 But verily I say unto you, that I have decreed a decree which my people shall ᵃrealize, inasmuch as they hearken from this very hour unto the ᵇcounsel which I, the Lord their God, shall give unto them.

6 Behold they shall, for I have decreed it, begin to ᵃprevail against mine ᵇenemies from this very hour.

7 And by ᵃhearkening to observe all the words which I, the Lord their God, shall speak unto them, they shall never cease to prevail until the ᵇkingdoms of the world are subdued under my feet, and the earth is ᶜgiven unto the saints, to ᵈpossess it forever and ever.

---

103 1a D&C 43:8; 82:9.
    b D&C 101:43 (43–62).
  2a D&C 101:1; 104:51;
    109:47.
    b Rom. 12:19 (17–20);
    Morm. 3:15 (9–15).
    TG Protection, Divine.
  3a Gen. 15:16; Matt. 23:32

(30–36); Alma 14:11
(10–11); 60:13.
  4a D&C 95:1. TG Chastening.
    b Lam. 1:5; D&C 101:2;
    105:9 (2–10). TG Disobedience.
  5a D&C 130:20.
    b TG Counsel.

6a Hosea 6:1.
    b Deut. 33:27.
  7a D&C 35:24. TG Obedience.
    b Dan. 2:44 (34–45).
    TG Earth, Destiny of;
    Kings, Earthly.
    c Dan. 7:27. TG Saints.
    d D&C 38:20.

8 But inasmuch as they *keep not my commandments, and hearken not to observe all my words, the kingdoms of the world shall prevail against them.

9 For they were set to be a *light unto the world, and to be the *saviors of men;

10 And inasmuch as they are not the saviors of men, they are as *salt that has lost its savor, and is thenceforth good for nothing but to be cast out and trodden under foot of men.

11 But verily I say unto you, I have decreed that your brethren which have been scattered shall return to the *lands of their inheritances, and shall *build up the waste places of Zion.

12 For after *much tribulation, as I have said unto you in a former commandment, cometh the blessing.

13 Behold, this is the blessing which I have promised after your tribulations, and the tribulations of your brethren—your redemption, and the redemption of your brethren, even their restoration to the land of Zion, to be established, no more to be thrown down.

14 Nevertheless, if they pollute their inheritances they shall be thrown down; for I will not spare them if they pollute their inheritances.

15 Behold, I say unto you, the *redemption of Zion must needs come by power;

16 Therefore, I will raise up unto my people a man, who shall *lead them like as Moses led the children of Israel.

17 For ye are the children of Israel, and of the *seed of Abraham, and ye must needs be *led out of *bondage by power, and with a stretched-out arm.

18 And as your fathers were *led at the first, even so shall the redemption of Zion be.

19 Therefore, let not your hearts faint, for I say not unto you as I said unto your fathers: Mine *angel shall go up before you, but not my *presence.

20 But I say unto you: Mine *angels shall go up before you, and also my *presence, and in time ye shall *possess the goodly land.

---

8 a Lev. 26:17 (16–17);
   1 Kgs. 8:33; Mosiah
   1:13 (13–14); D&C
   82:10.
9 a Ezek. 5:5; 1 Ne. 21:6;
   Alma 4:11; 39:11.
   TG Children of Light;
   Example; Light [noun].
   b Obad. 1:21.
10 a Matt. 5:13; D&C
   101:39 (39–41).
   TG Salt.

11 a D&C 101:18; 109:47.
   b Amos 9:14; D&C 84:3
   (2–5).
12 a John 16:33; Rev. 7:14
   (13–14); D&C 58:4;
   109:76; 112:13. TG Probation; Test.
15 a D&C 100:13; 105:1
   (1–16, 34).
16 a Ex. 3:10 (2–10); Mosiah
   7:19; Alma 36:28; D&C
   107:91 (91–92).

17 a TG Abrahamic Covenant; Seed of Abraham.
   b Ex. 13:21 (21–22).
   c TG Bondage, Physical.
18 a D&C 136:22 (18, 22).
19 a TG Angels.
   b Ex. 33:3 (1–4); D&C
   84:24 (23–28).
20 a Ex. 14:19 (19–20).
   b 1 Cor. 10:1.
   c D&C 100:13.

21 Verily, verily I say unto you, that my servant Joseph Smith, Jun., is the ᵃman to whom I likened the servant to whom the Lord of the ᵇvineyard spake in the parable which I have given unto you.

22 Therefore let my servant Joseph Smith, Jun., say unto the ᵃstrength of my house, my young men and the middle aged—Gather yourselves together unto the land of Zion, upon the land which I have bought with money that has been consecrated unto me.

23 And let all the churches send up wise men with their moneys, and ᵃpurchase lands even as I have commanded them.

24 And inasmuch as mine enemies come against you to drive you from my goodly ᵃland, which I have consecrated to be the land of Zion, even from your own lands after these testimonies, which ye have brought before me against them, ye shall curse them;

25 And whomsoever ye ᵃcurse, I will curse, and ye shall avenge me of mine enemies.

26 And my presence shall be with you even in ᵃavenging me of mine enemies, unto the third and fourth generation of them that hate me.

27 Let no man be afraid to lay down his ᵃlife for my sake; for whoso ᵇlayeth down his life for my sake shall find it again.

28 And whoso is not willing to lay down his life for my sake is not my disciple.

29 It is my will that my servant Sidney Rigdon shall lift up his voice in the congregations in the eastern countries, in preparing the churches to keep the commandments which I have given unto them concerning the restoration and redemption of Zion.

30 It is my will that my servant Parley P. Pratt and my servant Lyman Wight should not return to the land of their brethren, until they have obtained companies to go up unto the land of Zion, by tens, or by twenties, or by fifties, or by an hundred, until they have obtained to the number of five hundred of the ᵃstrength of my house.

31 Behold this is my will; ask and ye shall receive; but men do ᵃnot always do my will.

---

21 a D&C 101:44 (44, 55).
　 b TG Vineyard of the Lord.
22 a D&C 35:13 (13–14); 101:55; 105:16 (16, 29–30).
23 a D&C 42:35; 57:5 (5–7); 58:49 (49–51);

101:70 (68–74).
24 a D&C 28:9; 29:8 (7–8); 45:66 (64–66); 52:2 (2, 42); 57:1 (1–2).
25 a Deut. 30:7; D&C 124:93.
26 a D&C 97:22; 101:58; 105:30 (15, 30).

27 a Luke 14:33.
　 b Matt. 10:39; Luke 9:24; D&C 98:13 (13–15); 124:54.
30 a D&C 101:55.
31 a D&C 82:10.

32 Therefore, if you cannot obtain five hundred, seek diligently that peradventure you may obtain three hundred.

33 And if ye cannot obtain three hundred, seek diligently that peradventure ye may obtain one hundred.

34 But verily I say unto you, a commandment I give unto you, that ye shall not go up unto the land of Zion until you have obtained a hundred of the strength of my house, to go up with you unto the land of Zion.

35 Therefore, as I said unto you, ask and ye shall receive; pray earnestly that peradventure my servant Joseph Smith, Jun., may go with you, and preside in the midst of my people, and organize my kingdom upon the *consecrated land, and establish the children of Zion upon the laws and commandments which have been and which shall be given unto you.

36 All victory and glory is brought to pass unto you through your *diligence, faithfulness, and *prayers of faith.

37 Let my servant Parley P. Pratt journey with my servant Joseph Smith, Jun.

38 Let my servant Lyman Wight journey with my servant Sidney Rigdon.

39 Let my servant Hyrum Smith journey with my servant Frederick G. Williams.

40 Let my servant Orson Hyde journey with my servant Orson Pratt, whithersoever my servant Joseph Smith, Jun., shall counsel them, in obtaining the fulfilment of these commandments which I have given unto you, and leave the residue in my hands. Even so. Amen.

SECTION 104

Revelation given to Joseph Smith the Prophet, at or near Kirtland, Ohio, April 23, 1834, concerning the United Firm (see the headings to sections 78 and 82). The occasion was likely that of a council meeting of members of the United Firm, which discussed the pressing temporal needs of the Church. An earlier meeting of the firm on April 10 had resolved that the organization be dissolved. This revelation directs that the firm instead be reorganized; its properties were to be divided among members of the firm as their stewardships. Under Joseph Smith's direction, the phrase "United Firm" was later replaced with "United Order" in the revelation.

---

35 a D&C 84:3 (3–4, 31); 105:15.

36 a TG Dedication; Diligence; Steadfastness;

Trustworthiness.
b D&C 104:82 (79–82).

1–10, Saints who transgress against the united order will be cursed; 11–16, The Lord provides for His Saints in His own way; 17–18, Gospel law governs the care of the poor; 19–46, The stewardships and blessings of various brethren are designated; 47–53, The united order in Kirtland and the order in Zion are to operate separately; 54–66, The sacred treasury of the Lord is set up for the printing of the scriptures; 67–77, The general treasury of the united order is to operate on the basis of common consent; 78–86, Those in the united order are to pay all their debts, and the Lord will deliver them from financial bondage.

1 Verily I say unto you, my friends, I give unto you counsel, and a commandment, concerning all the *a*properties which belong to the order which I commanded to be organized and established, to be a *b*united order, and an everlasting order for the benefit of my *c*church, and for the salvation of men until I come—

2 With promise immutable and unchangeable, that inasmuch as those whom I commanded were faithful they should be blessed with a *a*multiplicity of blessings;

3 But inasmuch as they were not faithful they were nigh unto *a*cursing.

4 Therefore, inasmuch as some of my servants have not kept the commandment, but have broken the covenant through *a*covetousness, and with feigned words, I have *b*cursed them with a very sore and grievous curse.

5 For I, the Lord, have decreed in my heart, that inasmuch as any man belonging to the order shall be found a transgressor, or, in other words, shall break the *a*covenant with which ye are bound, he shall be cursed in his life, and shall be trodden down by whom I will;

6 For I, the Lord, am not to be *a*mocked in these things—

7 And all this that the innocent among you may not be condemned with the *a*unjust; and that the guilty among you may not escape; because I, the Lord, have promised unto you a *b*crown of glory at my *c*right hand.

8 Therefore, inasmuch as you are found transgressors, you cannot escape my wrath in your lives.

9 Inasmuch as ye are *a*cut off for transgression, ye cannot escape the *b*buffetings of *c*Satan until the day of redemption.

10 And I now give unto you power from this very hour, that if any man among you, of the order, is found a transgressor and repenteth not of the

---

104 1*a* D&C 104:19 (19–46).
   b D&C 78:3 (3–15); 96:8
    (6–9); 105:4 (4–5).
   c TG Jesus Christ, Second
    Coming.
  2*a* Luke 18:30.

3*a* Heb. 6:8.
4*a* TG Covet.
   b D&C 82:21. TG Curse.
5*a* Hosea 10:4; 3 Ne. 24:5.
6*a* Gal. 6:7 (7–9).
   TG Mocking.
7*a* TG Injustice; Justice.

   b Isa. 62:3; D&C 76:56
    (50–70). TG Glory.
   c D&C 76:20 (20–23).
9*a* TG Excommunication.
   b D&C 82:21; 132:26.
   c TG Devil.

evil, that ye shall *deliver him over unto the buffetings of Satan; and he shall not have power to *bring evil upon you.

11 It is wisdom in me; therefore, a commandment I give unto you, that ye shall organize yourselves and appoint every man his *stewardship;

12 That every man may give an account unto me of the stewardship which is appointed unto him.

13 For it is expedient that I, the Lord, should make every man *accountable, as a *steward over earthly blessings, which I have made and prepared for my creatures.

14 I, the Lord, stretched out the heavens, and *built the earth, my very *handiwork; and all things therein are mine.

15 And it is my purpose to provide for my saints, for all things are mine.

16 But it must needs be done in mine own *way; and behold this is the way that I, the Lord, have decreed to provide for my saints, that the *poor shall be exalted, in that the rich are made low.

17 For the *earth is full, and there is enough and to spare; yea, I prepared all things, and have given unto the children of men to be *agents unto themselves.

18 Therefore, if any man shall take of the *abundance which I have made, and impart not his portion, according to the *law of my gospel, unto the *poor and the needy, he shall, with the wicked, lift up his eyes in *hell, being in torment.

19 And now, verily I say unto you, concerning the *properties of the *order—

20 Let my servant Sidney Rigdon have appointed unto him the place where he now resides, and the lot of the tannery for his stewardship, for his support while he is laboring in my vineyard, even as I will, when I shall command him.

21 And let all things be done according to the counsel of the order, and united consent or voice of the order, which dwell in the land of Kirtland.

22 And this stewardship and blessing, I, the Lord, confer upon my servant Sidney Rigdon for a blessing upon him, and his seed after him;

10a 1 Tim. 1:20.
  b D&C 109:26 (25–27).
11a D&C 42:32. TG Stewardship.
13a TG Accountability.
  b D&C 72:3 (3–5, 16–22).
14a Isa. 42:5; 45:12. TG Creation.
  b Ps. 19:1; 24:1.

16a D&C 105:5. TG Welfare.
  b 1 Sam. 2:8 (7–8); Luke 1:52 (51–53); D&C 88:17.
17a Ps. 136:25; D&C 59:16 (16–20). TG Earth, Purpose of; Nature, Earth.
  b TG Agency.
18a Luke 3:11; James 2:16.

TG Selfishness.
  b D&C 42:30.
  c Job 29:12; Prov. 14:21; Mosiah 4:26; D&C 52:40.
  d Luke 16:23 (20–31).
19a D&C 104:1.
  b D&C 92:1.

23 And I will multiply blessings upon him, inasmuch as he will be humble before me.

24 And again, let my servant Martin Harris have appointed unto him, for his stewardship, the lot of land which my servant John Johnson obtained in exchange for his former inheritance, for him and his seed after him;

25 And inasmuch as he is faithful, I will multiply blessings upon him and his seed after him.

26 And let my servant Martin Harris devote his moneys for the proclaiming of my words, according as my servant Joseph Smith, Jun., shall direct.

27 And again, let my servant Frederick G. Williams have the place upon which he now dwells.

28 And let my servant Oliver Cowdery have the lot which is set off joining the house, which is to be for the printing office, which is lot number one, and also the lot upon which his father resides.

29 And let my servants Frederick G. Williams and Oliver Cowdery have the printing office and all things that pertain unto it.

30 And this shall be their stewardship which shall be appointed unto them.

31 And inasmuch as they are faithful, behold I will bless, and multiply blessings upon them.

32 And this is the beginning of the stewardship which I have appointed them, for them and their seed after them.

33 And, inasmuch as they are faithful, I will multiply blessings upon them and their ^aseed after them, even a multiplicity of blessings.

34 And again, let my servant John Johnson have the house in which he lives, and the inheritance, all save the ground which has been reserved for the ^abuilding of my houses, which pertains to that inheritance, and those lots which have been named for my servant Oliver Cowdery.

35 And inasmuch as he is faithful, I will multiply blessings upon him.

36 And it is my will that he should sell the lots that are laid off for the building up of the ^acity of my saints, inasmuch as it shall be made known to him by the ^bvoice of the Spirit, and according to the counsel of the order, and by the voice of the order.

37 And this is the beginning of the stewardship which I have appointed unto him, for a blessing unto him and his seed after him.

38 And inasmuch as he is faithful, I will multiply a multiplicity of blessings upon him.

---

33 a Ps. 112:2.   34 a D&C 94:3 (3, 10, 16).   36 a D&C 48:4; 51:16.
                                                              b TG Revelation.

39 And again, let my servant Newel K. Whitney have appointed unto him the houses and lot where he now resides, and the lot and building on which the mercantile establishment stands, and also the lot which is on the corner south of the mercantile establishment, and also the lot on which the ashery is situated.

40 And all this I have appointed unto my servant Newel K. Whitney for his stewardship, for a blessing upon him and his seed after him, for the benefit of the mercantile establishment of my order which I have established for my stake in the land of Kirtland.

41 Yea, verily, this is the stewardship which I have appointed unto my servant N. K. Whitney, even this whole mercantile establishment, him and his *agent, and his seed after him.

42 And inasmuch as he is faithful in keeping my commandments, which I have given unto him, I will multiply blessings upon him and his seed after him, even a multiplicity of blessings.

43 And again, let my servant Joseph Smith, Jun., have appointed unto him the lot which is laid off for the *building of my house, which is forty rods long and twelve wide, and also the inheritance upon which his father now resides;

44 And this is the beginning of the stewardship which I have appointed unto him, for a blessing upon him, and upon his father.

45 For behold, I have reserved an inheritance for his *father, for his support; therefore he shall be reckoned in the house of my servant Joseph Smith, Jun.

46 And I will multiply blessings upon the house of my servant Joseph Smith, Jun., inasmuch as he is faithful, even a multiplicity of blessings.

47 And now, a commandment I give unto you concerning Zion, that you shall no longer be bound as a *united order to your brethren of Zion, only on this wise—

48 After you are organized, you shall be called the United Order of the *Stake of Zion, the City of Kirtland. And your brethren, after they are organized, shall be called the United Order of the City of Zion.

49 And they shall be organized in their own names, and in their own name; and they shall do their business in their own name, and in their own names;

50 And you shall do your business in your own name, and in your own names.

---

41 a D&C 84:113.
43 a D&C 95:8.

45 a D&C 90:20; 124:19.
47 a D&C 82:12 (11–12, 20).

48 a D&C 68:26; 82:13;
    94:1; 96:1; 109:59.

51 And this I have commanded to be done for your salvation, and also for their salvation, in consequence of their being *driven out and that which is to come.

52 The *covenants being broken through transgression, by *covetousness and feigned words—

53 Therefore, you are dissolved as a united order with your brethren, that you are not bound only up to this hour unto them, only on this wise, as I said, by *loan as shall be agreed by this order in council, as your circumstances will admit and the voice of the council direct.

54 And again, a commandment I give unto you concerning your stewardship which I have appointed unto you.

55 Behold, all these properties are mine, or else your faith is vain, and ye are found hypocrites, and the *covenants which ye have made unto me are broken;

56 And if the properties are mine, then ye are *stewards; otherwise ye are no stewards.

57 But, verily I say unto you, I have appointed unto you to be stewards over mine house, even stewards indeed.

58 And for this purpose I have commanded you to organize yourselves, even to print *my words, the fulness of my scriptures, the revelations which I have given unto you, and which I shall, hereafter, from time to time give unto you—

59 For the purpose of building up my church and kingdom on the earth, and to *prepare my people for the time when I shall *dwell with them, which is nigh at hand.

60 And ye shall prepare for yourselves a place for a *treasury, and consecrate it unto my name.

61 And ye shall appoint one among you to keep the treasury, and he shall be ordained unto this blessing.

62 And there shall be a seal upon the treasury, and all the sacred things shall be delivered into the treasury; and no man among you shall call it his own, or any part of it, for it shall belong to you all with one accord.

63 And I give it unto you from this very hour; and now see to it, that

---

51 a D&C 101:1; 103:2 (2, 11); 109:47.
52 a TG Covenants.
 b TG Covet.
53 a D&C 51:11.
55 a TG Consecration.
56 a TG Stewardship.

58 a IE the Bible translation. D&C 94:10; 124:89; 133:60. TG Scriptures, Preservation of; Scriptures to Come Forth.
59 a TG Millennium, Preparing a People for.

 b D&C 1:36 (35–36); 29:11 (9–11); 45:59; 84:119 (118–19). TG Jesus Christ, Second Coming.
60 a 2 Kgs. 22:4 (4–7); 2 Chr. 34:9 (8–14).

ye go to and make use of the stewardship which I have appointed unto you, exclusive of the sacred things, for the purpose of printing these sacred things as I have said.

64 And the *avails of the sacred things shall be had in the treasury, and a seal shall be upon it; and it shall not be used or taken out of the treasury by any one, neither shall the seal be loosed which shall be placed upon it, only by the voice of the order, or by commandment.

65 And thus shall ye preserve the avails of the sacred things in the treasury, for sacred and holy purposes.

66 And this shall be called the *sacred treasury of the Lord; and a seal shall be kept upon it that it may be holy and consecrated unto the Lord.

67 And again, there shall be another treasury prepared, and a treasurer appointed to keep the treasury, and a seal shall be placed upon it;

68 And all moneys that you receive in your stewardships, by improving upon the properties which I have appointed unto you, in houses, or in lands, or in cattle, or in all things save it be the holy and sacred writings, which I have reserved unto myself for holy and sacred purposes, shall be cast into the treasury as fast as you receive moneys, by hundreds, or by fifties, or by twenties, or by tens, or by fives.

69 Or in other words, if any man among you obtain five dollars let him cast them into the treasury; or if he obtain ten, or twenty, or fifty, or an hundred, let him do likewise;

70 And let not any among you say that it is his own; for it shall not be called his, nor any part of it.

71 And there shall not any part of it be used, or taken out of the treasury, only by the voice and common consent of the order.

72 And this shall be the voice and common consent of the order—that any man among you say to the treasurer: I have need of this to help me in my stewardship—

73 If it be five dollars, or if it be ten dollars, or twenty, or fifty, or a hundred, the treasurer shall give unto him the sum which he requires to help him in his stewardship—

74 Until he be found a transgressor, and it is manifest before the council of the order plainly that he is an unfaithful and an *unwise steward.

75 But so long as he is in full fellowship, and is faithful and wise in his

---

64 *a* IE profits, or proceeds.   66 *a* TG Sacred.   74 *a* Luke 16:1 (1–12).

stewardship, this shall be his token unto the treasurer that the treasurer shall not withhold.

76 But in case of transgression, the treasurer shall be subject unto the council and voice of the order.

77 And in case the treasurer is found an unfaithful and an unwise steward, he shall be subject to the council and voice of the order, and shall be removed out of his place, and ^aanother shall be appointed in his stead.

78 And again, verily I say unto you, concerning your debts—behold it is my will that you shall ^apay all your ^bdebts.

79 And it is my will that you shall ^ahumble yourselves before me, and obtain this blessing by your ^bdiligence and humility and the prayer of faith.

80 And inasmuch as you are diligent and humble, and exercise the ^aprayer of faith, behold, I will soften the hearts of those to whom you are in debt, until I shall send means unto you for your ^bdeliverance.

81 Therefore write speedily to New York and write according to that which shall be dictated by my ^aSpirit; and I will soften the hearts of those to whom you are in debt, that it shall be taken away out of their minds to bring affliction upon you.

82 And inasmuch as ye are ^ahumble and faithful and ^bcall upon my name, behold, I will give you the ^cvictory.

83 I give unto you a promise, that you shall be delivered this once out of your ^abondage.

84 Inasmuch as you obtain a chance to loan money by hundreds, or thousands, even until you shall loan enough to deliver yourself from bondage, it is your privilege.

85 And pledge the properties which I have put into your hands, this once, by giving your names by common consent or otherwise, as it shall seem good unto you.

86 I give unto you this privilege, this once; and behold, if you proceed to do the things which I have laid before you, according to my commandments, all these things are mine, and ye are my stewards, and the master will not suffer his house to be ^abroken up. Even so. Amen.

---

77 a D&C 64:40; 107:99
    (99–100).
78 a D&C 42:54.
    b TG Debt.
79 a TG Humility.

b TG Diligence.
80 a James 5:15.
    b TG Deliver.
81 a TG God, Spirit of.
82 a Luke 14:11; D&C

67:10; 101:42.
    b D&C 103:36.
    c TG Objectives.
83 a TG Bondage, Physical.
86 a Matt. 24:43.

SECTION 105

Revelation given through Joseph Smith the Prophet, on Fishing River, Missouri, June 22, 1834. Under the leadership of the Prophet, Saints from Ohio and other areas marched to Missouri in an expedition later known as Zion's Camp. Their purpose was to escort the expelled Missouri Saints back to their lands in Jackson County. Missourians who had previously persecuted the Saints feared retaliation from Zion's Camp and preemptively attacked some Saints living in Clay County, Missouri. After the Missouri governor withdrew his promise to support the Saints, Joseph Smith received this revelation.

1–5, Zion will be built up by conformity to celestial law; 6–13, The redemption of Zion is deferred for a little season; 14–19, The Lord will fight the battles of Zion; 20–26, The Saints are to be wise and not boast of mighty works as they gather; 27–30, Lands in Jackson and adjoining counties should be purchased; 31–34, The elders are to receive an endowment in the house of the Lord in Kirtland; 35–37, Saints who are both called and chosen will be sanctified; 38–41, The Saints are to lift an ensign of peace to the world.

1 Verily I say unto you who have assembled yourselves together that you may learn my will concerning the *ᵃredemption of mine afflicted people—

2 Behold, I say unto you, were it not for the *ᵃtransgressions of my people, speaking concerning the church and not individuals, they might have been redeemed even now.

3 But behold, they have not learned to be obedient to the things which I required at their hands, but are full of all manner of evil, and do not *ᵃimpart of their substance, as becometh saints, to the poor and afflicted among them;

4 And are not *ᵃunited according to the union required by the law of the celestial kingdom;

5 And *ᵃZion cannot be built up *ᵇunless it is by the *ᶜprinciples of the *ᵈlaw of the celestial kingdom; otherwise I cannot receive her unto myself.

6 And my people must needs be *ᵃchastened until they learn *ᵇobedience, if it must needs be, by the things which they *ᶜsuffer.

---

105 1*a* D&C 100:13; 103:15.
   2*a* D&C 104:52 (1–18,
    52). TG Transgress.
   3*a* Acts 5:2 (1–11); D&C
    42:30. TG Consecration; Welfare.

4*a* D&C 78:3 (3–7,
   11–15); 104:1 (1,
   47–53).
5*a* TG Zion.
   b D&C 104:16 (15–16).
   c D&C 11:9.

   d D&C 51:2; 88:22.
6*a* Deut. 11:2 (1–8); D&C
   95:1. TG Chastening;
   Suffering.
   b TG Obedience.
   c Heb. 5:8.

7 I speak not concerning those who are appointed to lead my people, who are the *first elders of my church, for they are not all under this condemnation;

8 But I speak concerning my churches abroad—there are many who will say: Where is their God? Behold, he will *deliver them in time of trouble, otherwise we will not go up unto Zion, and will keep our moneys.

9 Therefore, in consequence of the *transgressions of my people, it is expedient in me that mine elders should wait for a little season for the *redemption of Zion—

10 That they themselves may be prepared, and that my people may be *taught more perfectly, and have experience, and know more perfectly concerning their *duty, and the things which I require at their hands.

11 And this cannot be brought to pass until mine *elders are *endowed with power from on high.

12 For behold, I have prepared a great endowment and blessing to be *poured out upon them, inasmuch as they are faithful and continue in humility before me.

13 Therefore it is expedient in me that mine elders should wait for a little season, for the redemption of Zion.

14 For behold, I do not require at their hands to fight the battles of Zion; for, as I said in a former commandment, even so will I fulfil—I will *fight your battles.

15 Behold, the *destroyer I have sent forth to destroy and lay waste mine *enemies; and not many years hence they shall not be left to pollute mine heritage, and to *blaspheme my name upon the lands which I have *consecrated for the gathering together of my saints.

16 Behold, I have commanded my servant Joseph Smith, Jun., to say unto the *strength of my house, even my warriors, my young men, and middle-aged, to gather together for the redemption of my people, and throw down the towers of mine enemies, and scatter their *watchmen;

17 But the strength of mine house have not hearkened unto my words.

18 But inasmuch as there are those who have hearkened unto my words,

---

7 a D&C 20:2 (2, 5);
  88:85. TG Leadership.
8 a 2 Kgs. 17:39; 2 Ne.
  6:17; D&C 108:8.
  TG Deliver.
9 a Lam. 1:5; D&C 101:2;
  103:4.
  b D&C 105:31.
10 a TG Teachable.
  b TG Duty.

11 a TG Elder, Melchizedek
  Priesthood.
  b D&C 38:32; 95:8.
12 a Zech. 12:10; D&C
  110:10.
14 a Josh. 10:14 (12–14);
  2 Chr. 20:15; Ps. 35:1;
  Isa. 49:25; D&C 98:37.
  TG Protection, Divine.
15 a D&C 1:13 (13–14).

b Ex. 23:22 (20–23);
  D&C 8:4; 136:40.
c Ps. 74:10; D&C 112:26
  (24–26).
d D&C 52:2; 58:57; 84:3
  (3–4, 31); 103:35.
16 a D&C 101:55; 103:22
  (22, 30). TG Strength.
  b TG Watchman.

I have prepared a blessing and an *endowment for them, if they continue faithful.

19 I have heard their prayers, and will accept their offering; and it is expedient in me that they should be brought thus far for a *trial of their *faith.

20 And now, verily I say unto you, a commandment I give unto you, that as many as have come up hither, that can stay in the region round about, let them stay;

21 And those that cannot stay, who have families in the east, let them tarry for a little season, inasmuch as my servant Joseph shall appoint unto them;

22 For I will counsel him concerning this matter, and all things whatsoever he shall appoint unto them shall be fulfilled.

23 And let all my people who dwell in the regions round about be very faithful, and prayerful, and humble before me, and reveal not the things which I have revealed unto them, until it is wisdom in me that they should be revealed.

24 Talk not of judgments, neither *boast of faith nor of mighty *works, but carefully gather together, as much in one region as can be, consistently with the feelings of the people;

25 And behold, I will give unto you favor and grace in their eyes, that you may rest in *peace and safety, while you are saying unto the people: Execute judgment and justice for us according to law, and redress us of our *wrongs.

26 Now, behold, I say unto you, my friends, in this way you may find favor in the eyes of the people, until the *army of Israel becomes very great.

27 And I will soften the hearts of the people, as I did the heart of *Pharaoh, from time to time, until my servant Joseph Smith, Jun., and mine elders, whom I have appointed, shall have time to gather up the strength of my house,

28 And to have sent *wise men, to fulfil that which I have commanded concerning the *purchasing of all the lands in Jackson county that can be purchased, and in the adjoining counties round about.

29 For it is my will that these lands should be purchased; and after they are purchased that my saints should possess them according to the *laws of consecration which I have given.

---

18 a D&C 110:9 (8–10).
19 a TG Probation; Test.
   b TG Faith.
24 a D&C 50:33 (32–33);
   84:73. TG Boast.

   b TG Good Works.
25 a TG Grace; Protection,
   Divine.
   b TG Injustice; Justice.
26 a Joel 2:11 (11, 25).

27 a Gen. 47:6 (1–12).
28 a D&C 101:73.
   b D&C 42:35.
29 a D&C 42:30.

30 And after these lands are purchased, I will hold the *armies of Israel guiltless in taking possession of their own lands, which they have previously purchased with their moneys, and of throwing down the towers of mine enemies that may be upon them, and scattering their watchmen, and *avenging me of mine enemies unto the third and fourth generation of them that hate me.

31 But first let my army become very great, and let it be *sanctified before me, that it may become fair as the sun, and clear as the *moon, and that her banners may be terrible unto all nations;

32 That the kingdoms of this world may be constrained to acknowledge that the kingdom of Zion is in very deed the *kingdom of our God and his Christ; therefore, let us become *subject unto her laws.

33 Verily I say unto you, it is expedient in me that the first elders of my church should receive their *endowment from on high in my house, which I have commanded to be built unto my name in the land of Kirtland.

34 And let those commandments which I have given concerning Zion and her *law be executed and fulfilled, after her redemption.

35 There has been a day of *calling, but the time has come for a day of choosing; and let those be chosen that are *worthy.

36 And it shall be *manifest unto my servant, by the voice of the Spirit, those that are *chosen; and they shall be *sanctified;

37 And inasmuch as they follow the *counsel which they receive, they shall have power *after many days to accomplish all things pertaining to Zion.

38 And again I say unto you, sue for *peace, not only to the people that have smitten you, but also to all people;

39 And lift up an *ensign of *peace, and make a proclamation of peace unto the ends of the earth;

40 And make proposals for peace unto those who have smitten you, according to the voice of the Spirit which is in you, and *all things shall work together for your good.

41 Therefore, be faithful; and behold, and lo, *I am with you even unto the end. Even so. Amen.

30a D&C 35:13 (13–14);
  101:55 (55, 58); 103:22
  (22, 26, 29).
 b D&C 97:22.
31a D&C 105:9. TG Sanctification.
 b Song 6:10; D&C 5:14;
  109:73.
32a Rev. 11:15. TG Kingdom of God, on Earth.
 b TG Governments;

Submissiveness.
33a D&C 95:8 (8–9).
34a D&C 42:2 (2, 18–69);
  78:3 (1–22).
35a TG Called of God.
 b TG Worthiness.
36a TG Guidance, Divine.
 b D&C 95:5 (5–6).
 c TG Man, New,
  Spiritually Reborn;
  Sanctification.

37a Prov. 15:22. TG Counsel.
 b D&C 101:62.
38a Deut. 20:10.
39a TG Ensign.
 b TG Peace; Peacemakers.
40a Rom. 8:28; D&C
  90:24; 100:15.
41a Matt. 28:20 (19–20).

SECTION 106

Revelation given through Joseph Smith the Prophet, at Kirtland, Ohio, November 25, 1834. This revelation is directed to Warren A. Cowdery, an older brother of Oliver Cowdery.

1–3, Warren A. Cowdery is called as a local presiding officer; 4–5, The Second Coming will not overtake the children of light as a thief; 6–8, Great blessings follow faithful service in the Church.

1 It is my will that my servant Warren A. Cowdery should be appointed and ordained a presiding high priest over my church, in the land of ᵃFreedom and the regions round about;

2 And should preach my ᵃeverlasting gospel, and lift up his voice and warn the people, not only in his own place, but in the adjoining counties;

3 And devote his whole time to this high and holy calling, which I now give unto him, ᵃseeking diligently the kingdom of heaven and its righteousness, and all things necessary shall be added thereunto; for the ᵇlaborer is worthy of his hire.

4 And again, verily I say unto you, the ᵃcoming of the Lord draweth nigh, and it overtaketh the world as a ᵇthief in the night—

5 Therefore, gird up your loins, that you may be the ᵃchildren of light, and that day shall not ᵇovertake you as a thief.

6 And again, verily I say unto you, there was joy in heaven when my servant Warren bowed to my scepter, and separated himself from the crafts of men;

7 Therefore, blessed is my servant Warren, for I will have mercy on him; and, notwithstanding the ᵃvanity of his heart, I will lift him up inasmuch as he will humble himself before me.

8 And I will give him ᵃgrace and assurance wherewith he may stand; and if he continue to be a faithful witness and a ᵇlight unto the church I have prepared a crown for him in the ᶜmansions of my Father. Even so. Amen.

---

106 1 *a* IE the city of Freedom, New York, and environs.
  2 *a* D&C 18:4.
  3 *a* Matt. 6:33. TG Kingdom of God, in Heaven.
   b Matt. 10:10; D&C 31:5. TG Reward; Wages.
  4 *a* James 5:8. TG Jesus Christ, Second Coming; Last Days.
   b 1 Thes. 5:2.
  5 *a* TG Children of Light.
   b Rev. 16:15 (15–16).
  7 *a* TG Vanity.
  8 *a* TG Grace.
   b TG Example; Light [noun].
   c John 14:2; Ether 12:32 (32–37); D&C 59:2; 76:111; 81:6; 98:18.

SECTION 107

Revelation on the priesthood, given through Joseph Smith the Prophet, at Kirtland, Ohio, about April 1835. Although this section was recorded in 1835, the historical records affirm that most of verses 60 through 100 incorporate a revelation given through Joseph Smith on November 11, 1831. This section was associated with the organization of the Quorum of the Twelve in February and March 1835. The Prophet likely delivered it in the presence of those who were preparing to depart May 3, 1835, on their first quorum mission.

1–6, There are two priesthoods: the Melchizedek and the Aaronic; 7–12, Those who hold the Melchizedek Priesthood have power to officiate in all offices in the Church; 13–17, The bishopric presides over the Aaronic Priesthood, which administers in outward ordinances; 18–20, The Melchizedek Priesthood holds the keys of all spiritual blessings; the Aaronic Priesthood holds the keys of the ministering of angels; 21–38, The First Presidency, the Twelve, and the Seventy constitute the presiding quorums, whose decisions are to be made in unity and righteousness; 39–52, The patriarchal order is established from Adam to Noah; 53–57, Ancient Saints assembled at Adam-ondi-Ahman, and the Lord appeared to them; 58–67, The Twelve are to set the officers of the Church in order; 68–76, Bishops serve as common judges in Israel; 77–84, The First Presidency and the Twelve constitute the highest court in the Church; 85–100, Priesthood presidents govern their respective quorums.

1 There are, in the church, two *priesthoods*, namely, the Melchizedek and *Aaronic*, including the Levitical Priesthood.

2 Why the first is called the *Melchizedek* Priesthood is because *Melchizedek* was such a great high priest.

3 Before his day it was called *the Holy *Priesthood*, after the *Order of the Son of God.*

4 But out of *respect or *reverence* to the name of the Supreme Being, to avoid the too frequent repetition of his name, they, the church, in ancient days, called that priesthood after Melchizedek, or the Melchizedek Priesthood.

5 All other authorities or offices in the church are *appendages to this priesthood.

---

107 1 *a* TG Priesthood.
  b TG Priesthood, Aaronic.
2 *a* TG Priesthood, Melchizedek.

BD Melchizedek.
  b JST Gen. 14:25–40 (Bible Appendix); Alma 13:14 (3–19); D&C 84:14.
3 *a* TG Jesus Christ,

Authority of.
  b D&C 76:57.
4 *a* TG Respect.
  b TG Reverence.
5 *a* D&C 84:29; 107:14.

6 But there are two divisions or grand heads—one is the Melchizedek Priesthood, and the other is the Aaronic or *Levitical Priesthood.

7 The office of an *elder comes under the priesthood of Melchizedek.

8 The *Melchizedek Priesthood holds the right of presidency, and has power and *authority over all the offices in the church in all ages of the world, to administer in spiritual things.

9 The *Presidency of the High Priesthood, after the order of Melchizedek, have a right to officiate in all the offices in the church.

10 *High priests after the order of the Melchizedek Priesthood have a *right to officiate in their own *standing, under the direction of the presidency, in administering spiritual things, and also in the office of an elder, *priest (of the Levitical order), teacher, deacon, and member.

11 An elder has a right to officiate in his stead when the high priest is not present.

12 The high priest and *elder are to administer in spiritual things, agreeable to the covenants and commandments of the church; and they have a right to officiate in all these offices of the church when there are no higher authorities present.

13 The second priesthood is called the *Priesthood of Aaron, because it was conferred upon Aaron and his seed, throughout all their generations.

14 Why it is called the lesser priesthood is because it is an *appendage to the greater, or the Melchizedek Priesthood, and has power in administering outward ordinances.

15 The *bishopric is the presidency of this priesthood, and holds the *keys or authority of the same.

16 No man has a legal right to this office, to hold the keys of this priesthood, except he be a *literal descendant of *Aaron.

17 But as a high priest of the *Melchizedek Priesthood has authority to officiate in all the lesser offices, he may officiate in the office of *bishop when no literal descendant of Aaron can be found, provided he is called and *set apart and ordained unto this power by the hands of the *Presidency of the Melchizedek Priesthood.

---

6 a Deut. 10:8 (8–9); 18:5.
7 a TG Elder, Melchizedek Priesthood.
8 a Acts 6:4.
  b TG Authority; Priesthood, Authority.
9 a D&C 81:2; 107:22 (22, 65–67, 91–92).
10 a TG High Priest, Melchizedek Priesthood.
  b D&C 20:38 (38–67); 121:36 (35–46).

c D&C 124:133 (133–36).
d TG Priest, Aaronic Priesthood.
12 a D&C 124:137. TG Elder, Melchizedek Priesthood.
13 a Ex. 27:21; 2 Chr. 26:18; D&C 27:8; 84:18 (18–27). TG Priesthood, Aaronic.
14 a D&C 20:52; 107:5.
15 a D&C 124:141.

TG Bishop.
  b TG Priesthood, Keys of.
16 a Ex. 40:15 (12–15); D&C 68:16 (14–24); 84:18 (18, 30); 107:69 (68–78).
  b Neh. 11:22.
17 a TG Priesthood, Melchizedek.
  b TG Bishop.
  c TG Setting Apart.
  d D&C 68:15; 81:2.

18 The power and authority of the higher, or Melchizedek Priesthood, is to hold the [a]keys of all the spiritual blessings of the church—

19 To have the privilege of receiving the [a]mysteries of the kingdom of heaven, to have the [b]heavens opened unto them, to commune with the [c]general assembly and church of the [d]Firstborn, and to enjoy the communion and [e]presence of God the Father, and Jesus the [f]mediator of the new covenant.

20 The [a]power and authority of the lesser, or [b]Aaronic Priesthood, is to hold the [c]keys of the ministering of angels, and to [d]administer in outward [e]ordinances, the letter of the gospel, the baptism of repentance for the [f]remission of sins, agreeable to the covenants and commandments.

21 Of necessity there are presidents, or presiding [a]officers growing out of, or appointed of or from among those who are ordained to the several offices in these two priesthoods.

22 Of the [a]Melchizedek Priesthood, three [b]Presiding High Priests, chosen by the body, appointed and ordained to that office, and [c]upheld by the confidence, faith, and prayer of the church, form a quorum of the Presidency of the Church.

23 The [a]twelve traveling councilors are called to be the Twelve [b]Apostles, or special [c]witnesses of the name of Christ in all the world—thus differing from other officers in the church in the duties of their calling.

24 And they form a quorum, [a]equal in authority and power to the three presidents previously mentioned.

25 The [a]Seventy are also called to [b]preach the gospel, and to be especial witnesses unto the Gentiles and in all the world—thus differing from other officers in the church in the duties of their calling.

26 And they form a quorum, equal in [a]authority to that of the Twelve special witnesses or Apostles just named.

---

18 a TG Priesthood, Keys of.
19 a Eph. 1:9; Alma 12:9 (9–11); D&C 63:23; 84:19 (19–22). TG Mysteries of Godliness.
  b Ezek. 1:1; Acts 7:56; 10:11.
  c Heb. 12:23 (22–24).
  d TG Jesus Christ, Firstborn.
  e TG God, Presence of; God, Privilege of Seeing.
  f TG Jesus Christ, Messenger of the Covenant.

20 a Lev. 7:35.
  b TG Priesthood, Aaronic.
  c D&C 13; 84:27 (26–27).
  d Num. 18:5 (1–6).
  e TG Ordinance.
  f TG Baptism; Remission of Sins; Repent.
21 a Num. 11:16; D&C 88:127; 124:123.
22 a TG Priesthood, Melchizedek.
  b D&C 68:15; 90:6; 107:9 (9, 65–67, 78–84,

91–92).
  c TG Sustaining Church Leaders.
23 a D&C 18:31 (31–37); 107:33 (33–35).
  b 2 Pet. 1:1. TG Apostles.
  c TG Witness.
24 a D&C 90:6.
25 a D&C 107:34. TG Seventy.
  b TG Missionary Work; Preaching.
26 a Luke 10:1 (1–12, 17–20).

27 And every decision made by either of these quorums must be by the *unanimous voice of the same; that is, every member in each quorum must be agreed to its decisions, in order to make their decisions of the same power or validity one with the other—

28 A majority may form a quorum when circumstances render it impossible to be otherwise—

29 Unless this is the case, their decisions are not entitled to the same blessings which the decisions of a quorum of three presidents were anciently, who were ordained after the order of Melchizedek, and were *righteous and holy men.

30 The decisions of these quorums, or either of them, are to be made in all *righteousness, in holiness, and lowliness of heart, meekness and *longsuffering, and in *faith, and *virtue, and knowledge, temperance, patience, godliness, brotherly kindness and charity;

31 Because the promise is, if these things abound in them they shall not be *unfruitful in the knowledge of the Lord.

32 And in case that any decision of these quorums is made in unrighteousness, it may be brought before a general assembly of the several quorums, which constitute the spiritual authorities of the church; otherwise there can be no *appeal from their decision.

33 The *Twelve are a *Traveling Presiding High Council, to officiate in the name of the Lord, under the direction of the Presidency of the Church, agreeable to the institution of heaven; to build up the church, and regulate all the affairs of the same in all nations, first unto the *Gentiles and secondly unto the Jews.

34 The *Seventy are to act in the name of the Lord, under the direction of the *Twelve or the traveling high council, in building up the church and regulating all the affairs of the same in all nations, first unto the Gentiles and then to the Jews—

35 The Twelve being *sent out, holding the keys, to open the door by the proclamation of the gospel of Jesus Christ, and first unto the Gentiles and then unto the Jews.

27 a TG Unity.
29 a Ex. 22:31; Alma 13:26; D&C 49:8.
30 a D&C 121:36.
  TG Priesthood, Magnifying Callings within; Righteousness.
  b TG Forbear.
  c 2 Pet. 1:5 (5–7).

d D&C 121:41 (41–46).
  TG Benevolence; Godliness; Kindness; Temperance; Virtue.
31 a 2 Pet. 1:8 (5–8).
32 a D&C 102:20 (12–34).
33 a D&C 107:23 (23–24, 38–39). TG Apostles.
  b D&C 124:139.

c 1 Ne. 13:42; 3 Ne. 16:7 (4–13); D&C 18:6 (6, 26); 19:27; 21:12; 90:9 (8–9); 112:4.
34 a D&C 107:25 (25, 38). TG Seventy.
  b D&C 112:21.
35 a Matt. 10:5 (5–42).

36 The standing *high councils, at the stakes of Zion, form a quorum equal in authority in the affairs of the church, in all their decisions, to the quorum of the presidency, or to the traveling high council.

37 The *high council in Zion form a quorum equal in authority in the affairs of the church, in all their decisions, to the councils of the Twelve at the stakes of Zion.

38 It is the duty of the traveling high council to call upon the *Seventy, when they need assistance, to fill the several calls for preaching and administering the gospel, instead of any others.

39 It is the duty of the *Twelve, in all large branches of the church, to ordain *evangelical ministers, as they shall be designated unto them by revelation—

40 The order of this priesthood was confirmed to be handed down from father to son, and rightly belongs to the literal descendants of the chosen seed, to whom the promises were made.

41 This *order was instituted in the days of *Adam, and came down by *lineage in the following manner:

42 From Adam to *Seth, who was *ordained by Adam at the age of sixty-nine years, and was blessed by him three years previous to his (Adam's) death, and received the promise of God by his father, that his posterity should be the chosen of the Lord, and that they should be *preserved unto the end of the earth;

43 Because he (Seth) was a *perfect man, and his *likeness was the express likeness of his father, insomuch that he seemed to be like unto his father in all things, and could be distinguished from him only by his age.

44 Enos was ordained at the age of one hundred and thirty-four years and four months, by the hand of Adam.

45 God called upon Cainan in the wilderness in the fortieth year of his age; and he met Adam in journeying to the place Shedolamak. He was eighty-seven years old when he received his ordination.

46 Mahalaleel was four hundred and ninety-six years and seven days old when he was ordained by the hand of Adam, who also blessed him.

47 Jared was two hundred years old when he was ordained under the hand of Adam, who also blessed him.

---

36 a D&C 102:30 (27–32).
37 a D&C 124:131.
38 a D&C 107:34 (34, 90–98).
39 a D&C 107:33 (33–35, 58).

b D&C 124:91 (91–92).
41 a D&C 84:16. TG Patriarch; Priesthood, History of.
b Gen. 5:4 (1–32).
c Moses 6:22 (10–25).

42 a Gen. 4:25.
b D&C 84:16; Moses 6:2.
c Gen. 45:7 (1–8); 2 Ne. 3:16.
43 a TG Perfection.
b Gen. 5:3.

48 ^aEnoch was twenty-five years old when he was ordained under the hand of Adam; and he was sixty-five and Adam blessed him.

49 And he ^asaw the Lord, and he walked with him, and was before his face continually; and he ^bwalked with God three hundred and sixty-five years, making him four hundred and thirty years old when he was translated.

50 Methuselah was one hundred years old when he was ordained under the hand of Adam.

51 Lamech was thirty-two years old when he was ordained under the hand of Seth.

52 Noah was ten years old when he was ^aordained under the hand of Methuselah.

53 Three years previous to the death of Adam, he called Seth, Enos, Cainan, Mahalaleel, Jared, Enoch, and Methuselah, who were all ^ahigh priests, with the residue of his posterity who were righteous, into the valley of ^bAdam-ondi-Ahman, and there bestowed upon them his last blessing.

54 And the Lord appeared unto them, and they rose up and blessed ^aAdam, and called him Michael, the prince, the archangel.

55 And the Lord administered comfort unto Adam, and said unto him: I have set thee to be at the head; a multitude of nations shall come of thee, and thou art a ^aprince over them forever.

56 And Adam stood up in the midst of the congregation; and, notwithstanding he was bowed down with age, being full of the Holy Ghost, ^apredicted whatsoever should befall his posterity unto the latest generation.

57 These things were all written in the book of ^aEnoch, and are to be testified of in due time.

58 It is the duty of the ^aTwelve, also, to ^bordain and set in order all the other officers of the church, agreeable to the revelation which says:

59 To the church of Christ in the land of Zion, in addition to the church ^alaws respecting church business—

60 Verily, I say unto you, saith the Lord of Hosts, there must needs be ^apresiding elders to preside over those who are of the office of an elder;

48a Moses 6:25 (see Moses
  6:21–7:69).
49a TG Jesus Christ, Ap-
  pearances, Antemortal.
  b Gen. 5:22; Heb. 11:5;
  Moses 7:69. TG Trans-
  lated Beings; Walking
  with God.
52a Moses 8:19.
53a TG High Priest,

Melchizedek Priest-
  hood.
  b Dan. 7:13 (13–14);
  D&C 78:15 (15–20);
  116.
54a 2 Ne. 9:21; D&C
  128:21. TG Adam.
55a D&C 78:16.
56a Moses 5:10.
57a Moses 6:46 (5, 46).

TG Scriptures, Lost.
58a D&C 107:39 (38–39).
  TG Apostles.
  b TG Priesthood, Ordination.
59a D&C 42:59; 43:2–9;
  72:9; 83:1; 103:35.
60a D&C 107:89 (89–90).

61 And also ^apriests to preside over those who are of the office of a priest;

62 And also teachers to preside over those who are of the office of a teacher, in like manner, and also the ^adeacons—

63 Wherefore, from deacon to teacher, and from teacher to priest, and from priest to elder, severally as they are appointed, according to the covenants and commandments of the church.

64 Then comes the High Priesthood, which is the greatest of all.

65 Wherefore, it must needs be that one be appointed of the ^aHigh Priesthood to preside over the priesthood, and he shall be called President of the High Priesthood of the Church;

66 Or, in other words, the ^aPresiding High Priest over the High Priesthood of the Church.

67 From the same comes the administering of ordinances and blessings upon the church, by the ^alaying on of the hands.

68 Wherefore, the office of a bishop is not equal unto it; for the office of a ^abishop is in administering all ^btemporal things;

69 Nevertheless a ^abishop must be chosen from the ^bHigh Priesthood, unless he is a ^cliteral descendant of Aaron;

70 For unless he is a ^aliteral descendant of Aaron he cannot hold the keys of that priesthood.

71 Nevertheless, a high priest, that is, after the order of Melchizedek, may be set apart unto the ministering of temporal things, having a ^aknowledge of them by the Spirit of truth;

72 And also to be a ^ajudge in Israel, to do the business of the church, to sit in ^bjudgment upon transgressors upon testimony as it shall be laid before him according to the laws, by the assistance of his ^ccounselors, whom he has chosen or will choose among the elders of the church.

73 This is the duty of a bishop who is not a literal descendant of Aaron, but has been ordained to the High Priesthood after the order of Melchizedek.

74 Thus shall he be a ^ajudge, even a common judge among the inhabitants of Zion, or in a stake of Zion, or in any branch of the church where he shall

---

61 a D&C 20:46; 84:111;
107:87.
62 a D&C 107:85 (85–86).
65 a TG Priesthood,
Melchizedek.
66 a D&C 107:91 (9, 22,
91–92).
67 a TG Blessing; Hands,
Laying on of; Ordinance.

68 a TG Bishop.
b Acts 6:3; D&C 70:11
(11–12).
69 a D&C 41:9; 72:9 (9–12).
b TG Priesthood,
Melchizedek.
c D&C 68:16 (14–24);
107:16 (13–17).
70 a Ex. 40:15 (12–15);
D&C 84:18 (18, 30).

71 a TG Holy Ghost, Mission of; Knowledge.
72 a D&C 58:17 (17–18);
64:40.
b TG Judgment.
c TG Counselor.
74 a Ex. 18:13; Mosiah 29:11
(11–44); Alma 46:4.

be ^{b}set apart unto this ministry, until the borders of Zion are enlarged and it becomes necessary to have other bishops or judges in Zion or elsewhere.

75 And inasmuch as there are other bishops appointed they shall act in the same office.

76 But a literal descendant of Aaron has a legal right to the presidency of this priesthood, to the ^{a}keys of this ministry, to act in the office of bishop independently, without counselors, except in a case where a President of the High Priesthood, after the order of Melchizedek, is tried, to sit as a judge in Israel.

77 And the decision of either of these councils, agreeable to the commandment which says:

78 Again, verily, I say unto you, the most important business of the church, and the most ^{a}difficult cases of the church, inasmuch as there is not satisfaction upon the decision of the bishop or judges, it shall be handed over and carried up unto the council of the church, before the ^{b}Presidency of the High Priesthood.

79 And the Presidency of the council of the High Priesthood shall have power to call other high priests, even twelve, to assist as counselors; and thus the Presidency of the High Priesthood and its counselors shall have power to decide upon testimony according to the laws of the church.

80 And after this decision it shall be had in remembrance no more before the Lord; for this is the highest council of the church of God, and a final decision upon controversies in spiritual matters.

81 There is not any person belonging to the church who is exempt from this council of the church.

82 And inasmuch as a President of the High Priesthood shall transgress, he shall be had in remembrance before the ^{a}common council of the church, who shall be assisted by twelve counselors of the High Priesthood;

83 And their decision upon his head shall be an end of controversy concerning him.

84 Thus, none shall be exempted from the ^{a}justice and the ^{b}laws of God, that all things may be done in ^{c}order and in solemnity before him, according to truth and righteousness.

85 And again, verily I say unto you, the duty of a president over the office of a ^{a}deacon is to preside over twelve deacons, to sit in council with them,

---

74 b TG Setting Apart.
76 a TG Priesthood, Keys of.
78 a D&C 102:28 (13–14, 28).

 b D&C 68:22.
82 a D&C 107:74 (74–76).
84 a TG God, Justice of; Justice.

 b TG God, Law of.
 c TG Order.
85 a TG Deacon.

and to *b*teach them their duty, *c*edifying one another, as it is given according to the covenants.

86 And also the duty of the president over the office of the *a*teachers is to preside over twenty-four of the teachers, and to sit in council with them, teaching them the duties of their office, as given in the covenants.

87 Also the duty of the president over the Priesthood of Aaron is to preside over forty-eight *a*priests, and sit in council with them, to teach them the duties of their office, as is given in the covenants—

88 This president is to be a *a*bishop; for this is one of the duties of this priesthood.

89 Again, the duty of the president over the office of *a*elders is to preside over ninety-six elders, and to sit in council with them, and to teach them according to the covenants.

90 This presidency is a distinct one from that of the seventy, and is designed for those who do not *a*travel into all the world.

91 And again, the duty of the President of the office of the High Priesthood is to *a*preside over the whole church, and to be like unto *b*Moses—

92 Behold, here is wisdom; yea, to be a *a*seer, a *b*revelator, a translator, and a *c*prophet, having all the *d*gifts of God which he bestows upon the head of the church.

93 And it is according to the vision showing the order of the *a*Seventy, that they should have seven presidents to preside over them, chosen out of the number of the seventy;

94 And the seventh president of these presidents is to preside over the six;

95 And these seven presidents are to choose other seventy besides the first seventy to whom they belong, and are to preside over them;

96 And also other seventy, until seven times seventy, if the labor in the vineyard of necessity requires it.

97 And these *a*seventy are to be *b*traveling ministers, unto the Gentiles first and also unto the Jews.

98 Whereas other officers of the church, who belong not unto the Twelve,

---

85 *b* Ex. 35:34; Moro. 10:9
   (9–10); D&C 38:23;
   88:77 (77–79, 118).
   c TG Edification.
86 *a* D&C 20:53 (53–60).
   TG Teacher, Aaronic
   Priesthood.
87 *a* TG Priest, Aaronic
   Priesthood.
88 *a* TG Bishop.

89 *a* TG Elder, Melchizedek
   Priesthood.
90 *a* D&C 124:137.
91 *a* D&C 90:13 (13,
   32–33); 107:66 (9, 22,
   65–67).
   b D&C 28:2; 103:16
   (16–21).
92 *a* Mosiah 8:16 (13–18).
   TG Seer.

b TG Revelation.
c D&C 21:1. TG Prophets, Mission of.
d TG God, Gifts of; Holy
   Ghost, Gifts of.
93 *a* D&C 107:38.
97 *a* TG Seventy.
   b D&C 124:138
   (138–39).

neither to the Seventy, are not under the responsibility to travel among all nations, but are to travel as their circumstances shall allow, notwithstanding they may hold as high and responsible offices in the church.

99 Wherefore, now let every man learn his ᵃduty, and to act in the office in which he is appointed, in all ᵇdiligence.

100 He that is ᵃslothful shall not be counted ᵇworthy to stand, and he that learns not his duty and shows himself not approved shall not be counted worthy to stand. Even so. Amen.

SECTION 108

Revelation given through Joseph Smith the Prophet, at Kirtland, Ohio, December 26, 1835. This section was received at the request of Lyman Sherman, who had previously been ordained a seventy and who had come to the Prophet with a request for a revelation to make known his duty.

1–3, Lyman Sherman forgiven of his sins; 4–5, He is to be numbered with the leading elders of the Church; 6–8, He is called to preach the gospel and strengthen his brethren.

1 Verily thus saith the Lord unto you, my servant Lyman: Your sins are forgiven you, because you have obeyed my ᵃvoice in coming up hither this morning to receive counsel of him whom I have appointed.

2 Therefore, let your soul be at ᵃrest concerning your spiritual standing, and resist no more my voice.

3 And arise up and be more careful henceforth in observing your ᵃvows, which you have made and do make, and you shall be blessed with exceeding great blessings.

4 Wait patiently until the ᵃsolemn assembly shall be called of my servants, then you shall be remembered with the ᵇfirst of mine elders, and receive right by ordination with the rest of mine elders whom I have chosen.

5 Behold, this is the ᵃpromise of the Father unto you if you continue faithful.

---

99 *a* Deut. 4:5 (5–8); Mal.
   2:7 (7–9). TG Duty;
   Leadership; Priesthood,
   Magnifying Callings
   within; Priesthood,
   Oath and Covenant.
   b TG Dedication; Diligence; Steadfastness;
   Zeal.

100 *a* Matt. 24:45; D&C
   58:26 (26–29); 84:86
   (85–86). TG Apathy;
   Idleness; Laziness.
   b TG Priesthood, Oath
   and Covenant; Worthi-
   ness.
108 1 *a* TG Counsel; Guidance,
   Divine; Inspiration.

2 *a* TG Peace of God.
3 *a* TG Integrity; Vow.
4 *a* D&C 88:70; 95:7;
   109:6 (6–10).
   b D&C 88:85; 105:7 (7,
   33).
5 *a* D&C 82:10.

6 And it shall be fulfilled upon you in that day that you shall have right to *preach my gospel wheresoever I shall send you, from henceforth from that time.

7 Therefore, *strengthen your brethren in all your conversation, in all your prayers, in all your exhortations, and in all your doings.

8 And behold, and lo, I am with you to bless you and *deliver you forever. Amen.

SECTION 109

Prayer offered at the dedication of the temple at Kirtland, Ohio, March 27, 1836. According to the Prophet's written statement, this prayer was given to him by revelation.

1–5, The Kirtland Temple was built as a place for the Son of Man to visit; 6–21, It is to be a house of prayer, fasting, faith, learning, glory, and order, and a house of God; 22–33, May the unrepentant who oppose the Lord's people be confounded; 34–42, May the Saints go forth in power to gather the righteous to Zion; 43–53, May the Saints be delivered from the terrible things to be poured out upon the wicked in the last days; 54–58, May nations and peoples and churches be prepared for the gospel; 59–67, May the Jews, the Lamanites, and all Israel be redeemed; 68–80, May the Saints be crowned with glory and honor and gain eternal salvation.

1 *Thanks be to thy name, O Lord God of Israel, who keepest *covenant and showest mercy unto thy servants who walk uprightly before thee, with all their hearts—

2 Thou who hast commanded thy servants to *build a house to thy name in this place [Kirtland].

3 And now thou beholdest, O Lord, that thy servants have done according to thy commandment.

4 And now we ask thee, Holy Father, in the name of Jesus Christ, the Son of thy bosom, in whose name alone salvation can be administered to the children of men, we ask thee, O Lord, to accept of this *house, the *workmanship of the hands of us, thy servants, which thou didst command us to build.

5 For thou knowest that we have done this work through great tribulation; and out of our poverty we have *given of our substance to build a

---

6a TG Missionary Work.
7a Luke 22:32.
8a Dan. 6:27; 2 Ne. 9:19
    (18–19); D&C 105:8.
    TG Deliver.

109 1a 1 Chr. 16:8 (7–36);
    Alma 37:37; D&C
    46:32.
    b 1 Kgs. 8:23 (22–61);
    Dan. 9:4 (4, 9).

2a D&C 88:119.
4a 1 Kgs. 9:1.
    b 2 Ne. 5:16.
5a Mark 12:44 (41–44).

^{b}house to thy name, that the Son of Man might have a place to ^{c}manifest himself to his people.

6 And as thou hast said in a ^{a}revelation, given to us, calling us thy friends, saying—Call your solemn assembly, as I have commanded you;

7 And as all have not faith, seek ye diligently and teach one another words of wisdom; yea, seek ye out of the best ^{a}books words of wisdom, seek learning even by study and also by faith;

8 Organize yourselves; ^{a}prepare every needful thing, and establish a house, even a ^{b}house of prayer, a house of fasting, a house of faith, a house of learning, a house of glory, a house of ^{c}order, a ^{d}house of God;

9 That your ^{a}incomings may be in the name of the Lord, that your outgoings may be in the name of the Lord, that all your salutations may be in the name of the Lord, with uplifted hands unto the Most High—

10 And now, Holy Father, we ask thee to assist us, thy people, with thy grace, in calling our ^{a}solemn assembly, that it may be done to thine honor and to thy divine acceptance;

11 And in a manner that we may be found worthy, in thy sight, to secure a fulfilment of the ^{a}promises which thou hast made unto us, thy people, in the revelations given unto us;

12 That thy ^{a}glory may rest down upon thy people, and upon this thy house, which we now dedicate to thee, that it may be sanctified and consecrated to be holy, and that thy holy presence may be continually in this house;

13 And that all people who shall enter upon the threshold of the Lord's house may feel thy power, and feel constrained to acknowledge that thou hast sanctified it, and that it is thy house, a ^{a}place of thy holiness.

14 And do thou grant, Holy Father, that all those who shall worship in this house may be taught words of wisdom out of the best ^{a}books, and that they may seek learning even by study, and also by faith, as thou hast said;

15 And that they may grow up in thee, and receive a fulness of the Holy Ghost, and be organized according to thy laws, and be prepared to obtain every needful thing;

16 And that this house may be a house of prayer, a house of fasting, a house of faith, a house of glory and of God, even thy house;

17 That all the incomings of thy people, into this house, may be in the name of the Lord;

---

5 b D&C 124:27 (27–28).
  c Lev. 16:2.
6 a D&C 88:117 (117–20).
7 a D&C 88:118.
8 a TG Skill.
  b TG Temple.

  c TG Order.
  d 1 Kgs. 8:17.
9 a D&C 88:120.
10 a TG Solemn Assembly.
11 a D&C 38:32; 105:33
   (11–12, 18, 33); 110:9.

12 a Ex. 40:34; 1 Kgs. 8:11
   (10–13); 2 Chr. 7:2
   (2–3); D&C 84:5;
   109:37.
13 a Lev. 16:23.
14 a D&C 88:118 (118–19).

18 That all their outgoings from this house may be in the name of the Lord;

19 And that all their salutations may be in the name of the Lord, with holy hands, uplifted to the Most High;

20 And that no *unclean thing shall be permitted to come into thy house to *pollute it;

21 And when thy people *transgress, any of them, they may speedily repent and return unto thee, and find favor in thy sight, and be restored to the blessings which thou hast ordained to be poured out upon those who shall *reverence thee in thy house.

22 And we ask thee, Holy Father, that thy servants may go forth from this house armed with thy power, and that thy *name may be upon them, and thy glory be round about them, and thine *angels have charge over them;

23 And from this place they may bear exceedingly great and glorious tidings, in truth, unto the *ends of the earth, that they may know that this is thy work, and that thou hast put forth thy hand, to fulfil that which thou hast spoken by the mouths of the prophets, concerning the last days.

24 We ask thee, Holy Father, to establish the people that shall worship, and honorably hold a name and standing in this thy house, to all generations and for eternity;

25 That no weapon *formed against them shall prosper; that he who diggeth a *pit for them shall fall into the same himself;

26 That no combination of wickedness shall have power to rise up and *prevail over thy people upon whom thy *name shall be put in this house;

27 And if any people shall rise against this people, that thine anger be kindled against them;

28 And if they shall smite this people thou wilt smite them; thou wilt *fight for thy people as thou didst in the day of battle, that they may be delivered from the hands of all their enemies.

29 We ask thee, Holy Father, to confound, and astonish, and to bring to *shame and confusion, all those who have spread *lying reports abroad, over the world, against thy servant or servants, if they will not repent, when the everlasting gospel shall be proclaimed in their ears;

20a Luke 19:46 (46–48);
   D&C 94:8 (8–9); 97:15
   (15–17).
 b TG Pollution.
21a 1 Kgs. 8:31 (31–34).
 b TG Reverence.
22a TG Jesus Christ, Power
   of; Jesus Christ, Taking

the Name of.
 b TG Angels; Protection,
   Divine.
23a D&C 1:2.
25a Isa. 54:17.
 b Prov. 26:27; 1 Ne. 14:3;
   22:14.
26a Matt. 16:18; D&C

98:22.
 b 1 Kgs. 8:29; D&C
   112:12 (11–12).
28a TG Protection, Divine.
29a TG Shame.
 b TG Lying.

30 And that all their works may be brought to naught, and be swept away by the *hail, and by the judgments which thou wilt send upon them in thine anger, that there may be an end to *lyings and slanders against thy people.

31 For thou knowest, O Lord, that thy servants have been innocent before thee in *bearing record of thy name, for which they have suffered these things.

32 Therefore we plead before thee for a full and complete *deliverance from under this *yoke;

33 Break it off, O Lord; break it off from the necks of thy servants, by thy power, that we may rise up in the midst of this generation and do thy work.

34 O Jehovah, have mercy upon this people, and as all men *sin, forgive the transgressions of thy people, and let them be blotted out forever.

35 Let the *anointing of thy ministers be sealed upon them with power from on high.

36 Let it be fulfilled upon them, as upon those on the day of Pentecost; let the gift of *tongues be poured out upon thy people, even *cloven tongues as of fire, and the interpretation thereof.

37 And let thy house be filled, as with a rushing mighty *wind, with thy *glory.

38 Put upon thy servants the *testimony of the covenant, that when they go out and proclaim thy word they may *seal up the law, and prepare the hearts of thy saints for all those judgments thou art about to send, in thy wrath, upon the inhabitants of the *earth, because of their transgressions, that thy people may not faint in the day of trouble.

39 And whatsoever city thy servants shall enter, and the people of that city *receive their testimony, let thy peace and thy salvation be upon that city; that they may gather out of that city the righteous, that they may come forth to *Zion, or to her stakes, the places of thine appointment, with songs of everlasting joy;

40 And until this be accomplished, let not thy judgments fall upon that city.

30a Ex. 9:18 (13–35); Isa. 28:17 (15–19); Mosiah 12:6; D&C 29:16 (16–21).
 b Ps. 109:2; 3 Ne. 21:19 (11, 19–21).
31a Rev. 12:17.
32a TG Deliver.
 b TG Bondage, Spiritual.

34a Rom. 3:23; 5:1–12, 21. TG Sin.
35a Ex. 25:6; Lev. 8:12 (12–13); D&C 68:20. TG Anointing.
36a TG Holy Ghost, Gifts of.
 b Acts 2:3.
37a Acts 2:2.

 b 2 Chr. 7:2 (2–3); D&C 84:5; 109:12. TG God, Manifestations of.
38a TG Testimony.
 b Isa. 8:16; D&C 1:8.
 c TG Earth, Cleansing of.
39a Matt. 10:13 (11–15).
 b Isa. 35:10.

41 And whatsoever city thy servants shall enter, and the people of that city receive not the testimony of thy servants, and thy servants warn them to save themselves from this untoward generation, let it be upon that city according to that which thou hast spoken by the mouths of thy prophets.

42 But deliver thou, O Jehovah, we beseech thee, thy servants from their hands, and ᵃcleanse them from their blood.

43 O Lord, we delight not in the destruction of our fellow men; their ᵃsouls are precious before thee;

44 But thy word must be fulfilled. Help thy servants to say, with thy ᵃgrace assisting them: Thy will be done, O Lord, and not ours.

45 We know that thou hast spoken by the mouth of thy prophets terrible things concerning the ᵃwicked, in the last days—that thou wilt pour out thy judgments, without measure;

46 Therefore, O Lord, deliver thy people from the calamity of the wicked; enable thy servants to seal up the law, and ᵃbind up the testimony, that they may be prepared against the day of burning.

47 We ask thee, Holy Father, to remember those who have been ᵃdriven by the inhabitants of Jackson county, Missouri, from the lands of their inheritance, and break off, O Lord, this ᵇyoke of affliction that has been put upon them.

48 Thou knowest, O Lord, that they have been greatly ᵃoppressed and afflicted by wicked men; and our ᵇhearts flow out with sorrow because of their grievous ᶜburdens.

49 O Lord, ᵃhow long wilt thou suffer this people to bear this affliction, and the ᵇcries of their innocent ones to ascend up in thine ears, and their ᶜblood come up in testimony before thee, and not make a display of thy testimony in their behalf?

50 Have ᵃmercy, O Lord, upon the wicked mob, who have driven thy people, that they may cease to spoil, that they may repent of their sins if repentance is to be found;

51 But if they will not, make bare thine arm, O Lord, and ᵃredeem that which thou didst appoint a Zion unto thy people.

52 And if it cannot be otherwise, that the cause of thy people may not fail

42 a TG Purification.
43 a TG Life, Sanctity of; Worth of Souls.
44 a TG God, Will of; Grace.
45 a TG Last Days; Wickedness.
46 a Isa. 8:16. TG Seal;

Sealing; Testimony.
47 a D&C 101:1; 103:2 (2, 11); 104:51.
  b TG Bondage, Physical.
48 a TG Oppression.
  b TG Compassion.
  c Ps. 81:6 (5–6).
49 a Ps. 13:2 (1–6); 74:10

(10–23).
  b Ex. 3:9 (7, 9); 2 Ne. 26:15; Mosiah 21:15.
  c TG Martyrdom.
50 a TG Mercy; Repent.
51 a D&C 100:13; 105:2.

before thee may thine anger be kindled, and thine ^aindignation fall upon them, that they may be wasted away, both root and branch, from under heaven;

53 But inasmuch as they will repent, thou art ^agracious and merciful, and wilt turn away thy wrath when thou lookest upon the face of thine Anointed.

54 Have mercy, O Lord, upon all the ^anations of the earth; have mercy upon the rulers of our land; may those principles, which were so honorably and nobly defended, namely, the ^bConstitution of our land, by our fathers, be established forever.

55 ^aRemember the kings, the princes, the nobles, and the great ones of the earth, and all people, and the churches, all the poor, the needy, and afflicted ones of the earth;

56 That their hearts may be softened when thy servants shall go out from thy house, O Jehovah, to bear testimony of thy name; that their prejudices may give way before the ^atruth, and thy people may obtain favor in the sight of all;

57 That all the ends of the earth may know that we, thy servants, have ^aheard thy voice, and that thou hast sent us;

58 That from among all these, thy servants, the sons of Jacob, may gather out the righteous to build a holy ^acity to thy name, as thou hast commanded them.

59 We ask thee to appoint unto Zion other ^astakes besides this one which thou hast appointed, that the gathering of thy ^bpeople may roll on in great power and majesty, that thy work may be cut ^cshort in righteousness.

60 Now these words, O Lord, we have spoken before thee, concerning the revelations and commandments which thou hast given unto us, who are identified with the ^aGentiles.

61 But thou knowest that thou hast a great love for the children of Jacob, who have been ^ascattered upon the ^bmountains for a long time, in a ^ccloudy and dark day.

62 We therefore ask thee to have mercy upon the children of Jacob, that ^aJerusalem, from this hour, may begin to be redeemed;

---

52 a TG God, Indignation of; Punish.
53 a TG Forgive; Grace.
54 a TG Governments; Nations.
  b 1 Pet. 2:13 (13–14); D&C 44:4; 51:6; 98:5 (5–7); 101:77 (77, 80).
55 a TG Compassion.

56 a TG Hardheartedness; Teachable; Truth.
57 a D&C 20:16; 76:14 (14, 22–24).
58 a D&C 28:9.
59 a Isa. 54:2; D&C 104:48.
  b D&C 86:11. TG Israel, Gathering of.
  c Matt. 24:22.

60 a 1 Ne. 13:4 (1–32); 15:13 (13–18).
61 a Hosea 1:6; 13:9 (9–14).
  b Gen. 49:26.
  c Ezek. 30:3.
62 a 3 Ne. 20:29. TG Jerusalem.

63 And the yoke of bondage may begin to be broken off from the house of *a*David;

64 And the children of *a*Judah may begin to return to the *b*lands which thou didst give to Abraham, their father.

65 And cause that the *a*remnants of Jacob, who have been cursed and smitten because of their transgression, be *b*converted from their wild and savage condition to the fulness of the everlasting gospel;

66 That they may lay down their weapons of bloodshed, and cease their rebellions.

67 And may all the scattered remnants of *a*Israel, who have been driven to the ends of the earth, come to a knowledge of the truth, believe in the Messiah, and be redeemed from *b*oppression, and rejoice before thee.

68 O Lord, remember thy servant, Joseph Smith, Jun., and all his afflictions and persecutions—how he has *a*covenanted with *b*Jehovah, and vowed to thee, O Mighty God of Jacob—and the commandments which thou hast given unto him, and that he hath sincerely striven to do thy will.

69 Have mercy, O Lord, upon his *a*wife and children, that they may be exalted in thy presence, and preserved by thy fostering hand.

70 Have mercy upon all their *a*immediate connections, that their prejudices may be broken up and swept away as with a flood; that they may be *b*converted and redeemed with Israel, and know that thou art God.

71 Remember, O Lord, the presidents, even all the presidents of thy church, that thy right hand may exalt them, with all their families, and their immediate connections, that their names may be perpetuated and had in everlasting remembrance from generation to generation.

72 Remember all thy church, O Lord, with all their families, and all their immediate connections, with all their sick and afflicted ones, with all the poor and meek of the earth; that the *a*kingdom, which thou hast set up without hands, may become a great mountain and fill the whole earth;

73 That thy *a*church may come forth out of the wilderness of darkness, and shine forth fair as the *b*moon, clear as the sun, and terrible as an army with banners;

---

63 a 1 Kgs. 11:39. TG Israel, Restoration of.
64 a Hosea 1:7; Zech. 12:6 (6–9); Mal. 3:4; D&C 133:35 (13, 35). TG Israel, Judah, People of.
 b Gen. 17:8 (1–8). TG Promised Lands.
65 a 2 Ne. 30:3; Alma 46:23 (23–24); 3 Ne. 20:16 (15–21); D&C 3:18; 10:48 (46–52); 19:27;

52:2; 87:5 (4–5). TG Israel, Remnant of.
 b 2 Ne. 30:6; 3 Ne. 21:25 (22–25); D&C 49:24. TG Conversion.
67 a TG Israel, Restoration of; Israel, Scattering of.
 b TG Bondage, Spiritual; Oppression.
68 a TG Covenants.
 b TG Jesus Christ, Jehovah.

69 a TG Family; Family, Eternal.
70 a IE close relatives.
 b TG Conversion.
72 a Dan. 2:44 (44–45); D&C 35:27; 65:2.
73 a TG Mission of Latter-day Saints.
 b Song 6:10; D&C 5:14; 105:31.

74 And be adorned as a bride for that day when thou shalt unveil the heavens, and cause the mountains to ᵃflow down at thy presence, and the ᵇvalleys to be exalted, the rough places made smooth; that thy glory may fill the earth;

75 That when the trump shall sound for the dead, we shall be ᵃcaught up in the cloud to meet thee, that we may ever be with the Lord;

76 That our garments may be pure, that we may be clothed upon with ᵃrobes of ᵇrighteousness, with palms in our hands, and ᶜcrowns of glory upon our heads, and reap eternal ᵈjoy for all our ᵉsufferings.

77 O Lord God Almighty, hear us in these our petitions, and answer us from heaven, thy holy habitation, where thou sittest enthroned, with ᵃglory, honor, power, majesty, might, dominion, truth, justice, judgment, mercy, and an infinity of fulness, from everlasting to everlasting.

78 O hear, O hear, O hear us, O Lord! And answer these petitions, and accept the ᵃdedication of this house unto thee, the ᵇwork of our hands, which we have built unto thy name;

79 And also this church, to put upon it thy ᵃname. And help us by the power of thy Spirit, that we may ᵇmingle our voices with those bright, shining ᶜseraphs around thy throne, with acclamations of ᵈpraise, singing Hosanna to God and the ᵉLamb!

80 And let these, thine ᵃanointed ones, be clothed with salvation, and thy saints ᵇshout aloud for joy. Amen, and Amen.

SECTION 110

Visions manifested to Joseph Smith the Prophet and Oliver Cowdery in the temple at Kirtland, Ohio, April 3, 1836. The occasion was that of a Sabbath day meeting. Joseph Smith's history states: "In the afternoon, I assisted the other Presidents in distributing the Lord's Supper to the Church, receiving it from the Twelve, whose privilege it was to officiate at the sacred desk this day. After having performed this service to my brethren, I retired to the pulpit,

74a Judg. 5:5; D&C 133:22
　　(21–22, 40); Moses
　　6:34.
　　b Isa. 40:4; Luke 3:5; Hel.
　　14:23; D&C 49:23.
75a 1 Thes. 4:17.
76a Lev. 8:7; 2 Ne. 9:14.
　　b TG Righteousness.
　　c TG Exaltation.
　　d Heb. 12:2 (1–11); D&C

58:4; 103:12 (11–14).
　e Heb. 11:40; JST Heb.
　　11:40 (Heb. 11:40 note
　　a). TG Suffering.
77a TG God, Glory of.
78a TG Dedication.
　　b TG Industry.
79a TG Jesus Christ, Taking
　　the Name of.
　　b D&C 20:16, 36

(35–36).
　c Isa. 6:2 (1–6).
　d Ezra 3:11 (11–13);
　　D&C 136:28.
　e TG Jesus Christ, Lamb
　　of God.
80a Ps. 18:50; 20:6.
　　TG Anointing; Salva-
　　tion.
　　b Ps. 132:16.

the veils being dropped, and bowed myself, with Oliver Cowdery, in solemn and silent prayer. After rising from prayer, the following vision was opened to both of us."

1–10, The Lord Jehovah appears in glory and accepts the Kirtland Temple as His house; 11–12, Moses and Elias each appear and commit their keys and dispensations; 13–16, Elijah returns and commits the keys of his dispensation as promised by Malachi.

1 The *a*veil was taken from our minds, and the *b*eyes of our *c*understanding were opened.

2 We *a*saw the Lord *b*standing upon the breastwork of the pulpit, before us; and under his feet was a paved work of pure *c*gold, in color like amber.

3 His *a*eyes were as a flame of fire; the hair of his head was white like the pure snow; his *b*countenance shone above the brightness of the sun; and his *c*voice was as the sound of the rushing of great waters, even the voice of *d*Jehovah, saying:

4 I am the *a*first and the last; I am he who *b*liveth, I am he who was slain; I am your *c*advocate with the Father.

5 Behold, your sins are *a*forgiven you; you are clean before me; therefore, lift up your heads and *b*rejoice.

6 Let the hearts of your brethren rejoice, and let the hearts of all my people rejoice, who have, with their might, *a*built this house to my name.

7 For behold, I have *a*accepted this *b*house, and my name shall be here; and I will *c*manifest myself to my people in mercy in this house.

8 Yea, I will *a*appear unto my servants, and speak unto them with mine own voice, if my people will keep my commandments, and do not *b*pollute this *c*holy house.

9 Yea the hearts of thousands and tens of thousands shall greatly rejoice in consequence of the *a*blessings which shall be poured out, and the *b*endowment with which my servants have been endowed in this house.

---

110 1 *a* TG Veil.
  b D&C 76:12 (10, 12, 19); 136:32; 138:11.
  c TG Understanding.
2 *a* TG God, Privilege of Seeing; Jesus Christ, Appearances, Postmortal.
  b 1 Sam. 3:10; 1 Ne. 1:11 (8–15); JS—H 1:17.
  c Ezek. 1:27 (26–28); Rev. 21:21; D&C 137:4.
3 *a* Rev. 1:14; 2:18. TG God, Body of, Corporeal Nature.
  b Ex. 34:29 (29–35); Rev.

1:16; Hel. 5:36; JS—H 1:32.
  c Ezek. 1:24; 43:2; Rev. 1:15; D&C 133:22.
  d TG Jesus Christ, Jehovah.
4 *a* TG Jesus Christ, Firstborn.
  b Deut. 5:24 (22–24); Zech. 13:6; D&C 45:52 (51–52).
  c TG God, Access to; Jesus Christ, Authority of; Jesus Christ, Relationships with the Father.

5 *a* Luke 5:21. TG Forgive.
  b TG Joy.
6 *a* D&C 109:4 (4–5).
7 *a* 2 Chr. 7:16. TG Dedication.
  b TG Temple.
  c TG God, Manifestations of.
8 *a* Ex. 19:11 (10–11); D&C 50:45.
  b D&C 88:134; 97:15 (15–17). TG Pollution.
  c TG Holiness.
9 *a* Gen. 12:3 (1–3); D&C 39:15; Abr. 2:11 (8–11).
  b D&C 95:8 (8–9).

10 And the fame of this house shall spread to foreign lands; and this is the beginning of the blessing which shall be *poured out upon the heads of my people. Even so. Amen.

11 After this *vision closed, the heavens were again *opened unto us; and *Moses appeared before us, and committed unto us the *keys of the *gathering of Israel from the four parts of the earth, and the leading of the ten tribes from the land of the *north.

12 After this, *Elias appeared, and committed the *dispensation of the *gospel of Abraham, saying that in us and our seed all *generations after us should be *blessed.

13 After this vision had closed, another great and glorious *vision burst upon us; for *Elijah the prophet, who was taken to heaven without tasting death, stood before us, and said:

14 Behold, the time has fully come, which was spoken of by the mouth of Malachi—testifying that he [Elijah] should be sent, before the great and dreadful day of the Lord come—

15 To *turn the *hearts of the fathers to the children, and the children to the fathers, lest the whole earth be smitten with a curse—

16 Therefore, the *keys of this *dispensation are committed into your hands; and by this ye may know that the great and dreadful *day of the Lord is near, even at the doors.

SECTION 111

Revelation given through Joseph Smith the Prophet, at Salem, Massachusetts, August 6, 1836. At this time the leaders of the Church were heavily in debt due to their labors in the ministry. Hearing that a large amount of money would be available to them in Salem, the Prophet, Sidney Rigdon, Hyrum

10a Zech. 12:10; D&C
   105:12.
11a TG Vision.
   b Ezek. 1:1.
   c Matt. 17:3; D&C
   133:55.
   d D&C 113:6. TG Priesthood, Keys of.
   e 1 Ne. 22:12 (10–12);
   Jacob 6:2; D&C 29:7;
   45:43; 127:6. TG Israel,
   Gathering of.
   f D&C 133:26. TG Israel, Ten Lost Tribes of.

12a BD Elias.
   b TG Dispensations.
   c Gal. 3:8 (6–29); D&C
   124:58. TG Abrahamic
   Covenant.
   d Gen. 18:18 (17–19).
   e TG Mission of Latter-day Saints.
13a TG Vision.
   b 1 Kgs. 17:1; Mal. 4:5
   (5–6); Matt. 17:3
   (1–4); Luke 4:25; 3 Ne.
   25:5 (5–6); D&C 2:1;
   35:4; 128:17; 138:46.

   TG Translated Beings.
15a JS—H 1:39 (38–39).
   b TG Family, Love
   within; Genealogy and
   Temple Work; Salvation
   for the Dead.
16a TG Authority; Priesthood, Keys of; Sealing.
   b TG Dispensations; Restoration of the Gospel.
   c Zeph. 1:14. TG Jesus
   Christ, Second Coming; Last Days.

Smith, and Oliver Cowdery traveled there from Kirtland, Ohio, to investigate this claim, along with preaching the gospel. The brethren transacted several items of Church business and did some preaching. When it became apparent that no money was to be forthcoming, they returned to Kirtland. Several of the factors prominent in the background are reflected in the wording of this revelation.

1–5, The Lord looks to the temporal needs of His servants; 6–11, He will deal mercifully with Zion and arrange all things for the good of His servants.

1 I, the Lord your God, am ªnot displeased with your coming this journey, notwithstanding your follies.

2 I have much ªtreasure in this city for you, for the benefit of Zion, and many people in this city, whom I will gather out in due time for the benefit of Zion, through your instrumentality.

3 Therefore, it is expedient that you should form ªacquaintance with men in this city, as you shall be led, and as it shall be given you.

4 And it shall come to pass in due time that I will ªgive this city into your hands, that you shall have power over it, insomuch that they shall not ᵇdiscover your secret parts; and its wealth pertaining to gold and silver shall be yours.

5 Concern not yourselves about your ªdebts, for I will give you power to pay them.

6 Concern not yourselves about Zion, for I will deal mercifully with her.

7 Tarry in this place, and in the regions round about;

8 And the place where it is my will that you should tarry, for the main, shall be signalized unto you by the ªpeace and power of my ᵇSpirit, that shall flow unto you.

9 This place you may obtain by hire. And inquire diligently concerning the more ancient inhabitants and founders of this city;

10 For there are more treasures than one for you in this city.

11 Therefore, be ye as ªwise as serpents and yet without ᵇsin; and I will order all things for your ᶜgood, as fast as ye are able to receive them. Amen.

---

111 1 *a* TG God, Mercy of.
2 *a* Acts 18:10 (9–11); Rom.
1:13. TG Treasure.
3 *a* TG Fellowshipping;
Missionary Work.

4 *a* TG Conversion.
b TG Shame.
5 *a* D&C 64:27 (27–29).
8 *a* Micah 5:5; D&C 27:16.
TG Peace of God.

b TG God, Spirit of.
11 *a* Matt. 10:16.
b Heb. 4:15.
c Rom. 8:28; D&C
100:15.

SECTION 112

Revelation given through Joseph Smith the Prophet to Thomas B. Marsh, at Kirtland, Ohio, July 23, 1837, concerning the Twelve Apostles of the Lamb. This revelation was received on the day Elders Heber C. Kimball and Orson Hyde first preached the gospel in England. Thomas B. Marsh was at this time President of the Quorum of the Twelve Apostles.

1–10, The Twelve are to send the gospel and raise the warning voice to all nations and people; 11–15, They are to take up their cross, follow Jesus, and feed His sheep; 16–20, Those who receive the First Presidency receive the Lord; 21–29, Darkness covers the earth, and only those who believe and are baptized will be saved; 30–34, The First Presidency and the Twelve hold the keys of the dispensation of the fulness of times.

1 Verily thus saith the Lord unto you my servant Thomas: I have heard thy prayers; and thine *a*alms have come up as a *b*memorial before me, in behalf of those, thy brethren, who were chosen to bear testimony of my name and to *c*send it abroad among all nations, kindreds, tongues, and people, and ordained through the instrumentality of my servants.

2 Verily I say unto you, there have been some few things in thine heart and with thee with which I, the Lord, was not well pleased.

3 Nevertheless, inasmuch as thou hast *a*abased thyself thou shalt be exalted; therefore, all thy sins are forgiven thee.

4 Let thy heart be of good *a*cheer before my face; and thou shalt bear record of my name, not only unto the *b*Gentiles, but also unto the Jews; and thou shalt send forth my word unto the ends of the earth.

5 *a*Contend thou, therefore, morning by morning; and day after day let thy *b*warning voice go forth; and when the night cometh let not the inhabitants of the earth slumber, because of thy *c*speech.

6 Let thy habitation be known in Zion, and *a*remove not thy house; for I, the Lord, have a great work for thee to do, in publishing my name among the children of men.

7 Therefore, *a*gird up thy loins for the work. Let thy feet be shod also, for thou art chosen, and thy path lieth among the mountains, and among many nations.

---

112 1*a* TG Almsgiving.
    b Acts 10:4.
    c D&C 18:28.
  3*a* Matt. 23:12; Luke 14:11.
4*a* Matt. 9:2; John 16:33.
    b 1 Ne. 13:42; D&C 18:6 (6–26); 19:27; 21:12; 90:9 (8–9); 107:33.
5*a* Jude 1:3.
    b Ether 12:3 (2–3). TG Zeal.
    c TG Missionary Work.
6*a* Ps. 125:1; Micah 4:2.
7*a* Eph. 6:15 (14–17).

8 And by thy word many high ones shall be brought low, and by thy word many low ones shall be *exalted.

9 Thy voice shall be a rebuke unto the transgressor; and at thy *rebuke let the tongue of the slanderer cease its perverseness.

10 Be thou *humble; and the Lord thy God shall *lead thee by the hand, and give thee answer to thy prayers.

11 I know thy heart, and have heard thy prayers concerning thy brethren. Be not partial towards them in love above many others, but let thy *love be for them as for thyself; and let thy love abound unto all men, and unto all who love my name.

12 And pray for thy brethren of the Twelve. *Admonish them sharply for my name's sake, and let them be admonished for all their sins, and be ye faithful before me unto my *name.

13 And after their *temptations, and much *tribulation, behold, I, the Lord, will feel after them, and if they harden not their hearts, and *stiffen not their necks against me, they shall be *converted, and I will heal them.

14 Now, I say unto you, and what I say unto you, I say unto all the Twelve: Arise and gird up your loins, take up your *cross, follow me, and *feed my sheep.

15 Exalt not yourselves; *rebel not against my servant Joseph; for verily I say unto you, I am with him, and my hand shall be over him; and the *keys which I have given unto him, and also to youward, shall not be taken from him till I come.

16 Verily I say unto you, my servant Thomas, thou art the man whom I have chosen to hold the *keys of my kingdom, as pertaining to the Twelve, abroad among all nations—

17 That thou mayest be my servant to unlock the door of the kingdom in all places where my servant Joseph, and my servant Sidney, and my servant Hyrum, *cannot come;

18 For on them have I laid the burden of all the churches for a little season.

19 Wherefore, whithersoever they shall send you, go ye, and I will be with

---

8 a Ezek. 17:24; Matt. 23:12; 2 Ne. 20:33.
9 a Luke 17:2; 2 Tim. 4:2.
10 a Prov. 18:12. TG Humility; Meek.
  b Isa. 57:18 (16–18). TG Guidance, Divine.
11 a Matt. 5:43 (43–48). TG Charity; Love.
12 a Rom. 15:14; 2 Thes. 3:15 (14–15).
  b TG Jesus Christ, Taking the Name of.
13 a TG Temptation; Test.
  b John 16:33; Rev. 7:14 (13–14); D&C 103:12. TG Tribulation.
  c TG Stiffnecked.
  d John 12:40; 2 Ne. 26:9; 3 Ne. 9:13 (13–14);
18:32. TG Conversion; Man, New, Spiritually Reborn.
14 a Matt. 16:24; Luke 9:23.
  b John 21:16 (15–17).
15 a TG Rebellion.
  b D&C 28:7.
16 a TG Priesthood, Keys of.
17 a Luke 10:1.

you; and in whatsoever place ye shall proclaim my name an ^aeffectual door shall be opened unto you, that they may receive my word.

20 Whosoever ^areceiveth my word receiveth me, and whosoever receiveth me, receiveth those, the First Presidency, whom I have sent, whom I have made counselors for my name's sake unto you.

21 And again, I say unto you, that whosoever ye shall send in my name, by the voice of your brethren, the ^aTwelve, duly recommended and ^bauthorized by you, shall have power to open the door of my kingdom unto any nation whithersoever ye shall send them—

22 Inasmuch as they shall humble themselves before me, and abide in my word, and ^ahearken to the voice of my Spirit.

23 Verily, verily, I say unto you, ^adarkness covereth the earth, and gross darkness the minds of the people, and all flesh has become ^bcorrupt before my face.

24 Behold, ^avengeance cometh speedily upon the inhabitants of the earth, a day of wrath, a day of burning, a day of ^bdesolation, of ^cweeping, of mourning, and of lamentation; and as a whirlwind it shall come upon all the face of the earth, saith the Lord.

25 And upon my ^ahouse shall it ^bbegin, and from my house shall it go forth, saith the Lord;

26 First among those among you, saith the Lord, who have ^aprofessed to know my ^bname and have not ^cknown me, and have ^dblasphemed against me in the midst of my house, saith the Lord.

27 Therefore, see to it that ye trouble not yourselves concerning the affairs of my church ^ain this place, saith the Lord.

28 But ^apurify your hearts before me; and then ^bgo ye into all the world, and preach my gospel unto every creature who has not received it;

29 And he that ^abelieveth and is ^bbaptized shall be saved, and he that believeth not, and is not baptized, shall be ^cdamned.

19a 1 Cor. 16:9.
20a D&C 84:35. TG Teachable.
21a D&C 107:34 (34–35).
 b TG Authority; Delegation of Responsibility.
22a TG God, Spirit of; Obedience.
23a Isa. 60:2; Micah 3:6; D&C 38:11 (11–12); Moses 7:61 (61–62). TG Apostasy of the Early Christian Church; Darkness, Spiritual.
 b Gen. 6:11 (5–6, 11–13);

Ps. 14:1; D&C 10:21 (20–23).
24a TG Day of the Lord; Retribution; Vengeance.
 b Mal. 4:5.
 c Matt. 8:12; D&C 101:91; 124:8. TG Mourning.
25a TG Chastening.
 b 1 Pet. 4:17 (17–18).
26a D&C 41:1; 50:4; 56:1. TG Hypocrisy.
 b TG Jesus Christ, Taking the Name of.
 c Hosea 8:2 (1–4); Luke

6:46; Mosiah 26:25 (24–27); 3 Ne. 14:23 (21–23).
 d D&C 105:15. TG Apostasy of Individuals; Blaspheme.
27a D&C 107:33 (33–39).
28a TG Purification; Purity.
 b Mark 16:15 (15–16); D&C 18:28.
29a Morm. 9:23 (22–24); D&C 20:25.
 b TG Baptism, Essential.
 c TG Damnation.

30 For unto you, the *Twelve, and those, the First Presidency, who are appointed with you to be your *counselors and your leaders, is the *power of this priesthood given, for the last days and for the last time, in the which is the dispensation of the *fulness of times,

31 Which power you hold, in connection with all those who have received a *dispensation at any time from the beginning of the creation;

32 For verily I say unto you, the *keys of the dispensation, which ye have received, have *come down from the fathers, and last of all, being sent down from heaven unto you.

33 Verily I say unto you, behold how great is your calling. *Cleanse your hearts and your garments, lest the blood of this generation be *required at your hands.

34 Be faithful until I come, for I *come quickly; and my reward is with me to recompense every man according as his *work shall be. I am Alpha and Omega. Amen.

SECTION 113

Answers to certain questions on the writings of Isaiah, given by Joseph Smith the Prophet, at or near Far West, Missouri, March 1838.

1–6, The Stem of Jesse, the rod coming therefrom, and the root of Jesse are identified; 7–10, The scattered remnants of Zion have a right to the priesthood and are called to return to the Lord.

1 Who is the *Stem of Jesse spoken of in the 1st, 2d, 3d, 4th, and 5th verses of the 11th chapter of Isaiah?

2 Verily thus saith the Lord: It is Christ.

3 What is the *rod spoken of in the first verse of the 11th chapter of Isaiah, that should come of the Stem of Jesse?

4 Behold, thus saith the Lord: It is a servant in the hands of Christ, who is partly a descendant of Jesse as well as of *Ephraim, or of the house of Joseph, on whom there is laid much *power.

---

30 *a* TG Apostles; Church Organization.
 b TG Counselor; Leadership.
 c TG Priesthood, Power of.
 d Eph. 1:10 (9–10); D&C 27:13; 76:106; 124:41. TG Restoration of the Gospel.
31 *a* TG Dispensations.

32 *a* TG Priesthood, Keys of.
 b Abr. 1:3. TG Priesthood, History of.
33 *a* Jacob 1:19; 2:2; D&C 88:85.
 b Ezek. 34:10; D&C 72:3.
34 *a* Rev. 3:11; 22:7 (7, 12); D&C 1:12.
 b TG Good Works; Reward.

113 1 *a* Isa. 11:1 (1–5). TG Jesus Christ, Davidic Descent of.
 3 *a* Ps. 110:2 (1–4).
 4 *a* Gen. 41:52 (50–52); D&C 133:34 (30–34). TG Israel, Joseph, People of.
 b D&C 110:16 (11–16).

5 What is the *root of Jesse spoken of in the 10th verse of the 11th chapter?

6 Behold, thus saith the Lord, it is a *descendant of Jesse, as well as of Joseph, unto whom rightly belongs the *priesthood, and the *keys of the kingdom, for an *ensign, and for the gathering of my people in the *last days.

7 Questions by Elias Higbee: What is meant by the command in Isaiah, 52d chapter, 1st verse, which saith: Put on thy strength, O Zion—and what people had Isaiah reference to?

8 He had reference to those whom God should call in the last days, who should hold the *power of *priesthood to bring again *Zion, and the redemption of Israel; and to put on her *strength is to put on the *authority of the *priesthood, which she, Zion, has a *right to by lineage; also to return to that power which she had lost.

9 What are we to understand by Zion loosing herself from the bands of her neck; 2d verse?

10 We are to understand that the *scattered *remnants are exhorted to *return to the Lord from whence they have fallen; which if they do, the promise of the Lord is that he will speak to them, or give them revelation. See the 6th, 7th, and 8th verses. The *bands of her neck are the curses of God upon her, or the remnants of Israel in their scattered condition among the Gentiles.

SECTION 114

Revelation given through Joseph Smith the Prophet, at Far West, Missouri, April 11, 1838.

1–2, Church positions held by those who are not faithful will be given to others.

1 Verily thus saith the Lord: It is wisdom in my servant David W. Patten, that he settle up all his business as soon as he possibly can, and make a disposition of his merchandise, that he may *perform a mission unto me next

---

5 a 2 Ne. 21:10 (10–12).
6 a Isa. 11:10.
  b TG Priesthood, Melchizedek.
  c D&C 110:11. TG Priesthood, Keys of.
  d Isa. 30:17; D&C 45:9. TG Ensign.
  e TG Israel, Gathering of; Last Days.
8 a TG Priesthood,

Power of.
  b D&C 86:8. TG Priesthood, Keys of.
  c TG Zion.
  d Isa. 45:24; 52:1; 1 Ne. 17:3; D&C 82:14. TG Israel, Restoration of; Strength.
  e TG Authority; Mission of Latter-day Saints; Priesthood, Authority.

f TG Priesthood, History of.
  g TG Birthright.
10 a TG Israel, Scattering of.
  b Micah 5:3. TG Israel, Remnant of.
  c Hosea 3:5; 2 Ne. 6:11.
  d Isa. 52:2 (2, 6–8). TG Bondage, Spiritual.
114 1 a D&C 118:5.

spring, in company with others, even twelve including himself, to testify of my name and bear glad tidings unto all the world.

2 For verily thus saith the Lord, that inasmuch as there are those among you who *deny my name, others shall be *planted in their *stead and receive their *bishopric. Amen.

SECTION 115

Revelation given through Joseph Smith the Prophet, at Far West, Missouri, April 26, 1838, making known the will of God concerning the building up of that place and of the Lord's house. This revelation is addressed to the presiding officers and the members of the Church.

1–4, The Lord names His church The Church of Jesus Christ of Latter-day Saints; 5–6, Zion and her stakes are places of defense and refuge for the Saints; 7–16, The Saints are commanded to build a house of the Lord at Far West; 17–19, Joseph Smith holds the keys of the kingdom of God on earth.

1 Verily thus saith the Lord unto you, my servant Joseph Smith, Jun., and also my servant Sidney Rigdon, and also my servant Hyrum Smith, and your *counselors who are and shall be appointed hereafter;

2 And also unto you, my servant *Edward Partridge, and his counselors;

3 And also unto my faithful servants who are of the high council of my *church in Zion, for thus it shall be called, and unto all the elders and people of my Church of Jesus Christ of Latter-day Saints, scattered abroad in all the world;

4 For thus shall *my *church be called in the last days, even The Church of Jesus Christ of Latter-day *Saints.

5 Verily I say unto you all: *Arise and shine forth, that thy *light may be a *standard for the *nations;

6 And that the *gathering together upon the land of *Zion, and upon her *stakes, may be for a defense, and for a *refuge from the storm, and from wrath when it shall be *poured out without mixture upon the whole earth.

2*a* TG Apostasy of Individuals.
  b 1 Sam. 2:35; D&C 118:1 (1, 6).
  c D&C 35:18; 42:10; 64:40.
  d Acts 1:20 (20–26).
115 1*a* D&C 81:1; 112:20; 124:91.
  2*a* D&C 64:17; 124:19.
  3*a* TG Jesus Christ, Head of the Church.

4*a* 3 Ne. 27:8.
  b 1 Cor. 1:10 (10–13); D&C 20:1 (1–4); 136:2 (2–8). TG Kingdom of God, on Earth.
  c TG Saints.
5*a* Isa. 60:1 (1–3). TG Mission of Latter-day Saints.
  b TG Light [noun]; Peculiar People.
  c Gen. 18:18 (17–19);

Isa. 11:12. TG Ensign; Example.
  d TG Nations.
6*a* TG Last Days.
  b TG Zion.
  c D&C 101:21; 115:18 (17–18). TG Stake.
  d Isa. 25:4 (3–5); D&C 45:66 (62–71). TG Refuge.
  e Rev. 14:10; D&C 1:13 (13–14).

7 Let the city, Far West, be a holy and consecrated land unto me; and it shall be called most holy, for the ground upon which thou standest is *a*holy.

8 Therefore, I command you to *a*build a house unto me, for the gathering together of my saints, that they may *b*worship me.

9 And let there be a beginning of this work, and a foundation, and a preparatory work, this following summer;

10 And let the beginning be made on the fourth day of July next; and from that time forth let my people *a*labor diligently to build a house unto my name;

11 And in *a*one year from this day let them re-commence laying the foundation of my *b*house.

12 Thus let them from that time forth labor diligently until it shall be finished, from the cornerstone thereof unto the top thereof, until there shall not anything remain that is not finished.

13 Verily I say unto you, let not my servant Joseph, neither my servant Sidney, neither my servant Hyrum, get in *a*debt any more for the building of a house unto my name;

14 But let a house be built unto my name according to the *a*pattern which I will show unto them.

15 And if my people build it not according to the pattern which I shall show unto their presidency, I will not accept it at their hands.

16 But if my people do build it according to the pattern which I shall show unto their presidency, even my servant Joseph and his counselors, then I will accept it at the hands of my people.

17 And again, verily I say unto you, it is my will that the city of Far West should be built up speedily by the gathering of my saints;

18 And also that other places should be appointed for *a*stakes in the regions round about, as they shall be manifested unto my servant Joseph, from time to time.

19 For behold, I will be with him, and I will sanctify him before the people; for unto him have I given the *a*keys of this kingdom and ministry. Even so. Amen.

---

7 *a* Ex. 3:5; Josh. 5:15;
     D&C 101:64.
8 *a* D&C 88:119; 95:8.
   b TG Worship.
10 *a* Neh. 4:6; D&C 52:39;

      75:3. TG Industry.
11 *a* D&C 118:5.
    b D&C 124:45 (45–54).
13 *a* D&C 104:86 (78–86).
14 *a* Num. 8:4; Heb. 8:5;

       D&C 97:10.
18 *a* D&C 101:21; 115:6.
      TG Stake.
19 *a* TG Priesthood, Keys of.

SECTION 116

Revelation given to Joseph Smith the Prophet, near Wight's Ferry, at a place called Spring Hill, Daviess County, Missouri, May 19, 1838.

1 Spring Hill is named by the Lord ^aAdam-ondi-Ahman, because, said he, it is the place where ^bAdam shall come to visit his people, or the Ancient of Days shall sit, as spoken of by Daniel the prophet.

SECTION 117

Revelation given through Joseph Smith the Prophet, at Far West, Missouri, July 8, 1838, concerning the immediate duties of William Marks, Newel K. Whitney, and Oliver Granger.

1–9, The Lord's servants should not covet temporal things, for "what is property unto the Lord?"; 10–16, They are to forsake littleness of soul, and their sacrifices will be sacred unto the Lord.

1 Verily thus saith the Lord unto my servant ^aWilliam Marks, and also unto my servant Newel K. Whitney, let them settle up their business speedily and journey from the land of Kirtland, before I, the Lord, ^bsend again the snows upon the earth.

2 Let them awake, and arise, and ^acome forth, and not tarry, for I, the Lord, command it.

3 Therefore, if they ^atarry it shall not be well with them.

4 Let them repent of all their sins, and of all their covetous desires, before me, saith the Lord; for what is ^aproperty unto me? saith the Lord.

5 Let the properties of Kirtland be turned out for ^adebts, saith the Lord. Let them go, saith the Lord, and whatsoever remaineth, let it remain in your hands, saith the Lord.

6 For have I not the fowls of heaven, and also the fish of the sea, and the beasts of the mountains? Have I not ^amade the earth? Do I not hold the ^bdestinies of all the armies of the nations of the earth?

---

116 1*a* Dan. 7:13 (13–14, 22);
　　　D&C 78:15 (15, 20);
　　　95:17; 107:53; 117:8 (8,
　　　11). Note that a song
　　　titled "Adam-ondi-
　　　Ahman," written by
　　　William W. Phelps, was
　　　sung at the Kirtland

　　　Temple dedication.
　b TG Adam.
117 1*a* D&C 124:79 (79–80).
　　b Job 37:6 (5–6); Ps.
　　　148:8; Hel. 11:17
　　　(13–17); Ether 2:24.
　2*a* IE from Kirtland.
　3*a* TG Disobedience;
　　　Procrastination.

　4*a* Mark 14:4 (3–4); D&C
　　　104:14.
　5*a* D&C 90:23 (22–23).
　6*a* TG Creation; God,
　　　Works of; Jesus Christ,
　　　Creator.
　b Isa. 45:1 (1–3); 1 Ne.
　　　17:37.

7 Therefore, will I not make ^asolitary places to bud and to ^bblossom, and to bring forth in abundance? saith the Lord.

8 Is there not room enough on the mountains of ^aAdam-ondi-Ahman, and on the plains of Olaha ^bShinehah, or the land where ^cAdam dwelt, that you should covet that which is but the drop, and neglect the more weighty matters?

9 Therefore, come up hither unto the land of my people, even Zion.

10 Let my servant William Marks be ^afaithful over a few things, and he shall be a ruler over many. Let him preside in the midst of my people in the city of Far West, and let him be blessed with the blessings of my people.

11 Let my servant Newel K. Whitney be ashamed of the ^aNicolaitane band and of all their ^bsecret abominations, and of all his littleness of soul before me, saith the Lord, and come up to the land of Adam-ondi-Ahman, and be a ^cbishop unto my people, saith the Lord, not in name but in deed, saith the Lord.

12 And again, I say unto you, I remember my servant ^aOliver Granger; behold, verily I say unto him that his name shall be had in sacred remembrance from generation to generation, forever and ever, saith the Lord.

13 Therefore, let him contend earnestly for the redemption of the First Presidency of my Church, saith the Lord; and when he falls he shall rise again, for his ^asacrifice shall be more sacred unto me than his increase, saith the Lord.

14 Therefore, let him come up hither speedily, unto the land of Zion; and in the due time he shall be made a merchant unto my name, saith the Lord, for the benefit of my people.

15 Therefore let no man despise my servant Oliver Granger, but let the blessings of my people be on him forever and ever.

16 And again, verily I say unto you, let all my servants in the land of Kirtland remember the Lord their God, and mine house also, to keep and preserve it holy, and to overthrow the moneychangers in mine own due time, saith the Lord. Even so. Amen.

7 a Isa. 35:1 (1–2).
  b D&C 35:24; 39:13;
     49:25. TG Earth,
     Renewal of.
8 a D&C 116.
  b Abr. 3:13.

  c TG Adam; Eden.
10 a Matt. 25:23.
11 a Rev. 2:6 (6, 15).
   b TG Secret Combina-
     tions.
   c D&C 72:8 (6–8).

12 a IE the agent left by the
      Prophet to settle his
      affairs in Kirtland.
13 a TG Self-Sacrifice.

SECTION 118

Revelation given through Joseph Smith the Prophet, at Far West, Missouri, July 8, 1838, in response to the supplication, "Show us thy will, O Lord, concerning the Twelve."

1–3, The Lord will provide for the families of the Twelve; 4–6, Vacancies in the Twelve are filled.

1 Verily, thus saith the Lord: Let a conference be held immediately; let the Twelve be organized; and let men be appointed to *a*supply the place of those who are fallen.

2 Let my servant *a*Thomas remain for a season in the land of Zion, to publish my word.

3 Let the residue continue to preach from that hour, and if they will do this in all *a*lowliness of heart, in meekness and humility, and *b*long-suffering, I, the Lord, give unto them a *c*promise that I will provide for their families; and an effectual door shall be opened for them, from henceforth.

4 And next spring let them depart to go over the great waters, and there promulgate my gospel, the fulness thereof, and bear record of my name.

5 Let them *a*take leave of my saints in the city of Far West, on the *b*twenty-sixth day of April next, on the building-spot of my house, saith the Lord.

6 Let my servant John Taylor, and also my servant John E. Page, and also my servant Wilford Woodruff, and also my servant Willard Richards, be appointed to fill the places of those who have *a*fallen, and be officially notified of their appointment.

SECTION 119

Revelation given through Joseph Smith the Prophet, at Far West, Missouri, July 8, 1838, in answer to his supplication: "O Lord! Show unto thy servants how much thou requirest of the properties of thy people for a tithing." The law of tithing, as understood today, had not been given to the Church previous to this revelation. The term tithing *in the prayer just quoted and in previous revelations (64:23; 85:3; 97:11) had meant not just one-tenth, but all free-will offerings, or contributions, to the Church funds. The Lord had previously given to the Church the law of consecration and stewardship of property,*

---

118 1*a* Acts 1:25 (23–26);
     D&C 114:2.
  2*a* IE Thomas B. Marsh.

3*a* Eph. 4:2.
  b TG Perseverance.
  c TG Promise.

5*a* D&C 114:1.
  b D&C 115:11.
6*a* D&C 114:2.

which members (chiefly the leading elders) entered into by a covenant that was to be everlasting. Because of failure on the part of many to abide by this covenant, the Lord withdrew it for a time and gave instead the law of tithing to the whole Church. The Prophet asked the Lord how much of their property He required for sacred purposes. The answer was this revelation.

1–5, The Saints are to pay their surplus property and then give, as tithing, one-tenth of their interest annually; 6–7, Such a course will sanctify the land of Zion.

1 Verily, thus saith the Lord, I require all their ^asurplus property to be put into the hands of the bishop of my church in Zion,

2 For the building of mine ^ahouse, and for the laying of the foundation of Zion and for the priesthood, and for the debts of the Presidency of my Church.

3 And this shall be the beginning of the ^atithing of my people.

4 And after that, those who have thus been ^atithed shall pay one-tenth of all their interest annually; and this shall be a standing law unto them forever, for my holy priesthood, saith the Lord.

5 Verily I say unto you, it shall come to pass that all those who gather unto the land of ^aZion shall be tithed of their surplus properties, and shall observe this law, or they shall not be found worthy to abide among you.

6 And I say unto you, if my people observe not this law, to keep it holy, and by this law sanctify the land of Zion unto me, that my statutes and my judgments may be kept thereon, that it may be most holy, behold, verily I say unto you, it shall not be a land of ^aZion unto you.

7 And this shall be an ensample unto all the ^astakes of Zion. Even so. Amen.

SECTION 120

Revelation given through Joseph Smith the Prophet, at Far West, Missouri, July 8, 1838, making known the disposition of the properties tithed as named in the preceding revelation, section 119.

1 Verily, thus saith the Lord, the time is now come, that ^ait shall be ^bdisposed of by a council, composed of the First Presidency of my Church, and of the bishop and his council, and by my high council; and by mine own voice unto them, saith the Lord. Even so. Amen.

---

119 1 *a* D&C 42:33 (33–34), 55; 51:13; 82:18 (17–19).
2 *a* 2 Chr. 3:3 (3–4); D&C

115:8 (8–13).
3 *a* D&C 42:30; 64:23; 120.
4 *a* TG Tithing.
5 *a* D&C 52:42 (42–43).

6 *a* TG Zion.
7 *a* D&C 82:13.
120 1 *a* D&C 119:1 (1–4).
b TG Accountability; Church Organization.

SECTION 121

Prayer and prophecies written by Joseph Smith the Prophet in an epistle to the Church while he was a prisoner in the jail at Liberty, Missouri, dated March 20, 1839. The Prophet and several companions had been months in prison. Their petitions and appeals directed to the executive officers and the judiciary had failed to bring them relief.

1–6, The Prophet pleads with the Lord for the suffering Saints; 7–10, The Lord speaks peace to him; 11–17, Cursed are all those who raise false cries of transgression against the Lord's people; 18–25, They will not have right to the priesthood and will be damned; 26–32, Glorious revelations promised those who endure valiantly; 33–40, Why many are called and few are chosen; 41–46, The priesthood should be used only in righteousness.

1 O God, *ᵃ*where art thou? And where is the pavilion that covereth thy *ᵇ*hiding place?

2 *ᵃ*How long shall thy hand be stayed, and thine eye, yea thy pure eye, behold from the eternal heavens the wrongs of thy people and of thy servants, and thine ear be penetrated with their cries?

3 Yea, O Lord, *ᵃ*how long shall they suffer these wrongs and unlawful *ᵇ*oppressions, before thine heart shall be softened toward them, and thy bowels be moved with *ᶜ*compassion toward them?

4 O Lord God *ᵃ*Almighty, maker of *ᵇ*heaven, earth, and seas, and of all things that in them are, and who controllest and subjectest the devil, and the dark and benighted dominion of Sheol—stretch forth thy hand; let thine eye pierce; let thy *ᶜ*pavilion be taken up; let thy *ᵈ*hiding place no longer be covered; let thine ear be inclined; let thine *ᵉ*heart be softened, and thy bowels moved with compassion toward us.

5 Let thine *ᵃ*anger be kindled against our enemies; and, in the fury of thine heart, with thy *ᵇ*sword *ᶜ*avenge us of our wrongs.

6 Remember thy *ᵃ*suffering saints, O our God; and thy servants will rejoice in thy name forever.

7 My son, *ᵃ*peace be unto thy soul; thine *ᵇ*adversity and thine afflictions shall be but a *ᶜ*small moment;

---

121 1 *a* Matt. 27:46.
 b Ps. 13:1 (1–2); 18:11;
  102:2; Isa. 45:15.
 2 *a* Ex. 5:22; Ps. 35:17
  (17–28); 89:46; Hab.
  1:2 (2–4).
 3 *a* Ps. 69:14 (1–2, 14);
  Alma 14:26 (26–29).
 b TG Cruelty;

Oppression; Persecu-
tion.
 c TG Compassion.
4 *a* TG God, Power of.
 b Gen. 1:1.
 c 2 Sam. 22:7.
 d D&C 101:89; 123:6.
 e TG Compassion; God,
  Mercy of.
5 *a* Ps. 119:84.

 b D&C 1:13 (13–14).
 c Ps. 35:1 (1–10); Luke
  18:7.
6 *a* D&C 122:5 (5–7).
 TG Suffering.
7 *a* Acts 23:11 (11–14).
 TG Comfort.
 b TG Adversity; Affliction.
 c Isa. 54:7.

8 And then, if thou *endure it well, God shall exalt thee on high; thou shalt triumph over all thy *foes.

9 Thy *friends do stand by thee, and they shall hail thee again with warm hearts and friendly hands.

10 Thou art not yet as Job; thy *friends do not contend against thee, neither charge thee with transgression, as they did Job.

11 And they who do charge thee with transgression, their hope shall be blasted, and their prospects shall *melt away as the hoar frost melteth before the burning rays of the rising sun;

12 And also that God hath set his hand and seal to change the *times and seasons, and to blind their *minds, that they may not understand his *marvelous workings; that he may *prove them also and take them in their own craftiness;

13 Also because their hearts are corrupted, and the things which they are willing to bring upon others, and love to have others suffer, may come upon *themselves to the very uttermost;

14 That they may be *disappointed also, and their hopes may be cut off;

15 And not many years hence, that they and their *posterity shall be *swept from under heaven, saith God, that not one of them is left to stand by the wall.

16 *Cursed are all those that shall lift up the *heel against mine *anointed, saith the Lord, and cry they have *sinned when they have not sinned before me, saith the Lord, but have done that which was meet in mine eyes, and which I commanded them.

17 But *those who cry transgression do it because they are the servants of sin, and are the *children of disobedience themselves.

18 And those who *swear *falsely against my servants, that they might bring them into bondage and death—

19 Wo unto them; because they have *offended my little ones they shall be severed from the *ordinances of mine house.

---

8 a 1 Pet. 2:20 (19–23).
    TG Perseverance; Probation.
  b TG Enemies.
9 a D&C 122:3.
    TG Friendship.
10 a Job 4:1 (1–8); 13:4;
    16:2.
11 a Ps. 58:7 (3–11); Jer. 1:19
    (7–19).
12 a Dan. 2:21 (19–22, 28);
    Acts 1:7; D&C 68:11
    (7–12). TG Time.

  b 2 Kgs. 6:18 (18–23).
    TG Mind.
  c Ex. 8:19; 1 Ne. 19:22;
    Alma 23:6; D&C 84:3.
  d TG Test.
13 a Prov. 28:10; 1 Ne. 14:3.
14 a 3 Ne. 4:10.
15 a Ps. 37:28; 109:13.
  b D&C 124:52.
16 a TG Curse.
  b Ps. 41:9; John 13:18.
    TG Prophets, Rejection
    of; Reviling.

  c 1 Sam. 26:9; Ps. 2:2
    (2–4); 105:15.
  d 2 Ne. 15:20; Moro. 7:14
    (14, 18); D&C 64:16.
17 a Rev. 12:10; Alma 15:15.
  b Eph. 5:6 (2–6).
18 a TG Swearing.
  b Mal. 3:5. TG Lying;
    Slander.
19 a Matt. 18:6. TG Offense.
  b TG Ordinance; Salvation.

20 Their *basket shall not be full, their houses and their barns shall perish, and they themselves shall be *despised by those that flattered them.

21 They shall not have right to the *priesthood, nor their posterity after them from generation to generation.

22 It had been *better for them that a millstone had been hanged about their necks, and they drowned in the depth of the sea.

23 Wo unto all those that *discomfort my people, and drive, and *murder, and testify against them, saith the Lord of Hosts; a *generation of vipers shall not escape the damnation of hell.

24 Behold, mine eyes *see and know all their works, and I have in reserve a swift *judgment in the season thereof, for them all;

25 For there is a *time *appointed for every man, according as his *works shall be.

26 God shall give unto you *knowledge by his *Holy Spirit, yea, by the unspeakable *gift of the Holy Ghost, that has not been *revealed since the world was until now;

27 Which our forefathers have awaited with *anxious expectation to be revealed in the last times, which their minds were pointed to by the angels, as held in reserve for the fulness of their glory;

28 A time to come in the which *nothing shall be withheld, whether there be *one God or many *gods, they shall be manifest.

29 All thrones and dominions, principalities and powers, shall be *revealed and set forth upon all who have endured *valiantly for the gospel of Jesus Christ.

30 And also, if there be *bounds set to the heavens or to the seas, or to the dry land, or to the sun, moon, or stars—

31 All the times of their revolutions, all the appointed days, months, and

---

20a Deut. 28:17 (15–26).
  b Prov. 24:24 (23–26).
21a Alma 13:4 (3–5).
    TG Priesthood, Quali-
    fying for.
22a Matt. 18:6; D&C 54:5.
23a D&C 101:1.
  b Esth. 3:13.
  c Matt. 12:34; 23:33.
24a Job 10:4; Ps. 139:1;
    Jonah 3:10. TG God,
    Omniscience of.
  b Ps. 109:7 (3–7); Hel.
    8:25; D&C 10:23
    (20–23).

25a D&C 122:9.
  b Job 7:1; Alma 12:27
    (26–28); D&C 42:48.
  c TG Good Works.
26a Dan. 2:28 (22–29,
    49); Amos 3:7; A of F
    1:9. TG Mysteries of
    Godliness; Revelation.
  b TG God, Spirit of.
  c TG Holy Ghost, Gift of.
  d Alma 12:10 (9–11);
    40:3. TG Scriptures to
    Come Forth.
27a Rom. 16:25; D&C 6:7
    (7–11); 42:65 (61–65).

28a D&C 42:61; 59:4; 76:7;
    98:12; 101:32.
  b Rom. 3:30 (28–31);
    1 Tim. 2:5.
  c Ps. 82:6; John 10:34;
    1 Cor. 8:6 (5–6); D&C
    76:58; Abr. 4:1 (1–31);
    5:1 (1–21).
29a D&C 101:32.
  b D&C 76:79. TG Dili-
    gence; Trustworthiness.
30a Job 26:10 (7–14);
    38:33 (1–41); Ps. 104:9
    (1–35); Acts 17:26
    (24–28).

years, and all the days of their days, months, and years, and all their ᵃglories, laws, and set times, shall be revealed in the days of the ᵇdispensation of the fulness of times—

32 According to that which was ᵃordained in the midst of the ᵇCouncil of the Eternal ᶜGod of all other gods before this ᵈworld was, that should be reserved unto the finishing and the end thereof, when every man shall enter into his eternal ᵉpresence and into his immortal ᶠrest.

33 How long can rolling waters remain impure? What ᵃpower shall stay the heavens? As well might man stretch forth his puny arm to stop the Missouri river in its decreed course, or to turn it up stream, as to ᵇhinder the ᶜAlmighty from pouring down ᵈknowledge from heaven upon the heads of the Latter-day Saints.

34 Behold, there are many ᵃcalled, but few are chosen. And why are they not chosen?

35 Because their ᵃhearts are set so much upon the things of this ᵇworld, and ᶜaspire to the ᵈhonors of men, that they do not learn this one lesson—

36 That the ᵃrights of the priesthood are inseparably connected with the powers of heaven, and that the powers of heaven cannot be ᵇcontrolled nor handled only upon the ᶜprinciples of righteousness.

37 That they may be conferred upon us, it is true; but when we undertake to ᵃcover our ᵇsins, or to gratify our ᶜpride, our vain ambition, or to exercise control or ᵈdominion or compulsion upon the souls of the children of men, in any degree of unrighteousness, behold, the heavens ᵉwithdraw themselves; the Spirit of the Lord is grieved; and when it is withdrawn, Amen to the priesthood or the authority of that man.

---

31 a Abr. 3:4 (2–10).
   TG Glory; God, Law of.
  b TG Dispensations.
32 a TG Earth, Purpose of.
  b TG Council in Heaven.
  c Deut. 10:17 (17–21);
   Dan. 11:36.
  d TG Earth, Destiny of;
   World.
  e TG Man, Potential to
   Become like Heavenly
   Father.
  f Ps. 95:11; Heb. 3:11;
   4:1; Alma 12:34; 3 Ne.
   27:19; D&C 84:24.
33 a Rom. 8:39 (35–39).
  b Dan. 4:35.
  c TG God, Power of.

  d Dan. 12:4. TG Knowl-
   edge.
34 a Matt. 20:16; 22:14
   (1–14); Luke 13:23;
   D&C 63:31; 95:5
   (5–6). TG Called of
   God.
35 a Luke 14:18 (18–20).
  b TG Selfishness; Worldliness.
  c TG Motivations.
  d Matt. 6:2; 2 Ne. 26:29;
   D&C 58:39. TG Honor.
36 a D&C 107:10.
   TG Priesthood, Author-
   ity; Priesthood, Keys of;
   Priesthood, Oath and
   Covenant; Priesthood,

   Power of.
  b TG Priesthood, Magni-
   fying Callings within.
  c D&C 107:30. TG Righ-
   teousness.
37 a Prov. 28:13. TG Apostasy of Individuals;
   Honesty; Hypocrisy.
  b TG Sin.
  c TG Haughtiness; Pride.
  d Gen. 1:26 (26–28);
   D&C 76:111 (110–12).
  e 1 Sam. 18:12; D&C
   1:33; 3:11; JS—H 1:46.
   TG Holy Ghost, Loss
   of.

38 Behold, ere he is aware, he is left unto himself, to *a*kick against the pricks, to *b*persecute the saints, and to *c*fight against God.

39 We have learned by sad experience that it is the *a*nature and disposition of almost all men, as soon as they get a little *b*authority, as they suppose, they will immediately begin to exercise *c*unrighteous dominion.

40 Hence many are called, but *a*few are chosen.

41 No *a*power or influence can or ought to be maintained by virtue of the *b*priesthood, only by *c*persuasion, by *d*long-suffering, by gentleness and meekness, and by love unfeigned;

42 By *a*kindness, and pure *b*knowledge, which shall greatly enlarge the *c*soul without *d*hypocrisy, and without *e*guile—

43 *a*Reproving betimes with *b*sharpness, when *c*moved upon by the Holy Ghost; and then showing forth afterwards an increase of *d*love toward him whom thou hast reproved, lest he esteem thee to be his enemy;

44 That he may know that thy faithfulness is stronger than the cords of *a*death.

45 Let thy *a*bowels also be full of charity towards all men, and to the household of faith, and let *b*virtue garnish thy thoughts unceasingly; then shall thy *c*confidence wax strong in the *d*presence of God; and the doctrine of the priesthood shall distil upon thy soul as the *e*dews from heaven.

46 The Holy Ghost shall be thy constant *a*companion, and thy scepter an unchanging scepter of *b*righteousness and truth; and thy *c*dominion shall be an everlasting dominion, and without compulsory means it shall flow unto thee forever and ever.

38*a* Acts 9:5; 26:14.
  b TG Persecution.
  c Micah 3:5; 1 Ne. 11:35 (34–36).
39*a* TG Man, Natural, Not Spiritually Reborn.
  b TG Authority.
  c 1 Kgs. 16:2. TG Leadership; Unrighteous Dominion.
40*a* Matt. 20:16; D&C 95:5.
41*a* TG Priesthood, Power of.
  b 1 Pet. 5:3 (1–3). TG Priesthood; Priesthood, Magnifying Callings within.

  c Prov. 25:15. TG Communication; Marriage, Husbands.
  d 2 Cor. 6:6. TG Forbear; Love; Meek; Patience.
42*a* TG Courtesy; Kindness.
  b 1 Pet. 3:7. TG Knowledge.
  c TG Understanding.
  d James 3:17.
  e TG Guile; Sincere.
43*a* TG Chastening; Reproof.
  b D&C 15:2.
  c TG Holy Ghost, Mission of.
  d TG Charity.
44*a* TG Dependability.

45*a* 1 Thes. 3:12; 1 Jn. 3:17 (16–17). TG Benevolence; Charity; Priesthood, Magnifying Callings within.
  b TG Chastity; Modesty; Virtue.
  c TG Trust in God.
  d TG God, Presence of; God, Privilege of Seeing.
  e Deut. 32:2; D&C 128:19.
46*a* TG Holy Ghost, Mission of; Spirituality.
  b TG Righteousness.
  c Dan. 7:14.

SECTION 122

The word of the Lord to Joseph Smith the Prophet, while a prisoner in the jail at Liberty, Missouri. This section is an excerpt from an epistle to the Church dated March 20, 1839 (see the heading to section 121).

1–4, The ends of the earth will inquire after the name of Joseph Smith; 5–7, All his perils and travails will give him experience and be for his good; 8–9, The Son of Man has descended below them all.

1 The ends of the earth shall inquire after thy ^aname, and fools shall have thee in ^bderision, and hell shall rage against thee;

2 While the pure in heart, and the wise, and the noble, and the virtuous, shall seek ^acounsel, and authority, and blessings constantly from under thy hand.

3 And thy ^apeople shall never be turned against thee by the testimony of traitors.

4 And although their influence shall cast thee into trouble, and into bars and walls, thou shalt be had in ^ahonor; and but for a small ^bmoment and thy voice shall be more terrible in the midst of thine enemies than the fierce ^clion, because of thy righteousness; and thy God shall stand by thee forever and ever.

5 If thou art called to pass through ^atribulation; if thou art in perils among false brethren; if thou art in ^bperils among robbers; if thou art in perils by land or by sea;

6 If thou art ^aaccused with all manner of false accusations; if thine enemies fall upon thee; if they tear thee from the society of thy father and mother and brethren and sisters; and if with a drawn sword thine enemies tear thee from the bosom of thy wife, and of thine offspring, and thine elder son, although but six years of age, shall cling to thy garments, and shall say, My father, my father, why can't you stay with us? O, my father, what are the men going to do with you? and if then he shall be thrust from thee by the sword, and thou be dragged to ^bprison, and thine enemies prowl around thee like ^cwolves for the blood of the lamb;

---

122 1 a JS—H 1:33.
  b Job 30:1; Ps. 119:51
    (49–52); Jer. 20:7 (7–9).
  2 a TG Counsel.
  3 a D&C 121:9. TG Friend-
    ship.

4 a TG Respect.
  b D&C 121:7 (7–8).
  c 3 Ne. 20:16 (16–21).
    TG Protection, Divine.
  5 a D&C 121:6. TG Tribu-
    lation.
  b 2 Cor. 11:26 (23–28).

6 a Job 8:6 (1–22).
  b Jer. 36:5; Acts 5:18
    (15, 18); 12:5; 16:23
    (19–40); Alma 14:22
    (22–28).
  c Luke 10:3.

7 And if thou shouldst be cast into the ^apit, or into the hands of murderers, and the sentence of death passed upon thee; if thou be cast into the ^bdeep; if the billowing surge conspire against thee; if fierce winds become thine enemy; if the heavens gather blackness, and all the elements combine to ^chedge up the way; and above all, if the very jaws of ^dhell shall gape open the mouth wide after thee, know thou, my son, that all these things shall give thee ^eexperience, and shall be for thy good.

8 The ^aSon of Man hath ^bdescended below them all. Art thou greater than he?

9 Therefore, ^ahold on thy way, and the priesthood shall ^bremain with thee; for their ^cbounds are set, they cannot pass. Thy ^ddays are known, and thy years shall not be numbered less; therefore, ^efear not what man can do, for God shall be with you forever and ever.

SECTION 123

Duty of the Saints in relation to their persecutors, as written by Joseph Smith the Prophet while a prisoner in the jail at Liberty, Missouri. This section is an excerpt from an epistle to the Church dated March 20, 1839 (see the heading to section 121).

1–6, The Saints should collect and publish an account of their sufferings and persecutions; 7–10, The same spirit that established the false creeds also leads to persecution of the Saints; 11–17, Many among all sects will yet receive the truth.

1 And again, we would suggest for your consideration the propriety of all the saints ^agathering up a knowledge of all the facts, and ^bsufferings and abuses put upon them by the people of this State;

2 And also of all the property and amount of damages which they have sustained, both of character and personal ^ainjuries, as well as real property;

3 And also the names of all persons that have had a hand in their ^aoppressions, as far as they can get hold of them and find them out.

---

7 a Gen. 37:24; Jer. 38:6 (6–13).
b Ps. 69:2 (1–2, 14); Jonah 2:3 (3–9); 2 Cor. 11:25.
c Lam. 3:7 (7–8). TG Despair.
d 2 Sam. 22:6 (5–7); JS—H 1:16 (15–16).
e Job 2:10 (10–13); 3:20 (20–26); 5:27; Eccl. 3:10 (9–10); Jer. 24:5;

2 Cor. 4:17; Heb. 12:10 (10–11); 1 Pet. 2:20 (20–21); 2 Ne. 2:11.
8 a TG Jesus Christ, Son of Man.
b Mark 14:37 (37, 40–41); Heb. 2:17 (9–18); D&C 76:107; 88:6.
9 a TG Steadfastness.
b D&C 13; 84:17; 90:3; 124:130.

c Deut. 32:8; Job 11:20 (19–20).
d D&C 121:25.
e Neh. 4:14; Ps. 56:4 (4, 11); 118:6; Jer. 1:17 (17–19); Luke 12:5 (4–5); 2 Ne. 8:7 (7–12); D&C 3:7; 98:14.
123 1 a D&C 69:8.
b Ezra 4:1 (1–24).
2 a TG Injustice.
3 a TG Oppression.

4 And perhaps a committee can be appointed to find out these things, and to take *statements and affidavits; and also to gather up the libelous publications that are afloat;

5 And all that are in the magazines, and in the encyclopedias, and all the libelous histories that are published, and are writing, and by whom, and present the whole concatenation of diabolical rascality and nefarious and murderous impositions that have been practiced upon this people—

6 That we may not only publish to all the world, but present them to the *heads of government in all their dark and hellish hue, as the last effort which is enjoined on us by our Heavenly Father, before we can fully and completely claim that promise which shall call him forth from his *hiding place; and also that the whole nation may be left without excuse before he can send forth the power of his mighty arm.

7 It is an imperative duty that we owe to God, to angels, with whom we shall be brought to stand, and also to ourselves, to our wives and *children, who have been made to bow down with grief, sorrow, and care, under the most damning hand of murder, tyranny, and *oppression, supported and urged on and upheld by the influence of that spirit which hath so strongly riveted the *creeds of the fathers, who have inherited lies, upon the hearts of the children, and filled the world with confusion, and has been growing stronger and stronger, and is now the very mainspring of all corruption, and the whole *earth groans under the weight of its iniquity.

8 It is an iron *yoke, it is a strong band; they are the very handcuffs, and chains, and shackles, and fetters of *hell.

9 Therefore it is an imperative duty that we owe, not only to our own wives and children, but to the *widows and fatherless, whose husbands and fathers have been *murdered under its iron hand;

10 Which dark and blackening deeds are enough to make hell itself *shudder, and to stand aghast and pale, and the hands of the very devil to tremble and palsy.

11 And also it is an imperative duty that we owe to all the rising generation, and to all the pure in heart—

12 For there are many yet on the earth among all sects, parties, and denominations, who are *blinded by the subtle *craftiness of men, whereby

---

4 a TG Record Keeping.
6 a Ezra 5:8 (8–17).
  b D&C 101:89; 121:4 (1, 4).
7 a TG Family, Children, Responsibilities toward.
  b TG Cruelty.

c Alma 24:7; JS—H 1:19.
  TG Traditions of Men.
d Isa. 33:9; Moses 7:49.
8 a TG Bondage, Physical; Bondage, Spiritual.
  b TG Hell.
9 a TG Children; Widows.

b D&C 98:13; 103:27 (27–28); 124:54.
10 a Isa. 14:9 (4–11).
12 a Col. 2:8; D&C 76:75.
  TG Spiritual Blindness.
  b TG False Doctrine; False Prophets.

they lie in wait to ^cdeceive, and who are only kept from the truth because they ^dknow not where to find it—

13 Therefore, that we should waste and ^awear out our lives in bringing to light all the ^bhidden things of darkness, wherein we know them; and they are truly manifest from heaven—

14 These should then be attended to with great ^aearnestness.

15 Let no man count them as small things; for there is much which lieth in futurity, pertaining to the saints, which depends upon these things.

16 You know, brethren, that a very large ship is ^abenefited very much by a very small helm in the time of a storm, by being kept workways with the wind and the waves.

17 Therefore, dearly beloved brethren, let us ^acheerfully ^bdo all things that lie in our power; and then may we stand still, with the utmost assurance, to see the ^csalvation of God, and for his arm to be revealed.

SECTION 124

Revelation given to Joseph Smith the Prophet, at Nauvoo, Illinois, January 19, 1841. Because of increasing persecutions and illegal procedures against them by public officers, the Saints had been compelled to leave Missouri. The exterminating order issued by Lilburn W. Boggs, governor of Missouri, dated October 27, 1838, had left them no alternative. In 1841, when this revelation was given, the city of Nauvoo, occupying the site of the former village of Commerce, Illinois, had been built up by the Saints, and here the headquarters of the Church had been established.

1–14, Joseph Smith is commanded to make a solemn proclamation of the gospel to the president of the United States, the governors, and the rulers of all nations; 15–21, Hyrum Smith, David W. Patten, Joseph Smith Sr., and others among the living and the dead are blessed for their integrity and virtues; 22–28, The Saints are commanded to build both a house for the entertainment of strangers and a temple in Nauvoo; 29–36, Baptisms for the dead are to be performed in temples; 37–44, The Lord's people always build temples for the performance of holy ordinances; 45–55, The Saints are excused from building the temple in Jackson County because of the oppression of their enemies; 56–83, Directions are given for the building of the Nauvoo

12 c Col. 2:18 (16–23).
  d 1 Ne. 8:21 (19–24).
    TG Mission of Latter-
    day Saints.
13 a TG Dedication.

  b 1 Cor. 4:5. TG Secret
    Combinations.
14 a TG Zeal.
16 a James 3:4; 1 Ne. 16:29;
    Alma 37:6 (6–8); D&C

    64:33.
17 a TG Cheerful.
  b TG Initiative.
  c Ex. 14:13; Isa. 30:15.

House; 84–96, Hyrum Smith is called to be a patriarch, to receive the keys, and to stand in the place of Oliver Cowdery; 97–122, William Law and others are counseled in their labors; 123–45, General and local officers are named, along with their duties and quorum affiliations.

1 Verily, thus saith the Lord unto you, my servant Joseph Smith, I am well pleased with your ªoffering and acknowledgments, which you have made; for unto this end have I raised you up, that I might show forth my ᵇwisdom through the ᶜweak things of the earth.

2 Your prayers are acceptable before me; and in answer to them I say unto you, that you are now called immediately to make a solemn ªproclamation of my gospel, and of this ᵇstake which I have planted to be a ᶜcornerstone of Zion, which shall be polished with the refinement which is after the similitude of a palace.

3 This proclamation shall be made to all the ªkings of the world, to the four corners thereof, to the honorable president-elect, and the high-minded governors of the nation in which you live, and to all the nations of the earth scattered abroad.

4 Let it be ªwritten in the spirit of meekness and by the power of the Holy Ghost, which shall be in you at the time of the writing of the same;

5 For it shall be ªgiven you by the Holy Ghost to know my ᵇwill concerning those ᶜkings and authorities, even what shall befall them in a time to come.

6 For, behold, I am about to call upon them to give heed to the light and glory of Zion, for the set time has come to favor her.

7 Call ye, therefore, upon them with loud proclamation, and with your testimony, fearing them not, for they are as ªgrass, and all their glory as the flower thereof which soon falleth, that they may be left also without excuse—

8 And that I may ªvisit them in the day of visitation, when I shall ᵇunveil the face of my covering, to appoint the portion of the ᶜoppressor among hypocrites, where there is ᵈgnashing of teeth, if they reject my servants and my testimony which I have revealed unto them.

124 1 *a* Rom. 12:1; 1 Tim. 2:3 (1–4); 1 Pet. 2:5.
 b TG God, Wisdom of.
 c 1 Cor. 1:27 (26–29); D&C 1:19; 35:13.
 2 *a* TG Mission of Latter-day Saints.
 b TG Stake.
 c TG Cornerstone.

3 *a* Ps. 119:46; 138:4 (1–5); Matt. 10:18; Acts 9:15; D&C 1:23.
 4 *a* TG Holy Ghost, Gifts of; Meek.
 5 *a* Dan. 2:22 (19–22, 28).
 b TG God, Will of.
 c Gen. 41:25; Dan. 2:21 (20–22). TG Kings, Earthly.

7 *a* Ps. 90:5; 103:15 (15–16); Isa. 40:6 (6–8); 1 Pet. 1:24.
 8 *a* Isa. 10:3 (1–4); 1 Pet. 2:12.
 b D&C 1:12. TG Veil.
 c TG Cruelty; Oppression.
 d D&C 29:15 (15–20); 101:91; 112:24.

9 And again, I will visit and soften their hearts, many of them for your good, that ye may find grace in their eyes, that they may come to the *light of truth, and the Gentiles to the exaltation or lifting up of Zion.

10 For the day of my visitation cometh speedily, in an *hour when ye think not of; and where shall be the safety of my people, and refuge for those who shall be left of them?

11 Awake, O kings of the earth! Come ye, O, come ye, with your *gold and your silver, to the help of my people, to the house of the daughters of Zion.

12 And again, verily I say unto you, let my servant Robert B. Thompson help you to write this proclamation, for I am well pleased with him, and that he should be with you;

13 Let him, therefore, hearken to your counsel, and I will bless him with a multiplicity of blessings; let him be faithful and true in all things from henceforth, and he shall be great in mine eyes;

14 But let him remember that his *stewardship will I require at his hands.

15 And again, verily I say unto you, blessed is my servant Hyrum Smith; for I, the Lord, love him because of the *integrity of his heart, and because he loveth that which is right before me, saith the Lord.

16 Again, let my servant John C. Bennett help you in your labor in sending my word to the kings and people of the earth, and stand by you, even you my servant Joseph Smith, in the hour of affliction; and his reward shall not fail if he receive *counsel.

17 And for his love he shall be great, for he shall be mine if he do this, saith the Lord. I have seen the work which he hath done, which I accept if he continue, and will crown him with blessings and great glory.

18 And again, I say unto you that it is my will that my servant Lyman Wight should continue in preaching for Zion, in the spirit of meekness, confessing me before the world; and I will bear him up as on *eagles' wings; and he shall beget glory and honor to himself and unto my name.

19 That when he shall finish his work I may *receive him unto myself, even as I did my servant David Patten, who is with me at this time, and also my servant *Edward Partridge, and also my aged servant Joseph Smith, Sen., who sitteth *with Abraham at his right hand, and blessed and holy is he, for he is mine.

---

9 a Isa. 60:3 (1–12).
   TG Light [noun].
10 a Matt. 24:44.
11 a Isa. 60:6 (6, 11–17);
   61:6 (4–6).

14 a TG Stewardship.
15 a TG Integrity; Sincere.
16 a TG Counsel.
18 a Ex. 19:4; Isa. 40:31.
19 a D&C 124:130.

b D&C 115:2 (2–6).
c Luke 16:22; D&C
   137:5.

20 And again, verily I say unto you, my servant George Miller is without *guile; he may be trusted because of the *integrity of his heart; and for the love which he has to my testimony I, the Lord, love him.

21 I therefore say unto you, I seal upon his head the office of a bishopric, like unto my *servant Edward Partridge, that he may receive the consecrations of mine house, that he may administer blessings upon the heads of the poor of my people, saith the Lord. Let no man despise my servant George, for he shall honor me.

22 Let my servant George, and my servant Lyman, and my servant John Snider, and others, build a *house unto my name, such a one as my servant Joseph shall show unto them, upon the place which he shall show unto them also.

23 And it shall be for a house for boarding, a house that strangers may come from afar to lodge therein; therefore let it be a good house, worthy of all acceptation, that the weary *traveler may find health and safety while he shall contemplate the word of the Lord; and the *cornerstone I have appointed for Zion.

24 This house shall be a healthful habitation if it be built unto my name, and if the governor which shall be appointed unto it shall not suffer any pollution to come upon it. It shall be holy, or the Lord your God will not *dwell therein.

25 And again, verily I say unto you, let all my saints *come from afar.

26 And send ye *swift messengers, yea, chosen messengers, and say unto them: Come ye, with all your *gold, and your silver, and your precious stones, and with all your antiquities; and with all who have *knowledge of antiquities, that will come, may come, and bring the *box tree, and the fir tree, and the pine tree, together with all the precious trees of the earth;

27 And with iron, with copper, and with brass, and with zinc, and with all your precious things of the earth; and build a *house to my name, for the Most High to *dwell therein.

28 For there is not a place found on earth that he may come to and *restore again that which was lost unto you, or which he hath taken away, even the fulness of the priesthood.

---

20 a TG Guile; Sincere.
  b Prov. 19:1. TG Integrity.
21 a D&C 41:9. TG Bishop.
22 a D&C 124:56 (56–82, 111–22).
23 a Lev. 25:35 (35–38); Deut. 31:12 (12–13); Matt. 25:35 (35, 38, 43–44).

  b D&C 124:2.
24 a Alma 7:21 (20–21).
25 a D&C 10:65.
26 a Isa. 18:2 (1–7).
  b 1 Kgs. 6:21 (21–22); 2 Ne. 5:15.
  c D&C 93:53.
  d Ex. 26:15; Isa. 41:19; 60:13.

27 a D&C 109:5. TG Temple.
  b Ex. 25:8; 1 Kgs. 6:13; D&C 97:16 (15–17); 104:59.
28 a TG Priesthood, Melchizedek; Restoration of the Gospel.

29 For a ᵃbaptismal font there is not upon the earth, that they, my saints, may be ᵇbaptized for those who are dead—

30 For this ordinance belongeth to my house, and cannot be acceptable to me, only in the days of your poverty, wherein ye are not able to build a house unto me.

31 But I command you, all ye my saints, to ᵃbuild a house unto me; and I grant unto you a sufficient time to build a house unto me; and during this time your baptisms shall be acceptable unto me.

32 But behold, at the end of this appointment your baptisms for your dead shall not be acceptable unto me; and if you do not these things at the end of the appointment ye shall be rejected as a church, with your dead, saith the Lord your God.

33 For verily I say unto you, that ᵃafter you have had sufficient time to build a house to me, wherein the ordinance of baptizing for the dead belongeth, and for which the same was instituted from before the foundation of the world, your baptisms for your dead cannot be acceptable unto me;

34 For therein are the ᵃkeys of the holy priesthood ordained, that you may receive honor and glory.

35 And after this time, your baptisms for the dead, by those who are scattered abroad, are not acceptable unto me, saith the Lord.

36 For it is ordained that in Zion, and in her stakes, and in Jerusalem, those places which I have appointed for ᵃrefuge, shall be the places for your baptisms for your dead.

37 And again, verily I say unto you, how shall your ᵃwashings be acceptable unto me, except ye perform them in a house which you have built to my name?

38 For, for this cause I commanded Moses that he should build a ᵃtabernacle, that they should bear it with them in the wilderness, and to build a house in the land of promise, that those ordinances might be revealed which had been hid from before the world was.

39 Therefore, verily I say unto you, that your ᵃanointings, and your washings, and your ᵇbaptisms for the dead, and your ᶜsolemn assemblies, and

29a D&C 76:51; 128:13.
  b 1 Cor. 15:29; D&C 127:6; 138:33. TG Baptism for the Dead; Salvation for the Dead.
31a 2 Chr. 3:1 (1–17); 2 Ne. 5:16 (15–17); D&C 84:5 (5, 31); 97:10.
33a IE Oct. 3, 1841.

34a D&C 110:16 (14–16).
36a Isa. 4:6 (4–6); D&C 133:13 (4–14).
37a Lev. 8:6; D&C 88:74. TG Wash.
38a Ex. 25:9 (1–9); 29:4; 33:7; 35:11; Ezek. 37:27. TG Temple.
39a Ex. 25:6; 29:7; Lev.

10:7; 14:28; Num. 18:8; D&C 68:21. TG Anointing.
  b TG Baptism for the Dead; Genealogy and Temple Work.
  c D&C 88:70 (70, 117). TG Solemn Assembly.

your [d]memorials for your [e]sacrifices by the sons of Levi, and for your [f]oracles in your most [g]holy places wherein you receive conversations, and your statutes and judgments, for the beginning of the revelations and foundation of Zion, and for the glory, honor, and endowment of all her municipals, are ordained by the ordinance of my holy house, which my people are always commanded to build unto my holy name.

40 And verily I say unto you, let this [a]house be built unto my name, that I may reveal mine ordinances therein unto my people;

41 For I deign to [a]reveal unto my church things which have been kept [b]hid from before the foundation of the world, things that pertain to the dispensation of the [c]fulness of times.

42 And [a]I will show unto my servant Joseph all things pertaining to this house, and the priesthood thereof, and the place whereon it shall be built.

43 And ye shall build it on the place where you have contemplated building it, for that is the spot which I have chosen for you to build it.

44 If ye labor with all your might, I will consecrate that spot that it shall be made [a]holy.

45 And if my people will hearken unto my voice, and unto the voice of my [a]servants whom I have appointed to lead my people, behold, verily I say unto you, they shall not be moved out of their place.

46 But if they will not [a]hearken to my voice, nor unto the voice of these men whom I have appointed, they shall not be blest, because they [b]pollute mine holy grounds, and mine holy ordinances, and charters, and my holy words which I give unto them.

47 And it shall come to pass that if you build a house unto my name, and do not do the things that I say, I will not perform the [a]oath which I make unto you, neither fulfil the promises which ye expect at my hands, saith the Lord.

48 For [a]instead of blessings, ye, by your own works, bring cursings, wrath, indignation, and judgments upon your own heads, by your follies, and by all your abominations, which you practice before me, saith the Lord.

49 Verily, verily, I say unto you, that when I give a commandment to any

39 d Ex. 12:14 (14–17); Lev. 2:2 (2, 9, 16).
  e Deut. 10:8; D&C 13; 84:31; 128:24; JS—H 1:69.
  f D&C 90:4.
  g Ex. 26:33; 1 Kgs. 6:16; Ezek. 41:4.

40 a TG Ordinance; Temple.
41 a A of F 1:9.
  b Alma 40:3; D&C 121:26 (26–31).
  c Eph. 1:10 (9–10); D&C 27:13; 76:106; 112:30.
42 a D&C 95:14 (14–17).
44 a TG Holiness.

45 a TG Leadership; Prophets, Mission of.
46 a TG Prophets, Rejection of.
  b TG Pollution.
47 a TG Oath; Promise.
48 a Deut. 28:15 (1–47).

of the sons of men to do a work unto my name, and those sons of men go with all their might and with all they have to perform that work, and cease not their *a*diligence, and their enemies come upon them and *b*hinder them from performing that work, behold, it behooveth me to *c*require that work no more at the hands of those sons of men, but to accept of their offerings.

50 And the iniquity and transgression of my holy laws and commandments I will *a*visit upon the heads of those who hindered my work, unto the third and fourth *b*generation, so long as they repent not, and hate me, saith the Lord God.

51 Therefore, for this cause have I accepted the offerings of those whom I commanded to build up a city and a *a*house unto my name, in Jackson county, Missouri, and were hindered by their enemies, saith the Lord your God.

52 And I will answer *a*judgment, wrath, and indignation, wailing, and anguish, and gnashing of teeth upon their heads, unto the third and fourth generation, so long as they repent not, and hate me, saith the Lord your God.

53 And this I make an *a*example unto you, for your consolation concerning all those who have been commanded to do a work and have been hindered by the hands of their enemies, and by *b*oppression, saith the Lord your God.

54 For I am the Lord your God, and will save all those of your brethren who have been *a*pure in heart, and have been *b*slain in the land of Missouri, saith the Lord.

55 And again, verily I say unto you, I command you again to build a *a*house to my name, even in this place, that you may *b*prove yourselves unto me that ye are *c*faithful in all things whatsoever I command you, that I may bless you, and crown you with honor, immortality, and eternal life.

56 And now I say unto you, as pertaining to my boarding *a*house which I have commanded you to build for the boarding of strangers, let it be built unto my name, and let my name be named upon it, and let my servant Joseph and his house have place therein, from generation to generation.

57 For this *a*anointing have I put upon his head, that his blessing shall also be put upon the head of his posterity after him.

---

49 *a* TG Diligence.
   b Ezra 4:21.
   c D&C 56:4.
50 *a* Jer. 9:9; Mosiah 12:1.
   TG Accountability.
   b Deut. 5:9. TG Procrastination; Repent.
51 *a* D&C 115:11.

52 *a* D&C 121:15 (11–23).
   TG Punish; Sorrow.
53 *a* Num. 26:10.
   b TG Oppression.
54 *a* TG Purity.
   b Matt. 10:39; D&C 98:13; 103:27 (27–28); 123:9 (7, 9).

55 *a* D&C 127:4.
   b Ex. 15:25 (23–26); D&C 98:14 (12–14); Abr. 3:25. TG Test.
   c 1 Kgs. 6:12 (11–13).
56 *a* D&C 124:22 (22–24).
57 *a* TG Anointing.

58 And as I said unto *a*Abraham concerning the kindreds of the earth, even so I say unto my servant Joseph: In thee and in thy *b*seed shall the kindred of the earth be blessed.

59 Therefore, let my servant Joseph and his seed after him have place in that house, from generation to generation, forever and ever, saith the Lord.

60 And let the name of that house be called *a*Nauvoo House; and let it be a delightful habitation for man, and a resting-place for the weary traveler, that he may contemplate the glory of Zion, and the glory of this, the cornerstone thereof;

61 That he may receive also the counsel from those whom I have set to be as *a*plants of renown, and as *b*watchmen upon her walls.

62 Behold, verily I say unto you, let my servant George Miller, and my servant Lyman Wight, and my servant John Snider, and my servant Peter Haws, organize themselves, and appoint one of them to be a president over their quorum for the purpose of building that house.

63 And they shall form a constitution, whereby they may receive stock for the building of that house.

64 And they shall not receive less than fifty dollars for a share of stock in that house, and they shall be permitted to receive fifteen thousand dollars from any one man for stock in that house.

65 But they shall not be permitted to receive over fifteen thousand dollars stock from any one man.

66 And they shall not be permitted to receive under fifty dollars for a share of stock from any one man in that house.

67 And they shall not be permitted to receive any man, as a stockholder in this house, except the same shall pay his stock into their hands at the time he receives stock;

68 And in proportion to the amount of stock he pays into their hands he shall receive stock in that house; but if he pays nothing into their hands he shall not receive any stock in that house.

69 And if any pay stock into their hands it shall be for stock in that house, for himself, and for his generation after him, from generation to generation, so long as he and his heirs shall hold that stock, and do not sell or convey the stock away out of their hands by their own free will and act, if you will do my will, saith the Lord your God.

70 And again, verily I say unto you, if my servant George Miller, and my servant Lyman Wight, and my servant John Snider, and my servant

---

58a Gen. 12:3; 22:18; Abr. 2:11. TG Abrahamic Covenant.
b D&C 110:12.
60a IE beautiful, delightful, as used in Isa. 52:7 in Hebrew.
61a Isa. 60:21; Ezek. 34:29.
b TG Watchman.

Peter Haws, receive any stock into their hands, in moneys, or in properties wherein they receive the real value of moneys, they shall not appropriate any portion of that stock to any other purpose, only in that house.

71 And if they do appropriate any portion of that stock anywhere else, only in that house, without the consent of the stockholder, and do not repay four-fold for the stock which they appropriate anywhere else, only in that house, they shall be accursed, and shall be moved out of their place, saith the Lord God; for I, the Lord, am God, and cannot be ᵃmocked in any of these things.

72 Verily I say unto you, let my servant Joseph pay stock into their hands for the building of that house, as seemeth him good; but my servant Joseph cannot pay over fifteen thousand dollars stock in that house, nor under fifty dollars; neither can any other man, saith the Lord.

73 And there are others also who wish to know my will concerning them, for they have asked it at my hands.

74 Therefore, I say unto you concerning my servant Vinson Knight, if he will do my will let him put stock into that house for himself, and for his generation after him, from generation to generation.

75 And let him lift up his voice long and loud, in the midst of the people, to ᵃplead the cause of the poor and the needy; and let him not fail, neither let his heart faint; and I will ᵇaccept of his offerings, for they shall not be unto me as the offerings of Cain, for he shall be mine, saith the Lord.

76 Let his family rejoice and turn away their hearts from affliction; for I have chosen him and anointed him, and he shall be honored in the midst of his house, for I will forgive all his sins, saith the Lord. Amen.

77 Verily I say unto you, let my servant Hyrum put stock into that house as seemeth him good, for himself and his generation after him, from generation to generation.

78 Let my servant Isaac Galland put stock into that house; for I, the Lord, love him for the work he hath done, and will forgive all his sins; therefore, let him be remembered for an interest in that house from generation to generation.

79 Let my servant Isaac Galland be appointed among you, and be ordained by my servant William Marks, and be blessed of him, to go with my servant Hyrum to accomplish the work that my servant Joseph shall point out to them, and they shall be greatly blessed.

80 Let my servant William Marks pay stock into that house, as seemeth him good, for himself and his generation, from generation to generation.

---

71 a Gal. 6:7.   75 a Prov. 22:23; 31:9.   b Gen. 4:4–5.

81 Let my servant Henry G. Sherwood pay stock into that house, as seemeth him good, for himself and his seed after him, from generation to generation.

82 Let my servant William Law pay stock into that house, for himself and his seed after him, from generation to generation.

83 If he will do my will let him not take his family unto the eastern lands, even unto Kirtland; nevertheless, I, the Lord, will build up *a*Kirtland, but I, the Lord, have a scourge prepared for the inhabitants thereof.

84 And with my servant Almon Babbitt, there are many things with which I am not pleased; behold, he aspireth to establish his counsel instead of the counsel which I have ordained, even that of the Presidency of my Church; and he setteth up a *a*golden calf for the worship of my people.

85 Let no man *a*go from this place who has come here essaying to keep my commandments.

86 If they live here let them live unto me; and if they die let them die unto me; for they shall *a*rest from all their labors here, and shall continue their works.

87 Therefore, let my servant William put his trust in me, and cease to fear concerning his family, because of the sickness of the land. If ye *a*love me, keep my commandments; and the sickness of the land shall *b*redound to your glory.

88 Let my servant William go and proclaim my everlasting gospel with a loud voice, and with great joy, as he shall be moved upon by my *a*Spirit, unto the inhabitants of Warsaw, and also unto the inhabitants of Carthage, and also unto the inhabitants of Burlington, and also unto the inhabitants of Madison, and await patiently and diligently for further instructions at my general conference, saith the Lord.

89 If he will do my *a*will let him from henceforth hearken to the counsel of my servant Joseph, and with his interest support the *b*cause of the poor, and publish *c*the new translation of my holy word unto the inhabitants of the earth.

90 And if he will do this I will *a*bless him with a multiplicity of blessings, that he shall not be forsaken, nor his seed be found *b*begging bread.

91 And again, verily I say unto you, let my servant William be appointed, ordained, and anointed, as counselor unto my servant Joseph, in the room

83 *a* D&C 117:16.
84 *a* Ex. 32:4.
85 *a* Luke 9:62; D&C 124:108 (87, 108–10).
86 *a* Rev. 14:13. TG Paradise.

87 *a* John 14:15.
   b D&C 121:8; 122:7.
88 *a* TG God, Spirit of.
89 *a* TG God, Will of.
   b D&C 78:3.
   c IE the Joseph Smith

Translation of the Bible. D&C 94:10.
90 *a* TG Blessing.
   b Ps. 37:25.

of my servant Hyrum, that my servant Hyrum may take the office of Priesthood and *a*Patriarch, which was appointed unto him by his father, by blessing and also by right;

92 That from henceforth he shall hold the keys of the *a*patriarchal blessings upon the heads of all my people,

93 That whoever he blesses shall be blessed, and whoever he *a*curses shall be cursed; that whatsoever he shall *b*bind on earth shall be bound in heaven; and whatsoever he shall loose on earth shall be loosed in heaven.

94 And from this time forth I appoint unto him that he may be a prophet, and a *a*seer, and a revelator unto my church, as well as my servant Joseph;

95 That he may act in concert also with my *a*servant Joseph; and that he shall receive counsel from my servant Joseph, who shall show unto him the *b*keys whereby he may ask and receive, and be crowned with the same blessing, and glory, and honor, and priesthood, and gifts of the priesthood, that once were put upon him that was my servant *c*Oliver Cowdery;

96 That my servant Hyrum may bear record of the things which I shall show unto him, that his name may be had in honorable remembrance from generation to generation, forever and ever.

97 Let my servant William Law also receive the keys by which he may ask and receive blessings; let him be *a*humble before me, and be without *b*guile, and he shall receive of my Spirit, even the *c*Comforter, which shall manifest unto him the truth of all things, and shall give him, in the very hour, what he shall say.

98 And these *a*signs shall follow him—he shall heal the *b*sick, he shall cast out devils, and shall be delivered from those who would administer unto him deadly poison;

99 And he shall be led in paths where the poisonous serpent *a*cannot lay hold upon his heel, and he shall mount up in the *b*imagination of his thoughts as upon eagles' wings.

100 And what if I will that he should *a*raise the dead, let him not withhold his voice.

101 Therefore, let my servant William cry aloud and spare not, with joy and rejoicing, and with hosannas to him that sitteth upon the throne forever and ever, saith the Lord your God.

---

91 *a* D&C 107:40 (39–40).
92 *a* TG Patriarch; Patriarchal Blessings.
93 *a* D&C 103:25; 132:47 (45–48). TG Curse.
　 b Matt. 16:19; 18:18. TG Priesthood, Keys of; Sealing.
94 *a* D&C 107:92. TG Seer.

95 *a* D&C 6:18 (18–19).
　 b D&C 6:28.
　 c See "Oliver Cowdery" in the Index for references to his callings.
97 *a* TG Teachable.
　 b TG Guile; Sincere.
　 c TG Holy Ghost, Comforter.

98 *a* Mark 16:17 (17–18). TG Holy Ghost, Gifts of.
　 b TG Heal; Sickness.
99 *a* Acts 28:3 (3–9); D&C 24:13; 84:72 (71–72).
　 b Isa. 40:31.
100 *a* TG Death, Power over.

102 Behold, I say unto you, I have a mission in store for my servant William, and my servant Hyrum, and for them alone; and let my servant Joseph tarry at home, for he is needed. The remainder I will show unto you hereafter. Even so. Amen.

103 And again, verily I say unto you, if my servant Sidney will serve me and be ^acounselor unto my servant Joseph, let him arise and come up and stand in the office of his calling, and humble himself before me.

104 And if he will offer unto me an acceptable offering, and acknowledgments, and remain with my people, behold, I, the Lord your God, will heal him that he shall be healed; and he shall lift up his voice again on the mountains, and be a ^aspokesman before my face.

105 Let him come and locate his family in the neighborhood in which my servant Joseph resides.

106 And in all his journeyings let him lift up his voice as with the sound of a trump, and warn the inhabitants of the earth to flee the wrath to come.

107 Let him assist my servant Joseph, and also let my servant William Law assist my servant Joseph, in making a solemn ^aproclamation unto the kings of the earth, even as I have before said unto you.

108 If my servant Sidney will do my will, let him not remove his family unto the ^aeastern lands, but let him change their habitation, even as I have said.

109 Behold, it is not my will that he shall seek to find safety and refuge out of the city which I have appointed unto you, even the city of Nauvoo.

110 Verily I say unto you, even now, if he will hearken unto my voice, it shall be well with him. Even so. Amen.

111 And again, verily I say unto you, let my servant Amos Davies pay stock into the hands of those whom I have appointed to build a house for boarding, even the Nauvoo House.

112 This let him do if he will have an interest; and let him hearken unto the counsel of my servant Joseph, and labor with his own hands that he may obtain the confidence of men.

113 And when he shall ^aprove himself faithful in all things that shall be ^bentrusted unto his care, yea, even a few things, he shall be made ruler over many;

114 Let him therefore ^aabase himself that he may be exalted. Even so. Amen.

103 a D&C 90:21.
104 a Ex. 4:16 (14–16); 2 Ne. 3:17 (17–18); D&C 100:9 (9–11).
107 a D&C 124:2.
108 a D&C 124:83.
113 a TG Test.
    b 1 Thes. 2:4.
114 a Matt. 23:12; D&C 101:42.

115 And again, verily I say unto you, if my servant Robert D. Foster will obey my voice, let him build a house for my servant Joseph, according to the contract which he has made with him, as the door shall be open to him from time to time.

116 And let him repent of all his *folly, and clothe himself with *charity; and *cease to do evil, and lay aside all his hard *speeches;

117 And pay stock also into the hands of the quorum of the Nauvoo House, for himself and for his generation after him, from generation to generation;

118 And hearken unto the counsel of my servants Joseph, and Hyrum, and William Law, and unto the authorities which I have called to lay the foundation of Zion; and it shall be well with him forever and ever. Even so. Amen.

119 And again, verily I say unto you, let no man pay stock to the quorum of the Nauvoo House unless he shall be a believer in the Book of Mormon, and the revelations I have given unto you, saith the Lord your God;

120 For that which is *more or less than this cometh of evil, and shall be attended with cursings and not blessings, saith the Lord your God. Even so. Amen.

121 And again, verily I say unto you, let the quorum of the Nauvoo House have a just recompense of wages for all their labors which they do in building the Nauvoo House; and let their wages be as shall be agreed among themselves, as pertaining to the price thereof.

122 And let every man who pays stock bear his proportion of their wages, if it must needs be, for their support, saith the Lord; otherwise, their labors shall be accounted unto them for stock in that house. Even so. Amen.

123 Verily I say unto you, I now give unto you the *officers belonging to my Priesthood, that ye may hold the *keys thereof, even the Priesthood which is after the order of Melchizedek, which is after the order of mine *Only Begotten Son.

124 First, I give unto you Hyrum Smith to be a *patriarch unto you, to hold the *sealing blessings of my church, even the Holy Spirit of *promise, whereby ye are *sealed up unto the day of redemption, that ye may not fall notwithstanding the *hour of temptation that may come upon you.

116a TG Foolishness.
  b Col. 3:14.
  c TG Self-Mastery.
  d TG Slander.
120a Deut. 28:14; Matt. 5:37.
123a D&C 107:21;
  124:143. TG Church

Organization; Delegation of Responsibility.
  b TG Priesthood, Keys of.
  c TG Jesus Christ, Authority of.
124a D&C 124:91. TG Patriarch.

  b TG Sealing.
  c D&C 76:53; 88:3
    (3–4); 132:19 (18–26).
  d Eph. 4:30.
  e Rev. 3:10.

125 I give unto you my servant Joseph to be a presiding elder over all my church, to be a translator, a revelator, a ᵃseer, and prophet.

126 I give him for ᵃcounselors my servant Sidney Rigdon and my servant William Law, that these may constitute a quorum and First Presidency, to receive the ᵇoracles for the whole church.

127 I give unto you my servant ᵃBrigham Young to be a president over the Twelve traveling council;

128 Which ᵃTwelve hold the keys to open up the authority of my kingdom upon the four corners of the earth, and after that to send my word to every ᵇcreature.

129 ᵃThey are Heber C. Kimball, Parley P. Pratt, Orson Pratt, Orson Hyde, William Smith, John Taylor, John E. Page, Wilford Woodruff, Willard Richards, George A. Smith;

130 David Patten I have ᵃtaken unto myself; behold, his ᵇpriesthood no man ᶜtaketh from him; but, verily I say unto you, another may be appointed unto the same calling.

131 And again, I say unto you, I give unto you a ᵃhigh council, for the cornerstone of Zion—

132 Namely, Samuel Bent, Henry G. Sherwood, George W. Harris, Charles C. Rich, Thomas Grover, Newel Knight, David Dort, Dunbar Wilson—Seymour Brunson I have taken unto myself; no man taketh his priesthood, but another may be appointed unto the same priesthood in his stead; and verily I say unto you, let my servant Aaron Johnson be ordained unto this calling in his stead—David Fullmer, Alpheus Cutler, William Huntington.

133 And again, I give unto you Don C. Smith to be a president over a quorum of high priests;

134 Which ordinance is instituted for the purpose of qualifying those who shall be appointed standing presidents or servants over different ᵃstakes scattered abroad;

135 And they may travel also if they choose, but rather be ordained for standing presidents; this is the office of their calling, saith the Lord your God.

136 I give unto him Amasa Lyman and Noah Packard for counselors,

---

125 a D&C 20:2; 21:1.
   TG Seer.
126 a D&C 68:15; 90:21;
   124:91. TG Counselor.
   b D&C 90:4 (4–5).
   TG Revelation.
127 a D&C 18:27; 107:23;

   126:1.
128 a TG Apostles.
   b Mark 16:15.
129 a See Index for reference
   to each name.
130 a D&C 124:19.
   b Heb. 5:6.

   c D&C 90:3. TG Priest-
   hood.
131 a D&C 102:30 (27–32);
   107:36 (36–37).
134 a TG Stake.

that they may preside over the quorum of high priests of my church, saith the Lord.

137 And again, I say unto you, I give unto you John A. Hicks, Samuel Williams, and Jesse Baker, which priesthood is to preside over the quorum of ^aelders, which quorum is instituted for standing ministers; nevertheless they may travel, yet they are ordained to be standing ministers to my church, saith the Lord.

138 And again, I give unto you Joseph Young, Josiah Butterfield, Daniel Miles, Henry Herriman, Zera Pulsipher, Levi Hancock, James Foster, to preside over the quorum of ^aseventies;

139 Which quorum is instituted for ^atraveling elders to bear record of my name in all the world, wherever the traveling high council, mine apostles, shall send them to prepare a way before my face.

140 The difference between this quorum and the quorum of elders is that one is to travel continually, and the other is to preside over the churches from time to time; the one has the responsibility of presiding from time to time, and the other has no responsibility of presiding, saith the Lord your God.

141 And again, I say unto you, I give unto you Vinson Knight, Samuel H. Smith, and Shadrach Roundy, if he will receive it, to preside over the ^abishopric; a knowledge of said bishopric is given unto you in the book of Doctrine and Covenants.

142 And again, I say unto you, Samuel Rolfe and his counselors for ^apriests, and the president of the teachers and his counselors, and also the president of the deacons and his counselors, and also the president of the stake and his counselors.

143 The above ^aoffices I have given unto you, and the keys thereof, for helps and for governments, for the work of the ministry and the ^bperfecting of my saints.

144 And a commandment I give unto you, that you should fill all these offices and ^aapprove of those names which I have mentioned, or else disapprove of them at my general conference;

145 And that ye should prepare rooms for all these offices in my ^ahouse when you build it unto my name, saith the Lord your God. Even so. Amen.

---

137 a D&C 20:38; 107:12 (11–12, 89–90). TG Elder, Melchizedek Priesthood.
138 a TG Seventy.
139 a D&C 107:33 (33, 93–98).

141 a D&C 68:14 (14–24); 107:15 (15–17), 68 (68–76).
142 a TG Deacon; Priest, Aaronic Priesthood; Teacher, Aaronic Priesthood.

143 a D&C 107:21; 124:23. b 1 Cor. 12:28; Eph. 4:11 (11–16).
144 a D&C 26:2. TG Common Consent; Sustaining Church Leaders.
145 a D&C 124:27 (27–28).

SECTION 125

Revelation given through Joseph Smith the Prophet, at Nauvoo, Illinois, March 1841, concerning the Saints in the territory of Iowa.

1–4, The Saints are to build cities and to gather to the stakes of Zion.

1 What is the will of the Lord concerning the saints in the Territory of Iowa?

2 Verily, thus saith the Lord, I say unto you, if those who ᵃcall themselves by my name and are essaying to be my saints, if they will do my will and keep my commandments concerning them, let them gather themselves together unto the places which I shall appoint unto them by my servant Joseph, and build up cities unto my name, that they may be prepared for that which is in store for a time to come.

3 Let them build up a city unto my name upon the land opposite the city of Nauvoo, and let the name of ᵃZarahemla be named upon it.

4 And let all those who come from the east, and the west, and the north, and the south, that have desires to dwell therein, take up their inheritance in the same, as well as in the city of ᵃNashville, or in the city of Nauvoo, and in all the ᵇstakes which I have appointed, saith the Lord.

SECTION 126

Revelation given through Joseph Smith the Prophet, in the house of Brigham Young, at Nauvoo, Illinois, July 9, 1841. At this time Brigham Young was President of the Quorum of the Twelve Apostles.

1–3, Brigham Young is commended for his labors and is relieved of future travel abroad.

1 Dear and well-beloved brother, ᵃBrigham Young, verily thus saith the Lord unto you: My servant Brigham, it is ᵇno more required at your hand to leave your family as in times past, for your offering is acceptable to me.

2 I have seen your ᵃlabor and toil in journeyings for my name.

3 I therefore command you to ᵃsend my word abroad, and take especial ᵇcare of your family from this time, henceforth and forever. Amen.

---

125 2 *a* TG Jesus Christ, Taking the Name of.
3 *a* Omni 1:14 (14, 18); Alma 2:26.
4 *a* IE Nashville, Lee

County, Iowa.
  b TG Stake.
126 1 *a* D&C 124:127; 136 heading.
  b D&C 18:28 (27–28).

2 *a* TG Good Works.
3 *a* D&C 107:38; 124:139.
  b TG Family, Children, Responsibilities toward; Family, Love within.

SECTION 127

An epistle from Joseph Smith the Prophet to the Latter-day Saints at Nauvoo, Illinois, containing directions on baptism for the dead, dated at Nauvoo, September 1, 1842.

1–4, Joseph Smith glories in persecution and tribulation; 5–12, Records must be kept relative to baptisms for the dead.

1 Forasmuch as the Lord has revealed unto me that my enemies, both in Missouri and this State, were again in the pursuit of me; and inasmuch as they pursue me without a ^acause, and have not the least shadow or coloring of justice or right on their side in the getting up of their prosecutions against me; and inasmuch as their pretensions are all founded in falsehood of the blackest dye, I have thought it expedient and wisdom in me to leave the place for a short season, for my own safety and the safety of this people. I would say to all those with whom I have business, that I have left my ^baffairs with agents and clerks who will transact all business in a prompt and proper manner, and will see that all my debts are canceled in due time, by turning out property, or otherwise, as the case may require, or as the circumstances may admit of. When I learn that the storm is fully blown over, then I will return to you again.

2 And as for the ^aperils which I am called to pass through, they seem but a small thing to me, as the ^benvy and wrath of man have been my common lot all the days of my life; and for what cause it seems mysterious, unless I was ^cordained from before the foundation of the world for some good end, or bad, as you may choose to call it. Judge ye for yourselves. God ^dknoweth all these things, whether it be good or bad. But nevertheless, deep water is what I am wont to swim in. It all has become a second nature to me; and I feel, like Paul, to glory in ^etribulation; for to this day has the God of my fathers delivered me out of them all, and will deliver me from henceforth; for behold, and lo, I shall triumph over all my enemies, for the Lord God hath spoken it.

3 Let all the saints rejoice, therefore, and be exceedingly glad; for Israel's ^aGod is their God, and he will mete out a just recompense of ^breward upon the heads of all their ^coppressors.

---

127 1*a* Job 2:3; Matt. 5:10 (10–12); 10:22 (22–23).
b TG Accountability.
2*a* Ps. 23:4 (1–6); 138:7. TG Persecution.
b TG Envy.

c Alma 13:3.
d TG God, Omniscience of; God, Perfection of.
e 2 Cor. 6:4 (4–5). TG Test.
3*a* Isa. 29:23 (22–24);

45:3; 3 Ne. 11:14; D&C 36:1.
b TG Reward.
c TG Oppression.

4 And again, verily thus saith the Lord: Let the work of my ᵃtemple, and all the works which I have appointed unto you, be continued on and not cease; and let your ᵇdiligence, and your perseverance, and patience, and your works be redoubled, and you shall in nowise lose your reward, saith the Lord of Hosts. And if they ᶜpersecute you, so persecuted they the prophets and righteous men that were before you. For all this there is a reward in heaven.

5 And again, I give unto you a word in relation to the ᵃbaptism for your dead.

6 Verily, thus saith the Lord unto you concerning your dead: When any of you are ᵃbaptized for your dead, let there be a ᵇrecorder, and let him be eye-witness of your baptisms; let him hear with his ears, that he may testify of a truth, saith the Lord;

7 That in all your recordings it may be ᵃrecorded in heaven; whatsoever you ᵇbind on earth, may be bound in heaven; whatsoever you loose on earth, may be loosed in heaven;

8 For I am about to ᵃrestore many things to the earth, pertaining to the ᵇpriesthood, saith the Lord of Hosts.

9 And again, let all the ᵃrecords be had in order, that they may be put in the archives of my holy temple, to be held in remembrance from generation to generation, saith the Lord of Hosts.

10 I will say to all the saints, that I desired, with exceedingly great desire, to have addressed them from the stand on the subject of baptism for the dead, on the following Sabbath. But inasmuch as it is out of my power to do so, I will write the word of the Lord from time to time, on that subject, and send it to you by mail, as well as many other things.

11 I now close my letter for the present, for the want of more time; for the enemy is on the alert, and as the Savior said, the ᵃprince of this world cometh, but he hath nothing in me.

12 Behold, my prayer to God is that you all may be saved. And I subscribe myself your servant in the Lord, prophet and ᵃseer of The Church of Jesus Christ of Latter-day Saints.

JOSEPH SMITH.

4a D&C 124:55 (25–48, 55).
  b TG Dedication; Diligence; Patience.
  c TG Hate; Malice; Reward.
5a TG Baptism for the Dead; Genealogy and

Temple Work; Salvation for the Dead.
6a 1 Cor. 15:29; D&C 124:29; 128:18 (13, 18).
  b D&C 128:2 (2–4, 7).
7a TG Book of Life.
  b TG Priesthood, Keys of.
8a TG Restoration of the

Gospel.
  b TG Priesthood, Melchizedek.
9a D&C 128:24. TG Record Keeping.
11a John 14:30. TG Satan.
12a D&C 124:125. TG Seer.

SECTION 128

An epistle from Joseph Smith the Prophet to The Church of Jesus Christ of Latter-day Saints, containing further directions on baptism for the dead, dated at Nauvoo, Illinois, September 6, 1842.

1–5, Local and general recorders must certify to the fact of baptisms for the dead; 6–9, Their records are binding and recorded on earth and in heaven; 10–14, The baptismal font is a similitude of the grave; 15–17, Elijah restored power relative to baptism for the dead; 18–21, All of the keys, powers, and authorities of past dispensations have been restored; 22–25, Glad and glorious tidings are acclaimed for the living and the dead.

1 As I stated to you in my letter before I left my place, that I would write to you from time to time and give you information in relation to many subjects, I now resume the subject of the *a*baptism for the dead, as that subject seems to occupy my mind, and press itself upon my feelings the strongest, since I have been pursued by my enemies.

2 I wrote a few words of revelation to you concerning a recorder. I have had a few additional views in relation to this matter, which I now certify. That is, it was declared in my former letter that there should be a *a*recorder, who should be eye-witness, and also to hear with his ears, that he might make a record of a truth before the Lord.

3 Now, in relation to this matter, it would be very difficult for one recorder to be present at all times, and to do all the business. To obviate this difficulty, there can be a recorder appointed in each ward of the city, who is well qualified for taking accurate minutes; and let him be very particular and precise in taking the whole proceedings, certifying in his record that he saw with his eyes, and heard with his ears, giving the date, and names, and so forth, and the history of the whole transaction; naming also some three individuals that are present, if there be any present, who can at any time when called upon certify to the same, that in the mouth of two or three *a*witnesses every word may be established.

4 Then, let there be a general *a*recorder, to whom these other records can be handed, being attended with certificates over their own signatures, certifying that the record they have made is true. Then the general church recorder can enter the record on the general church book, with the certificates and all the attending witnesses, with his own statement that he verily believes the above statement and records to be true, from his knowledge of the general character and appointment of those men by the church. And

---

128 1 *a* TG Baptism for the
Dead; Genealogy and

Temple Work.
2 *a* 1 Kgs. 4:3; D&C 127:6.
3 *a* D&C 6:28.

TG Witness.
4 *a* D&C 47:1 (1–4).

when this is done on the general church book, the record shall be just as holy, and shall answer the ordinance just the same as if he had seen with his eyes and heard with his ears, and made a record of the same on the general church book.

5 You may think this order of things to be very particular; but let me tell you that it is only to answer the will of God, by conforming to the ordinance and preparation that the Lord ordained and prepared before the foundation of the world, for the *salvation of the dead who should die without a *knowledge of the gospel.

6 And further, I want you to remember that John the Revelator was contemplating this very subject in relation to the dead, when he declared, as you will find recorded in Revelation 20:12—*And I saw the dead, small and great, stand before God; and the books were opened; and another book was opened, which is the book of life; and the dead were judged out of those things which were *written in the books, according to their works.*

7 You will discover in this quotation that the books were opened; and another book was opened, which was the book of life; but the dead were judged out of those things which were written in the books, according to their works; consequently, the books spoken of must be the books which contained the record of their works, and refer to the *records which are kept on the earth. And the book which was the *book of life is the record which is kept in heaven; the principle agreeing precisely with the doctrine which is commanded you in the revelation contained in the letter which I wrote to you previous to my leaving my place—that in all your recordings it may be recorded in heaven.

8 Now, the nature of this ordinance consists in the *power of the priesthood, by the revelation of Jesus Christ, wherein it is granted that whatsoever you *bind on earth shall be bound in heaven, and whatsoever you loose on earth shall be loosed in heaven. Or, in other words, taking a different view of the translation, whatsoever you record on earth shall be recorded in heaven, and whatsoever you do not record on earth shall not be recorded in heaven; for out of the books shall your dead be judged, according to their own works, whether they themselves have attended to the *ordinances in their own *propria persona,* or by the means of their own agents, according to the ordinance which God has prepared for their salvation from before the foundation of the world, according to the records which they have kept concerning their dead.

5a TG Salvation for the Dead.
b 1 Pet. 4:6; D&C 138:2.
6a Heb. 12:23.
7a D&C 21:1.

b Rev. 20:12; D&C 127:6 (6–7). TG Book of Life.
8a TG Priesthood, Power of.

b TG Priesthood, Keys of; Sealing.
c TG Ordinance.

9 It may seem to some to be a very bold doctrine that we talk of—a power which records or binds on earth and binds in heaven. Nevertheless, in all ages of the world, whenever the Lord has given a *a*dispensation of the priesthood to any man by actual revelation, or any set of men, this power has always been given. Hence, whatsoever those men did in *b*authority, in the name of the Lord, and did it truly and faithfully, and kept a proper and faithful record of the same, it became a law on earth and in heaven, and could not be annulled, according to the decrees of the great *c*Jehovah. This is a faithful saying. Who can hear it?

10 And again, for the precedent, Matthew 16:18, 19: *And I say also unto thee, That thou art Peter, and upon this *a*rock I will build my church; and the gates of hell shall not prevail against it. And I will give unto thee the keys of the kingdom of heaven: and whatsoever thou shalt bind on earth shall be bound in heaven; and whatsoever thou shalt loose on earth shall be loosed in heaven.*

11 Now the great and grand secret of the whole matter, and the *summum bonum* of the whole subject that is lying before us, consists in obtaining the *a*powers of the Holy Priesthood. For him to whom these keys are given there is no difficulty in obtaining a *b*knowledge of facts in relation to the *c*salvation of the children of men, both as well for the dead as for the living.

12 Herein is *a*glory and honor, and immortality and eternal life—The ordinance of baptism by water, to be *b*immersed therein in order to answer to the likeness of the dead, that one principle might accord with the other; to be immersed in the water and come forth out of the water is in the likeness of the resurrection of the dead in coming forth out of their graves; hence, this ordinance was instituted to form a relationship with the ordinance of baptism for the dead, being in likeness of the dead.

13 Consequently, the *a*baptismal font was instituted as a similitude of the grave, and was commanded to be in a place underneath where the living are wont to assemble, to show forth the living and the dead, and that all things may have their likeness, and that they may accord one with another—that which is earthly conforming to that which is *b*heavenly, as Paul hath declared, 1 Corinthians 15:46, 47, and 48:

14 *Howbeit that was not first which is spiritual, but that which is natural; and afterward that which is spiritual. The first man is of the earth, earthy; the second man is the Lord from heaven. As is the earthy, such are they also that are*

9*a* TG Dispensations.
 b TG Authority; Priesthood, Authority.
 c TG Jesus Christ, Jehovah.
10*a* Matt. 16:18 (18–19).

11*a* TG Priesthood, Power of.
 b TG Learn.
 c TG Salvation.
12*a* TG Glory; Honor; Immortality.

 b TG Baptism, Immersion.
13*a* Rom. 6:4 (3–5); D&C 76:51; 124:29.
 b TG Symbolism.

earthy; and as is the heavenly, such are they also that are heavenly. And as are the records on the earth in relation to your dead, which are truly made out, so also are the records in heaven. This, therefore, is the *a*sealing and binding power, and, in one sense of the word, the *b*keys of the kingdom, which consist in the key of *c*knowledge.

15 And now, my dearly beloved brethren and sisters, let me assure you that these are principles in relation to the dead and the living that cannot be lightly passed over, as pertaining to our salvation. For their *a*salvation is necessary and essential to our salvation, as Paul says concerning the fathers— that they without us cannot be made perfect—neither can we without our dead be made *b*perfect.

16 And now, in relation to the baptism for the dead, I will give you another quotation of Paul, 1 Corinthians 15:29: *Else what shall they do which are baptized for the dead, if the dead rise not at all? Why are they then baptized for the dead?*

17 And again, in connection with this quotation I will give you a quotation from one of the prophets, who had his eye fixed on the *a*restoration of the priesthood, the glories to be revealed in the last days, and in an especial manner this most glorious of all subjects belonging to the everlasting gospel, namely, the baptism for the dead; for Malachi says, last chapter, verses 5th and 6th: *Behold, I will send you* *b*Elijah *the prophet before the coming of the great and dreadful day of the Lord: And he shall turn the heart of the fathers to the children, and the heart of the children to their fathers, lest I come and smite the earth with a curse.*

18 I might have rendered a *a*plainer translation to this, but it is sufficiently plain to suit my purpose as it stands. It is sufficient to know, in this case, that the earth will be smitten with a *b*curse unless there is a welding *c*link of some kind or other between the fathers and the *d*children, upon some subject or other—and behold what is that subject? It is the *e*baptism for the dead. For we without them cannot be made perfect; neither can they without us be made perfect. Neither can they nor we be made perfect without those who have died in the gospel also; for it is necessary in the ushering in of the dispensation of the *f*fulness of times, which dispensation is now beginning to usher in, that a whole and complete and perfect union, and

---

14*a* TG Sealing.
   b TG Priesthood, Keys of.
   c Luke 11:52. TG Knowledge.
15*a* TG Mission of Latter-day Saints; Salvation, Plan of.
   b Heb. 11:40.

    TG Perfection.
17*a* TG Restoration of the Gospel.
   b 3 Ne. 25:5 (5–6); D&C 2:1; 35:4; 110:14 (13–16).
18*a* D&C 2:2 (1–3); JS—H 1:39 (36–39).

   b TG Curse.
   c TG Genealogy and Temple Work.
   d TG Family, Children, Duties of.
   e 1 Cor. 15:29; D&C 124:29 (28–29); 127:6.
   f D&C 138:53.

welding together of dispensations, and keys, and powers, and glories should take place, and be revealed from the days of Adam even to the present time. And not only this, but those things which never have been revealed from the ᵍfoundation of the world, but have been kept hid from the wise and prudent, shall be revealed unto ʰbabes and sucklings in this, the dispensation of the fulness of times.

19 Now, what do we hear in the gospel which we have received? A voice of ᵃgladness! A voice of mercy from heaven; and a voice of ᵇtruth out of the earth; glad tidings for the dead; a voice of gladness for the living and the dead; glad tidings of great ᶜjoy. How beautiful upon the mountains are the ᵈfeet of those that bring glad tidings of good things, and that say unto Zion: Behold, thy God reigneth! As the ᵉdews of Carmel, so shall the knowledge of God descend upon them!

20 And again, what do we hear? Glad tidings from ᵃCumorah! ᵇMoroni, an angel from heaven, declaring the fulfilment of the prophets—the ᶜbook to be revealed. A voice of the Lord in the wilderness of Fayette, Seneca county, declaring the three witnesses to ᵈbear record of the book! The voice of ᵉMichael on the banks of the Susquehanna, detecting the ᶠdevil when he appeared as an angel of ᵍlight! The voice of ʰPeter, James, and John in the wilderness between Harmony, Susquehanna county, and Colesville, Broome county, on the Susquehanna river, declaring themselves as possessing the ⁱkeys of the kingdom, and of the dispensation of the fulness of times!

21 And again, the voice of God in the chamber of old ᵃFather Whitmer, in Fayette, Seneca county, and at sundry times, and in divers places through all the travels and tribulations of this Church of Jesus Christ of Latter-day Saints! And the voice of Michael, the archangel; the voice of ᵇGabriel, and of Raphael, and of divers ᶜangels, from Michael or ᵈAdam down to the present time, all declaring their ᵉdispensation, their rights, their ᶠkeys, their honors, their majesty and glory, and the power of their priesthood; giving line upon line, ᵍprecept upon precept; here a little, and there a little;

---

18 g D&C 35:18.
  h Matt. 11:25; Luke
    10:21; Alma 32:23.
19 a TG Happiness; Joy.
  b Ps. 85:11 (9–11).
  c Luke 2:10.
  d Isa. 52:7 (7–10); Nahum 1:15; Mosiah 15:18 (13–18); 3 Ne. 20:40.
  e Deut. 32:2; Isa. 26:19; Hosea 14:5; D&C 121:45.

20 a JS—H 1:51 (51–52).
  b D&C 27:5 (5–16).
  c Isa. 29:11 (4, 11–14); 2 Ne. 27:6 (6–29).
  d D&C 17:3 (1–9).
  e D&C 27:11. TG Adam.
  f TG Devil.
  g 2 Cor. 11:14 (13–15).
  h Matt. 17:1; D&C 27:12.
  i TG Priesthood, History of; Priesthood, Keys of; Priesthood,

Melchizedek.
21 a D&C 30:4.
  b Dan. 8:16; Luke 1:19 (19, 26).
  c TG Angels.
  d 2 Ne. 9:21; D&C 107:54 (53–56).
  e TG Dispensations.
  f TG Priesthood, Keys of.
  g Isa. 28:10.

giving us consolation by holding forth that which is to come, confirming our *hope!

22 Brethren, shall we not go on in so great a cause? Go forward and not backward. *Courage, brethren; and on, on to the victory! Let your hearts rejoice, and be exceedingly glad. Let the earth break forth into *singing. Let the *dead speak forth anthems of eternal praise to the *King Immanuel, who hath ordained, before the world was, that which would enable us to *redeem them out of their *prison; for the prisoners shall go free.

23 Let the *mountains shout for joy, and all ye valleys cry aloud; and all ye seas and dry lands tell the wonders of your Eternal King! And ye rivers, and brooks, and rills, flow down with gladness. Let the woods and all the trees of the field praise the Lord; and ye solid *rocks weep for joy! And let the sun, moon, and the *morning stars sing together, and let all the sons of God shout for joy! And let the eternal creations declare his name forever and ever! And again I say, how glorious is the voice we hear from heaven, proclaiming in our ears, glory, and salvation, and honor, and *immortality, and eternal life; kingdoms, principalities, and powers!

24 Behold, the great *day of the Lord is at hand; and who can *abide the day of his coming, and who can stand when he appeareth? For he is like a *refiner's *fire, and like fuller's soap; and he shall sit as a *refiner and purifier of silver, and he shall purify the sons of *Levi, and purge them as gold and silver, that they may offer unto the Lord an *offering in righteousness. Let us, therefore, as a church and a people, and as Latter-day Saints, offer unto the Lord an offering in righteousness; and let us present in his holy temple, when it is finished, a book containing the *records of our dead, which shall be worthy of all acceptation.

25 Brethren, I have many things to say to you on the subject; but shall now close for the present, and continue the subject another time. I am, as ever, your humble servant and never deviating friend,

JOSEPH SMITH.

21 *b* 1 Cor. 15:19. TG Hope.
22 *a* TG Courage; Zeal.
  b Isa. 49:13.
  c Isa. 25:8; 26:19.
  d Isa. 7:14; Matt. 2:2;
    2 Ne. 10:14; Alma 5:50;
    Moses 7:53; Abr. 3:27.
  e TG Redemption; Salvation, Plan of.
  f Isa. 24:22; 49:9; D&C
    76:73 (72–74).
23 *a* Isa. 42:11 (10–14);
    44:23; 55:12.

  b Luke 19:40.
  c Job 38:7.
  d TG Eternal Life; Immortality.
24 *a* TG Day of the Lord.
  b Mal. 3:2 (1–3).
  c TG Earth, Cleansing of; Jesus Christ, Second Coming.
  d Num. 11:1 (1, 10);
    D&C 35:14; Moses 7:34.
  e Prov. 17:3; Zech. 13:9;

    3 Ne. 24:2 (2–3).
  f Deut. 10:8; 3 Ne. 24:3;
    D&C 13; 124:39.
  g D&C 84:31. TG Sacrifice.
  h Num. 1:18; D&C 127:9
    (5–10). TG Genealogy and Temple Work; Mission of Latter-day Saints; Salvation for the Dead.

SECTION 129

Instructions given by Joseph Smith the Prophet, at Nauvoo, Illinois, February 9, 1843, making known three grand keys by which the correct nature of ministering angels and spirits may be distinguished.

1–3, There are both resurrected and spirit bodies in heaven; 4–9, Keys are given whereby messengers from beyond the veil may be identified.

1 There are two kinds of beings in *a*heaven, namely: *b*Angels, who are *c*resurrected personages, having *d*bodies of flesh and bones—

2 For instance, Jesus said: *Handle me and see, for a spirit hath not *a*flesh and bones, as ye see me have.*

3 Secondly: the *a*spirits of *b*just men made *c*perfect, they who are not resurrected, but inherit the same glory.

4 When a messenger comes saying he has a message from God, offer him your hand and request him to shake hands with you.

5 If he be an angel he will do so, and you will feel his hand.

6 If he be the spirit of a just man made perfect he will come in his glory; for that is the only way he can appear—

7 Ask him to shake hands with you, but he will not move, because it is contrary to the *a*order of heaven for a just man to *b*deceive; but he will still deliver his message.

8 If it be the *a*devil as an angel of light, when you ask him to shake hands he will offer you his hand, and you will not *b*feel anything; you may therefore detect him.

9 These are three grand *a*keys whereby you may know whether any administration is from God.

SECTION 130

Items of instruction given by Joseph Smith the Prophet, at Ramus, Illinois, April 2, 1843.

1–3, The Father and the Son may appear personally to men; 4–7, Angels reside in a celestial sphere; 8–9, The celestial earth will be a great Urim and Thummim;

---

129 1 *a* TG Heaven.
    b TG Angels.
    c TG Resurrection.
    d Matt. 27:52 (52–53).
  2 *a* Luke 24:39.
  3 *a* TG Spirit Body; Spirits,

Disembodied.
    b Gen. 6:9; Heb. 12:23;
    D&C 76:69.
    c TG Man, Potential to
    Become like Heavenly
    Father.
  7 *a* TG Order.

    b TG Deceit; Lying.
  8 *a* 2 Cor. 11:14; 2 Ne.
    9:9. TG Spirits, Evil or
    Unclean.
    b D&C 131:8 (7–8).
  9 *a* 1 Jn. 4:1 (1–6). TG Discernment, Spiritual.

10–11, A white stone is given to all who enter the celestial world; 12–17, The time of the Second Coming is withheld from the Prophet; 18–19, Intelligence gained in this life rises with us in the Resurrection; 20–21, All blessings come by obedience to law; 22–23, The Father and the Son have bodies of flesh and bones.

1 When the Savior shall *ᵃappear we shall see him as he is. We shall see that he is a *ᵇman like ourselves.

2 And that same *ᵃsociality which exists among us here will exist among us there, only it will be coupled with *ᵇeternal glory, which glory we do not now enjoy.

3 John 14:23—The *ᵃappearing of the Father and the Son, in that verse, is a personal *ᵇappearance; and the idea that the Father and the Son *ᶜdwell in a man's heart is an old sectarian notion, and is false.

4 In answer to the question—Is not the reckoning of God's *ᵃtime, angel's time, prophet's time, and man's time, according to the planet on which they reside?

5 I answer, Yes. But there are no *ᵃangels who *ᵇminister to this earth but those who do belong or have belonged to it.

6 The angels do not reside on a planet like this earth;

7 But *ᵃthey reside in the *ᵇpresence of God, on a globe *ᶜlike a *ᵈsea of glass and *ᵉfire, where all things for their glory are manifest, past, present, and future, and are continually before the Lord.

8 The place where God resides is a great *ᵃUrim and Thummim.

9 This *ᵃearth, in its *ᵇsanctified and *ᶜimmortal state, will be made like unto *ᵈcrystal and will be a Urim and Thummim to the inhabitants who dwell thereon, whereby all things pertaining to an inferior kingdom, or all kingdoms of a lower order, will be manifest to those who dwell on it; and this earth will be *ᵉChrist's.

10 Then the white *ᵃstone mentioned in Revelation 2:17, will become a

130 1 a 1 Jn. 3:2. TG Jesus Christ, Second Coming.
b TG God, Body of, Corporeal Nature; Man, Potential to Become like Heavenly Father.
2 a TG Family, Eternal; Family, Love within; Marriage, Continuing Courtship in.
b TG Celestial Glory; Eternal Life.
3 a TG God, Privilege of Seeing.
b John 14:23 (21–23);

D&C 93:1. TG Revelation.
c Alma 34:36; D&C 130:22.
4 a Abr. 3:9 (4–10); 4:13 (13–14); 5:13. TG Time.
5 a TG Angels.
b D&C 7:6; 43:25; 129:3 (3, 6–7).
7 a Matt. 18:10; 25:31; 2 Thes. 1:7; D&C 76:21; 136:37.
b 1 Tim. 6:16; D&C 76:62, 94 (94, 119); 88:19. TG God, Presence of.

c Ezek. 1:4 (4, 26–28); Hel. 5:23; D&C 133:41; 137:2.
d Rev. 4:6; 15:2 (1–4).
e Isa. 33:14.
8 a TG Urim and Thummim.
9 a TG Earth, Destiny of.
b D&C 77:1.
c TG Immortality.
d Ezek. 1:22.
e TG Jesus Christ, King.
10 a TG Urim and Thummim.

Urim and Thummim to each individual who receives one, whereby things pertaining to a *b*higher order of kingdoms will be made known;

11 And a *a*white stone is given to each of those who come into the celestial kingdom, whereon is a new *b*name written, which no man knoweth save he that receiveth it. The new name is the key word.

12 I prophesy, in the name of the Lord God, that the commencement of the *a*difficulties which will cause much bloodshed previous to the coming of the Son of Man will be in South Carolina.

13 It may probably arise through the slave question. This a *a*voice declared to me, while I was praying earnestly on the subject, December 25th, 1832.

14 I was once praying very earnestly to know the time of the *a*coming of the Son of Man, when I heard a voice repeat the following:

15 Joseph, my son, if thou livest until thou art eighty-five years old, thou shalt see the face of the Son of Man; therefore *a*let this suffice, and trouble me no more on this matter.

16 I was left thus, without being able to decide whether this coming referred to the beginning of the millennium or to some previous appearing, or whether I should die and thus see his face.

17 I believe the coming of the Son of Man will not be any sooner than that time.

18 Whatever principle of *a*intelligence we attain unto in this life, it will rise with us in the *b*resurrection.

19 And if a person gains more *a*knowledge and intelligence in this life through his *b*diligence and obedience than another, he will have so much the *c*advantage in the world to come.

20 There is a *a*law, irrevocably decreed in *b*heaven before the foundations of this world, upon which all *c*blessings are predicated—

21 And when we obtain any *a*blessing from God, it is by *b*obedience to that law upon which it is predicated.

22 The *a*Father has a *b*body of flesh and bones as tangible as man's; the

---

10 *b* Abr. 3:3 (3–17).
11 *a* Rev. 2:17.
  b Isa. 62:2; 65:15; Mosiah 5:12 (9–14).
12 *a* D&C 38:29; 45:63 (26, 63); 87:2 (1–5). TG War.
13 *a* TG Revelation.
14 *a* TG Jesus Christ, Prophecies about; Jesus Christ, Second Coming.
15 *a* Matt. 24:36 (36–42); D&C 49:7.

18 *a* 2 Ne. 9:13 (13–14); D&C 93:36. TG Intelligence; Learn.
  b TG Resurrection.
19 *a* TG Education; Knowledge; Objectives.
  b TG Diligence.
  c Matt. 25:21 (14–29); Alma 12:10 (9–11).
20 *a* Jer. 26:4; D&C 82:10.
  b TG Council in Heaven; God, Law of.
  c Ex. 32:29; Deut. 11:27 (26–28); D&C 132:5.

21 *a* Deut. 6:24; Alma 45:16 (15–17). TG Blessing.
  b TG Obedience.
22 *a* TG Godhead; God the Father, Elohim; Man, Potential to Become like Heavenly Father.
  b John 4:24 (23–24); 14:9; Acts 17:28 (25–29); Heb. 1:3. TG God, Body of, Corporeal Nature; God, Knowledge about; God, Manifestations of.

Son also; but the Holy Ghost has not a body of flesh and bones, but is a personage of ^cSpirit. Were it not so, the Holy Ghost could not ^ddwell in us.

23 A man may receive the ^aHoly Ghost, and it may descend upon him and not ^btarry with him.

SECTION 131

Instructions by Joseph Smith the Prophet, given at Ramus, Illinois, May 16 and 17, 1843.

1–4, Celestial marriage is essential to exaltation in the highest heaven; 5–6, How men are sealed up unto eternal life is explained; 7–8, All spirit is matter.

1 In the ^acelestial glory there are three ^bheavens or degrees;

2 And in order to obtain the ^ahighest, a man must enter into this ^border of the ^cpriesthood [meaning the ^dnew and everlasting covenant of ^emarriage];

3 And if he does not, he cannot obtain it.

4 He may enter into the other, but that is the end of his kingdom; he cannot have an ^aincrease.

5 (May 17th, 1843.) The more sure word of ^aprophecy means a man's knowing that he is ^bsealed up unto ^ceternal life, by revelation and the spirit of prophecy, through the power of the Holy Priesthood.

6 It is impossible for a man to be ^asaved in ^bignorance.

7 There is no such thing as immaterial matter. All ^aspirit is matter, but it is more fine or pure, and can only be discerned by ^bpurer eyes;

8 We cannot ^asee it; but when our bodies are purified we shall see that it is all ^bmatter.

---

22 c TG Spirit Body.
  d 2 Tim. 1:14. TG Holy Ghost, Mission of.
23 a TG Holy Ghost, Gift of.
  b TG Holy Ghost, Loss of.
131 1 a D&C 76:70. TG Celestial Glory.
  b TG Heaven. BD Heaven.
2 a D&C 132:21 (5–21). TG Family, Eternal; Man, Potential to Become like Heavenly Father.
  b TG Genealogy and

Temple Work.
  c TG Priesthood, Melchizedek.
  d TG New and Everlasting Covenant.
  e TG Marriage, Celestial.
4 a Matt. 22:30 (23–33); D&C 132:16–17. TG Marriage, Fatherhood; Marriage, Motherhood.
5 a 2 Pet. 1:19 (3–21). TG Prophecy.
  b TG Election; Eternal Life; Sealing.

  c D&C 68:12; 88:4.
6 a TG Salvation.
  b Mal. 2:7 (7–9); D&C 90:15 (14–15); 107:99 (99–100). TG Apathy; Education; Ignorance; Knowledge; Learn.
7 a TG Spirit Body; Spirit Creation.
  b D&C 76:12; 97:16; Moses 1:11.
8 a D&C 129:8.
  b D&C 77:2; Moses 3:5 (5–9).

SECTION 132

Revelation given through Joseph Smith the Prophet, at Nauvoo, Illinois, recorded July 12, 1843, relating to the new and everlasting covenant, including the eternity of the marriage covenant and the principle of plural marriage. Although the revelation was recorded in 1843, evidence indicates that some of the principles involved in this revelation were known by the Prophet as early as 1831. See Official Declaration 1.

1–6, Exaltation is gained through the new and everlasting covenant; 7–14, The terms and conditions of that covenant are set forth; 15–20, Celestial marriage and a continuation of the family unit enable men to become gods; 21–25, The strait and narrow way leads to eternal lives; 26–27, The law is given relative to blasphemy against the Holy Ghost; 28–39, Promises of eternal increase and exaltation are made to prophets and Saints in all ages; 40–47, Joseph Smith is given the power to bind and seal on earth and in heaven; 48–50, The Lord seals upon him his exaltation; 51–57, Emma Smith is counseled to be faithful and true; 58–66, Laws governing plural marriage are set forth.

1 Verily, thus saith the Lord unto you my servant Joseph, that inasmuch as you have inquired of my hand to know and understand wherein I, the Lord, justified my servants Abraham, Isaac, and Jacob, as also Moses, David and Solomon, my servants, as touching the principle and doctrine of their having many *a*wives and *b*concubines—

2 Behold, and lo, I am the Lord thy God, and will answer thee as touching this matter.

3 Therefore, *a*prepare thy heart to receive and *b*obey the instructions which I am about to give unto you; for all those who have this law revealed unto them must obey the same.

4 For behold, I reveal unto you a new and an everlasting *a*covenant; and if ye abide not that covenant, then are ye *b*damned; for no one can *c*reject this covenant and be permitted to enter into my glory.

5 For all who will have a *a*blessing at my hands shall abide the *b*law which was appointed for that blessing, and the conditions thereof, as were instituted from before the foundation of the world.

6 And as pertaining to the *a*new and everlasting covenant, it was instituted

---

132 1*a* Ex. 21:10 (1, 7–11);
   Jacob 2:24 (23–30);
   D&C 132:38 (34,
   37–39). TG Marriage,
   Plural.
 b Gen. 25:6. TG Concu-
   bine.

3*a* Ezra 7:10; D&C 29:8;
   58:6; 78:7.
 b TG Obedience.
4*a* TG Covenants.
 b D&C 84:24. TG Dam-
   nation.
 c D&C 131:2 (1–4).

5*a* Ex. 32:29; D&C
   130:20; 132:11 (11, 28,
   32).
 b TG God, Law of.
6*a* D&C 66:2. TG New
   and Everlasting Cove-
   nant.

for the fulness of my *b*glory; and he that receiveth a fulness thereof must and shall abide the law, or he shall be damned, saith the Lord God.

7 And verily I say unto you, that the *a*conditions of this law are these: All covenants, contracts, bonds, obligations, *b*oaths, *c*vows, performances, connections, associations, or expectations, that are not made and entered into and *d*sealed by the Holy Spirit of promise, of him who is *e*anointed, both as well for time and for all eternity, and that too most holy, by *f*revelation and commandment through the medium of mine anointed, whom I have appointed on the earth to hold this *g*power (and I have appointed unto my servant Joseph to hold this *h*power in the last days, and there is never but one on the earth at a time on whom this power and the *i*keys of this priesthood are conferred), are of no efficacy, virtue, or force in and after the resurrection from the dead; for all contracts that are not made unto this end have an end when men are dead.

8 Behold, mine house is a house of *a*order, saith the Lord God, and not a house of confusion.

9 Will I *a*accept of an offering, saith the Lord, that is not made in my name?

10 Or will I receive at your hands that which I have not *a*appointed?

11 And will I appoint unto you, saith the Lord, except it be by law, even as I and my Father *a*ordained unto you, before the world was?

12 I am the Lord thy God; and I give unto you this commandment—that no man shall *a*come unto the Father but by me or by my word, which is my law, saith the Lord.

13 And everything that is in the world, whether it be ordained of men, by *a*thrones, or principalities, or powers, or things of name, whatsoever they may be, that are not by me or by my word, saith the Lord, shall be thrown down, and shall *b*not remain after men are dead, neither in nor after the resurrection, saith the Lord your God.

14 For whatsoever things remain are by me; and whatsoever things are not by me shall be shaken and destroyed.

6*b* D&C 76:70 (50–70, 92–96). TG Celestial Glory.
7*a* D&C 88:39 (38–39).
b TG Oath.
c TG Vow.
d TG Holy Ghost, Mission of; Holy Spirit; Sealing.
e TG Priesthood, Authority.
f TG Prophets, Mission of; Revelation.
g TG Priesthood, Power of.
h TG Priesthood, Authority.
i TG Priesthood, Keys of.
8*a* TG Order.
9*a* Lev. 7:18 (16–18); 17:8 (8–9); Moro. 7:6 (5–6). TG Sacrifice.
10*a* Lev. 22:20 (20–25); Moses 5:21.
11*a* D&C 49:15; 132:5 (5, 63).
12*a* Isa. 55:3; John 14:6. TG God, Access to.
13*a* TG Governments; Kings, Earthly.
b 3 Ne. 27:11 (10–11).

15 Therefore, if a *man marry him a wife in the world, and he marry her not by me nor by my word, and he covenant with her so long as he is in the world and she with him, their covenant and marriage are not of force when they are dead, and when they are out of the world; therefore, they are not bound by any law when they are out of the world.

16 Therefore, when they are out of the world they neither marry nor are given in *marriage; but are appointed angels in *heaven, which angels are ministering *servants, to minister for those who are worthy of a far more, and an exceeding, and an eternal weight of glory.

17 For these angels did not abide my law; therefore, they cannot be enlarged, but remain separately and singly, without exaltation, in their saved condition, to all eternity; and from henceforth are not gods, but are *angels of God forever and ever.

18 And again, verily I say unto you, if a man marry a wife, and make a covenant with her for time and for all eternity, if that *covenant is not by me or by my word, which is my law, and is not sealed by the Holy Spirit of promise, through him whom I have anointed and appointed unto this power, then it is not valid neither of force when they are out of the world, because they are not joined by me, saith the Lord, neither by my word; when they are out of the world it cannot be received there, because the angels and the gods are appointed there, by whom they cannot pass; they cannot, therefore, inherit my glory; for my house is a house of order, saith the Lord God.

19 And again, verily I say unto you, if a man *marry a wife by my word, which is my law, and by the *new and everlasting covenant, and it is *sealed unto them by the Holy Spirit of *promise, by him who is anointed, unto whom I have appointed this power and the *keys of this priesthood; and it shall be said unto them—Ye shall come forth in the first resurrection; and if it be after the first resurrection, in the next resurrection; and shall inherit *thrones, kingdoms, principalities, and powers, dominions, all heights and depths—then shall it be written in the Lamb's *Book of Life, that he shall commit no *murder whereby to shed innocent *blood, and if ye abide in

15 a TG Marriage, Husbands; Marriage, Interfaith; Marriage, Temporal; Marriage, Wives.
16 a Matt. 22:30 (23–33); Mark 12:25; Luke 20:35 (27–36). TG Marriage, Marry.
  b D&C 131:4 (1–4). TG Heaven.
  c TG Servant.
17 a Luke 20:36.
18 a D&C 132:7 (7, 46–47).
19 a TG Marriage, Celestial; Marriage, Wives.
  b TG New and Everlasting Covenant.
  c TG Sealing.
  d 2 Pet. 1:19; D&C 68:12; 76:53; 88:3 (3–4); 124:124; 132:49.
  e TG Priesthood, Keys of.
  f Ex. 19:6; Rev. 5:10; 20:6; D&C 76:56; 78:15 (15, 18).
  g TG Book of Life.
  h TG Murder.
  i Jer. 22:3. TG Blood, Shedding of; Life, Sanctity of.

my covenant, and commit no murder whereby to shed innocent blood, it shall be done unto them in all things whatsoever my servant hath put upon them, in time, and through all eternity; and shall be of full force when they are out of the world; and they shall pass by the angels, and the gods, which are set there, to their *j*exaltation and glory in all things, as hath been sealed upon their heads, which glory shall be a fulness and a continuation of the *k*seeds forever and ever.

20 Then shall they be gods, because they have no end; therefore shall they be from *a*everlasting to everlasting, because they continue; then shall they be above all, because all things are subject unto them. Then shall they be *b*gods, because they have *c*all power, and the angels are subject unto them.

21 Verily, verily, I say unto you, except ye abide my *a*law ye cannot attain to this glory.

22 For *a*strait is the gate, and narrow the *b*way that leadeth unto the exaltation and continuation of the *c*lives, and few there be that find it, because ye receive me not in the world neither do ye know me.

23 But if ye receive me in the world, then shall ye know me, and shall receive your exaltation; that *a*where I am ye shall be also.

24 This is *a*eternal lives—to *b*know the only wise and true God, and Jesus Christ, whom he hath *c*sent. I am he. Receive ye, therefore, my law.

25 *a*Broad is the gate, and wide the way that leadeth to the *b*deaths; and many there are that go in thereat, because they *c*receive me not, neither do they abide in my law.

26 Verily, verily, I say unto you, if a man marry a wife according to my word, and they are sealed by the *a*Holy Spirit of promise, according to mine appointment, and he or she shall commit any sin or transgression of the new and everlasting covenant whatever, and all manner of blasphemies, and if they *b*commit no murder wherein they shed innocent blood, yet they shall come forth in the first resurrection, and enter into their exaltation; but

---

19 *j* TG Celestial Glory;
    Election; Exaltation;
    Glory.
   k TG Family, Eternal;
    Family, Patriarchal.
20 *a* Rev. 22:5 (1–5).
   b Matt. 25:21; D&C
    132:37. TG Exaltation;
    Man, Potential to
    Become like Heavenly
    Father.
   c D&C 29:13 (12–13);
    50:27 (26–28); 76:95;
    78:5 (5–7); 84:38
    (35–39).

21 *a* TG God, Law of.
22 *a* Luke 13:24 (22–30);
    2 Ne. 33:9; Hel. 3:29
    (29–30).
   b Matt. 7:13–14, 23;
    JST Matt. 7:13–14
    (Bible Appendix); 2 Ne.
    9:41; 31:21 (17–21).
   c D&C 132:30 (30–31).
23 *a* John 14:3 (2–3).
24 *a* John 17:3. TG Eternal
    Life.
   b TG God, Knowledge
    about.
   c John 3:17 (16–17);

    D&C 49:5.
25 *a* Gen. 6:12; 2 Ne. 28:11;
    Hel. 6:31; 3 Ne. 14:13
    (13–15).
   b Matt. 7:13 (13–14).
    TG Death, Spiritual,
    First; Death, Spiritual,
    Second.
   c John 5:43.
26 *a* D&C 88:3 (3–4);
    132:19 (7, 19–20).
   b Alma 39:5 (5–6).
    TG Blood, Shedding of.

they shall be destroyed in the flesh, and shall be ʿdelivered unto the buffetings of ᵈSatan unto the day of ᵉredemption, saith the Lord God.

27 The ᵃblasphemy against the Holy Ghost, which shall ᵇnot be ʿforgiven in the world nor out of the world, is in that ye commit ᵈmurder wherein ye shed innocent blood, and assent unto my death, after ye have received my new and everlasting covenant, saith the Lord God; and he that abideth not this law can in nowise enter into my glory, but shall be ᵉdamned, saith the Lord.

28 I am the Lord thy God, and will give unto thee the ᵃlaw of my Holy Priesthood, as was ordained by me and my Father before the world was.

29 ᵃAbraham received all things, whatsoever he received, by revelation and commandment, by my word, saith the Lord, and hath entered into his exaltation and sitteth upon his throne.

30 ᵃAbraham received promises concerning his seed, and of the fruit of his loins—from whose ᵇloins ye are, namely, my servant Joseph—which were to continue so long as they were in the world; and as touching Abraham and his seed, out of the world they should continue; both in the world and out of the world should they continue as innumerable as the ʿstars; or, if ye were to count the sand upon the seashore ye could not number them.

31 This promise is yours also, because ye are of ᵃAbraham, and the promise was made unto Abraham; and by this law is the continuation of the works of my Father, wherein he glorifieth himself.

32 Go ye, therefore, and do the ᵃworks of Abraham; enter ye into my law and ye shall be saved.

33 But if ye enter not into my law ye cannot receive the promise of my Father, which he made unto Abraham.

34 God ᵃcommanded Abraham, and Sarah gave ᵇHagar to Abraham to wife. And why did she do it? Because this was the law; and from Hagar sprang many people. This, therefore, was fulfilling, among other things, the promises.

---

26 c 1 Tim. 1:20; D&C
   82:21; 104:9 (9–10).
   d TG Devil.
   e TG Redemption.
27 a TG Blaspheme; Holy
   Ghost, Unpardonable
   Sin against; Sin.
   b Matt. 12:32 (31–32);
   Heb. 6:6 (4–6); 10:29
   (26–29); D&C 42:18;
   76:34 (31, 34–35);
   84:41.
   c TG Death, Spiritual,
   Second; Forgive; Sons

   of Perdition.
   d TG Murder.
   e TG Damnation.
28 a Acts 17:26; D&C
   132:5.
29 a Gen. 26:5; D&C
   132:37; 133:55; 137:5;
   Abr. 2:11 (9–11).
30 a Gen. 12:3 (1–3); 13:16;
   Lev. 26:42; Gal. 3:14
   (7–14, 26–29); 2 Ne.
   29:14; D&C 84:34.
   TG Abrahamic Cove-
   nant; Seed of Abraham.

   b 2 Ne. 3:6 (6–16).
   c Gen. 15:5; 22:17; Deut.
   1:10; 1 Chr. 27:23;
   Neh. 9:23; Hosea 1:10.
31 a D&C 86:9 (8–11);
   110:12.
32 a John 8:39; Alma 5:24
   (22–24).
34 a Gen. 16:2 (1–3); Gal.
   4:22 (21–31); D&C
   132:65.
   b Gen. 25:12 (12–18).

35 Was Abraham, therefore, under condemnation? Verily I say unto you, Nay; for I, the Lord, ^acommanded it.

36 Abraham was ^acommanded to offer his son Isaac; nevertheless, it was written: Thou shalt not ^bkill. Abraham, however, did not refuse, and it was accounted unto him for ^crighteousness.

37 Abraham received ^aconcubines, and they bore him children; and it was accounted unto him for righteousness, because they were given unto him, and he abode in my law; as Isaac also and ^bJacob did none other things than that which they were commanded; and because they did none other things than that which they were commanded, they have entered into their ^cexaltation, according to the promises, and sit upon thrones, and are not angels but are gods.

38 David also received ^amany wives and concubines, and also Solomon and Moses my servants, as also many others of my servants, from the beginning of creation until this time; and in nothing did they sin save in those things which they received not of me.

39 ^aDavid's wives and concubines were ^bgiven unto him of me, by the hand of Nathan, my servant, and others of the prophets who had the ^ckeys of this power; and in none of these things did he ^dsin against me save in the case of ^eUriah and his wife; and, therefore he hath ^ffallen from his exaltation, and received his portion; and he shall not inherit them out of the world, for I ^ggave them unto another, saith the Lord.

40 I am the Lord thy God, and I gave unto thee, my servant Joseph, an ^aappointment, and restore all things. Ask what ye will, and it shall be given unto you according to my word.

41 And as ye have asked concerning adultery, verily, verily, I say unto you, if a man ^areceiveth a wife in the new and everlasting covenant, and if she be with another man, and I have not appointed unto her by the holy ^banointing, she hath committed ^cadultery and shall be destroyed.

42 If she be not in the new and everlasting covenant, and she be with another man, she has ^acommitted adultery.

35a Jacob 2:30 (24–30).
36a Gen. 22:2 (2–12).
  b Ex. 20:13.
  c Gen. 15:6; Jacob 4:5. TG Righteousness.
37a Gen. 25:6.
  b Gen. 30:4 (3–4); D&C 133:55.
  c TG Exaltation; Man, Potential to Become like Heavenly Father.
38a Ex. 21:10 (1, 7–11);

1 Sam. 25:43 (42–43); 2 Sam. 5:13; 1 Kgs. 11:3 (1–3); Jacob 1:15; D&C 132:1.
39a 1 Sam. 27:3; 2 Sam. 2:2; 1 Chr. 14:3; Jacob 2:24 (23–24).
  b 2 Sam. 12:8.
  c TG Priesthood, Keys of.
  d 2 Sam. 11:27. TG Adulterer; Sin.
  e 2 Sam. 11:4; 12:9

(1–15); 1 Kgs. 15:5; 1 Chr. 11:41.
  f Ps. 89:39. TG Punish.
  g Jer. 8:10.
40a JS—H 1:33 (18–20, 26, 33). TG Prophets, Mission of; Restoration of the Gospel.
41a D&C 132:19 (4–7, 19).
  b TG Anointing.
  c TG Adulterer.
42a D&C 42:24 (22–26).

43 And if her husband be with another woman, and he was under a ᵃvow, he hath broken his vow and hath committed adultery.

44 And if she hath not committed adultery, but is innocent and hath not broken her vow, and she knoweth it, and I reveal it unto you, my servant Joseph, then shall you have power, by the power of my Holy Priesthood, to take her and ᵃgive her unto him that hath not committed ᵇadultery but hath been ᶜfaithful; for he shall be made ruler over many.

45 For I have conferred upon you the ᵃkeys and power of the priesthood, wherein I ᵇrestore all things, and make known unto you all things in due time.

46 And verily, verily, I say unto you, that whatsoever you ᵃseal on earth shall be sealed in heaven; and whatsoever you ᵇbind on earth, in my name and by my word, saith the Lord, it shall be eternally bound in the heavens; and whosesoever sins you ᶜremit on earth shall be remitted eternally in the heavens; and whosesoever sins you retain on earth shall be retained in heaven.

47 And again, verily I say, whomsoever you bless I will bless, and whomsoever you curse I will ᵃcurse, saith the Lord; for I, the Lord, am thy God.

48 And again, verily I say, unto you, my servant Joseph, that whatsoever you give on earth, and to whomsoever you ᵃgive any one on earth, by my word and according to my law, it shall be visited with blessings and not cursings, and with my power, saith the Lord, and shall be without condemnation on earth and in heaven.

49 For I am the Lord thy God, and will be ᵃwith thee even unto the ᵇend of the world, and through all eternity; for verily I ᶜseal upon you your ᵈexaltation, and prepare a throne for you in the kingdom of my Father, with Abraham your ᵉfather.

50 Behold, I have seen your ᵃsacrifices, and will forgive all your sins; I have seen your ᵇsacrifices in obedience to that which I have told you. Go, therefore, and I make a way for your escape, as I ᶜaccepted the offering of Abraham of his son Isaac.

51 Verily, I say unto you: A commandment I give unto mine handmaid, Emma Smith, your wife, whom I have given unto you, that she stay herself

---

43 a TG Covenants; Marriage, Marry; Vow.
44 a TG Divorce.
  b TG Chastity.
  c Luke 16:10 (10–12); 19:26 (12–26).
45 a TG Priesthood, Keys of.
  b Acts 3:21; D&C 86:10. TG Restoration of the Gospel.
46 a TG Marriage, Celestial;

Sealing.
  b TG Priesthood, Authority.
  c TG Remission of Sins.
47 a Gen. 12:3 (1–3); D&C 103:25; 124:93.
48 a D&C 132:39.
49 a TG God, Presence of; Walking with God.
  b Matt. 28:20.
  c 2 Pet. 1:19; D&C

68:12; 132:19.
  d D&C 5:22. TG Election.
  e Gen. 17:4 (1–8); 2 Ne. 8:2; D&C 109:64.
50 a Luke 14:33 (28–33).
  b TG Sacrifice.
  c Gen. 22:12 (1–18); Gal. 3:6; D&C 52:15; 97:8; Moses 5:23.

and partake not of that which I commanded you to offer unto her; for I did it, saith the Lord, to ᵃprove you all, as I did Abraham, and that I might require an offering at your hand, by covenant and sacrifice.

52 And let mine handmaid, Emma Smith, ᵃreceive all those that have been given unto my servant Joseph, and who are virtuous and pure before me; and those who are not pure, and have said they were pure, shall be destroyed, saith the Lord God.

53 For I am the Lord thy God, and ye shall obey my voice; and I give unto my servant Joseph that he shall be made ruler over many things; for he hath been ᵃfaithful over a few things, and from henceforth I will strengthen him.

54 And I command mine handmaid, Emma Smith, to abide and ᵃcleave unto my servant Joseph, and to none else. But if she will not abide this commandment she shall be ᵇdestroyed, saith the Lord; for I am the Lord thy God, and will destroy her if she abide not in my law.

55 But if she will not abide this commandment, then shall my servant Joseph do all things for her, even as he hath said; and I will bless him and multiply him and give unto him an ᵃhundred-fold in this world, of fathers and mothers, brothers and sisters, houses and lands, wives and children, and crowns of ᵇeternal lives in the eternal worlds.

56 And again, verily I say, let mine handmaid ᵃforgive my servant Joseph his trespasses; and then shall she be forgiven her trespasses, wherein she has trespassed against me; and I, the Lord thy God, will bless her, and multiply her, and make her heart to ᵇrejoice.

57 And again, I say, let not my servant Joseph put his property out of his hands, lest an enemy come and destroy him; for ᵃSatan ᵇseeketh to destroy; for I am the Lord thy God, and he is my servant; and behold, and lo, I am with him, as I was with Abraham, thy father, even unto his ᶜexaltation and glory.

58 Now, as touching the law of the ᵃpriesthood, there are many things pertaining thereunto.

59 Verily, if a man be called of my Father, as was ᵃAaron, by mine own voice, and by the voice of him that ᵇsent me, and I have endowed him with

51 a Gen. 22:1; Ex. 15:25 (23–26); D&C 98:14 (12–14); 101:4; 124:55; Abr. 3:25. TG Test.
52 a D&C 132:65.
53 a Matt. 25:21 (14–28); D&C 52:13.
54 a D&C 42:22. TG Marriage, Husbands.

b Acts 3:23; D&C 25:15.
55 a Mark 10:30 (28–31).
b D&C 132:22 (22–24). TG Family, Eternal.
56 a Matt. 6:15 (12–15). TG Family, Love within; Forgive.
b Gen. 21:6; D&C 25:9.
57 a TG Devil; Enemies.

b Matt. 10:28; Rev. 12:12 (12–17).
c D&C 132:37.
58 a D&C 84:19 (19–26).
59 a Heb. 5:4 (1–6). TG Priesthood, Qualifying for.
b TG Jesus Christ, Authority of.

the ᶜkeys of the power of this priesthood, if he do anything in my name, and according to my law and by my word, he will not commit ᵈsin, and I will justify him.

60 Let no one, therefore, set on my servant Joseph; for I will justify him; for he shall do the sacrifice which I require at his hands for his transgressions, saith the Lord your God.

61 And again, as pertaining to the law of the priesthood—if any man espouse a virgin, and desire to espouse ᵃanother, and the first give her consent, and if he espouse the second, and they are virgins, and have vowed to no other man, then is he justified; he cannot commit adultery for they are given unto him; for he cannot commit adultery with that that belongeth unto him and to no one else.

62 And if he have ᵃten virgins given unto him by this law, he cannot commit adultery, for they belong to him, and they are given unto him; therefore is he justified.

63 But if one or either of the ten virgins, after she is espoused, shall be with another man, she has committed adultery, and shall be destroyed; for they are given unto him to ᵃmultiply and replenish the earth, according to my commandment, and to fulfil the promise which was given by my Father before the foundation of the world, and for their exaltation in the eternal worlds, that they may bear the souls of men; for herein is the work of my Father continued, that he may be ᵇglorified.

64 And again, verily, verily, I say unto you, if any man have a wife, who holds the keys of this power, and he teaches unto her the law of my priesthood, as pertaining to these things, then shall she believe and administer unto him, or she shall be destroyed, saith the Lord your God; for I will destroy her; for I will magnify my name upon all those who receive and abide in my law.

65 Therefore, it shall be lawful in me, if she receive not this law, for him to receive all things whatsoever I, the Lord his God, will give unto him, because she did not believe and administer unto him according to my word; and she then becomes the transgressor; and he is exempt from the law of Sarah, who administered unto Abraham according to the law when I commanded Abraham to take ᵃHagar to wife.

66 And now, as pertaining to this law, verily, verily, I say unto you, I will reveal more unto you, hereafter; therefore, let this suffice for the present. Behold, I am Alpha and Omega. Amen.

---

59 c TG Priesthood, Keys of.
  d 1 Jn. 5:18.
61 a TG Marriage, Plural.
62 a D&C 132:48. See also

OD 1.
63 a Gen. 1:22 (20–25);
  Jacob 2:30.
  b Moses 1:39.

65 a Gen. 16:2 (1–3); 25:12;
  Gal. 4:22; D&C 132:34
  (34, 61).

SECTION 133

Revelation given through Joseph Smith the Prophet, at Hiram, Ohio, November 3, 1831. Prefacing this revelation, Joseph Smith's history states, "At this time there were many things which the Elders desired to know relative to preaching the Gospel to the inhabitants of the earth, and concerning the gathering; and in order to walk by the true light, and be instructed from on high, on the 3rd of November, 1831, I inquired of the Lord and received the following important revelation." This section was first added to the book of Doctrine and Covenants as an appendix and was subsequently assigned a section number.

1–6, The Saints are commanded to prepare for the Second Coming; 7–16, All men are commanded to flee from Babylon, come to Zion, and prepare for the great day of the Lord; 17–35, He will stand on Mount Zion, the continents will become one land, and the lost tribes of Israel will return; 36–40, The gospel was restored through Joseph Smith to be preached in all the world; 41–51, The Lord will come down in vengeance upon the wicked; 52–56, It will be the year of His redeemed; 57–74, The gospel is to be sent forth to save the Saints and for the destruction of the wicked.

1 Hearken, O ye people of my church, saith the Lord your God, and hear the word of the Lord concerning you—

2 The Lord who shall suddenly *a*come to his temple; the Lord who shall come down upon the world with a curse to *b*judgment; yea, upon all the nations that *c*forget God, and upon all the ungodly among you.

3 For he shall make *a*bare his holy arm in the eyes of all the nations, and all the ends of the earth shall see the *b*salvation of their God.

4 Wherefore, prepare ye, prepare ye, O my people; sanctify yourselves; gather ye together, O ye people of my church, upon the land of Zion, all you that have not been commanded to *a*tarry.

5 Go ye out from *a*Babylon. Be ye *b*clean that bear the vessels of the Lord.

6 Call your *a*solemn assemblies, and *b*speak often one to another. And let every man call upon the name of the Lord.

7 Yea, verily I say unto you again, the time has come when the voice of

---

133 2 *a* Mal. 3:1; D&C 36:8.
    TG Jesus Christ, Second
    Coming.
   b D&C 1:36. TG Jesus
    Christ, Judge; Judg-
    ment, the Last.
   c 2 Kgs. 17:38; Alma

46:8.
3 *a* Isa. 52:10. TG God,
    Power of.
   b Isa. 12:2; 52:10. TG Sal-
    vation.
4 *a* D&C 62:4; 63:41 (24,
    39–41).
5 *a* Alma 5:57; D&C 1:16.

TG Worldliness.
   b Isa. 52:11; 2 Tim. 2:21;
    3 Ne. 20:41; D&C
    38:42. TG Body, Sanc-
    tity of; Cleanliness.
6 *a* TG Solemn Assembly.
   b Mal. 3:16 (16–18).

the Lord is unto you: Go ye out of Babylon; *a*gather ye out from among the nations, from the *b*four winds, from one end of heaven to the other.

8 Send forth the elders of my church unto the *a*nations which are afar off; unto the *b*islands of the sea; send forth unto foreign lands; call upon all nations, first upon the *c*Gentiles, and then upon the Jews.

9 And behold, and lo, this shall be their cry, and the voice of the Lord unto all people: Go ye forth unto the land of Zion, that the borders of my people may be enlarged, and that her *a*stakes may be strengthened, and that *b*Zion may go forth unto the regions round about.

10 Yea, let the cry go forth among all people: Awake and arise and go forth to meet the *a*Bridegroom; behold and lo, the Bridegroom cometh; go ye out to meet him. Prepare yourselves for the *b*great day of the Lord.

11 *a*Watch, therefore, for ye *b*know neither the day nor the hour.

12 Let them, therefore, who are *a*among the Gentiles flee unto *b*Zion.

13 And let them who be of *a*Judah flee unto *b*Jerusalem, unto the *c*mountains of the Lord's *d*house.

14 Go ye *a*out from among the nations, even from *b*Babylon, from the midst of *c*wickedness, which is spiritual Babylon.

15 But verily, thus saith the Lord, let not your flight be in *a*haste, but let all things be prepared before you; and he that goeth, let him *b*not look back lest sudden destruction shall come upon him.

16 Hearken and hear, O ye inhabitants of the earth. *a*Listen, ye elders of my church together, and hear the voice of the Lord; for he calleth upon all men, and he commandeth all men everywhere to *b*repent.

17 For behold, the Lord God hath *a*sent forth the angel crying through the midst of heaven, saying: Prepare ye the way of the Lord, and make his paths straight, for the hour of his *b*coming is nigh—

7*a* D&C 29:8. TG Israel,
  Gathering of; Mission
  of Latter-day Saints.
 b Zech. 2:6 (6–7).
8*a* TG Missionary Work;
  Nations.
 b Isa. 11:11; 51:5; 1 Ne.
  22:4; 2 Ne. 10:8 (8, 20);
  29:7.
 c Matt. 19:30; Acts
  13:46; D&C 18:26
  (26–27); 90:9 (8–9).
9*a* Isa. 54:2. TG Stake.
 b D&C 58:25 (25, 56);
  63:24; 101:68 (68–71).
  TG Zion.
10*a* Matt. 25:6; D&C 33:17

(17–18); 45:56 (54–59).
 b D&C 1:12. TG Day of
  the Lord.
11*a* Prov. 27:18; Mark 13:35
  (24–37); 1 Ne. 21:23;
  2 Ne. 6:13.
 b D&C 49:7.
12*a* Isa. 4:2; D&C 38:31
  (31, 42).
 b TG Jerusalem, New;
  Zion.
13*a* D&C 45:25 (24–25).
  TG Israel, Judah, People
  of.
 b TG Jerusalem.
 c Ezek. 38:8; Dan. 11:45;
  JS—M 1:13.

 d Ps. 122:1 (1–9).
14*a* TG Israel, Gathering of;
  Separation.
 b D&C 1:16.
 c TG Wickedness.
15*a* Isa. 52:12 (10–12);
  D&C 58:56. TG Haste.
 b Gen. 19:17; Luke 9:62;
  D&C 67:14.
16*a* D&C 1:1 (1–6).
 b TG Repent.
17*a* D&C 13; 27:5 (5–10);
  88:92.
 b Isa. 40:3 (3–5); Mal.
  3:1; Rev. 14:6 (6–8).
  TG Jesus Christ, Proph-
  ecies about.

18 When the ᵃLamb shall stand upon ᵇMount Zion, and with him a ᶜhundred and forty-four thousand, having his Father's name written on their foreheads.

19 Wherefore, prepare ye for the ᵃcoming of the Bridegroom; go ye, go ye out to meet him.

20 For behold, he shall ᵃstand upon the mount of Olivet, and upon the mighty ocean, even the great deep, and upon the islands of the sea, and upon the land of Zion.

21 And he shall ᵃutter his voice out of ᵇZion, and he shall speak from Jerusalem, and his ᶜvoice shall be heard among all people;

22 And it shall be a voice as the ᵃvoice of many waters, and as the voice of a great ᵇthunder, which shall ᶜbreak down the mountains, and the valleys shall not be found.

23 He shall command the great deep, and it shall be driven back into the north countries, and the ᵃislands shall become one land;

24 And the ᵃland of Jerusalem and the land of ᵇZion shall be turned back into their own place, and the ᶜearth shall be like as it was in the days before it was ᵈdivided.

25 And the Lord, even the Savior, shall ᵃstand in the midst of his people, and shall ᵇreign over all flesh.

26 And they who are in the ᵃnorth countries shall come in remembrance before the Lord; and their prophets shall hear his voice, and shall no longer stay themselves; and they shall ᵇsmite the rocks, and the ice shall flow down at their presence.

27 And an ᵃhighway shall be cast up in the midst of the great deep.

28 Their enemies shall become a prey unto them,

---

18 a Rev. 14:1.
  b D&C 84:2.
  c Rev. 7:4 (1–4).
19 a Matt. 25:6 (1–13);
    D&C 33:17 (17–18);
    88:92.
20 a Isa. 51:5 (3–6); Zech.
    14:4 (4–9); 3 Ne. 20:22;
    21:25 (23–25); D&C
    45:48 (48–53). TG Jesus
    Christ, Second Coming.
21 a Joel 3:16; Amos 1:2.
  b Isa. 2:3 (2–4).
  c D&C 45:49 (48–49).

22 a Ezek. 43:2; Rev. 1:15;
    19:6; D&C 110:3.
  b Ps. 77:18; Rev. 14:2.
  c Judg. 5:5; Isa. 40:4;
    64:1; Rev. 16:20
    (17–21); D&C 49:23;
    88:87; 109:74; Moses
    6:34.
23 a Rev. 6:14 (13–17).
24 a TG Israel, Land of.
  b TG Zion.
  c TG Earth, Destiny of.
  d Gen. 10:25. TG Earth,
    Dividing of; Earth,
    Renewal of.

25 a Isa. 12:6.
  b TG Jesus Christ, King;
    Jesus Christ, Second
    Coming; Millennium.
26 a Jer. 16:15 (14–15);
    D&C 110:11. TG Israel,
    Bondage of, in Other
    Lands; Israel, Ten Lost
    Tribes of.
  b Ex. 17:6 (6–7).
27 a Ex. 14:29; Isa. 11:16
    (15–16); 35:8 (8–10);
    51:11 (9–11); 62:10
    (10–12); 2 Ne. 21:16.
    TG Israel, Gathering of.

29 And in the ^abarren deserts there shall come forth pools of ^bliving water; and the parched ground shall no longer be a thirsty land.

30 And they shall bring forth their rich ^atreasures unto the children of Ephraim, my servants.

31 And the boundaries of the everlasting ^ahills shall tremble at their presence.

32 And there shall they fall down and be ^acrowned with glory, even in Zion, by the hands of the servants of the Lord, even the children of ^bEphraim.

33 And they shall be filled with ^asongs of everlasting joy.

34 Behold, this is the ^ablessing of the ^beverlasting God upon the ^ctribes of ^dIsrael, and the richer blessing upon the head of ^eEphraim and his fellows.

35 And they also of the tribe of ^aJudah, after their pain, shall be ^bsanctified in ^choliness before the Lord, to dwell in his ^dpresence day and night, forever and ever.

36 And now, verily saith the Lord, that these things might be known among you, O inhabitants of the earth, I have sent forth mine ^aangel flying through the midst of heaven, having the everlasting ^bgospel, who hath appeared unto some and hath committed it unto man, who shall appear unto ^cmany that dwell on the earth.

37 And this ^agospel shall be ^bpreached unto ^cevery nation, and kindred, and tongue, and people.

38 And the ^aservants of God shall go forth, saying with a loud voice: Fear God and give glory to him, for the hour of his judgment is come;

39 And ^aworship him that made heaven, and earth, and the sea, and the ^bfountains of waters—

29 a Isa. 35:7 (6–7).
  b TG Living Water.
30 a Isa. 60:9 (8–12).
  TG Treasure.
31 a Gen. 49:26; Hab. 3:6;
    D&C 49:25.
32 a Deut. 33:16 (13–17).
    TG Exaltation.
  b Gen. 48:20 (16–20);
    49:26 (22–26); Zech.
    10:7 (7–12). TG Israel,
    Joseph, People of;
    Mission of Latter-day
    Saints.
33 a Isa. 35:10 (8–10); 51:11;
    Jer. 31:12 (10–14);
    D&C 66:11. TG Sing-
    ing.
34 a TG Israel, Blessings of.

  b Gen. 21:33.
  c TG Israel, Twelve Tribes
    of.
  d TG Israel, Mission of.
  e Gen. 41:52 (50–52);
    48:14 (14–20); 1 Chr.
    5:1 (1–2); Jer. 31:9
    (6–9); Ether 13:7
    (7–10); D&C 113:4.
35 a Hosea 1:7; D&C
    109:64. TG Israel,
    Judah, People of.
  b Gen. 49:11.
  c TG Holiness.
  d TG God, Presence of.
36 a Rev. 14:6 (6–7); D&C
    20:6 (6–12); 133:17.
  b TG Restoration of the
    Gospel.

  c D&C 77:8; 88:103
    (103–4).
37 a Ps. 67:2 (1–2). TG Last
    Days.
  b TG Mission of
    Latter-day Saints;
    Preaching.
  c Gen. 12:3; D&C 42:58
    (58–60); 43:25 (23–
    27); 58:64 (63–64);
    88:84 (84, 87–92);
    90:10; Abr. 2:11 (9–11).
38 a Rev. 14:7. TG Mission-
    ary Work.
39 a Zech. 14:16. TG Wor-
    ship.
  b D&C 133:20 (20, 23).

40 Calling upon the name of the Lord day and night, saying: O that thou wouldst *rend the heavens, that thou wouldst come down, that the mountains might flow down at thy presence.

41 And it shall be answered upon their heads; for the presence of the Lord shall be *as the melting fire that burneth, and as the fire which causeth the waters to boil.

42 O Lord, thou shalt come down to make thy name known to thine adversaries, and all nations shall tremble at thy presence—

43 When thou doest *terrible things, things they look not for;

44 Yea, when thou comest down, and the mountains flow down at thy presence, thou shalt *meet him who rejoiceth and worketh righteousness, who remembereth thee in thy ways.

45 For since the beginning of the world have not men heard nor perceived by the ear, neither hath any eye seen, O God, besides thee, how great things thou hast *prepared for him that *waiteth for thee.

46 And it shall be said: *Who is this that cometh down from God in heaven with dyed *garments; yea, from the regions which are not known, clothed in his glorious apparel, traveling in the greatness of his strength?

47 And he shall say: *I am he who spake in *righteousness, mighty to save.

48 And the Lord shall be *red in his apparel, and his garments like him that treadeth in the wine-vat.

49 And so great shall be the glory of his presence that the *sun shall hide his face in shame, and the moon shall withhold its light, and the stars shall be hurled from their places.

50 And his *voice shall be heard: I have *trodden the wine-press alone, and have brought judgment upon all people; and none were with me;

51 And I have *trampled them in my fury, and I did tread upon them in mine anger, and their blood have I *sprinkled upon my garments, and stained all my raiment; for this was the *day of vengeance which was in my heart.

40 a Isa. 64:1 (1–8); D&C 88:95.
41 a Ex. 24:17; Job 41:31; Jer. 9:7; Hel. 5:23; D&C 130:7; 137:2. TG Earth, Cleansing of.
43 a Deut. 10:21.
44 a 1 Thes. 4:17 (15–18).
45 a Isa. 64:4; 1 Cor. 2:9.
 b Lam. 3:25 (25–26); 1 Ne. 21:23; 2 Ne. 6:7, 13; D&C 98:2.
46 a Isa. 63:1 (1–2).

 b Luke 22:44; Mosiah 3:7; D&C 19:18. TG Jesus Christ, Second Coming.
47 a 2 Ne. 8:12; D&C 136:22.
 b Dan. 9:16.
48 a Gen. 49:11 (11–12); Rev. 19:13 (11–15).
49 a Isa. 13:10 (9–13); 24:23; Joel 2:10; Amos 5:18; D&C 45:42; 88:87.

50 a Joel 2:11; D&C 35:21; 43:18 (17–25).
 b Isa. 63:3 (3–9); Rev. 19:15 (11–15); D&C 76:107; 88:106.
51 a Ps. 110:6 (1–7); 1 Cor. 15:27 (24–28); Heb. 10:13 (12–14).
 b Lev. 8:30; Num. 18:17; Isa. 63:3 (2–4).
 c TG Day of the Lord; Vengeance.

52 And now the year of my ªredeemed is come; and they shall mention the loving kindness of their Lord, and all that he has bestowed upon them according to his ᵇgoodness, and according to his loving kindness, forever and ever.

53 In all their ªafflictions he was afflicted. And the angel of his presence saved them; and in his ᵇlove, and in his pity, he ᶜredeemed them, and bore them, and carried them all the days of old;

54 Yea, and ªEnoch also, and they who were with him; the prophets who were before him; and ᵇNoah also, and they who were before him; and ᶜMoses also, and they who were before him;

55 And from ªMoses to Elijah, and from Elijah to John, who were with Christ in his ᵇresurrection, and the holy apostles, with Abraham, Isaac, and Jacob, shall be in the presence of the Lamb.

56 And the ªgraves of the ᵇsaints shall be ᶜopened; and they shall come forth and stand on the ᵈright hand of the Lamb, when he shall stand upon ᵉMount Zion, and upon the holy city, the New Jerusalem; and they shall ᶠsing the ᵍsong of the ʰLamb, day and night forever and ever.

57 And for this cause, that men might be made ªpartakers of the ᵇglories which were to be revealed, the Lord sent forth the fulness of his ᶜgospel, his everlasting covenant, reasoning in plainness and simplicity—

58 To ªprepare the ᵇweak for those things which are coming on the earth, and for the Lord's errand in the day when the weak shall ᶜconfound the ᵈwise, and the little one become a ᵉstrong ᶠnation, and two shall put their tens of thousands to ᵍflight.

59 And by the weak things of the earth the Lord shall ªthresh the nations by the power of his Spirit.

60 And for this cause these commandments were given; they were

52 a Isa. 63:4.
   b Isa. 63:7.
53 a Isa. 63:9; Lam. 3:33 (1–39).
   b TG Charity; Compassion; God, Love of.
   c TG Jesus Christ, Redeemer.
54 a Gen. 5:23; D&C 38:4; 45:11 (11–12).
   b Gen. 7:23 (1–24); 8:1 (1–22).
   c Ex. 3:8 (1–22).
55 a TG Dispensations.
   b Alma 40:20 (18–21). TG Jesus Christ, Resurrection.
56 a D&C 29:13.
   b TG Saints.

   c D&C 45:45 (45–46); 88:97 (96–97). TG Resurrection.
   d Matt. 25:34 (31–46). TG Exaltation.
   e Isa. 24:23; Heb. 12:22 (22, 24); Rev. 14:1; D&C 76:66; 84:2 (2, 18, 32).
   f Isa. 12:5 (1–6).
   g Rev. 15:3 (3–4); D&C 84:98 (98–102).
   h TG Jesus Christ, Lamb of God.
57 a D&C 93:22. TG Man, Potential to Become like Heavenly Father.
   b TG Celestial Glory; Glory; Telestial Glory;

   Terrestrial Glory.
   c TG Gospel; New and Everlasting Covenant; Restoration of the Gospel.
58 a TG Mission of Latter-day Saints.
   b D&C 35:13; 124:1.
   c Matt. 11:25; 1 Cor. 1:27; Alma 32:23; 37:7 (6–7).
   d Isa. 44:25; 1 Cor. 1:20.
   e Josh. 1:6 (6–9); Isa. 60:22; D&C 52:17; 66:8.
   f TG Kingdom of God, on Earth.
   g Deut. 32:30 (29–30).
59 a Micah 4:13 (11–13).

commanded to be kept from the world in the day that they were given, but now are to *go forth unto *all flesh—

61 And this according to the mind and will of the Lord, who ruleth over all flesh.

62 And unto him that repenteth and *sanctifieth himself before the Lord shall be given eternal life.

63 And upon them that *hearken not to the voice of the Lord shall be fulfilled that which was written by the prophet Moses, that they should be *cut off from among the people.

64 And also that which was written by the prophet *Malachi: For, behold, the *day cometh that shall *burn as an oven, and all the proud, yea, and all that do *wickedly, shall be stubble; and the day that cometh shall burn them up, saith the Lord of hosts, that it shall leave them neither root nor branch.

65 Wherefore, this shall be the answer of the Lord unto them:

66 In that day when I came unto mine own, no man among you *received me, and you were driven out.

67 When I called again there was none of you to answer; yet my *arm was not shortened at all that I could not redeem, neither my *power to deliver.

68 Behold, at my rebuke I *dry up the sea. I make the rivers a wilderness; their fish stink, and die for thirst.

69 I clothe the heavens with blackness, and make sackcloth their covering.

70 And *this shall ye have of my hand—ye shall lie down in sorrow.

71 Behold, and lo, there are none to deliver you; for ye *obeyed not my voice when I called to you out of the heavens; ye *believed not my servants, and when they were *sent unto you ye received them not.

72 Wherefore, they sealed up the testimony and bound up the law, and ye were delivered over unto *darkness.

73 These shall go away into outer darkness, where there is *weeping, and wailing, and gnashing of teeth.

74 Behold the Lord your God hath spoken it. Amen.

60a D&C 104:58.
  b D&C 1:2.
62a 2 Chr. 35:6; D&C
    88:74. TG Sanctifica-
    tion.
63a Deut. 28:15. TG Dis-
    obedience.
  b Acts 3:23; 1 Ne. 22:20
    (20–21); 3 Ne. 20:23;
    21:11; D&C 1:14;
    JS—H 1:40.
64a Mal. 4:1.
  b D&C 5:19; JS—H 1:37.
    TG Last Days.

  c Isa. 24:6; 66:15
    (15–16); Joel 2:5; 1 Ne.
    22:15; 3 Ne. 25:1; D&C
    29:9; 64:24. TG Earth,
    Cleansing of.
  d JS—M 1:4.
66a Matt. 23:38 (37–39);
    John 1:11.
67a 2 Ne. 28:32.
  b Isa. 50:2; Ezek. 37:12
    (11–14); Hosea 13:14.
68a Ex. 14:21 (1–31); Josh.
    3:17 (14–17); 2 Ne. 7:2.
    TG Drought.

70a Isa. 50:11.
71a TG Apostasy of Israel.
  b Luke 16:31. TG Proph-
    ets, Rejection of.
  c 2 Chr. 36:15; Jer. 44:4
    (4–5).
72a Isa. 8:16 (13–16); Matt.
    8:12 (11–12); D&C
    77:8. TG Darkness,
    Spiritual.
73a Luke 13:28; D&C 19:5;
    101:91 (90–91).

SECTION 134

A declaration of belief regarding governments and laws in general, adopted by unanimous vote at a general assembly of the Church held at Kirtland, Ohio, August 17, 1835. Many Saints gathered together to consider the proposed contents of the first edition of the Doctrine and Covenants. At that time, this declaration was given the following preamble: "That our belief with regard to earthly governments and laws in general may not be misinterpreted nor misunderstood, we have thought proper to present, at the close of this volume, our opinion concerning the same."

1–4, Governments should preserve freedom of conscience and worship; 5–8, All men should uphold their governments and owe respect and deference to the law; 9–10, Religious societies should not exercise civil powers; 11–12, Men are justified in defending themselves and their property.

1 We believe that ᵃgovernments were instituted of God for the benefit of man; and that he holds men ᵇaccountable for their acts in relation to them, both in making laws and administering them, for the good and safety of society.

2 We believe that no government can exist in ᵃpeace, except such laws are framed and held inviolate as will secure to each individual the ᵇfree exercise of ᶜconscience, the right and control of property, and the ᵈprotection of life.

3 We believe that all governments necessarily require ᵃcivil ᵇofficers and magistrates to enforce the laws of the same; and that such as will administer the law in equity and justice should be sought for and upheld by the voice of the people if a republic, or the will of the sovereign.

4 We believe that religion is instituted of God; and that men are amenable to him, and to him only, for the exercise of it, unless their religious opinions prompt them to infringe upon the rights and liberties of others; but we do not believe that human law has a right to interfere in prescribing rules of ᵃworship to bind the consciences of men, nor dictate forms for public or private devotion; that the civil magistrate should restrain crime, but never control conscience; should punish ᵇguilt, but never suppress the freedom of the soul.

---

134 1 *a* Jer. 27:6 (4–11); John
  19:11; Rom. 13:1
  (1–4); D&C 98:5
  (4–7); 101:77; A of F
  1:12. TG Citizenship;
  Governments.
 b TG Accountability;

Judgment.
2 *a* TG Peace.
 b TG Agency; Liberty.
 c TG Conscience.
 d Josh. 20:3; D&C 42:18
  (18–19).
3 *a* Ezra 7:25; 2 Pet. 2:13
  (13–17).

 b D&C 98:10 (8–10).
  TG Delegation of
  Responsibility.
4 *a* Matt. 22:21; Alma
  21:22 (21–22); D&C
  63:26; A of F 1:11.
  TG Worship.
 b TG Guilt; Punish.

5 We believe that all men are bound to *sustain and uphold the respective *governments in which they reside, while protected in their inherent and inalienable rights by the laws of such governments; and that sedition and *rebellion are unbecoming every citizen thus protected, and should be punished accordingly; and that all governments have a right to enact such laws as in their own judgments are best calculated to secure the public interest; at the same time, however, holding sacred the freedom of conscience.

6 We believe that every man should be *honored in his station, rulers and magistrates as such, being placed for the protection of the innocent and the punishment of the guilty; and that to the *laws all men owe *respect and deference, as without them peace and harmony would be supplanted by anarchy and terror; human laws being instituted for the express purpose of regulating our interests as individuals and nations, between man and man; and divine laws given of heaven, prescribing rules on spiritual concerns, for faith and worship, both to be answered by man to his Maker.

7 We believe that rulers, states, and governments have a right, and are bound to enact laws for the protection of all *citizens in the free exercise of their religious *belief; but we do not believe that they have a right in justice to deprive citizens of this privilege, or proscribe them in their opinions, so long as a regard and reverence are shown to the laws and such religious opinions do not justify sedition nor conspiracy.

8 We believe that the commission of crime should be *punished according to the nature of the offense; that murder, treason, robbery, theft, and the breach of the general peace, in all respects, should be punished according to their criminality and their tendency to evil among men, by the laws of that government in which the offense is committed; and for the public *peace and tranquility all men should step forward and use their ability in bringing *offenders against good laws to punishment.

9 We do not believe it just to *mingle religious influence with civil government, whereby one religious society is fostered and another proscribed in its spiritual privileges, and the individual rights of its members, as citizens, denied.

10 We believe that all religious societies have a right to deal with their members for disorderly conduct, *according to the rules and regulations

5 a TG Loyalty; Obedience; Order.
  b TG Citizenship; Governments.
  c TG Rebellion.
6 a Rom. 13:7.

  b D&C 58:21; 88:34.
  c TG Respect.
7 a TG Citizenship.
  b Micah 4:5; A of F 1:11.
8 a Alma 1:14 (11–18); D&C 42:84 (84–87).

  b TG Peace.
  c Ex. 18:22 (17–26).
    TG Offense.
9 a Alma 30:7 (7–11).
    TG Governments.
10 a D&C 42:81.

of such societies; provided that such dealings be for fellowship and good standing; but we do not believe that any religious society has *b*authority to try men on the right of property or life, to take from them this world's goods, or to put them in jeopardy of either life or limb, or to inflict any physical punishment upon them. They can only excommunicate them from their society, and withdraw from them their fellowship.

11 We believe that men should appeal to the civil law for redress of all *a*wrongs and grievances, where personal abuse is inflicted or the right of property or character infringed, where such laws exist as will protect the same; but we believe that all men are justified in *b*defending themselves, their friends, and property, and the government, from the unlawful assaults and encroachments of all persons in times of exigency, where immediate appeal cannot be made to the laws, and relief afforded.

12 We believe it just to *a*preach the gospel to the nations of the earth, and warn the righteous to save themselves from the corruption of the world; but we do not believe it right to interfere with *b*bond-servants, neither preach the gospel to, nor baptize them contrary to the will and wish of their masters, nor to meddle with or influence them in the least to cause them to be dissatisfied with their situations in this life, thereby jeopardizing the lives of men; such interference we believe to be unlawful and unjust, and dangerous to the peace of every government allowing human beings to be held in *c*servitude.

SECTION 135

Announcement of the martyrdom of Joseph Smith the Prophet and his brother, Hyrum Smith the Patriarch, at Carthage, Illinois, June 27, 1844. This document was included at the end of the 1844 edition of the Doctrine and Covenants, which was nearly ready for publication when Joseph and Hyrum Smith were murdered.

1–2, Joseph and Hyrum martyred in Carthage Jail; 3, The preeminent position of the Prophet is acclaimed; 4–7, Their innocent blood testifies of the truth and divinity of the work.

1 To seal the testimony of this book and the Book of Mormon, we announce the *a*martyrdom of Joseph Smith the Prophet, and Hyrum Smith

---

10 *b* TG Authority; Excommunication.
11 *a* TG Injustice; Malice; Oppression; Persecution.

b TG Deliver.
12 *a* TG Mission of Latter-day Saints; Warn.
b Philem. 1:10 (10–19). TG Bondage, Physical.

c TG Slavery.
135 1 *a* D&C 5:22; 6:30. TG Martyrdom.

the Patriarch. They were shot in Carthage jail, on the 27th of June, 1844, about five o'clock p.m., by an armed mob—painted black—of from 150 to 200 persons. *b*Hyrum was shot first and fell calmly, exclaiming: *I am a *c*dead man!* Joseph leaped from the window, and was shot dead in the attempt, exclaiming: *d*O Lord my God!* They were both shot after they were dead, in a brutal manner, and both received four balls.

2 John Taylor and Willard Richards, two of the Twelve, were the only persons in the room at the time; the former was wounded in a savage manner with four balls, but has since recovered; the latter, through the providence of God, escaped, without even a hole in his robe.

3 Joseph Smith, the *a*Prophet and *b*Seer of the Lord, has done more, *c*save Jesus only, for the salvation of men in this world, than any other man that ever lived in it. In the short space of twenty years, he has brought forth the Book of Mormon, which he translated by the gift and power of God, and has been the means of publishing it on two continents; has sent the *d*fulness of the everlasting gospel, which it contained, to the four quarters of the earth; has brought forth the revelations and commandments which compose this book of Doctrine and Covenants, and many other wise documents and instructions for the benefit of the children of men; gathered many thousands of the Latter-day Saints, founded a great city, and left a fame and name that cannot be slain. He lived great, and he died great in the eyes of God and his people; and like most of the Lord's anointed in ancient times, has sealed his mission and his works with his own *e*blood; and so has his brother Hyrum. In life they were not divided, and in death they were not *f*separated!

4 When Joseph went to Carthage to deliver himself up to the pretended requirements of the law, two or three days previous to his assassination, he said: "I am going like a *a*lamb to the slaughter; but I am calm as a summer's morning; I have a *b*conscience *c*void of offense towards God, and towards all men. I SHALL DIE INNOCENT, AND IT SHALL YET BE SAID OF ME—HE WAS MURDERED IN COLD BLOOD."—The same morning, after Hyrum had made ready to go—shall it be said to the slaughter? yes, for so it was—he read the following paragraph, near the close of the twelfth chapter of Ether, in the Book of Mormon, and turned down the leaf upon it:

---

1 *b* JS—H 1:4.
　c TG Death; Murder.
　d Ps. 38:21 (21–22);
　　71:12.
3 *a* TG Prophets, Mission
　　of.
　b TG Seer.

　c TG Jesus Christ, Savior;
　　Salvation.
　d D&C 35:17; 42:12.
　　TG Restoration of the
　　Gospel.
　e Mosiah 17:20; D&C
　　136:39. TG Blood,

　　Symbolism of.
　f 2 Sam. 1:23.
4 *a* Isa. 53:7; Jer. 11:19;
　　Mosiah 14:7.
　b TG Conscience.
　c TG Purity.

5 *And it came to pass that I prayed unto the Lord that he would give unto the Gentiles grace, that they might have charity. And it came to pass that the Lord said unto me: If they have not charity it mattereth not unto thee, thou hast been* ^a*faithful; wherefore thy garments shall be made* ^b*clean. And because thou hast seen thy weakness, thou shalt be made strong, even unto the sitting down in the place which I have prepared in the mansions of my Father. And now I . . . bid farewell unto the Gentiles; yea, and also unto my brethren whom I love, until we shall meet before the* ^c*judgment-seat of Christ, where all men shall know that my garments are not spotted with your blood.* The ^dtestators are now dead, and their ^etestament is in force.

6 Hyrum Smith was forty-four years old in February, 1844, and Joseph Smith was thirty-eight in December, 1843; and henceforward their names will be classed among the ^amartyrs of religion; and the reader in every nation will be reminded that the Book of Mormon, and this book of Doctrine and Covenants of the church, cost the best blood of the nineteenth century to bring them forth for the salvation of a ruined world; and that if the fire can scathe a ^bgreen tree for the glory of God, how easy it will burn up the dry trees to purify the vineyard of corruption. They lived for glory; they died for glory; and glory is their eternal ^creward. From age to age shall their names go down to posterity as gems for the sanctified.

7 They were innocent of any crime, as they had often been proved before, and were only confined in jail by the conspiracy of traitors and wicked men; and their *innocent blood* on the floor of Carthage jail is a broad seal affixed to "Mormonism" that cannot be rejected by any court on earth, and their *innocent blood* on the ^aescutcheon of the State of Illinois, with the broken faith of the State as pledged by the governor, is a witness to the truth of the everlasting gospel that all the world cannot impeach; and their *innocent blood* on the banner of liberty, and on the *magna charta* of the United States, is an ambassador for the religion of Jesus Christ, that will touch the hearts of honest men among all nations; and their *innocent blood,* with the innocent blood of all the martyrs under the ^baltar that John saw, will cry unto the Lord of Hosts till he avenges that blood on the earth. Amen.

---

5 a TG Loyalty; Steadfast-
　ness.
　b D&C 88:74 (74–75).
　c Ether 12:36–38.
　d 1 Tim. 2:6; Heb. 9:16

(16–17).
　e Heb. 9:17. TG Testi-
　mony.
6 a TG Martyrdom.
　b Luke 23:31.

c TG Reward.
7 a IE coat of arms.
　b Rev. 6:9.

SECTION 136

The word and will of the Lord, given through President Brigham Young at Winter Quarters, the camp of Israel, Omaha Nation, on the west bank of the Missouri River, near Council Bluffs, Iowa.

1–16, How the camp of Israel is to be organized for the westward journey is explained; 17–27, The Saints are commanded to live by numerous gospel standards; 28–33, The Saints should sing, dance, pray, and learn wisdom; 34–42, Prophets are slain so that they might be honored and the wicked condemned.

1 The Word and *ª*Will of the Lord concerning the Camp of *ᵇ*Israel in their journeyings to the West:

2 Let all the people of *ª*The Church of Jesus Christ of Latter-day Saints, and those who journey with them, be organized into companies, with a covenant and promise to *ᵇ*keep all the commandments and statutes of the Lord our God.

3 Let the companies be organized with captains of *ª*hundreds, captains of fifties, and captains of tens, with a president and his two counselors at their head, under the direction of the Twelve *ᵇ*Apostles.

4 And this shall be our *ª*covenant—that we will *ᵇ*walk in all the *ᶜ*ordinances of the Lord.

5 Let each company provide themselves with all the teams, wagons, provisions, clothing, and other necessaries for the journey, that they can.

6 When the companies are organized let them go to with their *ª*might, to prepare for those who are to tarry.

7 Let each company, with their captains and presidents, decide how many can go next spring; then choose out a sufficient number of able-bodied and expert men, to take teams, seeds, and farming utensils, to go as pioneers to prepare for putting in spring crops.

8 Let each company *ª*bear an equal proportion, according to the dividend of their property, in taking the poor, the *ᵇ*widows, the *ᶜ*fatherless, and the families of those who have gone into the army, that the cries of the widow and the *ᵈ*fatherless come not up into the ears of the Lord against this people.

9 Let each company prepare houses, and fields for raising *ª*grain, for those

---

136 1 *a* TG God, Will of.
   b D&C 133:32 (32–35);
     A of F 1:10.
  2 *a* D&C 20:1 (1–4); 115:4.
   b D&C 41:5 (5–6); 56:2
     (2–3).

3 *a* Ex. 18:21 (21–27).
   b TG Apostles.
4 *a* TG Covenants.
   b TG Walking with God.
   c TG Ordinance.
6 *a* Judg. 6:14.
8 *a* D&C 38:24 (24–27).

   b TG Poor; Widows.
   c Ps. 68:5; 146:9 (1–10);
     James 1:27 (25–27).
   d 3 Ne. 24:5.
9 *a* TG Bread; Self-
     Sacrifice.

who are to remain behind this season; and this is the will of the Lord concerning his people.

10 Let every man use all his influence and property to remove this people to the place where the Lord shall locate a ^astake of Zion.

11 And if ye do this with a pure heart, in all faithfulness, ye shall be blessed; you shall be ^ablessed in your flocks, and in your herds, and in your fields, and in your houses, and in your families.

12 Let my servants Ezra T. Benson and Erastus Snow organize a company.

13 And let my servants Orson Pratt and Wilford Woodruff organize a company.

14 Also, let my servants Amasa Lyman and George A. Smith organize a company.

15 And appoint presidents, and ^acaptains of hundreds, and of fifties, and of tens.

16 And let my servants that have been appointed go and ^ateach this, my will, to the saints, that they may be ready to go to a land of peace.

17 Go thy way and do as I have told you, and ^afear not thine enemies; for they shall not have power to stop my work.

18 Zion shall be ^aredeemed in mine own due time.

19 And if any man shall seek to build up himself, and seeketh not my ^acounsel, he shall have no power, and his ^bfolly shall be made manifest.

20 ^aSeek ye; and keep all your ^bpledges one with another; and ^ccovet not that which is thy brother's.

21 ^aKeep yourselves from evil to take the name of the Lord in vain, for I am the Lord your God, even the ^bGod of your fathers, the God of Abraham and of Isaac and of Jacob.

22 I am he who ^aled the children of Israel out of the land of Egypt; and my arm is stretched out in the last days, to ^bsave my people Israel.

23 Cease to ^acontend one with another; cease to speak ^bevil one of another.

---

10 a TG Stake; Zion.
11 a Gen. 26:12; Deut. 28:4 (1–14); Alma 34:20 (17–27). TG Blessing.
15 a Deut. 1:15.
16 a TG Teaching.
17 a TG Courage; Enemies; Fearful.
18 a D&C 100:13.
19 a TG Counsel; Problem-Solving.
  b TG Foolishness.

20 a IE Seek the Lord's counsel; see v. 19.
  b TG Honesty; Promise; Vow.
  c TG Covet.
21 a TG Profanity; Self-Mastery.
  b Ex. 3:6; Matt. 22:32; 1 Ne. 19:10.
22 a Gen. 15:14 (13–14); Ex. 13:18 (18, 20); Amos 3:1 (1–2); 1 Ne. 5:15;

D&C 103:18.
  b Isa. 9:12; Jer. 30:10; 32:17; Ezek. 20:34 (33–34); Hosea 13:9; D&C 38:33.
23 a Prov. 17:14; 2 Tim. 2:24; 3 Ne. 11:29 (29–30). TG Contention; Disputations; Strife.
  b D&C 20:54. TG Backbiting.

24 Cease *a*drunkenness; and let your words tend to *b*edifying one another.

25 If thou *a*borrowest of thy *b*neighbor, thou shalt *c*restore that which thou hast borrowed; and if thou canst not repay then go straightway and tell thy neighbor, lest he condemn thee.

26 If thou shalt find that which thy neighbor has *a*lost, thou shalt make diligent search till thou shalt *b*deliver it to him again.

27 Thou shalt be *a*diligent in *b*preserving what thou hast, that thou mayest be a wise *c*steward; for it is the free gift of the Lord thy God, and thou art his steward.

28 If thou art *a*merry, *b*praise the Lord with singing, with music, with *c*dancing, and with a *d*prayer of praise and *e*thanksgiving.

29 If thou art *a*sorrowful, call on the Lord thy God with supplication, that your souls may be *b*joyful.

30 Fear not thine *a*enemies, for they are in mine hands and I will do my pleasure with them.

31 My people must be *a*tried in all things, that they may be prepared to receive the *b*glory that I have for them, even the glory of Zion; and he that will not *c*bear chastisement is not worthy of my kingdom.

32 Let him that is *a*ignorant *b*learn *c*wisdom by *d*humbling himself and calling upon the Lord his God, that his *e*eyes may be opened that he may see, and his ears opened that he may hear;

33 For my *a*Spirit is sent forth into the world to enlighten the *b*humble and contrite, and to the *c*condemnation of the ungodly.

34 Thy brethren have rejected you and your testimony, even the nation that has *a*driven you out;

35 And now cometh the day of their calamity, even the days of sorrow,

---

24 a TG Drunkenness; Word of Wisdom.
  b 1 Pet. 1:15. TG Edification.
25 a TG Borrow; Debt; Honesty.
  b TG Neighbor.
  c Ps. 37:21; Mosiah 4:28.
26 a Lev. 6:4; Deut. 22:3.
  b TG Honesty.
27 a TG Diligence.
  b Prov. 21:20.
  c TG Stewardship.
28 a TG Happiness.
  b Ps. 33:1; 147:7; Isa. 12:4; Eph. 5:19 (19–20); 1 Ne. 18:16; Mosiah 2:20 (20–21);

Alma 26:8; D&C 25:11 (11–12); 109:79. TG Communication; Singing.
  c 2 Sam. 6:14.
  d TG Prayer.
  e 2 Chr. 5:13; D&C 97:13. TG Thanksgiving.
29 a 2 Sam. 22:7. TG Sorrow.
  b TG Joy.
30 a Deut. 30:7. TG Enemies.
31 a Gen. 22:1 (1–19); D&C 101:4. TG Adversity; Millennium, Preparing a People for; Test.
  b Rom. 8:18; D&C 58:4;

63:66. TG Celestial Glory.
  c Lam. 3:27 (24–27). TG Chastening.
32 a TG Ignorance.
  b TG Education; Learn.
  c TG Wisdom.
  d TG Humility; Teachable.
  e Gen. 3:5 (3–6); Mosiah 27:22; D&C 88:11 (11–13); 110:1.
33 a TG God, Spirit of.
  b TG Contrite Heart; Meek.
  c TG Chastening.
34 a TG Persecution.

like a woman that is taken in travail; and their ^asorrow shall be great unless they speedily repent, yea, very speedily.

36 For they ^akilled the prophets, and them that were sent unto them; and they have ^bshed innocent blood, which crieth from the ground against them.

37 Therefore, marvel not at these things, for ye are not yet ^apure; ye can not yet bear my glory; but ye shall behold it if ye are faithful in keeping all my words that I have ^bgiven you, from the days of Adam to Abraham, from Abraham to Moses, from Moses to Jesus and his apostles, and from Jesus and his apostles to Joseph Smith, whom I did call upon by mine ^cangels, my ministering servants, and by mine own voice out of the heavens, to bring forth my work;

38 Which ^afoundation he did lay, and was faithful; and I took him to myself.

39 Many have marveled because of his death; but it was needful that he should ^aseal his ^btestimony with his ^cblood, that he might be ^dhonored and the wicked might be condemned.

40 Have I not delivered you from your ^aenemies, only in that I have left a witness of my name?

41 Now, therefore, hearken, O ye people of my ^achurch; and ye elders listen together; you have received my ^bkingdom.

42 Be ^adiligent in keeping all my commandments, lest judgments come upon you, and your faith fail you, and your enemies triumph over you. So no more at present. Amen and Amen.

SECTION 137

A vision given to Joseph Smith the Prophet, in the temple at Kirtland, Ohio, January 21, 1836. The occasion was the administration of ordinances in preparation for the dedication of the temple.

1–6, The Prophet sees his brother Alvin in the celestial kingdom; 7–9, The doctrine of salvation for the dead is revealed; 10, All children are saved in the celestial kingdom.

---

35 a TG Punish; Sorrow.
36 a Zech. 1:4 (2–5).
  TG Prophets, Rejection of.
  b Rev. 19:2; Morm. 8:41 (40–41).
37 a TG Purity.
  b Hel. 8:18 (16–19).
  c Rev. 14:6; D&C 27:16;

110:11–16; 128:20 (19–21); 133:36; JS—H 1:30–47.
38 a D&C 135:3.
39 a Rev. 2:10; Mosiah 17:20; D&C 98:14; 135:3.
  b TG Testimony.
  c TG Martyrdom.

d TG Honor; Justice.
40 a Ex. 23:22 (20–23); D&C 8:4; 105:15.
41 a TG Jesus Christ, Head of the Church.
  b Dan. 7:27.
42 a TG Steadfastness.

1 The *heavens were *opened upon us, and I beheld the *celestial kingdom of God, and the glory thereof, whether in the *body or out I cannot tell.

2 I saw the transcendent *beauty of the *gate through which the heirs of that kingdom will enter, which was *like unto *circling flames of fire;

3 Also the *blazing *throne of God, whereon was seated the *Father and the *Son.

4 I saw the beautiful streets of that kingdom, which had the appearance of being paved with *gold.

5 I saw Father *Adam and *Abraham; and my *father and my mother; my brother *Alvin, that has long since *slept;

6 And *marveled how it was that he had obtained an *inheritance in that kingdom, seeing that he had departed this life before the Lord had set his hand to *gather Israel the second time, and had not been *baptized for the remission of sins.

7 Thus came the *voice of the Lord unto me, saying: All who have died *without a knowledge of this gospel, who would have received it if they had been permitted to tarry, shall be *heirs of the celestial kingdom of God;

8 Also all that shall die henceforth without a knowledge of it, who *would have received it with all their hearts, shall be heirs of that kingdom;

9 For I, the Lord, will *judge all men according to their *works, according to the *desire of their hearts.

10 And I also beheld that all *children who die before they arrive at the *years of accountability are *saved in the celestial kingdom of heaven.

---

137 1 a Acts 7:56 (55–56);
　　　1 Ne. 1:8; Hel. 5:48
　　　(45–49). TG Heaven.
　　 b JS—H 1:43.
　　 c TG Celestial Glory;
　　　Kingdom of God, in
　　　Heaven.
　　 d 2 Cor. 12:2 (2–4);
　　　Rev. 21:10; 1 Ne. 11:1;
　　　Moses 1:11.
　　2 a Rev. 21:19 (10–27);
　　　D&C 76:70. TG Beauty.
　　 b 2 Ne. 9:41.
　　 c Ex. 24:17; Isa. 33:14
　　　(14–15); Hel. 5:23;
　　　D&C 130:7; 133:41.
　　 d Ezek. 1:4 (4–25).
　　3 a Ezek. 1:27 (26–27);
　　　Dan. 7:9.
　　 b Isa. 6:1; Ezek. 1:26
　　　(26–28); D&C 76:108
　　　(106–8).
　　 c TG Godhead; God the

Father, Elohim.
　 d Acts 7:55 (55–56).
　4 a Rev. 21:21 (10–27);
　　　D&C 110:2.
　5 a TG Adam.
　 b D&C 132:29; Abr. 2:11
　　　(9–11).
　 c D&C 124:19. TG Fam-
　　　ily, Eternal.
　 d JS—H 1:4.
　 e 1 Cor. 15:20.
　6 a D&C 138:25.
　 b TG Salvation for the
　　　Dead.
　 c Isa. 11:11; 1 Ne. 22:12
　　　(10–12); Jacob 6:2.
　　　TG Israel, Gathering of;
　　　Israel, Restoration of.
　 d Luke 24:47; John 3:5
　　　(3–5); 2 Ne. 9:23; Ether
　　　4:18 (18–19); D&C
　　　76:52 (50–52); 84:74.
　　　TG Baptism, Essential.

7 a Hel. 5:30. TG Revela-
　　　tion.
　 b 1 Pet. 4:6; 2 Ne. 9:26
　　　(25–26); Mosiah 15:24;
　　　D&C 29:50.
　 c Heb. 9:15 (14–15);
　　　D&C 76:70 (50–70).
　　　TG Exaltation; Salva-
　　　tion for the Dead.
　8 a Alma 18:32; D&C 6:16.
　9 a Rev. 20:12 (12–14).
　　　TG God, Justice of;
　　　Judgment, the Last.
　 b TG Good Works;
　　　Justice.
　 c D&C 64:22 (22, 34).
　　　TG Agency; Motiva-
　　　tions.
　10 a TG Children.
　 b D&C 68:27 (25–27).
　 c TG Salvation of Little
　　　Children.

SECTION 138

A vision given to President Joseph F. Smith in Salt Lake City, Utah, on October 3, 1918. In his opening address at the 89th Semiannual General Conference of the Church, on October 4, 1918, President Smith declared that he had received several divine communications during the previous months. One of these, concerning the Savior's visit to the spirits of the dead while His body was in the tomb, President Smith had received the previous day. It was written immediately following the close of the conference. On October 31, 1918, it was submitted to the counselors in the First Presidency, the Council of the Twelve, and the Patriarch, and it was unanimously accepted by them.

1–10, President Joseph F. Smith ponders upon the writings of Peter and our Lord's visit to the spirit world; 11–24, President Smith sees the righteous dead assembled in paradise and Christ's ministry among them; 25–37, He sees how the preaching of the gospel was organized among the spirits; 38–52, He sees Adam, Eve, and many of the holy prophets in the spirit world who considered their spirit state before their resurrection as a bondage; 53–60, The righteous dead of this day continue their labors in the world of spirits.

1 On the third of October, in the year nineteen hundred and eighteen, I sat in my room *a*pondering over the scriptures;

2 And *a*reflecting upon the great *b*atoning *c*sacrifice that was made by the Son of God, for the *d*redemption of the world;

3 And the great and wonderful *a*love made manifest by the Father and the Son in the coming of the *b*Redeemer into the world;

4 That through his *a*atonement, and by *b*obedience to the principles of the gospel, mankind might be saved.

5 While I was thus engaged, my mind reverted to the writings of the apostle Peter, to the *a*primitive saints scattered abroad throughout *b*Pontus, Galatia, Cappadocia, and other parts of Asia, where the gospel had been *c*preached after the crucifixion of the Lord.

6 I opened the Bible and read the *a*third and fourth chapters of the first epistle of Peter, and as I read I was greatly *b*impressed, more than I had ever been before, with the following passages:

---

138 1 *a* TG Meditation; Scriptures, Study of.
  2 *a* JS—H 1:12.
    b Matt. 20:28. TG Jesus Christ, Atonement through.
    c TG Sacrifice.
    d TG Redemption.

3 *a* John 3:16 (14–17). TG God, Love of.
    b Isa. 63:9 (1–9). TG Jesus Christ, Redeemer.
  4 *a* 2 Ne. 25:23; A of F 1:3.
    b Matt. 7:21 (21–27). TG Obedience.
  5 *a* IE former-day saints.
    b 1 Pet. 1:1.

c Acts 16:6 (6–9); 19:26 (10–26).
  6 *a* See 1 Pet. 3:18–20 and 4:6 in the New Testament for additional notes and cross-references.
    b JS—H 1:12 (11–13).

7 "For Christ also hath once suffered for sins, the just for the unjust, that he might bring us to God, being put to death in the flesh, but quickened by the Spirit:

8 "By which also he went and preached unto the spirits in *prison;

9 "Which sometime were disobedient, when once the longsuffering of God waited in the days of Noah, while the ark was a preparing, wherein few, that is, eight souls were saved by water." (1 Peter 3:18–20.)

10 "For for this cause was the gospel preached also to them that are dead, that they might be judged according to men in the flesh, but live according to God in the spirit." (1 Peter 4:6.)

11 As I *pondered over these things which are *written, the *eyes of my *understanding were opened, and the Spirit of the Lord *rested upon me, and I saw the hosts of the *dead, both small and great.

12 And there were gathered together in one place an innumerable company of the spirits of the *just, who had been *faithful in the *testimony of Jesus while they lived in mortality;

13 And who had offered *sacrifice in the *similitude of the great sacrifice of the Son of God, and had suffered *tribulation in their Redeemer's *name.

14 All these had departed the mortal life, firm in the *hope of a glorious *resurrection, through the *grace of God the *Father and his *Only Begotten Son, Jesus Christ.

15 I beheld that they were filled with *joy and gladness, and were rejoicing together because the day of their *deliverance was at hand.

16 They were assembled awaiting the advent of the Son of God into the *spirit world, to declare their *redemption from the *bands of death.

17 Their sleeping *dust was to be *restored unto its *perfect frame, *bone to his bone, and the sinews and the flesh upon them, the *spirit and the body to be united never again to be divided, that they might receive a fulness of *joy.

8 a Isa. 61:1 (1–2); Luke
    4:18 (18–21); D&C
    76:73 (73–74); 88:99.
11 a D&C 76:19.
    b TG Scriptures, Value of.
    c Luke 24:31; Eph. 1:18;
    D&C 76:12 (10, 12,
    19); 110:1.
    d TG Understanding.
    e Num. 11:25; Isa. 11:2.
    f TG Spirits, Disembod-
    ied.
12 a Ezek. 18:9 (5–9); D&C
    76:69 (69–70).
    b D&C 6:13; 51:19; 76:52
    (51–53).
    c TG Testimony.

13 a TG Sacrifice.
    b TG Jesus Christ, Types
    of, in Anticipation;
    Jesus Christ, Types of,
    in Memory.
    c TG Persecution; Tribu-
    lation.
    d Matt. 5:11 (10–12).
14 a 1 Cor. 15:19 (18–21);
    Ether 12:4; Moro. 7:41
    (3, 40–48).
    b TG Resurrection.
    c TG Grace.
    d TG God the Father,
    Elohim.
    e TG Jesus Christ, Mis-
    sion of.

15 a Isa. 51:11; Alma 40:12
    (11–13).
    b TG Salvation.
16 a Luke 23:43; Alma
    40:20 (20–21). TG Par-
    adise.
    b TG Redemption.
    c Alma 36:18; Morm.
    9:13.
17 a Job 34:15.
    b 2 Ne. 9:13 (10–13);
    Alma 41:4 (3–5).
    c TG Perfection.
    d Ezek. 37:7 (1–14).
    e D&C 93:33 (33–34).
    f TG Joy.

18 While this vast multitude waited and conversed, rejoicing in the hour of their *deliverance from the chains of death, the Son of God appeared, declaring *liberty to the *captives who had been faithful;

19 And there he *preached to them the everlasting *gospel, the doctrine of the *resurrection and the redemption of mankind from the *fall, and from individual sins on conditions of *repentance.

20 But unto the *wicked he did not go, and among the ungodly and the unrepentant who had *defiled themselves while in the flesh, his voice was not raised;

21 Neither did the *rebellious who rejected the *testimonies and the warnings of the ancient *prophets behold his *presence, nor look upon his face.

22 Where these were, *darkness reigned, but among the righteous there was *peace;

23 And the saints rejoiced in their *redemption, and bowed the *knee and acknowledged the Son of God as their Redeemer and Deliverer from death and the *chains of *hell.

24 Their countenances *shone, and the *radiance from the presence of the Lord rested upon them, and they *sang praises unto his holy name.

25 I marveled, for I understood that the Savior spent about three years in his *ministry among the Jews and those of the house of Israel, endeavoring to *teach them the everlasting gospel and call them unto repentance;

26 And yet, notwithstanding his mighty works, and miracles, and proclamation of the truth, in great *power and authority, there were but *few who hearkened to his voice, and rejoiced in his presence, and received salvation at his hands.

27 But his ministry among those who were dead was limited to the *brief time intervening between the crucifixion and his resurrection;

28 And I wondered at the words of Peter—wherein he said that the Son of God preached unto the *spirits in prison, who sometime were disobedient,

18 a 2 Ne. 9:12.
  b TG Jesus Christ, Redeemer; Salvation for the Dead.
  c Isa. 61:1.
19 a D&C 76:73 (72–74). TG Preaching.
  b TG Gospel.
  c 2 Ne. 9:13 (4–22).
  d TG Fall of Man.
  e TG Repent.
20 a Alma 40:14 (13–14). TG Spirits in Prison; Wickedness.
  b 1 Ne. 10:21; D&C 138:37; Moses 6:57.

21 a Matt. 23:37. TG Rebellion.
  b D&C 76:82.
  c TG Prophets, Rejection of.
  d Moses 6:57.
22 a TG Darkness, Spiritual.
  b TG Peace of God.
23 a Heb. 9:12 (11–15). TG Joy; Redemption.
  b Rom. 14:11; Mosiah 27:31.
  c Alma 5:7.
  d TG Hell.
24 a Ex. 34:30 (29–30, 35); Hel. 5:36 (23–48);

JS—H 1:32 (31–32). TG Light [noun].
  b Ps. 104:2; Isa. 60:19; Rev. 22:5; JS—H 1:17.
  c 2 Chr. 29:30. TG Singing; Worship.
25 a TG Jesus Christ, Mission of.
  b TG Teaching.
26 a 1 Ne. 11:28 (28, 31).
  b Matt. 7:14 (13–14); 1 Ne. 11:31 (28–32); 14:12.
27 a Mark 8:31.
28 a TG Spirits in Prison.

when once the long-suffering of God waited in the days of Noah—and how it was possible for him to preach to those spirits and perform the necessary labor among them in so short a time.

29 And as I wondered, my eyes were opened, and my understanding *quickened, and I perceived that the Lord went not in person among the *wicked and the disobedient who had rejected the truth, to teach them;

30 But behold, from among the righteous, he *organized his forces and appointed *messengers, *clothed with power and authority, and *commissioned them to go forth and carry the light of the gospel to them that were in *darkness, even to *all the spirits of men; and thus was the gospel preached to the dead.

31 And the chosen messengers went forth to declare the *acceptable day of the Lord and proclaim *liberty to the captives who were bound, even unto all who would *repent of their sins and receive the gospel.

32 Thus was the gospel preached to those who had *died in their sins, without a *knowledge of the truth, or in *transgression, having *rejected the prophets.

33 These were taught *faith in God, repentance from sin, *vicarious baptism for the *remission of sins, the *gift of the Holy Ghost by the laying on of hands,

34 And all other principles of the gospel that were necessary for them to know in order to qualify themselves that they might be *judged according to men in the flesh, but live according to God in the spirit.

35 And so it was made known among the dead, both small and great, the unrighteous as well as the faithful, that redemption had been wrought through the *sacrifice of the Son of God upon the *cross.

36 Thus was it made known that our Redeemer spent his time during his sojourn in the world of *spirits, instructing and preparing the faithful spirits of the *prophets who had testified of him in the flesh;

---

29 a D&C 76:12.
   b D&C 138:20.
30 a TG Kingdom of God, in Heaven.
   b TG Missionary Work.
   c Luke 24:49. TG Delegation of Responsibility; Priesthood, Authority; Priesthood, Power of.
   d D&C 20:73.
   e TG Darkness, Spiritual.
   f D&C 1:2 (2, 11).

31 a Isa. 61:2; Luke 4:19.
   b TG Liberty.
   c TG Repent; Teachable.
32 a John 8:24 (21–24).
   b D&C 128:5. TG Knowledge.
   c TG Transgress.
   d D&C 76:74 (73–74).
33 a A of F 1:4. TG Faith.
   b D&C 124:33 (28–39). TG Baptism, Essential; Baptism for the Dead.

   c TG Remission of Sins.
   d TG Holy Ghost, Gift of.
34 a 1 Pet. 4:6. TG Judgment, the Last; Justice.
35 a Alma 34:14 (9–16). TG Jesus Christ, Atonement through; Sacrifice.
   b TG Jesus Christ, Crucifixion of.
36 a TG Paradise.
   b TG Prophets, Mission of.

37 That they might carry the message of redemption unto all the dead, unto whom he could not go personally, because of their ^arebellion and transgression, that they through the ministration of his servants might also hear his words.

38 Among the great and ^amighty ones who were assembled in this vast congregation of the righteous were Father ^bAdam, the ^cAncient of Days and father of all,

39 And our glorious ^aMother ^bEve, with many of her faithful ^cdaughters who had lived through the ages and worshiped the true and living God.

40 ^aAbel, the first ^bmartyr, was there, and his brother ^cSeth, one of the mighty ones, who was in the express ^dimage of his father, Adam.

41 ^aNoah, who gave warning of the flood; ^bShem, the great ^chigh priest; ^dAbraham, the father of the faithful; ^eIsaac, ^fJacob, and Moses, the great ^glaw-giver of Israel;

42 And ^aIsaiah, who declared by prophecy that the Redeemer was anointed to bind up the broken-hearted, to proclaim liberty to the ^bcaptives, and the opening of the ^cprison to them that were bound, were also there.

43 Moreover, Ezekiel, who was shown in vision the great valley of ^adry bones, which were to be ^bclothed upon with flesh, to come forth again in the resurrection of the dead, living souls;

44 Daniel, who foresaw and foretold the establishment of the ^akingdom of God in the latter days, never again to be destroyed nor given to other people;

45 ^aElias, who was with Moses on the Mount of Transfiguration;

46 And ^aMalachi, the prophet who testified of the coming of ^bElijah—of whom also Moroni spake to the Prophet Joseph Smith, declaring that he should come before the ushering in of the great and dreadful ^cday of the Lord—were also there.

---

37 a 1 Ne. 10:21; D&C 138:20; Moses 6:57.
38 a Abr. 3:22 (22–26).
  b Moses 1:34. TG Adam.
  c Dan. 7:9 (9–14); 2 Ne. 2:20; D&C 27:11.
39 a Moses 4:26.
  b Gen. 3:20; Moses 5:12 (4, 11–12).
  c Moses 5:2 (2–3). TG Sons and Daughters of God; Woman.
40 a Gen. 4:2 (1–8); Moses 5:17 (17–32).
  b TG Martyrdom.
c Gen. 4:25 (25–26); Moses 6:3 (2–13).
  d Gen. 5:3; Moses 6:10.
41 a Gen. 6:8 (1–22); Moses 8:13 (8–30).
  b Gen. 5:32.
  c TG High Priest, Melchizedek Priesthood; Priesthood, Melchizedek.
  d Gen. 17:5 (1–27).
  e Gen. 21:3 (1–8).
  f Gen. 35:10 (1–29).
  g TG Law of Moses.
42 a Isa. 1:1.
b Isa. 61:1 (1–2).
  c TG Spirits in Prison.
43 a Ezek. 1:3; 37:1 (1–14).
  b TG Resurrection.
44 a Dan. 2:44 (44–45). TG Kingdom of God, on Earth.
45 a BD Elias.
46 a Mal. 4:5 (5–6); JS—H 1:38 (36–39).
  b 1 Kgs. 17:1 (1–24); D&C 110:13 (13–15).
  c TG Day of the Lord.

47 The Prophet Elijah was to plant in the *hearts of the children the promises made to their fathers,

48 Foreshadowing the great work to be done in the *temples of the Lord in the *dispensation of the fulness of times, for the redemption of the dead, and the *sealing of the children to their parents, lest the whole earth be smitten with a curse and utterly wasted at his coming.

49 All these and many more, even the *prophets who dwelt among the Nephites and *testified of the coming of the Son of God, mingled in the vast assembly and waited for their deliverance,

50 For the *dead had looked upon the long absence of their *spirits from their bodies as a *bondage.

51 These the Lord taught, and gave them *power to come forth, after his resurrection from the dead, to enter into his Father's kingdom, there to be crowned with *immortality and eternal life,

52 And continue thenceforth their labor as had been promised by the Lord, and be partakers of all *blessings which were held in reserve for them that love him.

53 The Prophet Joseph Smith, and my father, Hyrum Smith, Brigham Young, John Taylor, Wilford Woodruff, and other choice *spirits who were *reserved to come forth in the *fulness of times to take part in laying the *foundations of the great latter-day work,

54 Including the building of the *temples and the performance of ordinances therein for the redemption of the *dead, were also in the spirit world.

55 I observed that they were also among the *noble and great ones who were *chosen in the beginning to be rulers in the Church of God.

56 Even before they were born, they, with many others, received their first *lessons in the world of spirits and were *prepared to come forth in the due *time of the Lord to labor in his *vineyard for the salvation of the souls of men.

---

47 *a* Mal. 4:6 (5–6); D&C 128:17; JS—H 1:39 (36–39).
48 *a* TG Genealogy and Temple Work; Salvation for the Dead.
  b TG Dispensations.
  c TG Family, Eternal; Sealing.
49 *a* TG Jesus Christ, Prophecies about.
  b Hel. 8:22 (19–22).
50 *a* Luke 1:79.

  b TG Spirits, Disembodied.
  c D&C 45:17.
51 *a* Rom. 8:11; 1 Cor. 6:14; Alma 40:20 (19–21).
  b D&C 29:43. TG Eternal Life.
52 *a* Deut. 7:13 (6–14); Isa. 64:4; 1 Cor. 2:9. TG Blessing.
53 *a* TG Man, Antemortal Existence of.
  b TG Foreordination.

  c D&C 128:18.
  d D&C 64:33.
54 *a* TG Temple.
  b TG Salvation for the Dead.
55 *a* Abr. 3:22 (22–24).
  b TG Foreordination.
56 *a* TG Earth, Purpose of; Learn.
  b Job 38:7 (1–7); Alma 13:3 (3–7).
  c Acts 17:26.
  d Jacob 6:2 (2–3).

57 I beheld that the faithful *a*elders of this dispensation, when they depart from mortal life, continue their labors in the *b*preaching of the *c*gospel of repentance and redemption, through the sacrifice of the Only Begotten Son of God, among those who are in darkness and under the bondage of sin in the great world of the *d*spirits of the dead.

58 The dead who *a*repent will be redeemed, through obedience to the *b*ordinances of the house of God,

59 And after they have paid the *a*penalty of their transgressions, and are *b*washed clean, shall receive a *c*reward according to their *d*works, for they are heirs of salvation.

60 Thus was the *a*vision of the redemption of the dead revealed to me, and I bear record, and I know that this *b*record is *c*true, through the blessing of our Lord and Savior, Jesus Christ, even so. Amen.

---

57 *a* TG Elder, Melchizedek
  Priesthood; Missionary
  Work.
  b TG Mission of Latter-
  day Saints.
  c TG Gospel.
  d TG Spirits in Prison.

58 *a* TG Redemption;
  Repent.
  b Matt. 16:19. TG Covenants; Ordinance.
59 *a* TG Punish.
  b Alma 5:21 (17–22).
  TG Forgive.

  c TG Justice; Reward.
  d TG Good Works.
60 *a* Rev. 20:12.
  b TG Testimony.
  c John 21:24. TG True.

OFFICIAL DECLARATION 1

The Bible and the Book of Mormon teach that monogamy is God's standard for marriage unless He declares otherwise (see 2 Samuel 12:7–8 and Jacob 2:27, 30). Following a revelation to Joseph Smith, the practice of plural marriage was instituted among Church members in the early 1840s (see section 132). From the 1860s to the 1880s, the United States government passed laws to make this religious practice illegal. These laws were eventually upheld by the U.S. Supreme Court. After receiving revelation, President Wilford Woodruff issued the following Manifesto, which was accepted by the Church as authoritative and binding on October 6, 1890. This led to the end of the practice of plural marriage in the Church.

To Whom It May Concern:

Press dispatches having been sent for political purposes, from Salt Lake City, which have been widely published, to the effect that the Utah Commission, in their recent report to the Secretary of the Interior, allege that plural marriages are still being solemnized and that forty or more such marriages have been contracted in Utah since last June or during the past year, also that in public discourses the leaders of the Church have taught, encouraged and urged the continuance of the practice of polygamy—

I, therefore, as President of The Church of Jesus Christ of Latter-day Saints, do hereby, in the most solemn manner, declare that these charges are false. We are not teaching polygamy or plural marriage, nor permitting any person to enter into its practice, and I deny that either forty or any other number of plural marriages have during that period been solemnized in our Temples or in any other place in the Territory.

One case has been reported, in which the parties allege that the marriage was performed in the Endowment House, in Salt Lake City, in the Spring of 1889, but I have not been able to learn who performed the ceremony; whatever was done in this matter was without my knowledge. In consequence of this alleged occurrence the Endowment House was, by my instructions, taken down without delay.

Inasmuch as laws have been enacted by Congress forbidding plural marriages, which laws have been pronounced constitutional by the court of last resort, I hereby declare my intention to submit to those laws, and to use my influence with the members of the Church over which I preside to have them do likewise.

There is nothing in my teachings to the Church or in those of my associates, during the time specified, which can be reasonably construed to inculcate or encourage polygamy; and when any Elder of the Church has used language which appeared to convey any such teaching, he has been promptly reproved. And I now publicly declare that my advice to the Latter-day Saints is to refrain from contracting any marriage forbidden by the law of the land.

Wilford Woodruff
President of The Church of Jesus Christ
of Latter-day Saints.

President Lorenzo Snow offered the following:

"I move that, recognizing Wilford Woodruff as the President of The Church of Jesus Christ of Latter-day Saints, and the only man on the earth at the present time who holds the keys of the sealing ordinances, we consider him fully authorized by virtue of his position to issue the Manifesto which has been read in our hearing, and which is dated September 24th, 1890, and that as a Church in General Conference assembled, we accept his declaration concerning plural marriages as authoritative and binding."

Salt Lake City, Utah, October 6, 1890.

EXCERPTS FROM THREE ADDRESSES BY PRESIDENT WILFORD WOODRUFF REGARDING THE MANIFESTO

The Lord will never permit me or any other man who stands as President of this Church to lead you astray. It is not in the programme. It is not in the mind of God. If I were to attempt that, the Lord would remove me out of my place, and so He will any other man who attempts to lead the children of men astray from the oracles of God and from their duty. (Sixty-first Semiannual General Conference of the Church, Monday, October 6, 1890, Salt Lake City, Utah. Reported in *Deseret Evening News,* October 11, 1890, p. 2.)

It matters not who lives or who dies, or who is called to lead this Church, they have got to lead it by the inspiration of Almighty God. If they do not do it that way, they cannot do it at all. . . .

I have had some revelations of late, and very important ones to me, and I will tell you what the Lord has said to me. Let me bring your minds to what is termed the manifesto. . . .

The Lord has told me to ask the Latter-day Saints a question, and He also told me that if they would listen to what I said to them and answer the question put to them, by the Spirit and power of God, they would all answer alike, and they would all believe alike with regard to this matter.

The question is this: Which is the wisest course for the Latter-day Saints to pursue—to continue to attempt to practice plural marriage, with the laws of the nation against it and the opposition of sixty millions of people, and at the cost of the confiscation and loss of all the Temples, and the stopping of all the ordinances therein, both for the living and the dead, and the imprisonment of the First Presidency and Twelve and the heads of families in the Church, and the confiscation of personal property of the people (all of which of themselves would stop the practice); or, after doing and suffering what we have through our adherence to this principle to cease the practice and submit to the law, and through doing so leave the Prophets, Apostles and fathers at home, so that they can instruct the people and attend to the duties of the Church, and also leave the Temples in the hands of the Saints, so that they can attend to the ordinances of the Gospel, both for the living and the dead?

The Lord showed me by vision and revelation exactly what would take place if we did not stop this practice. If we had not stopped it, you would have had no use for . . . any of the men in this temple at Logan; for all ordinances would be stopped throughout the land of Zion. Confusion would reign throughout Israel, and many men would be made prisoners. This trouble would have come upon the whole Church, and we should have been compelled to stop the practice. Now, the question is, whether it should be stopped in this manner, or in the way the Lord has manifested to us, and leave our Prophets and Apostles and fathers free men, and the temples in the hands of the people, so that the dead may be redeemed. A large number has already been delivered from the prison house in the spirit world by this people, and shall the work go on or stop? This is the question I lay before the Latter-day Saints. You have to judge for yourselves. I want you to answer it for yourselves. I shall not answer it; but I say to you that that is exactly the condition we as a people would have been in had we not taken the course we have.

. . . I saw exactly what would come to pass if there was not something done. I have had this spirit upon me for a long time. But I want to say this: I should have let all the temples go out of our hands; I should have gone to prison myself, and let every other man go there, had not the God of heaven commanded me to do what I did do; and when the hour came that I was commanded to do that, it was all clear to me. I went before the Lord, and I wrote what the Lord told me to write. . . .

I leave this with you, for you to contemplate and consider. The Lord is at work with us. (Cache Stake Conference, Logan, Utah, Sunday, November 1, 1891. Reported in *Deseret Weekly,* November 14, 1891.)

Now I will tell you what was manifested to me and what the Son of God performed in this thing. . . . All these things would have come to pass, as God Almighty lives, had not that Manifesto been given. Therefore, the Son of God felt disposed to have that thing presented to the Church and to the world for purposes in his own mind. The Lord had decreed the establishment of Zion. He had decreed the finishing of this temple. He had decreed that the salvation of the living and the dead should be given in these valleys of the mountains. And Almighty God decreed that the Devil should not thwart it. If you can understand that, that is a key to it. (From a discourse at the sixth session of the dedication of the Salt Lake Temple, April 1893. Typescript of Dedicatory Services, Archives, Church Historical Department, Salt Lake City, Utah.)

OFFICIAL DECLARATION 2

The Book of Mormon teaches that "all are alike unto God," including "black and white, bond and free, male and female" (2 Nephi 26:33). Throughout the history of the Church, people of every race and ethnicity in many countries have been baptized and have lived as faithful members of the Church. During Joseph Smith's lifetime, a few black male members of the Church were ordained to the priesthood. Early in its history, Church leaders stopped conferring the priesthood on black males of African descent. Church records offer no clear insights into the origins of this practice. Church leaders believed that a revelation from God was needed to alter this practice and prayerfully sought guidance. The revelation came to Church President Spencer W. Kimball and was affirmed to other Church leaders in the Salt Lake Temple on June 1, 1978. The revelation removed all restrictions with regard to race that once applied to the priesthood.

To Whom It May Concern:

On September 30, 1978, at the 148th Semiannual General Conference of The Church of Jesus Christ of Latter-day Saints, the following was presented by President N. Eldon Tanner, First Counselor in the First Presidency of the Church:

In early June of this year, the First Presidency announced that a revelation had been received by President Spencer W. Kimball extending priesthood and temple blessings to all worthy male members of the Church. President Kimball has asked that I advise the conference that after he had received this revelation, which came to him after extended meditation and prayer in the sacred rooms of the holy temple, he presented it to his counselors, who accepted it and approved it. It was then presented to the Quorum of the Twelve Apostles, who unanimously approved it, and was subsequently presented to all other General Authorities, who likewise approved it unanimously.

President Kimball has asked that I now read this letter:

June 8, 1978
To all general and local priesthood officers of The Church of Jesus Christ of Latter-day Saints throughout the world:

Dear Brethren:

As we have witnessed the expansion of the work of the Lord over the earth, we have been grateful that people of many nations have responded to the message of the restored gospel, and have joined the Church in ever-increasing numbers. This, in turn, has inspired us with a desire to extend to every worthy member of the Church all of the privileges and blessings which the gospel affords.

Aware of the promises made by the prophets and presidents of the Church who have preceded us that at some time, in God's eternal plan, all of our brethren who are worthy may receive the priesthood, and witnessing the faithfulness of those from whom the priesthood has been withheld, we have pleaded long and earnestly in behalf of these, our faithful brethren, spending many hours in the Upper Room of the Temple supplicating the Lord for divine guidance.

He has heard our prayers, and by revelation has confirmed that the long-promised day has come when every faithful, worthy man in the Church may receive the holy priesthood, with power to exercise its divine authority, and enjoy with his loved ones every blessing that flows therefrom, including the blessings of the temple. Accordingly, all worthy male members of the Church may be ordained to the priesthood without regard for race or color. Priesthood leaders are instructed to follow the policy of carefully interviewing all candidates for ordination to either the Aaronic or the Melchizedek Priesthood to insure that they meet the established standards for worthiness.

We declare with soberness that the Lord has now made known his will for the blessing of all his children throughout the earth who will hearken to the voice of his authorized servants, and prepare themselves to receive every blessing of the gospel.

Sincerely yours,

SPENCER W. KIMBALL
N. ELDON TANNER
MARION G. ROMNEY
The First Presidency

Recognizing Spencer W. Kimball as the prophet, seer, and revelator, and president of The Church of Jesus Christ of Latter-day Saints, it is proposed that we as a constituent assembly accept this revelation as the word and will of the Lord. All in favor please signify by raising your right hand. Any opposed by the same sign.

The vote to sustain the foregoing motion was unanimous in the affirmative.

Salt Lake City, Utah, September 30, 1978.

THE PEARL
OF GREAT PRICE

A SELECTION FROM THE REVELATIONS,
TRANSLATIONS, AND NARRATIONS OF
JOSEPH SMITH

FIRST PROPHET, SEER, AND REVELATOR TO
THE CHURCH OF JESUS CHRIST OF
LATTER-DAY SAINTS

CONTENTS

ABBREVIATIONS

Old Testament

Gen.	Genesis
Ex.	Exodus
Lev.	Leviticus
Num.	Numbers
Deut.	Deuteronomy
Josh.	Joshua
Judg.	Judges
Ruth	Ruth
1 Sam.	1 Samuel
2 Sam.	2 Samuel
1 Kgs.	1 Kings
2 Kgs.	2 Kings
1 Chr.	1 Chronicles
2 Chr.	2 Chronicles
Ezra	Ezra
Neh.	Nehemiah
Esth.	Esther
Job	Job
Ps.	Psalms
Prov.	Proverbs
Eccl.	Ecclesiastes
Song	Song of Solomon
Isa.	Isaiah
Jer.	Jeremiah
Lam.	Lamentations
Ezek.	Ezekiel
Dan.	Daniel
Hosea	Hosea
Joel	Joel
Amos	Amos
Obad.	Obadiah
Jonah	Jonah
Micah	Micah
Nahum	Nahum
Hab.	Habakkuk
Zeph.	Zephaniah
Hag.	Haggai
Zech.	Zechariah
Mal.	Malachi

New Testament

Matt.	Matthew
Mark	Mark
Luke	Luke
John	John
Acts	Acts
Rom.	Romans
1 Cor.	1 Corinthians
2 Cor.	2 Corinthians
Gal.	Galatians
Eph.	Ephesians
Philip.	Philippians
Col.	Colossians
1 Thes.	1 Thessalonians
2 Thes.	2 Thessalonians
1 Tim.	1 Timothy
2 Tim.	2 Timothy
Titus	Titus
Philem.	Philemon
Heb.	Hebrews
James	James
1 Pet.	1 Peter
2 Pet.	2 Peter
1 Jn.	1 John
2 Jn.	2 John
3 Jn.	3 John
Jude	Jude
Rev.	Revelation

Book of Mormon

1 Ne.	1 Nephi
2 Ne.	2 Nephi
Jacob	Jacob
Enos	Enos
Jarom	Jarom
Omni	Omni
W of M	Words of Mormon
Mosiah	Mosiah
Alma	Alma
Hel.	Helaman
3 Ne.	3 Nephi
4 Ne.	4 Nephi
Morm.	Mormon
Ether	Ether
Moro.	Moroni

Doctrine and Covenants

D&C	Doctrine and Covenants
OD	Official Declaration

Pearl of Great Price

Moses	Moses
Abr.	Abraham
JS—M	Joseph Smith—Matthew
JS—H	Joseph Smith—History
A of F	Articles of Faith

Other Abbreviations and Explanations

JST	Joseph Smith Translation
TG	Topical Guide
BD	Bible Dictionary
HEB	An alternate translation from the Hebrew
GR	An alternate translation from the Greek
IE	An explanation of idioms and difficult wording
OR	Alternate words that clarify the meaning of an archaic expression

INTRODUCTION

The Pearl of Great Price is a selection of choice materials touching many significant aspects of the faith and doctrine of The Church of Jesus Christ of Latter-day Saints. These items were translated and produced by the Prophet Joseph Smith, and most were published in the Church periodicals of his day.

The first collection of materials carrying the title Pearl of Great Price was made in 1851 by Elder Franklin D. Richards, then a member of the Council of the Twelve and president of the British Mission. Its purpose was to make more readily accessible some important articles that had had limited circulation in the time of Joseph Smith. As Church membership increased throughout Europe and America, there was a need to make these items available. The Pearl of Great Price received wide use and subsequently became a standard work of the Church by action of the First Presidency and the general conference in Salt Lake City on October 10, 1880.

Several revisions have been made in the contents as the needs of the Church have required. In 1878 portions of the book of Moses not contained in the first edition were added. In 1902 certain parts of the Pearl of Great Price that duplicated material also published in the Doctrine and Covenants were omitted. Arrangement into chapters and verses, with footnotes, was done in 1902. The first publication in double-column pages, with index, was in 1921. No other changes were made until April 1976, when two items of revelation were added. In 1979 these two items were removed from the Pearl of Great Price and placed in the Doctrine and Covenants, where they now appear as sections 137 and 138. In the present edition some changes have been made to bring the text into conformity with earlier documents.

Following is a brief introduction to the present contents:

1. *Selections from the Book of Moses.* An extract from the book of Genesis of Joseph Smith's translation of the Bible, which he began in June 1830.

2. *The Book of Abraham.* An inspired translation of the writings of Abraham. Joseph Smith began the translation in 1835 after obtaining some Egyptian papyri. The translation was published serially in the *Times and Seasons* beginning March 1, 1842, at Nauvoo, Illinois.

3. *Joseph Smith—Matthew.* An extract from the testimony of Matthew in Joseph Smith's translation of the Bible (see Doctrine and Covenants 45:60–61 for the divine injunction to begin the translation of the New Testament).

4. *Joseph Smith—History.* Excerpts from Joseph Smith's official testimony and history, which he and his scribes prepared in 1838–39 and which was published serially in the *Times and Seasons* in Nauvoo, Illinois, beginning on March 15, 1842.

5. *The Articles of Faith of The Church of Jesus Christ of Latter-day Saints.* A statement by Joseph Smith published in the *Times and Seasons* March 1, 1842, in company with a short history of the Church that was popularly known as the Wentworth Letter.

SELECTIONS FROM THE
BOOK OF MOSES

An extract from the translation of the Bible as revealed to Joseph Smith the Prophet, June 1830–February 1831.

CHAPTER 1

(June 1830)

God reveals Himself to Moses—Moses is transfigured—He is confronted by Satan—Moses sees many inhabited worlds—Worlds without number were created by the Son—God's work and glory is to bring to pass the immortality and eternal life of man.

1 The words of God, which he ^aspake unto Moses at a time when Moses was caught up into an exceedingly high ^bmountain,

2 And he ^asaw God ^bface to face, and he ^ctalked with him, and the ^dglory of God was upon Moses; therefore Moses could endure his presence.

3 And God spake unto Moses, saying: Behold, I am the Lord God ^aAlmighty, and ^bEndless is my ^cname; for I am without beginning of days or end of years; and is not this endless?

4 And, behold, thou art my son; wherefore ^alook, and I will show thee the ^bworkmanship of mine ^chands; but not all, for my ^dworks are without ^eend, and also my ^fwords, for they never cease.

5 Wherefore, no man can behold all my ^aworks, except he behold all my ^bglory; and no man can ^cbehold all my ^dglory, and afterwards remain in the flesh on the earth.

---

1 1a Alma 12:30; Moses 1:42.
   b Ex. 19:3; Ezek. 40:2; Rev. 21:10; Moses 1:42.
   2a Ex. 3:6; 33:20 (11–23); John 1:18; Ether 3:15; Moses 1:11. TG God, Privilege of Seeing; Jesus Christ, Appearances, Antemortal; Vision.
   b Num. 12:8; Deut. 34:10; D&C 17:1. TG God, Manifestations of.
   c Ex. 25:1. TG Communication.
   d Deut. 5:24; Moses 1:14

(13–14, 25). TG Glory; God, Glory of; Transfiguration.
   3a Rev. 19:6. TG Jesus Christ, Power of.
   b Isa. 63:16; D&C 19:10 (9–12); Moses 7:35. TG God, Eternal Nature of.
   c Ex. 3:15.
   4a Moses 7:4.
   b Job 9:12.
   c Moses 7:32 (32–37).
   d Ps. 40:5; 92:5; Morm. 9:16 (16–20); D&C

76:114. TG God, Power of.
   e Ps. 111:8 (7–8); 1 Ne. 14:7; D&C 29:33; Moses 1:38.
   f Ps. 33:11; 2 Ne. 9:16; D&C 1:38 (37–39).
   5a TG God, Works of.
   b TG Glory; Jesus Christ, Glory of.
   c TG God, Privilege of Seeing.
   d Ex. 24:17; John 12:41. TG Celestial Glory.

6 And I have a work for thee, Moses, my son; and thou art in the ^asimilitude of mine ^bOnly ^cBegotten; and mine Only Begotten is and shall be the ^dSavior, for he is full of ^egrace and ^ftruth; but there is ^gno God beside me, and all things are present with me, for I ^hknow them all.

7 And now, behold, this one thing I show unto thee, Moses, my son, for thou art in the world, and now I show it unto thee.

8 And it came to pass that Moses looked, and beheld the ^aworld upon which he was created; and Moses ^bbeheld the world and the ends thereof, and all the children of men which are, and which were created; of the same he greatly ^cmarveled and wondered.

9 And the ^apresence of God withdrew from Moses, that his ^bglory was not upon Moses; and Moses was left unto himself. And as he was left unto himself, he ^cfell unto the earth.

10 And it came to pass that it was for the space of many hours before Moses did again receive his natural ^astrength like unto man; and he said unto himself: Now, for this cause I know that ^bman is ^cnothing, which thing I never had supposed.

11 But now mine own eyes have ^abeheld God; but not my ^bnatural, but my ^cspiritual eyes, for my ^dnatural eyes could not have ^ebeheld; for I should have ^fwithered and ^gdied in his presence; but his ^hglory was upon me; and I beheld his ⁱface, for I was ^jtransfigured before him.

12 And it came to pass that when Moses had said these words, behold, ^aSatan came ^btempting him, saying: Moses, son of man, worship me.

13 And it came to pass that Moses looked upon Satan and said: Who art thou? For behold, I am a ^ason of God, in the similitude of his Only Begotten; and where is thy ^bglory, that I should worship thee?

6a Gen. 1:26; Deut. 18:15;
   Acts 3:22; 1 Ne. 22:21;
   Moses 1:16 (13–16).
 b Moses 1:33.
 c Moses 6:57.
 d 1 Ne. 13:40. TG Jesus
   Christ, Savior.
 e John 1:17 (14, 17);
   2 Ne. 2:6; Alma 13:9.
   TG Grace.
 f Moses 5:7.
 g Deut. 32:17; 1 Kgs. 8:60;
   Isa. 44:8; 45:5 (5–22);
   46:9.
 h Isa. 48:3 (3–7); 1 Ne.
   9:6; Moses 1:35. TG God,
   Foreknowledge of; God,
   Omniscience of.

8a Moses 2:1.
 b Moses 1:27.
 c Ps. 8:3 (3–4).
9a Job 10:12.
 b TG Glory.
 c Isa. 6:5; Acts 9:4; JS—H
   1:20.
10a Dan. 10:8 (8, 17); 1 Ne.
   17:47; 19:20; Alma 27:17.
 b TG Mortality.
 c Job 42:6 (1–6); Dan.
   4:35; Hel. 12:7; Ether
   3:2. TG Humility.
11a Moses 1:2. TG God, Privilege of Seeing.
 b Moses 6:36.
 c Moses 1:31.
 d Ex. 33:20.

e D&C 67:10 (10–13).
f Ex. 19:21; D&C 67:11
   (11–13).
g Ex. 20:19.
h TG Glory.
i Gen. 32:30; Moses 7:4.
j Matt. 17:2 (1–8); D&C
   137:1. TG Transfigura-
   tion.
12a Moses 4:4 (1, 4).
   TG Devil.
 b Luke 4:2 (1–13); 2 Cor.
   11:14 (13–15); Rev. 12:9
   (7–9); 2 Ne. 1:18 (17–18);
   Moses 1:21; 6:49.
13a Job 1:6; Isa. 14:12
   (12–15).
 b D&C 88:24.

14 For behold, I could not look upon God, except his *glory should come upon me, and I were transfigured before him. But I *can look upon thee in the natural man. Is it not so, surely?

15 Blessed be the name of my God, for his *Spirit hath not altogether withdrawn from me, or else where is thy glory, for it is darkness unto me? And I can judge between thee and God; for God said unto me: *Worship God, for him only shalt thou *serve.

16 Get thee hence, Satan; deceive me not; for God said unto me: Thou art after the *similitude of mine Only Begotten.

17 And he also gave me commandments when he *called unto me out of the burning *bush, saying: *Call upon God in the name of mine Only Begotten, and worship me.

18 And again Moses said: I will not cease to call upon God, I have other things to inquire of him: for his *glory has been upon me, wherefore I can judge between him and thee. *Depart hence, Satan.

19 And now, when Moses had said these words, *Satan cried with a loud voice, and ranted upon the earth, and commanded, saying: I am the *Only Begotten, worship me.

20 And it came to pass that Moses began to *fear exceedingly; and as he began to fear, he saw the bitterness of *hell. Nevertheless, *calling upon God, he received *strength, and he commanded, saying: Depart from me, Satan, for this one God only will I worship, which is the God of *glory.

21 And now Satan began to tremble, and the earth shook; and Moses received strength, and called upon God, saying: In the name of the Only Begotten, *depart hence, *Satan.

22 And it came to pass that Satan cried with a loud voice, with weeping, and wailing, and *gnashing of teeth; and he departed hence, even from the presence of Moses, that he beheld him not.

23 And now of this thing Moses bore record; but because of *wickedness it is *not had among the children of men.

---

14 a Moses 1:2 (2, 25).
  TG Glory.
 b Rev. 1:17.
15 a TG God, Spirit of.
 b Matt. 4:10. TG Worship.
 c 1 Sam. 7:3; 3 Ne. 13:24.
16 a Moses 1:6. TG God,
  Body of, Corporeal
  Nature.
17 a Ex. 19:3.
 b Ex. 3:2 (2–15).

 c Moses 5:8.
18 a TG Glory; Jesus Christ,
  Glory of.
 b Matt. 4:10.
19 a TG False Christs.
 b JS—M 1:6 (5–9).
20 a TG Fearful.
 b D&C 76:47 (44–47).
  TG Hell.
 c JS—H 1:16 (15–16).
  TG Prayer.

 d TG God, Power of;
  Strength.
 e TG Glory.
21 a Moses 1:12.
 b Matt. 10:1. TG Spirits,
  Evil or Unclean.
22 a Matt. 13:42 (41–42);
  Mosiah 16:2 (1–3).
23 a Luke 11:52. TG Record
  Keeping.
 b Moses 1:41.

24 And it came to pass that when Satan had departed from the presence of Moses, that Moses lifted up his eyes unto heaven, being filled with the *Holy Ghost, which beareth record of the Father and the Son;

25 And calling upon the name of God, he beheld his *glory again, for it was upon him; and he heard a *voice, saying: Blessed art thou, Moses, for I, the Almighty, have *chosen thee, and thou shalt be made stronger than many *waters; for they shall obey thy *command as if thou wert *God.

26 And lo, I am *with thee, even unto the end of thy days; for thou shalt *deliver my people from *bondage, even *Israel my *chosen.

27 And it came to pass, as the voice was still speaking, Moses cast his eyes and *beheld the earth, yea, even all of it; and there was not a particle of it which he did not behold, *discerning it by the *Spirit of God.

28 And he beheld also the inhabitants thereof, and there was not a *soul which he beheld not; and he discerned them by the Spirit of God; and their numbers were great, even numberless as the sand upon the sea shore.

29 And he beheld many lands; and each land was called *earth, and there were *inhabitants on the face thereof.

30 And it came to pass that Moses called upon God, saying: *Tell me, I pray thee, why these things are so, and by what thou madest them?

31 And behold, the glory of the Lord was upon Moses, so that Moses stood in the presence of God, and talked with him *face to face. And the Lord God said unto Moses: For mine own *purpose have I made these things. Here is *wisdom and it remaineth in me.

32 And by the *word of my power, have I created them, which is mine Only Begotten Son, who is full of *grace and truth.

33 And *worlds without number have I *created; and I also created them

---

24 *a* 3 Ne. 11:32 (32, 36);
     Moses 8:24.
25 *a* TG Glory.
    b Hel. 5:30; 3 Ne. 11:3.
    c Abr. 3:23.
    d Ex. 14:21.
    e TG Priesthood, Authority.
    f Ex. 4:16.
26 *a* TG Walking with God.
    b Ex. 3:10 (7–12). TG Israel, Deliverance of.
    c Ex. 20:2; Ps. 80:8; 1 Ne. 17:23 (23–25). TG Israel, Bondage of, in Egypt.
    d 1 Kgs. 8:53 (51, 53). TG Israel, Twelve

Tribes of.
    e Ps. 33:12.
27 *a* D&C 88:47 (45–47); Moses 1:8; 7:23; Abr. 3:21 (21–23). TG Vision.
    b TG Discernment, Spiritual; Holy Ghost, Mission of.
    c TG God, Spirit of.
28 *a* Moses 7:23.
29 *a* Gen. 1:10. TG Earth, Dividing of.
    b 1 Ne. 17:36.
30 *a* Moses 2:1.
31 *a* Deut. 5:4; Moses 1:11.
    b Isa. 45:18 (17–18); Eph. 3:11 (7–12); 2 Ne. 2:15

(14–30). TG Earth, Purpose of.
    c TG God, Intelligence of.
32 *a* John 1:3 (1–4); Heb. 1:2 (1–3); Rev. 19:13 (13–15); Jacob 4:9; Moses 2:1 (1, 5). TG Jesus Christ, Authority of.
    b Moses 5:7 (7–8). TG Grace.
33 *a* Job 9:9 (7–9); Ps. 8:3 (3–4); Amos 9:6; D&C 76:24; Moses 7:30 (29–31). TG Astronomy; Creation; God, Works of; World.
    b TG God, Creator.

for mine own purpose; and by the ^cSon I ^dcreated them, which is mine ^eOnly Begotten.

34 And the ^afirst man of all men have I called ^bAdam, which is ^cmany.

35 But only an account of this earth, and the inhabitants thereof, give I unto you. For behold, there are many worlds that have passed away by the word of my power. And there are many that now stand, and innumerable are they unto man; but all things are numbered unto me, for they are mine and I ^aknow them.

36 And it came to pass that Moses spake unto the Lord, saying: Be merciful unto thy servant, O God, and ^atell me concerning this earth, and the inhabitants thereof, and also the heavens, and then thy servant will be content.

37 And the Lord God spake unto Moses, saying: The ^aheavens, they are many, and they cannot be numbered unto man; but they are numbered unto me, for they are mine.

38 And as one earth shall pass away, and the heavens thereof even so shall another come; and there is no ^aend to my works, neither to my words.

39 For behold, this is my ^awork and my ^bglory—to bring to pass the ^cimmortality and ^deternal ^elife of man.

40 And now, Moses, my son, I will speak unto thee concerning this earth upon which thou standest; and thou shalt ^awrite the things which I shall speak.

41 And in a day when the children of men shall esteem my words as ^anaught and ^btake many of them from the ^cbook which thou shalt write, behold, I will raise up another ^dlike unto thee; and they shall be ^ehad again among the children of men—among as many as shall believe.

42 (These words were ^aspoken unto Moses in the mount, the name of which shall not be known among the children of men. And now they are spoken unto you. Show them not unto any except them that believe. Even so. Amen.)

---

33 c TG Jesus Christ, Divine
     Sonship; Jesus Christ,
     Jehovah.
   d TG Jesus Christ, Creator.
   e Moses 1:6.
34 a Moses 3:7.
   b Abr. 1:3. TG Adam.
   c 1 Cor. 15:45 (45–48);
     2 Ne. 2:20 (19–20);
     D&C 27:11; 76:24;
     138:38; Moses 4:26; 6:9.
35 a 1 Ne. 9:6; D&C 38:2;
     88:41; Moses 1:6; 7:36;
     Abr. 3:2 (1–16). TG God,
     Omniscience of.
36 a Moses 2:1.

37 a Gen. 1:1; Moses 2:1; Abr.
     4:1. TG Heaven.
38 a Moses 1:4.
39 a Ps. 90:16; Matt. 5:48;
     Rom. 8:17 (14–21); 2 Ne.
     2:15 (14–30); Alma
     42:26; D&C 29:43
     (42–44). TG God, Works
     of.
   b Micah 2:9; Mosiah
     4:12; D&C 81:4 (3–4).
     TG Glory; Jesus Christ,
     Glory of.
   c Moses 6:59. TG Immortality; Jesus Christ,
     Mission of; Resurrection.

   d TG Eternal Life; Man,
     Potential to Become like
     Heavenly Father.
   e TG Earth, Purpose of.
40 a Neh. 13:1 (1–3); 2 Tim.
     3:16; 2 Ne. 29:11
     (11–12).
41 a Moses 1:23.
   b 1 Ne. 13:26 (23–32).
   c Ex. 17:14; 1 Ne. 5:11;
     19:23.
   d 2 Ne. 3:9 (7–19).
   e 1 Ne. 13:32, 39–40;
     D&C 9:2.
42 a Moses 1:1.

CHAPTER 2

(June–October 1830)

God creates the heavens and the earth—All forms of life are created—God makes man and gives him dominion over all else.

1 And it came to pass that the Lord spake unto Moses, saying: Behold, I ^areveal unto you concerning this ^bheaven, and this ^cearth; ^dwrite the words which I speak. I am the Beginning and the End, the ^eAlmighty God; by mine ^fOnly Begotten I ^gcreated these things; yea, in the beginning I ^hcreated the ⁱheaven, and the earth upon which thou standest.

2 And the earth was without ^aform, and void; and I caused ^bdarkness to come up upon the face of the deep; and my ^cSpirit ^dmoved upon the face of the water; for I am God.

3 And I, God, said: Let there be ^alight; and there was light.

4 And I, God, saw the light; and that light was ^agood. And I, God, divided the ^blight from the darkness.

5 And I, God, called the light Day; and the darkness, I called Night; and this I did by the ^aword of my power, and it was done as I ^bspake; and the evening and the morning were the first ^cday.

6 And again, I, God, said: Let there be a ^afirmament in the midst of the water, and it was so, even as I spake; and I said: Let it divide the waters from the waters; and it was done;

7 And I, God, made the firmament and divided the ^awaters, yea, the great waters under the firmament from the waters which were above the firmament, and it was so even as I spake.

8 And I, God, called the firmament ^aHeaven; and the evening and the morning were the second day.

9 And I, God, said: Let the ^awaters under the heaven be gathered together

---

2 1 *a* Moses 1:30 (30, 36).
　b TG Heaven.
　c Moses 1:8.
　d D&C 76:80. TG Record Keeping; Scribe; Scriptures, Writing of.
　e 1 Ne. 1:14.
　f Moses 1:32; Abr. 4:1.
　g TG Creation; Jesus Christ, Creator.
　h TG God, Creator; God, Works of.
　i Gen. 1:1.
　2 *a* Jer. 4:23 (23–25).

　b TG Darkness, Physical.
　c TG God, Spirit of.
　d Gen. 1:2; Abr. 4:2.
　3 *a* D&C 88:7 (6–13). TG Light [noun].
　4 *a* Gen. 1:4; Abr. 4:4.
　b TG Light [noun].
　5 *a* Moses 1:32.
　b Ps. 33:9; 2 Cor. 4:6.
　c Gen. 1:5.
　6 *a* See Abr., fac. 2, fig. 4 concerning the firmament or expanse. See also Gen. 1:6 (6–8); Moses

2:14–18.
　7 *a* Amos 9:6; Abr. 4:9 (9–10).
　8 *a* IE The whole expanse around about the earth, its atmosphere, and beyond are generically here called "Heaven." The same word is also used sometimes to refer to paradise, to the dwelling place of God, and to the kingdoms of glory.
　9 *a* TG Earth, Dividing of.

unto *b*one place, and it was so; and I, God, said: Let there be dry land; and it was so.

10 And I, God, called the dry land *a*Earth; and the gathering together of the waters, called I the Sea; and I, God, saw that all things which I had made were good.

11 And I, God, said: Let the earth bring forth *a*grass, the herb yielding seed, the fruit tree yielding fruit, after his kind, and the tree yielding fruit, whose seed should be in itself upon the earth, and it was so even as I spake.

12 And the earth brought forth grass, every herb yielding seed after his kind, and the tree yielding fruit, whose seed should be in itself, after his *a*kind; and I, God, saw that all things which I had made were good;

13 And the evening and the morning were the third day.

14 And I, God, said: Let there be *a*lights in the firmament of the heaven, to divide the day from the night, and let them be for signs, and for seasons, and for days, and for years;

15 And let them be for lights in the firmament of the heaven to give light upon the earth; and it was so.

16 And I, God, made two great lights; the greater *a*light to rule the day, and the lesser light to rule the night, and the *b*greater light was the sun, and the lesser light was the moon; and the stars also were made even according to my word.

17 And I, God, set them in the firmament of the heaven to give light upon the earth,

18 And the *a*sun to rule over the day, and the moon to rule over the night, and to divide the light from the *b*darkness; and I, God, saw that all things which I had made were good;

19 And the evening and the morning were the fourth day.

20 And I, God, said: Let the waters bring forth abundantly the moving creature that hath life, and fowl which may fly above the earth in the open firmament of heaven.

21 And I, God, created great *a*whales, and every living creature that moveth, which the waters brought forth abundantly, after their kind, and every winged fowl after his kind; and I, God, saw that all things which I had created were good.

---

9 *b* Gen. 1:9; Abr. 4:9.
10 *a* IE The whole sphere or any of its parts above the seas is called "Earth."
11 *a* Gen. 1:11 (11–12); Abr.
4:11 (11–12).
12 *a* Gen. 1:12.
14 *a* Ps. 104:19.
16 *a* TG Light [noun].
  b Gen. 1:16.
18 *a* TG Astronomy.
  b TG Darkness, Physical.
21 *a* Gen. 1:21; Abr. 4:21.

22 And I, God, blessed them, saying: Be fruitful, and ^amultiply, and fill the waters in the sea; and let fowl multiply in the earth;

23 And the evening and the morning were the fifth day.

24 And I, God, said: Let the earth bring forth the living creature after his kind, cattle, and creeping things, and beasts of the earth after their kind, and it was so;

25 And I, God, made the beasts of the earth after their kind, and cattle after their kind, and everything which creepeth upon the earth after his kind; and I, God, saw that all these things were good.

26 And I, God, said unto mine ^aOnly Begotten, which was with me from the ^bbeginning: Let ^cus ^dmake man in our ^eimage, after our likeness; and it was so. And I, God, said: Let them have ^fdominion over the fishes of the sea, and over the fowl of the air, and over the cattle, and over all the earth, and over every creeping thing that creepeth upon the earth.

27 And I, God, created man in mine own ^aimage, in the image of mine Only Begotten created I him; male and female created I them.

28 And I, God, blessed them, and said unto them: Be ^afruitful, and ^bmultiply, and replenish the earth, and subdue it, and have dominion over the fish of the sea, and over the fowl of the air, and over every living thing that moveth upon the earth.

29 And I, God, said unto man: Behold, I have given you every herb bearing seed, which is upon the face of all the earth, and every tree in the which shall be the fruit of a tree yielding seed; to you it shall be for ^ameat.

30 And to every beast of the earth, and to every fowl of the air, and to everything that creepeth upon the earth, wherein I grant life, there shall be given every clean herb for meat; and it was so, even as I spake.

31 And I, God, saw everything that I had made, and, behold, all things which I had made were very ^agood; and the evening and the morning were the ^bsixth day.

---

22 a Gen. 1:22 (20–25); D&C
   45:58; 132:63 (55–56,
   63); Abr. 4:22.
26 a TG Jesus Christ, Divine
   Sonship.
   b TG Jesus Christ, Firstborn.
   c TG Jesus Christ, Creator.
   d TG Man, Physical Creation of.

   e Gen. 1:26 (26–28);
   Moses 6:9 (8–10); Abr.
   4:26 (26–31).
   f Gen. 1:26 (26–28); D&C
   76:111 (110–12); 121:37
   (34–46); Moses 5:1; Abr.
   4:26 (26–28).
27 a TG God, Body of, Corporeal Nature.
28 a TG Birth Control.

   b Moses 5:2. TG Marriage,
   Fatherhood.
29 a Gen. 1:29 (29–30); Ps.
   136:25; D&C 104:17
   (15–18); Abr. 4:29
   (29–30).
31 a Gen. 1:31; Moro. 7:12;
   D&C 59:17 (16–20).
   b Ex. 20:11 (8–11); 31:17;
   Mosiah 13:19; Abr. 4:31.

CHAPTER 3

(June–October 1830)

God created all things spiritually before they were naturally upon the earth—He created man, the first flesh, upon the earth—Woman is a help meet for man.

1 Thus the *a*heaven and the earth were finished, and all the *b*host of them.

2 And on the seventh day I, God, ended my work, and all things which I had made; and I *a*rested on the *b*seventh day from all my work, and all things which I had made were finished, and I, God, saw that they were good;

3 And I, God, *a*blessed the seventh day, and *b*sanctified it; because that in it I had rested from all my *c*work which I, God, had created and made.

4 And now, behold, I say unto you, that these are the generations of the heaven and of the earth, when they were *a*created, in the day that I, the Lord God, made the *b*heaven and the earth,

5 And every plant of the field before it was in the earth, and every herb of the field before it grew. For I, the Lord God, *a*created all things, of which I have spoken, *b*spiritually, before they were *c*naturally upon the face of the earth. For I, the Lord God, had not caused it to rain upon the face of the earth. And I, the Lord God, had *d*created all the children of men; and not yet a man to till the *e*ground; for in *f*heaven *g*created I them; and there was not yet flesh upon the earth, neither in the water, neither in the air;

6 But I, the Lord God, spake, and there went up a *a*mist from the earth, and watered the whole face of the ground.

7 And I, the Lord God, formed man from the *a*dust of the ground, and breathed into his nostrils the *b*breath of life; and *c*man became a living *d*soul, the *e*first flesh upon the earth, the first man also; nevertheless, all things were before created; but spiritually were they created and made according to my word.

---

3 1 *a* TG Creation.
   b Gen. 2:1; D&C 29:36; 38:1; 45:1; Abr. 5:1.
 2 *a* Gen. 2:2 (1–3); Abr. 5:2 (1–3). TG Rest.
   b TG Sabbath.
 3 *a* Ex. 20:11; Mosiah 13:19; D&C 77:12.
   b Abr. 5:3 (1–3).
   c Ex. 31:15 (14–15); Mosiah 13:18 (16–19).

4 *a* Gen. 2:4 (4–5); Abr. 5:4 (4–5).
   b Neh. 9:6.
 5 *a* Moses 6:51. TG Creation; God, Creator.
   b D&C 29:31–34; Abr. 3:23. TG Life, Sanctity of; Spirit Creation.
   c Moses 3:9. TG Man, Physical Creation of.
   d TG Man, a Spirit Child of Heavenly Father.

   e Gen. 2:5.
   f TG Heaven.
   g TG Man, Antemortal Existence of.
 6 *a* Gen. 2:6.
 7 *a* Gen. 2:7; Moses 4:25 (25–29); 6:59; Abr. 5:7.
   b TG Breath of Life.
   c TG Adam.
   d Isa. 57:16. TG Soul.
   e Moses 1:34.

8 And I, the Lord God, planted a garden eastward in *Eden, and there I put the man whom I had formed.

9 And out of the ground made I, the Lord God, to grow every tree, *naturally, that is pleasant to the sight of man; and man could behold it. And it became also a *living soul. For it was spiritual in the day that I created it; for it remaineth in the sphere in which I, God, created it, yea, even all things which I prepared for the use of man; and man saw that it was good for food. And I, the Lord God, planted the *tree of life also in the midst of the garden, and also the tree of knowledge of good and evil.

10 And I, the Lord God, caused a river to go out of *Eden to water the garden; and from thence it was parted, and became into four *heads.

11 And I, the Lord God, called the name of the first Pison, and it compasseth the whole land of *Havilah, where I, the Lord God, created much gold;

12 And the gold of that land was good, and there was bdellium and the *onyx stone.

13 And the name of the second river was called Gihon; the same that compasseth the whole land of *Ethiopia.

14 And the name of the third river was Hiddekel; that which goeth toward the east of Assyria. And the fourth river was the Euphrates.

15 And I, the Lord God, took the man, and put him into the Garden of *Eden, to dress it, and to keep it.

16 And I, the Lord God, commanded the man, saying: Of every tree of the garden thou mayest freely eat,

17 But of the tree of the *knowledge of good and evil, thou shalt not eat of it, nevertheless, thou mayest *choose for thyself, for it is given unto thee; but, remember that I *forbid it, for in the *day thou eatest thereof thou shalt surely *die.

18 And I, the Lord God, said unto mine *Only Begotten, that it was not good that the man should be *alone; wherefore, I will make an *help meet for him.

8a Isa. 51:3. TG Eden.
9a Moses 3:5.
 b TG Life, Sanctity of.
 c Gen. 2:9; 1 Ne. 11:25;
   15:22 (22, 28, 36); Alma
   42:5 (2–6); Moses 4:28
   (28, 31); Abr. 5:9.
10a TG Eden.
 b Gen. 2:10.
11a Gen. 2:11.
12a Ex. 25:7.

13a IE In the area of Eden
   and Adam-ondi-Ahman
   there were rivers and
   lands that received names
   that were later attached
   to other lands and rivers.
   As to the location of
   Eden and its environs,
   see D&C 117:8–9. Gen.
   2:13.
15a TG Eden.

17a TG Knowledge.
 b Moses 7:32. TG Agency.
 c 2 Ne. 2:15.
 d Abr. 5:13.
 e Gen. 2:17; Moses 4:17
   (17–19). TG Mortality.
18a TG Jesus Christ, Divine
   Sonship.
 b TG Family, Eternal.
 c Gen. 2:18; Abr. 5:14.

19 And out of the ground I, the Lord God, formed every *beast of the field, and every fowl of the air; and commanded that they should come unto Adam, to see what he would call them; and they were also living souls; for I, God, breathed into them the *breath of life, and commanded that whatsoever Adam called every living creature, that should be the name thereof.

20 And Adam gave *names to all cattle, and to the fowl of the air, and to every beast of the field; but as for Adam, there was not found an help meet for him.

21 And I, the Lord God, caused a deep sleep to fall upon Adam; and he slept, and I took one of his ribs and closed up the flesh in the stead thereof;

22 And the rib which I, the Lord God, had taken from man, made I a *woman, and brought her unto the man.

23 And *Adam said: This I know now is bone of my bones, and *flesh of my flesh; she shall be called Woman, because she was taken out of man.

24 Therefore shall a man leave his father and his mother, and shall *cleave unto his *wife; and *they shall be *one flesh.

25 And they were both naked, the man and his wife, and were not ashamed.

CHAPTER 4

(June–October 1830)

How Satan became the devil—He tempts Eve—Adam and Eve fall, and death enters the world.

1 And I, the *Lord God, spake unto Moses, saying: That *Satan, whom thou hast commanded in the name of mine Only Begotten, is the same which was from the *beginning, and he came before me, saying—Behold, here am I, send me, I will be thy son, and I will *redeem all mankind, that one soul shall not be lost, and surely *I will do it; wherefore *give me thine honor.

19 a Prov. 12:10; D&C 29:24
     (24–25); 49:19 (18–21);
     77:2. TG Creation.
   b TG Breath of Life.
20 a TG Language.
22 a TG Creation; Woman.
23 a TG Adam.
   b Gen. 2:23; Jacob 2:21;

       Abr. 5:17.
24 a Gen. 2:24 (23–24);
     D&C 42:22; 49:15
     (15–16); Abr. 5:18
     (17–18).
   b TG Family, Love within.
   c Eccl. 4:9 (9–12).
   d TG Divorce; Marriage,

       Celestial.
4 1 a Moses 5:58.
     b D&C 29:36 (36–39);
       76:25 (25–26); Abr. 3:27.
     c Moses 5:24.
     d TG Redemption.
     e Isa. 14:13 (12–15).
     f TG Selfishness.

2 But, behold, my Beloved ^aSon, which was my Beloved and ^bChosen from the beginning, said unto me—^cFather, thy ^dwill be done, and the ^eglory be thine forever.

3 Wherefore, because that ^aSatan ^brebelled against me, and sought to destroy the ^cagency of man, which I, the Lord God, had given him, and also, that I should give unto him mine own power; by the power of mine Only Begotten, I caused that he should be ^dcast down;

4 And he became ^aSatan, yea, even the ^bdevil, the father of all ^clies, to ^ddeceive and to blind men, and to lead them ^ecaptive at his will, even as many as would not ^fhearken unto my voice.

5 And now the serpent was more ^asubtle than any beast of the field which I, the Lord God, had made.

6 And ^aSatan put it into the heart of the serpent, (for he had drawn away ^bmany after him,) and he sought also to ^cbeguile Eve, for he ^dknew not the ^emind of God, wherefore he sought to destroy the world.

7 And he said unto the woman: Yea, hath God said—Ye shall not eat of every tree of the garden? (And he spake by the mouth of the serpent.)

8 And the woman said unto the serpent: We may eat of the fruit of the trees of the garden;

9 But of the fruit of the tree which thou beholdest in the midst of the garden, God hath said—Ye shall not eat of it, neither shall ye touch it, lest ye die.

10 And the serpent said unto the ^awoman: Ye shall not surely die;

11 For God doth know that in the day ye eat thereof, then your ^aeyes shall be opened, and ye shall be as gods, ^bknowing good and evil.

12 And when the woman saw that the tree was good for food, and that it became pleasant to the eyes, and a tree to be ^adesired to make her wise, she took of the ^bfruit thereof, and did ^ceat, and also gave unto her husband with her, and he did eat.

2 a TG Jesus Christ, Divine Sonship; Witness of the Father.
 b Moses 7:39; Abr. 3:27. TG Foreordination; Jesus Christ, Authority of; Jesus Christ, Foreordained; Jesus Christ, Messenger of the Covenant; Jesus Christ, Messiah.
 c TG God the Father, Elohim.
 d Luke 22:42. TG God, the Standard of Righteousness.
 e Ps. 96:8; John 7:18. TG Glory.
3 a TG Sons of Perdition.
 b Abr. 3:28. TG Council in Heaven; Rebellion.
 c TG Agency.
 d D&C 76:25 (25–27).
4 a Moses 1:12.
 b TG Devil.
 c 2 Ne. 2:18; D&C 10:25. TG Honesty; Lying.
 d 1 Thes. 3:5; D&C 29:39 (39–40, 47). TG Deceit.
 e TG Bondage, Spiritual.
 f TG Disobedience.
5 a Gen. 3:1; Mosiah 16:3;
    Alma 12:4; D&C 123:12.
6 a TG Devil.
 b D&C 29:36.
 c TG Honesty.
 d John 16:3 (1–3).
 e 1 Cor. 2:16. TG Mind.
10 a 1 Tim. 2:14.
11 a Gen. 3:5 (3–6); D&C 76:12 (12, 19); Moses 5:10.
 b Alma 12:31. TG Knowledge.
12 a Gen. 3:6; 1 Ne. 8:12 (10–15); 15:36.
 b D&C 29:40.
 c TG Fall of Man.

13 And the eyes of them both were opened, and they knew that they had been *naked. And they sewed fig leaves together and made themselves *aprons.

14 And they heard the voice of the Lord God, as they were *walking in the garden, in the cool of the day; and Adam and his wife went to hide themselves from the *presence of the Lord God amongst the trees of the garden.

15 And I, the Lord God, called unto Adam, and said unto him: Where *goest thou?

16 And he said: I heard thy voice in the garden, and I was afraid, because I beheld that I was naked, and I hid myself.

17 And I, the Lord God, said unto Adam: Who told thee thou wast naked? Hast thou eaten of the tree whereof I commanded thee that thou shouldst not eat, if so thou shouldst surely *die?

18 And the man said: The woman thou gavest me, and commandest that she should remain with me, she gave me of the fruit of the tree and I did eat.

19 And I, the Lord God, said unto the woman: What is this thing which thou hast done? And the woman said: The serpent *beguiled me, and I did eat.

20 And I, the Lord God, said unto the serpent: Because thou hast done this thou shalt be *cursed above all cattle, and above every beast of the field; upon thy belly shalt thou go, and dust shalt thou eat all the days of thy life;

21 And I will put *enmity between thee and the woman, between thy seed and her seed; and he shall *bruise thy head, and thou shalt bruise his heel.

22 Unto the woman, I, the Lord God, said: I will greatly multiply thy sorrow and thy conception. In *sorrow thou shalt bring forth children, and thy desire shall be to thy *husband, and he shall rule over thee.

23 And unto Adam, I, the Lord God, said: Because thou hast hearkened unto the voice of thy wife, and hast eaten of the fruit of the tree of which I commanded thee, saying—Thou shalt not eat of it, *cursed shall be the ground for thy sake; in *sorrow shalt thou eat of it all the days of thy life.

13 *a* Gen. 2:25; 2 Ne. 9:14.
  b TG Apparel.
14 *a* Gen. 3:8.
  b Jonah 1:3.
15 *a* Gen. 3:9.
17 *a* Moses 3:17.
19 *a* Gen. 3:13 (1–13); 2 Ne.

9:9; Mosiah 16:3; Ether 8:25.
20 *a* Gen. 3:14 (13–16).
21 *a* Gen. 3:15.
  b Ps. 68:21; Rom. 16:20; Heb. 2:14.
22 *a* Gen. 3:16. TG Pain.

  b TG Marriage, Husbands; Marriage, Wives.
23 *a* Job 14:1; Moses 8:9. TG Earth, Curse of.
  b TG Suffering.

24 Thorns also, and thistles shall it bring forth to thee, and thou shalt eat the herb of the field.

25 By the *a*sweat of thy *b*face shalt thou eat bread, until thou shalt return unto the ground—for thou shalt surely die—for out of it wast thou taken: for *c*dust thou wast, and unto dust shalt thou return.

26 And Adam called his wife's name Eve, because she was the mother of all living; for thus have I, the Lord God, called the first of all women, which are *a*many.

27 Unto Adam, and also unto his wife, did I, the Lord God, make coats of *a*skins, and *b*clothed them.

28 And I, the Lord God, *a*said unto mine Only Begotten: Behold, the *b*man is become as one of us to *c*know good and evil; and now lest he put forth his hand and *d*partake also of the *e*tree of life, and eat and live forever,

29 Therefore I, the Lord God, will send him forth from the Garden of *a*Eden, to till the ground from whence he was taken;

30 For as I, the Lord God, liveth, even so my *a*words cannot return void, for as they go forth out of my mouth they must be fulfilled.

31 So I drove out the man, and I placed at the east of the Garden of *a*Eden, *b*cherubim and a flaming sword, which turned every way to keep the way of the tree of life.

32 (And these are the words which I spake unto my servant Moses, and they are true even as I will; and I have spoken them unto you. See thou show them unto no man, until I command you, except to them that believe. Amen.)

CHAPTER 5

(June–October 1830)

Adam and Eve bring forth children—Adam offers sacrifice and serves God—Cain and Abel are born—Cain rebels, loves Satan more than God, and becomes Perdition—Murder and wickedness spread—The gospel is preached from the beginning.

---

25 a Gen. 3:19 (17–19).
  TG Mortality.
 b Moses 5:1.
 c Gen. 2:7; Job 10:9; Ps.
  104:29; Alma 42:30;
  Moses 3:7; 6:59; Abr. 5:7.
26 a Moses 1:34; 6:9.
27 a Gen. 27:16; Alma 49:6.

 b TG Apparel; Clothing;
  Modesty.
28 a Gen. 3:22.
 b TG Man, Potential to
  Become like Heavenly
  Father.
 c TG Knowledge; Probation.

 d Alma 42:5 (4–5).
 e Gen. 2:9; 1 Ne. 11:25;
  Moses 3:9; Abr. 5:9.
29 a TG Eden.
30 a 1 Kgs. 8:56; Jer. 44:28.
31 a TG Eden.
 b Alma 42:3. TG Cherubim.

1 And it came to pass that after I, the Lord God, had driven them out, that Adam began to till the earth, and to have ^adominion over all the beasts of the field, and to eat his bread by the sweat of his ^bbrow, as I the Lord had commanded him. And Eve, also, his wife, did ^clabor with him.

2 And ^aAdam knew his wife, and she bare unto him ^bsons and ^cdaughters, and they began to ^dmultiply and to replenish the earth.

3 And from that time forth, the sons and ^adaughters of Adam began to divide two and two in the land, and to till the land, and to tend flocks, and they also begat sons and daughters.

4 And Adam and Eve, his wife, ^acalled upon the name of the Lord, and they heard the voice of the Lord from the way toward the Garden of ^bEden, speaking unto them, and they saw him not; for they were shut out from his ^cpresence.

5 And he gave unto them commandments, that they should ^aworship the Lord their God, and should offer the ^bfirstlings of their ^cflocks, for an offering unto the Lord. And Adam was ^dobedient unto the commandments of the Lord.

6 And after many days an ^aangel of the Lord appeared unto Adam, saying: Why dost thou offer ^bsacrifices unto the Lord? And Adam said unto him: I know not, save the Lord commanded me.

7 And then the angel spake, saying: This thing is a ^asimilitude of the ^bsacrifice of the Only Begotten of the Father, which is full of ^cgrace and ^dtruth.

8 Wherefore, thou shalt do all that thou doest in the ^aname of the Son, and thou shalt ^brepent and ^ccall upon God in the name of the Son forevermore.

9 And in that day the ^aHoly Ghost fell upon Adam, which beareth record of the Father and the Son, saying: I am the ^bOnly Begotten of the Father from the beginning, henceforth and forever, that as thou hast ^cfallen thou mayest be ^dredeemed, and all mankind, even as many as will.

---

5 1 a Moses 2:26.
  b Moses 4:25.
  c TG Labor.
2 a Gen. 5:4 (3–32).
  b Gen. 4:1 (1–2); Moses 5:16 (16–17).
  c D&C 138:39.
  d Gen. 9:1; Moses 2:28.
3 a Gen. 4:17; Moses 5:28.
4 a Gen. 4:26; Moses 6:4.
  b TG Eden.
  c Alma 42:9.
5 a TG Worship.
  b Ex. 13:12 (12–13);

Num. 18:17; Mosiah 2:3. TG Firstborn.
  c Moses 5:19 (19–20).
  d TG Obedience.
6 a TG Angels.
  b TG Ordinance; Sacrifice.
7 a TG Jesus Christ, Types of, in Anticipation.
  b Gen. 4:5 (3–7); 1 Chr. 6:49; Alma 34:10 (10–15); Moses 5:21 (20–26). TG Blood, Symbolism of; Jesus Christ, Atonement through.
  c Moses 1:32. TG Grace.

d Moses 1:6.
8 a Moses 1:17.
  b Moses 6:57; 7:10. TG Repent.
  c TG Prayer.
9 a TG Holy Ghost, Baptism of.
  b TG Jesus Christ, Divine Sonship.
  c TG Death, Spiritual, First; Fall of Man.
  d Ps. 49:15; Mosiah 27:24 (24–26); D&C 93:38; A of F 1:3. TG Redemption; Salvation, Plan of.

10 And in that day Adam blessed God and was ^afilled, and began to ^bprophesy concerning all the families of the earth, saying: Blessed be the name of God, for because of my ^ctransgression my ^deyes are opened, and in this life I shall have ^ejoy, and again in the ^fflesh I shall see God.

11 And Eve, his wife, heard all these things and was glad, saying: Were it not for our transgression we never should have had ^aseed, and never should have ^bknown good and evil, and the joy of our redemption, and the eternal life which God giveth unto all the obedient.

12 And Adam and ^aEve blessed the name of God, and they made all things ^bknown unto their sons and their daughters.

13 And ^aSatan came among them, saying: I am also a son of God; and he commanded them, saying: ^bBelieve it; and they believed it not, and they ^cloved Satan more than God. And men began from that time forth to be ^dcarnal, sensual, and devilish.

14 And the Lord God called upon men by the ^aHoly Ghost everywhere and commanded them that they should repent;

15 And as many as ^abelieved in the Son, and repented of their sins, should be ^bsaved; and as many as believed not and repented not, should be ^cdamned; and the words went forth out of the mouth of God in a firm decree; wherefore they must be fulfilled.

16 And Adam and Eve, his wife, ceased not to call upon God. And Adam knew Eve his wife, and she conceived and bare ^aCain, and said: I have gotten a man from the Lord; wherefore he may not reject his words. But behold, Cain ^bhearkened not, saying: Who is the Lord that I should ^cknow him?

17 And she again conceived and bare his brother Abel. And Abel ^ahearkened unto the voice of the Lord. And ^bAbel was a keeper of sheep, but Cain was a tiller of the ground.

18 And Cain ^aloved Satan more than God. And Satan commanded him, saying: ^bMake an offering unto the Lord.

10 a TG Man, New, Spiritually Reborn.
  b D&C 107:56 (41–56).
  c TG Transgress.
  d Gen. 3:5 (3–6); D&C 76:12 (12, 19); Moses 4:11 (10–13).
  e TG Joy.
  f Job 19:26; 2 Ne. 9:4.
11 a 2 Ne. 2:23 (22–25).
  TG Birth Control; Family; Marriage,

Motherhood.
  b Gen. 3:22.
12 a Gen. 3:20; D&C 138:39.
  b Deut. 4:9 (9–10).
13 a TG Devil.
  b TG Spiritual Blindness; Unbelief.
  c Moses 5:28; 6:15.
  d TG Carnal Mind; Man, Natural, Not Spiritually Reborn.
14 a John 14:26 (16–26).

15 a TG Faith.
  b TG Jesus Christ, Savior.
  c D&C 42:60.
16 a Gen. 4:1 (1–2).
  b 1 Sam. 3:13; 1 Ne. 2:12 (12–13); Mosiah 27:8 (7–37).
  c Ex. 5:2; Alma 9:6.
17 a Heb. 11:4.
  b D&C 138:40.
18 a D&C 10:21 (20–21).
  b D&C 132:9 (8–11).

19 And in process of time it came to pass that Cain brought of the ^afruit of the ground an offering unto the Lord.

20 And Abel, he also brought of the ^afirstlings of his flock, and of the fat thereof. And the Lord had ^brespect unto Abel, and to his ^coffering;

21 But unto Cain, and to his ^aoffering, he had not respect. Now Satan knew this, and it ^bpleased him. And Cain was very wroth, and his countenance fell.

22 And the Lord said unto Cain: Why art thou wroth? Why is thy countenance fallen?

23 If thou doest well, thou shalt be ^aaccepted. And if thou doest not well, sin lieth at the door, and Satan ^bdesireth to have thee; and except thou shalt hearken unto my commandments, I will ^cdeliver thee up, and it shall be unto thee according to his desire. And thou shalt ^drule over him;

24 For from this time forth thou shalt be the father of his ^alies; thou shalt be called ^bPerdition; for thou wast also ^cbefore the world.

25 And it shall be said in time to come—That these abominations were had from ^aCain; for he rejected the greater counsel which was had from God; and this is a ^bcursing which I will put upon thee, except thou repent.

26 And Cain was wroth, and listened not any more to the voice of the Lord, neither to Abel, his brother, who walked in holiness before the Lord.

27 And Adam and his wife ^amourned before the Lord, because of Cain and his brethren.

28 And it came to pass that Cain took one of his brothers' daughters to ^awife, and they ^bloved Satan more than God.

29 And Satan said unto Cain: ^aSwear unto me by thy throat, and if thou tell it thou shalt die; and swear thy brethren by their heads, and by the living God, that they tell it not; for if they tell it, they shall surely die; and this that thy father may not know it; and this day I will deliver thy brother Abel into thine hands.

30 And Satan sware unto Cain that he would do according to his ^acommands. And all these things were done in secret.

31 And Cain said: Truly I am Mahan, the master of this great ^asecret, that

---

19 a Moses 5:5.
20 a Mosiah 2:3.
   b TG Respect.
   c TG Sacrifice.
21 a Gen. 4:5 (3–7); Moses 5:7 (4–8).
   b Moses 7:26.
23 a Gen. 4:7; D&C 52:15;

97:8; 132:50.
   b Gen. 4:7.
   c TG Bondage, Spiritual.
   d Moses 5:30.
24 a TG Honesty.
   b D&C 76:26, 32 (32–48). TG Sons of Perdition.
   c Moses 4:1.

25 a Hel. 6:27 (26–28).
   b Moses 5:36. TG Curse.
27 a TG Mourning.
28 a Moses 5:3 (2–3).
   b Moses 5:13.
29 a Matt. 5:36.
30 a Moses 5:23.
31 a Deut. 27:24.

I may *b*murder and get *c*gain. Wherefore Cain was called Master *d*Mahan, and he gloried in his wickedness.

32 And Cain went into the field, and Cain talked with Abel, his brother. And it came to pass that while they were in the field, Cain rose up against Abel, his brother, and slew him.

33 And Cain *a*gloried in that which he had done, saying: I am free; surely the *b*flocks of my brother falleth into my hands.

34 And the Lord said unto Cain: Where is Abel, thy brother? And he said: I know not. Am I my brother's *a*keeper?

35 And the Lord said: What hast thou done? The voice of thy brother's *a*blood cries unto me from the ground.

36 And now thou shalt be *a*cursed from the earth which hath opened her mouth to receive thy brother's blood from thy hand.

37 When thou tillest the ground it shall not henceforth yield unto thee her *a*strength. A *b*fugitive and a vagabond shalt thou be in the earth.

38 And Cain said unto the Lord: Satan *a*tempted me because of my brother's flocks. And I was wroth also; for his offering thou didst accept and not mine; my *b*punishment is greater than I can bear.

39 Behold thou hast driven me out this day from the face of the Lord, and from thy face shall I be hid; and I shall be a fugitive and a vagabond in the earth; and it shall come to pass, that he that findeth me will slay me, because of mine iniquities, for these things are not hid from the Lord.

40 And I the Lord said unto him: Whosoever slayeth thee, vengeance shall be taken on him sevenfold. And I the Lord set a *a*mark upon Cain, lest any finding him should kill him.

41 And Cain was *a*shut out from the *b*presence of the Lord, and with his wife and many of his brethren dwelt in the land of Nod, on the east of Eden.

42 And Cain knew his wife, and she conceived and bare Enoch, and he also begat many sons and daughters. And he builded a city, and he called the name of the *a*city after the name of his son, Enoch.

43 And unto Enoch was born Irad, and other sons and daughters. And

31 *b* TG Murder.
   c Deut. 27:25.
   d IE "Mind," "destroyer," and "great one" are possible meanings of the roots evident in "Mahan."
33 *a* TG Boast.
   b TG Covet.
34 *a* Gen. 4:9 (8–15).

35 *a* TG Life, Sanctity of.
36 *a* D&C 29:41. TG Curse.
37 *a* TG Strength.
   b Gen. 4:12 (11–12).
38 *a* TG Covet; Temptation.
   b TG Punish.
40 *a* Gen. 4:15; Alma 3:7 (7–16).
41 *a* TG Bondage, Spiritual.
   b Moses 6:49.

42 *a* IE There was a man named Enoch in Cain's lineage, and a city by that name among his people. Do not confuse these with the Enoch of the righteous line of Seth and with his city, Zion, also called "City of Enoch."

Irad begat Mahujael, and other sons and daughters. And Mahujael begat Methusael, and other sons and daughters. And Methusael begat Lamech.

44 And Lamech took unto himself two wives; the name of one being Adah, and the name of the other, Zillah.

45 And Adah bare Jabal; he was the father of such as dwell in ªtents, and they were keepers of cattle; and his brother's name was Jubal, who was the father of all such as handle the harp and organ.

46 And Zillah, she also bare Tubal Cain, an instructor of every artificer in brass and iron. And the sister of Tubal Cain was called Naamah.

47 And Lamech said unto his wives, Adah and Zillah: Hear my voice, ye wives of Lamech, hearken unto my speech; for I have slain a man to my wounding, and a young man to my hurt.

48 If Cain shall be avenged sevenfold, truly Lamech shall be ªseventy and seven fold;

49 For ªLamech having entered into a covenant with Satan, after the manner of Cain, wherein he became Master Mahan, master of that great secret which was administered unto Cain by Satan; and Irad, the son of Enoch, having known their secret, began to reveal it unto the sons of Adam;

50 Wherefore Lamech, being angry, slew him, not like unto Cain, his brother Abel, for the sake of getting gain, but he slew him for the ªoath's sake.

51 For, from the days of Cain, there was a secret ªcombination, and their works were in the dark, and they knew every man his brother.

52 Wherefore the Lord ªcursed Lamech, and his house, and all them that had covenanted with Satan; for they kept not the commandments of God, and it displeased God, and he ministered not unto them, and their works were abominations, and began to spread among all the ᵇsons of men. And it was among the sons of men.

53 And among the daughters of men these things were not spoken, because that Lamech had spoken the secret unto his wives, and they rebelled against him, and declared these things abroad, and had not compassion;

54 Wherefore Lamech was despised, and cast out, and came not among the sons of men, lest he should die.

55 And thus the works of ªdarkness began to prevail among all the sons of men.

---

45 a Moses 6:38; 7:5 (5–6).
48 a IE Lamech presumptively boasted that far more would be done for him than for Cain. The

reasons for his assumption are given in verses 49 and 50.
49 a Gen. 4:24.
50 a TG Oath.

51 a TG Secret Combinations.
52 a TG Curse.
  b Moses 8:14 (14–15, 19).
55 a TG Darkness, Spiritual.

56 And God ^acursed the earth with a sore curse, and was angry with the wicked, with all the sons of men whom he had made;

57 For they would not ^ahearken unto his voice, nor believe on his Only Begotten Son, even him whom he declared should ^bcome in the meridian of time, who was ^cprepared from before the foundation of the world.

58 And thus the ^aGospel began to be ^bpreached, from the beginning, being declared by ^choly ^dangels sent forth from the presence of God, and by his own voice, and by the gift of the Holy Ghost.

59 And thus all things were confirmed unto ^aAdam, by an holy ordinance, and the Gospel preached, and a decree sent forth, that it should be in the world, until the end thereof; and thus it was. Amen.

CHAPTER 6
(November–December 1830)

Adam's seed keep a book of remembrance—His righteous posterity preach repentance— God reveals Himself to Enoch—Enoch preaches the gospel—The plan of salvation was revealed to Adam—He received baptism and the priesthood.

1 And Adam hearkened unto the voice of God, and called upon his sons to repent.

2 And Adam knew his wife again, and she bare a son, and he called his name ^aSeth. And Adam glorified the name of God; for he said: God hath appointed me another seed, instead of Abel, whom Cain slew.

3 And God revealed himself unto ^aSeth, and he rebelled not, but offered an acceptable ^bsacrifice, like unto his brother Abel. And to him also was born a son, and he called his name Enos.

4 And then began these men to ^acall upon the name of the Lord, and the Lord blessed them;

5 And a ^abook of ^bremembrance was kept, in the which was recorded, in the ^clanguage of Adam, for it was given unto as many as called upon God to write by the spirit of ^dinspiration;

56 a TG Earth, Curse of.
57 a TG Disobedience; Unbelief.
  b Moses 7:46. TG Jesus Christ, Birth of.
  c TG Jesus Christ, Authority of.
58 a TG Gospel.
  b TG Preaching.

  c Alma 12:29 (28–30); Moro. 7:25 (25, 31).
  d Acts 7:53.
59 a TG Adam.
6 2 a Gen. 4:25.
3 a D&C 138:40.
  b TG Sacrifice.
4 a Gen. 4:26; Moses 5:4. TG Prayer.

5 a Abr. 1:28 (28, 31). TG Scriptures, Lost; Scriptures, Writing of.
  b TG Book of Remembrance.
  c Moses 6:46.
  d TG Guidance, Divine; Inspiration.

6 And by them their ^achildren were taught to read and write, having a ^blanguage which was ^cpure and undefiled.

7 Now this same ^aPriesthood, which was in the beginning, shall be in the end of the world also.

8 Now this prophecy Adam spake, as he was moved upon by the ^aHoly Ghost, and a ^bgenealogy was kept of the ^cchildren of God. And this was the ^dbook of the generations of Adam, saying: In the day that God created man, in the likeness of God made he him;

9 In the ^aimage of his own ^bbody, male and female, ^ccreated he them, and blessed them, and called their ^dname Adam, in the day when they were created and became living ^esouls in the land upon the ^ffootstool of God.

10 And ^aAdam lived one hundred and thirty years, and begat a son in his own likeness, after his own ^bimage, and called his name Seth.

11 And the days of Adam, after he had begotten Seth, were eight hundred years, and he begat many sons and daughters;

12 And all the days that Adam lived were nine hundred and thirty years, and he died.

13 Seth lived one hundred and five years, and begat Enos, and ^aprophesied in all his days, and taught his son Enos in the ways of God; wherefore Enos prophesied also.

14 And Seth lived, after he begat Enos, eight hundred and seven years, and begat many sons and daughters.

15 And the children of ^amen were numerous upon all the face of the land. And in those days ^bSatan had great ^cdominion among men, and raged in their hearts; and from thenceforth came ^dwars and bloodshed; and a man's hand was against his own brother, in administering death, because of ^esecret ^fworks, seeking for ^gpower.

---

6 a TG Education; Family, Children, Responsibilities toward.
  b TG Language.
  c Zeph. 3:9.
7 a TG Priesthood; Priesthood, History of; Priesthood, Melchizedek.
8 a Ex. 4:12 (12–16); 2 Pet. 1:21; D&C 24:6 (5–6); 28:4; Moses 6:32.
  b TG Genealogy and Temple Work.
  c TG Sons and Daughters

of God.
  d Gen. 5:1.
9 a Gen. 1:26 (26–28); Moses 2:26 (26–29); Abr. 4:26 (26–31).
  b TG God, Body of, Corporeal Nature.
  c TG Man, Physical Creation of.
  d Moses 1:34; 4:26.
  e TG Soul.
  f Moses 6:44; Abr. 2:7.
10 a D&C 107:41 (41–56).
  b IE Seth was in the

likeness and image of Adam, as Adam was in the image of God. Gen. 5:3; D&C 107:42–43; 138:40.
13 a Moses 5:23.
15 a Moses 8:14 (13–15).
  b 3 Ne. 6:15.
  c Moses 5:13.
  d TG War.
  e TG Conspiracy.
  f TG Secret Combinations.
  g Ether 8:23. TG Selfishness.

16 All the days of Seth were nine hundred and twelve years, and he died.

17 And Enos lived ninety years, and begat ªCainan. And Enos and the residue of the people of God came out from the land, which was called Shulon, and dwelt in a land of promise, which he called after his own son, whom he had named ᵇCainan.

18 And Enos lived, after he begat Cainan, eight hundred and fifteen years, and begat many sons and daughters. And all the days of Enos were nine hundred and five years, and he died.

19 And Cainan lived seventy years, and begat Mahalaleel; and Cainan lived after he begat Mahalaleel eight hundred and forty years, and begat sons and daughters. And all the days of ªCainan were nine hundred and ten years, and he died.

20 And Mahalaleel lived sixty-five years, and begat Jared; and Mahalaleel lived, after he begat Jared, eight hundred and thirty years, and begat sons and daughters. And all the days of Mahalaleel were eight hundred and ninety-five years, and he died.

21 And Jared lived one hundred and sixty-two years, and begat ªEnoch; and Jared lived, after he begat Enoch, eight hundred years, and begat sons and daughters. And Jared ᵇtaught Enoch in all the ways of God.

22 And this is the genealogy of the sons of Adam, who was the ªson of God, with whom God, himself, conversed.

23 And they were ªpreachers of ᵇrighteousness, and spake and ᶜprophesied, and called upon all men, everywhere, to repent; and ᵈfaith was ᵉtaught unto the children of men.

24 And it came to pass that all the days of Jared were nine hundred and sixty-two years, and he died.

25 And Enoch lived sixty-five years, and begat Methuselah.

26 And it came to pass that Enoch journeyed in the land, among the people; and as he journeyed, the ªSpirit of God descended out of heaven, and abode upon him.

27 And he heard a ªvoice from heaven, saying: ᵇEnoch, my son, ᶜprophesy unto this people, and say unto them—Repent, for thus saith the Lord: I am ᵈangry with this people, and my fierce anger is kindled against them; for

17 a D&C 107:45, 53.
 b Moses 6:41.
19 a Gen. 5:14 (4–24); D&C
    107:45 (45, 53).
21 a Gen. 5:22 (5–24); Moses
    7:69; 8:1 (1–2).
 b Moses 6:41.

22 a Luke 3:38.
23 a Moses 6:13. TG Preach-
    ing.
 b TG Righteousness.
 c Moses 8:3, 16. TG Proph-
    ets, Mission of.
 d TG Faith.

 e TG Education.
26 a TG God, Spirit of.
27 a TG Guidance, Divine.
 b Jude 1:14 (14–16).
 c Moses 8:19.
 d Deut. 32:21; 2 Ne. 15:25;
    D&C 63:32.

their hearts have waxed *hard, and their *ears are dull of hearing, and their eyes *cannot see afar off;

28 And for these many generations, ever since the day that I created them, have they gone astray, and have *denied me, and have sought their own counsels in the dark; and in their own abominations have they devised murder, and have not kept the commandments, which I gave unto their father, Adam.

29 Wherefore, they have foresworn themselves, and, by their oaths, they have brought upon themselves death; and a *hell I have prepared for them, if they repent not;

30 And this is a decree, which I have sent forth in the beginning of the world, from my own mouth, from the foundation thereof, and by the mouths of my servants, thy fathers, have I decreed it, even as it shall be sent forth in the world, unto the ends thereof.

31 And when Enoch had heard these words, he *bowed himself to the earth, before the Lord, and spake before the Lord, saying: *Why is it that I have found favor in thy sight, and am but a lad, and all the people *hate me; for I am *slow of speech; wherefore am I thy servant?

32 And the Lord said unto Enoch: Go forth and do as I have commanded thee, and no man shall pierce thee. Open thy *mouth, and it shall be filled, and I will give thee utterance, for all flesh is in my hands, and I will do as seemeth me good.

33 Say unto this people: *Choose ye *this day, to serve the Lord God who made you.

34 Behold my *Spirit is upon you, wherefore all thy words will I justify; and the *mountains shall flee before you, and the *rivers shall turn from their course; and thou shalt abide in me, and I in you; therefore *walk with me.

35 And the Lord spake unto Enoch, and said unto him: Anoint thine eyes with *clay, and wash them, and thou shalt see. And he did so.

36 And he beheld the *spirits that God had created; and he beheld also things which were not visible to the *natural eye; and from thenceforth

27 e TG Hardheartedness.
  f Ps. 78:1; 2 Ne. 9:31; Mosiah 26:28; D&C 1:14 (2, 11, 14).
  g Prov. 7:9; Alma 10:25; 14:6; Moses 7:26.
28 a TG Rebellion.
29 a Moses 7:37. TG Hell.
31 a Ex. 34:8.
  b Ex. 3:11 (10–21).
  c Jer. 11:19; Matt. 10:22;

JS—H 1:20. TG Hate.
  d Ex. 4:10; Jer. 1:6 (6–9).
32 a Ex. 4:12 (12–16); D&C 24:6 (5–6); 28:4; Moses 6:8; 7:13. TG Prophets, Mission of.
33 a TG Agency.
  b TG Procrastination.
34 a TG Teaching with the Spirit.
  b Judg. 5:5; Matt. 17:20;

D&C 109:74; 133:22 (21–22, 40).
  c Moses 7:13.
  d Gen. 5:24; Moses 7:69. TG Walking with God.
35 a John 9:6 (6, 15).
36 a TG Man, Antemortal Existence of; Spirit Body; Spirit Creation.
  b Moses 1:11.

came the saying abroad in the land: A ᶜseer hath the Lord raised up unto his people.

37 And it came to pass that Enoch went forth in the land, among the people, standing upon the hills and the high places, and cried with a loud voice, testifying against their works; and all men were ᵃoffended because of him.

38 And they came forth to hear him, upon the high places, saying unto the ᵃtent-keepers: Tarry ye here and keep the tents, while we go yonder to behold the seer, for he prophesieth, and there is a strange thing in the land; a ᵇwild man hath come among us.

39 And it came to pass when they heard him, no man laid hands on him; for ᵃfear came on all them that heard him; for he ᵇwalked with God.

40 And there came a man unto him, whose name was Mahijah, and said unto him: Tell us plainly who thou art, and from whence thou comest?

41 And he said unto them: I came out from the land of ᵃCainan, the land of my fathers, a land of ᵇrighteousness unto this day. And my father ᶜtaught me in all the ways of God.

42 And it came to pass, as I journeyed from the land of Cainan, by the sea east, I beheld a vision; and lo, the heavens I saw, and the Lord spake with me, and gave me commandment; wherefore, for this cause, to keep the commandment, I speak forth these words.

43 And Enoch continued his speech, saying: The Lord which spake with me, the same is the God of heaven, and he is my God, and your God, and ye are my brethren, and why ᵃcounsel ye yourselves, and deny the God of heaven?

44 The heavens he made; the ᵃearth is his ᵇfootstool; and the foundation thereof is his. Behold, he laid it, an host of men hath he brought in upon the face thereof.

45 And death hath come upon our fathers; nevertheless we know them, and cannot deny, and even the first of all we know, even ᵃAdam.

46 For a book of ᵃremembrance we have ᵇwritten among us, according to the pattern given by the finger of God; and it is given in our own ᶜlanguage.

---

36 c TG Seer.
37 a Matt. 11:6; 1 Ne. 16:2
   (1–3); Mosiah 13:7.
38 a Moses 5:45; 7:5 (5–6).
   b Gen. 16:12; Matt. 3:4
   (1–12).
39 a Luke 7:16; Alma 19:25
   (24–27).
   b TG God, Privilege of

Seeing; Walking with
   God.
41 a Moses 6:17.
   b TG Righteousness.
   c Moses 6:21.
43 a Prov. 1:25 (24–33); D&C
   56:14 (14–15).
44 a Deut. 10:14; 1 Ne. 11:6;
   2 Ne. 29:7; D&C 55:1.

b Moses 6:9; Abr. 2:7.
45 a TG Adam.
46 a TG Book of Remem-
   brance; Genealogy and
   Temple Work.
   b TG Scriptures, Writing
   of.
   c Moses 6:5.

47 And as Enoch spake forth the words of God, the people trembled, and could not ᵃstand in his presence.

48 And he said unto them: Because that Adam ᵃfell, we are; and by his fall came ᵇdeath; and we are made partakers of misery and woe.

49 Behold Satan hath come among the children of men, and ᵃtempteth them to ᵇworship him; and men have become ᶜcarnal, ᵈsensual, and devilish, and are shut out from the ᵉpresence of God.

50 But God hath made known unto our fathers that all men must repent.

51 And he called upon our father Adam by his own voice, saying: I am God; I ᵃmade the world, and ᵇmen ᶜbefore they were in the flesh.

52 And he also said unto him: If thou wilt turn unto me, and hearken unto my voice, and believe, and repent of all thy transgressions, and be ᵃbaptized, even in water, in the name of mine Only Begotten Son, who is full of ᵇgrace and truth, which is ᶜJesus Christ, the only ᵈname which shall be given under heaven, whereby ᵉsalvation shall come unto the children of men, ye shall receive the gift of the Holy Ghost, asking all things in his name, and whatsoever ye shall ask, it shall be given you.

53 And our father Adam spake unto the Lord, and said: Why is it that men must repent and be baptized in water? And the Lord said unto Adam: Behold I have ᵃforgiven thee thy transgression in the Garden of Eden.

54 Hence came the saying abroad among the people, that the ᵃSon of God hath ᵇatoned for original guilt, wherein the sins of the parents cannot be answered upon the heads of the ᶜchildren, for they are ᵈwhole from the foundation of the world.

55 And the Lord spake unto Adam, saying: Inasmuch as thy children are ᵃconceived in sin, even so when they begin to grow up, ᵇsin conceiveth in their hearts, and they taste the ᶜbitter, that they may know to prize the good.

---

47 a 1 Ne. 17:48 (48–55).
48 a 2 Ne. 2:25. TG Fall of Man.
  b TG Death; Mortality.
49 a Moses 1:12. TG Temptation.
  b TG Worship.
  c Mosiah 16:3 (3–4); Moses 5:13. TG Carnal Mind; Man, Natural, Not Spiritually Reborn.
  d TG Sensuality.
  e Gen. 4:16; Moses 5:41.
51 a Moses 3:5.

b TG Man, a Spirit Child of Heavenly Father.
  c TG Spirit Creation.
52 a 3 Ne. 11:26 (23–26). TG Baptism, Essential.
  b TG Grace.
  c TG Jesus Christ, Messiah.
  d Acts 4:12. TG Jesus Christ, Authority of; Name.
  e TG Jesus Christ, Savior; Salvation.
53 a TG Forgive.
54 a TG Jesus Christ, Divine

Sonship.
  b Mosiah 3:16. TG Jesus Christ, Atonement through.
  c TG Children.
  d TG Salvation of Little Children.
55 a TG Conceived in Sin.
  b TG Death, Spiritual, First; Man, Natural, Not Spiritually Reborn.
  c D&C 29:39. TG Opposition.

56 And it is given unto them to know good from evil; wherefore they are *agents unto themselves, and I have given unto you another law and commandment.

57 Wherefore teach it unto your children, that all men, everywhere, must *repent, or they can in nowise inherit the kingdom of God, for no *unclean thing can dwell there, or *dwell in his *presence; for, in the language of Adam, *Man of Holiness is his name, and the name of his Only Begotten is the *Son of Man, even *Jesus Christ, a righteous *Judge, who shall come in the meridian of time.

58 Therefore I give unto you a *commandment, to *teach these things freely unto your *children, saying:

59 That by reason of transgression cometh the fall, which fall bringeth death, and inasmuch as ye were born into the world by water, and blood, and the *spirit, which I have made, and so became of *dust a living soul, even so ye must be *born again into the kingdom of heaven, of *water, and of the Spirit, and be cleansed by blood, even the blood of mine Only Begotten; that ye might be sanctified from all sin, and *enjoy the *words of *eternal life in this world, and eternal life in the world to come, even immortal *glory;

60 For by the *water ye keep the commandment; by the Spirit ye are *justified, and by the *blood ye are *sanctified;

61 Therefore it is given to abide in you; the *record of heaven; the *Comforter; the *peaceable things of immortal glory; the truth of all things; that which quickeneth all things, which maketh alive all things; that which knoweth all things, and hath all *power according to wisdom, mercy, truth, justice, and judgment.

56a Gal. 5:1; 2 Ne. 2:27
   (26–27); Hel. 14:30
   (29–30). TG Agency.
57a 1 Cor. 6:9 (9–10); Moses
   5:8; 7:10. TG Baptism,
   Qualifications for;
   Repent.
  b Lev. 15:31. TG Chas-
   tity; Cleanliness; God,
   Perfection of; Modesty;
   Uncleanness.
  c Ps. 15:1 (1–5); 24:3
   (3–4); 27:4; 1 Ne. 10:21;
   15:33 (33–36); Mosiah
   15:23 (19–26); Morm.
   7:7; D&C 76:62 (50–62).
  d TG God, Presence of.
  e Moses 7:35.

  f Matt. 20:28; John 3:13
   (13–14).
  g TG Jesus Christ, Prophecies about.
  h TG God, Justice of; Jesus
   Christ, Judge.
58a TG Authority.
  b TG Education.
  c TG Family, Children,
   Responsibilities toward.
59a 1 Jn. 5:8.
  b Gen. 2:7; Moses 3:7; 4:25
   (25–29); Abr. 5:7.
  c TG Holy Ghost, Baptism
   of; Man, New, Spiritually
   Reborn.
  d TG Baptism; Baptism,
   Essential.

  e 2 Ne. 4:15 (15–16).
  f John 6:68.
  g Abr. 2:11.
  h TG Celestial Glory;
   Glory.
60a Moro. 8:25.
  b TG Justification.
  c TG Blood, Shedding of;
   Blood, Symbolism of.
  d TG Sanctification.
61a TG Holy Ghost, Source
   of Testimony.
  b TG Holy Ghost, Com-
   forter.
  c TG Peace of God.
  d TG Jesus Christ, Power
   of.

62 And now, behold, I say unto you: This is the *plan of salvation unto all men, through the *blood of mine *Only Begotten, who shall come in the meridian of time.

63 And behold, all things have their *likeness, and all things are created and made to *bear record of me, both things which are temporal, and things which are spiritual; things which are in the heavens above, and things which are on the earth, and things which are in the earth, and things which are under the earth, both above and beneath: all things bear record of me.

64 And it came to pass, when the Lord had spoken with Adam, our father, that Adam cried unto the Lord, and he was *caught away by the Spirit of the Lord, and was carried down into the water, and was laid under the *water, and was brought forth out of the water.

65 And thus he was baptized, and the Spirit of God descended upon him, and thus he was *born of the Spirit, and became quickened in the *inner man.

66 And he heard a voice out of heaven, saying: Thou art baptized with *fire, and with the Holy Ghost. This is the *record of the Father, and the Son, from henceforth and forever;

67 And thou art after the *order of him who was without beginning of days or end of years, from all eternity to all eternity.

68 Behold, thou art *one in me, a son of God; and thus may all become my *sons. Amen.

CHAPTER 7

(December 1830)

Enoch teaches, leads the people, and moves mountains—The city of Zion is established—Enoch foresees the coming of the Son of Man, His atoning sacrifice, and the resurrection of the Saints—He foresees the Restoration, the Gathering, the Second Coming, and the return of Zion.

---

62 a TG Gospel; Salvation, Plan of.
  b TG Blood, Symbolism of.
  c TG Jesus Christ, Birth of.
63 a Heb. 8:5; D&C 77:2.
  b Alma 30:44; D&C 88:47 (45–47).
64 a 1 Kgs. 18:12; 2 Kgs. 2:16.

TG Holy Ghost, Mission of.
  b TG Baptism, Immersion.
65 a TG Man, New, Spiritually Reborn.
  b Mosiah 27:25; Alma 5:14 (12–15).
66 a D&C 19:31.
  b 2 Ne. 31:18 (17–21);

3 Ne. 28:11.
67 a TG Priesthood, Melchizedek.
68 a John 17:21; 1 Jn. 1:3; D&C 35:2.
  b John 1:12 (9–13); Mosiah 27:25 (24–26); D&C 34:3. TG Sons and Daughters of God.

1 And it came to pass that Enoch continued his speech, saying: Behold, our father Adam taught these things, and many have believed and become the ^asons of God, and many have believed not, and have perished in their sins, and are looking forth with ^bfear, in torment, for the fiery indignation of the wrath of God to be poured out upon them.

2 And from that time forth Enoch began to prophesy, saying unto the people, that: As I was journeying, and stood upon the place Mahujah, and cried unto the Lord, there came a voice out of heaven, saying—Turn ye, and get ye upon the mount ^aSimeon.

3 And it came to pass that I turned and went up on the mount; and as I stood upon the mount, I beheld the heavens open, and I was clothed upon with ^aglory;

4 And I ^asaw the Lord; and he stood before my face, and he talked with me, even as a man talketh one with another, ^bface to face; and he said unto me: ^cLook, and I will ^dshow unto thee the world for the space of many generations.

5 And it came to pass that I beheld in the valley of Shum, and lo, a great people which dwelt in ^atents, which were the people of Shum.

6 And again the Lord said unto me: Look; and I looked towards the north, and I beheld the people of ^aCanaan, which dwelt in tents.

7 And the Lord said unto me: Prophesy; and I prophesied, saying: Behold the people of Canaan, which are numerous, shall go forth in battle array against the people of Shum, and shall slay them that they shall utterly be destroyed; and the people of Canaan shall divide themselves in the land, and the land shall be barren and unfruitful, and none other people shall dwell there but the people of Canaan;

8 For behold, the Lord shall ^acurse the land with much heat, and the ^bbarrenness thereof shall go forth forever; and there was a ^cblackness came upon all the children of Canaan, that they were despised among all people.

9 And it came to pass that the Lord said unto me: Look; and I looked, and I beheld the land of Sharon, and the land of Enoch, and the land of Omner, and the land of Heni, and the land of Shem, and the land of Haner, and the land of Hanannihah, and all the inhabitants thereof;

10 And the Lord said unto me: Go to this people, and say unto them— ^aRepent, lest I come out and smite them with a curse, and they die.

---

7 1 a TG Sons and Daughters of God.
b Alma 40:14 (11–14).
2 a The Hebrew equivalent of Simeon is *Shim'on*, which means "hearing."
3 a TG Transfiguration.
4 a TG God, Privilege of Seeing; Jesus Christ, Appearances, Antemortal.
b Gen. 32:30; Deut. 5:4; Moses 1:11 (2, 11, 31).
c Moses 1:4.
d TG God, Omniscience of; Revelation.
5 a Moses 5:45; 6:38.
6 a Abr. 1:21.
8 a TG Earth, Curse of.
b TG Barren.
c 2 Ne. 26:33.
10 a Moses 5:8; 6:57.

11 And he gave unto me a commandment that I should *baptize in the name of the Father, and of the Son, which is full of *grace and truth, and of the Holy Ghost, which beareth record of the Father and the Son.

12 And it came to pass that Enoch continued to call upon all the people, save it were the people of Canaan, to repent;

13 And so great was the *faith of Enoch that he led the people of God, and their enemies came to battle against them; and he *spake the word of the Lord, and the earth trembled, and the *mountains fled, even according to his command; and the *rivers of water were turned out of their course; and the roar of the lions was heard out of the wilderness; and all nations feared greatly, so *powerful was the word of Enoch, and so great was the power of the language which God had given him.

14 There also came *up a land out of the depth of the sea, and so great was the fear of the enemies of the people of God, that they fled and stood afar off and went upon the land which came up out of the depth of the sea.

15 And the *giants of the land, also, stood afar off; and there went forth a *curse upon all people that fought against God;

16 And from that time forth there were wars and bloodshed among them; but the Lord came and *dwelt with his people, and they dwelt in righteousness.

17 The *fear of the Lord was upon all nations, so great was the *glory of the Lord, which was upon his people. And the Lord blessed the *land, and they were blessed upon the mountains, and upon the high places, and did flourish.

18 And the Lord called his people *Zion, because they were of *one heart and one mind, and dwelt in righteousness; and there was no poor among them.

19 And Enoch continued his preaching in righteousness unto the people of God. And it came to pass in his days, that he built a city that was called the City of Holiness, even Zion.

20 And it came to pass that Enoch talked with the Lord; and he said unto the Lord: Surely *Zion shall dwell in safety forever. But the Lord said unto Enoch: Zion have I blessed, but the *residue of the people have I cursed.

21 And it came to pass that the Lord showed unto Enoch all the inhabitants of the earth; and he beheld, and lo, *Zion, in process of time, was

11 a TG Baptism, Essential.
  b TG Grace.
13 a TG Faith.
  b Moses 6:32.
  c Matt. 17:20; Luke 17:6 (5–6).
  d Moses 6:34.
  e TG Priesthood, Power of.
14 a 3 Ne. 9:8.

15 a Num. 13:33; Moses 8:18.
  b Ps. 83:17 (2–17); 2 Ne. 25:14; D&C 71:7.
16 a TG God, Presence of.
17 a Ex. 23:27 (27–28); Alma 14:26; D&C 64:43.
  b TG Glory.
  c 1 Chr. 28:8 (7–8); 1 Ne. 2:20.

18 a D&C 38:4. TG Zion.
  b 2 Chr. 30:12; Acts 4:32 (31–32); Philip. 2:1–4. TG Unity.
20 a Moses 7:63 (62–63). TG Jerusalem, New.
  b Moses 7:28.
21 a Moses 7:31.

*b*taken up into heaven. And the Lord said unto Enoch: Behold mine abode forever.

22 And Enoch also beheld the residue of the people which were the sons of Adam; and they were a mixture of all the seed of Adam save it was the seed of Cain, for the seed of Cain were *a*black, and had not place among them.

23 And after that Zion was taken up into *a*heaven, Enoch *b*beheld, and lo, *c*all the nations of the earth were before him;

24 And there came generation upon generation; and Enoch was high and *a*lifted up, even in the bosom of the Father, and of the Son of Man; and behold, the power of Satan was upon all the face of the earth.

25 And he saw angels descending out of heaven; and he heard a loud voice saying: Wo, wo be unto the inhabitants of the earth.

26 And he beheld Satan; and he had a great *a*chain in his hand, and it veiled the whole face of the earth with *b*darkness; and he looked up and *c*laughed, and his *d*angels rejoiced.

27 And Enoch beheld *a*angels descending out of heaven, bearing *b*testimony of the Father and Son; and the Holy Ghost fell on many, and they were caught up by the powers of heaven into Zion.

28 And it came to pass that the God of heaven looked upon the *a*residue of the people, and he wept; and Enoch bore record of it, saying: How is it that the heavens weep, and shed forth their tears as the rain upon the mountains?

29 And Enoch said unto the Lord: How is it that thou canst *a*weep, seeing thou art holy, and from all eternity to all eternity?

30 And were it possible that man could number the particles of the earth, yea, millions of *a*earths like this, it would not be a beginning to the number of thy *b*creations; and thy curtains are stretched out still; and yet thou art there, and thy bosom is there; and also thou art just; thou art merciful and kind forever;

31 And thou hast taken *a*Zion to thine own bosom, from all thy creations, from all eternity to all eternity; and naught but peace, *b*justice, and truth is

21 *b* Moses 7:47, 69.
22 *a* 2 Ne. 26:33.
23 *a* TG Heaven.
  b TG Vision.
  c D&C 88:47 (45–47);
    Moses 1:28 (27–29); Abr.
    3:21 (21–23).
24 *a* 2 Cor. 12:2 (1–4).
26 *a* Prov. 5:22; 2 Tim. 2:26

(24–26); Alma 12:11
(10–11).
  b Isa. 60:2 (1–3); Alma
    10:25; 14:6; Moses 6:27.
  c Moses 5:21.
  d 2 Pet. 2:4; Jude 1:6;
    D&C 29:37 (36–45).
27 *a* TG Angels.
  b TG Testimony.

28 *a* Moro. 7:32; Moses 7:20.
29 *a* Isa. 63:9 (7–10).
30 *a* Job 9:9 (7–9); Ps. 8:3
    (3–4); D&C 76:24; Moses 1:33. TG Astronomy.
  b TG Creation.
31 *a* Moses 7:21.
  b TG God, Justice of.

the habitation of thy throne; and mercy shall go before thy face and have no end; how is it thou canst ^cweep?

32 The Lord said unto Enoch: Behold these thy brethren; they are the workmanship of mine own ^ahands, and I gave unto them their ^bknowledge, in the day I created them; and in the Garden of Eden, gave I unto man his ^cagency;

33 And unto thy brethren have I said, and also given commandment, that they should ^alove one another, and that they should choose me, their Father; but behold, they are without affection, and they ^bhate their own blood;

34 And the ^afire of mine ^bindignation is kindled against them; and in my hot displeasure will I send in the ^cfloods upon them, for my fierce anger is kindled against them.

35 Behold, I am God; ^aMan of Holiness is my name; Man of Counsel is my name; and Endless and Eternal is my ^bname, also.

36 Wherefore, I can stretch forth mine hands and hold all the ^acreations which I have made; and mine eye can pierce them also, and among all the workmanship of mine hands there has not been so great ^bwickedness as among thy brethren.

37 But behold, their sins shall be upon the heads of their fathers; Satan shall be their father, and misery shall be their doom; and the whole heavens shall weep over them, even all the workmanship of mine hands; wherefore should not the heavens weep, seeing these shall suffer?

38 But behold, these which thine eyes are upon shall perish in the floods; and behold, I will shut them up; a ^aprison have I prepared for them.

39 And ^athat which I have chosen hath pled before my face. Wherefore, he ^bsuffereth for their sins; inasmuch as they will repent in the day that my ^cChosen shall return unto me, and until that day they shall be in ^dtorment;

40 Wherefore, for this shall the heavens weep, yea, and all the workmanship of mine hands.

41 And it came to pass that the Lord spake unto Enoch, and ^atold Enoch all the doings of the children of men; wherefore Enoch knew, and looked upon their wickedness, and their misery, and wept and stretched forth his

---

31 c Moses 7:37 (37, 40).
32 a Moses 1:4.
  b TG God, Intelligence of;
    Knowledge.
  c TG Agency.
33 a TG Love.
  b Gen. 6:11. TG Hate.
34 a Num. 11:1 (1, 10); D&C
    35:14.
  b Ps. 106:40.

  c Gen. 7:10 (4, 10); Moses
    8:17 (17, 24). TG Flood.
35 a Moses 6:57.
  b Ex. 3:15; Moses 1:3.
36 a D&C 38:2; 88:41; Moses
    1:35 (35–37). TG God,
    Omniscience of.
  b Gen. 6:5 (5–6); 3 Ne.
    9:9; Morm. 4:12 (10–12);
    D&C 112:23; Moses

    8:22 (22, 28–30).
38 a 1 Pet. 3:20 (18–21).
    TG Spirits in Prison.
39 a IE the Savior.
  b Ezek. 33:11.
  c Moses 4:2; Abr. 3:27.
  d TG Damnation.
41 a TG God, Omniscience
    of.

arms, and his *b*heart swelled wide as eternity; and his bowels yearned; and all eternity shook.

42 And Enoch also saw Noah, and his *a*family; that the posterity of all the sons of Noah should be saved with a temporal salvation;

43 Wherefore Enoch saw that Noah built an *a*ark; and that the Lord smiled upon it, and held it in his own hand; but upon the residue of the wicked the *b*floods came and swallowed them up.

44 And as Enoch saw this, he had *a*bitterness of soul, and wept over his brethren, and said unto the heavens: I will refuse to be *b*comforted; but the Lord said unto Enoch: Lift up your heart, and be glad; and look.

45 And it came to pass that Enoch looked; and from Noah, he beheld all the families of the earth; and he cried unto the Lord, saying: When shall the day of the Lord come? When shall the blood of the Righteous be shed, that all they that mourn may be *a*sanctified and have eternal life?

46 And the Lord said: It shall be in the *a*meridian of time, in the days of wickedness and vengeance.

47 And behold, Enoch *a*saw the day of the coming of the Son of Man, even in the flesh; and his soul rejoiced, saying: The Righteous is lifted up, and the *b*Lamb is slain from the foundation of the world; and through *c*faith I am in the bosom of the Father, and behold, *d*Zion is with me.

48 And it came to pass that Enoch looked upon the *a*earth; and he heard a voice from the bowels thereof, saying: Wo, wo is me, the mother of men; I am *b*pained, I am weary, because of the wickedness of my children. When shall I *c*rest, and be *d*cleansed from the *e*filthiness which is gone forth out of me? When will my Creator sanctify me, that I may rest, and righteousness for a season abide upon my face?

49 And when Enoch heard the earth mourn, he wept, and cried unto the Lord, saying: O Lord, wilt thou not have compassion upon the earth? Wilt thou not bless the children of Noah?

50 And it came to pass that Enoch continued his cry unto the Lord, saying: I ask thee, O Lord, in the name of thine Only Begotten, even Jesus Christ, that thou wilt have mercy upon Noah and his seed, that the earth might never more be covered by the *a*floods.

41 *b* Mosiah 28:3. TG Compassion.
42 *a* Gen. 8:16; Moses 8:12.
43 *a* Gen. 6:14–22; Ether 6:7 (6–8).
  b TG Flood; Punish.
44 *a* Job 10:1; Isa. 38:15.
  b Ps. 77:2; Ether 15:3.

45 *a* TG Sanctification.
46 *a* Moses 5:57.
47 *a* TG Jesus Christ, Appearances, Antemortal.
  b TG Jesus Christ, Lamb of God; Passover.
  c TG Faith.
  d Moses 7:21.

48 *a* TG Earth, Purpose of.
  b TG Pain.
  c Moses 7:64 (54, 58, 64).
  d TG Earth, Cleansing of.
  e TG Filthiness.
50 *a* TG Flood.

51 And the Lord could not withhold; and he *a*covenanted with Enoch, and sware unto him with an oath, that he would stay the *b*floods; that he would call upon the children of Noah;

52 And he sent forth an unalterable decree, that a *a*remnant of his seed should always be found among all nations, while the earth should stand;

53 And the Lord said: Blessed is he through whose seed Messiah shall come; for he saith—I am *a*Messiah, the *b*King of Zion, the *c*Rock of Heaven, which is broad as *d*eternity; whoso cometh in at the gate and *e*climbeth up by me shall never fall; wherefore, blessed are they of whom I have spoken, for they shall come forth with *f*songs of everlasting *g*joy.

54 And it came to pass that Enoch cried unto the Lord, saying: When the Son of Man cometh in the flesh, shall the earth rest? I pray thee, show me these things.

55 And the Lord said unto Enoch: Look, and he looked and beheld the *a*Son of Man lifted up on the *b*cross, after the manner of men;

56 And he heard a loud voice; and the heavens were *a*veiled; and all the creations of God mourned; and the earth *b*groaned; and the rocks were rent; and the *c*saints arose, and were *d*crowned at the *e*right hand of the Son of Man, with crowns of glory;

57 And as many of the *a*spirits as were in *b*prison came forth, and stood on the right hand of God; and the remainder were reserved in chains of darkness until the judgment of the great day.

58 And again Enoch wept and cried unto the Lord, saying: When shall the earth *a*rest?

59 And Enoch beheld the Son of Man ascend up unto the Father; and he called unto the Lord, saying: Wilt thou not come again upon the earth? Forasmuch as thou art God, and I know thee, and thou hast sworn unto me, and commanded me that I should ask in the name of thine Only Begotten; thou hast made me, and given unto me a right to thy throne, and not of myself, but through thine own grace; wherefore, I ask thee if thou wilt not come again on the earth.

60 And the Lord said unto Enoch: As I live, even so will I come in the

---

51 *a* Moses 7:60.
  b Ps. 104:9.
52 *a* Moses 8:2.
53 *a* TG Jesus Christ, Messiah.
  b Matt. 2:2; 2 Ne. 10:14;
     Alma 5:50; D&C 128:22
     (22–23).
  c Ps. 71:3; 78:35; Hel.
     5:12. TG Cornerstone;
     Rock.

d TG Eternity.
e 2 Ne. 31:19 (19–20).
f TG Singing.
g TG Joy.
55 *a* TG Jesus Christ, Prophecies about.
  b 3 Ne. 27:14. TG Jesus
     Christ, Crucifixion of.
56 *a* TG Veil.
  b Matt. 27:51 (45, 50–51).

c TG Saints.
d TG Exaltation.
e Matt. 25:34.
57 *a* TG Spirits, Disembodied.
  b D&C 76:73 (71–74);
     88:99. TG Salvation
     for the Dead; Spirits in
     Prison.
58 *a* Dan. 12:8 (8–13).

^alast days, in the days of wickedness and vengeance, to fulfil the ^boath which I have made unto you concerning the children of Noah;

61 And the day shall come that the earth shall ^arest, but before that day the heavens shall be ^bdarkened, and a ^cveil of darkness shall cover the earth; and the heavens shall shake, and also the earth; and great tribulations shall be among the children of men, but my people will I ^dpreserve;

62 And ^arighteousness will I send down out of heaven; and truth will I send forth out of the earth, to bear ^btestimony of mine Only Begotten; his ^cresurrection from the dead; yea, and also the resurrection of all men; and righteousness and truth will I cause to sweep the earth as with a flood, to ^dgather out mine elect from the four quarters of the earth, unto a place which I shall prepare, an Holy City, that my people may gird up their loins, and be looking forth for the time of my coming; for there shall be my tabernacle, and it shall be called ^eZion, a ^fNew Jerusalem.

63 And the Lord said unto Enoch: Then shalt thou and all thy ^acity meet them there, and we will ^breceive them into our bosom, and they shall see us; and we will fall upon their necks, and they shall fall upon our necks, and we will kiss each other;

64 And there shall be mine abode, and it shall be Zion, which shall come forth out of all the creations which I have made; and for the space of a ^athousand years the ^bearth shall ^crest.

65 And it came to pass that Enoch saw the ^aday of the ^bcoming of the Son of Man, in the last days, to dwell on the earth in righteousness for the space of a thousand years;

66 But before that day he saw great tribulations among the wicked; and he also saw the sea, that it was troubled, and men's hearts ^afailing them, looking forth with fear for the ^bjudgments of the Almighty God, which should come upon the wicked.

67 And the Lord showed Enoch all things, even unto the end of the world; and he saw the day of the righteous, the hour of their redemption, and received a fulness of ^ajoy;

---

60 a TG Last Days.
   b Moses 7:51.
61 a TG Rest.
   b Micah 3:6; D&C 38:11
    (11–12); 112:23.
   c TG Veil.
   d 1 Ne. 22:17 (15–22);
    2 Ne. 30:10. TG Protection, Divine.
62 a TG Righteousness.

   b TG Testimony.
   c TG Jesus Christ, Resurrection.
   d TG Israel, Gathering of.
   e TG Zion.
   f TG Jerusalem, New.
63 a Rev. 21:10 (9–11); D&C
    45:12 (11–12); Moses
    7:20 (20–21).
   b Rev. 14:13 (12–13).

64 a TG Millennium.
   b TG Earth, Destiny of.
   c Moses 7:48. TG Earth,
    Purpose of.
65 a 1 Cor. 5:5.
   b Jude 1:14.
66 a Isa. 13:7.
   b TG Judgment, the Last.
67 a TG Joy.

68 And all the days of *a*Zion, in the days of Enoch, were three hundred and sixty-five years.

69 And Enoch and all his people *a*walked with God, and he dwelt in the midst of Zion; and it came to pass that Zion was not, for God received it up into his own bosom; and from thence went forth the saying, Zion is Fled.

CHAPTER 8
(February 1831)

Methuselah prophesies—Noah and his sons preach the gospel—Great wickedness prevails—The call to repentance is unheeded—God decrees the destruction of all flesh by the Flood.

1 And all the days of *a*Enoch were four hundred and thirty years.

2 And it came to pass that Methuselah, the son of Enoch, was *a*not taken, that the covenants of the Lord might be fulfilled, which he made to Enoch; for he truly covenanted with Enoch that Noah should be of the fruit of his loins.

3 And it came to pass that Methuselah *a*prophesied that from his loins should spring all the kingdoms of the earth (through Noah), and he took glory unto himself.

4 And there came forth a great *a*famine into the land, and the Lord *b*cursed the earth with a sore curse, and many of the inhabitants thereof died.

5 And it came to pass that Methuselah lived one hundred and eighty-seven years, and begat Lamech;

6 And Methuselah lived, after he begat Lamech, seven hundred and eighty-two years, and begat sons and daughters;

7 And all the days of Methuselah were nine hundred and sixty-nine years, and he died.

8 And Lamech lived one hundred and eighty-two years, and begat a son,

9 And he called his name Noah, saying: This son shall comfort us concerning our work and toil of our hands, because of the ground which the Lord hath *a*cursed.

10 And Lamech lived, after he begat Noah, five hundred and ninety-five years, and begat sons and daughters;

68*a* Gen. 5:23; Moses 8:1.   **8** 1*a* Moses 7:68–69.   4*a* TG Famine.
69*a* Gen. 5:24; Moses 6:34.   2*a* Moses 7:52 (51–52).   *b* TG Curse.
   TG Walking with God.   3*a* Moses 6:23.   9*a* Moses 4:23. TG Curse.

11 And all the days of Lamech were seven hundred and seventy-seven years, and he died.

12 And Noah was four hundred and fifty years old, and *begat Japheth; and forty-two years afterward he begat *Shem of her who was the mother of Japheth, and when he was five hundred years old he begat *Ham.

13 And *Noah and his sons hearkened unto the Lord, and gave heed, and they were called the *sons of God.

14 And when these men began to multiply on the face of the earth, and daughters were born unto them, the *sons of men saw that those daughters were fair, and they took them *wives, even as they chose.

15 And the Lord said unto Noah: The daughters of thy sons have sold themselves; for behold mine anger is kindled against the sons of men, for they will not *hearken to my voice.

16 And it came to pass that Noah *prophesied, and taught the things of God, even as it was in the beginning.

17 And the Lord said unto Noah: My Spirit shall not always *strive with man, for he shall know that all *flesh shall die; yet his days shall be an *hundred and twenty years; and if men do not repent, I will send in the *floods upon them.

18 And in those days there were *giants on the earth, and they sought Noah to take away his *life; but the Lord was with Noah, and the *power of the Lord was upon him.

19 And the Lord *ordained *Noah after his own *order, and commanded him that he should go forth and *declare his Gospel unto the children of men, even as it was given unto Enoch.

20 And it came to pass that Noah called upon the children of men that they should *repent; but they hearkened not unto his words;

21 And also, after that they had heard him, they came up before him, saying: Behold, we are the sons of God; have we not taken unto ourselves

---

12 *a* Gen. 5:32; 9:18 (18–27).
  b 1 Chr. 1:4.
  c Abr. 1:11 (11–27).
13 *a* Gen. 6:8; 7:5; D&C
    138:41. TG Obedience.
  b TG Sons and Daughters
    of God.
14 *a* Moses 5:52; 6:15.
  b TG Marriage, Interfaith;
    Marriage, Marry.
15 *a* TG Disobedience.

16 *a* Moses 6:23.
17 *a* 2 Ne. 26:11; Ether 2:15.
    TG God, Access to.
  b Gen. 6:3; 2 Ne. 9:4
    (4–8). TG Flesh and
    Blood.
  c Gen. 6:3.
  d Gen. 7:10 (4, 10); Moses
    7:34.
18 *a* Gen. 6:4; Num. 13:33;
    Deut. 2:20; Josh. 17:15;

Moses 7:15 (14–15).
  b Moses 8:26.
  c TG Priesthood, Power of.
19 *a* D&C 107:52. TG Priest-
    hood, Ordination.
  b Abr. 1:19.
  c TG Priesthood, Melchize-
    dek.
  d TG Missionary Work.
20 *a* Gen. 5:29. TG Repent.

the daughters of men? And are we not ^aeating and drinking, and marrying and giving in marriage? And our wives bear unto us children, and the same are mighty men, which are like unto men of old, men of great renown. And they hearkened not unto the words of Noah.

22 And God saw that the ^awickedness of men had become great in the earth; and every man was lifted up in the ^bimagination of the thoughts of his heart, being only evil continually.

23 And it came to pass that Noah continued his ^apreaching unto the people, saying: Hearken, and give heed unto my words;

24 ^aBelieve and repent of your sins and be ^bbaptized in the name of Jesus Christ, the Son of God, even as our fathers, and ye shall receive the Holy Ghost, that ye may have all things made ^cmanifest; and if ye do not this, the floods will come in upon you; nevertheless they hearkened not.

25 And it ^arepented Noah, and his heart was pained that the Lord had made man on the earth, and it grieved him at the heart.

26 And the Lord said: I will ^adestroy man whom I have created, from the face of the earth, both man and beast, and the creeping things, and the fowls of the air; for it repenteth Noah that I have created them, and that I have made them; and he hath called upon me; for they have sought his ^blife.

27 And thus Noah found ^agrace in the eyes of the Lord; for Noah was a just man, and ^bperfect in his generation; and he ^cwalked with God, as did also his three sons, Shem, Ham, and Japheth.

28 The ^aearth was ^bcorrupt before God, and it was filled with violence.

29 And God looked upon the earth, and, behold, it was corrupt, for all flesh had corrupted its ^away upon the earth.

30 And God said unto Noah: The end of all flesh is come before me, for the earth is filled with violence, and behold I will ^adestroy all flesh from off the earth.

---

21 a Matt. 24:38; JS—M
   1:41. TG Disobedience.
22 a Gen. 6:5 (5–6); 3 Ne.
   9:9; Morm. 4:12 (10–12);
   D&C 112:23; Moses
   7:36 (36–37).
   b Alma 12:14 (3, 7, 14);
   D&C 124:99.
23 a TG Preaching.
24 a TG Baptism,

   Qualifications for.
   b TG Baptism, Essential.
   c 2 Ne. 32:5 (2–5); Moses
   1:24.
25 a Gen. 6:6; Ps. 106:45.
26 a TG Earth, Cleansing of.
   b Moses 8:18.
27 a TG Grace.
   b Gen. 6:9; D&C 129:3 (3,
   6).

   c TG Walking with God.
28 a Rev. 6:3 (3–4); D&C
   77:7.
   b Gen. 6:11 (11–13); D&C
   10:21; 112:23.
29 a Gen. 6:12; D&C 82:6.
30 a Gen. 6:13; 7:23; D&C
   56:3; 64:35.

A FACSIMILE FROM THE BOOK OF ABRAHAM

No. 1

EXPLANATION

Fig. 1. The Angel of the Lord.

Fig. 2. Abraham fastened upon an altar.

Fig. 3. The idolatrous priest of Elkenah attempting to offer up Abraham as a sacrifice.

Fig. 4. The altar for sacrifice by the idolatrous priests, standing before the gods of Elkenah, Libnah, Mahmackrah, Korash, and Pharaoh.

Fig. 5. The idolatrous god of Elkenah.

Fig. 6. The idolatrous god of Libnah.

Fig. 7. The idolatrous god of Mahmackrah.

Fig. 8. The idolatrous god of Korash.

Fig. 9. The idolatrous god of Pharaoh.

Fig. 10. Abraham in Egypt.

Fig. 11. Designed to represent the pillars of heaven, as understood by the Egyptians.

Fig. 12. Raukeeyang, signifying expanse, or the firmament over our heads; but in this case, in relation to this subject, the Egyptians meant it to signify Shaumau, to be high, or the heavens, answering to the Hebrew word, Shaumahyeem.

THE BOOK OF ABRAHAM

TRANSLATED FROM THE PAPYRUS, BY JOSEPH SMITH

A Translation of some ancient Records that have fallen into our hands from the catacombs of Egypt. The writings of Abraham while he was in Egypt, called the Book of Abraham, written by his own hand, upon papyrus.

CHAPTER 1

Abraham seeks the blessings of the patriarchal order—He is persecuted by false priests in Chaldea—Jehovah saves him—The origins and government of Egypt are reviewed.

1 In the land of the *a*Chaldeans, at the residence of my fathers, I, *b*Abraham, saw that it was needful for me to obtain another place of *c*residence;

2 And, finding there was greater *a*happiness and peace and rest for me, I sought for the blessings of the fathers, and the right whereunto I should be ordained to administer the same; having been myself a follower of *b*righteousness, desiring also to be one who possessed great *c*knowledge, and to be a greater follower of righteousness, and to possess a greater knowledge, and to be a father of many *d*nations, a prince of peace, and *e*desiring to receive instructions, and to keep the commandments of God, I became a rightful heir, a *f*High Priest, holding the right belonging to the fathers.

3 It was *a*conferred upon me from the fathers; it came down from the fathers, from the beginning of time, yea, even from the beginning, or before the foundation of the earth, down to the present time, even the right of the *b*firstborn, or the first man, who is *c*Adam, or first father, through the fathers unto me.

4 I sought for mine *a*appointment unto the Priesthood according to the appointment of God unto the *b*fathers concerning the seed.

5 My *a*fathers, having turned from their righteousness, and from the holy commandments which the Lord their God had given unto them, unto the worshiping of the *b*gods of the *c*heathen, utterly refused to hearken to my voice;

---

1 1 *a* Abr. 1:20 (20–30); 2:4 (1, 4).
b Gen. 11:26 (10–26); Hel. 8:18 (16–19).
c Acts 7:3 (2–4).
2 *a* TG Happiness; Priesthood, Qualifying for; Rest; Righteousness.
b TG God, the Standard of

Righteousness.
c Prov. 19:2; D&C 42:61.
d Gen. 12:2; 17:6; 18:18.
e Gen. 13:4.
f TG High Priest, Melchizedek Priesthood; Priesthood, History of; Priesthood, Melchizedek.
3 *a* D&C 84:14 (6–17).

TG Authority; Patriarch.
b D&C 68:17. TG Firstborn.
c Moses 1:34. TG Adam.
4 *a* TG Birthright.
b D&C 84:14 (6–17).
5 *a* Gen. 12:1.
b Josh. 24:14.
c TG Heathen.

6 For their *a*hearts were set to do *b*evil, and were wholly turned to the god of ⸵Elkenah, and the god of Libnah, and the god of Mahmackrah, and the god of Korash, and the god of Pharaoh, king of Egypt;

7 Therefore they turned their hearts to the sacrifice of the *a*heathen in offering up their children unto these dumb idols, and hearkened not unto my voice, but endeavored to take away my *b*life by the hand of the priest of Elkenah. The priest of Elkenah was also the priest of Pharaoh.

8 Now, at this time it was the custom of the priest of Pharaoh, the king of Egypt, to offer up upon the altar which was built in the land of Chaldea, for the offering unto these strange gods, men, women, and children.

9 And it came to pass that the priest made an offering unto the god of Pharaoh, and also unto the god of Shagreel, even after the manner of the Egyptians. Now the god of Shagreel was the sun.

10 Even the thank-offering of a child did the *a*priest of Pharaoh offer upon the altar which stood by the hill called Potiphar's Hill, at the head of the plain of Olishem.

11 Now, this priest had offered upon this altar three virgins at one time, who were the daughters of Onitah, one of the royal descent directly from the loins of *a*Ham. These virgins were offered up because of their virtue; they would not *b*bow down to worship gods of wood or of stone, therefore they were killed upon this altar, and it was done after the manner of the Egyptians.

12 And it came to pass that the priests laid violence upon me, that they might slay me also, as they did those virgins upon this altar; and that you may have a knowledge of this altar, I will refer you to the representation at the commencement of this record.

13 It was made after the form of a bedstead, such as was had among the Chaldeans, and it stood before the gods of Elkenah, Libnah, Mahmackrah, Korash, and also a god like unto that of Pharaoh, king of Egypt.

14 That you may have an understanding of these gods, I have given you the fashion of them in the figures at the beginning, which manner of figures is called by the Chaldeans Rahleenos, which signifies hieroglyphics.

15 And as they lifted up their hands upon me, that they might offer me up and take away my life, behold, I lifted up my voice unto the Lord my God, and the Lord *a*hearkened and heard, and he filled me with the vision

---

6a TG Hardheartedness.
  b Alma 40:13.
  c IE the "gods," as illustrated in Abr., fac. 1.
7a TG Heathen.
  b Abr. 1:15, 17, 30.
10a TG False Priesthoods.
11a Moses 8:12.
  b Dan. 3:18 (1–23).
15a Mosiah 9:18 (17–18); D&C 35:3.

of the Almighty, and the angel of his presence stood by me, and immediately [b]unloosed my bands;

16 And his voice was unto me: [a]Abraham, Abraham, behold, my [b]name is Jehovah, and I have heard thee, and have come down to deliver thee, and to take thee away from thy [c]father's house, and from all thy kinsfolk, into a strange [d]land which thou knowest not of;

17 And this because they have turned their [a]hearts away from me, to worship the god of Elkenah, and the god of Libnah, and the god of Mahmackrah, and the god of Korash, and the god of Pharaoh, king of Egypt; therefore I have come down to [b]visit them, and to destroy him who hath lifted up his hand against thee, Abraham, my son, to take away thy life.

18 Behold, I will lead thee by my hand, and I will take thee, to put upon thee my name, even the Priesthood of thy father, and my power shall be over thee.

19 As it was with [a]Noah so shall it be with thee; but through thy ministry my [b]name shall be known in the earth [c]forever, for I am thy God.

20 Behold, Potiphar's Hill was in the land of [a]Ur, of Chaldea. And the Lord broke down the altar of Elkenah, and of the gods of the land, and utterly destroyed them, and smote the priest that he died; and there was great mourning in Chaldea, and also in the court of Pharaoh; which Pharaoh signifies king by royal blood.

21 Now this king of Egypt was a descendant from the [a]loins of [b]Ham, and was a partaker of the blood of the [c]Canaanites by birth.

22 From this descent sprang all the Egyptians, and thus the blood of the [a]Canaanites was preserved in the land.

23 The land of [a]Egypt being first discovered by a woman, who was the daughter of Ham, and the daughter of Egyptus, which in the Chaldean signifies Egypt, which signifies that which is forbidden;

24 When this woman discovered the land it was under water, who afterward settled her sons in it; and thus, from Ham, sprang that race which preserved the curse in the land.

---

15 b Abr. 2:13; 3:20.
16 a "Abram" in 1:16–17; 2:3, 6, 14, 17, in *Times and Seasons*, March 1, 1842, but "Abraham" in all publications since *Millennial Star*, July 1842.
    b Jer. 16:21. TG Jesus Christ, Jehovah.
    c Gen. 12:1.

d TG Promised Lands.
17 a TG Worship.
    b 1 Ne. 13:34; D&C 124:8.
19 a Moses 8:19.
    b Gen. 12:3 (1–3); Abr. 2:6 (6–11).
    c Ps. 48:14; D&C 20:12.
20 a Gen. 11:28; Abr. 1:1; 2:4 (1–4).

21 a Gen. 10:6 (6–8); Abr. 1:25 (20–25).
    b Ps. 78:51; Moses 8:12.
    c Ps. 105:23; Moses 7:6 (6–8).
22 a Gen. 10:15 (6–20); Moses 7:7 (6–8).
23 a Gen. 10:6; Ps. 105:23.

25 Now the first ªgovernment of Egypt was established by Pharaoh, the eldest son of Egyptus, the daughter of Ham, and it was after the manner of the government of Ham, which was patriarchal.

26 Pharaoh, being a righteous man, established his kingdom and judged his people wisely and justly all his days, seeking earnestly to imitate that ªorder established by the fathers in the first generations, in the days of the first patriarchal reign, even in the reign of Adam, and also of Noah, his father, who blessed him with the ᵇblessings of the earth, and with the blessings of wisdom, but cursed him as pertaining to the Priesthood.

27 Now, Pharaoh being of that lineage by which he could not have the right of ªPriesthood, notwithstanding the Pharaohs would fain ᵇclaim it from Noah, through Ham, therefore my father was led away by their idolatry;

28 But I shall endeavor, hereafter, to delineate the chronology running back from myself to the beginning of the creation, for the ªrecords have come into my hands, which I hold unto this present time.

29 Now, after the priest of Elkenah was smitten that he died, there came a fulfilment of those things which were said unto me concerning the land of Chaldea, that there should be a ªfamine in the land.

30 Accordingly a famine prevailed throughout all the land of Chaldea, and my father was sorely tormented because of the famine, and he repented of the evil which he had determined against me, to take away my ªlife.

31 But the ªrecords of the fathers, even the patriarchs, concerning the right of Priesthood, the Lord my God preserved in mine own hands; therefore a knowledge of the beginning of the creation, and also of the ᵇplanets, and of the stars, as they were made known unto the fathers, have I kept even unto this day, and I shall endeavor to write some of these things upon this ᶜrecord, for the benefit of my posterity that shall come after me.

CHAPTER 2

Abraham leaves Ur to go to Canaan—Jehovah appears to him at Haran—All gospel blessings are promised to his seed and through his seed to all—He goes to Canaan and on to Egypt.

---

25 *a* TG Governments.
26 *a* TG Order.
   b TG Blessing.
27 *a* TG Priesthood, Qualifying for.
   b TG Unrighteous

Dominion.
28 *a* Moses 6:5. TG Scriptures, Writing of.
29 *a* Abr. 2:1, 17. TG Famine.
30 *a* Abr. 1:7 (7, 12).
31 *a* TG Record Keeping;

Scriptures, Preservation of.
   b Abr. 3:2 (1–21). TG Astronomy.
   c TG Book of Remembrance.

1 Now the Lord God caused the *famine to wax sore in the land of Ur, insomuch that *Haran, my brother, died; but *Terah, my father, yet lived in the land of Ur, of the Chaldees.

2 And it came to pass that I, Abraham, took *Sarai to wife, and *Nahor, my brother, took Milcah to wife, who was the *daughter of Haran.

3 Now the Lord had *said unto me: Abraham, get thee out of thy country, and from thy kindred, and from thy father's house, unto a land that I will show thee.

4 Therefore I left the land of *Ur, of the Chaldees, to go into the land of Canaan; and I took Lot, my brother's son, and his wife, and Sarai my wife; and also my *father followed after me, unto the land which we denominated Haran.

5 And the famine abated; and my father tarried in Haran and dwelt there, as there were many flocks in Haran; and my father turned again unto his *idolatry, therefore he continued in Haran.

6 But I, Abraham, and Lot, my brother's son, prayed unto the Lord, and the Lord *appeared unto me, and said unto me: Arise, and take Lot with thee; for I have purposed to take thee away out of Haran, and to make of thee a *minister to bear my *name in a strange *land which I will give unto thy seed after thee for an everlasting possession, when they hearken to my voice.

7 For I am the Lord thy God; I dwell in *heaven; the earth is my *footstool; I stretch my hand over the sea, and it obeys my voice; I cause the wind and the fire to be my *chariot; I say to the mountains—Depart hence—and behold, they are taken away by a whirlwind, in an instant, suddenly.

8 My *name is Jehovah, and I *know the end from the beginning; therefore my hand shall be over thee.

9 And I will make of thee a great *nation, and I will *bless thee above

2 1a Abr. 1:29.
 b Gen. 11:28.
 c Gen. 11:24 (24–26); 1 Chr. 1:26.
2a Gen. 11:29; 12:5.
 b Gen. 11:27; 22:23 (20–24).
 c Gen. 20:12 (12, 16).
3a Gen. 12:1; 20:13; Acts 7:2 (1–8, 16).
4a Neh. 9:7; Abr. 1:1, 20, 29–30.
 b Gen. 11:31 (31–32).
5a Josh. 24:2 (2–3).
6a Gen. 17:1; 48:3; Ex.
 6:2–3; D&C 107:54; Abr. 3:11. TG God, Manifestations of; Jesus Christ, Appearances, Antemortal.
 b TG Delegation of Responsibility.
 c Gen. 12:3; Abr. 1:19.
 d Gen. 13:15; 17:8; 48:4; Ex. 33:1; 1 Ne. 10:3; Abr. 2:19. TG Israel, Land of.
7a Moses 6:42.
 b Lam. 2:1; 1 Ne. 17:39; D&C 38:17; Moses 6:9, 44.
 c 2 Kgs. 2:11; Isa. 66:15 (15–16).
8a Jer. 16:21.
 b TG God, Foreknowledge of; God, Omniscience of.
9a 2 Sam. 7:23; Neh. 9:23; Isa. 9:3; 26:15; Acts 13:26; Abr. 3:14.
 b Gen. 12:2 (1–3); 49:26; Ps. 105:10 (8–10); 1 Ne. 17:40; 2 Ne. 29:14; 3 Ne. 20:27; Morm. 5:20. TG Seed of Abraham.

measure, and make thy name great among all nations, and thou shalt be a blessing unto thy seed after thee, that in their hands they shall bear this ministry and ᶜPriesthood unto all nations;

10 And I will ᵃbless them through thy name; for as many as receive this ᵇGospel shall be called after thy ᶜname, and shall be accounted thy ᵈseed, and shall rise up and bless thee, as their ᵉfather;

11 And I will ᵃbless them that bless thee, and ᵇcurse them that curse thee; and in thee (that is, in thy Priesthood) and in thy ᶜseed (that is, thy Priesthood), for I give unto thee a promise that this ᵈright shall continue in thee, and in thy seed after thee (that is to say, the literal seed, or the seed of the body) shall all the families of the earth be blessed, even with the blessings of the Gospel, which are the blessings of salvation, even of life eternal.

12 Now, after the Lord had withdrawn from speaking to me, and withdrawn his face from me, I said in my heart: Thy servant has ᵃsought thee earnestly; now I have found thee;

13 Thou didst send thine angel to ᵃdeliver me from the gods of Elkenah, and I will do well to hearken unto thy voice, therefore let thy servant rise up and depart in peace.

14 So I, Abraham, departed as the Lord had said unto me, and Lot with me; and I, Abraham, was ᵃsixty and two years old when I departed out of Haran.

15 And I took Sarai, whom I took to wife when I was in Ur, in Chaldea, and Lot, my brother's son, and all our substance that we had gathered, and the souls that we had ᵃwon in Haran, and came forth in the way to the land of Canaan, and dwelt in tents as we came on our way;

16 Therefore, ᵃeternity was our covering and our ᵇrock and our salvation, as we journeyed from Haran by the way of ᶜJershon, to come to the land of Canaan.

17 Now I, Abraham, built an ᵃaltar in the land of Jershon, and made an

---

9 c D&C 84:17 (17–19);
  Moses 6:7.
10 a TG Israel, Blessings of.
  b Acts 15:14; Gal. 3:8
    (7–9).
  c Gen. 12:2 (2–3); Isa.
    44:5.
  d Gen. 13:16 (14–16);
    Rom. 4:11; Gal. 3:29
    (26–29); 2 Ne. 30:2.
  e TG Patriarch.
11 a TG Israel, Blessings of.
  b TG Curse.

  c Isa. 49:3; 61:9.
  d TG Birthright; Israel,
    Mission of; Priesthood,
    Melchizedek.
12 a Jer. 29:13; D&C 88:63.
13 a Abr. 1:15 (15–17).
14 a Gen. 12:4.
15 a Gen. 12:5. TG Conver-
    sion.
16 a TG Eternity.
  b TG Rock.
  c IE There is a possibility
    that Abram traveled

southward on the ancient route by way of Damascus to the site of ancient Jerash (Jershon), thence down the Jabbok, across the Jordan, and up the Wadi Farah to Sechem (also spelled Shechem, Sichem, and Sychem).
17 a Gen. 12:7 (7–8); 1 Ne.
    2:7.

offering unto the Lord, and prayed that the ^b^famine might be turned away from my father's house, that they might not perish.

18 And then we passed from Jershon through the land unto the place of Sechem; it was situated in the plains of Moreh, and we had already come into the borders of the land of the ^a^Canaanites, and I offered ^b^sacrifice there in the plains of Moreh, and called on the Lord devoutly, because we had already come into the land of this idolatrous nation.

19 And the Lord ^a^appeared unto me in answer to my prayers, and said unto me: Unto thy seed will I give this ^b^land.

20 And I, Abraham, arose from the place of the altar which I had built unto the Lord, and removed from thence unto a mountain on the east of ^a^Bethel, and pitched my tent there, Bethel on the west, and ^b^Hai on the east; and there I built another ^c^altar unto the Lord, and ^d^called again upon the name of the Lord.

21 And I, Abraham, journeyed, going on still towards the south; and there was a continuation of a famine in the land; and I, Abraham, concluded to go down into Egypt, to sojourn there, for the famine became very grievous.

22 And it came to pass when I was come near to enter into Egypt, the Lord ^a^said unto me: Behold, Sarai, thy wife, is a very fair woman to look upon;

23 Therefore it shall come to pass, when the Egyptians shall see her, they will say—She is his wife; and they will kill you, but they will save her alive; therefore see that ye do on this wise:

24 Let her say unto the Egyptians, she is thy sister, and thy soul shall live.

25 And it came to pass that I, Abraham, told Sarai, my wife, all that the Lord had said unto me—Therefore say unto them, I pray thee, thou art my ^a^sister, that it may be well with me for thy sake, and my soul shall live because of thee.

CHAPTER 3

Abraham learns about the sun, moon, and stars by means of the Urim and Thummim—The Lord reveals to him the eternal nature of spirits—He learns of pre-earth life, foreordination, the Creation, the choosing of a Redeemer, and the second estate of man.

---

17 *b* Abr. 1:29; 2:1.
18 *a* Gen. 12:6.
   b TG Sacrifice.
19 *a* D&C 107:54 (53–54).
   b Gen. 11:31 (27–31);
     13:15; 17:8 (1–27); Ex.

3:8 (1–10); Num. 34:2
(1–29). TG Promised
Lands.
20 *a* Gen. 28:19.
   b Gen. 13:3.
   c Gen. 13:4.

d Gen. 12:8.
22 *a* Gen. 12:11.
25 *a* Gen. 12:13 (9–20);
    20:12.

1 And I, Abraham, had the ªUrim and Thummim, which the Lord my God had given unto me, in Ur of the Chaldees;

2 And I saw the ªstars, that they were very great, and that one of them was nearest unto the throne of God; and there were many great ones which were near unto it;

3 And the Lord said unto me: These are the governing ones; and the name of the great one is ªKolob, because it is near unto me, for I am the Lord thy God: I have set this one to govern all those which belong to the same order as that upon which thou standest.

4 And the Lord said unto me, by the Urim and Thummim, that Kolob was after the manner of the Lord, according to its ªtimes and seasons in the revolutions thereof; that one revolution was a ᵇday unto the Lord, after his manner of reckoning, it being one thousand ͨyears according to the time appointed unto that whereon thou standest. This is the reckoning of the Lord's ͩtime, according to the reckoning of Kolob.

5 And the Lord said unto me: The planet which is the lesser light, lesser than that which is to rule the day, even the night, is above or ªgreater than that upon which thou standest in point of reckoning, for it moveth in order more slow; this is in order because it standeth above the earth upon which thou standest, therefore the reckoning of its time is not so many as to its number of days, and of months, and of years.

6 And the Lord said unto me: Now, Abraham, these ªtwo facts exist, behold thine eyes see it; it is given unto thee to know the times of reckoning, and the set time, yea, the set time of the earth upon which thou standest, and the set time of the greater light which is set to rule the day, and the set time of the lesser light which is set to rule the night.

7 Now the set time of the lesser light is a longer time as to its reckoning than the reckoning of the time of the earth upon which thou standest.

8 And where these two facts exist, there shall be another fact above them, that is, there shall be another planet whose reckoning of time shall be longer still;

9 And thus there shall be the reckoning of the time of one ªplanet above another, until thou come nigh unto Kolob, which Kolob is after the reckoning of the Lord's time; which Kolob is set nigh unto the throne of God,

---

3 1 *a* Ex. 28:30; Mosiah 8:13 (13–19); 28:13 (13–16); JS—H 1:35. TG Urim and Thummim.
2 *a* Moses 1:35 (35–37); 7:36; Abr. 1:31.

3 *a* See also Abr., fac. 2, figs. 1–5. Abr. 3:16; 5:13. TG Astronomy.
4 *a* Dan. 2:21.
b Abr. 5:13.
c Ps. 90:4; 2 Pet. 3:8.

d TG Time.
5 *a* IE It rotates on its axis more slowly. See also v. 7.
6 *a* Abr. 3:16 (16–19).
9 *a* TG Astronomy.

to govern all those planets which belong to the same *b*order as that upon which thou standest.

10 And it is given unto thee to know the set time of all the stars that are set to give light, until thou come near unto the throne of God.

11 Thus I, Abraham, *a*talked with the Lord, face to face, as one man talketh with another; and he told me of the works which his hands had made;

12 And he said unto me: My son, my son (and his hand was stretched out), behold I will show you all these. And he put his hand upon mine eyes, and I saw those things which his hands had made, which were many; and they multiplied before mine eyes, and I could not see the end thereof.

13 And he said unto me: This is Shinehah, which is the sun. And he said unto me: Kokob, which is star. And he said unto me: Olea, which is the moon. And he said unto me: Kokaubeam, which signifies stars, or all the great lights, which were in the firmament of heaven.

14 And it was in the night time when the Lord spake these words unto me: I will *a*multiply thee, and thy *b*seed after thee, like unto these; and if thou canst count the *c*number of sands, so shall be the number of thy seeds.

15 And the Lord said unto me: Abraham, I *a*show these things unto thee before ye go into Egypt, that ye may declare all these words.

16 If *a*two things exist, and there be one above the other, there shall be greater things above them; therefore *b*Kolob is the greatest of all the Kokaubeam that thou hast seen, because it is nearest unto me.

17 Now, if there be two things, one above the other, and the moon be above the earth, then it may be that a planet or a star may exist above it; and there is nothing that the Lord thy God shall take in his heart to do but what he will *a*do it.

18 Howbeit that he made the greater star; as, also, if there be two *a*spirits, and one shall be more intelligent than the other, yet these two spirits, notwithstanding one is more intelligent than the other, have no beginning; they existed before, they shall have no end, they shall exist after, for they are *b*gnolaum, or eternal.

19 And the Lord said unto me: These two facts do exist, that there are two spirits, one being more intelligent than the other; there shall be another

---

9 *b* D&C 77:3; 88:42
(37–42). TG Order.
11 *a* Gen. 17:1; Abr. 2:6 (6, 8,
19). TG God, Access to;
God, Manifestations of;
God, Privilege of Seeing.
14 *a* Abr. 2:9.

b Gen. 13:16; D&C
132:30.
c Gen. 22:17; Hosea 1:10.
15 *a* TG Guidance, Divine.
16 *a* Abr. 3:6 (6, 8).
b Abr. 3:3.
17 *a* Job 9:4 (4–12).

18 *a* TG Spirit Body; Spirit
Creation.
b *Gnolaum* is a transliter-
ation of a Hebrew word
meaning eternal.

more intelligent than they; I am the Lord thy God, I am ^amore intelligent than they all.

20 The Lord thy God sent his angel to ^adeliver thee from the hands of the priest of Elkenah.

21 I dwell in the midst of them all; I now, therefore, have come down unto thee to declare unto thee the ^aworks which my hands have made, wherein my ^bwisdom excelleth them all, for I ^crule in the heavens above, and in the earth beneath, in all wisdom and prudence, over all the intelligences thine eyes have seen from the beginning; I came down in the beginning in the midst of all the intelligences thou hast seen.

22 Now the Lord had shown unto me, Abraham, the ^aintelligences that were organized before the world was; and among all these there were many of the ^bnoble and great ones;

23 And God saw these souls that they were good, and he stood in the midst of them, and he said: These I will make my rulers; for he stood among those that were spirits, and he saw that they were good; and he said unto me: Abraham, thou art one of them; thou wast ^achosen before thou wast born.

24 And there stood ^aone among them that was like unto God, and he said unto those who were with him: We will go down, for there is space there, and we will take of these materials, and ^bwe will make an earth whereon these may ^cdwell;

25 And we will ^aprove them herewith, to see if they will ^bdo all things whatsoever the Lord their God shall command them;

26 And they who ^akeep their first ^bestate shall be added upon; and they who keep not their first estate shall not have glory in the same kingdom with those who keep their first estate; and they who keep their second ^cestate shall have ^dglory added upon their heads for ever and ever.

27 And the ^aLord said: Whom shall I ^bsend? And one answered like unto

19 a Isa. 55:9 (8–9). TG God, Intelligence of; God, Omniscience of; Intelligence.
20 a Abr. 1:15.
21 a D&C 88:47 (45–47); Moses 1:27 (27–28); 7:23.
    b Job 12:13 (7–25); 2 Ne. 9:8.
    c TG God, Perfection of; Kingdom of God, in Heaven.

22 a TG Council in Heaven; Intelligence; Man, Antemortal Existence of; Man, a Spirit Child of Heavenly Father; Spirit Creation.
    b D&C 138:55.
23 a Isa. 49:1 (1–5); Jer. 1:5; Moses 1:25; 3:5. TG Election; Foreordination.
24 a TG Jesus Christ, First-born.
    b TG Jesus Christ, Creator.

    c TG Earth, Purpose of.
25 a D&C 98:14 (12–14); 124:55. TG Agency; Salvation, Plan of; Test.
    b TG Obedience.
26 a TG Dependability.
    b Jude 1:6.
    c TG Mortality.
    d Titus 1:2. TG Glory; Reward.
27 a TG God the Father, Elohim.
    b Moses 7:39.

the Son of Man: Here am I, send me. And ᶜanother answered and said: Here am I, send me. And the Lord said: I will ᵈsend the first.

28 And the ᵃsecond was angry, and kept not his first ᵇestate; and, at that day, many followed after him.

CHAPTER 4

The Gods plan the creation of the earth and all life thereon—Their plans for the six days of creation are set forth.

1 And then the Lord said: Let us go down. And they went down at the beginning, and they, that is the ᵃGods, ᵇorganized and formed the ᶜheavens and the earth.

2 And the earth, after it was formed, was empty and desolate, because they had not formed anything but the earth; and ᵃdarkness reigned upon the face of the deep, and the Spirit of the Gods ᵇwas brooding upon the face of the waters.

3 And they (the Gods) said: Let there be light; and there was light.

4 And they (the Gods) comprehended the light, for it was ᵃbright; and they divided the light, or caused it to be divided, from the darkness.

5 And the Gods called the light Day, and the darkness they called Night. And it came to pass that from the evening until morning they called ᵃnight; and from the morning until the evening they called day; and this was the first, or the beginning, of that which they called day and night.

6 And the Gods also said: Let there be an ᵃexpanse in the midst of the waters, and it shall divide the waters from the waters.

7 And the Gods ordered the expanse, so that it divided the waters which were under the expanse from the waters which were above the expanse; and it was so, even as they ordered.

8 And the Gods called the expanse, Heaven. And it came to pass that it was from evening until morning that they called night; and it came to pass that it was from morning until evening that they called day; and this was the second ᵃtime that they called night and day.

9 And the Gods ordered, saying: Let the ᵃwaters under the heaven be

---

27 c Moses 4:1 (1–2).
    d TG Jesus Christ, Authority of; Jesus Christ, Foreordained; Jesus Christ, Messenger of the Covenant; Jesus Christ, Messiah; Jesus Christ, Mission of.

28 a TG Devil.
    b TG Sons of Perdition.
4 1 a Gen. 1:1; Moses 2:1.
       TG Jesus Christ, Creator.
    b Prov. 3:19 (19–20).
    c Moses 1:37 (36–38).
2 a TG Darkness, Physical.
    b Gen. 1:2; Moses 2:2.

4 a Gen. 1:4; Moses 2:4.
5 a Gen. 1:5.
6 a Gen. 1:6.
8 a Gen. 1:8.
9 a Amos 9:6; Moses 2:7 (6–9).

gathered together unto *b*one place, and let the earth come up dry; and it was so as they ordered;

10 And the Gods pronounced the dry land, Earth; and the gathering together of the waters, pronounced they, *a*Great Waters; and the Gods saw that they were obeyed.

11 And the Gods said: Let us prepare the earth to bring forth *a*grass; the herb yielding seed; the fruit tree yielding fruit, after his kind, whose seed in itself yieldeth its own likeness upon the earth; and it was so, even as they ordered.

12 And the Gods organized the *a*earth to bring forth grass from its own seed, and the herb to bring forth herb from its own seed, yielding seed after his kind; and the earth to bring forth the tree from its own seed, yielding fruit, whose seed could only bring forth the same in itself, after his kind; and the Gods saw that they were obeyed.

13 And it came to pass that they numbered the days; from the evening until the morning they called night; and it came to pass, from the morning until the evening they called day; and it was the third time.

14 And the Gods organized the *a*lights in the expanse of the heaven, and caused them to divide the day from the night; and organized them to be for signs and for seasons, and for days and for years;

15 And organized them to be for lights in the expanse of the heaven to give light upon the earth; and it was so.

16 And the Gods organized the two great lights, the *a*greater light to rule the day, and the lesser light to rule the night; with the lesser light they set the stars also;

17 And the Gods set them in the expanse of the heavens, to give light upon the earth, and to rule over the day and over the night, and to cause to divide the light from the *a*darkness.

18 And the Gods watched those things which they had *a*ordered until they obeyed.

19 And it came to pass that it was from evening until morning that it was night; and it came to pass that it was from morning until evening that it was day; and it was the fourth time.

20 And the Gods said: Let us prepare the waters to bring forth abundantly

---

9 *b* Gen. 1:9.
10 *a* Gen. 1:10; Abr. 4:22.
11 *a* Gen. 1:11 (11–12); Moses 2:11 (11–12).
12 *a* Ex. 9:29; D&C 14:9; 15:2.
14 *a* D&C 88:7 (7–11).
16 *a* Gen. 1:16; D&C 76:71
(70–71); 88:45.
17 *a* TG Darkness, Physical.
18 *a* TG Order.

the moving creatures that have life; and the fowl, that they may fly above the earth in the open expanse of heaven.

21 And the Gods prepared the waters that they might bring forth great *whales, and every living creature that moveth, which the waters were to bring forth abundantly after their kind; and every winged fowl after their kind. And the Gods saw that they would be obeyed, and that their plan was good.

22 And the Gods said: We will bless them, and cause them to be fruitful and multiply, and fill the waters in the seas or *great waters; and cause the fowl to multiply in the earth.

23 And it came to pass that it was from evening until morning that they called night; and it came to pass that it was from morning until evening that they called day; and it was the fifth time.

24 And the Gods prepared the earth to bring forth the living creature after his kind, cattle and creeping things, and beasts of the earth after their kind; and it was so, as they had said.

25 And the Gods organized the earth to bring forth the beasts after their kind, and cattle after their kind, and every thing that creepeth upon the earth after its kind; and the Gods saw they would obey.

26 And the Gods took *counsel among themselves and said: Let us go down and *form man in our *image, after our likeness; and we will give them dominion over the fish of the sea, and over the fowl of the air, and over the cattle, and over all the earth, and over every creeping thing that creepeth upon the earth.

27 So the *Gods went down to organize man in their own *image, in the image of the Gods to form they him, male and female to form they them.

28 And the Gods said: We will bless them. And the Gods said: We will cause them to be fruitful and multiply, and replenish the earth, and subdue it, and to have dominion over the fish of the sea, and over the fowl of the air, and over every living thing that moveth upon the earth.

29 And the Gods said: Behold, we will give them every herb bearing seed that shall come upon the face of all the earth, and every tree which shall have fruit upon it; yea, the fruit of the tree yielding seed to them we will give it; it shall be for their *meat.

30 And to every beast of the earth, and to every fowl of the air, and to every thing that creepeth upon the earth, behold, we will give them

---

21 a Gen. 1:21; Moses 2:21.
22 a Abr. 4:10.
26 a TG Counsel.
  b TG Man, Physical

Creation of.
  c Moses 6:9 (8–10).
27 a Gen. 1:26; Abr. 5:7.
  b TG God, Body of,

Corporeal Nature.
29 a Gen. 1:29 (29–30).

life, and also we will give to them every green herb for meat, and all these things shall be thus organized.

31 And the Gods said: We will do everything that we have said, and organize them; and behold, they shall be very obedient. And it came to pass that it was from evening until morning they called night; and it came to pass that it was from morning until evening that they called day; and they numbered the *a*sixth time.

CHAPTER 5

The Gods finish Their planning of the creation of all things—They bring to pass the Creation according to Their plans—Adam names every living creature.

1 And thus we will finish the heavens and the earth, and all the *a*hosts of them.

2 And the Gods said among themselves: On the seventh time we will end our work, which we have counseled; and we will *a*rest on the *b*seventh time from all our work which we have counseled.

3 And the Gods concluded upon the seventh time, because that on the seventh time they would *a*rest from all their *b*works which they (the Gods) counseled among themselves to form; and *c*sanctified it. And thus were their decisions at the time that they counseled among themselves to form the heavens and the earth.

4 And the Gods came down and formed these the generations of the heavens and of the earth, when they were formed in the day that the *a*Gods formed the earth and the heavens,

5 According to all that which they had said concerning every plant of the field before it was in the *a*earth, and every herb of the field before it grew; for the Gods had not caused it to rain upon the earth when they counseled to do them, and had not formed a man to till the ground.

6 But there went up a mist from the earth, and watered the whole face of the ground.

7 And the *a*Gods formed man from the *b*dust of the ground, and took his *c*spirit (that is, the man's spirit), and put it into him; and breathed into his nostrils the breath of life, and man became a living *d*soul.

---

31 *a* Ex. 31:17; Mosiah 13:19.
5 1 *a* D&C 38:1; 45:1.
   2 *a* TG Rest.
     b TG Sabbath.
   3 *a* Ex. 20:8 (8–11).
     b Ex. 31:15 (15–16); Mosiah 13:18 (16–19).

c Mosiah 13:19 (16–19); D&C 77:12.
   4 *a* Neh. 9:6.
   5 *a* TG Spirit Creation.
   7 *a* Abr. 4:27 (26–31).
     b Moses 4:25 (25–29); 6:59.

c Gen. 2:7; 2 Ne. 9:26; D&C 77:2; 93:33.
   TG Man, Antemortal Existence of; Spirit Body.
   d TG Soul.

8 And the Gods planted a garden, eastward in ^aEden, and there they put the man, whose spirit they had put into the body which they had formed.

9 And out of the ground made the Gods to grow every tree that is pleasant to the sight and good for food; the ^atree of life, also, in the midst of the garden, and the tree of knowledge of good and evil.

10 There was a river running out of Eden, to water the garden, and from thence it was parted and became into four heads.

11 And the Gods took the man and put him in the Garden of Eden, to dress it and to keep it.

12 And the Gods commanded the man, saying: Of every tree of the garden thou mayest freely eat,

13 But of the tree of knowledge of good and evil, thou shalt not eat of it; for in the time that thou eatest thereof, thou shalt surely die. Now I, Abraham, saw that it was after the Lord's ^atime, which was after the time of ^bKolob; for as yet the Gods had not appointed unto Adam his reckoning.

14 And the Gods said: Let us make an help meet for the man, for it is not good that the man should be alone, therefore we will form an help meet for him.

15 And the Gods caused a deep sleep to fall upon Adam; and he slept, and they took one of his ribs, and closed up the flesh in the stead thereof;

16 And of the rib which the Gods had taken from man, formed they a ^awoman, and brought her unto the man.

17 And Adam said: This was bone of my bones, and ^aflesh of my flesh; now she shall be called Woman, because she was taken out of man;

18 Therefore shall a man leave his father and his mother, and shall ^acleave unto his wife, and they shall be ^bone flesh.

19 And they were both naked, the man and his wife, and were not ^aashamed.

20 And out of the ground the Gods formed every beast of the field, and every fowl of the air, and brought them unto Adam to see what he would call them; and whatsoever ^aAdam called every living creature, that should be the name thereof.

21 And Adam gave ^anames to all ^bcattle, to the fowl of the air, to every beast of the field; and for Adam, there was found an ^chelp meet for him.

8 a TG Eden.
9 a 1 Ne. 11:25; Moses 4:28, 31.
13 a Abr. 3:4, 10. TG Time.
  b Abr. 3:3 (2–4).
16 a TG Woman.

17 a Jacob 2:21.
18 a D&C 42:22; 49:15 (15–16).
  b TG Divorce; Marriage, Celestial.
19 a TG Shame.

20 a TG Adam.
21 a TG Language.
  b Enos 1:21; Ether 9:18.
  c Abr. 5:14.

EXPLANATION

Fig. 1. Kolob, signifying the first creation, nearest to the celestial, or the residence of God. First in government, the last pertaining to the measurement of time. The measurement according to celestial time, which celestial time signifies one day to a cubit. One day in Kolob is equal to a thousand years according to the measurement of this earth, which is called by the Egyptians Jah-oh-eh.

Fig. 2. Stands next to Kolob, called by the Egyptians Oliblish, which is the next grand governing creation near to the celestial or the place where God resides; holding the key of power also, pertaining to other planets; as revealed from God to Abraham, as he offered sacrifice upon an altar, which he had built unto the Lord.

Fig. 3. Is made to represent God, sitting upon his throne, clothed with power and authority; with a crown of eternal light upon his head; representing also the grand Key-words of the Holy Priesthood, as revealed to Adam in the Garden of Eden, as also to Seth, Noah, Melchizedek, Abraham, and all to whom the Priesthood was revealed.

Fig. 4. Answers to the Hebrew word Raukeeyang, signifying expanse, or the firmament of the heavens; also a numerical figure, in Egyptian signifying one thousand; answering to the measuring of the time of Oliblish, which is equal with Kolob in its revolution and in its measuring of time.

Fig. 5. Is called in Egyptian Enish-go-on-dosh; this is one of the governing planets also, and is said by the Egyptians to be the Sun, and to borrow its light from Kolob through the medium of Kae-e-vanrash, which is the grand Key, or, in other words, the governing power, which governs fifteen other fixed planets or stars, as also Floeese or the Moon, the Earth and the Sun in their annual revolutions. This planet receives its power through the medium of Kli-flos-is-es, or Hah-ko-kau-beam, the stars represented by numbers 22 and 23, receiving light from the revolutions of Kolob.

Fig. 6. Represents this earth in its four quarters.

Fig. 7. Represents God sitting upon his throne, revealing through the heavens the grand Key-words of the Priesthood; as, also, the sign of the Holy Ghost unto Abraham, in the form of a dove.

Fig. 8. Contains writings that cannot be revealed unto the world; but is to be had in the Holy Temple of God.

Fig. 9. Ought not to be revealed at the present time.

Fig. 10. Also.

Fig. 11. Also. If the world can find out these numbers, so let it be. Amen.

Figures 12, 13, 14, 15, 16, 17, 18, 19, 20, and 21 will be given in the own due time of the Lord.

The above translation is given as far as we have any right to give at the present time.

A FACSIMILE FROM THE BOOK OF ABRAHAM

No. 3

ENG. BY R. REDLOCK

EXPLANATION

Fig. 1. Abraham sitting upon Pharaoh's throne, by the politeness of the king, with a crown upon his head, representing the Priesthood, as emblematical of the grand Presidency in Heaven; with the scepter of justice and judgment in his hand.

Fig. 2. King Pharaoh, whose name is given in the characters above his head.

Fig. 3. Signifies Abraham in Egypt as given also in Figure 10 of Facsimile No. 1.

Fig. 4. Prince of Pharaoh, King of Egypt, as written above the hand.

Fig. 5. Shulem, one of the king's principal waiters, as represented by the characters above his hand.

Fig. 6. Olimlah, a slave belonging to the prince.

Abraham is reasoning upon the principles of Astronomy, in the king's court.

JOSEPH SMITH—MATTHEW

An extract from the translation of the Bible as revealed to Joseph Smith the Prophet in 1831: Matthew 23:39 and chapter 24.

CHAPTER 1

Jesus foretells the impending destruction of Jerusalem—He also discourses on the Second Coming of the Son of Man, and the destruction of the wicked.

1 ^aFor I say unto you, that ye shall not see me henceforth and know that I am he of whom it is written by the prophets, until ye shall say: Blessed is he who ^bcometh in the name of the Lord, in the clouds of heaven, and all the holy angels with him. Then understood his disciples that he should come again on the earth, after that he was glorified and ^ccrowned on the right hand of God.

2 And Jesus went out, and departed from the temple; and his disciples came to him, for to ^ahear him, saying: Master, show us concerning the buildings of the temple, as thou hast said—They shall be thrown down, and left unto you desolate.

3 And Jesus said unto them: See ye not all these things, and do ye not understand them? Verily I say unto you, there shall not be left here, upon this temple, one ^astone upon another that shall not be thrown down.

4 And Jesus left them, and went upon the Mount of Olives. And as he sat upon the Mount of Olives, the disciples came unto him privately, saying: Tell us when shall these things be which thou hast said concerning the destruction of the temple, and the Jews; and what is the ^asign of thy ^bcoming, and of the ^cend of the world, or the destruction of the ^dwicked, which is the end of the world?

5 And Jesus answered, and said unto them: Take heed that no man deceive you;

6 For many shall come in my name, saying—I am ^aChrist—and shall deceive many;

7 Then shall they deliver you up to be ^aafflicted, and shall kill you, and ye shall be ^bhated of all nations, for my name's sake;

---

1 1 *a* Matt. 23:39.
　b Ps. 118:26 (24–26);
　　Matt. 26:64; Acts 1:11.
　c TG Jesus Christ, Relationships with the Father.
2 *a* Matt. 24.

3 *a* Luke 19:44 (41–44).
4 *a* Luke 21:7 (7–36); D&C
　　45:16 (16–75). TG Last
　　Days.
　b TG Jesus Christ, Second
　　Coming.
　c TG World, End of.

　d Mal. 4:1; D&C 133:64
　　(64–74).
6 *a* Moses 1:19. TG False
　　Christs.
7 *a* 1 Pet. 4:13 (12–16).
　b TG Hate; Malice.

8 And then shall many be ^aoffended, and shall betray one another, and shall hate one another;

9 And many ^afalse prophets shall arise, and shall deceive many;

10 And because iniquity shall abound, the ^alove of many shall wax cold;

11 But he that remaineth ^asteadfast and is not overcome, the same shall be saved.

12 When you, therefore, shall see the ^aabomination of ^bdesolation, spoken of by Daniel the prophet, concerning the destruction of ^cJerusalem, then you shall stand in the ^dholy place; whoso readeth let him understand.

13 Then let them who are in Judea flee into the ^amountains;

14 Let him who is on the housetop flee, and not return to take anything out of his house;

15 Neither let him who is in the field return back to take his clothes;

16 And wo unto them that are with ^achild, and unto them that give suck in those days;

17 Therefore, pray ye the Lord that your flight be not in the winter, neither on the Sabbath day;

18 For then, in those days, shall be great ^atribulation on the ^bJews, and upon the inhabitants of ^cJerusalem, such as was not before sent upon Israel, of God, since the beginning of their kingdom until this time; no, nor ever shall be sent again upon Israel.

19 All things which have befallen them are only the beginning of the sorrows which shall come upon them.

20 And except those days should be shortened, there should none of their flesh be ^asaved; but for the elect's sake, according to the ^bcovenant, those days shall be shortened.

21 Behold, these things I have spoken unto you concerning the Jews; and again, after the tribulation of those days which shall come upon Jerusalem, if any man shall say unto you, Lo, here is Christ, or there, believe him not;

22 For in those days there shall also arise false ^aChrists, and false prophets, and shall show great signs and wonders, insomuch, that, if possible, they shall deceive the very elect, who are the elect according to the covenant.

23 Behold, I speak these things unto you for the ^aelect's sake; and you also

8 a Ezek. 32:9 (7–9). TG Offense.
9 a TG False Prophets.
10 a D&C 45:27.
11 a 2 Pet. 3:17.
12 a JS—M 1:32.
  b TG Abomination of Desolation.
c TG Jerusalem.
  d D&C 101:22 (22–25).
13 a D&C 133:13 (9–13).
16 a Luke 23:29 (29–31).
18 a Dan. 12:1; JS—M 1:36.
  b TG Israel, Judah, People of.
  c Zech. 12:3 (1–14); 14:2
(1–5).
20 a D&C 97:25 (21–28).
  b 2 Ne. 30:2; 3 Ne. 21:22–24.
22 a TG False Christs.
23 a D&C 29:7 (7–23).

shall hear of *b*wars, and rumors of wars; see that ye be not troubled, for all I have told you must come to pass; but the end is not yet.

24 Behold, I have told you before;

25 Wherefore, if they shall say unto you: Behold, he is in the desert; go not forth: Behold, he is in the secret chambers; believe it not;

26 For as the light of the morning cometh out of the *a*east, and shineth even unto the west, and covereth the whole earth, so shall also the coming of the Son of Man be.

27 And now I show unto you a parable. Behold, wheresoever the *a*carcass is, there will the eagles be *b*gathered together; so likewise shall mine elect be gathered from the four quarters of the earth.

28 And they shall hear of wars, and rumors of wars.

29 Behold I speak for mine elect's sake; for nation shall rise against nation, and kingdom against kingdom; there shall be *a*famines, and pestilences, and earthquakes, in divers places.

30 And again, because iniquity shall abound, the love of men shall wax *a*cold; but he that shall not be overcome, the same shall be saved.

31 And again, this *a*Gospel of the Kingdom shall be preached in all the world, for a witness unto all *b*nations, and then shall the end come, or the destruction of the wicked;

32 And again shall the *a*abomination of desolation, spoken of by Daniel the prophet, be fulfilled.

33 And immediately after the tribulation of those days, the *a*sun shall be *b*darkened, and the moon shall not give her light, and the *c*stars shall fall from heaven, and the powers of heaven shall be shaken.

34 Verily, I say unto you, this *a*generation, in which these things shall be shown forth, shall not pass away until all I have told you shall be fulfilled.

35 Although, the days will come, that heaven and earth shall pass away; yet my *a*words shall not pass away, but all shall be fulfilled.

36 And, as I said before, after the *a*tribulation of those days, and the powers of the heavens shall be shaken, then shall appear the sign of the Son of Man in heaven, and then shall all the tribes of the earth *b*mourn; and they

23 *b* D&C 45:26 (18–59).
26 *a* Ezek. 43:2 (1–9).
27 *a* Deut. 28:26.
  b Ps. 74:1 (1–2); Matt.
    24:28; 1 Ne. 19:16
    (15–16); D&C 35:25.
29 *a* Joel 1:10; D&C 43:25
    (24–25); 87:6 (1–8).

30 *a* Isa. 9:19; Mosiah 9:2.
31 *a* Matt. 9:35; D&C 84:80
    (79–80).
  b TG Nations.
32 *a* JS—M 1:12.
33 *a* Joel 2:10; D&C 29:14.
  b Amos 5:18.
  c Ezek. 32:7 (7–9).

34 *a* Matt. 24:34; D&C
    45:31.
35 *a* D&C 1:38; 29:33.
36 *a* JS—M 1:18. TG Tribulation.
  b TG Mourning.

shall see the ᶜSon of Man ᵈcoming in the clouds of heaven, with power and great glory;

37 And whoso ᵃtreasureth up my word, shall not be deceived, for the Son of Man shall ᵇcome, and he shall send his ᶜangels before him with the great sound of a trumpet, and they shall gather together the ᵈremainder of his elect from the four winds, from one end of heaven to the other.

38 Now learn a parable of the ᵃfig tree—When its branches are yet tender, and it begins to put forth leaves, you know that summer is nigh at hand;

39 So likewise, mine elect, when they shall see all these things, they shall know that he is near, even at the doors;

40 But of that day, and hour, no one ᵃknoweth; no, not the angels of God in heaven, but my Father only.

41 But as it was in the days of ᵃNoah, so it shall be also at the coming of the Son of Man;

42 For it shall be with them, as it was in the days which were before the ᵃflood; for until the day that Noah entered into the ark they were eating and drinking, marrying and giving in marriage;

43 And ᵃknew not until the flood came, and took them all away; so shall also the coming of the Son of Man be.

44 Then shall be fulfilled that which is written, that in the ᵃlast days, two shall be in the field, the one shall be taken, and the other ᵇleft;

45 Two shall be grinding at the mill, the one shall be taken, and the other left;

46 And what I say unto one, I say unto all men; ᵃwatch, therefore, for you know not at what hour your Lord doth come.

47 But know this, if the good man of the house had known in what watch the thief would come, he would have watched, and would not have suffered his house to have been broken up, but would have been ready.

48 Therefore be ye also ᵃready, for in such an hour as ye think not, the Son of Man cometh.

49 Who, then, is a ᵃfaithful and wise servant, whom his lord hath made ruler over his household, to give them meat in due season?

36 c TG Millennium.
    d Matt. 25:31.
37 a TG Scriptures, Study of;
    Study; Treasure.
    b TG Jesus Christ, Second
    Coming.
    c D&C 29:11 (11–15);
        Moses 7:25 (25–26).
    d TG Israel, Remnant of.
38 a D&C 35:16.
40 a D&C 39:21 (20–22);
        49:7.
41 a Gen. 6:5.
42 a TG Flood.
43 a TG Apathy.
44 a TG Earth, Cleansing of.
    b Zech. 13:8.
46 a TG Watch.
48 a TG Procrastination.
49 a TG Trustworthiness.

50 Blessed is that *servant whom his lord, when he cometh, shall find so doing; and verily I say unto you, he shall make him ruler over all his goods.

51 But if that evil servant shall say in his heart: My lord *delayeth his coming,

52 And shall begin to smite his fellow-servants, and to eat and drink with the drunken,

53 The lord of that servant shall come in a day when he looketh not for him, and in an hour that he is not aware of,

54 And shall cut him asunder, and shall appoint him his portion with the hypocrites; there shall be weeping and *gnashing of teeth.

55 And thus cometh the *end of the wicked, according to the prophecy of Moses, saying: They shall be cut off from among the people; but the end of the earth is not yet, but by and by.

---

50 a TG Millennium, Preparing a People for.
51 a D&C 45:26.

54 a Matt. 8:12.
55 a Ps. 36:11–12; 73:17
   (3–17); 2 Ne. 30:10;

D&C 1:9 (9–10); 29:17.
TG World, End of.

JOSEPH SMITH—HISTORY

EXTRACTS FROM THE HISTORY OF
JOSEPH SMITH, THE PROPHET

CHAPTER 1

Joseph Smith tells of his ancestry, family members, and their early abodes—An unusual excitement about religion prevails in western New York—He determines to seek wisdom as directed by James—The Father and the Son appear, and Joseph is called to his prophetic ministry. (Verses 1–20.)

1 Owing to the many reports which have been put in circulation by evil-disposed and designing persons, in relation to the rise and progress of ^aThe Church of Jesus Christ of Latter-day Saints, all of which have been designed by the authors thereof to militate against its character as a Church and its progress in the world—I have been induced to write this history, to disabuse the public mind, and put all inquirers after truth in possession of the ^bfacts, as they have transpired, in relation both to myself and the Church, so far as I have such facts in my possession.

2 In this history I shall present the various events in relation to this Church, in truth and righteousness, as they have transpired, or as they at present exist, being now [1838] the ^aeighth ^byear since the organization of the said Church.

3 ^aI was born in the year of our Lord one thousand eight hundred and five, on the twenty-third day of December, in the town of Sharon, Windsor county, State of Vermont. . . . My father, ^bJoseph Smith, Sen., left the State of Vermont, and moved to Palmyra, Ontario (now Wayne) county, in the State of New York, when I was in my tenth year, or thereabouts. In about four years after my father's arrival in Palmyra, he moved with his family into Manchester in the same county of Ontario—

4 His family consisting of eleven souls, namely, my father, Joseph Smith; my ^amother, Lucy Smith (whose name, previous to her marriage, was Mack, daughter of Solomon Mack); my brothers, ^bAlvin (who died November 19th, 1823, in the 26th year of his age), ^cHyrum, myself, ^dSamuel Harrison, William, Don Carlos; and my sisters, Sophronia, Catherine, and Lucy.

---

1 1 *a* TG Restoration of the Gospel.
  b Luke 1:4 (1–4).
 2 *a* JS—H 1:60.

b D&C 20:1.
3 *a* TG Joseph Smith.
  b 2 Ne. 3:15.
4 *a* JS—H 1:20 (7, 20).
  b D&C 137:5 (5–6);

JS—H 1:56.
 c D&C 11:23 (1–30);
   135:1 (1–4).
 d D&C 23:4 (3–5).

5 Some time in the second year after our removal to Manchester, there was in the place where we lived an unusual excitement on the subject of religion. It commenced with the Methodists, but soon became general among all the sects in that region of country. Indeed, the whole district of country seemed affected by it, and great multitudes united themselves to the different religious parties, which created no small stir and division amongst the people, some crying, *"Lo, here!" and others, "Lo, there!" Some were contending for the Methodist faith, some for the Presbyterian, and some for the Baptist.

6 For, notwithstanding the great *love which the converts to these different faiths expressed at the time of their conversion, and the great zeal manifested by the respective clergy, who were active in getting up and promoting this extraordinary scene of religious feeling, in order to have everybody converted, as they were pleased to call it, let them join what sect they pleased; yet when the converts began to file off, some to one party and some to another, it was seen that the seemingly good feelings of both the priests and the converts were more *pretended than real; for a scene of great confusion and bad feeling ensued—priest contending against priest, and convert against convert; so that all their good feelings one for another, if they ever had any, were entirely lost in a strife of words and a contest about opinions.

7 I was at this time in my fifteenth year. My father's family was proselyted to the Presbyterian faith, and four of them joined that church, namely, my mother, Lucy; my brothers Hyrum and Samuel Harrison; and my sister Sophronia.

8 During this time of great excitement my mind was called up to serious reflection and great uneasiness; but though my feelings were deep and often poignant, still I kept myself aloof from all these parties, though I attended their several meetings as often as occasion would permit. In process of time my mind became somewhat partial to the Methodist sect, and I felt some desire to be united with them; but so great were the confusion and *strife among the different denominations, that it was impossible for a person young as I was, and so unacquainted with men and things, to come to any certain conclusion who was *right and who was wrong.

9 My mind at times was greatly excited, the cry and tumult were so great and incessant. The Presbyterians were most decided against the Baptists and Methodists, and used all the powers of both reason and sophistry to prove their errors, or, at least, to make the people think they were in error.

5 *a* Matt. 24:23.   *b* TG Guile; Hypocrisy.   *b* D&C 101:95 (93–95).
6 *a* 1 Pet. 1:22.   8 *a* TG Strife.

On the other hand, the Baptists and Methodists in their turn were equally zealous in endeavoring to establish their own tenets and disprove all others.

10 In the midst of this war of words and tumult of opinions, I often said to myself: What is to be done? Who of all these parties are right; or, are they all wrong together? If any one of them be *right, which is it, and how shall I know it?

11 While I was laboring under the extreme difficulties caused by the contests of these parties of religionists, I was one day reading the *Epistle of James, first chapter and fifth verse, which reads: *If any of you lack *wisdom, let him ask of God, that giveth to all men liberally, and upbraideth not; and it shall be given him.*

12 Never did any passage of *scripture come with more power to the heart of man than this did at this time to mine. It seemed to enter with great force into every feeling of my heart. I reflected on it again and again, knowing that if any person needed *wisdom from God, I did; for how to act I did not know, and unless I could get more wisdom than I then had, I would never know; for the teachers of religion of the different sects *understood the same passages of scripture so differently as to destroy all confidence in settling the question by an appeal to the Bible.

13 At length I came to the conclusion that I must either remain in *darkness and confusion, or else I must do as James directs, that is, ask of God. I at length came to the determination to "ask of God," concluding that if he gave wisdom to them that lacked wisdom, and would *give liberally, and not upbraid, I might venture.

14 So, in accordance with this, my determination to ask of God, I retired to the *woods to make the attempt. It was on the morning of a *beautiful, clear day, early in the spring of eighteen hundred and twenty. It was the first time in my life that I had made such an attempt, for amidst all my anxieties I had never as yet made the attempt to *pray *vocally.

15 After I had retired to the place where I had previously designed to go, having looked around me, and finding myself alone, I kneeled down and began to offer up the desires of my heart to God. I had scarcely done so, when immediately I was *seized upon by some power which entirely overcame me, and had such an astonishing influence over me as to bind

---

10a TG Truth.
11a James 1:5 (1–7).
   b 1 Kgs. 3:12; 2 Ne. 28:15;
     Jacob 6:12.
12a D&C 138:6.

b TG Guidance, Divine.
c 1 Cor. 2:11 (10–16).
13a Micah 7:8.
   b TG Communication.
14a Matt. 14:23.

b TG Beauty.
c TG Prayer.
d Ps. 77:1.
15a Eph. 6:12 (11–18).

my tongue so that I could not speak. Thick *b*darkness gathered around me, and it seemed to me for a time as if I were doomed to sudden destruction.

16 But, exerting all my powers to *a*call upon God to deliver me out of the power of this enemy which had seized upon me, and at the very moment when I was ready to sink into *b*despair and abandon myself to destruction—not to an imaginary ruin, but to the power of some actual being from the unseen world, who had such marvelous power as I had never before felt in any being—just at this moment of great alarm, I saw a pillar of *c*light exactly over my head, above the brightness of the *d*sun, which descended gradually until it fell upon me.

17 It no sooner appeared than I found myself *a*delivered from the enemy which held me bound. When the light rested upon me I *b*saw two *c*Personages, whose brightness and *d*glory defy all description, *e*standing above me in the air. One of them spake unto me, calling me by name and said, pointing to the other—*This is My *f*Beloved *g*Son. Hear Him!*

18 My object in going to *a*inquire of the Lord was to know which of all the sects was right, that I might know which to join. No sooner, therefore, did I get possession of myself, so as to be able to speak, than I asked the Personages who stood above me in the light, which of all the sects was right (for at this time it had never entered into my heart that all were wrong)—and which I should join.

19 I was answered that I must join none of them, for they were all *a*wrong; and the Personage who addressed me said that all their creeds were an abomination in his sight; that those *b*professors were all *c*corrupt; that: "they *d*draw near to me with their lips, but their *e*hearts are far from me, they teach for doctrines the *f*commandments of men, having a form of godliness, but they deny the *g*power thereof."

20 He again forbade me to join with any of them; and many other things did he say unto me, which I cannot write at this time. When I came to

15 *b* Gen. 15:12 (1–21).
   TG Darkness, Physical.
16 *a* Moses 1:20.
   b Isa. 6:5 (1–7). TG Despair.
   c Acts 26:13.
   d Rev. 1:16.
17 *a* TG Deliver.
   b TG God, Privilege of Seeing; Vision.
   c Jer. 10:10; 1 Jn. 4:12 (7–21); JS—H 1:25. TG God, Manifestations of; Godhead; God the Father, Elohim; Jesus

Christ, Appearances, Postmortal; Restoration of the Gospel; Revelation.
   d TG Jesus Christ, Glory of.
   e 1 Sam. 3:10.
   f Matt. 3:17; 17:5; 3 Ne. 11:7. TG Witness of the Father.
   g TG Jesus Christ, Divine Sonship.
18 *a* Ex. 18:15; 1 Sam. 9:9; Alma 27:10 (7, 10); D&C 6:11; 46:7.

19 *a* TG Apostasy of the Early Christian Church.
   b Jude 1:4. TG False Prophets.
   c TG False Doctrine.
   d Isa. 29:13; Ezek. 33:31 (30–33); Luke 6:46.
   e Jer. 3:10. TG Apostasy of Individuals; Hardheartedness; Hypocrisy.
   f Col. 2:22 (18–22); Titus 1:14; D&C 3:6 (6–7); 45:29; 46:7.
   g 2 Tim. 3:5.

myself again, I found myself *a*lying on my back, looking up into heaven. When the light had departed, I had no strength; but soon recovering in some degree, I went home. And as I leaned up to the fireplace, *b*mother inquired what the matter was. I replied, "Never mind, all is well—I am well enough off." I then said to my mother, "I have learned for myself that Presbyterianism is not true." It seems as though the *c*adversary was aware, at a very early period of my life, that I was destined to prove a disturber and an annoyer of his kingdom; else why should the powers of darkness combine against me? Why the *d*opposition and persecution that arose against me, almost in my infancy?

Some preachers and other professors of religion reject the account of the First Vision—Persecution is heaped upon Joseph Smith—He testifies of the reality of the vision. (Verses 21–26.)

21 Some few days after I had this vision, I happened to be in company with one of the Methodist preachers, who was very active in the before mentioned religious excitement; and, conversing with him on the subject of religion, I took occasion to give him an account of the vision which I had had. I was greatly surprised at his behavior; he treated my communication not only lightly, but with great contempt, saying it was all of the devil, that there were no such things as *a*visions or *b*revelations in these days; that all such things had ceased with the apostles, and that there would never be any more of them.

22 I soon found, however, that my telling the story had excited a great deal of prejudice against me among professors of religion, and was the cause of great *a*persecution, which continued to increase; and though I was an *b*obscure boy, only between fourteen and fifteen years of age, and my circumstances in life such as to make a boy of no consequence in the world, yet men of high standing would take notice sufficient to excite the public mind against me, and create a bitter persecution; and this was common among all the sects—all united to persecute me.

23 It caused me serious reflection then, and often has since, how very strange it was that an obscure *a*boy, of a little over fourteen years of age,

---

20 *a* Dan. 10:9; 1 Ne. 1:7;
　　Moses 1:9.
　 b JS—H 1:4. TG Family,
　　Love within.
　 c TG Devil.
　 d Jer. 11:19; Matt. 10:22;

　　Moses 6:31 (31–37).
21 *a* 1 Sam. 3:1.
　 b TG Revelation.
22 *a* James 5:10 (10–11);
　　Mosiah 17:13 (10–20);
　　Alma 14:26 (20–27).

　 b 1 Sam. 17:33 (32–51);
　　1 Chr. 29:1.
23 *a* Amos 7:14 (14–15); Acts
　　5:38 (38–39).

and one, too, who was doomed to the necessity of obtaining a scanty maintenance by his daily *b*labor, should be thought a character of sufficient importance to attract the attention of the great ones of the most popular sects of the day, and in a manner to create in them a spirit of the most bitter *c*persecution and *d*reviling. But strange or not, so it was, and it was often the cause of great sorrow to myself.

24 However, it was nevertheless a fact that I had beheld a *a*vision. I have thought since, that I felt much like Paul, when he made his defense before King Agrippa, and related the account of the vision he had when he saw a light, and heard a voice; but still there were but few who believed him; some said he was dishonest, others said he was *b*mad; and he was ridiculed and reviled. But all this did not destroy the reality of his vision. He had seen a vision, he knew he had, and all the *c*persecution under heaven could not make it otherwise; and though they should persecute him unto death, yet he knew, and would know to his latest breath, that he had both seen a light and heard a voice speaking unto him, and all the world could not make him think or believe otherwise.

25 So it was with me. I had actually seen a light, and in the midst of that light I saw two *a*Personages, and they did in reality speak to me; and though I was *b*hated and *c*persecuted for saying that I had seen a vision, yet it was true; and while they were persecuting me, reviling me, and speaking all manner of evil against me *d*falsely for so saying, I was led to say in my heart: Why persecute me for telling the truth? I have actually seen a vision; and who am I that I can withstand God, or why does the world think to make me deny what I have actually seen? For I had seen a vision; I knew it, and I knew that God knew it, and I could not *e*deny it, neither dared I do it; at least I knew that by so doing I would offend God, and come under condemnation.

26 I had now got my mind satisfied so far as the sectarian world was concerned—that it was not my duty to join with any of them, but to continue as I was until further *a*directed. I had found the testimony of James to be true—that a man who lacked wisdom might ask of God, and obtain, and not be *b*upbraided.

---

23 *b* TG Industry.
　c Jer. 1:19 (6–19). TG Malice; Persecution.
　d TG Reviling.
24 *a* Ezek. 1:1; 1 Ne. 1:16. TG Vision.

　b Acts 26:24 (1–32).
　c 1 Thes. 3:3.
25 *a* JS—H 1:17.
　b TG Hate.
　c TG Adversity.
　d TG Injustice.

　e TG Courage; Honesty; Integrity.
26 *a* JS—H 1:33 (33–50).
　b Ps. 20:6; James 1:5.

Moroni appears to Joseph Smith—Joseph's name is to be known for good and evil among all nations—Moroni tells him of the Book of Mormon and of the coming judgments of the Lord and quotes many scriptures—The hiding place of the gold plates is revealed—Moroni continues to instruct the Prophet. (Verses 27–54.)

27 I continued to pursue my common vocations in life until the twenty-first of September, one thousand eight hundred and twenty-three, all the time suffering severe persecution at the hands of all classes of men, both religious and irreligious, because I continued to *a*affirm that I had seen a vision.

28 During the space of time which intervened between the time I had the vision and the year eighteen hundred and twenty-three—having been forbidden to join any of the religious sects of the day, and being of very tender years, and persecuted by those who ought to have been my *a*friends and to have treated me kindly, and if they supposed me to be deluded to have endeavored in a proper and affectionate manner to have reclaimed me—I was left to all kinds of *b*temptations; and, mingling with all kinds of society, I frequently fell into many foolish *c*errors, and displayed the weakness of youth, and the foibles of human nature; which, I am sorry to say, led me into divers temptations, offensive in the sight of God. In making this confession, no one need suppose me guilty of any great or malignant sins. A disposition to commit such was never in my nature. But I was guilty of *d*levity, and sometimes associated with jovial company, etc., not consistent with that character which ought to be maintained by one who was *e*called of God as I had been. But this will not seem very strange to any one who recollects my youth, and is acquainted with my native *f*cheery temperament.

29 In consequence of these things, I often felt condemned for my weakness and imperfections; when, on the evening of the above-mentioned twenty-first of September, after I had retired to my bed for the night, I betook myself to *a*prayer and supplication to Almighty God for forgiveness of all my sins and follies, and also for a manifestation to me, that I might know of my state and standing before him; for I had full *b*confidence in obtaining a divine manifestation, as I previously had one.

30 While I was thus in the act of calling upon God, I discovered a *a*light appearing in my room, which continued to increase until the room was lighter than at noonday, when immediately a *b*personage appeared at my bedside, standing in the air, for his feet did not touch the floor.

---

27 *a* 2 Cor. 1:12.
28 *a* TG Friendship.
  b TG Temptation.
  c Ps. 25:7; D&C 20:5.

d TG Levity.
e TG Called of God.
f TG Cheerful.
29 *a* TG Prayer.

b James 1:6 (5–7).
30 *a* 1 Ne. 1:6.
  b TG Angels.

31 He had on a loose robe of most exquisite ᵃwhiteness. It was a whiteness beyond anything earthly I had ever seen; nor do I believe that any earthly thing could be made to appear so exceedingly white and brilliant. His hands were naked, and his arms also, a little above the wrist; so, also, were his feet naked, as were his legs, a little above the ankles. His head and neck were also bare. I could discover that he had no other clothing on but this robe, as it was open, so that I could see into his bosom.

32 Not only was his robe exceedingly white, but his whole person was ᵃglorious beyond description, and his countenance truly like ᵇlightning. The room was exceedingly light, but not so very bright as immediately around his person. When I first looked upon him, I was ᶜafraid; but the ᵈfear soon left me.

33 He called me by ᵃname, and said unto me that he was a ᵇmessenger sent from the presence of God to me, and that his name was Moroni; that God had a work for me to do; and that my name should be had for ᶜgood and evil among all nations, kindreds, and tongues, or that it should be both good and evil spoken of among all people.

34 He said there was a ᵃbook deposited, written upon gold plates, giving an account of the former inhabitants of this continent, and the source from whence they sprang. He also said that the ᵇfulness of the everlasting Gospel was contained in it, as delivered by the Savior to the ancient inhabitants;

35 Also, that there were two stones in silver bows—and these stones, fastened to a ᵃbreastplate, constituted what is called the ᵇUrim and Thummim—deposited with the plates; and the possession and use of these stones were what constituted ᶜ"seers" in ancient or former times; and that God had prepared them for the purpose of translating the book.

36 After telling me these things, he commenced quoting the prophecies of the Old Testament. He first quoted part of the ᵃthird chapter of Malachi; and he quoted also the fourth or last chapter of the same prophecy, though with a little variation from the way it reads in our Bibles. Instead of quoting the first verse as it reads in our books, he quoted it thus:

---

31 a Acts 10:30 (30–33);
  1 Ne. 8:5; 3 Ne. 11:8.
32 a TG Glory.
  b Ex. 34:29 (29–35); Hel.
  5:36; D&C 110:3.
  c Ex. 3:6; Ether 3:6 (6–8,
  19).
  d Dan. 10:12; Hel. 5:26;

D&C 68:6; 98:1.
33 a Ex. 33:12 (12, 17); Isa.
  45:3 (3–4).
  b JS—H 1:26.
  c Isa. 5:20.
34 a TG Book of Mormon;
  Scriptures, Preservation
  of.

  b Rom. 15:29. TG Restoration of the Gospel.
35 a Ex. 25:7; Lev. 8:8 (7–9).
  b Ex. 28:30. TG Urim and
  Thummim.
  c 1 Sam. 9:9.
36 a Mal. 3–4.

37 For behold, the *day cometh that shall *burn as an oven, and all the proud, yea, and all that do wickedly shall burn as *stubble; for they that come shall burn them, saith the Lord of Hosts, that it shall leave them neither root nor branch.

38 And again, he quoted the fifth verse thus: *Behold, I will reveal unto you the *Priesthood, by the hand of *Elijah the prophet, before the coming of the great and dreadful day of the *Lord.

39 He also quoted the next verse differently: *And he shall plant in the hearts of the *children the *promises made to the fathers, and the hearts of the children shall turn to their fathers. If it were not so, the whole earth would be utterly wasted at his coming.*

40 In addition to these, he quoted the *eleventh chapter of Isaiah, saying that it was about to be fulfilled. He quoted also the third chapter of Acts, twenty-second and twenty-third verses, precisely as they stand in our New Testament. He said that that *prophet was Christ; but the day had not yet come when "they who would not hear his voice should be *cut off from among the people," but soon would come.

41 He also quoted the *second chapter of Joel, from the twenty-eighth verse to the last. He also said that this was not yet fulfilled, but was soon to be. And he further stated that the fulness of the *Gentiles was soon to come in. He quoted many other passages of scripture, and offered many explanations which *cannot be mentioned here.

42 Again, he told me, that when I got those plates of which he had spoken— for the time that they should be obtained was not yet fulfilled—I should not show them to any person; neither the breastplate with the Urim and Thummim; only to those to whom I should be commanded to show them; if I did I should be *destroyed. While he was conversing with me about the plates, the vision was opened to my *mind that I could see the place where the plates were deposited, and that so clearly and distinctly that I knew the place again when I visited it.

43 After this communication, I saw the light in the room begin to gather immediately around the person of him who had been speaking to me, and

37 *a* TG Day of the Lord.
  b Isa. 9:5 (5, 18–19); 3 Ne. 25; D&C 64:23 (23–24). TG Earth, Cleansing of; World, End of.
  c Ex. 15:7 (7–8); Nahum 1:10; 1 Ne. 22:23 (15, 23); 2 Ne. 26:6 (4–6); D&C 29:9.
38 *a* TG Priesthood;

Priesthood, Keys of.
  b Mal. 4:5 (5–6); D&C 27:9; 110:13–16; 138:46.
  c TG Millennium.
39 *a* TG Genealogy and Temple Work; Salvation for the Dead.
  b Gal. 3:5, 8, 18, 29.
40 *a* Isa. 11:10 (1–16).
  b Deut. 18:15 (15–19); Acts

3:22 (22–23); 7:37.
  c 3 Ne. 20:23; 21:20.
41 *a* Joel 2:28 (28–32); Acts 2:16 (16–21).
  b Isa. 42:6; Rom. 11:25 (11–27); D&C 88:84 (84–85). TG Gentiles.
  c 2 Cor. 12:4.
42 *a* JS—H 1:59.
  b TG Mind.

it continued to do so until the room was again left dark, except just around him; when, instantly I saw, as it were, a conduit open right up into heaven, and he ªascended till he entirely disappeared, and the room was left as it had been before this heavenly light had made its appearance.

44 I lay musing on the singularity of the scene, and marveling greatly at what had been told to me by this extraordinary messenger; when, in the midst of my ªmeditation, I suddenly discovered that my room was again beginning to get lighted, and in an instant, as it were, the same heavenly messenger was again by my bedside.

45 He commenced, and ªagain related the very same things which he had done at his first visit, without the least variation; which having done, he informed me of great ᵇjudgments which were coming upon the earth, with great desolations by ᶜfamine, ᵈsword, and pestilence; and that these grievous judgments would come on the earth in this generation. Having related these things, he again ascended as he had done before.

46 By this time, so deep were the impressions made on my mind, that sleep had fled from my eyes, and I lay overwhelmed in ªastonishment at what I had both seen and heard. But what was my surprise when again I beheld the same messenger at my bedside, and heard him rehearse or repeat over again to me the same things as before; and added a caution to me, telling me that Satan would try to ᵇtempt me (in consequence of the indigent circumstances of my father's family), to get the plates for the purpose of getting ᶜrich. This he forbade me, saying that I must have no other object in view in getting the plates but to glorify God, and must not be influenced by any other ᵈmotive than that of building his kingdom; otherwise I could not get them.

47 After this third visit, he again ascended into heaven as before, and I was again left to ªponder on the strangeness of what I had just experienced; when almost immediately after the heavenly messenger had ascended from me for the third time, the cock crowed, and I found that day was approaching, so that our interviews must have occupied the whole of that night.

48 I shortly after arose from my bed, and, as usual, went to the necessary labors of the day; but, in attempting to work as at other times, I found my ªstrength so exhausted as to render me entirely unable. My father, who was laboring along with me, discovered something to be wrong with me, and

---

43 a Acts 1:9.
44 a D&C 76:19. TG Meditation.
45 a Ezek. 2:3 (1–10); 3:4 (1–27).
  b TG Judgment.

c TG Famine.
d Deut. 32:25; 1 Ne. 1:13; Alma 10:22.
46 a Dan. 8:27.
  b TG Temptation.
  c TG Sacrilege.

d Luke 11:34 (34–36); D&C 121:37.
47 a TG Meditation.
48 a TG Strength.

told me to go home. I started with the intention of going to the house; but, in attempting to cross the fence out of the field where we were, my strength entirely failed me, and I *b*fell helpless on the ground, and for a time was quite unconscious of anything.

49 The first thing that I can recollect was a voice speaking unto me, calling me by name. I looked up, and beheld the same messenger standing over my head, surrounded by light as before. He then again related unto me all that he had related to me the previous night, and commanded me to go to my *a*father and tell him of the vision and commandments which I had received.

50 I obeyed; I returned to my *a*father in the field, and rehearsed the whole matter to him. He *b*replied to me that it was of God, and told me to go and do as commanded by the messenger. I left the field, and went to the place where the messenger had told me the plates were deposited; and owing to the distinctness of the vision which I had had concerning it, I knew the place the instant that I arrived there.

51 Convenient to the village of Manchester, Ontario county, New York, stands a *a*hill of considerable size, and the most elevated of any in the neighborhood. On the west side of this hill, not far from the top, under a stone of considerable size, lay the plates, deposited in a stone box. This stone was thick and rounding in the middle on the upper side, and thinner towards the edges, so that the middle part of it was visible above the ground, but the edge all around was covered with earth.

52 Having removed the earth, I obtained a lever, which I got fixed under the edge of the stone, and with a little exertion raised it up. I looked in, and there indeed did I behold the *a*plates, the *b*Urim and Thummim, and the breastplate, as stated by the messenger. The box in which they lay was formed by laying stones together in some kind of cement. In the bottom of the box were laid two stones crossways of the box, and on these stones lay the plates and the other things with them.

53 I made an attempt to take them out, but was forbidden by the messenger, and was again informed that the time for bringing them forth had not yet arrived, neither would it, until four years from that time; but he told me that I should come to that place precisely in one year from that time, and that he would there meet with me, and that I should continue to do so until the time should come for obtaining the plates.

---

48 *b* Acts 9:4 (4–8).
49 *a* TG Family, Love within.
50 *a* TG Honoring Father and

Mother.
b TG Counsel.
51 *a* D&C 128:20.

52 *a* Morm. 6:6; Ether 4:5
(4–7); D&C 17:1.
b TG Urim and Thummim.

54 Accordingly, as I had been commanded, I went at the end of each year, and at each time I found the same messenger there, and received instruction and intelligence from him at each of our interviews, respecting what the Lord was going to do, and how and in what manner his *a*kingdom was to be conducted in the last days.

Joseph Smith marries Emma Hale—He receives the gold plates from Moroni and translates some of the characters—Martin Harris shows the characters and translation to Professor Anthon, who says, "I cannot read a sealed book." (Verses 55–65.)

55 As my father's worldly circumstances were very limited, we were under the necessity of *a*laboring with our hands, hiring out by day's work and otherwise, as we could get opportunity. Sometimes we were at home, and sometimes abroad, and by continuous *b*labor were enabled to get a comfortable maintenance.

56 In the year 1823 my father's family met with a great *a*affliction by the death of my eldest brother, *b*Alvin. In the month of October, 1825, I hired with an old gentleman by the name of Josiah Stoal, who lived in Chenango county, State of New York. He had heard something of a silver mine having been opened by the Spaniards in Harmony, Susquehanna county, State of Pennsylvania; and had, previous to my hiring to him, been digging, in order, if possible, to discover the mine. After I went to live with him, he took me, with the rest of his hands, to dig for the silver mine, at which I continued to work for nearly a month, without success in our undertaking, and finally I prevailed with the old gentleman to cease digging after it. Hence arose the very prevalent story of my having been a money-digger.

57 During the time that I was thus employed, I was put to board with a Mr. Isaac Hale, of that place; it was there I first saw my wife (his daughter), Emma Hale. On the 18th of January, 1827, we were married, while I was yet employed in the service of Mr. Stoal.

58 Owing to my continuing to assert that I had seen a vision, *a*persecution still followed me, and my wife's father's family were very much opposed to our being married. I was, therefore, under the necessity of taking her elsewhere; so we went and were married at the house of Squire Tarbill, in South Bainbridge, Chenango county, New York. Immediately after my marriage, I left Mr. Stoal's, and went to my father's, and *b*farmed with him that season.

54*a* TG Kingdom of God, on Earth.
55*a* TG Industry.
b TG Work, Value of.
56*a* TG Affliction.
b JS—H 1:4.
58*a* TG Hate; Persecution.
b TG Industry.

59 At length the time arrived for obtaining the plates, the Urim and Thummim, and the breastplate. On the twenty-second day of September, one thousand eight hundred and twenty-seven, having gone as usual at the end of another year to the place where they were deposited, the same heavenly messenger delivered them up to *me with this charge: that I should be *responsible for them; that if I should let them go carelessly, or through any *neglect of mine, I should be cut off; but that if I would use all my endeavors to *preserve them, until he, the messenger, should call for them, they should be protected.

60 I soon found out the reason why I had received such strict charges to keep them safe, and why it was that the messenger had said that when I had done what was required at my hand, he would call for them. For no sooner was it known that I had them, than the most strenuous exertions were used to *get them from me. Every stratagem that could be invented was resorted to for that purpose. The persecution became more bitter and severe than before, and multitudes were on the alert continually to get them from me if possible. But by the wisdom of God, they remained safe in my hands, until I had accomplished by them what was required at my hand. When, according to arrangements, the messenger called for them, I delivered them up to him; and he has them in his charge until this *day, being the second day of May, one thousand eight hundred and thirty-eight.

61 The excitement, however, still continued, and rumor with her thousand tongues was all the time employed in circulating *falsehoods about my father's family, and about myself. If I were to relate a thousandth part of them, it would fill up volumes. The persecution, however, became so intolerable that I was under the necessity of leaving Manchester, and going with my wife to Susquehanna county, in the State of Pennsylvania. While preparing to start—being very poor, and the persecution so heavy upon us that there was no probability that we would ever be otherwise—in the midst of our afflictions we found a friend in a gentleman by the name of *Martin Harris, who came to us and gave me fifty dollars to assist us on our journey. Mr. Harris was a resident of Palmyra township, Wayne county, in the State of New York, and a farmer of respectability.

---

59 a Isa. 29:12.
  b TG Dependability; Trustworthiness.
  c JS—H 1:42.

d TG Scriptures, Preservation of.
60 a TG Stealing.
  b JS—H 1:2.

61 a TG Injustice.
  b D&C 5:1 (1–32).

62 By this timely aid was I enabled to reach the place of my destination in Pennsylvania; and immediately after my arrival there I commenced copying the characters off the plates. I copied a considerable number of them, and by means of the *Urim and Thummim I translated some of them, which I did between the time I arrived at the house of my wife's father, in the month of December, and the February following.

63 Sometime in this month of February, the aforementioned Mr. Martin Harris came to our place, got the characters which I had drawn off the plates, and started with them to the city of New York. For what took place relative to him and the characters, I refer to his own account of the circumstances, as he related them to me after his return, which was as follows:

64 "I went to the city of New York, and presented the characters which had been translated, with the translation thereof, to Professor Charles Anthon, a gentleman celebrated for his literary attainments. Professor Anthon stated that the translation was correct, more so than any he had before seen translated from the Egyptian. I then showed him those which were not yet translated, and he said that they were Egyptian, Chaldaic, Assyriac, and Arabic; and he said they were true characters. He gave me a certificate, certifying to the people of Palmyra that they were true characters, and that the translation of such of them as had been translated was also correct. I took the certificate and put it into my pocket, and was just leaving the house, when Mr. Anthon called me back, and asked me how the young man found out that there were gold plates in the place where he found them. I answered that an angel of God had revealed it unto him.

65 "He then said to me, 'Let me see that certificate.' I accordingly took it out of my pocket and gave it to him, when he took it and tore it to pieces, saying that there was no such thing now as ministering of *angels, and that if I would bring the plates to him he would translate them. I informed him that part of the plates were *sealed, and that I was forbidden to bring them. He replied, 'I cannot read a sealed book.' I left him and went to Dr. Mitchell, who sanctioned what Professor Anthon had said respecting both the characters and the translation."

---

62 a TG Urim and Thummim.
65 a TG Angels, Ministering.

b Isa. 29:11 (11–12); Dan.
12:9; 1 Ne. 14:26; 2 Ne.

27:10; Ether 4:5 (4–7);
D&C 35:18.

· · · · · · ·

Oliver Cowdery serves as scribe in translating the Book of Mormon—Joseph and Oliver receive the Aaronic Priesthood from John the Baptist—They are baptized, ordained, and receive the spirit of prophecy. (Verses 66–75.)

66 On the 5th day of April, 1829, *a*Oliver Cowdery came to my house, until which time I had never seen him. He stated to me that having been teaching school in the neighborhood where my father resided, and my father being one of those who sent to the school, he went to board for a season at his house, and while there the family related to him the circumstances of my having received the plates, and accordingly he had come to make inquiries of me.

67 Two days after the arrival of Mr. Cowdery (being the 7th of April) I commenced to translate the Book of Mormon, and he began to *a*write for me.

· · · · · · ·

68 We still continued the work of translation, when, in the ensuing month (May, 1829), we on a certain day went into the woods to pray and inquire of the Lord respecting *a*baptism for the *b*remission of sins, that we found mentioned in the translation of the plates. While we were thus employed, praying and calling upon the Lord, a messenger from heaven descended in a *c*cloud of light, and having laid his *d*hands upon us, he *e*ordained us, saying:

69 *Upon you my fellow servants, in the name of Messiah, I confer the* *a*Priesthood of *b*Aaron, which holds the keys of the ministering of angels, and of the gospel of repentance, and of *c*baptism by immersion for the remission of sins; and this shall never be taken again from the earth until the sons of *d*Levi do offer again an offering unto the Lord in *e*righteousness.*

70 He said this Aaronic Priesthood had not the power of laying on hands for the gift of the Holy Ghost, but that this should be conferred on us hereafter; and he commanded us to go and be baptized, and gave us directions that I should baptize Oliver Cowdery, and that afterwards he should baptize me.

---

66 a D&C 6:14–16; 8:1
    (1–12).
67 a D&C 9:1. TG Scriptures,
    Writing of.
68 a TG Baptism; Baptism,
    Essential; Baptism,
    Immersion.
   b TG Remission of Sins.

c Num. 11:25; Ether 2:4
   (4–5, 14); D&C 34:7
   (7–9).
d A of F 1:5. TG Hands,
   Laying on of.
e TG Priesthood, Authority; Priesthood, History
   of.

69 a TG Restoration of the
    Gospel.
   b TG Priesthood, Aaronic.
   c TG Baptism.
   d Deut. 10:8; D&C 13;
    124:39.
   e TG Righteousness.

71 Accordingly we went and were baptized. I *baptized him first, and afterwards he baptized me—after which I laid my hands upon his head and ordained him to the Aaronic Priesthood, and afterwards he laid his hands on me and ordained me to the same Priesthood—for so we were commanded.*

72 The *messenger who visited us on this occasion and conferred this Priesthood upon us, said that his name was John, the same that is called *bJohn the Baptist in the New Testament, and that he acted under the direction of *cPeter, James and John, who held the keys of the Priesthood of Melchizedek, which Priesthood, he said, would in due time be conferred on us, and that I should be called the first *dElder of the Church, and he (Oliver Cowdery) the second. It was on the fifteenth day of May, 1829, that we were ordained under the hand of this messenger, and baptized.

73 Immediately on our coming up out of the water after we had been baptized, we experienced great and glorious blessings from our Heavenly Father. No sooner had I baptized Oliver Cowdery, than the Holy Ghost fell upon him, and he stood up and *aprophesied many things which should shortly come to pass. And again, so soon as I had been baptized by him, I also had the spirit of prophecy, when, standing up, I prophesied concerning the rise of this Church, and many other things connected with the Church, and this generation of the children of men. We were filled with the Holy Ghost, and rejoiced in the God of our salvation.

---

* Oliver Cowdery describes these events thus: "These were days never to be forgotten—to sit under the sound of a voice dictated by the inspiration of heaven, awakened the utmost gratitude of this bosom! Day after day I continued, uninterrupted, to write from his mouth, as he translated with the Urim and Thummim, or, as the Nephites would have said, 'Interpreters,' the history or record called 'The Book of Mormon.'

"To notice, in even few words, the interesting account given by Mormon and his faithful son, Moroni, of a people once beloved and favored of heaven, would supersede my present design; I shall therefore defer this to a future period, and, as I said in the introduction, pass more directly to some few incidents immediately connected with the rise of this Church, which may be entertaining to some thousands who have stepped forward, amid the frowns of bigots and the calumny of hypocrites, and embraced the Gospel of Christ.

71a Mosiah 18:13–15; 3 Ne. 19:10–13.
72a Luke 3:4.
  b Matt. 3:1 (1–12).

c D&C 7:7 (5–7); 27:12.
  TG Priesthood, Keys of;
  Priesthood, Melchizedek.
  d TG Elder.

73a TG Holy Ghost, Gifts of;
  Holy Ghost, Mission of.

74 Our minds being now enlightened, we began to have the *a*scriptures laid open to our understandings, and the *b*true meaning and intention of their more *c*mysterious passages revealed unto us in a manner which we never could attain to previously, nor ever before had thought of. In the meantime we were forced to keep secret the circumstances of having received the Priesthood and our having been baptized, owing to a spirit of persecution which had already manifested itself in the neighborhood.

75 We had been threatened with being mobbed, from time to time, and this, too, by professors of religion. And their intentions of mobbing us were only counteracted by the influence of my wife's father's family (under Divine providence), who had become very *a*friendly to me, and who were opposed to mobs, and were willing that I should be allowed to continue the work of translation without interruption; and therefore offered and promised us protection from all unlawful proceedings, as far as in them lay.

"No men, in their sober senses, could translate and write the directions given to the Nephites from the mouth of the Savior, of the precise manner in which men should build up His Church, and especially when corruption had spread an uncertainty over all forms and systems practiced among men, without desiring a privilege of showing the willingness of the heart by being buried in the liquid grave, to answer a 'good conscience by the resurrection of Jesus Christ.'

"After writing the account given of the Savior's ministry to the remnant of the seed of Jacob, upon this continent, it was easy to be seen, as the prophet said it would be, that darkness covered the earth and gross darkness the minds of the people. On reflecting further it was as easy to be seen that amid the great strife and noise concerning religion, none had authority from God to administer the ordinances of the Gospel. For the question might be asked, have men authority to administer in the name of Christ, who deny revelations, when His testimony is no less than the spirit of prophecy, and His religion based, built, and sustained by immediate revelations, in all ages of the world when He has had a people on earth? If these facts were buried, and carefully concealed by men whose craft would have been in danger if once permitted to shine in the faces of men, they were no longer to us; and we only waited for the commandment to be given 'Arise and be baptized.'

"This was not long desired before it was realized. The Lord, who is rich in mercy, and ever willing to answer the consistent prayer of the humble, after we had called upon Him in a fervent manner, aside from the abodes of men, condescended

---

74 *a* D&C 32:4.
  b John 16:13.

c TG Mysteries of Godliness.

75 *a* TG Friendship.

to manifest to us His will. On a sudden, as from the midst of eternity, the voice of the Redeemer spake peace to us, while the veil was parted and the angel of God came down clothed with glory, and delivered the anxiously looked for message, and the keys of the Gospel of repentance. What joy! what wonder! what amazement! While the world was racked and distracted—while millions were groping as the blind for the wall, and while all men were resting upon uncertainty, as a general mass, our eyes beheld, our ears heard, as in the 'blaze of day'; yes, more—above the glitter of the May sunbeam, which then shed its brilliancy over the face of nature! Then his voice, though mild, pierced to the center, and his words, 'I am thy fellow-servant,' dispelled every fear. We listened, we gazed, we admired! 'Twas the voice of an angel from glory, 'twas a message from the Most High! And as we heard we rejoiced, while His love enkindled upon our souls, and we were wrapped in the vision of the Almighty! Where was room for doubt? Nowhere; uncertainty had fled, doubt had sunk no more to rise, while fiction and deception had fled forever!

"But, dear brother, think, further think for a moment, what joy filled our hearts, and with what surprise we must have bowed, (for who would not have bowed the knee for such a blessing?) when we received under his hand the Holy Priesthood as he said, 'Upon you my fellow-servants, in the name of Messiah, I confer this Priesthood and this authority, which shall remain upon earth, that the Sons of Levi may yet offer an offering unto the Lord in righteousness!'

"I shall not attempt to paint to you the feelings of this heart, nor the majestic beauty and glory which surrounded us on this occasion; but you will believe me when I say, that earth, nor men, with the eloquence of time, cannot begin to clothe language in as interesting and sublime a manner as this holy personage. No; nor has this earth power to give the joy, to bestow the peace, or comprehend the wisdom which was contained in each sentence as they were delivered by the power of the Holy Spirit! Man may deceive his fellow-men, deception may follow deception, and the children of the wicked one may have power to seduce the foolish and untaught, till naught but fiction feeds the many, and the fruit of falsehood carries in its current the giddy to the grave; but one touch with the finger of his love, yes, one ray of glory from the upper world, or one word from the mouth of the Savior, from the bosom of eternity, strikes it all into insignificance, and blots it forever from the mind. The assurance that we were in the presence of an angel, the certainty that we heard the voice of Jesus, and the truth unsullied as it flowed from a pure personage, dictated by the will of God, is to me past description, and I shall ever look upon this expression of the Savior's goodness with wonder and thanksgiving while I am permitted to tarry; and in those mansions where perfection dwells and sin never comes, I hope to adore in that day which shall never cease."—*Messenger and Advocate,* vol. 1 (October 1834), pp. 14–16

THE ARTICLES OF FAITH
OF THE CHURCH OF JESUS CHRIST
OF LATTER-DAY SAINTS

1 We *believe in *God, the Eternal Father, and in His *Son, Jesus Christ, and in the *Holy Ghost.

2 We believe that men will be *punished for their *own sins, and not for *Adam's transgression.

3 We believe that through the *Atonement of Christ, all *mankind may be *saved, by obedience to the laws and ordinances of the Gospel.

4 We believe that the first principles and *ordinances of the Gospel are: first, *Faith in the Lord Jesus Christ; second, *Repentance; third, *Baptism by *immersion for the *remission of sins; fourth, Laying on of *hands for the *gift of the Holy Ghost.

5 We believe that a man must be *called of God, by *prophecy, and by the laying on of *hands by those who are in *authority, to *preach the Gospel and administer in the *ordinances thereof.

6 We believe in the same *organization that existed in the Primitive Church, namely, apostles, *prophets, *pastors, *teachers, *evangelists, and so forth.

7 We believe in the *gift of *tongues, *prophecy, *revelation, *visions, *healing, *interpretation of tongues, and so forth.

---

1 1 *a* TG Believe.
  b TG Godhead; God the Father, Elohim.
  c TG Jesus Christ, Divine Sonship.
  d TG Holy Ghost.
2 *a* TG Punish.
  b Ex. 32:33; Deut. 24:16; Ezek. 18:20 (1–20). TG Accountability; Agency.
  c TG Fall of Man.
3 *a* TG Jesus Christ, Atonement through.
  b Jude 1:3.
  c Ps. 49:15; Mosiah 27:24 (24–26); D&C 93:38;

Moses 5:9. TG Salvation.
4 *a* TG Ordinance.
  b D&C 138:33. TG Baptism, Qualifications for; Faith.
  c TG Repent.
  d TG Baptism.
  e TG Baptism, Immersion.
  f TG Remission of Sins.
  g TG Hands, Laying on of.
  h TG Holy Ghost, Gift of.
5 *a* Num. 27:16 (15–20). TG Called of God; Priesthood, Qualifying for.
  b TG Prophecy.
  c TG Hands, Laying on of.
  d TG Authority; Priesthood, Authority.

e D&C 11:15 (15–21). TG Preaching.
  f Alma 13:16 (8–16).
6 *a* TG Church Organization.
  b TG Prophets, Mission of.
  c TG Bishop.
  d TG Teacher; Teacher, Aaronic Priesthood.
  e TG Patriarch.
7 *a* TG Holy Ghost, Gifts of.
  b TG Language.
  c TG Prophecy.
  d TG Revelation.
  e TG Vision.
  f TG Heal.
  g 1 Cor. 12:10; Morm. 9:7.

8 We believe the *Bible to be the *word of God as far as it is translated *correctly; we also believe the *Book of Mormon to be the word of God.

9 We believe all that God has *revealed, all that He does now reveal, and we believe that He will yet *reveal many great and important things pertaining to the Kingdom of God.

10 We believe in the literal *gathering of Israel and in the restoration of the *Ten Tribes; that *Zion (the New Jerusalem) will be built upon the American continent; that Christ will *reign personally upon the earth; and, that the earth will be *renewed and receive its *paradisiacal *glory.

11 We claim the *privilege of worshiping Almighty God according to the *dictates of our own *conscience, and allow all men the same privilege, let them *worship how, where, or what they may.

12 We believe in being *subject to *kings, presidents, rulers, and magistrates, in *obeying, honoring, and sustaining the *law.

13 *We believe in being *honest, true, *chaste, *benevolent, virtuous, and in doing *good to all men; indeed, we may say that we follow the admonition of Paul—We believe all things, we *hope all things, we have endured many things, and hope to be able to *endure all things. If there is anything *virtuous, *lovely, or of good report or praiseworthy, we seek after these things.

JOSEPH SMITH.

8 a TG Bible; Revelation; Scriptures, Preservation of; Scriptures, Value of; Scriptures, Writing of.
b Isa. 8:20 (16–22).
c 1 Ne. 13:26 (20–40); 14:21 (20–26).
d TG Book of Mormon.
9 a TG Revelation.
b Dan. 2:28 (22–29, 49); Amos 3:7; D&C 121:26 (26–33). TG Scriptures to Come Forth.
10 a Isa. 49:22 (20–22); 60:4; 1 Ne. 19:16 (16–17). TG Israel, Gathering of.
b TG Israel, Ten Lost Tribes of.
c Ether 13:6 (2–11); D&C

42:9; 45:66 (66–67); 84:2 (2–5); Moses 7:62. TG Jerusalem, New; Zion.
d Micah 4:7. TG Jesus Christ, Millennial Reign.
e TG Earth, Cleansing of; Earth, Renewal of; Eden.
f IE a condition like the Garden of Eden; see Isa. 11:1–9; 35; 65:17–25; Ezek. 36:35 (1–38); 2 Ne. 8:1–3. TG Paradise.
g TG Glory.
11 a Alma 21:22 (21–22); D&C 93:19; 134:4 (1–4).
b TG Agency.
c TG Conscience.

d Micah 4:5; D&C 134:7 (4, 7). TG Worship.
12 a D&C 134:1 (1–11). TG Citizenship; Governments.
b TG Kings, Earthly.
c TG Obedience.
d D&C 58:21 (21–23).
13 a Philip. 4:8.
b TG Honesty; Integrity.
c TG Chastity.
d TG Benevolence.
e TG Good Works.
f TG Hope.
g TG Perseverance; Steadfastness.
h TG Modesty; Virtue.
i TG Beauty.